THE COUNTER-REVOLUTION
OF 1836

THE COUNTER-REVOLUTION OF 1836

Texas Slavery & Jim Crow and the Roots of American Fascism

By Gerald Horne

INTERNATIONAL PUBLISHERS, New York

Gerald Horne is Moores Professor of History & African American Studies at the University of Houston. He has published more than three dozen books including "White Supremacy Confronted: US Imperialism & Anticommunism vs the Liberation of Southern Africa from Rhodes to Mandela", "The Apocalypse of Settler Colonialism: The Roots of Slavery, and White Supremacy and Capitalism in 17th Century North America and the Caribbean" and "The Bittersweet Science"

International Publishers, NY 10011

Printed in the United States

ISBN 10: 0-7178-00016   ISBN-13 978-07178-00018
Typeset by Amnet Systems, Chennai, India

Table of Contents

Author's Note

This is a book shaped by Covid-19. After returning from research in France in early 2020 I had intended more travel but the virus grounded me. However, that turned me toward other sources, e.g., U.S. State Department records on microfilm; oral histories, dissertations and the like online, much of which is reflected in these pages. Still, readers should bear with me if—assuming the pandemic recedes—I decide to pursue this project with further archival digging.

THE COUNTER-REVOLUTION
OF 1836

Introduction

Where the Old South Meets the Wild West

In 1859 Texas was a bleeding sore. Or so thought Robert Neighbors, a so-called "Indian Agent" toiling on Washington's behalf. There was a clique led by John Baylor, soon to bathe in infamy during the forthcoming Civil War for demanding "extermination" of Indigenes, who sought to accelerate this deadly process. This clique formed an organized conspiracy against the Indian policy of the federal government which emphasized a "reserve"—or reservation—in the Lone Star State. No, insisted these opponents, Indigenes should be simply liquidated. To demonstrate their utter seriousness—and in anticipation of the Civil War—they launched "frequent attacks on the United States military," bloodthirstiness which, said Neighbors, "exceeds all the brutality attributed to the wild Comanches," the ultimate target.[1]

Neighbors was informed by a confidant in Waco of a "secret move among some of the leading men upon the frontier to resist the removal of the Indians"—but, instead, "to kill them."[2] This gruesomely macabre turn was hardly happenstance: Baylor's brother George listed himself in an official document as an "Indian Killer."[3]

However, his startling profession was likely exceeded by that of his better known brother, the hefty 6'3" and 230-pound blue-eyed John Baylor, who had the build of a linebacker and the mien of a murderer.[4] His deeds were backed by inflammatory words as the publisher of what has been termed fairly as "the worst Indian condemnatory sheet in all history," the tellingly titled "The White Man." Reputedly, this genocidal call, said a pro-settler chronicler, "appealed

---

1. Robert S. Neighbors, Supervising Agent Texas Indians to Honorable J.W. Denver, Commission of Indian Affairs, Washington, D.C., 1859, 226-8, Cleon Eugene Heflin Papers, U of Oklahoma-Norman (abbrev. Heflin Papers), (University of Oklahoma-Norman abbrev. UOk-N).

2. E.J. Gurley to R.S. Neighbors, 5 May 1859, 274-5, Heflin Papers.

3. Doug J. Swanson, *Cult of Glory: The Bold and Brutal History of the Texas Rangers*, New York: Viking, 2020, 222 (abbrev. Swanson).

4. Donald Shaw Frazier, "Blood and Treasure: Confederate Imperialists in the American Southwest," Ph.D. dissertation, Texas Christian U, 1992, 65 (abbrev. Frazier), (Texas Christian University abbrev. TCU).

to Americans more, perhaps, than any other theme in all Texas border history" in its cry for "advocating extermination of the Indians and Unionists alike...."[5]

As suggested by his seeking to place Indigenes on reservations—not to mention his status as a slaveholder—Neighbors was no radical. Yet, that did not save him. By September 1859 he was murdered: "contemporaries believed the assassins," said a 20th-century analyst, "resented his defense of the Indians...."[6] Although in favor of illicit land grabs and enslavement, he was out of step with the ascending politics of Texas, soon-to-be the palisade of the continent, where the Old South met the Wild West, where genocidal impulse suffused genocidal reality.

Even a mainstream Texas historian felt compelled to acknowledge that Washington "never formally adopted the policy of massacre authorized" by Texas, where it was "permissible to kill all males twelve years and older" by the 1850s and where the vaunted Texas Rangers were little more than death squads of a type that came to characterize U.S. foreign policy by the mid-20th century. Conflict over "Indian" policy generated momentum for Texas's second secession following the bolting from Mexico in 1836: this time from the U.S. itself in 1861. Texas entered the U.S. as the 28th state in 1845 (this after existence as an independent republic), and part of the deal was control of its vast public lands, providing local authorities with more leeway in routing Indigenes in comparison to other states.[7]

The land of Indigenes and Mexicans was the premium desired ravenously by poorer settlers, which was part of the epoxy binding class collaboration between them and their "betters." Enlistees in the 1846 war with Mexico who completed 12 months' service were promised a whopping 160 acres of land.[8]

The martyrdom of Neighbors was reflective of a larger point: there were many reasons for the soon to erupt U.S. Civil War, but among this lengthy list was the genocidal drive in the then largest state, the anchor of slaveholding, which also faced a formidable opponent

---

5. Rupert Norval Richardson, *The Frontier of Northwest Texas, 1846 to 1876: Advance and Defense by the Pioneer Settlers of the Cross Timbers and Prairies*, Glendale: Clark, 1963, 198, 211, 235 (abbrev. R.N. Richardson).

6. Kenneth Neighbours, "Indian Exodus out of Texas in 1859," *West Texas Historical Association Yearbook*, 36 (October 1960): 80-97, 95, 274-5, Heflin Papers.

7. Patrick George Williams, "Redeemer Democrats and the Roots of Modern Texas, 1872-1884," Columbia U, Ph.D. dissertation, 1996, 7.

8. Peter Guardino, *The Dead March: A History of the Mexican-American War*, Cambridge: Harvard U Press, 2017, 349 (abbrev. Guardino).

in Mexico and some of the more fearsome Indigenes—especially Comanches, Caddoes and Apaches. Yet there was serious doubt among the European settlers in Texas that Washington was up to the task of liquidating Indigenes, seen as critical to the confrontation with Mexico, and corralling rambunctious Africans.

In essence Texas had a problem not encountered by other slave societies on the continent: an abolitionist nation along the border—which mandated enhanced militarism. Thus, it was in 1840, while Texas remained independent, that the U.S. Secretary of State was told that "during the last six months...parties of Indians have arrived in this city [Matamoros along the border]," including "Cherokees, Delawares, Kickapoos and Caddoes...all of whom it would seem have entered into Mexican service" and, thus, "furnished with arms [and] ammunition...." Busily, they had "killed all the Texians" encountered en route, and "stripped them of their clothing and effects...."[9]

This created more openings for the African to gain allies—much more so than elsewhere in Dixie. There were not only Mexicans, but Germans and Czechs too, some refugees from the failed revolutions of 1848 and with abolitionist impulses. The Africans in Texas also had a wider range of jobs, not only in cotton but rice, sugar, timber, cattle ranching and shipping. As slavery was decomposing in 1864-1865, many enslavers due east began flooding into Texas, enlarging the enslaved population, providing more political heft. As well, enslaved Africans continued to be landed in Galveston even after this official commerce had ended—ostensibly. Thus, official figures suggest there were 58,161 Africans in Texas in 1851 but 182,566 a decade later[10]—and even more by 1870.

Texas was so unsettled by the slew of problems it faced that steps were taken then that today seem startlingly incongruous. In 1842 there was a bloody revolt of the Mayas in Yucatan, Mexico—a "caste war"—which, it was thought, "threatened to destroy white civilization." So, the navy of Texas intervened—on behalf of Indigenes,[11] the

---

9. D.W. Smith to Secretary of State John Forsyth, 14 January 1840, Reel 2, Despatches from U.S. Consuls in Matamoros, Mexico, National Archives and Records Administration, College Park, Maryland (abbrev. NARA).

10. Alan Govenar, compiler, *The Blues Come to Texas: Paul Oliver and Mack McCormick's Unfinished Book*, College Station: Texas A&M U Press, 2019, 49, 210 (abbrev. Govenar), Texas A&M University (abbrev. TA&MU).

11. Lynda Sanderford Morrison, "The Life and Times of José Canuto Yela: Yucatecan Priest and Patriot (1802-1859), Ph.D. dissertation, U of Alabama, 1993, vii, viii, 132 (abbrev. Morrison).

same force they were battling at home, as they were determined to weaken the prime foe: Mexico.

As Texas lurched from Mexican province festooned with rapacious Euro-American settlers in the 1820s to pro-slavery secession in 1836 to the premier *casus belli* U.S. state in 1845 to bulwark of Confederate secession in 1861 to the vanguard of racist counter-revolution by the 1870s, the then largest state was setting the pace for North American reaction more generally. Size mattered. Texas's 400,000 square miles, argued one opponent in 1845, was equal to "fifty states the size of Massachusetts... more than twice as large as all New England and all the Middle States taken collectively,"[12] all of which did not bode well for the ultimate political direction of the House of Representatives. With the slaveholders' land grab in Texas, reflexively detractors thought this should be countervailed by snatching Canada,[13] the prospect of which only propelled further antagonism between London and Washington. Edward Everett Hale in 1845 posed the query that has yet to be answered definitively: "How to Conquer Texas before Texas Conquers Us?"[14]

In the same vein, scholar Sam Haynes argued that "nowhere in North America did cultural chauvinism reach such hysterical proportion than in Texas, where the Revolution [*sic*] appeared to portend the inexorable advance of the white race across the continent."[15] The sons of 1776 may have dissented, but this only illustrates the accord between the two epochal processes and underscores why the sons of 1836 averred that their secession was "the Second Coming of the American Revolution"[16]—or what I term the Second Counter-Revolution,

12. Stephen C. Phillips, "An Address on the Annexation of Texas and the Aspect of Slavery in the United States in Connection therewith; Delivered in Boston, November 14 and 18, 1845," Boston: Crosby and Nichols, 1845, Oberlin College-Ohio (abbrev. Phillips). This document can also be found at the New York Historical Society in Manhattan (abbrev. NYHS).

13. Citizens of New York State to Congress, January and February 1844, Box No. N.A. of LC 136, 137, 138, RG 233, Records of U.S. House of Representatives, 26th-28th Congress, 1840-1845, National Archives and Records Administration-Washington, D.C. (abbrev. NARA-DC).

14. Edward Everett Hale, "How to Conquer Texas Before Texas Conquers Us," Boston: Redding & Co., 17 March 1845 (abbey. Hale), University of California-Berkeley (abbrev. UC-B).

15. Sam W. Haynes, "The Somervell and Mier Expeditions: The Political and Diplomatic Consequences of Frontier Adventurism in the Texas Republic, 1842-1844," Ph.D. dissertation, U of Houston, 1988, 9-10 (abbrev. Haynes, Somervell).

16. Bryan Burrough, et al., *Forget the Alamo: The Rise and Fall of an American Myth*, New York: Penguin, 2021, 73 (abbrev. Burrough).

both driven by the passion for slavery and land grabs.[17] It was only to be expected that the name for the birthplace of the 1836 republic was "Washington-on-the-Brazos."[18]

As shall be seen, it was then that the seeds were planted and watered for the 21st-century flowering of a unique brand of U.S. fascism. Yet, dialectically, the good news is that what served to drive Texas in this daunting direction was precisely the strength of the many foes it faced—initially Indigenous polities, then Mexico, and Africans (who as of this writing, are more populous in Texas than anywhere else in the U.S.), and these latter groupings may very well have the final say on the state and nation's evolution.

* * *

Neighbors's status as a master of bondage should have led him to realize, in the prelude to the U.S. Civil War, that those who presided over a slave society—soon to be liquidated as a class—were noticeably jumpy and trigger-happy. After all, it was in September 1856 in Colorado County, Texas, that the press reported breathlessly about "well organized and systematized plans for the murder of our entire white population" by enslaved Africans, "with the exception of the young ladies who were to be taken captives and made the wives of the diabolical murderers of their parents and friends"; in fact, "found in their possession" were a "number of pistols, Bowie knives, guns and ammunition," not to mention their chilling "motto[:] 'leave not a shadow behind.'" The plan was to "fight their way to a 'Free State,'" a plot that understandably generated "intense excitement" since "more than two hundred Negroes had violated the law," the "penalty of which is death...." However, this was Texas—the only slave society with an immediate abolitionist neighbor—and, thus, worryingly "without exception, every Mexican in the county was implicated." Likewise, "they were arrested and ordered to leave the county within five days" and ordered brusquely "never again to return," too "under the penalty of death." The conclusion reached

---

17. Gerald Horne, *The Counter-Revolution of 1776: Slave Resistance and the Origins of the United States of America*, New York: New York U Press, 2014 (abbrev. Horne, *Counter-Revolution of 1776*), New York University (abbrev. NYU).

18. Caroline Levander, "Sutton Griggs and the Borderlands of Empire" (abbrev. Levander), in Tess Chakkalakal and Kenneth W. Warren, eds., *Jim Crow, Literature, and the Legacy of Sutton E. Griggs*, Athens: U of Georgia Press, 2013, 21-48. 34 (abbrev. Chakkalakal and Warren).

was hardly comforting: "the lower class of the Mexican population are incendiaries in any country where slaves are held."[19]

Another contemporary observer detected "dreadful scenes of St. Domingo" at play in this "attempted Negro insurrection." "Two or three hundred able bodied slaves held in secret" a "conclave" to devise "this murderous plan...." Fleeing to Mexico was their related "aim" where then being debated was a "new constitution" that argued that the state "shall ever[more]...will give protection to all slaves that migrate to their country and will not treat with any nation for their delivery...."[20]

It would have been folly for enslavers to dismiss the significance of this plot for it was in 1835, just before Texas's secession, that founding father Stephen F. Austin, in the midst of—again—confronting Mexico, was apprised that "the Negroes on Brazos made an attempt to rise" and consequently "near 100 had been taken up [with] many whip[ped] nearly to death" and "some hung." At the same time "Carancawa [Karankawa] Indians" were exceedingly restive, complicating matters. But it was African unrest that had seized imaginations: they had decided to "divide...all the cotton farms and they intended to ship the cotton to New Orleans and make the white man serve them in turn...."[21]

Again, enslavers in Texas had to take more seriously such plots because of the looming presence of Mexico. As Euro-American settlers began flocking there in the 1820s, Mexico was developing an abolitionist policy that was rivaling that of the hemispheric champion, whose very name commanded fear and respect: Haiti. This was not only for humanitarian reasons but also because Mexico saw an advantage in undermining the nation from whom they had gained their own independence—Spain—not least by sponsoring revolts of the enslaved in nearby Cuba. Especially after Texas secession from Mexico in 1836, followed by the U.S. war of aggression against its southern neighbor in 1846, the Foreign Ministry had little reason to accommodate U.S. enslavers, leading to thousands of the enslaved finding refuge by heading southward.[22]

---

19. *Galveston News*, 9 September 1856, Texas Slave Laws Collection, University of Texas-Austin (abbrev. UT-A).

20. H. McBride Pridgen, "People of Texas on the Protection of Slave Property," Austin, 1859, Harvard U, Cambridge, Massachusetts (abbrev. Pridgen).

21. B.J. White to Stephen F. Austin, 17 October 1835, in Eugene Barker, ed., *The Austin Papers, October 1834-January 1837, Volume III*, Washington: Government Printing Office, 1924-1928, 190 (abbrev. Austin Papers).

22. Alice Baumgartner, "Abolition from the South: Mexico and the Road to U.S. Civil War, 1821-1867," Ph.D. dissertation, Yale U, 2018, 6, 51 (abbrev.

Indeed, even as Euro-American settlers led by Austin were flooding into Mexican territory, Secretary of War José María Tornel y Mendivil—among a coterie of officialdom said to hold "distinctly anti-United States views"—apparently felt that the presence, then emancipation of the enslaved, would serve to checkmate potential secessionists.[23] This was prescience on his part in that just as the transformative 1846 war of aggression waged by the U.S. on Mexico was declared, leading to the seizure of such lush prizes as California, rumors flooded Mexico to the effect that Mexicans were being seized and branded and sold in the slave markets of New Orleans; after all, why wouldn't Washington impose on its latest victim what it had imposed on Africans?[24]

As early as 1826 this fraught matter was capturing the attention of future U.S. president James Buchanan. As hemispheric nations were about to confer in Panama, he noticed that Cuba could be "invaded by Colombia and Mexico and pass under their dominion," an abolitionist coup by the latter nation in particular since "Mexico is destined to become our rival. She already feels it and knows it. She already looks to war between us and the Southern Republics."[25] This nightmare scenario of spawning abolition in Cuba, thought one Texan writer of that era, was "recalling the dreadful scenes of St. [sic] Domingo," dystopia for enslavers.[26]

Relations between the quarreling republics were complicated further when Texas enslavers took matters into their own hands and began crossing the border to snatch Africans for purposes of bondage. Just before the murder of Neighbors in 1859, a U.S. envoy recounted how a "free Mexican Negro servant" sued a Euro-American in Mexico "for wages due him" and in response, the latter miscreant "collected a party of eight armed Americans on the Texas side of the [border] came over and the Negro who was at the time standing at the door of the Court House and attempted to carry him off" and a "running fight was kept up until the Americans reached the river"; a

---

Baumgartner). The author also argues that the date 1837 rather than 1829 should be seen as the year of abolition in Mexico—still, well before 1865.

23. Fane Downs, "The History of Mexicans in Texas, 1820-1845," Ph.D. dissertation, Texas Tech U, 1970, 214 (abbrev. Downs), (Texas Tech University abbrev. TTU).

24. Guardino, 219.

25. Speech, 11 April 1826, in John Bassett Moore, ed., *The Works of James Buchanan, Comprising His Speeches, State Papers and Private Correspondence, Volume I, 1813-1830*, London: Lippincott, 1908, 184-206, 200-201 (abbrev. J.B. Moore).

26. Pridgen.

"large number of shots were fired" as the would-be kidnappers were detained[27]—practically the reverse of what would have occurred in Texas.

Ultimately, capital flight, in the form of enslaved Africans, scurried to Mexico in the thousands, and says scholar James David Nichols, "in a very real sense African American runaways from slavery began driving Mexico and Anglo Texans toward a conflict"[28]—and Texas and Dixie versus a Washington thought to be suspect too. In some ways, the U.S. victorious war of aggression over Mexico was a catastrophic success for Washington, reanimating the sectional divide over slavery in the territories—especially in California where Texans wielded early influence—leading to the unsatisfying Compromise of 1850, a capitulation to enslavers in essence, which further strained sectionalism to the point of rupture about a decade later.[29]

The 1846 war, according to a recent study, ignited a "'Greater Reconstruction'...adding peoples and territory whose incorporation nullified the old balance between North and South and reoriented national policy toward Latin America and the Pacific,"[30] a process that continues.

Yet another process that continues is U.S. imperialism, thought to have been fomented post-1898 with the knockout blow delivered to the tottering Spanish Empire in the Philippines and Cuba.[31] However, if one posits, as has the scholar Tim De Wit, that even the pre-1898 U.S. was a "prison of nations,"[32] then the squashing by European settlers of countless Indigenous nations, along with the ransacking of Mexico, was at least a dress rehearsal for imperialism. It was also the case that the unremitting pressure placed on nations—Mexico,

27. David Diffenderfer to Sir, July 1859, Reel 1, Despatches from U.S. Consuls in Paseo del Norte, Mexico, NARA.

28. James David Nichols, *The Limits of Liberty: Mobility and the Making of the Eastern U.S. Mexican Border*, Lincoln: U of Nebraska Press, 2018, 59 (abbrev. Nichols 2018).

29. Stephen E. Maizlish, *A Strife of Tongues: The Compromise of 1850 and the Ideological Foundations of the American Civil War*, Charlottesville: U of Virginia Press, 2018.

30. Thomas G. Connors and Raúl Isaí Muñoz, "Looking for the North American Invasion in Mexico City," *American Historical Review* 125 (No. 2, April 2020): 498-518, 500 (abbrev. Connors and Muñoz). See also Elliott West, "Reconstructing Race," *Western Historical Quarterly*, 34 (No. 1, 2003): 6-26.

31. J.A. Hobson, *Imperialism: A Study*, New York: Gordon Press, 1975. V.I. Lenin, *On Imperialism and Imperialists*, Moscow: Progress, 1973.

32. Tim de Wit, "Land of Conspiracies: Pan-Indian Conspiracy Fears in the Union Government and the American Civil War in the Indian Territory, 1861-1866," date unclear, Faculty of Humanities, Vrije Universiteit van Amsterdam, (abbrev. de Wit), Box 13, Division of Manuscripts Collection, UOk-N.

Cherokee, Creek, *et al.*—impelled civil wars amongst them, weakening these opponents of U.S. settlers that then created momentum and dynamics that eventuated in the U.S. Civil War.

That was not all. Assuredly, the military praxis and tactics honed on what came to be U.S. soil proved quite useful overseas.[33] Similarly, it was not only "White Supremacist Democrats" who noticed that their Republican antagonists in the late 19th century were "enthusiastically supporting an openly racist imperialism."[34] Simultaneously, this undercut their purported sympathy for the formerly enslaved, as it was fueled by brutal conflicts with Indigenes.

Propelling this cycle of violence was not only the racism that generated land grabs and the desire for enslaved labor, it was also the lack of confidence in the U.S. itself, as exemplified by the flight beyond then U.S. borders by the Church of Latter Day Saints [Mormons], the anti-republican animus in Canada backed by their potent London ally, slave revolts, the continuing uprisings of Comanches and their allies, etc.[35]

Civil wars among Cherokees and Creeks and other Indigenes generated by pressure from settlers eventuated in the "Black Hawk" war and wars with Seminoles, then war with Mexico—which served as a training ground and a precipitant for the U.S. Civil War, i.e., how to divide the spoils between wings of the ruling class.[36]

*   *   *

Even before 1857 and the infamously pivotal *Dred Scott* case which, *inter alia*, denied African-Americans' citizenship,[37] U.S. envoys had arrived at this inglorious conclusion. It was in 1855 that James Pickett, soon to be a Confederate, from his perch in Vera Cruz, conceded that "The Negro Question...has been the theme of much

33. Katherine Bjork, *Prairie Imperialists: The Indian Country Origins of American Empire*, Philadelphia: U of Pennsylvania Press, 2019. See also Gerrit John Dirmaat, "Enemies Foreign and Domestic: U.S. Relations with Mormons in the U.S. Empire in North America, 1844-1854," Ph.D. dissertation, U of Colorado, 2010, 21 (abbrev. Dirkmaat).

34. Sam Erman, *Almost Citizens: Puerto Rico, the U.S. Constitution and Empire*, New York: Cambridge U Press, 2019, 30-31 (abbrev. Erman).

35. Thomas W. Richards, Jr., "The Texas Moment: Breakaway Republics and Contested Sovereignty in North America," Ph.D. dissertation, Temple U, 2016 (abbrev. Richards).

36. Felice Flanery Lewis, *Trailing Clouds of Glory: Zachary Taylor's Mexican War Campaign and His Emerging Civil War Leaders*, Tuscaloosa: U of Alabama Press, 2010 (abbrev. Lewis).

37. Earl M. Maltz, *Dred Scott and the Politics of Slavery*, Lawrence: U Press of Kansas, 2007.

correspondence and conversation" with his Mexican interlocutors. "Persons of the African race," he sniffed "are not recognized as 'citizens of the USA.'" Mexico asserted that if you were on their territory for a month you must receive a *"carta de Seguro"*—a kind of visa—but, countered Pickett, if given to a "colored person it would be necessary to describe" said persons as "citizens of the United States," where he thought they "would always be regarded as minors."[38]

The prominent James Gadsden, who gave his name to yet another territorial cession from Mexico, did not object, anticipating Pickett by grousing about "those who seek abroad what would not be acknowledged at home," meaning citizenship. "There are a large number of this caste," he carped, "who are increasing to a fearful extent"; making it plain, he added nervously, "I allude to the Africans who are flocking in number from the United States to Mexico"[39] and had proven they were capable of providing intelligence and military aid besides to their adopted homeland.

The very terrain conspired against warm relations between the two neighbors. Just before this 1859 contretemps, a Texas farmer along the border found that a shift in river currents—an "avulsion"—meant that the "property which he had on his plantation" was now on Mexican soil and was deemed to be "contraband" and was "immediately seized," i.e., "confiscated," which was not an unusual occurrence.[40]

*   *   *

Like their republican peers in Washington, Texas too was disadvantaged in the battle to win hearts and minds among Africans. As early as 1789, Spain offered refuge to any slave fleeing the U.S. with republicans objecting to no avail. By 1805, in a maneuver imitated relentlessly by other republican antagonists, Spain threatened to spawn revolts of the enslaved in the U.S. if the new nation encroached further on its territory—a tactic later emulated by Mexico.[41] The enslaved from Louisiana and points east sought asylum

---

38. James Pickett to Secretary of State William Marcy, 21 February 1855, Reel 6, Despatches from U.S. Consuls in Vera Cruz, NARA. The city (and the state of the same name) are now normally spelled as one word, Veracruz.

39. James Gadsden to U.S. Consuls in Mexico, 28 June 1854, Reel 6, Despatches from U.S. Consuls in Vera Cruz, NARA.

40. Peter Seuzeneau to Lewis Cass, 4 April 1858, Reel 3, Despatches from U.S. Consuls in Matamoros, Mexico, NARA.

41. Sue Clark Wortham, "The Role of the Negro on the Texas Frontier, 1821-1836," M.A. thesis, Texas State U-San Marcos, 1970, 8, 86.

in the borderlands where Mexicans prevailed, which was hardly unusual.[42]

However, the 1810 revolt in Mexico, which in no small measure was a revolt of the Indigenous against the horrors of centuries of Spanish colonialism, induced many Spaniards to flee, which in turn created an opening for Euro-American settlers.[43] Subsequently, Alphonse Du Bois de Saligny, the French envoy in independent Texas, concluded what was then obvious: allowing Euro-Americans to settle northern Mexico was a "great mistake" that leaders "should have been able to foresee,"[44] as settlers deployed their rapidly developing strategy of "squatter sovereignty"—flooding a territory with a Pan-European bloc of settlers who then through force of arms and the patina of "democracy" claimed total control.

This perceptive Frenchman was among the legions of his countrymen who had not relinquished a fond hope of regaining a foothold on the continent, after being ousted from what is now Quebec, then the vast Louisiana Territory. France was the first nation to recognize Texas's secession, said a French envoy triumphantly[45]—trumping Washington—then sought to seize Mexico decades later as the U.S. Civil War erupted. During this latter tumultuous era, Paris's envoy in Galveston claimed that all members of the Catholic clergy there were French and were bolstered by a steady stream from their comrades in New Orleans.[46]

Enslavers looked longingly to France, particularly after the reversal of the late 18th-century abolition decree in Paris and the continuation of the peculiar institution in their domain until the mid-19th century. Thus, as late as 1856, Jefferson Davis, soon to spearhead secession from the U.S., acknowledged admiringly that "the occupation of Algeria by the French presents a case having much parallelism to that of our own western frontier and affords us the opportunity of

---

42. Paul Andres Barba, "Enslaved in Texas: Slavery, Migration and Identity in Native Country," Ph.d. dissertation, U of California-Santa Barbara, 2016, 370 (abbrev. Barba).

43. Charles J. Folsom, *Mexico in 1842: A Description of the Country, its Natural and Political Features...*, New York: Folsom, 1842, 12, 63.

44. Alphonse Du Bois de Saligny to Monsieur le Comte, Houston, 3 March 1839, Box 1, Alphonse Du Bois de Saligny Translation Project Records, Austin Public Library-Texas (abbrev. Saligny), Austin Public Library (abbrev. APL).

45. Consul to French Ambassador in Washington, 22 July 1862, Galveston Consulate, Diplomatic Archives-Paris, France (abbrev. Galveston Consulate).

46. Report, 20 December 1865, Galveston Consulate.

profiting by their experience."[47] Less than a decade later, his fellow secessionist, Wade Hampton—post-Appomattox—was commenting on a movement centered in Texas unwilling to surrender; "escape this train of horrors," he counseled, adding with realism: "we can hold Texas…[dispatch] men who will fight to Texas," then "seek refuge" in French controlled "Mexico, rather than [rejoin] the Union."[48]

For less than a year before Hampton issued this clarion call, a U.S. envoy in Tampico, Mexico—perhaps the key port keeping Confederates afloat—said wondrously that "this place has been more like a colony to [secessionists]."[49] Tampico was linked inexorably to Matamoros—the twin of Brownsville, Texas—and during the civil war these Mexican cities kept not only Texas afloat but, especially after the fall of New Orleans in 1862, the entire secession, with manufactured goods and munitions too.[50]

By June 1865, there were—according to the envoy—"over 1000 African troops" (meaning those who had arrived from Colonized Africa, e.g., Sudan and Algeria) fighting for France in Tamaulipas and, it was added glumly and prematurely, "will doubtless turn the balance of power in the hands of the imperials once more…."[51] By September, Washington was told that France had just landed "350 infantry belonging to the 2nd African battalion…recently arrived on this coast from Algiers…."[52] As shall be seen, some of those Africans deserted and—who knows?—may have ended up in the U.S.

The religious sectarianism that had characterized Catholic France, colonial Mexico and then—to a degree—was inherited by the republic, did not deter Moses Austin and his enterprising son Stephen. They and other potential migrants had other concerns, as exemplified by the fact that the elder Austin had built a lead mining and manufacturing enterprise in Virginia built on the backs of enslaved

---

47. Jefferson Davis to Franklin Pierce, 1 December 1856, in Duncan Rowland, ed., *Jefferson Davis, Constitutionalist: His Letters, Papers and Speeches, Volume 3,* Jackson: Mississippi Department of Archives and History, 1923, 75 (abbrev. Rowland).

48. Wade Hampton to Jefferson Davis, 19 April 1865, in Rowland, Volume 6, 552-553.

49. Franklin Chase, Consul, to Frederick W. Seward, 26 September 1864, Reel 4, Despatches from U.S. Consuls in Tampico, NARA.

50. James Daddysman, *The Matamoros Trade: Confederate Commerce, Diplomacy and Intrigue,* Newark: U of Delaware Press, 1984.

51. Franklin Chase to William Hunter, State Department, 16 June 1865, Reel 4, Despatches from U.S. Consuls in Tampico, NARA.

52. Franklin Chase to Secretary of State William Seward, 26 September 1865, Reel 4, Despatches from U.S. Consuls in Tampico, NARA.

labor.[53] Upon arriving in Texas in the early 1820s, the younger Austin—short and slight with curly hair and the requisite fair complexion[54]—mirrored his father.

Although these newcomers hailed from the U.S., James Buchanan, a future president, was among those who thought that the Republic of Texas had the potential to become a rival to Washington—"and must of necessity attach herself to some foreign nation"[55]—with dire consequences for the U.S. itself. The Lone Star republic could, for example, ally with the real or imagined foes of Washington, be they Mormons or Indigenes or Frenchmen—or some other real or imagined foe of the U.S. in the 21st century.

These alliances were mandatory since Texas—under whatever flag—faced unremitting hostility from Africans, Indigenes and Mexicans, at times combined.[56] By 1842 they were worrying about the "Grappes," or those defined as Caddo Indigenes, who were said to be "nearly black, with 'kinky hair,'" i.e., "'free men of color.'" Mexico, it was said, "gave them a tract of country" in Texas,[57] a recipe for conflict. Unsurprisingly, given the penchant in Texas to enslave those of their hue, a subsequent scholar limned the "influence of the Caddoes over other tribes," which "was mentioned frequently in early Texas official records;" they "exercise[d] a controlling influence over…Wacoes, Twachenes, Keechies, Iones and Pawnees" and, thus, said officialdom, were "eminently injurious to Texas.…"[58]

The Caddoes, asserted another analyst "achieved a level of cultural development unsurpassed by other Texas Indians" and were the "most important of the state's natives from several points of view."[59]

---

53. Barba, 389.

54. Lawrence Wright, *God Save Texas: A Journey into the Soul of the Lone Star State*, New York: Random House, 2018, 76 (abbrev. L. Wright).

55. Speech, 14 February 1845, in J.B. Moore, Volume 6, 87, 107.

56. Kenneth Wiggins Porter, "Negroes and Indians on the Texas Frontier, 1831-1876," *Journal of Negro History*, 41 (July 1956): 185-214. Kenneth Wiggins Porter, "Negroes and Indians on the Texas Frontier, 1831-1876, Part 2," *Journal of Negro History*, 41 (1956): 285-310.

57. U.S. Congress, House of Representatives, 27th Congress, 2nd Session, Rep. No. 1035, The Caddo Indian Treaty, 20 August 1842, Huntington Library-San Marino, California (abbrev. Huntington Library).

58. Mildred S. Gleason, *Caddo: A Survey of Caddo Indians in Northeast Texas and Marion County, 1541-1840*, Jefferson, Texas: Marion County Historical Commission, 1981, 60, 61 (abbrev. Gleason).

59. W.W. Newcomb, Jr., *Indians of Texas*, Austin: U of Texas Press, 1961, 279 (abbrev. Newcomb).

The Caddoes, said historian Francis H. Galan, "were even more anti-Texas in March 1836," the time of secession, "than the Cherokees and more amenable to the Mexican agents...."[60]

Like the Indigenes of Florida known as the Seminoles, to a degree Caddo too had merged with Africans. But this meant they could be redefined as "Free Negro," who were treated inhospitably in Texas. In sovereign Texas in 1840 no Free Negro was allowed and even those of this group from other jurisdictions, e.g., the British Caribbean, faced harassment or enslavement upon arriving in Galveston.[61]

A visitor to Texas in the year of union with Washington in 1845 saw "great numbers of blacks wearing shawl turbans, which seem well-suited to their pseudo-Moorish character" and were said to be "superior in intelligence to the Indians, who mostly have recourse to them in their intercourse with the whites...." The "Africans" were "said to acquire the different Indian languages with great facility...."[62]

This was a widespread trait continentally and represented a formidable bloc of opposition to settlers[63] that began to be smashed

---

60. Francis H. Galan, "A Tainted Leadership: The Betrayal of Tejanos in the Republic of Texas," in Kenneth W. Howell and Charles Swanlund, eds., *Single Star of the West: The Republic of Texas, 1836-1845*, Denton: U of North Texas Press, 2017, 437-482, 474 (abbrev. Howell and Swanlund), University of North Texas (abbrev. UNT).

61. Andrew Forest Muir, "The Free Negro in Galveston County, Texas," *Negro History Bulletin*, 22 (December 1958): 68-70, Box 14, Kenneth Wiggins Porter Papers, Schomburg Center for Research in Black Culture, New York Public Library (abbrev. Porter Papers).

62. John Galvin, ed., James W. Abert, *Through the Country of the Comanche Indians in the Fall of the Year 1845, the Journal of a U.S. Army Expedition...*, San Francisco: Howell, 1970, 64 (abbrev. Abert).

63. Patrick Minges, "Beneath the Underdog: Race, Religions and the Trail of Tears," *American Indian Quarterly*, 25 (2002): 453-479: By the late 1700s, settlers feared a "Black-Red" alliance and legislated to bar their interaction, followed by forced removal of Indigenes, then Africans to Liberia. See also Charles J. Kappler, compiler, *Indian Affairs. Laws and Treaties, Volume II*, Washington, D.C.: Government Printing Office, 1904: The Sioux Treaty of 1815 included a signatory "Warchesunsapa, the Negro." See also Emil Schlup "Tarhe-the Crane," *Ohio Archeological and Historical Quarterly*, 14 (1905): 132-138: A Negro, Jonathan Pointer, served as an interpreter for the Wyandot. Africans worked as interpreters for Creeks: John R. Swanton, "The Green Corn Dance," *Chronicles of Oklahoma*, 10 (1932): 170-195. Africans also worked as interpreters for Seminoles, seen as a branch of Creeks: Carolyn Thomas Foreman, "The Jumper Family of the Seminole Nation," *Chronicles of Oklahoma* 34 (1956): 272-286. A man of African descent translated for Florida Indigenes at the signing of the Treaty of Fort Dade in 1837: Kenneth Wiggins Porter, "Abraham," *Phylon*, 22 (1941): 105-116. This same translator returned from Indian Territory

with the defeat of slaveholders and halting steps toward citizenship for Africans, which was sufficient to woo them, then turn them as a sledgehammer against their former allies in the form of the "Buffalo Soldiers" assaulting Indigenes, an entity that represents one of the most disgraceful episodes of African-American history.[64]

Black leaders and intellectuals of that era did not seem to grasp wholly what a modern scholar depicted in 2020: it was "required that every step toward Black freedom be compensated with a step toward Indian annihilation."[65]

Still, enslaving of Africans was hardly unknown among certain Indigenes, especially the Cherokees, an unsteady foundation for an alliance.[66] Yet the hysterically anti-Indigene writer J.W. Wilbarger

---

[Oklahoma] by 1852 to interpret during the Third Seminole War: Kenneth Wiggins Porter, "The Negro Abraham," *Florida Historical Quarterly*, 25 (1946): 1-43. Henry Mills, a Negro, worked as an interpreter for the Blackfeet Indigenes, then married into the grouping, and his son became one of their key leaders: Hugh A. Dempsey, "Black White Man," *Alberta Historical Review*, 6 (1958): 7-11. See the story of David Mills, who married a member of the same grouping in the late 1800s: Adolph Hungry Wolf, *The Blood People: A Division of the Blackfoot Confederacy*, New York: Harper and Row, 1977. During the 1830s a Negro led the Crow into battle: Zenas Leonard, *Narrative of the Adventures of Zenas Leonard*, Chicago: Lakeside Press, 1934. In Colorado a Negro served as a court interpreter for both Indigenes and Mexicans: D.B. McCue, "John Taylor—Slave Born Colorado Pioneer," *The Colorado Magazine*, 18 (1941): 161-168. Taylor ultimately married a Ute woman: Virginia McConnell Simmons, *The Ute Indians of Utah, Colorado and New Mexico*, Boulder: U of Colorado Press, 2000. Later Matthew Henson, a Negro, became the only member of a U.S. force to the Far North who chose to learn Inuit: S. Allen Counter, *North Pole Legacy: Black, White and Eskimo*, Amherst: U of Massachusetts Press, 1991. See also Arthur T. Burton, *Black, Red and Deadly: Black and Indian Gunfighters of the Indian Territories*, Fort Worth: Eakin, 1991, 164, 218: "Blacks made a greater effort to understand the Native American languages…the two races were very compatible…." (abbrev. Burton, *Black*). Grant Johnson, a Negro lawman there, spoke fluent Creek.

64. See e.g., Paul H. Carlson, "William R. Shafter and the Finale to the Red River War," *Red River Valley Historical Review*, 3 (1978): 247-258: Shamefully, these Negroes routed Comanches, Kiowas and Cheyennes. Yes, a Negro interpreter perished alongside George Custer at the seismic defeat of U.S. forces at the Little Big Horn in 1876: Roland McConnell, "Isaiah Dorman and the Custer Expedition," *Journal of Negro History*, 33 (1948): 344-353.

65. Walter Johnson, *The Broken Heart of America: St. Louis and the Violent History of the United States*, New York: Basic, 2020, 163 (abbrev. W. Johnson).

66. Daniel F. Littlefield and Lonnie E. Underhill, "'Slave Revolt' in the Cherokee Nation, 1842," *American Indian Quarterly*, 3 (1977): 121-133. Yet even a leading Cherokee official—like so many other Indigenous leaders—had an African (a young girl, in his case) as an interpreter: "James' Account

found that in Texas "during the days of slavery the Indians very seldom killed a Negro. They preferred to capture them, in the hopes of obtaining a high ransom" and given their value, "they were not often disappointed,"[67] which reinforced the tendency. But there may have been something else at play since a U.S. military man during the apex of the genocidal war against Indigenes in the late 19th century was stunned to ask, "why colored soldiers are never scalped...." He spent considerable time in Texas and concluded, "an Indian will never take the scalp of a colored soldier, nor does he give any reason for it...."[68]

Another tendency that the enslaved and Africans generally brought to Texas was a fervent Anglophilia that complicated security for Washington especially. This "infatuation with Britain,"[69] as one student described it, skyrocketed after London banned slavery

---

of S.H. Long's Expedition, 1819-1820," in Reuben Goldthwaites, ed., *Early Western Travels, 1748-1846*, Cleveland: Clark, 1906. Yet another Negro interpreter for the Cherokees was spotted in 1838: James Kimmins Greer, *Colonel Jack Hays: Texas Frontier Leader and California Builder*, New York: Dutton, 1952. The Choctaws who too were forced to relocate to today's Oklahoma were akin to the Cherokees in bondage. See William G. McLoughlin, "The Choctaw Slave Burning: A Crisis in Mission Work Among the Indians," *Journal of the West*, 13 (1974): 113-127: In 1859 some Choctaws burned an enslaved woman at the stake after being accused of instigating another slave to kill a slaveholder. Still, Choctaw slaveholders tended to be of partial European descent and wealthier: C. Calvin Smith, "The Oppressed Oppressors: Negro Slavery Among the Choctaw Indians of Oklahoma," *Red River Valley Historical Quarterly*, 2 (Summer 1975): 240-253. A similar tendency was found among the Creeks, i.e., an acceptance of enslavement of Africans among the racially mixed—but this split northern and southern Creeks: Claudio Saunt, "'The English Has Now a Mind to Make Slaves of them All': Creeks, Seminoles and the Problem of Slavery," *American Indian Quarterly*, 22 (1998): 157-180.

67. J.W. Wilbarger, *Indian Depredations in Texas. Reliable Accounts of Battles, Wars, Adventures, Forays, Murders, Massacres, etc. Together with Biographical Sketches of Many of the Most Noted Fighters and Frontiersmen of Texas*, Austin: Hutchings, 1889, 269 (abbrev. Wilbarger). The author found that Indigenous groupings attacking settlers included Africans as attackers with the latter at times serving as leaders.

68. Colonel Richard Irving Dodge, *Our Wild Indians: Thirty Three Years of Personal Experience Among the Red Men of the Great West, a Popular Account*, Washington, D.C.: Worthington, 1882, xxvii, 517.

69. Daniel Kilbride, *Being American in Europe, 1750-1860*, Baltimore: Johns Hopkins U Press, 2013, 162 (abbrev. Kilbride).

in the 1830s as Texas was seceding in order to perpetuate it. In turn this heightened antipathy toward Africans perceived them not only as rebels but subversives too, yet another tendency that has yet to dissipate.

However, because settlers were so dependent upon the labor of enslaved Africans, they continued to specialize in their importation. It may not be accidental that the African Slave Trade skyrocketed—and no less to Cuba and Brazil—during the time of Texas independence: 1836-1845.[70]

Yet this would-be republican rival to Washington found it difficult to prosper, given pressure from abolitionist Britain and Haiti, attacks from Indigenes often aided by Africans—not to mention Mexico, which had yet to reconcile to the idea of a successful secession. Moreover, there were those in the U.S. itself who felt that the idea of Texas as a state was a non-starter. The prominent Judge William Jay was among these, warning in 1843 that such a Union member would mean "farewell to every hope of freeing our country from the plague of slavery," extending this "plague" to Panama. "Dissolution" of the Union was his preferred option if Texas were to become a member of this exclusive club since this would mean that "we of the North will become the serf of the slaveholders."[71]

John Quincy Adams was even more dramatic, averring that "the treaty for the annexation of Texas to this union was this day sent to the Senate; and with it went the freedom of the human race."[72] From the other shore, the militant Carolinian, J.H. Hammond—months later—instructed his fellow Palmetto State comrade, John C. Calhoun, that Texas annexation "could not be a better pretext" for the "Union to break" in two, since with the Lone Star regime "the slave

70. Gerald Horne, *The Deepest South: The United States, Brazil and the African Slave Trade*, New York: NYU Press, 2007; Gerald Horne, *Race to Revolution: The United States and Cuba During Slavery and Jim Crow*, New York: Monthly Review Press, 2014 (abbrev. Horne, *Race to Revolution*).

71. Judge William Jay to Liberty Press, 21 October 1843, in Annie Heloise Abel and Frank J. Klingberg, eds., *A Side Light on Anglo-American Relations, 1839-1858, Furnished by the Correspondence of Lewis Tappan and Others with the British and Foreign Anti-Slavery Foreign Society*, Lancaster, Pennsylvania: Association for the Study of Negro Life and History, 1927 (abbrev. Abel and Klingberg): ASNLH, 12-13.

72. Entry, April 1844, in Charles Francis Adams, ed., *Memoirs of John Quincy Adams Comprising Portions of His Diary from 1795 to 1848, Volume 12*, Philadelphia: Lippincott, 13 (abbrev. C.F. Adams).

states would form a territory large enough for a *first rate power*"[73] able to stand up to London and Washington alike [emphasis-original].

Still, what was serving to drive events was a force not necessarily under the control of Jay nor Adams nor Hammond. Once war was launched against Mexico, a reigning symbol of the bellicosity was the presence of a formerly enslaved African of Sam Houston himself who became an officer in the Mexican military.[74]

Yet again, the Mexicans and Pueblo Indigenes too had a vote on unfolding events and by January 1847 they cast their ballot decisively when they erupted, and murdered every U.S. national in Taos, New Mexico (later a haunt of Euro-American bohemians), including the occupier's chief delegate, whose body was chopped into small bits.[75]

This was preceded by a Christmas conspiracy in 1846 by a similar association which threatened the death of all Euro-Americans and their fellow Texas interlopers in the territory.[76] This too was a harbinger of conflict to come, this time stoked by the new U.S. state of Texas, which by 1850 threatened secession and war unless its outsized claims to New Mexico territory were recognized.[77]

* * *

This odiously brisk commerce in Africans was of a piece with Texas's hemispheric dreams. Texans were prominent in the "Knights of the Golden Circle," which sought to expand hegemony southward. Sam Houston—a founder of the Lone Star republic—was said to have a "threefold 'Grand Plan'" involving the swallowing of Mexico, somehow settling the sectional conflict, then following his friend Andrew Jackson as U.S. president. Evidently he was not the head of KGC although, says historian Ollinger Crenshaw, others had reason to

---

73. J.H. Hammond to John C. Calhoun, 10 May 1844, in J. Franklin Jameson, ed., *Correspondence of John C. Calhoun*, Washington, D.C., 1899, 953 (abbrev. Jameson).

74. Mekala Shadd-Sartor Audain, "Mexican Canaan: Fugitive Slaves and Free Blacks on the American Frontier, 1804-1867," Ph.D. dissertation, Rutgers U, 2014, 106 (abbrev. Audain).

75. Note in Stella M. Drum, ed., *Down the Santa Fe Trail and Into Mexico: The Diary of Susan Shelby Magoffin, 1846-1847*, Lincoln: U of Nebraska Press, 1962, 190 (abbrev. Drum).

76. Keith William Cox, "Conflicts of Interest: Race, Class, Mexicanidad and the Negotiation of Rule in U.S. Occupied Mexico, 1846-1848," Ph.D. dissertation, U of California-Riverside, 2007, 127 (abbrev. Cox).

77. Walter Louis Buenger, "Stilling the Voice of Reason: Texas and the Union," Ph.D. dissertation, Rice U, 1979, 6 (abbrev. Buenger).

think he was. Thus, many within the KGC found the U.S. Civil War to be a diversion from the necessary work of attacking southward.[78]

Predictably, Texas—an outgrowth of Mexico—provided the strongest support for the KGC; one of its central nodes was in San Antonio, and the largest number of "Knights" were in the state.[79] In early 1865 Francis P. Blair of Missouri, with Washington's knowledge, came to Richmond and conferred with "President" Jefferson Davis, and proposed that the combatants unite to attack Mexico, a quintessential KGC idea.[80] Again, this was an anticipation of a full-blown U.S. imperialism in which Texas was instrumental.

*   *   *

As Jefferson Davis struggled to reach Texas in 1865 for the rebels' final stand in conjunction with French-backed Mexico, Major General Gordon Granger approached Galveston with a Union force thought to be comprised of upwards of 75% Negro troops.[81]

The composition of this force made sense not only because, as the Spanish had discovered decades earlier, these troops were more determined than most to fight—a quality that was desperately required in light of the depth of the challenge—but, as well, they were ideal to vouchsafe the order issued on 19 June reiterating the legality of abolition, or what came to be known as "Juneteenth." For Davis and his fellow desperados thought they could rally the erstwhile "Lost Cause" from their new residence in Mexico, then retake Texas and the Southwest, and as one student bluntly put it, "they could launch raids and continue to kill Yankees (Jefferson Davis's loose plan when he fled)"—or alternatively akin to Texan slaveholder, Frank McMullen, one could flee all the way to Brazil and form "New Texas" in a slaveholding empire that could challenge Washington diplomatically, perhaps militarily.[82]

78. Ollinger Crenshaw, "The Knights of the Golden Circle," *American Historical Review*, 47 (No. 1, October 1941): 23-50, 42 (abbrev. Crenshaw).

79. Charles David Grear, "Texans to the Front: Why Texans Fought the Civil War," Ph.D. dissertation, TCU, 2005, 97 (abbrev. Grear).

80. Note in Douglas Southall Freeman, ed., *Lee's Dispatches: Unpublished Letters of General Robert E. Lee, CSA, to Jefferson Davis and the War Department of the Confederate States of America, 1862-1865*, New York: Putnam's Sons, 1957, 333-334.

81. *Houston Chronicle*, 15 June 2021.

82. Christopher L. Jones, "Deserting Dixie: A History of Emigres, Exiles and Dissenters from the American South, 1866-1925," Brown U, Ph.D. dissertation, 2009, 23, 56.

But most rebels chose to simply cross the border from Texas into Mexico—at times with their erstwhile human property in tow.[83] As matters evolved, it did seem that "Juneteenth" was a pivotal date— for it was on 19 June 1867 that the French puppet in Mexico, the so-called emperor Maximilian, was executed,[84] a severe setback to the scheme of rebels to convert this nation into a rear base from which to reclaim Texas for slavery.

Again, there was often little daylight separating Unionists from traitors in terms of swallowing Mexico. John Russell Young, one of General U.S. Grant's closest companions, wrote breezily postwar that "now that slavery is out of the way there could be no better future for Mexico than absorption in the United States...."[85] To be fair to Young, this was nothing new: in the aftermath of the smashing conquest of Mexican soil in 1848, an "All Mexico Movement" arose which advocated absorbing the entire nation and not just its northern half. This movement gained more traction in the North than the South, as Dixie balked at the thought of "racial mixing" with Mexicans, which in turn argued for stark imperialism:[86] economic exploitation bolstered by political domination.

However, it was then that what seemed to be a rosy dawn of freedom was swiftly drowned in death as Texas solidified its already extant role as the continental epicenter of counter-revolution. Between 1865 and 1868, as the reborn nation was struggling to solidify a new birth of freedom, Texas led the nation in total number of homicides.[87] Historian Fawn Brodie, in her study of abolitionist hero Thaddeus Stevens, concluded morosely that at that point Texas "Negroes were worse off in that state than any other...."[88] Not unrelated is the point that there

---

83. Note in Ramón Eduardo Ruiz, ed., *An American in Maximilian's Mexico, 1865-1866: The Diaries of William Marshall Anderson*, Huntington Library, 1959, 57 (abbrev. R.E. Ruiz).

84. "Introduction," in William A. Link, ed., *United States Reconstruction Across the Americas*, Gainesville: U Press of Florida, 2019, 1-10, 7.

85. John Russell Young, *Around the World with General Grant, Volume 2*, New York: American News Company, 1879, 448.

86. Adrienne Helene Caughfield, *Mothers of the West: Women in Texas and their Roles in Manifest Destiny, 1820-1860*, TCU, 2002, 135 (abbrev. Caughfield).

87. Bearington Cecil Curtis, "A Sisyphean Task: Reevaluating Reconstruction in Texas Under the Command of Major General Charles Griffin," M.A. thesis, TA&MU, 2020, 8 (abbrev. B.C. Curtis). See also John Pressley Carrier, "A Political History of Texas During the Reconstruction, 1865-1874," Ph.D. dissertation, Vanderbilt U, 1971.

88. Fawn M. Brodie, *Thaddeus Stevens, Scourge of the South*, New York: Norton, 1959, 235; Robert Walter Shook, "Federal Occupation and Administration of Texas," Ph.D. dissertation, UNT, 1970, 207 (abbrev. Shook).

was a lesser amount of property confiscation in Texas compared to other slave giants, e.g., Virginia, South Carolina and Georgia.[89]

A reason for the reign of terror inflicted on Texas Africans exposed the dialectic of why the state generated such a fierce response—because it faced a fierce challenge. It was in November 1866, when the die of Ku Klux Klan ascendancy was hardly cast, when the man who became known as Governor James Throckmorton of Texas announced portentously: "The Negroes are drilling [in] many localities in this state. They are armed."[90]

Nevertheless, the fate of Negroes was bound up with Union "allies" who seemed to outdo the most genocidal Texans. Shonda Buchanan, a self-proclaimed "Black Indian" of Choctaw and Cherokee ancestry, had not forgotten in 2019 that General Philip Sheridan of the U.S. military announced dreadfully back then in words that continue to alarm that "the only good Indians I ever saw were dead."[91] Such an "ally" was bound to produce a violent political climate that could only harm the newly freed and would compel the Negroes to align against Indigenes with whom they had shared a trench quite recently.

In this fluid post-1865 atmosphere just north of Texas in "Indian Territory," Richard Morgan, a Negro born in Virginia in 1854 and who married a Choctaw, reminded an inquirer in 1937 that "Negro slaves of Choctaws received forty acres" post-slavery, unlike those he had left behind in the Cradle of the Confederacy: "the government paid the Choctaws for land given the Negro."[92]

"Indian Territory" reflected the dialectic of radical reform vs. reaction in a manner as profound as its southern neighbor, Texas. One analyst has observed that what became Oklahoma at that juncture had "more bandits, horse thieves, counterfeiters, whisky peddlers and train robbers per square mile...than any other place in the United States"; it "wasn't uncommon...for travelers to disappear and never be heard from again...." At the same time "Black Deputy Marshals...in the Indian Territory...had the authority to arrest whites and defend their lives in doing so...they had the authority to kill whites...if the situation called for it," which was "unique for the United States at the time...." Nevertheless, the "allies" of the Negro liquidated "Indian Territory," then by 1907 established the state

89. Shook, 244-245.

90. James Throckmorton to General Kidoo, Box 2H 28, James Throckmorton Papers, UT-A (abbrev. Throckmorton Papers).

91. Shonda Buchanan, *Black Indian: A Memoir*, Detroit: Wayne State U Press, 2019, vii.

92. Oral History, Richard Morgan, 14 April 1937, Indian Pioneer Papers, UOk-N (abbrev. IPP).

of Oklahoma—whose initial bills imposed Jim Crow.[93] The Sooner State has been described as resembling a meat cleaver lurking above Texas, its blade dripping with the blood of the Red River. But the implicit threat of the foregoing rise of Negroes tended to dissipate after Indian Territory was largely dissolved.[94]

Similarly problematic is the betrayal of Africa itself involved in this post-1865 marriage of convenience with the Union. The man who became known as Sir Henry Stanley, a Confederate warrior—he was taken prisoner at Shiloh—by 1867 was battling Comanches and Kiowas on behalf of the U.S., before decamping to Abyssinia, where his British homeland was then enmeshed in hostilities. Of course he had a "fever of admiration" for Confederate military hero P.G.T. Beauregard, accorded discredit by leading the attack on Fort Sumter in 1861.[95] Stunningly, "Sir Henry" confessed bluntly that "lessons derived from the near extinction of the Indian are very applicable to Africa," as he went on to praise the virtues of "breech-loading rifles…."[96]

Texas Negroes had a small margin for error: sharing a frontline with the likes of Sir Henry was a prescription for catastrophe. For in 1868, as he was en route to the Horn of Africa, the Freedmen's Bureau, an early social welfare agency reported morosely from Austin, Texas, about the "bitterness of the prejudice which still exists against the education of the colored people…upon subject of the education of the freedmen there is but little difference in sentiment among the great mass of the people between those who are loyal and those who are not"—i.e., settler rebels and patriots. Schoolhouses were torched, schoolteachers were assaulted, along with schoolchildren. The only recommendation proffered then was "send us some male teachers" as "they would be less exposed to insult or outrage"—or even "murder"[97]—but this would only reinforce patriarchal hierarchies to the overall detriment of the community.

*   *   *

93. Burton, 161, 164, 214.

94. Russell Cobb, *The Great Oklahoma Swindle: Race, Religion and Lies in America's Weirdest State*, Lincoln: U of Nebraska Press, 2020, 74 (abbrev. Cobb).

95. Dorothy Stanley, ed., *The Autobiography of Sir Henry Morton Stanley*, Boston: Houghton Mifflin, 1909, 186, 235, 445 (abbrev. D. Stanley).

96. Henry M. Stanley, *My Early Travels and Adventures in America and Asia*, London: Low, Marston, 1895, x.

97. Austin Bureau to Major J.J. Reynolds, 17 October 1868, Reel 1, Records of the Assistant Commissioner for the State of Texas, Bureau of Refugees, Freedmen and Abandoned Land, 1865-1869, U of Houston-Texas (abbrev. FBR).

It was in 1867 when the coiner of the "Lost Cause," the mythical rationalization of Dixie defeat, conceded on the last page of his 752-page tome that the war settled only the issue of union and abolition—but not "Negro Equality" nor "Negro Suffrage."[98] This became the mantra not just of unrepentant rebels but was the underpinning of what was to emerge in ultra-right and proto-fascist movements that soon emerged.

William Cowper Brann of Austin and Waco was among the most vitriolic, adding contemptuously, "if the South is ever to rid herself of the negro-rape fiend she must take a day off and kill every member of the accursed race that declines to leave the country...."[99] Negroes should have realized that genocide against Indigenes only prepared the ground for genocide against themselves.

But, again, the ferocity of reaction was so strident since the ruling class faced a uniquely redoubtable challenge. Thus, the Negro William Goyens had migrated to Nacogdoches by 1820 and controlled 13,000 acres of land by 1856, while the Ashworth brothers, arguably the wealthiest of Free Negroes regionally, controlled 2000 acres and other assets. The percentage of Negro landowners increased by a magnitude of 14 between 1870 and 1890, and as late as 1924 Texas had a disproportionately large number of Black property and landowners.[100] The momentum generated by pre-existing Spanish and Mexican rule, which stressed religious adherence—Catholicism— while the incoming settlers stressed "race,"[101] both uplifted some Negroes while impelling the latest Negrophobes to resist ever more stoutly further gains. Texas had more land than other states in any case, and the powerful resistance of Indigenes and the role of the "Buffalo Soldiers" created conditions for land concessions to Negroes. Hence, in northeast Texas, the heart of the "Black Belt," there were a shocking 46 Negroes lynched between 1883 and 1923—which began to decline because, as one analysis posited, "Blacks began to fight back." There were armed pitched battles in Simsboro, for example, between "armed Blacks" and their opponents, reminiscent of 1866. It was back then that a group of Negroes told Washington poignantly,

---

98. Edward A. Pollard, *The Lost Cause: A New Southern History of the War of the Confederates*, New York: E.B. Treat, 1866, 752 (abbrev. Pollard).

99. William Cowper Brann, *A Collection of Writings of W.C. Brann, Volume 1*, Waco: Herz, 1905, 27, 24 (abbrev. Brann).

100. Levander, 21-48, 40.

101. Gerald Horne, *The Dawning of the Apocalypse: The Roots of Slavery, White Supremacy, Settler Colonialism and Capitalism in the Long 16th Century*, New York: Monthly Review Press, 2020 (abbrev. Horne, *Dawning*).

"we would prefer to live by ourselves rather than scattered among the whites." Thus, landownership rose more vertiginously in Texas than in any other Southern state. In 1870 only 1.8% of the state's Black farmers owned land, but by 1890, this figure had risen to 26% and peaked at 31% by the turn of the century.[102]

The very strength of Africans mandated that maximum strength had to be deployed to keep this rebellious and cheap labor force in check. Thus, by some measures the "Slocum Massacre" in East Texas in 1910 was more fatal for Negroes than better-known pogroms in Tulsa and Rosewood, Florida, and was dubbed "one of the largest mass murders of blacks in American history," an "act of genocide," in sum, an emblem of an emerging fascism.[103]

In the following pages, I will trace this dialectic between repression and resistance. Texas, which has been a leader in genocide,[104] enslavement, chauvinism of various sorts, dispossession, demagogy, wars of aggression, shameless patriarchy, instrumentalized religion, battered labor facilitated by class collaboration in the Pan-European community—and worse—even today is a harbinger of what could become a full-blown U.S. fascism: unless its historic adversaries intervene.

---

102. Thad Sitton and James H. Conrad, *Freedom Colonies: Independent Black Texans in the Time of Jim Crow*, Austin: U of Texas Press, 2005, 168, 170, 179, 2 (abbrev. Sitton and Conrad).

103. E.R. Bills, *The 1910 Slocum Massacre: An Act of Genocide in East Texas*, Charleston, S.C.: History Press, 2014, 115-116 (abbrev. E.R. Bills).

104. See Paul Burba, *Country of the Cursed and the Driven: Slavery and the Texas Borderlands*, Lincoln: University of Nebraska Press, 2021, 8: "Prior to the latter half of the nineteenth century, Texas was, at its core, a series of Indigenous homelands, the home of Conchos, Sumas, Cocoyames, Mesquites, Cacalotes, Opoxmes, Conejos, Polacmes, Puliques, Poxsalmes, Payayas, Pastias, Pampopas, Cacaxtles, Pacuaches, Ijibas, Apaysis, Apes, Yoricas, Ocanas, Sampanals, Xarames, Ervipiames, Avavares, Cantonas, Mandones, Chalomes, Sanas, Emets, Cavas, Tohos, Mariames, Tohahas, Pansius, Panequos, Apasams, Muruams, Manams, Naamans, Caisquetebanas, Mayeyes, Biskatronges, Kironas, Palaquechares, Teaos, Yojuanes, Simaomas, Tusonibis, Cascosis, Coapites, Cujanes, Clamcoehs, Temerlouans, Querechos, Escanjaques, Vaqueros, Llaneros, Natagés, Lipanes, Mescaleros, Hasinais, Nabedaches, Nacogdoches, Nadacos, Neches, Nasonis, Caddohadachos, Natchitoches, Adais, Guascos, Tonkawas, Taovayas, Tawakonis, Wichitas, Iscanis, Cocos, Orcoquizas, Bidais, Deadoses, Attacapas, Opelousas, and others."

Chapter 1

Before the Counter-Revolution, 1750-1829

Like many regions that were to comprise the United States, Texas too was wracked with instability and unrest before joining the Union. The slayer of Alexander Hamilton, Aaron Burr, had plans as early as 1806 to establish an independent republic in northern Mexico—farming a mere 40,000 acres under Spanish aegis was his version of the story. The intense contestation between the new republic and Madrid proceeded apace, though Spain had boosted its rival into independence post-1776 as a blow against London.

What is remarkable about this skein of events was how flexible the United States was in pursuing its continental objectives. Thus, in the early 19th century, the republic actually armed Comanches in order to undermine colonial Spain[1]—before turning on this Indigenous grouping with a vengeance once Madrid was ousted. The maladroitness of their opponents was a factor too in insuring republican victory. Bernardo de Gálvez, who bequeathed his name to the once premier port that was Galveston and was christened as the "Spanish Hero of the American Revolution," early on called for "total extermination" of the Apaches, which anticipated and gave sustenance to the genocidal republican battle cry.[2]

Part of the problem for Indigenes was that the influx of settlers placed pressure on these original inhabitants to migrate—which often brought them into conflict and competition with others in this category. As they migrated, they often had been weakened by the hammering blows administered by colonizers: the Indigenous population south of the border in "New Spain" declined by a reputed 85% in the century following the initial 16th-century invasion. It was

---

1. Ed Bradley, "Forgotten Filibusters: Private Hostile Expeditions from the United States into Spanish Texas, 1812-1821," Ph.D. dissertation, U of Illinois, 1999, 35 (abbrev. Bradley).

2. Gonzalo M. Quintero Saravia, *Bernardo de Gálvez: Spanish Hero of the American Revolution*, Chapel Hill: U of North Carolina Press, 2018, 309.

unusual for two countries that shared a common border to share fewer commonalities than the U.S. and Mexico—but the history of bludgeoning Indigenes was a commonality, which worked to the disadvantage of the soon to be plundered Mexico.[3]

Even as Mexico was striding toward independence, it was waging war against Comanches[4]—who had appeared in New Mexico in the early 18th century; and in the early 19th century, Alabama Coushatta and Choctaw alike migrated to Texas. When intimidating Comanche proceeded to best Spanish invaders in San Saba, Texas, and on the Red River in 1758, this may have incited Gálvez's aforementioned blood-curdling demand. Moving south from Kansas into Texas were the Taovaya, the Wichita, the Tonkawa (pushed out of northwestern Oklahoma by 1601, then further south by the Apaches by 1700), and the Tawakoni (from Oklahoma to Texas), while the Hasinai moved from Texas to Oklahoma. Virtually all of these peoples were decimated—minimally, as a direct result of the arrival of repeated waves of European settlers—and this lengthy list included the Xarame and the Xaranames, along with the Bidais and Orcoquizas and others wiped out, leaving fewer traces. Gálvez notwithstanding, by the late 18th century there was a Spanish-Comanche alliance against the Lipan Apache, then perceived to be as menacing as Madrid's temporary ally.

Wiser Comanches and Lipan began to ally by 1794, and by 1803 more Indigenes were fleeing helter-skelter upon the arrival of the victorious republicans from the east, already with a well-deserved reputation for grisliness. Choctaws, Atakapas and Coushatta were among those who petitioned to move into Texas. Although the Texas census of 1783 listed 36 Negroes, and that of 1785 showed merely 41, regulations to bar an uprising of the enslaved were rigorous—as it was recognized that this class was quite prone to upend the status quo. It is likely that these figures did not include a growing number of bonded laborers from Louisiana fleeing from New Orleans due west.

However, the authorities would have done well to pay more attention to the credible rumors about an influx of Euro-Americans into Texas, especially given the downturn in relations between Madrid and the republicans.[5]

---

3. Comment: Gilbert M. Joseph and Timothy Henderson, eds., *The Mexico Reader: History, Culture, Politics*, Durham: Duke U Press, 2002, 3, 120 (abbrev. Joseph and Henderson).

4. Letter, 19 April 1815, Box 6, José Marcos Mugarrieta Papers, UC-B (abbrev. Mugarrieta Papers).

5. Odie B. Faulk, "The Last Years of Spanish Texas, 1778-1821," Ph.D. dissertation, TTU, 1962, 34, 86, 88, 94, 108-9, 157, 191, 195, 200-1 (abbrev. Faulk).

It was not just the Comanches who were pushed into Texas. From Wyoming others were forced to move by the pressure of the Lakota [Sioux]. Many proved willing to consort with Euro-Americans but were justifiably hostile to the Euro-Texans. The Kiowas were pushed into Texas from Montana at the behest of the Cheyenne and Arapaho and out of the Black Hills by the Lakota. This commonness brought them closer to the Comanches. Choctaws and Chickasaws who wound up in Indian Territory were mutually hostile, catnip for settlers. Indigenes with deeper roots in Texas, e.g., the Karankawas, were hostile to the arrival of settlers and thus were deemed to be treacherous and worthy of liquidation. The same held true for the Wacos, Tahaucanos, Bidais, Aranama, Tonkawas—though the latter were viewed more benignly by settlers than the Karankawas.[6]

This benignity toward certain Indigenes too did not survive, for after presiding over their degradation, Stephen F. Austin dismissed them contemptuously as "great beggars,"[7] a process of humiliation that Negroes—post-1865—came to know all too well. Not long after setting up shop in Texas, the younger Austin launched what was called an "all-out war of extermination" against those he later derided. Since 90% of his fellow settlers came from the slaveholding regions of the U.S.—with Louisiana, Alabama and Arkansas accounting for more than half of the settlers—he was able to back up his brash actions and words with fire and the sword.[8]

Spain, then Mexico, had immense difficulty in combating daunting Indigenes, not least since their adherents were often grossly outnumbered, a reality buttressed by compelling settlers to profess at least nominal Catholicism at a time when anti-Vatican sentiment continentally was hardly absent. The non-Indigenous, non-enslaved population in Texas in 1809 was said to be a mere 4155, while in 1819 the Indigenous population was reportedly 12,000—likely a gross undercount—with Comanches the largest amongst this diverse grouping. The 1792 census included 34 Africans and 414 defined

---

Note: for the convenience of readers I will use geographic designations, e.g., "Oklahoma" before such terms were cognizable legally.

6. M.P. Mayhall, "Indian Relations in Texas, 1820-1835," n.d., Box 2 B 112, Eugene Barker Papers, UT-A (abbrev. Mayhall).

7. Kelly Frank Himmel, "Anglo-Texans, Karankawas and Tonkawas, 1821-1859: A Sociological Analysis of Conquest," Ph.D. dissertation, UT-A, 1995, 102 (abbrev. Himmel).

8. Andrew J. Torget, *Seeds of Empire: Cotton, Slavery and the Transformation of the Texas Borderlands, 1800-1850*, Chapel Hill: U of North Carolina Press, 2015, 93, 85 (abbrev. Torget, *Seeds*).

as "mulatto."[9] At that point in Coahuila, the Mexican province with which Texas was to be yoked, 18.5% of the urban node that was Monterrey was also deemed to be "mulatto" and 50.2% were "*castas*," which could include people with some African ancestry. In Nacogdoches 28% then were said to be "Afro-mestizo";[10] the good news was that the heterogeneity south of Texas was to serve as a stumbling block for many of Washington's racially minded expansionists. It would require a shifting of settler requisites from religion to "race"—Pan-Europeanism, in sum, that pointedly did not exclude French Catholics—that could attract the gross numbers to overwhelm Indigenes and Africans to produce the wealth to attract them likewise.

This shift was both propelled and shaped by the Treaty of Fort Adams in 1801 between the Choctaw and the U.S., when the former at gunpoint were compelled to cede over 2 million acres, including a good deal of Mississippi, which provided momentum for the Indian Removal Act of 1830 that wounded Cherokees severely.[11] These massive land grabs then necessitated the need for more settlers and enslaved laborers to develop this territory.

Texas's neighbor, Louisiana, was replete with Catholics: thus, Frenchmen as of the early 1800s dominated the slaveholding class. Even the aforementioned affluent Negro settler, William Goyens, who owned six enslaved persons, was reportedly Catholic.[12]

Heavily Protestant London also sought to insert itself into continental affairs, fittingly given its foothold in Canada. Yet one of the major reasons why Indigenes were unable to prevail was because of their difficulty in brokering a consistent alliance with this global power, which had been adumbrated when the Cherokees and Creeks dispatched an envoy to London in the late 18th century.[13]

The Cherokees thought they had made a wise bet when many of them led by Billy Bowles moved to Texas in 1824, but that only set

9. Bradley, 62.

10. Audain, 37.

11. S. Charles Bolton, *Fugitivism: Escaping Slavery in the Lower Mississippi Valley, 1820-1860*, Fayetteville: U of Arkansas Press, 2019, 50 (abbrev. Bolton).

12. James M. McReynolds, "Family Life in a Borderland Community: Nacogdoches, Texas, 1779-1861," Ph.D. dissertation, TTU, 1978, 180 (abbrev. McReynolds). See also Linda E. Devereaux, "William Goyens: Black Leader in Early Texas," *East Texas Historical Journal*, 45 (No. 1, 2007): 52-57, 54.

13. Benjamin Baynton, *Authentic Memoirs of William Augustus Bowles, Esquire: Ambassador from the United Nations of Creeks and Cherokees to the Court of London*, London: Faulder, 1791.

them on a path to conflict with not only the U.S. but secessionist Texas too.[14]

Still, the Kickapoo and redcoats jointly defeated the U.S. at Prairie du Chien in today's Wisconsin, slowing down the settlers.[15] Moreover, the Creeks, who were pro-London during the 1812 war, also owned enslaved Africans, which in the long run likely weakened their overall posture.[16]

On the other hand, the Cherokees were to emerge as leading enslavers among Indigenes and assimilated as much as any to the dominant culture of the slaveholders' republic, pledging not to join the "Pan-Indian" army of the great Tecumseh, perhaps the final opportunity to mount an effective challenge to the invaders.[17]

Nonetheless, Andrew Jackson, who earned credibility among settlers because of his ironfisted approach to Indigenes, concluded early on that Indigenes would have been more easily defeated but for the external aid rendered not only by London but what was thought to be an "Anglo-Spanish alliance" besides. This was a critical factor in explicating the difficulty of the U.S. in seizing Indigenous land; another was the heavy reliance in neighboring Louisiana on enslaved workers who as of 1810 were said to comprise 55.2% of the total population of the state. (This figure declined to 51.8% by 1820 but had risen to an all-time high of 58.5% by 1830 before plummeting thereafter in nervous reaction to the Nat Turner slave revolt in Virginia in 1831: Governor A.B. Roman of the Pelican State pointed to this population disparity then and its manifest downside.)[18]

Less than a decade earlier Roman was among the settlers who were startled by the news from St. Martinville in a region still larded with the Atakapa ethnic group, that Mexico's constitution was guaranteeing freedom and equality for Africans: predictably the Africans

---

14. Donaly E. Brice, *The Great Comanche Raid: Boldest Indian Attack on the Texas Republic*, Austin: Eakin, 1987, 3 (abbrev. Brice).

15. Jennifer Kirsten Stinson, "Black Bondspeople, White Masters and Mistresses and the Americanization of the Upper Mississippi River Lead District," *Journal of Global Slavery*, 1 (2016): 165-195, 171.

16. W. Craig Gaines, *The Confederate Cherokees: John Drew's Regiment of Mounted Rifles*, Baton Rouge: Louisiana State U Press, 1989, 16 (W.C. Gaines), Louisiana State University (abbrev. LSU).

17. John Sedgwick, *Blood Moon: An American Epic of War and Splendor in the Cherokee Nation*, New York: Simon & Schuster, 2018, 99 (abbrev. Sedgwick).

18. Roland McConnell, *Negro Troops of Antebellum Louisiana: A History of the Battalion of Free Men of Color*, Baton Rouge: LSU Press, 1968, 102 (abbrev. McConnell, *Negro Troops*).

immediately fled westward, further complicating Louisiana's security. The Plan of Iguala in 1821 too guaranteed all inhabitants the same; then Mexico refused to ratify a commercial treaty with the United States until the provision of return of runaway enslaved Africans was removed[19]—which incurred the wrath of its northern neighbor.

The Plan of Iguala was bound to upset the slaveholders' republic, insofar as it foreshadowed equality and abolition, which was viewed in the slaveholders' republic the way the creation of a socialist Cuba was viewed in the U.S. in the 20th century.[20] "When I speak of Americans," said Agustín de Iturbide with prescience, "I speak not only of those persons born in [the] Americas but the Europeans, Africans and Asians who reside here," speaking of Mexico. Equating Africans, routinely treated like cattle north of his homeland, with Europeans was like flashing a red flag in the face of a bull.[21]

Historian John Sedgwick asserted that Andrew Jackson, the military hero, espied "two classes of humanity he most reviled—the British and any Indians who collaborated with them...."[22] Jackson earned his stripes by besting London at the Battle of New Orleans in 1815 and had firsthand experience with the presence on U.S. soil of ebony redcoats dispatched from Jamaica and the resultant ripples in the Gulf of Mexico[23]; about two decades earlier he acknowledged that the southern states could secede unless the other prong of insecurity—Indigenes—were vanquished or controlled, an issue that bubbled to the surface in Texas on the eve of civil war, as Robert Neighbors was slain. The 1812 war had hardly been concluded before the U.S. pressed Indigenes—especially Wyandots, Delawares, Shawnees, Senekas [sic] and Miamis—to assist the slaveholders' republic in soon-to-come wars with other foes. The pact with the Creeks specifically demanded that they "abandon all communication" with London and Madrid.[24]

---

19. Bolton, 84.

20. Levander, 21-48, 36.

21. Agustín de Iturbide, "Plan of Iguala," in Joseph and Henderson, 192-195, 192.

22. Sedgwick, 100.

23. Gerald Horne, *Negro Comrades of the Crown: African Americans and the British Empire Fight the U.S. Before Emancipation*, New York: NYU Press, 2013 (abbrev. Horne, *Negro Comrades*).

24. "Message from the President of the United States...Ratified Treaties... with the Several Tribes of Indians Called Wyandots, Delawares, Shawnees, Senekas and Miamis; the Other on Ninth of August 1814 with the Creek

Even James Wilkinson, with whom Jackson had clashed, termed the Comanches the "most powerful nation of savages on this continent,"[25] whose presence in Texas complicated mightily the U.S.'s manifest desire to expand westward, along with their unsteady existence in Louisiana. A 20th century study declared flatly that "in warfare no one surpassed them...." However, the colonizers had multiple tools at their disposal, bullets and disease among them, with the latter exacting a heavy toll by 1816.[26] Nevertheless, the consensus is that settlers had more to fear from Comanches than any other Indigenous grouping.[27]

Yet indicative of the strategic dilemma faced by invaders, it was Wilkinson who in 1806, speaking from the Arkansas River, mused emphatically if "the greater danger is not to be comprehended from the <u>Pawnee</u> [not the Comanches]...than any other nation of savages in <u>Louisiana</u> not only owing to their intercourse with the Mexicans proper but to their friendship for the Spaniards, who have regular factors amongst them."[28] [emphasis in original]

The existence of the state to which Wilkinson referred—Louisiana—was made more complex and unbalanced when the African Slave Trade was barred officially in 1807-1808,[29] which made more valuable the Africans then fleeing into alien territory.

Just before then, Jackson expressed the Washington consensus when he snapped, "I hate the Dons [Spaniards]. I would delight to see Mexico reduced,"[30] an opinion formed doubtlessly by incipient abolitionism south of the border—a movement symbolized by the president of African descent, born in 1782, Vicente Guerrero, who in 1829 presided over emancipation.[31]

Nation of Indians....23 February 1815," Washington: Way, 1815, Huntington Library.

25. Brian DeLay, *War of a Thousand Deserts*, New Haven: Yale U Press, 2008, 7 (abbrev. DeLay).

26. Ernest Wallace and E.A. Hoebel, *The Comanches: Lords of the South Plains*, Norman: U of Oklahoma Press, 1952, 34 (abbrev. Wallace and Hoebel).

27. Mayhall.

28. James Wilkinson to Dear Sir, 26 October 1806, Carton 46, Herbert Bolton Papers, UC-B (abbrev. Bolton Papers).

29. Audain, 33.

30. Andrew Jackson to W.C. Claiborne, 12 November 1806, in John Spencer Bassett, ed., *The Correspondence of Andrew Jackson*, Washington, D.C.: Carnegie, 1926, 153 (abbrev. Bassett).

31. Eugene Wilson Harrell, "Vicente Guerrero and the Birth of Modern Mexico, 1821-1831," Ph.D. dissertation, Tulane U, 1976.

Thus Jackson—Guerrero's counterpoint—asserted prematurely, "add Mexico either to the union or by an alliance" which would "add to the growing greatness of America," i.e., "punishing the Dons and adding Mexico to the United States."[32]

There was reason for Jackson's ire. As early as 1758 and proceeding briskly thereafter, runaways from various regions were reaching the borders of what was soon to become independent Mexico, thereby weakening the lands from which they fled.[33] There had been a similar problem in Spanish Florida for decades[34]—if not centuries[35]—which led to the successful effort to grab this key peninsula, as Mexico was surging toward independence. The slaveholders' republic, said historian Alan Taylor, disliked Florida's laws that "protected slaves from abuse." Of course, Miguel Hidalgo, the vector of independence in "New Spain"—unlike the Founding Father for whom slaveholders named their capital—actually wanted to ban slavery.[36]

Those defined as "mulatto" were in the vanguard of the revolt against Spanish rule early in the century and were among those who demanded that slavery be proscribed forever—unlike the anti-colonial movement in their northern neighbor.[37]

Hidalgo's abolitionism was made easier by the decline of the peculiar institution in Mexico. It was virtually extinct beyond Vera Cruz and as late as 1793—when the slaveholders' republic was heading in the opposite direction—there were about 10,000 enslaved in the entire nation, and this number continued on its downward slide until it was euthanized in 1829, an event which became a source of tension with Texas settlers compelling secession.[38]

---

32. Andrew Jackson to Daniel Smith, 12 November 1806, Bassett, 154.

33. Maria Esther Hammack, "The Other Underground Railroad: Hidden Histories of Slavery and Freedom Across the Porous Frontiers of Nineteenth Century United States, Mexico and the Caribbean," M.A. thesis, East Carolina U, 2015, 41 (abbrev. Hammack).

34. Gerald Horne, *The Counter-Revolution of 1776: Slave Resistance and the Origins of the United States of America*, New York: NYU Press, 2014.

35. Horne, *Dawning*.

36. Alan Taylor, *American Republics: A Continental History of the United States, 1783-1850*, New York: Norton, 2021, 127, 128, 301.

37. José M. Morelos, "Sentiments of the Nation...." Joseph and Henderson, 189-191, 190.

38. Lester Gladstone Bugbee, "Slavery in Early Texas," *Political Science Quarterly*, 13 (1898): 389-412, 648-668, 389 (abbrev. Bugbee, Slavery).

Even Spanish-dominated Nacogdoches had few slaves by the 1820s.[39] By 1828 the Cherokees, not renowned for their abolitionist views, announced in their primary periodical that "one great advantage which New Spain [Mexico] enjoys over her neighbors, both to the north and south" was the relative dearth of the enslaved.[40]

* * *

By 1813 the redcoats were accused credibly of organizing a guerrilla army in Florida of Indigenes and Africans, supplied from the Bahamas and Jamaica, spreading terror north to Georgia and west to Louisiana, which fueled rumors of an imminent revolt of the enslaved along the Gulf of Mexico. At that point there were bases on Amelia Island off the coast of Georgia, and Galveston too, of armed Africans—the slaveholders' nightmare. The panicked republic responded to this angst-ridden environment by sending thousands of troops to the frontier, suggesting its vulnerability and how the U.S. could be thrown off-kilter by a small deployment from London. Jefferson, then Madison, had conducted their own covert actions, sponsoring filibustering to Florida and Texas too. A so-called Republic of Texas was proclaimed as early as 1813 in San Antonio.[41]

However, their French comrades acted similarly, seeking to install Joseph Bonaparte in power in Mexico.[42] These lancing thrusts were so complexifying that in 1818 even the slaveholders' republic passed an anti-filibustering bill,[43] observed in the breach, naturally.

The choppy gulf waters were roiled further by the anti-Madrid eruptions then coursing through Mexico, which contributed to the development of the potent slave port that was Galveston. Magnetically operating in tandem was the voracious appetite in Louisiana

---

39. Lauren A. Kattner, "Ethnicity Plus: Historical Roots of Slavery for the Germans of Louisiana and East Texas, 1719-1830," Ph.D. dissertation, UT-A, 1997, 35 (abbrev. Kattner).

40. *Cherokee Phoenix & Indians' Advocate*, 15 October 1828.

41. Curtis Wilgus, "Spanish American Patriot Activity Along the Gulf Coast of the United States, 1811-1822," *Louisiana Historical Quarterly*, 4 (1925): 193-215, 199.

42. Rafe Blaufarb, *Bonapartists in the Borderlands: French Exiles and Refugees on the Gulf Coast, 1815-1835*, Tuscaloosa: U of Alabama Press, 2005, 52, 70, 81 (abbrev. Blaufarb).

43. Steven Hahn, *A Nation Without Borders: The United States and Its World in an Age of Civil Wars, 1830-1910*, New York: Penguin, 2017 (abbrev. Hahn).

for bonded labor with the plunder of such pirates as Jean Lafitte sold almost openly in the streets of New Orleans, with this French corsair—consonant with the era—declaring Galveston to be a republican province, as the ineffable tie between flesh peddling and anti-monarchism became more evident.[44]

By 1818 Lafitte was engaged in ferocious warfare with Karankawas in Galveston, as—typically—republicans were seeking to make the island safe for slavery.[45] Shortly thereafter settlers intensified their effort to—as one scholar put it—"exterminate" the Karankawa as "water ran red with [their] blood,"[46] as the path was eased for the arrival of more of the enslaved.

The final decade of Spanish rule in Texas, says one analyst, involved a labyrinth of "shadowy conspiracies and actual invasions, of bloody revolts and bloodless counter-revolution, of comic opera humor and tragic seriousness." Lafitte was not the only Frenchman playing a starring role in this morbidly serious opera bouffe, though he had top billing given his offensive behavior in restive Yucatan and Natchez and his dabbling in a takeover in Nacogdoches by 1819. Yet another Frenchman, Louis Michel Aury, was plotting from New Orleans by 1816 as he mulled over meddling in Venezuela.[47]

Still, Aury, who incorporated Free Negroes into his ranks, clashed on Amelia Island off the coast of Georgia with the so-called "American party" of Jared Irwin and Ruggles Hubbard. The issue was not necessarily slavery vs. anti-slavery but more that Aury's crew was willing to share the booty of slave trading with the men of color in his ranks. It could not have been reassuring that the flag of Mexico was raised over this island, a reversal of what was to come: the U.S. flag flying over Mexican soil.[48] The larger point was the porousness of the purported ban on non-domestic slave trading, which boded well for the future secessionists in Texas.

Nacogdoches, featuring affluent Negroes—the legacy of Spanish rule—was bound to be a center of instability as their reality clashed sharply with the worldview of arriving Euro-American settlers. By 1826 they anticipated 1836 by seeking to secede from Mexico, but they

---

44. Press account of 1918 speech by Eugene Barker, *Slavery Scrapbook*, UT-A. See also William Richard Bridgewater, "Jean Lafitte," M.A. thesis, Rice University [Institute] (abbrev. Rice U), 1930, 46. He hailed from Bordeaux, born in 1780, a region that produced an unhealthy share of enslavers.

45. Mayhall.

46. Himmel, 10.

47. Faulk, 220, 227, 229, 233.

48. Blaufarb, 66, 67.

were unable to win over Indigenes—or Stephen F. Austin, for that matter. Nonetheless, the failure of this "Fredonia Rebellion" infuriated countless Euro-Americans, not least given the pivotal role of Indigenes in squashing a settlers' revolt[49]—a dangerous signal generally contrary to the continental model of development. Apparently, the rebels thought that Indigenes hostile to Mexico could be co-opted, though as a contemporary saw things, the "principal objection of the Fredonians to the Mexican government was the prohibition of slavery [sic]."[50]

Likewise, Mexico too began to look askance at the arrival of these U.S. migrants, which only enhanced the mutual alienation between the parties. Washington was hardly indifferent to this precursor of 1836: their envoy in faraway Vera Cruz reported to Secretary of State Henry Clay in the spring of 1827 that the "disturbances...have been quieted."[51]

The preceding arrival of future Texas secessionists, the Bowie brothers—John, Rezin and James, the latter a notorious knife fighter—also contributed to this destructive trend. Lafitte and the Bowies collaborated, consonant with capitalism, they launched marketing innovations, selling the enslaved for a dollar a pound.[52] Soon they were reaping thousands of dollars by smuggling enslaved Africans into Louisiana and Mississippi, and doing the same in Galveston—contrary to the emerging Mexican ethos. By late 1822 Mexico was debating what would soon become law: no sale or purchase of the enslaved,[53] a blow to this odious profiteering and another step toward dismantling Mexico in commercial revenge.

The early U.S. invaders of Texas were rather footloose. David G. Burnet, first president of the sovereign republic, was born in Newark, New Jersey, in 1788, but by 1806 was freebooting in Venezuela in search of fame and fortune, surrounded by men his biographer said "were from the best American families...." Such environs did not save him from barely escaping death by yellow fever. Then it was a

---

49. N. Doran Maillard, *The History of the Republic of Texas....*, London: Smith, Elder, 1842, 55 (abbrev. Maillard).

50. W.B. Dewees, *Letters from an Early Settler of Texas*, Louisville: Morton & Griswold, 1852, 71-72 (abbrev. Dewees).

51. William Taylor, Consul to Secretary of State Clay, 26 April 1827, Reel 1, Despatches from U.S. Consuls in Vera Cruz, NARA.

52. Bradley, 253.

53. Fred Robbins, "The Origin and Development of the African Slave Trade in Galveston, Texas and Surrounding Areas from 1816 to 1836," *East Texas Historical Journal*, 9 (No. 2, October 1971): 153-161, 156, 157 (abbrev. Robbins).

decade among the Comanches along the Colorado River, providing valuable intelligence for coming conquests.[54]

This rag-tag bunch of settlers, also included, *primus inter pares*, Moses Austin. Earlier he had been in Spanish-controlled Missouri and perambulating on a Spanish passport, then, ruined by the Panic of 1819, like others of his ilk, he migrated southward.[55] Just before he expired in June 1821, he was still trading in enslaved Africans, in conjunction with his entrepreneurial son, Stephen Austin, in a manner that came to be the settlers' hallmark.[56]

The elder Austin cooked up the notion of U.S. nationals flooding into Texas, the ultimate real estate deal, with Indigenous land offered to settlers willing to countenance—or execute—genocide. He had operated with wiliness as a Philadelphia merchant before operating lead mines in Virginia; the younger Austin was born in 1793 and four years later was seeking to stare down the Osage—described as "hostile"—in what was to become the state of Missouri, then "Upper Louisiana." The younger Austin studied in Connecticut and Kentucky, but by 1813 was elected to office in what was to become the "Show Me" State and was regularly elected until 1819, as he began to move southward. But he left with the camaraderie of the influential Thomas Hart Benton, with whom he shared public office in Missouri. The departure of the Austins was inevitably motivated by financial setbacks in that the father was a substantial shareholder in the Bank of St. Louis, which just before 1819 suffered immense setbacks, meaning ruin. Though Mexican independence was ignited in 1810, it was declared formally in 1821, and the younger Austin arrived in Mexico City then, ignorant of the primary languages spoken there. Wracked by instability, the new nation was not in a fortuitous position to consider the immensity of signing off on the Austins' real estate speculation.[57]

---

54. A.M. Hobby, *The Life and Times of David G. Burnet, First President of the Republic of Texas*, Galveston: Steam Book and Job Office of the Galveston News, 1871, 13, 15, 17.

55. Michael Rugeley Moore, "Settlers, Slaves, Sharecroppers and Stockhands: A Texas Plantation Ranch, 1824-1896," M.A. thesis, U of Houston, 2001, 19 (abbrev. M.R. Moore).

56. Receipt for enslaved person, Richmond, 22 January 1821, Box 2B 111, Eugene Barker Collection, UT-A: "...received from Moses Austin a Negro man by the name of Richmond the property of Stephen Fuller Austin...." (abbrev. Barker Collection UT-A).

57. "The Austins and the Beginning of Anglo-American Settlement," n.d., Box 2B 111, Eugene Barker Papers, UT-A. In the same box, see the File on Land Speculation, 1819-1821.

For Austin sought to attract settlers by promising that their newly minted abodes would be exempt from seizure by ravenous creditors. This was a winning appeal, by arbitrage attracting settlers from neighboring jurisdictions, especially Tennessee and Mississippi, as the Panic of 1819 was followed by that of 1837. Crowning the appeal was independent Texas's decision to enact the first homestead exemption law, exempting basic items of personal property from attachment and later elevating this measure to constitutional status, compelling states like Mississippi to do so in order to avoid leaking settlers.[58]

Settlers were also pouring in next door in Arkansas. Their numbers more than doubled from about 14.2 thousand in 1820 to 30.3 thousand a decade later, with the prospect of what was soon to become Indian Territory in close proximity not slowing down their numbers.[59]

With settlers arrived the enslaved, but with British and Haitian pressure, smuggling them into Galveston was becoming more difficult. So, speaking from London, John Scobie counseled that Mexico's exiting from the slave trade officially as of 1824 along with the aforementioned pressure would impel the "slave breeding states"—especially Virginia—to "want Texas as a slave market, to which they can send their surplus population for sale." Eventually this would mean more of the enslaved arriving from Cuba, especially since these workers could cost as little as $300 on the island and as much as $1000 in Texas.[60]

Thus, it was in early 1824 that Secretary of State John Quincy Adams was informed nervously of the animated discussion in Mexico City "in favour [sic] of the abolition of the slave trade."[61] Ineluctably, it was in 1825 that the State Department began to clamor for Mexico to return escaped Africans,[62] a nettlesome and explosive issue for the slaveholders' republic since its founding.

---

58. Joseph A. Ranney, *A Legal History of Mississippi: Race, Class and the Struggle for Opportunity*, Jackson: U Press of Mississippi, 2019, 69.

59. Kelly Houston Jones, *A Weary Land: Slavery on the Ground in Arkansas*, Athens: U of Georgia Press, 2021, 17 (abbrev. K.H. Jones).

60. John Scobie, "Texas: Its Claims to be Recognized as an Independent Power by Great Britain; Examined in a Series of Letters," London: Harvey and Darnton, 1839, Huntington Library (abbrev. Scobie).

61. Santiago Smith Wilcocks to Secretary of State Adams, 8 February 1824, Reel 1, Despatches from U.S. Consuls in Mexico City, NARA.

62. Jose Maria Herrera, "The Blueprint for Hemispheric Hegemony: Joel Roberts Poinsett and the First United Diplomatic Mission to Mexico," Ph.D. dissertation, Purdue U, 2007, 135 (abbrev. Herrera).

Retrospectively, as early as 1824 it would have been possible to foresee a seismic rift between Mexico and its growing abolition-ism and the arriving Euro-American settlers who saw slavery as an emblem of the "freedom" they celebrated. It was in 1823, then reiterated forcefully in 1824, that Mexico declared, "there can be no sale or purchase of slaves which may be introduced…the children of slaves born in [Mexico] shall be free at fourteen years of age,"[63]—as their prime laboring years were beginning, as slaveholders scoffed. More to the point, it was by 1824 that Mexico banned the slave trade foreign and domestic, but contrary to their northern neighbor, this measure was enforced strenuously.[64]

Edward Stiff, a self-described "Texas Emigrant," was dismissive of this effort. "As early as 1823," he said, "the nominal government of Mexico had turned its attention to [the] subject of Negro Slavery" but, he said gleefully, "this decree was easily evaded, particularly in the province of Texas," which led to more stringent laws in 1824, then 1825, "abolishing all future traffic in slaves"—and then the cul-mination, he concluded scornfully, abolition,[65]which in turn spurred London in the same direction in 1833, while the slaveholders' repub-lic remained stubbornly hostile.

Similarly, unlike in the anti-London struggle of the late 18th cen-tury in North America, enslaved Africans in "New Spain" had little reason to join Madrid's side and, instead, were incentivized to fight the royalists. Tellingly, Vicente Guerrero, the president of African descent who in 1829 spearheaded abolition, sided with anti-royalist rebels in 1810.[66]

Slavery, says one scholar, was "almost dead by independence" in 1821 and was banned "without any opposition"[67]—contrary to the so-called "revolutionary republic" to the north. Thus, as Mexico was sprinting toward abolition in the 1820s, the new nation appealed to Free Negroes to come to Texas and, to a degree, fugitive slaves too,[68] which was bound to inflame tensions with pre-existing settlers there.

---

63. "Address to the Reader of the Documents Relating to the Galveston Bay & Texas Land Company….," New York: Hopkins, 1 January 1831, Hun-tington Library.

64. Bugbee, Slavery, 397.

65. Colonel Edward Stiff, The Texas Emigrant: A Narration of the Adventures of the Author in Texas…., Cincinnati: Conclin, 1840, 212 (abbrev. Stiff).

66. Audain, 62.

67. Hammack, 22, 25.

68. Audain, 52.

Anticipating President Guerrero, José M. Tornel introduced a bill two years before his decree for total abolition, which was received with stormy applause in the legislature. The custom in Mexico had been to spend on Independence Day to buy out slaveholders, but the enslaved had become so rare in the capital—unlike Washington—there was difficulty in rounding up a number sufficient to give resonance to the solemn ceremony.[69]

In the prelude to 1829, the state of Coahuila, then yoked to Texas, thoughtfully mandated in 1827 that "manumission...shall not take place when the masters or his heirs are poisoned or assassinated by one of their slaves...."[70]

Ironically, the continuing challenge provided by Spanish royalists was taken advantage of by so-called republicans due north who—purportedly—were anti-monarchy but more than this were pro-slavery and anti-abolition. As late as January 1828 the dual Mexican state of Coahuila and Texas deemed "native Spaniards" to be "dangerous persons," along with those "partial to a monarchical or central form of government."[71] Still, Washington seemed to benefit in 1829 as the envoy in Vera Cruz reported on the "expulsion of the Spaniards...," for the ouster of powerful European nations was a strategic objective of the U.S. so as to reserve exploitation of the hemisphere for itself. In the same sentence he happily told of the "considerable increase of American tonnage" that was "occasioned" by this draconian maneuver.[72]

Mexico was faced with a dual counter-revolutionary threat: one embodied by the likes of Stephen F. Austin, who sought to revolt against abolitionism, and the other symbolized by dead-end Spaniards who longed for a return to monarchy. This contributed to the growing sentiment in Mexico City that both forces could be resisted by overthrowing the local source: the Spanish slavocracy in Havana, a prospect which frightened Washington. The reverse had occurred in

---

69. Lester Gladstone Bugbee, "Slavery in Early Texas," Boston: Ginn, 1899, Baylor University, Waco, Texas I(abbrev. Baylor U). See also Bugbee, "Slavery in Early Texas," *Political Science Quarterly*, 13 (1898).

70. Decree Number 41, 17 January 1828, in J.P. Kimball, translator, *Laws and Decrees of the State of Coahuila and Texas in Spanish and English to which is added the Constitution of Said State: Also the Colonization Law of the State of Tamaulipas and Naturalization Law of the General Congress. By Order of the Secretary of State*, Houston: Telegraph Power Press, 1839, 63 (abbrev. Kimball).

71. Kimball, 96.

72. Report from William Taylor, Consul, July 1829, Reel 1, Despatches from U.S. Consuls in Vera Cruz, NARA.

Havana too, so by 1828 the authorities in Coahuila/Texas were contemplating the necessity to "repel the invasion preparing in Havana by the tyrannical King of Spain for the re-conquest of Mexico...."[73]

*   *   *

In sum, enslaved Africans had little reason to engage in class collaboration and stand beside their enslavers in the face of an external threat to the latter from Indigenes or European powers, for that matter, and this mandated that the U.S. offer more incentives to attract settlers to countervail this conundrum. Simultaneously, the sprawling land south of the border was rapidly becoming an abolitionist lodestar which gave more incentive for the slaveholders' republic to defenestrate it.

Like manna from heaven for the settlers, the man who restored slavery in the French Caribbean was defeated at Waterloo in 1815—and 30,000 of Napoleon's countrymen headed to the U.S., many of them landing in the Deep South. "At no time was American Anglo-phobia more pronounced than in the period 1815-18," and these immigrants did little to tamp down this sentiment. Some of them quickly joined the burgeoning filibuster movement to seize "New Spain." Speeding to the Gulf Coast, from Mobile to New Orleans, were not only French but Polish, Swiss, Italian, Belgian, Dutch, Irish, Spanish and Germans who too had been pro-Napoleon. In Alabama they adapted to enslaving like whales to water. By 1817 these refugees demanded land recently taken from the Choctaw between the Mississippi and Tombigbee rivers.[74]

As should be evident by the pivotal role of New Orleans in the Deep South, the open and notorious secret of the endurance of the inhumane system of enslavement was the instrumental role of the steady infusion of French migrants, many embittered and traumatized by the world historic transformation delivered by the Haitian Revolution. As early as 1819, according to one observer, "the coast of the Red River from the mouth up to Alexandria is inhabited mostly by Creole French. Some of them are wealthy planters."[75]

It was par for the course that leading the charge at Fort Sumter in 1861 was P.G.T. Beauregard, who grew up in Louisiana speaking

---

73. Decree Number 59, 14 May 1828, in Kimball, 101.

74. Blaufarb, 38, 46, 52, 99, 120. As should be evident thus far, for the sake of the reader's clarity I am using terms, e.g., "Italian" or even "Mexican" and "Dixie" that may not have been cognizable at the time.

75. Dewees, 12.

French.[76] The "people of the Confederacy idolized him into a great popular hero, second not even to [Robert E.] Lee," says his biographer, not least since he "fired the opening gun of the great drama at Fort Sumter...."[77]

The slaveholders' republic was gobbling territory rapidly, necessitating more of the enslaved and more settlers to preside over them. However, conflict and discord inhered in this jerry-built system. Those dispossessed were embittered, which then led to cries for "extermination" of them, creating more conflict. Those enslaved had little incentive to stand beside ruling enslavers, creating tremendous opportunities for leverage for those like the Seminoles of Florida or Britain—or Mexico—which meant they too had to be confronted. It was a kind of domino theory, with one land grab seeming to mandate the next. Seizing Louisiana created a backdoor escape for the enslaved to Texas, which meant taking this vast territory. New Orleans was the largest city in the South by 1861 and the most important commercial center there, en route to becoming the planet's largest exporting port (often cotton produced by sullen enslaved).[78] Colonizing Georgia in 1733 created a backdoor escape to Florida, which meant taking this vast territory. Seizing one territory necessitated taking a next-door neighbor, for slavery induced insecurity.[79] The most adamant belligerents thought that taking Florida should have included Cuba too, extending the cordon sanitaire protecting the slaveholders' republic across the Florida Straits.

*   *   *

As settlers from the U.S. in the 1820s were trickling into Texas, a premier Indigenous grouping was inadvertently weakening their own position, which could only aid the more adventurous settlers. It was in 1824 that the Cherokees, then residing in the southeastern quadrant of the continent—a decade or so before their unceremonious expulsion to what is now Oklahoma along the infamous "Trail of Tears"—ordered that "intermarriage between negro slaves and Indians, or whites, shall not be lawful...that any male Indian or white

---

76. Mark F. Bielski, *The Mortal Blow to the Confederacy: The Fall of New Orleans, 1862*, El Dorado Hills, California: Savas Beatie, 2021, 10 (abbrev. Bielski).

77. T. Harry Williams, *P.G.T. Beauregard: Napoleon in Gray*, Baton Rouge: LSU Press, 1955, 1.

78. Bielski, xi, xvii.

79. Junius, "Annexation of Texas," New York: Greeley & McElrath, 1844, Oberlin College (abbrev. Junius).

man marrying a negro woman slave, he or they shall be punished with fifty-nine stripes on the bare back and any Indian or white woman marrying a negro man slave, shall be punished with twenty five stripes on her or their back."

Many Cherokees tried mightily to accommodate themselves to settler cant: professing Christianity, practicing agriculture consonant with settler praxis, developing an alphabet for the production of newspapers, adopting settler sartorial customs—and, yes, owning enslaved Africans. More than these other factors, the latter weakened their position in the eyes of many Mexicans, then on the fast track to abolition and rivaling Haiti in this glorious competition, while alienating too many Negroes, who often wrongly imputed Cherokee pro-slavery praxis to all Indigenes.

Thus, it was also proclaimed by the Cherokee that it "shall not be lawful for negro slaves to possess property in horses, cattle or hogs and that those slaves now possessing property of that description, be required to dispose of…same in twelve months from this date…." To be sure, the Cherokee were only emulating "best practices" among white supremacists, who seemed to be in concert with the tides of history. But in the long run, what they promulgated was terribly undermining: they invidiously targeted Negroes in their Constitution, announcing that "all free male citizens (excepting negroes and descendants of white and Indian men by negro women who may have been set free) who shall have attained the age of eighteen years, shall be equally entitled to vote in all public elections…."[80] Routinely, in their periodical, the *Cherokee Phoenix & Indians' Advocate*, Negroes were disparaged and compared derogatorily to other groups.[81]

---

80. *Laws of the Cherokee Nation Adopted by the Council at Various Periods*, Tahlequah, Indian Territory: Cherokee Advocate Office, 1852, Huntington Library, 38, 39, 118-130. The Cherokee rejected the praxis of the nascent Church of Latter Day Saints, declaring that it would be "unlawful for a white man (citizen of the United States) living in the Nation to have more than one wife…neither shall he make use of the woman's [his wife's] property without her consent….," 171. The Cherokee also legislated that "no citizen or citizens of the Cherokee nation shall receive in their employment any citizen or citizens of the United States, or negro slaves belonging to citizens of the United States, without first obtaining a permit…," 34. Cf. William S. Pugsley and Marilyn P. Duncan, eds., *The Laws of Slavery in Texas: Historical Documents and Essays*, Austin: U of Texas Press, 2010, and Jason A. Gillmer, *Slavery and Freedom in Texas: Stories from the Courtroom, 1821-1871*, Athens: U of Georgia Press, 2017.

81. *Cherokee Phoenix & Indians' Advocate*, 21 May 1828.

Again, it would be an error to assume that the benighted posture of these Cherokee provisions was symptomatic of a consensus among Indigenes generally, just as it would be a gross mistake to assume praxis among Danes implicates Russians or Slovenians. As the Cherokees were formulating these laws, a visitor noticed a differing trend not far away, speaking of other Indigenes, whereby "the chiefs and influential men in some of the tribes object to intermarriages with the whites on account of the aberration from this standard color, which is exhibited in the offspring; white being regarded characteristic of effeminacy and cowardice...next in order to themselves, some class the whites, while others suppose the blacks to be superior to them...."[82]

Despite their repetitive flaying of Negroes legislatively and otherwise, even the Cherokees—in the pages of their journal—apprised their readers of views of the enslaved often at odds with settler renderings. With sympathy they recounted the affecting story from Natchez of a 67-year-old African—"Prince...Ibrahim"—freed and allowed to return home after negotiations with Tangiers.[83]

This journal cited the leading Negro periodical, *Freedom's Journal*, when discussing colonization—or deporting Free Negroes en masse[84]—unlike many settler enterprises. In their expansive coverage of slavery,[85] this newspaper carried heartrending stories on slavery, e.g., a case of Free Negroes arrested in Kentucky due to an outmoded law who faced being sold into slavery: "surely this is a free country" where this should be disallowed, cried the writer. Instead, it was insisted, "restore [them] to the land of his father at the public expense," a "small return for the injury which has been done to him or his ancestors" but by all means, resist "consigning them to the horrors of slavery...."[86] This was the case, it was reported, since even slavery in Cuba was "less severe" than in the slaveholders' republic.[87] Despite

---

82. John D. Hunter, *Manners and Customs of Several Indian Tribes Located West of the Mississippi*, Philadelphia: Maxwell, 1823, 201-202.

83. *Cherokee Phoenix & Indians' Advocate*, 11 June 1828. See the same periodical of 3 December 1828: another article on "Abduhl Rahhahman" of Natchez, the "Moorish Prince." The periodical seemed to lament the fact that the "Prince" was unable to ransom his children who remained in Mississippi.

84. Ibid., 1 April 1829.

85. Ibid., 11 March 1828.

86. Ibid., 15 April 1829.

87. Ibid., 22 April 1829.

the Cherokee nation's own role in enslavement, this journal did not shrink in reporting sympathetically about slave rebellion.[88]

What is remarkable about early U.S. history is how united the settlers were in pursuit of mutual gain by any means necessary under the banner of white supremacy and how fragmented Indigenes were, apparently unaware that a page of history had turned and they were confronting an antagonist of the new type. For not far distant from the Cherokee redoubt there existed an interlocking directorate with Africans, leading to what has been described as the "longest and most expensive Indian war the United States government was to wage"; yet, the fact that they too were subjected to expulsion suggests that even the Seminoles of Florida could have utilized more external aid to resist encroachment. William P. Duval, the first civilian governor of Florida, succeeding Andrew Jackson, stressed *"breaking up of the runaway slaves and outlaw Indians"* [emphasis-original] and saw both as potential allies of foreign powers (akin to the 1812 war). Still, as so often happened, the pressure for removal emerged from settler grassroots, as much as leaders. The victors did grant the "concession" that the Seminoles could head west without selling their African allies into slavery, as some settlers demanded.[89]

The 1812 war reportedly cost the settler state $90 million, while three years of war in Florida cost $40 million[90]—the looming incubus

88. Ibid., 23 September 1829: A slave trader and "two other white men" were traveling through Kentucky "with a drove of 60 Negroes" en route from "Maryland to Mississippi." The chattel were "handcuffed and chained together" but they managed to cut the chains, "killed" two captors and beat their chief, who they assumed was dead. He was not and "rallied" his remaining forces, "capturing" a number who were then to be tried for "murder."

89. George Klos, "Blacks and the Seminole Removal Debate, 1821-1835," *Florida Historical Quarterly*, 68 (No. 1, 1989): 55-78, 58, 66, 69 (abbrev. Klos). Many of these Africans "could 'speak English' as well as Indian" and "from their understanding of both languages possess considerable influence with their masters," thus becoming "influential in Indian councils...." A number of "slave disputes between Seminoles and whites frequently went unresolved because the [Negro] interpreters in these negotiations sometimes were former slaves themselves." William P. Duval felt that African Seminoles were "much more hostile to the white people than their masters," which enabled them to "artfully represent" whites as hostile to people of color.

90. *Albany Evening Journal*, n.d., and Julius Rubens Ames and Benjamin Lundy, *The Anti-Texass Legion Protest of Some Free Men, States and Presses Against the Texass Rebellion Against the Laws of Nature and Nations*, Albany, 1844 (abbrev. Ames and Lundy), NYHS.

for Washington was the possibility of London and Indigenes combining more consistently.

The wider point is that the seeming inability of Indigenes to execute Tecumseh's vision of a "Pan-Indian" confederacy was one explanation for their ultimate continental setback and in Texas more specifically.[91]

Besides Indigenous fissures, Washington was well aware of similar rifts in Mexico. Just as the Cherokee were formulating their anti-Negro laws in 1824, the U.S. envoy in Vera Cruz instructed Secretary of State John Quincy Adams that the "hostility against Mexican Spaniards is deep and more firmly fixed than ever...."[92] This hostility against the residue of centuries of oppressive colonial rule underpinned the instability that allowed Washington to take advantage of this neighbor.[93]

But like Canada, Mexico was gaining an identity in juxtaposition to the abject hypocrisy of the slaveholders' republic. Besides, it made good strategic sense for Mexico to position itself favorably in concert with a major threat to U.S. national security—the ever growing population of African descent, which tended toward unity vis-à-vis slaveholders, unlike diverse Indigenes. Then just across the Florida Straits was yet another enslaved population that was thought to be influenced by the ultimate bête noire—neighboring Haiti. By 1826 the future president, James Buchanan (chief executive, 1857-1861) was fretting openly as a hemispheric gathering was being organized in Panama. "During the last summer," he averred, "it was apprehended...that France was about to invade the island of Cuba. We were then instantly called upon to redeem our pledge and protect that island against the fleet and army of France," no minor matter as Indigenes were on the march in Florida. Furthermore, trade with Cuba "is, at present, more valuable to the United States, than that of all the Southern Republics united." Yet what was really chilling was the dire prospect of "servile war" in Cuba replicating the "dreadful scenes of St. Domingo" which could materialize if Mexico—as threatened—perpetrated an abolitionist intervention. "There are portions of this Union," he concluded bitterly, "in which, if you emancipate your slaves, they will become

---

91. William Brattle Gannett, "The American Invasion of Texas, 1820-1845: Patterns of Conflict Between Settlers and Indians," Ph.D. dissertation, Cornell U, 1984.

92. William Taylor, Consul to Secretary of State John Quincy Adams, 22 June 1824, Reel 1, Despatches from U.S. Consuls in Vera Cruz, NARA.

93. See also Timo H. Schaefer, *Liberalism as Utopia: The Rise and Fall of Legal Rule in Post-Colonial Mexico, 1820-1900*, New York: Cambridge U Press, 2017.

masters. There can be no middle course,"[94] a subject to which this future Secretary of State (1845-1849) turned repeatedly.[95]

This latter point underscores the point often lost today: à la Haiti, there was a real fear that the enslaved could revolt—what did they have to lose but their chains?—and seize power.

Foremost on Buchanan's mind was a case involving an enslaved African in Pensacola named Henry, a mere 14, meaning his optimal laboring years were beginning. In 1814 redcoats invaded, then carried him to an allied Negro bastion in Apalachicola, and from thence he was seen among the Creeks, then to Tampa Bay and from there on a fishing vessel to Havana, depriving his owner of the investment.[96] What would occur if Mexico were to seize this valuable island? Would Florida be drained of Africans with a domino effect then stretching into Georgia and points north?

Buchanan was reflecting the parlous strategic position endured by the slaveholders' republic, surrounded by territory controlled by London—Canada, Bermuda, the Bahamas, etc.—and now republican Mexico which was flexing its abolitionist muscles. "As to Cuba and Puerto Rico," he spat out, "I would not agree that any nation on earth should wrest those islands from the dominion of Spain...with the exception of England, there is no government in existence that I would not rather see in possession of them than the government of Mexico."[97]

U.S. officialdom was almost clinically paranoid to the point that envoy Joel Poinsett insisted that Scottish Masons ran Mexico in London's behalf.[98] There was coruscating suspicion in Washington that Mexico would be aided in liberating Cuba by the nation that contained Cartagena, which had a merited reputation as a citadel of African resistance to oppression. Even a Cherokee scribe, from a polity which countenanced slavery, thought that what is now Colombia "put to the blush the tardy and heartless" enslavers of Washington.[99]

The slaveholders' republic posture on Cuba revealed the contradictions in its hemispheric strategy. Purportedly, the U.S. was favorable to anti-colonialism in the hemisphere because of its own origins—or at least since it removed a Spanish competitor, per the "Monroe Doctrine," allowing Washington to feast more readily. Yet

---

94. Speech, 11 April 1826, in J.B. Moore, 184-206, 191, 200-201, 202.
95. Ibid., Speech 18 April and 20 April 1826, 206.
96. Ibid., On the Case of Manuel del Barco, 4 January 1830, 427.
97. Ibid., Remarks, 27 March 1826, 179-182, 181.
98. Jose Maria Herrera, "The Blueprint for Hemispheric Hegemony," 342.
99. *Cherokee Phoenix & Indians' Advocate*, 5 August 1829.

the U.S. was hotly opposed to Mexico and Colombia seizing Cuba from Spain despite the obvious anti-colonial implications, not least since Madrid's control of the island maintained relentless pressure on Mexico, especially in the Yucatan and Vera Cruz. Similarly, though Indigenes overwhelmingly were the mortal enemy of Washington whose land they desired, U.S. merchants were trafficking weapons to these same Indigenes especially in northern Mexico, which had the added benefit of diluting opposition to Texas secessionists. By 1827 the U.S. had a whopping 11 consulates in Mexico, including two in Texas,[100] providing plenty of opportunity for mischief.

The 1812 war showed that confronting London was then beyond the ken of Washington, but Mexico was another story, a reality aided by fractiousness there between the detritus of Spanish monarchy and republicans and the latter often confronting abolitionists consonant with the philosophy of the northern neighbor.

And then there was London, which already was creeping toward an abolitionist alliance with Haiti,[101] with Mexico thought to be next on the list. As early as 1824, Secretary of State John Quincy Adams was being informed by his colleague in Vera Cruz about growing concern about British loans to Mexico.[102] Then his successor Henry Clay, yet another presidential aspirant, was informed nervously when London "concluded a treaty of commerce with this government,"[103] speaking of Mexico.

Finally, the U.S. consul, William Taylor, could no longer conceal his upset, warning ominously that the "Mexican government" was now "husbanding their resources for defense at home or to meet their engagements [to] the English Jews [sic], of whom they have made heavy loans…who Shylock like will certainly demand the forfeiture of their bonds…." Then "speculating about Cuba," he advised that it was "again reported that that island is to be invaded by a Mexican force,"[104] to the detriment of the slaveholders' republic. Taylor, who had been a self-described "U.S. agent [at] Port-au-Prince," for

---

100. Herrera, 161, 223.

101. Gerald Horne, *Confronting Black Jacobins: The U.S., the Haitian Revolution and the Origins of the Dominican Republic*, New York: Monthly Review Press, 2015, (abbrev. Horne, *Confronting Black Jacobins*).

102. William Taylor, Consul to Secretary of State Adams, 9 December 1824, Reel 1, Despatches from U.S. Consuls in Vera Cruz, NARA.

103. Ibid., William Taylor, Consul to Secretary of State Clay, 9 May 1825.

104. Ibid., William Taylor, Consul to Secretary of State Clay, 8 January 1826.

Haiti—for "many years residence"[105]—had firsthand knowledge of what was wracking his brain. Fortunately for the slaveholders, the steady arrival of settlers in Texas provided enormous leverage to be wielded against Mexico.

Taylor and those like him had much reason for worry. Arguably, the tariff placed on imported U.S. cotton in the 1820s, as this crop was expanding given the land grabs in Alabama and Mississippi to East Texas, could be interpreted as a subtle abolitionist measure and certainly hostile to the hegemonic line of "free trade."[106]

And it was not just Texas that was in the crosshairs. As early as 1825, Washington's man in Mazatlán was confiding that "several American vessels...have been for the last two years carrying on an intercourse with the Californias in direct opposition to a law of this Republic," risking "confiscation of vessel and cargo,"[107] underlining its importance.

As valued as the enslaved were, there were other commodities in Mexico and Texas that were attracting the riveting attention of settlers. This category included Joel Roberts Poinsett, a U.S. negotiator with Mexico who kept a close eye on silver mines south of the border.[108] But even mines could be fruitfully exploited with enslaved labor, which is one reason why, by 1826, where Austin settled, there were 443 bonded laborers among about 1400 settlers.[109]

Mexico, which had its own problems in confronting Indigenes, made a strategic blunder when allowing migrants from their predatory neighbor to settle in Texas. As Mexico was still reeling from the dislocation delivered by a complex struggle against Spain, it still had enough sense to move toward abolition; however, these interlopers were moving in an opposing direction and, not unlike 1776, these enslaving settlers rebelled—and triumphed.

---

105. Ibid., William Taylor, Consul to Sir, 18 November 1830.

106. Ibid., William Taylor, Consul to Secretary of State Clay, 4 January 1827.

107. James Lenox Kennedy, Consul to Secretary of State Clay, 8 April 1825, Reel 1, Despatches from U.S. Consuls in Mazatlán, Mexico, NARA.

108. Joel Roberts Poinsett to Leroy Bayard & Co., 6 December 1825, College of Charleston, South Carolina (abbrev. CCSC).

109. Kattner, 35.

Chapter 2

On the Cusp of Counter-Revolution, 1829-1836

Like counter-revolutionaries generally—or revolutionaries for that matter—there is a felt desire to spread the gospel and example. In the case of the slaveholders' republic, this felt need was even more urgent given the example provided by Mexico, which as of abolition in 1829 was led by a leader—Vicente Guerrero—of African descent, a leadership feat not attained by the so-called "revolutionary republic" to the north until the 21st century. The secession from Mexico anticipated and resembled the better known model of 1861, with the "freedom" to enslave Africans being at the heart of the matter.

A central irony of the past 250 years in North America was that the overthrow of monarchy meant the rise of republicans, often federalists in Mexico, who were open to slavery's continuance, not least in Texas, while their centralizing foes were often found on the other side of the barricades.[1] Ironic, as well, is that one of the reasons why 1861 failed miserably was because of the secessionists' energy over the decades in importing so many Africans, who then delivered the knockout blow to secession—quite appropriately. Texas had been similarly energetic but barely had begun to attract settlers before deciding that Mexican abolition was not compatible with their crude tastes and, thus, were spared the ignominy of being vanquished by "their property." Nonetheless, as annexation to the U.S. approached in 1845, independent Texas was highly vulnerable to the same forces that upended its Confederate peer, as exemplified when the Irish patriot, Daniel O'Connell, in 1839 called for a colony of Free Negroes in northern Mexico designed to destroy the "piratical society called the state of Texas."[2]

*   *   *

---

1. Andrew John Torget, "Cotton Empire: Slavery and the Texas Borderlands, 1820-1837," Ph.D. dissertation, U of Virginia, 2009, 108 (abbrev. Torget, *Cotton*). See also Torget, *Seeds*.

2. Torget, *Cotton*, 236.

O'Connell's counsel was welcome but he was pushing on an open door in that Africans from various sections of the slaveholders' republic were fleeing south of the border. There was Nicholas Drouet, for example, a Free Negro from Louisiana who arrived in Matamoros around 1830. He had lived in New Orleans, may have spent time in Haiti, whose very name was akin to waving holy water beneath the nose of the devil. He was accompanied by a number of runaways and Indigenes too who joined Mexican forces in their repeated jousting with Texas in the tumultuous decade of the 1830s.[3]

This factor, as much as any other, made more thorny bilateral ties between the two republics—one abolitionist, the other enslaving—especially when Mexico balked at returning runaways from Texas and points eastward, a damaging capital loss.[4]

Drouet was preceded by John Bird of Virginia, yet another pro-Mexico Negro who settled along the border.[5] The perception was that not only Mexico but even Texas—because of Mexican influence—was more of a beacon of opportunity than the U.S. itself or even the post 1836 republic.[6] Their arrival was echoed by the attempted revolt of the enslaved in Texas in March 1829.[7]

Like iron filings to a magnet, Africans were drawn to Mexico—especially after President Guerrero issued his earthshaking abolitionist decree of 15 September 1829: even before this measure, Africans were saluting this southern neighbor, for the decree was more like a crowning glory than a radical departure. José María Tornel, a member of the Mexican elite as an army general and leading politician, not only saw this as a humanitarian gesture but reflected his (and his class's) spiraling opposition to the northern neighbor. The decree was an implicit recognition of what was obvious: slavery was the national security Achilles heel of the U.S., just as the scuttlebutt was that Mexico was in the midst of brokering a "secret alliance" with Haiti, which could then include Cuba.[8]

---

3. John C. Gassner, "African American Fugitive Slaves and Freemen in Matamoros, Tamaulipas, 1820-1865," M.A. thesis, U of Texas-Pan American, 2004, 21, 26 (abbrev. Gassner), University of Texas-Pan American (abbrev. UT-PA).

4. Herrera, 307.

5. Levander, 36.

6. Jodella Dorothea Kite, "A Social History of the Anglo-American Colonies in Mexican Texas, 1821-1835," Ph.D. dissertation, TTU, 1990, 200 (abbrev. Kite).

7. McConnell, 103.

8. Bugbee.

Yet, Mexico's antagonists too had their own pressure points that could be squeezed to disable this Haitian ally in that as the decree was promulgated, the nation was threatened with a Spanish invasion.[9] Tampico, the port on the eastern coast, was targeted by the royalists,[10] at a time when U.S. envoys there were monitoring closely the comings and goings from there of Mexican military men.[11] Even the U.S. consul in Tampico—by his own admission—was "alarmed for our persons in property...send a sufficient force for our protection" was his instruction to Secretary of State Edward Livingston—illustrating the objective alliance between destabilization in Mexico and opportunities created for the slaveholders' republic.[12]

By the early 1830s there was yet another uprising in nearby Vera Cruz, which coincidentally was helpful to companion ferment in Texas.[13] "This country is in a state of revolt against the government,"[14] was the exhortation from the U.S. envoy in Vera Cruz. Promptly a naval squadron from the U.S. menacingly showed the flag in this troubled port, which happened to have a sizable population of African descent.[15]

Even a Cherokee writer sensed that the unrest in the Yucatan in early 1830 was tied to the spreading anti-abolitionist animosity targeting Guerrero; ominously, a U.S. warship had just left this region.[16] Soon Guerrero himself was liquidated, an early victory for anti-abolitionist counter-revolution, which was prefigured when the U.S. envoy, Joel Poinsett, unaccustomed to dealing with Africans with power, expressed resentment at his "temper."[17]

---

9. Baumgartner, 64, 66.

10. Leslie Alice Jones Wagner, "Disputed Territory: Rio Grande/Rio Bravo Borderlands, 1838-1840," M.A. thesis, U of Texas-Arlington, 1998, 39 (abbrev. Wagner), University of Texas-Arlington (abbrev. UT-Arl).

11. William Taylor to Sir, 25 September 1829, Reel 1, Despatches from U.S. Consuls in Vera Cruz, NARA.

12. George Robertson, Consul to Secretary of State Edward Livingston, 20 September 1832, Reel 1, Despatches from U.S. Consuls in Tampico, NARA.

13. Beauford Chambless, "The First President of Texas: The Life of David Gouverneur Burnet," Rice U, Ph.D. dissertation, 1954, 42 (abbrev. Chambless).

14. James A. Cameron to Secretary of State Livingston, 5 January 1832, Reel 2, Despatches from U.S. Consuls in Vera Cruz, NARA.

15. Ibid., J.A. Cameron, Consul to Secretary of State Livingston, 2 February 1832.

16. *Cherokee Phoenix & Indians' Advocate,* 10 March 1830.

17. Herrera, 258.

The section of Mexico where Guerrero's abolitionist decree was met with dollops of anxiousness and anger alike was Texas, the restive province that may have been the ultimate target of this measure,[18] though he sought to carve out an exemption for this province in his far-reaching decree of December 1829.[19] Despite widespread support for this measure, not accidentally Guerrero was ousted from power shortly after it was coming into effect—then executed, an event that met with few tears in the corridors of power in Washington.[20]

It also met with fewer tears still in similar corridors in Texas, where it was greeted with derision among slaveholders, who often made sure it was neither published, nor enforced. In San Antonio, in a sign of things to come, both settlers and many Tejanos [those of Mexican origin] alike were in stern opposition. That some enslaved Africans heard of this measure and immediately fled, enhanced opposition.[21]

By 1828 General Manuel de Mier y Terán decided to inspect Texas, this increasingly problematic colony. By 1829 General Terán was stating the obvious: "the most persistent goal for this colony," he said of Texas, "is to obtain [further] permission for the introduction of slaves." Futilely, this led to an 1830 law seeking to bar both the enslaved and settlers in Texas.[22] Austin and his fellow enslavers were seeking to hide the number of slaves, which was not easy when a single settler owned 150. However, General Terán unintentionally revealed a presumed weakness, and settler strength, when he lamented, "the North Americans understand war with the savages better than do our Mexicans," since the former were "striking back ten times for every blow they received. If [Indigenes] killed a settler, a large party of settlers would set out to hunt and kill ten of the tribe, of any age or sex. By such behavior they have reduced the tribe of Tarancahuases [Karankawas] such that no one speaks of it today because it seems to have been exterminated...." Then there was the Gross [Groce]" family, "the richest property owner in the Austin

---

18. Bugbee, 649.

19. Note in Ronnie C. Tyler and Lawrence R. Murphy, eds., *The Slave Narratives of Texas*, Austin: Encino, 1974, xx (abbrev. Tyler and Murphy).

20. Kristopher Paschal, "'Texas Must be a Slave Country:' The Development of Slavery in Mexican Texas and the Institution's Role in the Coming of Revolution, 1821-1836," M.A. thesis, Southern Methodist U, 2010, 57 (abbrev. Paschal), Southern Methodist University (abbrev. SMU).

21. Torget, *Cotton*, 213, 215.

22. Paschal, 59.

colony. He has 105 slaves" with the "main crop" being cotton, much of it sold to the British ally.[23]

This family, like so many others in slave territory, profited handsomely from enslaved labor, as they resided sumptuously in one of the most luxurious log homes in the settlement, thanks to the skill and ingenuity of enslaved artisans.[24] General Terán, writing from Nacogdoches, acknowledged to the Ministry of Foreign Affairs that the unabated duress imposed upon Indigenes was impacting Mexico, particularly as they fled southward in escape, which like a chain reaction imposed duress on Mexicans of various stripes.[25]

Nacogdoches proved to be instructive for General Terán. Like the settlement as a whole, it attracted all manner of disreputable figures, as escaping from nearby Louisiana meant residence in a separate jurisdiction and nation, likely escaping extradition: ideal for criminals and scoundrels. Though Mexico sought to evade a crackdown on slavery in Texas after abolition, Louisianans provided helpful instruction on how to provide pointers on identifying this "property" as indentured servants, contributing to the overall disrespect for Mexico,[26] which responded vigorously seeking to puncture this fiction—while stiffening regulations on sale or purchase of remaining enslaved in the prelude to abolition in 1829—and that only contributed to the overall secessionist sentiment.[27]

This upset the plans and temperament of settlers. One Alabaman was in New Orleans en route to Texas with his human property when he received the disconsolate news about abolition. So he obtained crude signatures of the enslaved on articles of indenture, which bound them to serve him for 99 years[28]—the preferred option post-1865 when other enslavers were headed from defeated Texas deep

---

23. Jack Jackson, ed., *Texas by Terán: The Diary Kept by General Manuel de Mier y Terán on His 1828 Inspection of Texas*, Austin: U of Texas Press, 2000, 33, 34, 144.

24. Kite, 54.

25. General Terán to Minister of Foreign Affairs, 5 July 1828, H/200 & 72: 73 1 L-E-1076 (V), Fol. 52 1828 Fol. 53, Archivo Histórico de la Secretaría de Relaciones Exteriores, in W. L. Anderson, et.al., eds., *Guide to Cherokee Documents in Foreign Archives*, Metuchen, N.J.: Scarecrow Press, 1983, 517 (abbrev. Anderson).

26. Kite, 10, 33.

27. Robbins, 153-161, 157.

28. *A Visit to Texas: Being the Journal of a Traveller Through Those Parts Most Interesting to American Settlers with Descriptions of Scenery, Habits…Containing a Sketch of the Late War*, New York: Van Nostrand, 1836.

into Mexico. Part of what was happening—in addition to "breeding" Africans in the Upper South—was that there was so much Indigenous land seized east of Texas as a result of expulsions that the need for the enslaved concomitantly increased. Thus, the number of enslaved doubled in Mississippi and Louisiana from 1820-1830 and almost tripled in Alabama.[29]

Mexico has been accused not without cause of being harsh toward Indigenes within its borders, but officialdom there seemed to be shocked by the atrocities visited upon Cherokees particularly as the Indian Removal Act of 1830 was instigated,[30] an early form of "ethnic cleansing." Even Thomas Jefferson, no opponent of land grabs, just before passing from the scene, met early one morning with an interlocutor who said the former president was "decidedly opposed to the Georgia claim" of Cherokee land, especially since the Peach State contained those who were "the most greedy of…any State in the Union."[31]

It is possible that the rapidly expiring former president may have had Austin in mind. He was veritably the absolute ruler in the colony from 1821-1828, and was garlanded by a staggering 70,000 acres of land in return for delivering 200 families, who in turn received handsome emoluments, soon to be burnished by an equally staggering arrival of enslaved Africans to work on their behalf. Naturally, these later arrivals grumbled and accused Austin of speculation—which was like accusing Satan of being diabolical—since he skimmed a healthy percentage of these settlers' payments. Suspicions almost eventuated in a revolt, though the presence of unsettled Indigenes and Africans who could take advantage of their Pan-European unrest served as a damper on their agitation—although one settler opportunistically abandoned the settlement and proposed to incite Indigenes against his erstwhile fellow colonists. Inevitably, ill feelings existed between Austin's colony and that of Martin de León, comprised of Mexicans (many of the former did not comprehend Spanish). Austin had ill feeling toward de León, whom he accused of harboring these dissidents, along with a man described as "the mulatto Drake," whom Austin previously had beaten and chased from the settlement.[32]

---

29. Torget, *Cotton*, 4.

30. José María Fornet to Minister of Foreign Affairs, 1 September 1830, H/510 (73.0) " 830"/1 5-2-7828. Fol. 27 in Anderson, 517.

31. Interview with Thomas Jefferson conducted by Samuel Whitcomb, Monday morning, 31 May 1824, between 8-9 A.M., University of Virginia-Charlottesville (abbrev. UVa-C).

32. Lester Bugbee, "Some Difficulties of a Texas Empresario," Harrisburg, Pennsylvania: Southern Historical Association, 1899, Huntington Library.

Ultimately, it is dispiriting and politically desiccating to recognize that murderous bellicosity "worked" in Texas, in terms of emptying the land of Indigenes, bringing in enslaved African labor to develop the economy and allowing enough European migrants to profit to the point where this dystopian scenario was shrouded subsequently.

Part of the problem may have been naivety of Austin's actual opponents in accepting his oleaginous words. By 1830 there had been Mexican abolition, the Indian Removal Act upsetting certain Indigenes, gathering Mexican ties to Haiti and Britain, unrest in the Yucatan, the negative example of French seizure of Algeria—and more. It was then that Austin reassured Mexican officialdom, asserting with mock sincerity that "various rumors have upset public opinion concerning the colonies of Texas; rumors without the least foundation in fact, although not without a specious basis...." To the contrary, he insisted, "the idea that the colonists of Texas wish to separate from Mexico is entirely mistaken; there is not & never has been such an idea," he avowed. Presumably barely keeping a straight face as he wrote, he contended that it was "not to the interest of Texas to be separated from Mexico," and "these colonists, dear sir, are not discontented or dissatisfied...." What was animating his anxious and faux genuineness were "alarming rumors concerning the excitement which was said to have been manifested against them [U.S. settlers] in Mexico," including the proliferating stories that "a large expedition was coming here to destroy them. The injurious effect of such rumors,"[33] was the propellant driving his sly deceptiveness, an embossed stamp of settler colonialism.

*　*　*

Again, the Cherokees compromised their position by their emulation of settlers, up to and including enslavement. One study has found that the "development of plantation slavery and the adoption of the 1827 Constitution helped create, for the first time, two distinct classes within Cherokee society"—with slave-owning plutocrats frequently at the top of the heap.[34]

Nevertheless, unlike their settler neighbors in Georgia, then others further west and due north, the Cherokees indulged critiques of the

---

33. Stephen F. Austin to Mexico City officialdom. 13 July 1830, Box 2B 211, Barker Collection UT-A.

34. Joyce Ann Kievit, "Dissension in the Cherokee Nation, 1860 to 1866," M.A. thesis, U of Houston-Clear Lake, 1992, 10 (abbrev. Kievit).

barbarism that was slavery. Slavery in Washington, D.C., and circumscribing Free Negroes in Michigan were termed "revolting and disgraceful" and a "foul blot upon the national escutcheon...."[35] As Black people were chased from Cincinnati in 1830, augmenting the "African colony" in Canada, the Cherokee journal warned threateningly that "in case of a collision between the English and American governments," these forced migrants "will powerfully strengthen the English...."[36] Harking back to the bygone days of Tecumseh and the 1812 war, "English opinions on the Indian Question" were contrasted with those of the slaveholders' republic.[37] (Tecumseh was lauded in its pages: his mother was Cherokee was the message to readers.)[38] Expulsion of Free Negroes from Louisiana did not meet with their approval,[39] nor did the ongoing slave trade from West Africa.[40] Although a gag order in the Deep South sought to illegalize the simple discussion of abolitionism, the Cherokee periodical reported on an important abolitionist meeting in Leeds.[41]

For purposes here, consider a lengthy report on Mexico appearing on the front page in May 1831. "Indians & Mestizos, Negroes and Mulattoes are equally free citizens and voters," it was noted in contrast to what was unfolding due north. "Negroes are few," but wondrously "there is a Negro General in the army." Adding the obvious, it was observed that "this is considered great improvement over our federal constitution, which acknowledges all men are free and equal yet allows...Negro slavery and Indian oppression...." More, "slavery has been happily abolished without difficulty" in Mexico, where even proclaiming abolition in the "revolutionary republic" could bring sanction—or worse. Still, the perceptive writer detected that Mexico's emphasis on religion and the U.S.'s stressing on "race" was a crucial difference, for in the former land "bigoted Spaniards and priests once called all heretic strangers, English and Americans, by the name of *Judeos* or Jews!"[42]

As the Indian Removal Act began to bite, the Cherokee stepped up their reporting on discriminatory contrasts between Mexico and the

35. *Cherokee Phoenix & Indians' Advocate*, 22 May 1830.
36. Ibid., 1 May 1830.
37. Ibid., 8 May 1830.
38. Ibid., 12 May 1832.
39. Ibid., 5 August 1830.
40. Ibid., 3 December 1829.
41. Ibid., 10 March 1830.
42. Ibid., 28 May 1831.

U.S., which could only have incited more anger within the latter republic with untoward consequences for the former. Joel Poinsett, sent to negotiate/pressure Mexico, was singled out for derision. The U.S. was encouraging "outlaws...Comanches and other predatory tribes" to attack Mexico, it was charged—a policy that could backfire since these "tribes'" weapons could just as easily be turned against settlers in Texas. The latter had the audacious temerity, it was said, to "buy" the "spoils" taken from Mexico, including "stolen mules and even *Mexican freemen* [Africans] who are bought as slaves and some mulattos and Indians held as such in Louisiana..." [emphasis-original]. This was a perilous policy to pursue since London was encouraging Mexico to "invade Louisiana, declare all the Negroes free [and] expel all the American settlers from Texas," the bruiting of which "staggered... friends of North America...," while the "bad treatment of the Indians" was seen as a *casus belli*. Forebodingly, the writer advised that "the nearest states to Mexico have a large slave population" and are "very easy to rouse by an offer of complete freedom"; besides, "borders of the two countries are filled with Indian tribes" who had yet to reconcile to the ongoing reality of settler invasion. Many, e.g., the Comanches, had been forced to migrate to the borderlands by settler encroachment where they were "very unwisely concentrated"—and "would join the Mexican army which are nearly all Indians...."[43] More than many U.S. abolitionists, the Cherokee analyst noticed that in Mexico "there is no slavery to weaken the social system...."[44]

As the U.S. accelerated their oppressive maneuvers against the Cherokee, the latter turned increasingly to praising Mexico,[45] especially regarding the fraught matter of abolition. In 1832 their reporter conversed with a former Mississippi enslaver who had been residing in Matamoros for a decade, who proceeded to describe in detail how manumission functioned there and how it might work in the Magnolia State.[46] Such press coverage was complemented in 1833 by reportage on abolition of Caribbean slavery by London.[47]

The Cherokee were joined on the "Trail of Tears" by yet another Indigenous grouping that countenanced enslavement. An onlooker then watched how members of a Christian denomination "in the Chickasaw wilderness" worshipped: "about two thirds of the members of

---

43. Ibid., 4 June 1831.
44. Ibid., 6 November 1831.
45. Ibid., 9 July 1831.
46. Ibid., 3 March 1832.
47. Ibid., 17 August 1833.

the church are of African descent..." and "mostly understand English" and "on account of that are more accessible than the Chickasaws...." Remarkably, "the meeting was conducted wholly by *Christian slaves* in the Chickasaw language..."[48] [emphasis-original]. (Similarly, a Texas settler thought Comanche songs were "similar to that common among Negro minstrels....")[49]

But how could Mexicans be expected to sympathize with the plight of the Chickasaws when they were willing to tolerate enslavement of Africans in Texas? On the other hand, arguably forcing so many Indigenes west to Texas's neighborhood placed more pressure on the region, inducing more instability and unsteadiness; minimally— enslavement aside—it placed on Texas's northern border, in what became Oklahoma, more disgruntled Indigenes subject to being manipulated by Mexico.

On the other hand, Chickasaws proved to be closer to the Cherokees as slaveholders than the settlers—putatively irrelevant, but material when in negotiating with Chickasaws in the early 1830s, Washington was keen to underscore how a settler "had stolen from him by a negro slave of the Chickasaws, a box containing one thousand dollars," a fortune for a Negro then (even now).[50]

Nonetheless, Negroes fled Chickasaw enslavers, their alleged benefaction notwithstanding. Advertisements appeared in an Arkansas periodical in 1831 seeking the retrieval of a Negro man, his wife and two children, all of whom spoke Chickasaw and had escaped from Chickasaw territory in Mississippi.[51]

Still, many Indigenes shared the skepticism of the Osage ethnic group toward bedrock settler notions: "What makes white men so anxious to get money?" a chief inquired querulously, and "why do the whites make the Negroes slave?" the ally to the prior supposition.[52] This Osage rebuke was a derivative of the reality, up until the

---

48. Christopher C. Dean, *Letters on the Chickasaw and Osage Missions...*, Boston: Massachusetts Sabbath School Union, 1831, 9. 10 (abbrev. Dean).

49. Nelson Lee, *Three Years Among the Comanches: The Narrative of Nelson Lee, the Texas Ranger*, [originally published Albany: Baker Taylor, 1859], Norman: U of Oklahoma Press, 1957, 122 (abbrev. Lee).

50. "Treaty Between the United States of America and the Chickasaw Nation of Indians, 1834, Article 4, Supplementary," 24 May 1834, UVa-C.

51. Bolton, 154.

52. Dean, 99.

early 19th century, that they were able to deal with European invaders and settlers as relative equals.[53]

Thus, given his inspection tour, the perceptive among General Terán's comrades should not have been overly surprised by secession. It was not only the conflict between abolitionism in Mexico versus unabashed enthusiasm for enslavement in Texas—a yawning chasm that could not be bridged—but the genocidal thrust against Indigenes exhibited a startling bloodthirstiness that could easily be directed against forces to the south. Another visitor shortly thereafter brought more troubling news. "Osages are perpetually at war with the Comanches and the hatred between these two people is so fierce that neither side ever takes prisoners",[54] *inter alia*, this was suggestive of the pressure placed upon Texas by the ferocious velocity generated by settler colonialism, with again this fungible ferocity being turned easily against Mexico.

In the prelude to the Counter-Revolution of 1836—a naked revolt against Mexican abolition and in favor of a gargantuan land grab— Choctaws and Chickasaws were said to be mutually antagonistic, unable to muster the adhesiveness delivered by "whiteness" and white supremacy. A band of Floridians—described as Seminoles and Africans—had gathered on the border near Eagle Pass, Texas, an intrusive presence unsettling for all sides. On the other side of the state, there were Cherokees associated with the ill-fated Fredonia Rebellion of 1826-1827, a dress rehearsal for 1836, compromising that Indigenous group's attempt to garner support in Mexico City. Still, there were numerous other groupings, resolved to resist settler incursion in Texas—albeit inconsistently—including Karankawas, Tonkawas, Wacos, Tahaucanos or Keechai, Bidais, Aranamas, Coushattas, Hasinai or Caddos, and others, most of whom were then subjected to systemic annihilation. A troubling sign appeared in 1830 when escaped Negro property, fleeing Cherokee enslavers, turned up near San Antonio. This made all the more pressing the iron necessity of settlers to attract more of their kind, with the land of those soon to be vanquished dangled as bait.[55]

53. Willard Hughes Rollings, "Prairie Hegemony: An Ethno-historical Study of the Osage, From Early Time to 1840," Ph.D. dissertation, TTU, 1983, 335.

54. John C. Ewers, ed., Jean Louis Berlandier, *The Indians of Texas in 1830*, Washington: Smithsonian, 1969, 140.

55. Mayhall.

Ultimately, in this three-cornered struggle among and between Indigenes, slaves and settlers, the latter, with more to offer recruits based on the looting of the former two, prevailed. Still, when the U.S. abolitionist press linked enslavement to expulsion of the Indigenes— lust for land conjoined with desire for enslaved labor—it was a signal that these natural allies would not surrender easily.[56]

But the dialectic in Texas was that massive resistance of the oppressed, buttressed frequently by state power in Mexico, was met with ever more brutal massive force, creating the soil for more land grabs, more enslavement—and, finally, the roots of fascism. In this context, the 1830s were determining, not only because of the 1836 counter-revolution and expulsion of Indigenous, and the ripples created by the 1831 Nat Turner revolt of the enslaved, but also because this vital decade marked a turning point in assaults on U.S. abolitionists. There were "merely" 21 such attacks in 1820s and 7 in the preceding decades—but a breathtaking 115 such incidents in the 1830s.[57] This phenomenon was hardly unknown in Texas but, as with the emerging pattern, it is also the case that real and justified fears of slave revolts were particularly prominent in the period preceding secession in 1836 and the immediate aftermath.[58] The prime exhibit in this regard were the uproarious events of October 1835, when scores of enslaved Africans in the Lower Brazos Valley rebelled but were defeated by armed opponents, who lynched suspected leaders and whipped others.[59] The rebels' far-reaching plans were said to include dividing the plantations among themselves and to enslave their erstwhile masters.[60] They would then ship the cotton the newly enslaved picked through the port of New Orleans.[61]

---

56. John Matthew Teutsch, "'We Wish to Plead Our Own Cause': Rhetorical Links Between Native Americans and African Americans During the 1820s and 1830s," Ph.D. dissertation, U of Louisiana-Lafayette, 2014, 8.

57. Kellie Carter Jackson, *Force and Freedom: Black Abolitionists and the Politics of Violence*, Philadelphia: U of Pennsylvania, 2019, 28.

58. Barba, 433.

59. Alwyn Barr, "Freedom and Slavery in the Republic: African American Experiences in the Republic of Texas," in Howell and Swanlund, 423-436, 425 (abbrev. Barr). See also Sean Kelley, "'Mexico in His Head': Slavery and the Texas-Mexico Border, 1810-1860," *Journal of Social History*, 37 (No. 3, Spring 2004): 709-723, 716.

60. Tom V. Watson, "A Study of Agriculture in Colonial Texas, 1821-1836," M.A. thesis, TTU, 1935, 85 (abbrev. Watson).

61. Paschal, 74.

It was only to be expected what one 19th-century observer saw: "the Slave Trade was perhaps never so extensively prosecuted as in the year 1832," due partially to the growing conflict between U.S slave traders and a London pressed toward abolition, which seemed to energize the former to newer heights of brigandage. Foremost among the brigands was the Kentuckian Monroe Edwards. who traded Africans to Brazil by 1832, then, being a farsighted rascal, invested the proceeds in Texas,[62]a growingly important sunny site for ever shadier scamps. Thus, before settling in Texas, Edwards made it to Africa itself, which likely facilitated his aggressive slave trading in the settlement. His fellow Texas settler, James Fannin, a hero of 1836, only made it to Cuba, where he too became a major slave trader to Texas.[63]

Nelson Lee, an early Texas Ranger—a kind of proto-death squad targeting Indigenes—also had sojourned for suspect reasons in Brazil in the 1830s before heading northward to fight in the bloodstained Blackhawk War during the same decade in today's U.S. Midwest. He managed to squeeze in fighting Indigenes in Florida too before arriving in Galveston, then it was on to gory meddling in the Yucatan to draw Mexican attention away from Texas.[64]

Also making it to Brazil was James Kirker, born in 1793 in war-torn Belfast—a launching pad for some of the more violent settlers in North America—who wound up in South America until 1813, before making it to Mexico by 1824, then to the borderlands, where he earned a well-merited reputation as an anti-Indigenous cutthroat.[65]

As Indian Removal proceeded in this disastrous decade, historian Claudio Saunt detected the "steepest slide" to violence[66] in 1836. However, as the latter date suggests, it was the Deep South's closest neighbor—Texas—that was the none too silent partner in this hideously accelerating process.

This dialectic—or two sidedness—was embodied in Stephen F. Austin, who at once suspected that annexation to the U.S. could encrust slavery in Texas (prescient in retrospect) but as early as 1831

62. Anonymous, *The Life and Adventures of the Accomplished Forger and Swindler, Colonel Monroe Edwards,* New York: Long, 1848.

63. Robbins, 153-161, 157.

64. Lee, 8, 12.

65. Report on James Kirker, n.d., from *St. Louis Post,* Box 11, Kathleen Stoes Papers, New Mexico State U-Las Cruces (abbrev. Stoes Papers).

66. Claudio Saunt, *Unworthy Republic: The Dispossession of Native Americans and the Road to Indian Territory,* New York: Norton, 2020, 232 (abbrev. Saunt).

also suspected that this would mean a "large part of America will be Santo Domingoized in 100 or 200 years," which managed dialectically to be wildly optimistic about the prevalence of enslavement but exhibiting the gift of prophecy when considering the armed Negroes who materialized in 1863. This anguish was expressed during Austin's bout of pessimism in the immediate aftermath of Mexican abolition. He then feared that Africans would outnumber Europeans in Texas to the latter's detriment, i.e., a kind of "race war," a repetitive worry north of the border. "Satan entered the sacred garden in the shape of a serpent," he advised devilishly, and "if he is allowed to enter Texas in the shape of Negroes, it will share the fate of Eden."[67]

In any case, his moment of ambivalence about slavery dissolved rather soon, as was the case in the slaveholders' republic generally.[68] "Texas must be slave country," was his emphatic demand in May 1833.[69]

That was not the only bad news faced by Mexico. George Erath was born in Vienna in 1813 but wound up as a staunch Texas patriot by the 1830s. He was aware of what he was to term "revolutionary times: the insurrection of 1830 drove the Bourbons from the throne of France...Poland revolted against Russia" and "France sent troops to Rome to protect the Pope...."[70] His litany did not include the event of moment for his new homeland: it was in 1830 that France seized control of Algeria,[71] which was to serve as a template for controlling Texas, up to and including the sending of North Africans to Mexico in the 1860s to assist the French puppet regime there. In retrospect, it is difficult to ascertain if Paris was taking instruction from Texas (or the U.S.) in terms of settler colonialism—or vice versa.[72]

Thus, as these dual horrific processes were unfolding, the son of the Texas Republic's first governor was telling his "dear father" about the need to "learn...by example or experience. The long wars the French carried on in Algeria cost vast amounts of blood and treasure; and on a larger scale, they are the same as our Indian wars on the plains, the same half desert and entire desert...same roving, crafty enemy...." One lesson: "French did very little towards

---

67. Torget, *Cotton*, 228.

68. Zoie Odom Newsome, "Antislavery Sentiment in Texas, 1821-1861," M.A. thesis, TTU, 1968, 27 (abbrev. Newsome).

69. Paschal, 69.

70. *Memoirs of George Erath*, Austin: Texas State Historical Association, 1923, 4 (abbrev. Erath).

71. Blaufarb, 168.

72. Saunt, xvi.

reducing the wild Arabs until they emploid [*sic*] the nativs [*sic*] against them," which augured intensified internecine conflict among Texas Indigenes. Already, he said, "friendly Indians" were "becoming very useful as guides and had been for a long time...."[73] Settlers continued to cooperate with Frenchmen, including the continuing efforts to import enslaved Africans from the Caribbean colony that was Martinique.[74]

Before being ousted by London in the mid-18th century from today's Canada, French settlers often were willing to cut deals with Indigenes in a manner seemingly alien to their British—or "Anglo"—counterparts.[75] Thus, Greenwood Le Flore, an affluent Choctaw slaveholder, had considerable French ancestry, and Levi Colbert, a Chickasaw leader, was not the only Indigene who spoke French. When the former died, 400 enslaved Africans were freed.[76]

Perhaps it was their enslaving proclivities that induced the Choctaws when faced with expulsion to capitulate and move to Texas rather than Indian Country. By February 1833, hundreds of them passed through Natchitoches, then settled within miles of Nacogdoches with Creeks following in their footsteps. But Texas settlers were displeased,[77] contributing to the overall malaise leading to both genocide and secession—not unlike the prelude to 1861.

These forced migrations were generating instability, as Indigenes were moving to and fro, futilely seeking to avoid settler depredations while often coming into conflict with other Indigenes as a result. Many Delaware fled the U.S. for Texas in the 1820s, then fled to Kansas in 1835 as Texas was in revolt, then to Indian Territory [Oklahoma] by 1867,[78] encountering disputatiousness all the while.

---

73. Raymond Estep, "Lieutenant William E. Burnett: Notes on Removal of Indians from Texas to Indian Territory," Chronicles of Oklahoma, William Kay Kendall Papers, UOk-N (abbrev. Kendall Papers).

74. Sean Kelley, "Blackbirders and Bozales: African Born Slaves on the Lower Brazos River of Texas in the Nineteenth Century," *Civil War History*, 54 (December 2008): 406-423, 412.

75. See e.g., Thomas Flanagan, *Louis 'David' Riel: Prophet of the New World*, Toronto: U of Toronto Press, 1996.

76. Saunt, 134-135, 109.

77. Grant Foreman, *Indian Removal: The Emigration of the Five Civilized Tribes of Indians*, Norman: U of Oklahoma Press, 1953, 96.

78. Lena Clara Koch, "The Federal Indian Policy in Texas, 1845-1860," *Southwestern Historical Quarterly*, 28 (No. 4, April 1925): 223-234, 229 (abbrev. Koch).

Still, President Andrew Jackson, who had expressed ambivalence about the settler project in Texas, by 1834 was mulling the possibility to take advantage of the situation by—as a close aide put it—striving to "populate the borders" of the still Mexican province with those, it was stressed, who were *"part French and the exiled Polanders."* This plot was "conducted in the most secret manner"[79] and was a step toward taking over Texas altogether. Although Germans generally have received credit for abolitionist stances, this was more true of the post-1848 refugees than those before, for in the early 1830s, one study concludes that "extermination" of Indigenes—as with settlers largely—was "on the minds of many Germans."[80] In the Third Ward of New Orleans—the urban capital of slavery—the German language was spoken so commonly that even the pigs were said to "grunt in that language."[81]

If Mexico had been a tad more farsighted in handling negotiations with Indigenes, together they may have been able to thwart Texas secessionists. Those described as "Alabamas and Coushattas," who relied heavily on the land, assumed an aggressive stance toward settler invasions and, along with the Cherokees, appealed to Mexico in 1831 for an official title to the land they occupied between the Neches and Trinity rivers, not far distant from today's Dallas. This was a throwback to events of the early days of post-1821 independence when Agustín de Iturbide, an early leader, granted certain Indigenes various privileges. But then some of these Indigenes, according to historian Sheri Marie Shuck, dismissed the 1836 secession as "a white man's war,"[82] an evaluation that redounded to their detriment, reflective of a dearth of strategic vision.

Yet the parlous position of Texas settlers was reflected in the point that although the regime was desperately in need of colonizers who could be defined as "white," even those arriving from the storm-tossed French Caribbean were not necessarily reliable politically. Thus, George Jeannet wound up in Texas, after playing a role in effectuating slave emancipation. He was said to have sought to spark an uprising among Africans against the regime in Guadeloupe

---

79. Anthony Butler to President Jackson, 7 March 1834, in Bassett, Volume 5, 1931, 249.

80. Adam J. Pratt, *Toward Cherokee Removal: Land, Violence and the White Man's Chance*, Athens: U of Georgia Press, 2020, 122.

81. Bolton, 134.

82. Sheri Marie Shuck, "Voices from the Southern Borderlands: The Alabamas and Coushattas, 1500-1859," Ph.D. dissertation, Auburn U, 2000, 134, 140 (abbrev. Shuck).

in conjunction with Titus Bigard and other Free Negroes; their fleet—and plan—was to disembark hundreds of armed men, burn plantations, murder settlers and destroy the regime.[83] Jeannet's presence exposed how vulnerable Texas was, dependent as it was upon a fundamental white supremacist qualification for settlement, that was hardly foolproof. On the other hand, according to one source, there were in 1830 "more Anglo-Americans in Texas than there were Mexicans and Indians combined."[84] This was unfortunate for Indigenes, who in 1832 were on the verge of one of their most significantly profound uprisings to that point.[85]

Yet, by 1833 a settler was writing of the previous months that the Comanches "hurt the Mexicans and murder them without mercy,"[86] suggesting the coordination of settler opponents was not smooth. By 1834, like a chess grandmaster, Mexico granted Cherokees a land to the north of Austin's colony,[87] which if exploited could have meant checkmate.

Prior to this there was another possibility for Mexico to have checked—potentially—the increasingly frisky settlers in Texas. The Utopian Socialist and philanthropist Robert Owen was in Mexico City in 1829 in conversation with President Guerrero about forming a district, 150 miles "broad," said the Welshman, "along the whole of frontier bordering on the U. States...for the purpose of establishing a new political and moral system of government." Such a settlement could have jeopardized the fortunes of secessionist Texas. Proceedings in increasingly abolitionist London prompted Owen to sail westward for his "well received" dialogue with Guerrero. That he stopped in Haiti along the way was a telling signal for this regime then often treated contemptuously like a polecat, prompted by Paris and Washington. In Vera Cruz he conferred with Richard Exeter, "the head of one of the first English [merchant] houses in the city" and "one of the largest proprietors in Texas," giving ballast to

---

83. Vanessa Mongey, *Rogue Revolutionaries: The Fight for Legitimacy in the Greater Caribbean*, Philadelphia: U of Pennsylvania Press, 2020. See also Blaufarb, 170.

84. Newcomb, 340.

85. P.E. Pearson, *Sketch of the Life of Judge Edwin Waller Together with some of the More Important Events of the Early Texas Revolution, in which he Participated Such as the Battle of Velasco...*,Galveston: Steam Book, 1874, 12.

86. Mary Austin Holley, *Texas. Observations, Historical, Geographical and Descriptive in a Series of Letters, Written During a Visit to Austin's Colony...in the Autumn of 1831...*, Baltimore: Armstrong & Plaskitt, 1833, 91.

87. Dewees, 151.

the persistent rumors that London had abolitionist plans for Austin's regime. As for President Guerrero, he admitted, "we separated apparently mutually pleased with each other," a confession bound to attract negative attention north of the border. Similarly unsettling was his description of his confab with Antonio López de Santa Anna, soon to be the dominant shaper of Mexico's often fractious politics for decades to come. "When I was about to leave," said Owen, "General Santa Anna...had become interested in a very extraordinary degree by this conversation" with Guerrero. He instructed Owen that "he would henceforth do whatever was in his power, to promote these objects...; he added [tantalizingly]: tell Mr. Owen that I wish he would consider me his agent in this country, to carry his plans into execution."[88]

The general who was to become a nettlesome annoyance for the slaveholders' republic was in the U.S. crosshairs early on, with the envoy in Vera Cruz in early 1832 expressing distaste for this Mexican's "desire" that "the American merchants of Vera Cruz should pay a whole or a part of what they owed...for duties."[89] The unease created by his evident "desire" was manifested when it was repeated days later,[90] suggesting that the slaveholders' republican objection to certain taxes proved generative in 1836 as it had proven to be in 1776.

The east coast of Mexico was proving to be as troublesome as the northern border, or so Washington was told. It was also in 1832 that U.S. national, Dr. John Baldwin, was summoned in Minatitlán by an official and, said the former's spouse, "he immediately went" and instantaneously was subjected to a "torrent of abuse" and was "ordered to the stocks" despite the abused feeling that the matter in controversy was minor. Yet a "number of armed French & Creoles" were "approaching" to rescue him from "bloodthirstiness" when Dr. Baldwin somehow "loaded his gun to prepare to defend himself"

---

88. "Robert Owen's Opening Speech and His Reply to the Rev. Alex Campbell, in the Recent Public Discussion in Cincinnati...also, Mr. Owen's Memorial to the Republic of Mexico and a Narrative of the Proceedings Thereon, Which Led to the Promise of the Mexican Government to Place a District One Hundred and Fifty Miles Broad, Along the Whole of the Frontier Bordering on the U. States Under Mr. Owen's Jurisdiction for the Purpose of Establishing a New Political and Moral System of Government...," Cincinnati: Owen, 1829, Filson Historical Society-Louisville.

89. J.A. Cameron, Consul to Colonel Vasquez, 19 April 1832, Reel 2, Despatches from U.S. Consuls in Vera Cruz, NARA.

90. Ibid., J.A. Cameron, Consul to State Department, 11 May 1832.

but wound up being "confined to the prison..."[91] His leg was badly damaged and, interestingly, "two American men" were pressed into service to aid him and a "Negro man"—not often accorded the descriptor of "American" north of the border—was prominent in this regard: "Isaac Reives..."[92] The latter's presence and prominence was suggestive of an increasing migration of U.S. Negroes to this vicinity, including Peter Hazur, described as "a man of colour, carpenter and native of New Orleans [who] died here...."[93]

This brightening horizon unveiled by Owen quickly darkened. Owen demanded religious tolerance,[94] a bridge too far for potent clerical forces in Mexico, who inherited from Spain a blinding Catholicism that had handicapped Madrid from the inception of settler colonialism,[95] a major factor explicating why His Catholic Majesty could not move northward from Florida post-1565 and had to yield to English invaders by 1607. Moreover, London—the ultimate guarantor—was overstretched in British India and the Caribbean, where increasingly the Africans were driving the agenda. Could it afford yet another tussle with the slaveholders' republic after the stalemate of the 1812 war?

As time passed in the 1830s, Mexico sensed correctly that Texas settlers' secessionist plans were proceeding at breakneck speed. Juan Almonte—a Mexican leader, soldier and diplomat, who wound up fighting the secessionists on the battlefield—was told by a U.S. sympathizer that "some of my slaveholding and insatiable countrymen cherish...wresting from your country the noble and beautiful province of Texas...." As David Lee Child wrote, "Hutchins Burton, formerly a representative in Congress from North Carolina & subsequently governor" had just "made a purchase of 40, 000 acres of land in Texas" in anticipation that the province "was soon to be annexed." Then President Jackson had the "intention to make said Burton the first governor of the new territory...." A major reason? "They want Texas as a market for their increasing <u>herds</u> of human creatures, raised only to be turned into cash"[96] [emphasis-original].

---

91. Ibid., Report by Isabella Baldwin, 3 January 1832.

92. Ibid., Isabella Baldwin to Respected Sir, 11 January 1832.

93. Ibid., Peter Cullen to State Department, 1 August 1834.

94. Wilbert H. Timmons, "Robert Owen's Texas Project," *Southwestern Historical Quarterly*, 52 (No. 3, January 1949): 286-293, 287. See also Edward A. Lukes, *De Witt Colony of Texas*, Austin: Pemberton, 1976.

95. Horne, *Dawning*.

96. David Lee Child to Juan Almonte, 15 September 1834, Carton 46, Bolton Papers.

With dreams of a tsunami of dollars dancing in their heads, one spectator then noticed that Texas had "become a kind of deport for malefactors, not only from the United States" but also from "the West India islands" as the debris of the slaveholding class there fled to greener pastures, often with actually freed Africans in tow, as "many a stolen Negro and many a free one" were dragged along to this sink of iniquity.[97] Things had gotten so bad that in 1828, Washington issued an official report about the problem created by "fugitives from the United States to Mexico [Texas]," along with the related issue "respecting the boundary line between the United States and the province of Texas," as the suspicion arose that this flow of roughnecks was not accidental but part of Texas's visionary plan of becoming a rival of the U.S.[98]

One hand washed another, since early on Austin demonically accepted enslaved Africans as payment for land[99]—which hyped the market for both. Early on, for each enslaved person owned, the arriving enslaver could receive an additional 160 acres—seized illicitly from Indigenes[100]—or at least 50 acres.[101]

Yes, Washington was watching Mexico's response to this treachery carefully. Reporting from Vera Cruz not long after Owen's departure, the U.S. envoy reported with apparent anxiety that "Texas is another topic which has engaged the attention of the government during the last three months of its administration. It was next in importance to the regulation of internal affairs,"[102] a project made difficult by restiveness by clerics, Indigenes and Spaniards alike.

Nevertheless, it was evident early on that a secessionist Texas—like its descendant, the so-called Confederate States of America—could be wielded against Washington, though enslavers predominated there too. Early in 1831 President Andrew Jackson expressed mordant

---

97. Stiff, 213.

98. "Fugitives From United States to Mexico...Message from the President of the United States...Respecting the Recovery of Debts...in the Mexican States from Persons Absconding from the United States: Also Respecting the Boundary Line Between the United States and the Province of Texas," 20th Congress, Doc. No. 61, House of Representatives, 15 January 1828, Washington: Gales & Seaton, 1828, Williams Research Center, Historic New Orleans Collection (abbrev. Historic New Orleans).

99. Audain, 55.

100. Paschal, 23.

101. Torget, *Cotton*, 81.

102. Report from the U.S. Consul, 7 May 1830, Reel 1, Despatches from U.S. Consuls in Vera Cruz, NARA.

"fear that a project is already on foot by adventurers from the United States, acting in concert with disaffected citizens of Mexico to take possession of Texas and declare it an independent republic"—a mischievous project he swore to "defeat."[103]

Why would an infamous land grabber and enslaver be suspicious of his comrades in Texas? These latest secessionists might have been rivals as much as comrades, willing to engage in arbitrage in league with major powers contrary to the interest of the original secessionist. The ambitious Austin and his comrades tended to think they could build a credible rival to the U.S.[104]

Then again, independent Texas could prove to be exceedingly vulnerable, leading to pressure from the major powers it could not withstand, thereby jeopardizing Louisiana and points eastward. Hence, before this intervention, President Jackson wondered about the "influence which the population of Texas is fast acquiring and which there is reason to fear on account of the liberating of their slaves"—certainly not the intention of the enslavers but possible because of pressure exerted by abolitionists in Mexico, Haiti, Britain, Indigenous nations, and, of course, the enslaved themselves. Thus, the settlement was enmeshed "in a state of considerable disaffection." The knock-on impact on the slaveholders' republic sited in Washington could be catastrophic.[105]

What to do? President Jackson's envoy in Mexico, Anthony Butler, revealed the way out in early 1832 when he told his boss: "I presume you are still as anxious to procure Texas to be added to the U. States as you were two years ago," scheming against a close neighbor, incompatible with diplomacy as traditionally understood. As a result, Butler labored under "disadvantages" in Mexico, to be expected as delegate of a piratical regime: the "weight of prejudice, suspicion and bad feeling" stalked his every maneuver there. This was a continuation of the "odium engendered against my predecessor[,] all of which was transferred to me in advance...." Mexicans, he wailed, "attack my character, misrepresent the objects of my mission and identify me in the hate they bore toward Mr. Poinsett," his predecessor. Though he was studying the "Castilian language," he conceded that he was a "stranger to the language of the country,"[106] perhaps his premier "disadvantage."

---

103. President Jackson to Anthony Butler, 15 February 1831, in Bassett, Volume 4, 1929, 243.

104. Torget, Cotton, 12.

105. President Jackson to Anthony Butler, 23 March 1830, in Bassett, Volume 4, 129.

106. Anthony Butler to President Jackson, 2 January 1832 in Bassett, Volume 4, 390.

* * *

Empowering these settler land grabs and mass enslavement was a peculiarly malignant form of racism, distinct from others in the Old South in that it was charged with national chauvinism vis-à-vis Mexicans. It also crossed gender lines in that it was early settler Mary S. Helm who charged that "Mexicans are…the debris of several inferior and degraded races; African and Indian crossed and mixed and even the old Spanish blood was mixed with the Moorish and demoralized by a long course of indolence and political corruption," i.e., the "very antithesis of the Anglo-American."[107] This chauvinistic swagger was underlined in pre-1836 Texas when it was declared that "five Indians will chase twenty Mexicans but five Americans (that is from the United States of the North) will chase twenty Indians…."[108] Such propaganda was useful in creating the requisite psychosis needed to execute genocide and lay the foundation for fascism.

Au contraire, argued many settlers, including Nelson Lee, an early Texas Ranger: as he saw things, many Indigenes—for some reason—tended to "cherish an inveterate hatred of the white race, whom they regard as usurpers"; thus, he cried, "hundreds of our people," meaning settlers, "are captured yearly, enslaved and barbarously put to death."[109] That is—dialectically—the pre-existing martial skills of the Comanches, in particular, confronted the rapacity of the settlers, creating a hellscape needed to foment an all-encompassing "ethnic cleansing" that created today's Texas and laid the foundation for a nascent fascism.

But the Texas settlers anticipated their republican descendants by making room in their enterprise for quislings, among whom was Lorenzo de Zavala, born in the strife-ridden Yucatan, notorious for seemingly endemic conflict between the Indigenous and their opponents, who wound up as a vice president of the secessionist Republic of Texas in 1836. In 1831 he was listed as one of three "empresarios" of the "Galveston Bay & Texas Land Company," equivalent to getting in on the ground floor of a munificent 21st-century initial public offering.[110] Before that, he was accused of leaking confidential Mexican

---

107. Mary S. Helm, *Scraps from Texas History, 1828 to 1843*, Austin: Author, 1884, 52.

108. Kite, 35.

109. Lee, 139-140.

110. *Address to the Reader of the Documents Relating to the Galveston Bay & Texas Land Company…Translation of the Colonization of the United Mexican*

negotiating points to U.S. envoy Poinsett in 1826.[111] Zavala—as late as 1821, when Mexico was surging to independence from Spain—represented the turbulent Yucatan in the official representative body in Spain.[112]

According to Edward Stiff, this former Mexican Minister to France "engaged in a treasonable correspondence with the war party in Texas and also with the French government, as well as individuals in the United States...." Recalled by Mexico, he then sailed to France to confer with confederates there, then it was on to New Orleans, refuge for numerous French conspirers, before decamping further west, where he united with the victorious Texans—and wound up being the Mexican figleaf on an otherwise "Anglo" white supremacist project.[113]

Proficient in English by his own admission and actually born in the seat of racist conflict—the Yucatan—in 1778, he was to refer to "the colored people" as the "Jews of North America...this situation is not very natural in a country where they profess the principles of the widest liberty," which was either terribly naïve or utterly cynical. Like Judas denying selling out early Christians, he adamantly denied selling out Mexico.[114]

Zavala was the template for the rising of a disturbing trend: the man of "Hispanic" origin who throws in his lot with "Anglo" reactionaries, a development that reaches a kind of apogee with the ascension of Santos Benavides, a wealthy born Spanish national who became a colonel in the so-called Confederate States of America—after doing similar dirty work in the borderlands.[115] Those like Zavala were essential to the "success" of the Counter-Revolution of 1836.

States and of the State of Coauila and Texas, as Published by Stephen F. Austin, New York: Hopkins, 1831.

111. Herrera, 248.

112. Paschal, 32.

113. Stiff, 264.

114. Lorenzo de Zavala, *Journey to the United States of America*, Austin: Shoal Creek, 1980, xv, 109, 96.

115. John Denny Riley, "Santos Benavides: His Influence in the Lower Rio Grande, 1823-1891," Ph.D. dissertation, TCU, 1976, 6 (abbrev. J.D. Riley).

Chapter 3

The Counter-Revolution of 1836

The man described as "an old negro" saw a Euro-American man in Texas who looked familiar. He was not wrong. William F. Gray had been driven out of Virginia by a sharp economic downturn and, like so many so affected, he moved to Texas. By the time of this encounter—October 1835—the opening gun had sounded marking the onset of anti-Mexican secession, but the man who then answered to "Colonel Gray" recalled that he and the "old negro" whom he had seen had espied each other previously in the Cavalier State, since this "old Negro" "had belonged to General Minor's estate in Fredericksburg"[1] and like so many enslaved Africans in the Upper South, was dumped in Texas.

Colonel Gray's presence was a token of a catastrophic war, which was to be punctuated by a number of now mythical landmarks, including the siege of the Alamo in February 1836, the equivalent of 4 July 1776 (speaking of 2 March 1836) and the companion to the Battle of Yorktown signaling settler victory, speaking of 21 April 1836 and the Battle of San Jacinto.[2]

And preceding it all was the Battle of Velasco of 1832—just as the Battle of Lexington preceded 1776—when armed settlers attacked the Mexican military, which was an episode in a chain of turmoil, especially uproars over slavery. Typical was the story of Joel W. Robinson, born in Georgia in 1815, who accompanied his father to Texas in 1831 and soon was expectedly battling Mexicans. "Both my father

---

1. Note and entry in *From Virginia to Texas 1835: Diary of Col. William F. Gray, Giving Details of His Journey to Texas and Return in 1835-1836 and Second Journey to Texas in 1837*, Houston: Young, 1965 [originally published 1909], iii, 23 (abbrev. *From Virginia*), Virginia Historical Society-Richmond (abbrev. VaHS-R).

2. William C. Binkley, *The Texas Revolution*, Baton Rouge: LSU Press, 1952, and Sam W. Haynes, et al., eds., *Contested Empire: Rethinking the Texas Revolution*, College Station: TA&MU Press, 2015. See also William Campbell Binkley, *The Expansionist Movement in Texas, 1836-1850*, Berkeley: U of California Press, 1925.

and myself," he said, "were engaged in the attack upon the Mexican fort at Velasco in June 1832."[3] One scholar who asserts flatly that the "Texas Revolution [*sic*] was outright defense of slavery," also observes that in September 1835, during a conflict with the Comanches at "De Witt's Colony," a major settlement, fired then were the "first...shots...of the Texas Revolution...."[4]

Just as Robert Neighbors, a federal agent, was slain by a Texas patriot in 1859 because of a perceived lassitude in massacring Indigenes, the U.S. envoy in Texas in August 1836 argued that the then crisis with Mexico was driven by the supposed "refusal upon the part of Mexico to protect the colonial settlements from the depredations of the Indian tribes...."[5]

Austin, on an apparent fund-raising junket in Louisville in March 1836, was full-throated in militant defense of the "Anglo-Saxon Race" then consummating sovereignty, whom he correctly analogized to "our forefathers in '76 [who] flew to arms for much less." Lulling his fellow Southerners, he proclaimed that the rebels' aim was independence or annexation to the U.S.—London or Paris was likely to receive only the former message. But his main point was that their declaration *cum* war justification of 7 November 1835 was needed to thwart the dreaded "servile war"—code for an African and/or Indigenous uprising—propelled by "wild fanatics" whose real goal was "intervention in the domestic concerns of the South" itself. Like the 1776 Declaration, that of 2 March 1836, harangued Mexico as Britain was denounced, since "through its emissaries, [Mexico City] incited the merciless savage, with the tomahawk and scalping knife."[6]

Given its birth in the toxically amniotic fluid of white supremacy and shameless profiteering, was it possible for Texas to pursue any other course besides one leading hypnotically to fascism?

However, as the presence of the "old Negro" tended to suggest, all who had arrived in this battleground were not necessarily there voluntarily and, as scholars have suggested, a number were aware

---

3. Statement by Joel W. Robinson, ca. 1832, Kendall Papers.

4. Paschal, iv, 74.

5. "Condition of Texas...Message from the President of the United States...," 22, 24 December 1836, U.S. Congress. House of Representatives, 24th Congress, 2nd Session, Doc. No. 35, Huntington Library (abbrev. "Condition of Texas").

6. "Address of the Honorable William H. Wharton, Delivered in New York on Tuesday April 25, 1836, Also Address of the Honorable Stephen F. Austin Delivered in Louisville, Kentucky, on the 7th March 1836...," New York: Colyer, 1836, NYHS.

of the abolitionist stakes at play and more specifically, that Colonel Gray and many of his comrades had taken up arms against a government that objected to enslavement of Africans.[7] Indeed, as one scholarly study argued, "if the documents are to be believed, literally thousands of Texas negroes either fled or participated in an organized attempt at rebellion"[8]—as settlers were launching their own revolt. It was unavoidable that Texas was in a state of flux and decomposition as 1836 approached, which happened to be ideal conditions for the enslaved to engage in self-determination.

Shortly before hostilities commenced in October 1835, settler authorities were keen to guard against insurrections of the enslaved. Austin was told hurriedly that an invasion from the sea by Mexico would mean "great danger from the negroes should a large Mexican force come so near...."[9]

As with 1776,[10] Texas settlers were on a buying spree of enslaved Africans as the moment for armed confrontation arrived, perhaps high on their own supply and assuming that these Negroes were simply unpaid labor at little or no socio-political cost and not potential gravediggers willing to bury the secessionist project. Settler hero James W. Fannin alone had delivered more than 150 enslaved Africans from Cuba to Texas in August 1835.[11] At the same time, yet another settler hero was enmeshed as well in slave trading.[12] Between 1833 and 1835, one contemporary source asserts that four boatloads of Africans had been brought to Texas via Cuba and the source actually saw some of these arrivals in the borderlands.[13]

But it was not just Cuba. Edwin Waller, a counter-revolutionary stalwart and the first mayor of the ostentatiously named Austin, Texas—the eventual capital—went directly to the beleaguered

---

7. Kite, 3-4.

8. Note in Tyler and Murphy, xxxvii.

9. See Matagorda Resolutions, 30 September 1835; Report, 30 September 1835; Josiah Bell to Stephen F. Austin, 6 October 1835; and Thomas J. Pilgrim to Stephen F. Austin, 6 October 1835, in *Austin Papers*, Volume III, 143, 161, 162.

10. Horne, *Counter-Revolution of 1776*.

11. M.R. Moore, 91.

12. Marjorie Denise Brown, "Diplomatic Ties: Slavery and Diplomacy in the Gulf Coast Region, 1836-1845," Ph.D. dissertation, Vanderbilt U, 2017, 52 (abbrev. M.D. Brown).

13. Note in Paul Lack, ed., "The Diary of William Fairfax Gray: From Virginia to Texas, 1835," Dallas: De Golyer Library, Clements Center, SMU, 1997, 230 (abbrev. William Fairfax Gray).

continent to ensnare enslaved Africans. Understandably, they escaped promptly and remained at large for a year. The years of Texas unrest, 1836-1838, also proved to be the time when African-born enslaved were among the most repetitive and ferociously resistant runaways.[14]

Stephen F. Austin himself had reason to suspect what was occurring under his nose. As if he were shocked by gambling occurring in a casino, he confided in 1836 that "extensive projects are in contemplation to introduce African negro slaves into this country by citizens of the United States."[15] The operative words may be the final two, as if what actually rankled him was that this putative rival was reaping the windfall rather than his fellow freebooters.

As if there were cause and effect, it was also in August 1835 that Caleb Green, Jr., in nearby southwestern Louisiana, worriedly told his father of an impending insurrection of the enslaved: "there is no doubt," he declared "[that]a widely extended conspiracy has embraced the whole southwestern country...." Stating the blindingly obvious, he concluded, "[I] feel as if we [are] upon a dormant volcano—I never retire to bed without examining our [security measures]."[16]

The question for today is whether settlers have engaged in a kind of repressed memory syndrome, audaciously ejecting from consciousness the fearful idea of being overtaken by furious Africans, yet still operating with this danger subconsciously or even intentionally motivating Negrophobia.

Critical to the success of the secessionist project was a man—Robert Mills, the "Duke of Brazoria"—who happened to be one of the wealthiest men in antebellum Texas and the South, having a fortune approaching a stunning $5 million. He not only owned more enslaved Africans than any enslaver in Texas, forced to free 800 of them in 1865, but this Kentuckian was also a financier of the counter-revolution and, given the potential impact on his pocketbook, this was understandable. He stood as a major reason why between the formal onset of counter-revolution in 1835 and 1847—in the immediate aftermath of Texas joining the Union—the enslaved population skyrocketed from 4000 to 39,000, then to a stunning 183,000 by 1860. The "Duke" was related via marriage to William Moody—a Virginian by birth—one of the richest and most powerful men in the

---

14. Ibid., 267.

15. Stephen F. Austin, 16 December 1836, in Kenneth R. Stevens, ed., *The Texas Legation Papers*, Fort Worth: TCU Press, 2012, 54 (abbrev. Stevens).

16. Caleb Green, Jr. to Caleb Green, Sr., 29 August 1835, Caleb Green Letters, Historic New Orleans.

antebellum South and gung-ho on 1861 secession: his daughter married Mills's grandnephew.[17]

As indicated by the promiscuous presence on the frontlines of Texas of Kentuckians and Virginians, this hostile takeover of Texas was substantially a product of the slaveholders' republic to the east. It was in 1835 that William Fairfax Gray was informed that "in five years...two-thirds of the negroes of South Carolina will be moved off to this or some other Southern state," en route to the final destination: Texas. This realization fed a speculative boom, he said: "the negotiations for land and negroes continues with unabated ardor"; the premier speculative investment was, it was said, "buy cotton land on the coast and stock it with Negroes from Cuba...plenty of good land may now be bought in Texas for twenty five cents per acre...."[18]

Thus, it was not just enslaved Africans who were arriving en masse as Texas settlers geared up for secession. As annexation was becoming an accomplished fact in 1845, lips were loosened, and it was admitted that just prior to 1836, Stephen A. Austin himself had snuck into New Orleans with the aim of borrowing a hefty $200,000 for secessionist purposes. During the pivotal battles, transports were continuously departing this commercial center for slavery filled with armed volunteers headed toward the battlefield that was then northern Mexico. The authorities turned a blind eye, which ostensibly violated "neutrality" laws since President Jackson himself was reported to be providing a wink and a nod in assent, not least since regulars of his own Democratic Party were in the vanguard. But even London was said to be waffling, contrary to their seemingly reflexive opposition to the slaveholders' republic, since financier Baring Brothers at the apex of the City of London were said to be in league with counter-revolutionary pillar Benjamin Rush Milam, who supposedly stood to gain a breathtaking one million acres of prime property if his side prevailed.[19]

Again, the land grab from Indigenes and Mexicans facilitated further enslavement of Africans, and these factors in concert led to a

---

17. Robert Stuart Shelton, "Waterfront Workers of Galveston, Texas, 1838-1920," Ph.D. dissertation, Rice U, 2001, 48, 65, 66, 76 (abbrev. Shelton).

18. Entry, 13 December 1835, in William Fairfax Gray, 50.

19. Report, 4 February 1845, in George Edward Ellis, ed., *Letters Upon the Annexation of Texas, Addresses to Hon. John Quincy Adams, as Originally Published in the Boston Atlas Under the Signature of Lisle*, Boston: White, Lewis & Porter, 1845 (abbrev. Ellis), American Antiquarian Society, Worcester, Massachusetts (abbrev. AAS).

resurgence of the slave trade to the vicinity.[20] One scholar goes as far as suggesting that what drove settlers to rebel was Mexico intercepting slave ships to Texas.[21]

This factor was disruptive to the political economy of New Orleans, which is one reason some of the most enthusiastic backing for secession emerged precisely from this town. By October 1834 Austin was informed happily about the "excitement of the Public Mind" there; the pro-secession "meeting was the largest ever known in New Orleans"; and this was not just the sound and fury signifying nothing, for promptly dispatched westward to the battleground were "two divisions of about 60 men each...."[22]

But it was not just this Louisiana metropolis that was shuttling material aid to the rebels. A Mexican official in October 1835 told the U.S. Secretary of State that New York vessels were headed to Louisiana—"not less than twelve in number"—but really bound for Texas in order to "introduce into that colony arms and munitions of war" for the purpose of "insurrection...."[23]

Soon Austin was involved in a scheme to bring 1000 families to the settlement from Great Britain in return for land grants, which would have the added benefit of creating leverage against London.[24]

À la 1776, investments in land were not the only asset at issue. Again, on the brink of annexation, more detail emerged about the illicit importing of the enslaved not only from further east but the U.S. too. "All are aware of the desire of [many in] France to extinguish slavery in her colonies," leading to fire-sale prices as the enslaved from Martinique were dumped on the market. The "value of slaves

---

20. M.D. Brown, 8.

21. Greg Grandin, *The End of the Myth: From the Frontier to the Border Wall in the Mind of America*, New York: Holt, 2019, 84 (abbrev. Grandin).

22. James Ramage to Stephen F. Austin, 21 October 1835, in *Austin Papers*, Volume III, 198.

23. Mr. J.M. Castillo y Lanzas to Secretary of State John Forsyth, 29 October 1835, in *Examination and Review of a Pamphlet Printed and Secretly Circulated by M.D. Gorostiza, Late Envoy Extraordinary from Mexico: Previous to His Departure from the United States and by Him Entitled 'Correspondence Between the Legation Extraordinary of Mexico and the Department of State of the United States Respecting the Passage of the Sabine, by the Troops Under the Command of General Gaines*, Washington, D.C.: Force, 1837, 43-44, NYHS (abbrev. *Examination and Review*).

24. J.E. Savage to Stephen F. Austin, 18 March 1836, in *Austin Papers*, Volume III, 308.

in Texas will be, for many years, greater than in these United States," said one financial analyst, as the feeding frenzy of 1835 ensued.[25]

Also, as with 1776, the cascading and influx of the enslaved into Texas on the brink of war were not necessarily the asset for secessionists that importers may have imagined initially. Many arrived from Cuba—or worse, for enslavers, Africa—and were justifiably disgruntled. Some of these Africans were not only fluent in various Indigenous languages based on pre-existing experience on the continent but Spanish (based on experience in Cuba) or French (sojourning in Martinique or Guadeloupe or even Louisiana). "I know I was born in Morocco," said the once enslaved woman Silvia King, then she moved on to France: this remark was made after she was emancipated.[26]

In March 1836 a settler spoke of a settler patriarch who had "staying with him four young African negroes, two males, two females. They were brought here from the West Indies by a Mr. Monroe Edwards…[they were] native Africans for they can speak not a word of English, French or Spanish" and, not unrelated, "their habits are beastly,"[27] he maintained.

This linguistic facility could not only mean facilitation of escape by pretending to be "free" or a foreigner—one runaway used his fluency with Indian languages to further his expedition to the Creek Nation—it could also mean facilitation of anti-settler espionage.[28]

Retrospectively, this linguistic facility should be seen as unsurprising. The historian Vincent Brown has reminded that West Africans in the Americas not only "learned…new mores and customs" but "second and third languages" as well, as a matter of sheer survival.[29]

Sheer survival indeed, for conditions on the frontier in Texas for the enslaved may have been even harsher than Virginia, an early and persistent site of roughhewn pitilessness. William Fairfax Gray, the former Virginian who turned up in Texas just in time to fight Mexicans, said as much. "The log huts of the poor Negroes [in Texas]," he lamented "are more open than the log stables in Virginia and some of them have no chimney. No wonder they sicken and die," he cried; "the wonder is that any of them live."[30]

25. Report, 22 February 1845, in Ellis.

26. Oral History, Silvia King, circa 1937, in Tyler and Murphy, 3.

27. Entry, 25 March 1836, in William Fairfax Gray.

28. Paul Dean Lack, "Urban Slavery in the Southwest," Ph.D. dissertation, TTU, 1973, 248 (abbrev. Lack).

29. Vincent Brown, *Tacky's Revolt: The Story of an Atlantic Slave War*, Cambridge: Harvard U Press, 2020, 99.

30. Entry, 7 April 1837, in William Fairfax Gray, 220.

Of course, multilingualism was hardly unusual in neighboring Louisiana and may have been the sieve leaking intelligence in French into the eager ears of the enslaved. It was in early 1836 that the Virginian *cum* Texan made his way to the legislative assembly in the Pelican State. "Some of the members speak French," he noted just after the visit. "When one speaks in French an interpreter renders it into English"—convenient for any Negro "servants" in earshot—"and *vice versa.*"[31]

Befitting his roots in Virginia, Gray was swayed by racialist views. Like post-1865 rationalizations of secession, he—and others of his ilk—argued that constitutionalism was the issue in 1836, not land and labor. Thus, in Louisiana he found that "this place is much divided on the questions of adhering to the Mexican Constitution of 1824"—purported justification for secession—and "much excitement prevailed" as a result. But like the post-1865 rationalizers of secession, Gray was also revealing in his unsparingly describing one side of this battle: the "Constitutional Party have enlisted on their side *all* the Mexicans, or Native Texans, who are a swarthy, dirty looking people much resembling our mulattos, some of them nearly black but having straight hair..."[32] [emphasis-original].

(Of course, certain enslavers had difficulty in separating their material interest in preserving the system of human property from opposition to Santa Anna's desire to upend federalists—who often were more open to enslavement.[33] Jousting over constitutional pettifoggery cannot obscure the ampler point that secession was driven by an unsated appetite for land and enslaved labor more than words on a piece of paper.[34])

Those Africans flooding into Texas from Cuba may have received news in Spanish that was circulating in the borderlands in the run-up to 1836, i.e., that General Santa Anna wanted to emancipate the enslaved but slaveholders were balking.[35] (Days after the epochal Alamo battle, Santa Anna issued a decree freeing slaves in Texas—which was translated. Coincidentally, the only male survivor of this battle was a man of African descent,[36] the (then) property of settler

---

31. Ibid., Entry, 5 January 1836.

32. Entries, 5 January 1836, and 1 February 1836, *From Virginia*, 67.

33. Torget, *Cotton*, 202. See also Carlos E. Castaneda, translator, *The Mexican Side of the Texas Revolution. By the Chief Mexican Participants...*, Dallas: Turner, 1928.

34. Cf. Torget, Cotton, 122.

35. DeLay, 73.

36. George Nelson, *The Alamo: An Illustrated History*, Uvalde, Texas: Aldine, 2009 (abbrev. G. Nelson). For more on this episode, see *Telegraph & Texas Register*, 8 June 1837.

champion William Travis.)[37] A leader of the counter-revolution, Benjamin Milam warned further that Santa Anna sought to stoke a slave revolt to thwart the settler overthrow of the existing regime.[38] His comrade, Thomas Pilgrim, wondered nervously, "would there not be great danger from the Negroes should a large Mexican force... come so near?"[39]

Of course, Santa Anna as villainous abolitionist was useful in bringing enslavers from points eastward to Texas, including the influential John Quitman, who left his Mississippi to join the fray in order to quell what was to be described as a "suspected Tejano-Indian uprising," with possible devastating consequences for slavery and settler colonialism continentally;[40] he was also greeted by rumors of a brewing slave rebellion along the Brazos River and credible stories about the enslaved fleeing into the arms of the Mexican military. Apparently, Santa Anna contacted Mexico City seeking sanction for emancipating the enslaved as a key component of squashing the rebellion.[41]

Mexico aimed a double-barreled weapon at the settlers, not only seeking to spawn revolts of the enslaved, but pushing Indigenes in a similar direction.[42] Coincidentally enough, 1835 marks the onset of ever more hostile raids by Indigenes targeting settlements.[43] Washington tried to help, brokering a treaty with the Cherokees in December 1835, but since so many were still smarting from being forced to embark on the "Trail of Tears," it is unclear how much this aided the Texas settlers.[44]

Yet Cherokee had reason to distrust Mexico City, since as early as the 1820s many of them had migrated to Texas and thought they had received a promise for clear title to an immense territory—but, it was thought, this promise was unfulfilled.[45] Then there were the Caddo, who by 1835 Washington felt their land grant from Mexico had been

37. Entry, 20 March 1836, in *From Virginia*, 136-137.

38. Note in Tyler and Murphy, xxxvii.

39. Paschal, 74.

40. Note, William Fairfax Gray, 229.

41. Torget, *Cotton*, 244.

42. Benjamin Milam to Francis Johnson, 5 July 1835, in *Austin Papers*, Volume III, 82.

43. Wallace and Hoebel, 292.

44. "Supplementary Articles to a Treaty With the Cherokees," 29 December 1835, UOk-N.

45. "A Bloody Christmas Eve: How the Death of Richards Fields and Lauerac Caused the Collapse of the Fredonian Republic," from Memoirs of John P. Simpson 1838-1841 (abbrev. Simpson), originally from Steen Library,

honored; thus, the U.S. War Department was told by an official at Fort Jessup just across the border near Natchitoches, "these Indians are more attached to the Spaniards [*sic*] than to the Americans...."[46]

Both the settlers and Mexico vied for support from diverse Indigenous groupings—but the latter were divided, making it difficult for them to multiply their leverage. Mexican agents were energetic in lobbying the Comanches and Wichita, neither of which required much encouragement to combat invading settlers.[47] But Chickasaw warned settlers about approaching Waco in November 1830 with malign intentions.[48] One settler, a self-described "Indian trader" in Texas in 1836, was organizing "Creeks, Delawares" and other Indigenes to "act against the Western Indians, who are in the Mexican interest and are becoming troublesome...." His aims were modest then compared to the subsequently massive "ethnic cleansing" and "extermination." Then William Fairfax Gray found it "practicable to remove all the Indians from this part of the state and place them on the head waters of the Brazos, Colorado, etc. on the east side of the mountain, which forms the western boundary of Texas [*sic*] and thus make them a barrier against the Comanches...."[49]

The aforementioned deviltry notwithstanding, apparently there were terribly misguided Free Negroes who fought against Mexico beginning in 1835, indicating that not only were certain Indigenes misled.[50] Again, it is remarkable how united the diverse Pan-European settlers stood, especially compared to those they were seeking to undo.

Often Indigenes were also divided internally, e.g., the Creeks, who often relied upon Negro interpreters but who waged war against the settlers and their own internal foes in the so-called "Red Stick" warfare,[51] one of many continental civil wars fed by struggles that

---

Stephen F. Austin State U, Box 4, Gary Anderson Papers, UOk-N (abbrev. Anderson Papers).

46. Report to D. Kurtz, Acting Commissioner of Indian Affairs, War Department, 6 January 1835, Box 1, Heflin Papers.

47. Elizabeth Ann Harper, "The Taovayas Indians in Frontier Trade and Diplomacy," *Panhandle Plains Historical Review*, 26 (1953): 41-72, 68, Box 4, Anderson Papers.

48. Statement by Joel W. Robinson, circa 1832, Kendall Papers.

49. Entry, circa 1836, William Fairfax Gray, 50.

50. Audain, 80.

51. Angela Pulley Hudson, *Creek Paths and Federal Roads: Indians, Settlers and Slaves in the Making of the American South*, Chapel Hill: U of North Carolina Press, 2010, 24.

mirrored the eventuating U.S. Civil War. One sector of the Creeks with roots in Alabama, but then ousted by 1835, were—said a Mexican envoy—"now emigrating and establishing itself in lands belonging to Mexico"[52]—but, alas, not for long.

Simultaneously, numerous settlers had honed their own warfare skills by battling in the Blackhawk War in the U.S. Midwest of the 1830s and similar warring in Florida and elsewhere.[53] "I expect to proceed to Florida in a few weeks and remain this winter as usual," said R.B. Hicks of Virginia, who was not referring to vacationing on the beach. "Should the Indian war in Florida be brought to a speedy close," he continued in 1836, "I may pay Texas a visit,"[54] indicating the pro-slavery solidarity that had blossomed by 1861. However, he may have been detained in the Sunshine State by the likes of Abraham, the Indigenous leader of African descent, described complimentarily as a man with the "crouch and the spring of panther"; he was accorded the accolade that he was "like a Frenchman of the old school. His countenance is one of great cunning and penetration...."[55]

Besides, the French comrades who flexed their muscles in Texas, then again by 1861, had endured warfare particularly in North Africa, that also came in handy.[56] Ironically, Mexico upon independence was imbued with the laudable goals of the French Revolution; this inspired their 1824 measure to bar further introduction of the enslaved, which brought so much grief to the regime.[57] The problem here was the counter-revolution launched by Napoleon Bonaparte, which led directly to colonizing Algeria and seeking to seize Mexico eventually.

George Erath was born in Vienna and seemingly was inspired by the dispatching of French troops to Rome decades before Texas secession. By 1832 he was headed across the Atlantic to New Orleans, finding it was cheaper to go there than New York. Soon he was fighting Mexicans and Indigenes in Texas, where he noticed that battling was more intense against the Comanches in the western portion of

---

52. J.M. Castillo y Lanzas to Asbury Dickins, 14 October 1835, in *Examination and Review*.

53. William Preston Johnston, *The Life of General Albert Sidney Johnston*, New York: Appleton, 1878, 25 (abbrev. W.P. Johnston).

54. R.B. Hicks to Thomas Jefferson Green, 4 October 1836, Thomas Jefferson Green Papers, U of North Carolina-Chapel Hill (abbrev. Green Papers), University of North Carolina-Chapel Hill (abbrev. UNC-CH).

55. Klos, 55-78, 69.

56. Blaufarb, 5.

57. Downs, 211.

the territory than elsewhere. By the fall of 1836 he was still in the thick of things, motivated by material incentive: he was promised a then considerable $25 monthly and a still considerable 1280 acres of land for every 12 months' service. This future Texas republic legislator for whom today's Erath County was named, certainly profited from this venture.[58] But it would be mistaken to see this as the norm. Texas's real estate speculation play was akin to a Ponzi scheme. Recruits received "land certificates" that often were sold for a song—or less. "They would let merchants have 320 acre certificates for a [pair] of pants" or another necessity.[59]

Nonetheless, Texas secession was a goldmine for Europeans of various stripes, since the bounty was dished out on a racist basis, consonant with continental praxis but heightened in Texas, then facing an enraged neighbor in Mexico, sullen enslaved, and battle-hardened Indigenes. At once, this determined that Texas would become an even more extremist version of the slaveholders' republic and, thus, would have to yield even more emoluments to attract Europeans—or whoever could pass for "white." Thus, when Mexican forces slaughtered 400 Texas volunteers at Goliad in March 1836, the massacred included Poles, British, Canadians, Germans and the like. There were no Mexican surnames affixed to the dead, suggestive of how Mexicans—Zavala notwithstanding—were being ousted from the hallowed halls of "whiteness." Austin himself made it plain when he proclaimed that the war was targeting a "Mongrel Spanish-Indian and negro race, against civilization and the Anglo-American race"—Poles not excluded from this flexible category, of course.[60] Apparently, Jewish Americans were not barred either, since Moses Albert Levy of Virginia (also known as Albert Moses Levy) became the chief surgeon of the secessionists[61]— then committed suicide in 1848.

These elements of "race war" may account for the savagery of Austin's forces: thus, the ornithologist and graphic artist John James Audubon—tellingly, born in the nation that became Haiti, principal site of slaveholders' nightmares—decapitated Mexican bodies after the culminating Battle of San Jacinto of 1836 and sent the heads to the phrenologist Samuel George Morton, in order to prove the alleged "superiority of white Europeans."[62]

58. Erath, 4, 7, 9, 33, 46.

59. *The Narrative of Robert Hancock Hunter*, Austin: Encino, 1966, 26.

60. Jay A. Stout, *Slaughter at Goliad: The Mexican Massacre: The Massacre of 400 Texas Volunteers*, Annapolis: Naval Institute Press, 2008 (abbrev. Stout).

61. Moses Albert Levy, "Letters of a Texas Patriot," ca. 1956, VaHS-R.

62. *Washington Post*, 4 August 2020.

Audubon, who had a "touch of the tarbush"—i.e., partial African ancestry—and was also a slaveholder himself, embodied the combination of hostility and anxiety that thrust secession in motion, then nurtured it. Thus, in March 1836, when it seemed secession was a done deal, Henry Austin—a scion of the pioneering family of the same surname—advised sending family members to safety in New Orleans since in motion was a "possible rising of the negroes and the danger that the Indians," would revolt similarly.[63]

Hence, the scholar William Dean Carrigan was among those who argued that settlers feared in 1835 that as Santa Anna's forces marched northward, they would free the enslaved to destabilize the revolt.[64] What made Santa Anna such a reviled figure among settlers, according to British abolitionist Joseph Sturges, was his seeking to enforce anti-slavery laws.[65]

It was comprehensible why Mexico's abolition plans may have been inexpertly circulated and lost in translation. The constitution in Coahuila and Texas barred slavery—but there was a gaping loophole, as the recent Texan William Fairfax Gray noted in his diary: the Africans were compelled to "serve others for a term of years. In this way Negroes have been held in Texas [and] a great many are introduced here and held without that formality. There is a general desire to hold slaves and it is permitted by common consent, no one being willing to prosecute for the violation of the law...."[66]

*   *   *

One lesson of counter-revolution is that the chances for success are enhanced with the aid of a potent ally. France played that role in 1776 (and to a degree in 1836), and the slaveholders' republic played a likeminded role in 1836. In December 1835 in Tampico the U.S. envoy calmly reported the arrival of an "expedition fitted out in New Orleans," comprised of "two hundred men"; it was true that after

---

63. Henry Austin to James F. Perry, 5 March 1836 in *Austin Papers*, Volume III, xxv.

64. William Dean Carrigan, "Slavery on the Frontier: The Peculiar Institution in Central Texas," in Bruce A. Glasrud and Deborah M. Liles, eds., *African Americans in Central Texas History: From Slavery to Civil Rights*, College Station: TA&MU, 2019, 41-69, 44 (abbrev. Carrigan).

65. Sturges quoted in Ames and Lundy. See also Benjamin Lundy, *The Life, Travels and Opinions of Benjamin Lundy, Including his Journeys to Texas and Mexico...*, Philadelphia: Parrish, 1847.

66. Entry, 5 January 1836 in William Fairfax Gray, 57.

"fighting for about an hour," the invaders "were dispersed in every direction" but the message was clear: if Mexico sent troops northward, the nation ran the risk of being overrun. Worse, the invaders were "commanded by a General Mejia and Colonel Peraza both of the Mexican army but who were sent out of this country about two years since...." Still, there was a downside for the enslavers: "excitement exists in this country against all Americans, first caused by their difficulties in the colony of Texas and secondly, by the recent invasion from New Orleans...." The remedy proposed by the consul, George Robertson, was akin to dousing flames with gasoline, since backed by local U.S. merchants, he demanded that Washington dispatch "some force to appear off this port...."[67]

What was sparking the consul's imaginative powers was that a few months earlier a New Orleans vessel suspiciously was "captured" in Galveston by a "Mexican armed schooner" and was "brought into this port...."[68] When this outlaw ship was "condemned"—expropriated—by Mexico, this exacerbated bilateral relations.[69]

The rampant unrest generated by the Texas revolt and the slaveholders' threat may shed light on what unfolded in nearby Vera Cruz earlier in 1835. The "tranquility of Mexico is again interrupted," said the U.S. envoy there, as troops had revolted and captured a fort.[70]

As the above suggests, and not coincidentally, the ongoing revolt in Texas had negative consequences for the rest of Mexico, contributing, said a U.S. diplomat, to "civil discord" as he freely admitted that "certain measures adopted by the Texians [sic]" were "inimical to the policy" of Mexico.[71] Unfortunately, the unrest in Mexico—including Texas—represented ripples from independence in 1821, including enslavers versus abolitionists, and centralizers versus federalists, that had not been resolved wholly by the 1830s.[72]

Unrest in Mexico was coupled inexorably with animosity toward the northern neighbor, with consequences that continue to reverberate. By December 1835 the U.S. found Vera Cruz to be "extremely unsettled" in that "the feeling of the people against foreigners and their prejudice more especially as it regards citizens of the United

---

67. George Robertson to Secretary of State John Forsyth, 9 December 1835, Reel 1, Despatches from U.S. Consuls in Tampico, NARA.

68. Report to Secretary of State Forsyth, 21 June 1835, Reel 2, Despatches from U.S. Consuls in Vera Cruz, NARA.

69. Ibid., Report to Secretary of State Forsyth, 23 July 1835.

70. Ibid., Report to Secretary of State Forsyth, 7 March 1835.

71. Ibid., Report to Secretary of State Forsyth, 11 November 1835.

72. *The Texas Navy*, Washington, D.C.: Naval History Department, 1968.

States prevails to an alarming degree...." The disquieting slogan "Death to all foreigners" [emphasis-original] virtually invited London to intervene further to distract antipathy northward rather than toward themselves. Even then, militarism was seen as the answer for a political question. The "state of excitement" was such that "I conceive," said the envoy in Vera Cruz, "that the property of American citizens at this place, requires for its protection the presence of physical force." The situation was deteriorating rapidly in that "acts of violence" were "jeopardizing...property of the American citizens, if not [their] personal security in this country...."[73]

Mexico City was contending with like forces: this was the discomfiting message to President Jackson in December 1835. "This country is in a perfect tempest of passion in consequence of the Revolt in Texas," said Anthony Butler "and all breathe vengeance against that devoted country," meaning points due north. "Santa Anna is perfectly furious," not a good sign; he was "charging our government and people with promoting and supporting that Revolt with sinister views," i.e., "with the view of acquiring the [vast] Territory" known as Texas, which upon settler victory stretched northward as far as Wyoming and westward as far as New Mexico. It was reported with emphasis: Santa Anna promised to "*chastise us*,"[74] dragging the slaveholders' republic into yet another war when it was still combating Indigenes, and intense squabbling with London still loomed. In the buildup to the defining battle at the Alamo in early February 1836, secessionist agents in New Orleans had reason to fear that chastisement was in the offing. "Santa Anna is at Saltillo with 7000 men, waiting provisions, which are very scarce"; he "issued a proclamation...threatening extermination of all Texians [sic] who opposed him" and to "treat as pirates all American vessels....conveying arms or provisions to Texas...."[75]

As so often happened in the slaveholders' republic, the impetus for land seizures and further enslavement was not always emerging from Washington or the continental elite in the first instance. In a sense, Texas settlers were driving the agenda, as they hungered for increased

73. Report to Secretary of State Forsyth, 3 December 1835, Reel 2, Despatches from U.S. Consuls in Vera Cruz, NARA.

74. Anthony Butler to President Jackson, 19 December 1835, in Bassett, *Volume 5*, 381. See also José Enrique de la Peña, *With Santa Anna in Texas: A Personal Narrative of the Revolution*, College Station: TA&MU Press, 1975.

75. William Bryant, Agency Office-New Orleans to "His Ex[cellency] the Governor & Hon [sic] Council of Texas," 6 February 1835, Box 2-9/1, Records of Texas Republic Secretary of State, Texas State Archives-Austin (abbrev. Texas Republic SoS).

wealth. It was in August 1835, just as the flames of war began to leap, in one of his more infamous quotes, that Austin exhorted, "Texas must become a slave country. It is no longer a matter of doubt. The interests of Louisiana requires that it should be" since "a population of fanatical abolitionists in Texas would have a very pernicious and dangerous influence on the overgrown slave population of state." Texas must escape the clutches of abolitionist Mexico so that it could help "defend the key of the western world—the mouths of the Mississippi...." It was also true that "a great immigration from Kentucky, Tennessee, etc., each man with his rifle or musket would be of great use to us— very great indeed" since, he insisted, "my object has always been to fill up Texas with a North American population."[76]

Austin's project was a premature version of "squatter sovereignty" wherein invaders created new "facts on the ground," then demanded autonomy and ouster altogether of pre-existing Indigenes. Some of the key enslavers hailed from Virginia, arguably the most important state, including Jared Groce, one of the wealthiest slaveholders. One scholar has estimated that 90% of the settlers came from Louisiana, Arkansas, Alabama, etc. accounting for an outsized percentage of Texas's settler population. This is one reason why Texas created what the Confederacy sought to create, building upon 1776: a slavocracy.[77]

However, Virginia—as in 1861—was heavily represented in this secession too. Sam Houston was born near Lexington, and Stephen Fuller Austin was born in Wythe County. Appropriately, 17 Virginians were at the tip of the spear at the Alamo and 13 of them died in battle.[78]

Texas settlers, especially during the war against Mexico, also arrived from other slaveholding states, e.g., North Carolina. "Backwoods and towns sent pistol belted horsemen and heavy bearded homesteaders toting long rifles in answer to Texas' call.... Lincoln, North Carolina was the birth place of J. Pinckney Henderson, first governor of Texas following annexation...; he was the republic's

---

76. Stephen F. Austin to Mary Austin Holley, 21 August 1835, in *Austin Papers*, Volume III, Austin: U of Texas Press, 1928, 101.

77. Torget, *Cotton*, 120, 250.

78. Vertical File, "Virginians in Texas": Sam Houston Dixon and Louis Wiltz Kemp, *The Heroes of San Jacinto*, Houston: Anson Jones Press, 1932, and "Leaders of the Revolution," "Virginia Historical Society-Richmond," n.d. At the same site see also Bill Groneman, *Alamo Defenders, A Genealogy: The People and their Words*, Austin: Eakin, n.d. See also James E. Winston, "Virginia and the Independence of Texas," *Southwestern Historical Quarterly*, 16 (No. 1, 1913): 277-284.

minister to France and England [and] fought with General Zachary Taylor...against Mexico..." was the claim in a 1936 centenary celebration. Naturally, he "was brilliant in the Confederate army." And "of the 52 names signed to the Declaration of Independence" of Texas in March 1836, "nine came from North Carolina...."[79]

The antiwar preacher William Channing, who took umbrage at the idea that "adherence to the Catholic religion was required as the condition of settlement" in northern Mexico, was no less impressed with the fact that in 1836 "in the army of eight hundred men [in] the victory which scattered the Mexican force...not more than fifty were citizens of Texas...." Reflecting a growing sentiment that was to deepen sectional cleavages, the Reverend Channing argued that "the Texans in this warfare are a little more than a name, a cover, under which selfish adventurers from another country have prosecuted their work of plunder.... Texas is a country conquered by our citizens," he insisted. It was "the beginning of conquests which, unless arrested and beaten back...will only stop at the Isthmus of Darien," which was barely mistaken. Looking into his crystal ball, he sensed that "to annex Texas is to declare perpetual war with Mexico" and, in essence, was "the first step to Mexico['s]" annexation. He knew that annexation in whatever instance was "for the very purpose of extending slavery" and "extension to the slave trade," meaning "collision with the West Indies,"[80] i.e., colliding with a steely London.

But then Channing's view was not hegemonic. Instead, consider Samuel H. Walker, born in enslaving Maryland and who fought in enslaving Florida in the 1830s before becoming an arms purchaser in New York for Texas secessionists, indicative of how 1836 helped to develop an infrastructure for 1861. As for Walker, Samuel Colt himself named his new revolver after him, which was essential in massacring Indigenes and "winning the West." Then he fell in battle in 1847 fighting Mexicans.[81]

Also garnering valuable experience fighting Negroes and Seminoles in Florida was the premier Confederate secessionist of Texas, Louis Wigfall, whose roots were in Edgefield, South Carolina, notorious for containing a hardy corps of obstreperous Africans and Gullah.[82]

---

79. "Texas Centennial" dateline, circa 1936, Samuel Asbury Papers, UNC-CH.

80. William Channing, "A Letter...on the Annexation of Texas to the United States," Boston: Munroe, 1837, Huntington Library.

81. See "Diary of Samuel H. Walker," UNC-CH.

82. Alvy Leon King, "Louis T. Wigfall: The Stormy Petrel," Ph.D. dissertation, TTU, 1967, 25, 12-13, 14 (abbrev. King).

Then there was Felix Huston, who traipsed from Natchez by 1836 and fittingly—and agilely—positioned himself to the right of Austin. He was close to fellow Mississippian—and temporary Texan—John Quitman, who actually had left his post as governor, before then turning his rapacious attention to Cuba. But it was Huston who advised invading Mexico upon arrival and similarly had sought to purge Texas of Tejanos, though some were more than willing to support secession. This slave trader appropriately became the first commanding general of the military of the expansionist Republic of Texas.[83]

Combatants descended upon Texas from Tuscaloosa,[84] New Orleans (with "235 kegs of powder" but "few muskets," a solvable issue)[85] and further points eastward. Critical expertise was brought by "highly recommended" Benjamin Austin, a surgeon who served 15 years in the U.S. Navy.[86] Texas's "purchasing agent" in New Orleans affirmed by June 1836 that "my duty has been to purchase all articles for the Government...and charter all vessels, furnish transportation to all emigrants (volunteers),"[87] of which there were many.

Even after the apparent victory of the secessionists, they were dispatching agents to the U.S. "to raise a body of emigrants for our new country," as one leader was told.[88] It was not as if this were a covert action, shrouded in darkness. Those interfering in this Mexican internal affair openly broadcast their putative illegality.[89] It is likely that the rough economic times Louisiana had been enduring were encouraging certain denizens to seek greener pastures in any case.[90]

These supplies were needed for some time to come—even after San Jacinto—for Mexico was hardly reconciled to defeat. By June 1836 Texas authorities "received intelligence that the Mexicans were advancing upon us again with increased numbers and doubtless increased fury," meaning the "army must be fed and clothed and they

---

83. Matthew Dungain Campbell, "Attempts at Southern Expansion: The Campaigns of Felix Huston," M.A. thesis, Mississippi College, 2020, no pagination.

84. "We the undersigned volunteers...," 20 March 1836, Box 2-9/1, Texas Republic SoS.

85. Ibid., Report to "His Excellency," 31 March 1836.

86. Ibid., Report to "President of the Republic," 8 April 1836.

87. Ibid., Purchasing Agent to President Burnet, 17 June 1836.

88. Ibid., Report to Thomas Toby, 24 September 1836.

89. *A Vindication of the Conduct of the Agency of Texas in New Orleans...*, New Orleans: Advertiser, 1836, Historic New Orleans.

90. W.P. Johnston, 51.

must have arms and ammunition...." Unavoidably they looked long-ingly eastward for "succor"—and more. Typically, these saviors were not above taking advantage, sending "damaged and very indifferent powder, some of it really too worthless and inefficient to be used," according to one with reason to know—but few other options were then available.[91]

Others from the Slave South were not so sure about Texas seces-sion. The "Committee on Foreign Relations" in South Carolina demanded "strict neutrality with all foreign nations and especially with Mexico in her contest with Texas; and that we are the last peo-ple who should set an example of impertinent interference with the internal concerns of other states...." (Of course, this may have been misdirection for external consumption.) Anticipating aftershocks, it was underlined that "a war at this time between the United States and Mexico" would be a "calamity greatly to be deprecated"—and, as events demonstrated, sure to ensue.[92]

As for the Tennessean—President Jackson—he seemed to warm to the idea of Texas sovereignty, unwilling to be outflanked by London and Paris, who could establish a toehold there to Washington's det-riment. In fact, he reverted to the older argument that Texas never was Mexican land in the first place, it "was once claimed as part of our property," he claimed, a result of negotiations with Spain as it was in halting retreat from the hemisphere in recent years. Thus, he anticipated with satisfaction the "prospect of the reunion of the ter-ritory to our country..."—so, he was hesitant to accord diplomatic recognition to a republic that his own nation claimed for itself.[93]

The new republic of Texas was no naïf in the high-stakes game of big-power politics. Shortly after it came clear that secession had succeeded—an encouragement of 1861—Secretary of State John For-syth was told that this would "awaken the attention of some of the European powers against the slave trade, which her [Texas] citizens will carry now," a prophetic analysis.[94] Their pressure on Texas could easily bleed into enhanced pressure on Washington—but it could also cause the older republic to rush to the younger's defense.

Mexico, said Washington's man in Texas, "has already proposed a treaty of alliance with those tribes, the consideration for which, in

---

91. Report to Thomas Toby, Texas Agent, 20 June 1836, Box 2-9/1, Texas Republic SoS.

92. Statement #98, 1836, Committee on Foreign Relations, South Carolina Department of Archives and History-Columbia.

93. "Condition of Texas."

94. Ibid., Henry Morfit to Secretary of State Forsyth, 24 September 1836.

the event of success is that the Indians shall possess" chits to cash in, maybe inimical to the interests of Washington. Concern was expressed about the "Comanches, who are the largest tribe in the country and more numerous than all the rest together, having about 2000 warriors, or 8000 souls"—but also inciting ire were the "Conshattees [Coushatta] and Alabamas...." Inevitably "negroes...about 5000 in number" had to be taken into account.[95]

In short, if settlers were weakened in Texas vis-à-vis Indigenes and Africans, it could threaten Louisiana, a point buttressed further when a prominent memoirist discerned in April 1836 that the Caddo were in the process of "entering Texas" in order to "act against the citizens of that state under the auspices of the Mexican authorities."[96] This repetitive theme—Mexico allying with Indigenes—undergirded the eventual war with Mexico and the presumed need to continue grabbing more land as a buffer to protect slavery.

Moreover, if Texas were to ascend truly to the eminent role of "rival" to the U.S., it could impair possible subversion by the jealous older sibling by making sure that the latter too could suffer if the Lone Star Republic were subverted.

By December 1836, Austin had assayed an "essential improvement" in the military situation, despite "rumors of an invasion by land and water"; critical to this strategy were the Caddo—often interlocked with Negroes—who were "decidedly hostile and have committed many depredations." They, along with—specifically—"Cherokees of the Nacogdoches district," the "Comanches and all the small tribes who were under their influence, except the Shawnees, had actually entered into a combination to join the Mexicans...and were preparing to do so, when they heard of the defeat at San Jacinto...." Revealing the dependence on Washington that compromised the ambitious plan to become a rival of the latter, Austin counseled as a result that "American troops should be continued at Nacogdoches and the number increased...."[97]

---

95. Ibid., Henry Morfit to Secretary of State Forsyth, 27 August 1836.

96. Robert Mayo, *Political Sketches of Eight Years in Washington; in Four Parts with Annotations to Each...*, Baltimore: Lucas, 1839, 120 (abbrev. Mayo). See also Henry C. Corbin and F.T. Wilson, *Federal Aid in Domestic Disturbances, 1787-1903:* Washington, D.C.: Government Printing Office, 1903, 60: "Mexican government...sent envoys to the Indians residing along the borders of Louisiana to arouse and entice them to join the war against Texas"—these "rumors were well founded."

97. Stephen F. Austin to William Wharton, 10 December 1836, in *Annual Report of the American Historical Association for the Year 1907...*, Volume II,

These troops were needed, since on the eve of the replica of Yorktown—San Jacinto—military leader Sam Houston was almost overthrown by mutinous forces of his own.[98] They were also needed since Negro restiveness had yet to be squelched altogether, as evidenced by the fact that during the secessionist war, Mexican leader Juan Almonte, who was present at the Alamo battle, utilized African Americans for reconnaissance. This scorned grouping experienced far less racism in Almonte's nation than in their homeland, especially from officialdom well-schooled in the asset that was anti-Yanqui sentiment. Anti-Negro sentiment—as Guerrero's example showed—was less salient in Mexico, handing an incalculable advantage to the latter nation.[99]

So, despite these multiple problems with Indigenes, the republic's 1836 constitution denied citizenship to Native Americans. Republic leader Mirabeau Lamar—yes, of French Huguenot descent, albeit born in Georgia—was not alone among fellow settlers in Indian-hating. Following Sam Houston as republican president, he sought extermination of these "sanguinary savages" and "wild cannibals" but, consonant with the ideology of white supremacy, he was not above seeking to pit Lipan Apaches vs. Comanches, Mexicans and Cherokees. Interestingly, the Lipan deployed women diplomats, the Comanches too, whereas the purportedly civilized enslavers did not.[100]

This manipulation continued in December 1836 when Austin announced, "extensive projects are in contemplation to introduce African Negros into this country by citizens of the United States...on the seashore bank of the Sabine [River]"[101]—as if Texans were both helpless to stop it or otherwise uninvolved in this odious commerce. Secretary of State John Forsyth of the elder republic, knew of this ongoing plan, which involved landing the smuggled enslaved from Cuba and elsewhere first in U.S. territory—before they could then be brought to Texas, which was technically legal.[102] In other words,

---

Diplomatic Correspondence of the Republic of Texas, Part I, Washington, D.C.: Government Printing Office, 1908, 149-150.

98. Haynes, Somervell, 52, 288, 335.

99. Nichols 2018, 13.

100. Neal McDonald Hampton, "A Dark Cloud Rests Upon our Nation: Lipan Sovereignty and Relations with Mexico, the United States and the Republic of Texas," M.A. thesis, U of Central Oklahoma, 2015, 6, 58, 62 (abbrev. Hampton).

101. Stephen F. Austin to William Wharton, 16 December 1836 in Stevens, 55.

102. Secretary of State Forsyth to Memucan Hunt, 24 July 1837, Box 5, Records of Texas Legation to U.S., Texas State Archives-Austin (abbrev. Texas Legation).

the "sovereign" Texas republic became an open backdoor through which the enslaved could be smuggled, with Washington disclaiming responsibility and Austin seemingly not culpable.

Thus, Washington had cards to play too. By late 1836, a U.S. "man of war" had arrived in Northern California with their man in San Diego reporting that the aim was to "force Californians to put themselves under the protection of the United States." This maneuver, if extended eastward from San Diego, would allow for an encirclement of Texas, an undermining of Mexico, preempting a similar move by the new republic and a wrong-footing of European powers, especially London and Paris, who had their own designs on this rich territory.[103]

Days later, just after Christmas 1836, a U.S. naval officer was chortling about the "recent revolution in Upper California...." Converging on the future Golden State was a flotilla sent "from the Sandwich Islands [Hawaii]," including "eight other American vessels of war [now] on the coast...." Seemingly approaching a Texas replay due west, claims of *ultra vires* plans for California were denied adamantly—"false impressions," it was said—while pointing to the hundreds of "American citizens in Upper California"; and (it was observed pointedly) that such a figure could "probably...produce another Texas affair" on the Pacific, the steppingstone to the ample Chinese market.[104]

Dated auspiciously 7 November 1836—coinciding with a similar Texas document precisely a year earlier—the self-styled "Declaration of Independence of the Citizens of Upper California" issued from Monterey in a Spanish-language original, sought a middle range between the sectarianism of Mexico and the free exercise of the newest republic: "religion shall be the Roman Catholic Apostolic forbidding the public exercise of any other, although the government shall not molest anyone for his particular religious opinions...."[105]

At times it seemed that Washington found it hard to believe that those like the Cherokee, whom they battered from pillar to post, could ever be friendly to them—so, they had to keep punishing them as a hedge against their becoming unfriendly. Hence, in June 1836, as the embers of war had yet to be extinguished, John Ross and his Indigenous comrades informed the U.S. Congress that "said

---

103. Frederick Becker, San Diego, to William D. Jones, Consul, 20, 25 December 1836, Despatches from U.S. Consuls in Mexico City, NARA.

104. Rick Waldron, Captain of U.S. ship "Peacock" to "Sir," 30 December 1836, Reel 1, Despatches from U.S. Consuls in Mazatlan, NARA.

105. Ibid., Translated "Declaration of Dependence of the Citizens of Upper California," 7 November 1836.

Cherokee nation will not hold any treaty with any foreign power," i.e., renouncing a potent weapon, while acknowledging "valuable gold mines were discovered upon the Cherokee lands...." He assured that the "Cherokee population [of] 18,000...have become civilized and adopted the Christian religion...." The assimilationist announced that he and his nation had been "taught to think and feel as the American citizen," accepting the reality of forced expropriation.[106]

Such opinions contributed to what amounted to a civil war among Cherokees, one of a number that surged into the U.S. Civil War—with these Indigenes split once more, some leaders siding with the Confederates. This was even more striking since the Cherokees, broadly speaking, instead of rampaging in small bands, the normative approach of the Comanches, were able to mobilize an army against settlers.[107]

So, counter-revolution prevailed, given external assistance from Washington, strict solidarity among settlers, and fissiparousness among their many foes: this was not to be the end of this distasteful recipe.

106. "Memorial and Protest of the Cherokee Nation to the Honourable the Senate and House of Representatives of the United States of North America, in Congress Assembled," 21 June 1836, Signed by John Ross, et al., Huntington Library.

107. Stout, 68. On "Cherokee civil wars" see e.g., Colin G. Calloway, *Pen & Ink Witchcraft: Treaties and Treaty Making in American Indian History*, New York: Oxford U Press, 153.

Chapter 4

After the Counter-Revolution,
1836-1838

The secessionists felt sufficiently confident to issue their "Declaration of Independence" on 2 March 1836.[1] This may have seemed premature at the time in the face of continuing combativeness from Mexicans, rebelliousness among Indigenes and insurrectionism among enslaved Africans, but with the backing of allies in Washington, the deed was done.

Consciously walking in the footsteps of 1776, the proclamation was issued from "Washington-on-the-Brazos," though this misdeed also anticipated 1861 and gives a hint of what that secession—if successful—would have delivered: more slave trading, more expansionism, more bloody conflict. But exiting from informed speculation, it remains true that like the victory over London in the late 18th century, a prickly bilateral relationship was preordained between victor and vanquished when haggling took place over whether Mexico would agree to return escaped formerly enslaved property[2]—pronto. It was on 28 May 1836 that Santa Anna and David Burnet on behalf of the secessionists, bandied about language to resolve the immediate conflict; in Article V it was said "that all private property, including cattle, horses, negro slaves…which may have been taken by a part of the Mexican army or which should have taken refuge in said army…

---

1. For the text of the "Unanimous Declaration of Independence of the Delegates of the people of Texas…," see e.g., John Niles, *History of South America and Mexico…*, Hartford: Huntington, 1839, 300-303 (abbrev. Niles). This pro-secessionist book was penned by a U.S. Senator from Connecticut, though it had been suspected that Northerners generally were hostile to this pro-slavery project. However, this exposes the debility of ignoring the Indigenous Question, still bestirring continentally. Thus, in referring angrily to the "Carancahua Indians," Niles indicted Mexico which—per the 1776 accusation of Britain—"incited the merciless savage with the tomahawk and scalping knife."

2. Barr, 423-36, 426.

shall be returned...."[3] There were about 3500 enslaved Africans in Texas, said an early historian, and as 1836 approached, half fled or "joined the Mexican army...but were subsequently restored to their respective owners"; this allegation is best interpreted as reflecting the then often hysterical reaction to the internal threat presented by the enslaved and the felt desire of slaveholders to recover lost "property."[4]

A protractedly negotiated contemporaneous treaty between the old republic and Mexico sought to compel each party to keep Indigenes within their borders on a tight leash, and allowed the U.S. to "occupy a portion of the contiguous Mexican territory" if the latter republic was seen as derelict, which was foreseen, since already "Mexican officers were exciting the Indians to hostilities against the United States...."[5] As years passed, slave runaways and the seeming reluctance of Mexico to rein in Indigenes, were to afflict the three cornered relation between the two slaveholding republics and their abolitionist neighbor.

Mexico's envoy in Washington, who frankly acknowledged his imperfect acquaintance with the English language, still managed to interpose objection to what he saw as a crude U.S. interference in his nation's internal affairs in allowing nationals from their nation to aid secession.[6] Washington had its own complaints. Lewis Cass of the appropriately named U.S. Department of War, turned the tables, denouncing the "many Indian tribes whose habitual predisposition to engage in war is well known" and the "efforts...made to induce these Indian tribes to join the Mexican troops...."[7]

Slavery continued to bedevil the relationship with Sam Houston himself—a slaveholder—as early as 1837 lamenting the arrival in Texas of "thousands of Africans" from Cuba and often onward to Texas itself.[8]

---

3. Article V, 28 May 1836, in General Vicente Filisola, *Evacuation of Texas, Translation of the Representation to the Supreme Government...in Defence of His Honor...Explanation of His Operations as Commander-in-Chief of the Army Against Texas*, Columbia, Texas: Borden, 1837, 56-58, NYHS.

4. Maillard, 260.

5. Department of State to M.D. Gorostiza, 13 October 1836, in *Examination and Review*.

6. Ibid., M.D. Gorostiza to Secretary of State Forsyth, 20 April 1836.

7. Ibid., Lewis Cass to Sir, 25 April 1836.

8. President Houston's Speech to the Senate and House of Representatives of the Republic of Texas, 5 May 1837, NYHS. Earl Wesley Fornell, "Island City: The Story of Galveston on the Eve of Secession, 1850-1860," Ph.D. dissertation, Rice U, 1955, 332 (abbrev. Fornell).

As with the assassination of federal agent Robert Neighbors in 1859, patriot William Wharton, born in Virginia and son-in-law of the new republic's largest slaveholder, days before proclamation of Texas sovereignty accused Mexico too of failing to deal aggressively with Indigenes. "Not a Mexican soldier ever aided in expelling these Indians," he screeched—though by 1859 expulsion was insufficient when extermination was on offer. Then there was the 1830 Mexican statute which he found noticeably objectionable since "by this law, North Americans, and they alone, were forbidden admission into Texas," which flew in the face of his supposition that "the Anglo-American race are destined to be forever proprietors of this land...." Irony unbounded, he proclaimed that Mexican authorities "want to 'enslave' this race...." He concluded accurately, however, arguing that the "people of Texas [are] strugglers for the sacred principles of the American [Revolution]...."[9]

Even the differences between the dual counter-revolutions were more apparent than real. Beginning in 1836 to annexation in 1845, the new republic issued countless resolutions, laws and decrees and, according to one study, 19 pertained to slavery or Free Negroes, while the legendary U.S. Constitution tended to shroud the visible stain that was enslavement.[10] In response, by 1837 Mexico stiffened further its abolitionism[11]—a stern slap in the face against secession.

Still, when Stephen F. Austin reached Senator Lewis F. Linn of Missouri in early May 1836, his words underscored the fragility of the new republic. "A war of extermination is raging in Texas," he decried, "a war of barbarism and despotic principles," even worse conducted by "mongrel[Mexicans]." Their "avowed intention is to excite the Indians and negroes and crimson the waters of the Mississippi and make it the eastern boundary of Mexico...for such an intention has been avowed," he instructed the Senator, whose state bordered this critical artery. This "must bring the bloody tide of savage war and the horrors of negro insurrection within its limits," he declaimed, not shy about generating hysteria. It was not just the "Texians" who were at risk, since "exterminating the American population in Texas and filling that country with Indians and negroes...

---

9. "Address of the Honorable William H. Wharton, Delivered in New York on Tuesday April 26, 1836...," New York: Colyer, 1836, NYHS.

10. Kelly Ray, "Houston in Chains: Slaves and Free Blacks in the Texas Courts, 1845-1867," M.A. thesis, U of Houston, 2011, 90 (abbrev. Ray). See also Paschal, 79: "The Texas document used the word [slave or slavery] no fewer than eleven times."

11. Torget, *Cotton*, 251.

will form an impenetrable barrier from the Sabine River to the Rio del Norte and thus restore the old Spanish policy, which was 'to prevent even a bird from crossing the Sabine River'"[12]—thus, hemming in the old republic's border.

Senator Linn, representing the gateway westward, hardly needed convincing. From Camp Sabine, Louisiana, he received the report that "we are fifty or sixty miles from those large planters who have so large a number of negroes that it would require a garrison near[by] to prevent their negroes from rising" and inflicting "violence." Then there was the potential for an Indigenous revolt too, which raised the looming specter of London. His correspondent recalled the 1812 war and the killing on the battlefield of a pro-London Indigenous leader, who was buried respectfully, an indicator—it was thought—of a continuing alliance.[13]

This likely worked to Texas's advantage since the new republic was quite energetic in repressing Indigenes, Africans and their Mexican allies that Washington was so concerned about. Also reporting from Missouri was one of the most battle-scarred military men in the old republic. Edmund Gaines had fought in the 1812 war, against Seminoles, against the Sauk in the epochal Black Hawk War, against Mexicans in the 1840s and, thus, his words were taken seriously. "From the mouth of the Sabine to [the] Red River…to the Arkansas River" was territory that was "by far the most vital and important section of the whole inland frontier of the [U.S.] because it is threatened by the most powerful and savage nations"—the Comanches, for example—and not far distant from the mighty Mississippi River, the spine of the continent. The exports and imports flowing from this vital region were "wealth enough to excite the cupidity and tempt the aggression" of other nations—London, for example. A "Tecumseh, an Osceola or even a pirate such as Lafitte," especially if allied with "abolitionists," could wreak havoc against republics old and new.[14]

---

12. Stephen F. Austin to Senator Lewis F. Linn, 4 May 1836 in *Austin Papers*, Volume III, 344.

13. B. Riley, Major in U.S. Army to Hon. Lewis Linn, in "Western Frontier Correspondence on the Subject of the Western Frontier Presented to the House…by Mr. Harrison of Missouri," U.S. Congress. House of Representatives, 25th Congress, 2nd Session, Document No. 76, Huntington Library.

14. Report by Major General Edmund Gaines, 28 February 1838, in "Defence of the Western Frontier, a Plan for the Defence of the Western Frontier…," U.S. Congress, House of Representatives, 25th Congress, 2nd Session, Doc. No. 311, Huntington Library.

Gaines the military man continuously rang a loud alarm about challenges to his republic. Santa Anna's "plan is to put to death all he finds in arms," as "Indians...will unite with him in his war of extermination"—so early on he demanded more troops in response.[15] Specifically, Gaines's contention was that Manuel Flores, "a Mexican Spaniard" then in Natchitoches, was "enticing the Indians...to join them in the war of extermination now raging in Texas"; this had "produced excitement among the Caddo" and bid fair, he emphasized, to "place the white settlements *on both sides of the* [state] *line wholly within the power of these savages.*"[16]

Speaking to the Texas Congress in May 1837, President Houston— who was thought to be close to the Cherokees, with whom he once consorted—was explicit in castigating the Caddo, then "inhabiting a portion of our northeastern frontier...." This grouping, thought to have Negro leadership at various levels, were responsible for "the principal aggressions" inflicted painfully on settlers." He thought that it was the "U.S. agent," perhaps seeking to stunt the rise of a rival, who was "furnishing them the means of further injury" and "issued the warriors, rifles and ammunition." In sum, he thought that the U.S., which was not exactly stable itself, preferred to direct Caddo militancy away from Louisiana. Mexico in turn had entertained a "delegation" of "twenty northern Indians" in Matamoros and "had stipulated with the Mexican authorities to furnish...three thousand warriors, well armed...[to] invade Texas...."[17] The two slaveholding republics were panicking and were each willing to act against the interests of the other.

This panic was comprehensible since a contemporaneous estimate was that there were 80,000 Indigenes in Texas, with the number of those defined as "white" exaggerated wildly in order to give momentum to sovereignty, and those present disproportionately comprised of "habitual liars, drunkards, blasphemers and slanderers; sanguinary gamesters and cold blooded assassins,"[18] with only the latter

15. General Gaines, Headquarters, Western Department, Natchitoches to Sir, 8 April 1836, in *Examination and Review.*

16. Ibid.

17. President Houston's Speech to the Senate and House of Representatives of the Republic of Texas, 5 May 1837, NYHS.

18. Maillard, 203, 206, 224. See e.g., James Edward Barbee, "A Brief History of the Early Barbee Families of Smith County, Texas," n.d., CCSC (abbrev. Barbee). Major Edward Barbee was born in Orange County, N.C., in 1793—"he fought the Indians in Tennessee as a young man and came to Texas in 1837." He was of French Huguenot ancestry. At the same site see

capable of becoming part of an effective fighting force—heightening the need for Texas to offer ever more Indigenous land to attract settlers from the east, which in turn generated ever more war in an endless feedback loop.

Reporting from Natchez, thought to be far from the frontlines of war, William Parker looked west and was struck by what he sensed: The Sabine was destined to be "the seat of an Indian war...." It was certain that "[Chief] Bowles, the Cherokee chief, is determined to obey the commands of the Mexicans. He says he is a colonel in the Mexican army and will obey their orders.... if however," he advised with requisite grisliness, "Bowles falls into the hands of General Gaines, I think he will Jackson-ize him a little—at least, hang him up to dry...."[19]

Even in faraway Mexico City, the U.S. consul in early 1838 reminded that the Indigenous Delaware then residing in Missouri, were seeking refuge in Mexico,[20] bringing along unresolved grievances.

Despite Austin's frenzy of enragement, it was not by chance that rebels prevailed in 1836. It was not just the avid backing from New Orleans, it was also the aforementioned splits among Indigenes—and Mexicans too. José Antonio Navarro signed the Declaration of Independence of March 1836, then sent his son Ángel to Harvard; he was pro-Confederate later and a leading white supremacist during Reconstruction—though, as scholar Arnoldo de León put it, he nonetheless "defended the cause of La Raza [Chicano/as]on numerous occasions." This group only numbered—excluding soldiers—about 2200 in 1821 and about 4000 by 1836—but by that date the self-described "Anglos" outnumbered Tejanos by ten to one.[21] Navarro was joined in this hall of shame by Emily West, also known as Emily Morgan

---

also Kenneth Kesselus, ed., *A Memoir of Capt'n C.R. Perry of Johnson City, Texas, a Texas Veteran*, Austin: Jenkins, 1990, 4, 6. Perry was born in Tuscaloosa but arrived in Texas by 1834; his father fought Mexico by 1836, whereas the son fought "both hostile Indians and warring Mexicans"—especially the Comanches by 1839, wherein he admitted to scalping. See also Niles, 226: In the conquest of Texas, said this U.S. Senator elatedly, "every state in the Union has contributed...Tennessee perhaps the largest share," reflecting Sam Houston's role in both territories, "and Kentucky would probably come next; Georgia and Alabama have latterly contributed most largely." Of necessity, many settlers harbored "diseased morals."

19. William Parker to Dear Sir, 4 August 1836, in *Examination and Review*.

20. W. Jones to Ministry of Foreign Affairs, 23 March 1838, Reel 1, Despatches from U.S. Consuls in Mexico City, NARA.

21. Arnoldo De León, *The Tejano Community, 1836-1900*, Dallas: SMU, 1997, xxii, 4 (abbrev. De León).

or "The Yellow Rose of Texas," a kind of "Malinche" who traduces Santa Anna to benefit settlers—or so it was said—before fleeing the new republic by 1837.[22] Odes celebrating her continued to be belted out in the 21st century.

No, Navarro was not necessarily emblematic of Tejanos, for he stood in contrast to Vicente Córdova who had been prominent in Nacogdoches but—wisely—was loath to back secession. In August 1838 he negotiated with Chief Bowles and the Cherokees leading to a de facto alliance—but their incipient rebellion was suppressed. Accompanied by fellow Tejanos and some Africans, Córdova attempted to flee to Matamoros but was confronted—appropriately—in Waterloo (today's Austin) and he and stragglers limped into Mexico.[23] According to one scholar, even a flock of "alienated Anglos" sided with Córdova.[24] The aforementioned Nicholas Drouet, a Free Negro who may have had roots in the predecessor regime in Haiti before settling in Louisiana, made it to Matamoros—likely after joining Córdova.[25]

Nacogdoches, which continued to harbor Free Negroes dangerously close to Louisiana, was also eyed by Mexico. This southern neighbor continued to dicker with Indigenes to turn them against settlers, offering returned land seized illicitly. According to London's man in Galveston, "Cherokees had opened negotiations with the Mexican government" and were to gain territory "provided they succeeded in ejecting" settlers: "they had formed a league with the Mexican population about Nacogdoches to attack simultaneously the Anglo-American inhabitants...." He asserted, a "considerable quantity of arms and ammunition had been procured and numbers of Cherokees, Creeks and Seminoles [were] invited from the United States into Texas...."[26]

John Salmon "Rip" Ford, one of the most renowned 19th-century Texans (born in South Carolina with Virginia roots) was said to be "fearful at the thought of a Cherokee-Mexican coalition."[27]

The foregoing and the "Córdova Rebellion" notwithstanding, it is difficult to describe adequately the depths to which Tejanos sunk, post 1836: land grabs, evisceration of political power, precipitous

22. Caughfield, 141.

23. McReynolds, 39.

24. Shuck, 148.

25. Gassner, 26.

26. William Kennedy, Esq., *Texas: The Rise, Progress and Prospects of the Republic of Texas, Volume II*, London: Hastings, 1841, 313, 314 (abbrev. Kennedy).

27. William John Hughes, "'Rip' Ford, Texan: The Public Life and Services of John Salmon Ford, 1836-1883," Ph.D. dissertation, TTU, 1958, 8 (abbrev. W.J. Hughes).

decline in socio-economic standing—even enslavement in certain cases when they were "mistaken" for Negroes. There were also those like Manuel Sabriego of Goliad, who fought beside his Mexican comrades, departed with the military—and ultimately lost his land. He returned with intended vengeance in 1838. Like many Cherokees, many Tejanos sought neutrality during secession—but suffered pulverizing losses nonetheless.[28]

As Sabriego's return suggested, even objective observers thought that Mexico was seeking to keep Texas off balance to hamper attacking to the south. The simultaneous "Trail of Tears" had stirred up numerous U.S. Indigenes, at any rate, and their arrival north of the Red River created numerous destabilizing opportunities—and false flag opportunities too. For Mexico later charged that in Kerr County, Texas, a "large party of American citizens…under the disguise of Indians have been perpetrating"—in the aftermath of 1836—"the most atrocious crimes."[29]

This may have been accurate, but giving this misdirection resonance was the reality that Indigenes continued to be outraged by the invasion of their homelands. An anonymous visitor to Texas in 1837 sensed as much. The new republic barely contained a "formidable enemy within her borders in numerous tribes of Indians. These tribes consist of the Comanches, Caddoes, Wacoes, Tawakonis, Karankawas, Tonkawas, Quapaws and several others…. these savages…are rendered still more restless and sanguinary by those Indians of the north which the policy of the United States has removed west of the Mississippi…." In short, Washington's infamous "Trail of Tears" had the perhaps not accidental impact of placing added pressure on the budding "rival" that was Texas. These latest antagonists included "Choctaw, the Chickasaw, the Alabama-Coushatta, the Kickapoo, the Potawatomi, the Creek and the Cherokee…." At one sketched "Indian Council," this observer was struck that the "person who attracted the greatest attention was a large negro who was looked upon with great respect by the tribe and seemed to hold undisputed dominion with the chief himself…." The "success" of the settlers was certified not least because of their unity, with the prospect of mutual gain via "whiteness"—inviting Poles, French and others into "Anglo"

---

28. Galan, in Howell and Swanlund, 437-482, 438.

29. *Report of the Committee of Investigation Sent in 1873 by the Mexican Government to the Frontier of Texas*, New York: Baker & Godwin, 1875, 321, 344 (abbrev. *Report of the Committee of Investigation 1873*).

identity—being the glue of solidarity. The "mighty frauds of the land speculator" impelled their "unappeasable hunger for Texan land."[30]

A spectator saw fleeing Mexican leaders in 1836-1837 on—it was said—a "skiff whose oars were manned by two negroes...."[31] In this land of ironies, by the 1870s, the formerly enslaved, rechristened as "Buffalo Soldiers," administered the final rites to numerous Indigenes—which simultaneously was a devastating blow to themselves—although they thought they were enacting the price of citizenship, which they were.

Still, though Mexico continued to attract Indigenes to Coahuila, the reigning symbol of this conflicted era was the spectacle of so many Indigenes—Cherokees, Kickapoos, some Seminoles, some Caddo and even some Tonkawa and Lipan Apaches—targeting Comanche warriors for death. This was occurring, even as Cherokee leaders, e.g., Chief Bowles, were collaborating with Santa Anna to the point where settlers feared a "fifth column" composed of revenge-seeking Indigenes in concert with Mexicans. Thus, in 1837 some Cherokee aided the Mexican military in snaring fleeing Texas prisoners.[32]

On the other hand, as secession was on the road on success, Free Africans and enslaved alike began to flood into Mexico, especially from New Orleans, including mechanics and marksmen. This was understandable since an early historian asserted that the enslaved in Texas were chiefly owned—if not financed—by "New Orleans cotton brokers."[33] Many of those fleeing Louisiana wound up in Tampico, which was to emerge as a Confederate stronghold but would have been even more deadly but for the presence of so many Black refugees. For Mexicans determined early on that these newcomers were harder to bribe by the northern republics and became some of the most dedicated soldiers in Mexico. The consensus in Mexico was that they were the "natural enemies of the Americans...."[34]

However, the "Americans"—meaning the settlers—could well be considered the "natural enemies" of those who were not in their privileged category. This was notably the case in 1838 when the Georgian slave trader Mirabeau Lamar—of French ancestry— followed Sam Houston as president of the republic; this occurred after two prominent challengers, Peter Grayson (with Virginia roots)

---

30. Andrew Forest Muir, *Texas in 1837, an Anonymous Contemporary Narrative*, Austin: U of Texas Press, 1958, 168, 47, 137, 138. See also *From Virginia*.

31. Chambless, 123.

32. Nichols 2018, 146.

33. Maillard, 210.

34. Nichols 2018, 119, 124, 121, 122, 124, 126, 145, 150.

and James Collinsworth (Tennessee roots), fell victim to suicide—the latter in mysterious circumstances.[35]

Houston was perceived widely by settlers as a tad too pro-Indigene, a descriptor that could hardly be affixed to his successor. Houston, said the influential Briton William Kennedy, embodied a "policy...with regard to the Cherokees and other north-eastern tribes" that "to many of the settlers...gave great dissatisfaction... "[36] Lamar on cue repudiated many of Houston's pacts with the Chero-kees and other Indigenes and proceeded to massacre or expel many of them.[37]

President Lamar was a harbinger of future leaders of the old republic who heedlessly and brazenly entered ever more macabre wars. For while brutalizing Indigenes and embracing conflict with Mexico, he turned thumbs down on annexation by Washington, which would have buttressed his outrageousness. In his inaugural address in 1838 he had the audacity to criticize the holy U.S. Constitution because of its "serious and alarming errors."[38] Lamar's rise was hardly accidental. A trademark of secession had been unalloyed hostility toward Indigenes[39]—essential to land grabs, then slavery—and Lamar was the embodiment of this unendurable trait.

He was not singular, sadly enough. Even before Lamar assumed office, his comrades were dissecting Indigenes like amateur anthro-pologists, probing for weaknesses that could profitably be exploited. The target were the "Caddo, Ioni, Anadarko, Abadoche, among whom are dispersed the Ais and Necogcoche Indians [who] speak a similar language [and] are descended from the old Caddo nation and with the exception of the Caddo are natives of this country" who were seen as coming from across the Sabine River. "All understand and speak the Castilian language," easing alliance with Mexico. Looming above all were the Comanche whom they confessed they knew "but little"—except they were the "natural enemies of the Mexicans," not a universally shared view. At least they acknowl-edged what some considered obvious, however: "no part of said

---

35. M.D. Brown, 104.

36. Kennedy, 311.

37. Galan, in Howell and Swanlund, 459.

38. The Inaugural Address of Mirabeau Lamar, President of the Republic of Texas, to Both Houses of Congress, by Order of Congress. Houston, 1838, NYHS.

39. *Journals of the Consultations Held at San Felipe Austin, October 16, 1835,* Houston: Published by Order of Congress, 1838, NYHS.

tribes have been our friends in War...."[40] Still, the Chickasaw had collaborated with the settlers against the Waco in the prelude to counter-revolution.[41]

However, the difference between his predecessors and Lamar and his retinue was akin to the difference between hardcore conservatives— and proto-fascists. Lamar, the exemplar of this latter category, saw Texas as challenging the old republic, but this ambition was tempered by the hornet's nest he stirred with his hard line toward Indigenes and his disreputable enslaving mania. He was determined to extend Texas's jurisdiction to the Pacific (also a goal of Washington), along with slavery.[42]

For Lamar, liquidating Indigenes was crucial to this wicked scheme: "We have long suspected that the Cherokees were our secret enemies, that while we [were] treating them with kindness...they were holding dark councils with the Mexicans...." But now Lamar and his crew were woke: these "vipers...must go," Lamar argued passionately.[43]

This chilling ukase placed inordinate pressure on the Cherokees. About six months later, a U.S. general concluded bluntly, "civil war in the Cherokee nation is almost certain."[44] Before that, the compensation they were slated to receive for acting as mediators with the Seminoles was questioned by Joel Poinsett, speaking for the U.S. Department of War.[45] This after Cherokee leaders were instructed to travel to Florida to "induce the Seminoles to comply" with yet another dictate and "remove to the lands allotted to them west of the Mississippi...;" the choices were either this dictated "peace" or a "resort...to arms."[46]

The Cherokees countenanced slavery yet found themselves in the middle of controversies about this property, winning no favors,

---

40. Report of the Standing Committee on Indian Affairs, 12 October 1837, in Dorman H. Winfrey, ed., *Texas Indian Papers, 1825-1843, Edited From the Original Manuscript Copies in the Texas State Archives*, Austin: Texas State Library, 1959, 22-28, 23, 24 (abbrev. Winfrey).

41. Statement by Joel W. Robinson, circa 1829-30, Kendall Papers. See also *The Rachel Plummer Narrative: A Stirring Narrative of Adventures, Hardship and Privation in the Early Days of Texas, Depicting Struggles with the Indians and Other Adventures*, 1926, Huntington Library.

42. M.D. Brown, 109.

43. Mirabeau Lamar to Linney, May 1839, in Winfrey, 66-67.

44. General Arbuckle to John Ross, 17 July 1839, Box 6, John Ross Collection, Division of Manuscripts Collection, UOk-N (abbrev. Ross Collection).

45. Ibid., Joel Poinsett to John Ross, 17 March 1838.

46. Ibid., Joel Poinsett to John Ross, 20 Match 1838.

just before Lamar was inaugurated, signaling a new dispensation: Poinsett questioned Chief John Ross about "two negroes which were improperly claimed...and removed from Alabama with the Cherokees"; he demanded that they be returned forthwith, so the matter could be adjudicated "before a judicial tribunal" dominated by the U.S., guaranteeing a dearth of impartiality.[47]

The Cherokees and other Indigenes were slated for Indian Territory—today's Oklahoma—a site that one scholar has written amounted to a "dumping ground" for Indigenes. Their capitulations to slavocracy, e.g., promulgating that all adult males could vote—except Negroes—did not assuage settlers' bloodlust. U.S. pressure had helped to induce a Creek civil war—the "Red Stick War" of 1813-1814—with no real victors. Then there was what amounted to a Cherokee civil war, when the Ross faction executed a good deal of the John Ridge faction, blamed for massive land cessions.[48]

Again, there were no real victors. Even the settlers "lost" insofar as this abject weakening of Indigenes did not sate their bottomless appetite for land, and the federals' alleged inability to oust Native Americans with more rapidity—as in Texas in 1859—fed the desire to construct a new government by 1861, just as it did something similar in 1836. The Cherokees, who bent as much as any other Indigenous grouping to the ways and whims of settlers—even reportedly scheming with settlers during the Fredonia Revolt of 1826-1827 against the interests of Mexico—may have been the biggest loser when Lamar initiated his explicit "extermination" policy toward Indigenes.[49] The settler recently arrived from Vienna, George Erath, seemed nonplussed by what he termed the "declaration of President Lamar to carry on war of extermination...."[50]

The Comanches were a major target not only subjected to fire and the sword but also nonstop pressure as the regime compelled many Indigenes in East Texas—Wichita, Waco, Tawakonies, Tonkawa and

---

47. Ibid., Joel Poinsett to John Ross, 17 December 1838.

48. de Wit, 44, 51, 53. On the internal ruckus within the Cherokee Nation, see e.g., "U.S. Congress. House of Representatives, 25th Congress, 2nd Session, Doc. No. 99, Memorial of a Delegation of the Cherokee Nation, Remonstrations Against the Instrument of Writing (Treaty) of December 1835," Huntington Library. See also Edward Everett Dale and Gaston Litton, *Cherokee Cavaliers: Forty Years of Cherokee History as Told in the Correspondence of the Ridge-Waite-Boudinot Family*, Norman: U of Oklahoma Press, 1939.

49. Helen Hornbeck Tanner, *The Territory of the Caddo Tribe of Oklahoma...*,New York: Garland, 1974, 79, 84 (abbrev. Tanner).

50. Erath, 58.

Lipan Apaches—into Comanche territory.[51] Clearing East Texas of original inhabitants did no favor for Negroes, allowing more of them to be enslaved there, just as clearing Indigenes by "Buffalo Soldiers" in the 1870s brought no surcease to the persecution of Africans.

Ross had performed mighty service to the settler state. After Texas independence he contacted the Seminoles unctuously, informing them that "I am of the aboriginal race of red men of this great island— and are you...." But the era was changing, in that "time was when our ancestors smoke the pipe of peace together" but "bad news" had descended, "it makes me feel sorry" to say. "Cherokees are also in trouble," which was accurate. "Since our arrival here [Washington] we have met with delegations of red m[e]n from several of the northern tribes"; thus, "we have seen Black Hawk" of the Sauk, for example. Now he wanted the Seminoles and Sauk to follow him on the sellout road with Ross serving as "mediator"[52]—before the rug was pulled out from under his feet too.

Thus, despite the service of Ross and other Indigenous leaders to Washington, this proved unavailing in white supremacist states— the U.S. now joined by Texas. It was in 1838 in Fannin County—like many of Texas's landmarks bearing the name of a prominent enslaver—that a settler stared with self-satisfaction as "the dark Indian staggered and fell dead"; the "next morning he was examined and found to be a woolly-headed negro,"[53] meaning that the color of their skin often conspired against Indigenes.

Hence, it was in early 1838 that settler Cassandra Sawyer Lockwood stood at what she described as a "considerable branch of the Arkansas [river]," not far from Indian Territory. "Here for the first time I beheld Cherokees, the shore being lined with Indians & negroes. The negroes were the slaves of the Indians...some wore handkerchiefs in the form of turbans...." Revealingly, she was "introduced to a black woman who was the only person among them, who could talk English."[54] This vignette exposed how the Cherokee surrendered to the settlers on the keystone matter of enslaving Africans—yet still were expelled, as they often remained reliant on this property with linguistic skill. The Cherokees lost though they were often treated as

---

51. Wallace and Hoebel, 229.

52. John Ross to Chief Headmen and Warriors of Seminoles, 18 October 1837, Box 1, Ross Collection.

53. *Simpson*, 1880, originally from Stephen F. Austin U at Nacogdoches, Anderson Papers.

54. Letter from Cassandra Sawyer Lockwood, 2 February 1838, Roberta Robey Collection, UOk-N (abbrev. Robey Collection).

being superior to other Indigenes, not least because of their assimilation policy. Lockwood also advised "respected young ladies" that "the character of the poor Osages differs materially from the Cherokees. They are many degrees lower in the scale of human beings," she stressed, because of the "baneful" impact of alcohol and "white traders."[55] She could have added what another observer noticed: The Caddo—along with the Comanches, Public Enemy Number 1 among settlers—were increasingly crossing the border into the U.S. from Texas "to avoid the Osages of whom they stood in fear," perhaps because their bellicosity was fueled by spirits, bountifully supplied by "white traders."[56]

Thus, despite the internal splits among Cherokees that led some to surrender to settlers and others to pursue an opposing course, a similar result ensued in both instances: defeat. Interviewed in 1936, the formerly enslaved Eliza Whitmire of Estella, Oklahoma, recalled when Cherokees were routed in Georgia: "on the heels of the retreating Indians came greedy whites to pillage the Indians' homes[,] drive off their cattle, horses, and hogs and they even rifled the graves for any jewelry or other ornaments that might have been buried with the dead...."[57]

But as President Jackson and his circle surveyed the landscape, as he began packing to leave the White House and return to his Tennessee plantation amply larded with enslaved Africans, there was remarkable sanguinity. Shortly before ascending to the highest court in the land, fellow Tennessean John Catron chose to "congratulate you" since the "Indian disturbances will afford the occasion for removal of this population" whereas "our relations with Texas, resting on our great slave and Indian border may be so settled as to leave no further cause of apprehension from the *poor* Mexicans or the (much to be dreaded) *English*...[emphasis-original]." In fact, he continued, "there is much [more] danger of Texas conquering Mexico than the reverse;" thus, signaling diplomatic recognition, he asserted that "any member of Congress should vote against Texas independence his political prospects would be ruined...." As of June 1836, Catron, who had visited Louisiana and Mississippi of late, felt that if Mexico sought to continue hostilities, "an army from the west," meaning

---

55. Letter of Cassandra Lockwood Sawyer, 7 March 1839, Robey Collection.

56. Remark by Joseph Valentin in U.S. Congress. House of Representatives, 27th Congress, 2nd Session, Rep. No. 1035, "The Caddo Indian Treaty," Historic New Orleans.

57. Oral History, Eliza Whitmire, 14 February 1936, IPP.

this southern region, "will march upon the city of Mexico"—which occurred about a decade later. If this further invasion occurred, then Mexico would demand intervention by London, which could mean this power seizing the vast area surrounding the Gulf of Mexico, though he insisted, "no European power should be permitted to gain a footing in Mexico." He saw no immediate need for annexation of the new republic since Mexico—"this feeble and worthless people is our safest neighbor" and "if the independence of Texas is recognized by our government, then Texas can be controlled by us...."[58] The president, supposedly endorsing "strict neutrality" in what amounted to a Mexican Civil War over slavery—anticipating 1861—then told one of his leading generals (as if he expected the correspondence to be published): "Mexicans have charged your soldiers with fighting the battle and defeating them at San Jacinto."[59]

In an appeal that reached the president, Austin continued his histrionics, claiming that Mexico was waging a "war against heretics"—meaning Protestants—"exciting the Comanches and other Indians" since, he exhorted, "this is a war of barbarism against civilization," i.e., "of Mexicans against Americans...a war in which every free American, who is not a fanatical abolitionist or a cold hearted recreant" must take a side.[60] The president, perhaps sensing the rise of a rival, disagreed.[61]

President Jackson also sensed that the hotheads in Texas had bungled their way into a quagmire sucking in countless U.S. nationals, but needed rescue—yet had not relinquished dreams of rivaling the rescuer. By February 1837 President Jackson knew that Texas was simultaneously courting London and Paris, which could be wielded like a cudgel against the would-be rescuer.[62]

Yet reservations aside, it was during Jackson's presidential tenure that a blow was said to be struck for Texas, meaning the admission of Arkansas as a state in June 1836, which provided more of a rationale for Washington pursuing Texas runaways and combative Indigenes alike.[63]

58. John Catron to President Jackson, 8 June 1836, in Bassett, Volume 5, 401.

59. Ibid., President Jackson to Brigadier General Edmund P. Gaines, 4 September 1836, 423-424.

60. Ibid., "Appeal by Stephen F. Austin," 15 April 1836, 397.

61. Ibid., Note from President Jackson, ca. April 1836, 398.

62. Ibid., President Jackson to Brigadier General Benjamin Howard, 2 February 1837, 456-457.

63. K.H. Jones, 31.

Then again, Arkansas statehood could have been seen in "Washington-on-the-Brazos" as another step toward encirclement of the presumed rival, which was sucking away U.S. nationals while consorting with London and other foes. Giving weight to this supposition was the 1838 invasion of Natchitoches supposedly to "chastise the Caddo," according to an insider.[64]

The emissary of the London foe was in New Orleans in 1837, the lever for Texas sovereignty. Joseph Crawford felt that within the older republic initial enthusiasm for Texas annexation was waning, for upon sober "reflection" the "interests" of the two "are at variance" since Texas "soil" was capable of "producing as much if not more cotton than is grown in America" (meaning the U.S.). Thus, as of late May 1837 Crawford perceived that next door in Texas "opinion...has changed and they are very anxious to have a separate, free and independent government to trade directly with other nations...." The complication was—"I lament to say...slaves have been imported directly into Texas.... there is still one or more American vessels employed in this most detestable traffic...landing the slaves on the east side of the Sabine and so evading the laws of Texas," while bringing the enslaved from Cuba. He predicted that "in twelve months from this time, the slave population of Texas will probably be doubled" because of the arrival of more settlers. And despite London's proud abolitionist tradition, he was optimistic that British manufacturers would do well.[65]

But abolitionists were hardly impotent in the British Isles, especially when it came to payback against their hypocritical spawn that shrieked endlessly about liberty while busily decapitating Indigenes and enslaving Africans. The leading Irish patriot Daniel O'Connell was among those who stridently opposed diplomatic recognition of sovereign Texas—unless Mexico consented (unlikely) and slavery and the slave trade barred (unlikely)—and he argued further that a Free Negro colony be formed along the border.[66] Yet the new republic

---

64. J. Cable to Hon. R. Garland, 1 December 1838 in "Message from the President of the United States...in Relation to the Invasion of the Southwestern Frontier by an Armed Force from the Republic of Texas...," 25th Congress, House of Representatives, Doc. No. 71, Historic New Orleans.

65. Joseph Crawford, Consul to Lord Pakenham, 26 May 1837, Box 2-23/755, Texas Republic SoS, Box 2-23/755, Barker Collection UT-A. Lord Pakenham had lived in Mexico for several years. See Eugene Maissin, *The French in Mexico and Texas, 1838-1839*, Salado, Texas: Anson Jones Press, 1961, 115 (abbrev. Maissin).

66. Vernon Stafford, "The Diplomatic Service of William Kennedy to Texas," M.A. Thesis, TTU, 1950, 6.

subtly manipulated London during its nine-year experiment with independence, dangling itself as a counterweight to Washington, while sneakily marching toward annexation. This was unfortunate, especially since even Andrew Jackson knew as early as 1838—if not before—that there were powerful forces in the U.S. who were firmly opposed to annexation on anti-slavery grounds.[67]

Texas—at least among some in the elite—was akin to a potential mate who "plays the field" in order to induce jealousy and intense interest on the part of the preferred partner: the U.S. So, James Pinckney Henderson, one of the new republic's chief emissaries abroad, alarmed Washington by seeming to be willing to cut deals with London. This was not altogether artificial since Texas's finances were abysmal early on, and London had a deep pocket. Henderson was wealthy and thus appreciated this factor; he had lived in Cuba and thus had the potential to frighten Mexico by consorting with Spaniards. Plus Cuba proved to be a fertile source of imports of enslaved Africans. But London had to worry if the Texas example would further inspire secessionism in Canada, while seeking to fend off the internal abolitionist lobby. The latter was hard to assuage when their own envoy, Joseph Crawford, reported that Texas's "slave population will probably be doubled" relatively soon, with Cuba being the major transmission point. Nor would this lobby be assuaged when Sam Houston told an inquiring reporter that Texas was simply unable to end the traffic in the enslaved. Just as the 1776 rebels repeatedly blamed London for the presence of the enslaved in the old republic, Henderson blamed Mexico. Still, his peregrinations in Paris were hampered by his lack of facility in French and a similar deficiency in English on the part of his interlocutors. But the influential Lewis Cass, the U.S. envoy to France, often lent him a hand. France recognized the secessionist state well before Britain, which placed pressure on London to act likewise.[68]

However, London had an obstacle to recognition that dwarfed similar blockages in Paris or Washington: perhaps the strongest organized abolitionist movement in the North Atlantic community.

For while Austin was waving the bloody shirt of anxiety *cum* revenge, by late May 1836, a U.S. vessel in Vera Cruz was apprised

67. Francis P. Blair to Andrew Jackson, 19 October 1838, in Bassett, Volume 5, 567.

68. Steven Grady Gamble, "James Pinckney Henderson in Europe: The Diplomacy of the Republic of Texas, 1837-1840," Ph.D. dissertation, TTU, 1976, 20, 22, 30, 44, 47, 71, 75, 77, 94, 108, 143, 170, 176, 225, 248, 284. On Houston and the reporter, see e.g., *Telegraph and Texas Register*, 5 May 1837.

of a smashing rebel victory led by Sam Houston: "the unexpected reverse of affairs act like an electric shock on the minds of the [Mexican] military," engendering a "high decree of excitement against our country," said the U.S. consul.[69] The response in Mexico was not just shock: later that year the "authorities," said the consul, engaged in "seizures" of U.S. vessels, including the appropriately entitled "Fourth of July" of Baltimore,[70] which served to worsen bilateral relations. This was not just supposition since the consul then objected vehemently to the most "recent outrage committed on the persons of citizens of the United States,"[71] yet another step toward war which was to erupt a decade later.

Still, despite the bloodcurdling yelps from Austin, which also happened to encourage an even more muscular intervention from the older republic, Southerners continued to arrive in Texas. The Panic of 1837 was a factor.[72] This latest economic downturn also may have slowed down the movement in the older republic toward annexation;[73] battling Seminoles in Florida and the Blackhawk war in the Midwest and other expensively murderous tussles may have played a role too. However, for various reasons—abolitionist sentiment especially—there was early resistance to annexing the new republic. One Congressman in 1837 declared that "the annexation of Texas to the Union is the first step to the conquest of all Mexico, of the West Indies, of a maritime, colonizing, slave tainted monarchy and extinguishment of freedom...."

However, Euro-Americans and Europeans were voting with their feet, albeit many were debtors fleeing the debris of the 1837 Panic.[74] "Many families are preparing to move to Texas," said a local scribe. "Emigrants to Texas are now entitled to 640 acres of land if single men, to 1280 if married"—while a steady stream of arriving enslaved Africans guaranteed a labor force and profitability.[75] In October, there was a typical story: "A large number of emigrants from the

---

69. M. Burrough, Consul to Sir, 27 May 1836, Reel 2, Despatches from U.S. Consuls in Vera Cruz, NARA.

70. Ibid., M. Burrough to Secretary of State Forsyth, 17 November 1836.

71. Ibid., M. Burrough to Secretary of State Forsyth, 1 December 1836.

72. M.D. Brown, 106.

73. Baumgartner, 103.

74. Clarence R. Wharton, *The Republic of Texas: A Brief History of Texas from the First American Colonies in 1821 to Annexation in 1846*, Houston: Young, 1922, 220, 221 (abbrev. Wharton).

75. *Telegraph & Texas Register*, 2 May 1837, Box 2b/123, Barker Collection UT-A.

United States have just arrived in Galveston bay,"[76] the prime port. In December there was a forbiddingly typical story: "[A] large number of emigrants are continually arriving from the United States. We notice with pleasure that most of them are well supplied with rifles,"[77] which were bound to be put to promiscuous use. During the summer and autumn of 1837, it was reported that 6000 of these "emigrants" had entered Texas via the Sabine River—alone, to the exclusion of other points of entry—attracted hypnotically by the dream of landowning.[78]

These "emigrants" from the U.S. were not finished. As so often happens, the success of aggression is self-perpetuating. By early 1837 the U.S. envoy in Mexico City was gleefully reporting on the "insurrection" in "San Diego, Upper California" in which, he said euphemistically, "some American citizens...took an active part."[79]

Mexico hardly had reconciled to this stinging defeat, this theft of a good deal of territory in order to perpetuate enslavement of Africans forevermore. From the grassroots in Mexico City came a groundswell of fury, as the residences of U.S. nationals—and their French allies—were stoned, a protest that was suppressed with fatalities by the authorities, leaving wounded "bayoneted."[80]

Then the U.S. was enraged when this older republic thought it had reason to believe that Mexico "in secret" was pushing a "project to dispose of Texas and as far south as necessary to the British," at the rock-bottom price of "five cents per acre in order to pay off the British debt."[81] Meanwhile, U.S. nationals were fleeing Mexico City in helter-skelter fashion in the face of unalloyed hostility. When the U.S. took steps to recognize the bastard republic in 1837, the response from Mexico was said to be "full of invective" with anguished cries charging "duplicity."[82] Though mutual vociferation was becoming normalized, the decibels seemed to reach new levels of intensity when word leaked that London was seeking to purchase "Upper California,"[83] thwarting the race by both republics to the Pacific.

76. Ibid., *Telegraph & Texas Register*, 7 October 1837.

77. Ibid., *Telegraph & Texas Register*, 2 December 1837.

78. Chambless, 170.

79. W. Jones, Consul to Secretary of State Forsyth, 8 February 1837, Reel 2, Despatches from U.S. Consuls in Mexico City, NARA.

80. Ibid., W. Jones, Consul to Secretary of State Forsyth, 14 March 1837.

81. Ibid., W. Jones to Secretary of State Forsyth, 28 March 1837.

82. Ibid., W. Jones to Secretary of State Forsyth, 2 April 1837.

83. Ibid., W. Jones to Secretary of State Forsyth, 18 April 1837.

By February 1837 policymakers in Richmond were clamoring for diplomatic recognition of Texas. One self-interested legislator was busily buying land in the republic, wagering on a price rise. Supposedly the incoming president Martin Van Buren dissented, but the tides of secession were hard to resist. The example of Henry Clay in the recognition of South American nations' independence was cited in contrast, though it was acknowledged that if the momentous step of recognition were to be taken, Mexico—already enduring secessionist urges in California and elsewhere—would be upset, all for the benefit of a "band of land speculators"[84] (and slave traders too). Thus, by 1838 one account avers that in that year alone, 15,000 of the enslaved were landed in Texas, many from parts of Africa dominated by France.[85]

Weeks after this Virginia colloquy, Richmond was heard in Washington, as a tariff bill deemed as favorable to Texas moved toward passage. Reverberations were felt in Vera Cruz, where the U.S. emissary reported that "the measure was denounced as an act of ill faith on the part of [Washington] toward a friendly nation...." But the State Department knew that Mexico's options for retaliation were limited as "the French are urging their claims against Mexico by the presence of physical force"; they were then menacing "this port" with a "frigate and two brigs of war" bristling with weapons.[86] Soon Paris upped the ante, dispatching a frigate with 60 guns to bolster a demand that Mexico repay swiftly an assumed debt of $800,000, including "indemnity claims in behalf of French subjects." Paris meant business since a "blockade" was imposed on Vera Cruz. London also revealed its scavenging instincts when arriving soon was "part of the English squadron for the Gulf of Mexico"—whose time would have been better spent chasing down slavers—which was tasked with "the adjustment of pending claims with Mexico...." In a sense, Washington did not have to lift a finger in order to coax its neighbor into line, which may not have been in the long-term interest of Paris or London.[87]

---

84. Speech of Joseph Segar, Esq. on the Motion of Mr. Chapman of Monroe. To Instruct the Senators and Request the Representatives in Congress from the State of Virginia to Vote for the Immediate Recognition of the Independence of Texas. Delivered in the House of Delegates of Virginia, 23 February 1837, Huntington Library.

85. Govenar, 49.

86. Report, 13 April 1837, Reel 3, Despatches from U.S. Consuls in Vera Cruz, NARA.

87. Ibid., M. Burrough, Consul to State Department, 24 March 1838.

So, the old republic joined in the fray, sending—said the U.S. consul in Mexico City—"armed vessels" to aid France's "blockading brig" with ample "provisions."[88] driven by continuing complaints about Mexico seizing the property of U.S. nationals.[89] Yet this move may not have been in the long-term interest of Washington, as the Civil War seizure of Mexico by France indicated. Both Mexico and the old republic alike should have been concerned when in 1838 Texas voted to develop its own navy. Soon this military branch was placed in the hands of rebels in the Yucatan, in order to subvert Mexico, then passed into the armada of Washington upon annexation—where they could be used to confront London.[90]

Paris likely was not threatened by this turn of events; their pressure on Vera Cruz certainly aided Texas', keeping Mexico on the back foot. Objectively French subversion of Algeria aided Texas' undermining of Mexico.[91]

But the U.S. was bound to be splattered by the resultant reaction, which arrived shortly: "feeling against foreigners is daily becoming more alarming," said the U.S. envoy.[92] Like a chain reaction, this response had to be suppressed by the aggressors, as the French squadron then "attacked the castle of San Juan de Ulloa," which "continued without intermission about five hours" and "hoisted their flag." Then U.S. naval commander David Farragut arrived, to rescue his nation's nationals and "innocent foreigners without distinction,"[93] said the consul, which Mexico hardly embraced.

Then in 1837, there was a full-scale leap toward renewed war with Mexico when reports emerged about a "Revolution" brewing in New Mexico—where Texas claimed a good deal of territory. Somehow 22 leaders there were "decapitated" with the weapon wielders seeking to flee to Washington and, as it was put, "treat with that government for annexation...." It is doubtful if Secretary of State

88. Memorandum from William Jones, Consul, 14 September 1838, Reel 3, Despatches from U.S. Consuls in Mexico City, NARA.

89. "Message from the President of the United States. U.S. Congress, House of Representatives, 25th Congress, 2nd Session, Doc. No. 351, United States and Mexico," Huntington Library.

90. Mollie Evelyn Moore Davis, *Under Six Flags: The Story of Texas*, Boston: Ginn, 1897, 120.

91. Maissin, xi, 27.

92. M. Burrough to "Sir," 17 April 1838, Reel 3, Despatches from U.S. Consuls in Vera Cruz, NARA.

93. Ibid., L.E. Hargous, Consul to Secretary of State Forsyth, 29 November 1838. See also, Chambless, 171.

John Forsyth, the recipient of this report, really believed what he was reading: "American citizens of Santa Fe refused to take any part in the matter"—though even the consul had to concede that there was a "difference of opinion" as to this latter point.[94]

Though Washington was far away from the lapping flames of the borderlands, even the most obtuse legislator could sense this crisis could ensnare the old republic: annexation of Texas was combined with the domestic slave trade and the horror of slavery in the District of Columbia, the self-asserted citadel of liberty, which did not enhance the reputation of the new republic.[95]

As this swirl of events was unfolding, the future abolitionist solon Charles Sumner arrived in Paris in March 1838, determined to "study" the "French language...."[96] Though overseas, he could not evade problems in his homeland, informing fellow abolitionist William Channing about his encounter in Paris with "Mr. Gibbs of South Carolina, a resident for some years. He is a slaveholder"—though like many, posed as being antislavery.[97] After several months of residence, Sumner headed home "with the liveliest regret.... I have been a learner daily" and was "longing to stay here": "I must return," he insisted.[98]

He did return to abolitionist fervor, which was needed more than ever in light of secession. As time passed, it also came clear that France was becoming ever more important to the fortunes of enslavement in the slaveholders' republics.

---

94. W. Jones to Secretary of State Forsyth, 22 September 1837, Reel 2, Despatches from U.S. Consuls in Mexico City, NARA.

95. "Speech of the Hon. Samuel Prentiss of Vermont upon the Reception of the Vermont Resolutions on the Subject of the Admission of Texas, the Domestic Slave Trade and Slavery in the District of Columbia, Delivered in the Senate...January 16, 1838," Washington: Gales and Seaton, 1838, NYHS.

96. Memorandum, 30 March 1838, in Edward Pierce, ed., *Memoir and Letters of Charles Sumner, Volume I*, London: Low, Marston, Searle & Rivington, 1878, 277 (abbrev. Pierce).

97. Ibid., Charles Sumner to the Reverend Dr. William Channing, 21 May 1838, 295-296.

98. Ibid., Charles Sumner to Judge Story, 14 May 1838, 294-295.

Chapter 5

Approaching Annexation, 1839-1840

As the 1830s were lurching to a close, sovereign Texas was beset with a passel of problems: restive Africans, rebellious Indigenes, revanchist Mexicans—and a depleting treasury, tied irrevocably to combating the foregoing. The new republic was not wholly trusted by the older sibling—at least not at the elite level: as ever in this "democracy," where one's ability to climb the greasy pole of success often involved climbing rungs comprised of cadavers of Indigenes, there was "grassroots" backing by Euro-Americans eager to join the land rush in Texas. Ostensibly, London was opposed to the accretion of enslavement but was outmaneuvered since it put too much stock into the narrative that Texas would stand as a rival to Washington, providing the Empire with leverage, while Paris too was flummoxed when annexation occurred in 1845, further fattening and emboldening Washington.

* * *

In retrospectively scrutinizing this fraught era, it is wise not to be distracted by the ultimate outcome—triumph of the settlers and enslavers—since this was hardly inevitable. In 1839 Texas was buzzing about proposals emanating from London about making the new republic an abolitionist settlement, even a version of Haiti.[1]

With abolition taking hold in the Caribbean, there were rampant predictions of a "Confederation of Negro Republics" stretching from Cuba to Trinidad—inspired by Haiti.[2] The formation of the British and Foreign Anti-Slavery Society in 1839, unbeknownst to all worldwide, began the accelerated countdown of slavery's terminal phase. So moved, both Daniel O'Connell and Harriet Beecher Stowe assailed pro-slavery forces amongst the Irish, especially in North

---

1. *Telegraph & Texas Register*, 4 December 1839. See also Gerald Horne, *Negro Comrades*.

2. Maissin, 221.

America, pushing back against their frequent disrupting of anti-slavery meetings and providing added impetus for abolitionism.[3]

Ashbel Smith, an avid secessionist in both 1836 and 1861—and, strategically, fluent in French[4]—was aghast at the idea that O'Connell in 1839 would introduce a parliamentary measure that would convert Texas's "unoccupied territory...near its northern border" to an asylum for "Her Majesty's subjects who may be desirous to emigrate"; this "free state" would also act as a "refuge and rendezvous for runaway Negroes from the southern states" and a "festering thorn in the side of the United States on their most exposed flank...." Smith, who served variously as Secretary of State of the new republic and its envoy to Paris and London, managed to attend abolitionist meetings in the latter capital—albeit for malign purposes. He lamented "plans" for "using Texas as a catspaw for undermining the border states;" that "aimed at the abolition of slavery in Texas" since "every Englishman is opposed to slavery...."[5]

This final point was inflated with yeast but it was intended to convey the message that Washington had an interest in aiding the new republic, rivalry notwithstanding; however, as matters evolved, it signaled that annexation of Texas by the old republic was not necessarily a sign of enslavement's strength but instead—as settlers might put it—it was a case of the enslavers circling the wagons to deflect a powerful onslaught from abolitionism.

In any event, Mexico creatively adapted Smith's nightmare in the 1840s when it was said to have collaborated with Comanche raids on Texas,[6] then began to form a kind of buffer zone on its northern border by inviting Kickapoo and Seminoles, as well as some Cherokee, Shawnee and Delaware to settle in Coahuila. As early as May 1840 the U.S. consul in Matamoros reported anxiously that "Comanche Indians approached within two leagues of this city, killed some of the inhabitants on the opposite side of the river and afterwards made their escape with several captives and a number of horses, mules," etc.[7]

---

3. Comment, Abel and Klingberg, 3, 31.

4. Maissin, 141.

5. Ashbel Smith, "Reminiscences of the Texas Republic, Annual Address Delivered Before the Historical Society of Galveston," 15 December 1875, Huntington Library (abbrev. A. Smith).

6. Brice, 1,2.

7. D.W. Smith to Secretary of State John Forsyth, 26 May 1840, Reel 2, Despatches from U.S. Consuls in Matamoros, NARA.

However, Texas had a potent card to play: it was the state—before and after annexation—that controlled public lands, not the federal government as was the case elsewhere.[8] This gave the local elite a powerful magnet by which settlers could be attracted continentally and globally, creating in rapid succession, more militia and Texas Rangers by which the land could be "cleansed." It also allowed for adept manipulation as when big landowners at one point effectively blocked inward migration as they waited for prices to rise[9]—though the downside risk was not having enough battlers to confront Indigenes and Africans. It could also slow the influx of the enslaved to work the land and gum up the entire economy based on land and unpaid labor; thus for the longest time in Texas the enslaved were accepted as payment for land at a rate of exchange equivalent to cattle—a cow and a calf for a hundred acres or a Negro woman and a child for same.[10]

Although it was recognized dimly at the time, as long as Indigenes were being massacred, land would be seized, providing more room for enslavement to grow. Thus, it was also in 1839 that Chief Bowles, a Cherokee leader, who despite his partial European ancestry, often stood tall against settlers, was slain—a devastating blow to Indigenes. He and his comrades were long suspected of aligning with Mexico and he was thought to have accepted an official commission from this state in the aftermath of the ill-fated Fredonia Revolt in 1827. Chief Bowles and his colleague, Big Mush [Gatunwali] turned toward Mexico when the Texas Congress turned thumbs down on a pact negotiated by President Houston, distrusted because of previous associations with Cherokees, leading to the ascension of the genocidal President Lamar. In any case, this Cherokee setback in 1839 induced many of this group to abandon Texas and cross the Red River.[11]

It is unclear if the survivors who fled included runaway slaves of Texas and about 80 Kickapoo, an ethnic group who were to become among the most militant of the many opponents of the colonizers.[12]

For President Lamar demanded an "absolute expulsion" of the "barbarian race"—meaning Indigenes—though this terrorism seemed downright liberal compared to his subsequent view that

---

8. Janne Lahti, *Wars for Empire: Apaches, the United States and the Southwest Borderlands*, Norman: U of Oklahoma Press, 2019, 112, 113 (abbrev. Lahti).

9. Maissin, 200.

10. Watson, 80.

11. Note in Grant Foreman, ed., *A Traveler in Indian Territory: The Journal of Ethan Allen Hitchcock*, Norman: U of Oklahoma Press, 1996, 213 (abbrev. Foreman, *Traveler*).

12. Nichols 2018, 150.

"extermination" was the preferred option. Even some Comanches began to retreat across the Red River, with many of those remaining reduced to consuming their horses by the 1870s. But this was an expensive crusade, accelerating an already staggering debt incurred by the war with Mexico, leaving few alternatives except annexation.[13] President Lamar, who had experience in routing Indigenes in Georgia, applied his gruesome expertise to Texas.[14]

This was ironic in that Lamar was among those who sought to carve out a separate path for Texas, not necessarily in the old republic's ensnarement. But his maneuvers bespoke a desperation, e.g., alliance with rebels in Yucatan, perceived widely as hostile to European incursions generally, of which those of Lamar and Co. were exemplary. But this was seen as a fitting response to the Comanche-Mexico tie. Comanche attitudes hardly improved when they began to negotiate in 1839 for a meeting the following year with settlers—that eventuated in the so-called "Council House Fight" disemboweling politically the Penateka Comanches, but hardening many of this group in their antipathy to double-dealing settlers.[15] The settlers pulled one of their oldest tricks: inviting antagonists to a meeting then detaining and killing them upon arrival.

The aggressive settler shift toward Lamar instigated their devaluation of his predecessor, Houston, despite his being a slaveholder. This in turn soiled the reputation of former President Jackson, one of Houston's closest comrades. It was also in 1839 that a well-connected analyst went so far as to link the two with the late Aaron Burr and his schemes to seize Spanish land and create a rump republic—which, after all, Houston actually did. "Many of the surviving confederates of Burr," charged Robert Mayo, "were the aiders and abettors of... Houston."[16]

The rise of Lamar was not the only setback endured by Indigenes. The debilitating conditions they had to endure made them more vulnerable to a smallpox epidemic, which too ensued in 1839, interacting mortally with the cholera and syphilis delivered by the invaders, which was particularly baneful for Comanches.[17]

Unfortunately, the frail diplomatic arms of Indigenes combined with the pre-existing ethnocentrism of European powers to delimit

---

13. Carol Lipscomb, "'Sorrow Whispers in the Wind: The Republic of Texas' Comanche Indian Policy, 1836-1846," M.A. thesis, UNT, 1994, 68, 117.

14. Brice, 2.

15. Himmel, 124, 125.

16. Mayo, 154, 155.

17. Wallace and Hoebel, 149.

the external aid the original inhabitants of the continent could have received. London's man, William Kennedy, observed that in 1839 that "hostilities...commenced between the Comanches and the united tribes of Lipan and Tokewas [Tonkawas]on the Upper Colorado,"[18] the latter grouping often allied with settlers. In this land of ironies, the Lipan Apache and the Comanches, major foes of settlers, were often at war with each other. The Lipan were so hard-pressed that they temporarily sought refuge among settlers. The Caranchua—or Karankawa—once thickly populated the region stretching from Galveston to Corpus Christi, but they too were perpetually at war with other Indigenes.[19] And as settlers invaded, Indigenes were often pushed onto the territory of others, fomenting conflict.

Settlers hardly escaped unscathed. Subsequently, the prominent settler Joseph Robertson recalled the events of 1839 when his "plantation on the Colorado River within Bastrop County was attacked by a considerable body of hostile Indians and my [sic] Negroes"; he was "forcibly taken" before finding sanctuary with Jesse Chisholm, a "half breed Cherokee...."[20]

Exacerbating the climate overall was the robust interventionism practiced by their competitors, which hindered Mexican aid to Indigenes. It was also in 1839 that 300 Euro-American men arrived in Tampico—soon to be a fortress of Confederate solidarity—to aid

---

18. Kennedy, Volume II, 340-341.

19. Wilbarger, 144, 1, 66: The "Caranchua," says the author, referred to as "'the Cronks'...differed in many respects from all the other native tribes of Texas.... they were the Ishmaelites of Texas...sometimes professed to be friendly to the whites...but no one had any faith in their sincerity.... physically they were much superior to any of the native tribes of Texas.... they never suffered from want of food...fish, oyster, clams...." But soon they were "exterminated" with remnants straggling into Mexico. "The Comanche Indians were to Texas what the Pequot Indians were to New England and what the Sioux were to the traders and trappers of the west.... the Comanche Indians are (or perhaps I should say were) one of the most warlike tribes on the American continent and were greatly dreaded by Americans, Mexicans and other Indians.... as a general rule the Lipans were unreliable, deceitful and treacherous. They always professed to be friendly to the whites, but it is well known that they frequently depredated upon their property...would occasionally take a scalp when they thought they could so with impunity. The tribe is now extinct," he added with a macabre smirk.

20. Joseph Robertson to James S. Mayfield, 7 April 1841, in Winfrey, 122-123.

Mexican allies in regime change.[21] This was later claimed to be an "entire falsehood"[22] in Mexico City but bolstered in a message to Tampico itself where "three hundred Americans" had "arrived...from New Orleans" to join "pro-French forces."[23] Adding to the unease was a report from Mazatlán, Mexico, pointing to an impending "invasion from Texas in combination with discontented [Mexican] federalists," which tended to "cause some sensation."[24]

Simultaneously in "Alta California," soon to be seized by the old republic, the U.S. consul in Oahu while there had noticed a "most distracted state; revolutions are every day taking place," unavoidably involving a "large number of American citizens, as almost an immense amount of American property are [sic] hereby exposed to insult, oppression and plunder...." Making a request with a preordained affirmative response, the consul "earnestly hoped that the government of the United States may extend her arm of power for the protection of the citizens in that quarter of the globe."[25]

Actually, according to the report weeks later from Mazatlán also on the Pacific coast, "'both of the Californias' are in a very unsettled state"; in fact, there was an "unsettled state of all this country bordering on the Pacific"; the "war with France" was a factor in creating this unrest but it made this expansive region ripe for the plucking by Washington.[26] By late 1839 British and French vessels had visited Galveston,[27] contributing to the miasma of nervousness.

Those like Texas diplomat and operative Anson Jones likely welcomed the Gallic visitors. He was close to the Marquis de Rumigny,[28] then French ambassador to Spain with the latter nation still scheming

---

21. William Jones, Consul to Sir, 27 February 1839, Reel 3, Despatches from U.S. Consuls in Mexico City, NARA.

22. Ibid., Report to William Jones, 14 March 1839.

23. W.D. Jones, Consul to John G. McCall and John McCall to Secretary of State Forsyth, 23 March 1839, Reel 1, Despatches from U.S. Consuls in Tampico, NARA.

24. John Parrott, Consul to Secretary of State Forsyth, 18 December 1839, Reel 1, Despatches from U.S. Consuls in Mazatlan, NARA.

25. Report from John Jones, Consul in Oahu, 23 January 1839, Reel 3, Despatches from U.S. Consuls in Mexico City, NARA.

26. John Parrott, Consul to Secretary of State, 26 February 1839, Reel 1, Despatches from U.S. Consuls in Mazatlan, NARA.

27. Kennedy, 346-347.

28. Christopher Hughes to Anson Jones, 24 April 1840, in Anson Jones, *Memoranda and Official Correspondence Relating to the Republic of Texas, its History and Annexation*, New York: Appleton, 1859, 155 (abbrev. A. Jones).

relentlessly for a comeback in the Americas in order to bolster Cuba. As for London, Jones's fellow Texas patriot Ashbel Smith was contemptuous, renouncing her "chiefly violent abolitionists" imbued with "Jesuitical fanaticism...." Singled out in this inflamed context was a hardy phenomenon, a *rara avis* scarcely spotted in Texas: a Euro-American abolitionist, Stephen Andrews.[29]

Hence, by September 1839 a report reached Washington from Mexico City that included tantalizingly a map of "Upper California" with words appended outlining the "vast importance that country might some day...come to the U.S." since it was "very rich and fertile" replete with "timber" along with "gold and silver to be found here in great abundance...." There were "rich resources...very little known to the world"; carefully sketched was the "fortification" guarding San Francisco with the alluring detail that "passage from California to China is from forty to fifty days."[30]

The race between Texas and the U.S. to the Pacific was on, but the new republic was hindered by its abysmal financial crisis, impelled in part by wasteful wars with ferocious Indigenes, especially the Caddo and Comanche. Texas's reach may have exceeded its grasp in that it was dependent beyond the short term on the beneficence of the U.S., in keeping Mexico in check, for example, or crushing Indigenes along the borders with Arkansas, Indian Territory, and Louisiana, but then it was openly seeking to outstrip this same benefactor. John C. Calhoun, the hawkish Vice President then Secretary of State, was not alone in ripping Texas with its bottomless begging bowl yet possessing "the ambition of Rome and the avarice of Carthage," all with the goal of becoming "the real empire...of the country."[31]

Likely Calhoun took note when President Lamar sent hundreds of Texans into New Mexico in search of a trade route in order to divert trade from the U.S. and also of his overweening idea of seizing two-thirds of Mexican land, an expanse then larger than the U.S. at that moment.[32] It was unavoidable that Washington was aware when Memucan Hunt, the new republic's envoy to the U.S., expressed a

---

29. Ashbel Smith to Anson Jones, 2 August 1843, in A. Jones, 236-237.

30. Report to State Department, 26 September 1839, Reel 4, Despatches from U.S. Consuls in Mexico City, NARA. See also Rose Marie Beebe and Robert M. Senkewicz, eds., *Lands of Promise and Despair: Chronicles of Early California, 1535-1846*, Berkeley: Heyday, 2001.

31. Levander, 35.

32. Haynes, Somervell, 4, 5.

felt desire for extending his realm to the Pacific—and was backed by his colleagues in power.[33]

However, these were not the only two competitors in the race to plunder Mexico. Indigenes would get a vote. Russia was creeping down the Pacific Coast. Then there was London—and especially Paris, which already was intimidating Mexico and was well-entrenched in Texas. If Texas could be plied away from Mexico, then why not California? Their legation in Texas was led by Alphonse Du Bois de Saligny, described as a "dandified little French whippersnapper who smoked expensive cigars, kept a stableful of fine horses and drank fine French wines and cognac instead of the local firewater," leaving a fine aroma in his wake and, possibly, cloudy thinking too. Maybe that is why "everyone knows he reneged on his hotel bill [and] had his servant shoot a number of the pigs of his former landlord...."[34]

Yet the Frenchman's mind was sufficiently uncloudy to realize that during the struggle for Texas culminating in sovereignty the rebels "every day received new reinforcements from the United States," including "New Orleans, Charleston, New York, Baltimore, Washington and other large cities" while "meetings favorable to the Texians were called by the most influential men." Even "Lorenzo de Zavala, former Minister from Mexico to France" jumped ship and "was elected Vice President" of Texas.[35] Zavala, according to another source, gifted U.S. envoy in Mexico Joel Poinsett a staggering 100,000 acres in Texas and, thinking that secession then annexation would enhance the value of his own holdings, joined the 1835 revolt but was not admitted to a share of the windfall commensurate with his eminent role, and "died of disappointment and chagrin...."[36] Still, says scholar Jose Maria Herrera coyly, the Poinsett-Zavala "fruitful friendship went far beyond politics."[37]

Unless France could dispatch nationals across the Atlantic—not easy given the troubles in Algeria—or denude Quebec and Louisiana

33. Kevin Waite, "The Slave South in the Far West: California, the Pacific and Proslavery Visions of Empire," Ph.D. dissertation, U of Pennsylvania, 2016, 28 (abbrev. Waite).

34. Nancy Barker, "New Documents for the Study of Texas History, the French Correspondence Concerning Texas, 1839-1846," n.d., Box 1, Saligny.

35. Ibid., Alphonse Du Bois de Saligny to Monsieur le Comte, 3 March 1839.

36. "Probus," *The Texan Revolution...a Letter from Washington on the Annexation of Texas and the Late Outrage in California*, 1842, Huntington Library (abbrev. Probus).

37. Herrera, 235.

of Frenchmen (which was likely insufficient in any case), Paris was doomed to lose the race for California too and end up more disappointed than Zavala. Instead, France joined Texas in pressuring Mexico and not only was one of the first to recognize secession diplomatically but supposedly influenced Belgium likewise.[38] Paris may have felt it needed leverage against Washington in that Daniel Webster himself, one of the old republic's staunchest advocates, told his Senate colleagues that French wines were "consumed extensively in the South and West" so "why should wines not pay a duty?"[39]

And his alleged fondness for alcohol notwithstanding, this French envoy could sense the waves of history as well as any. What was happening in Mississippi was not unique to the Magnolia State. But biting there by April 1839, he said, was a "financial crisis" that had ignited what seemed like a "complete revolution" as "some inhabitants, burdened with debt, pursued by creditors that they cannot satisfy, guns in hand, have opposed the seizing of their slaves and have brought them to Texas, leaving as the only guarantee to their creditors the land which had not been paid for"; resultantly, "different reasons... must bring a very large part of the population of the Southern States to this country," and "ten years from now, the cotton produced by Texas will equal half the crop in the United States...."[40] In the aftermath of the failed second secession in 1861, the Frenchman's musings materialized, as enslavers fled en masse to Texas, often with their "property" in tow, creating a population dynamic that was to roil the entire nation. Moreover, his musings to Paris helped to shape an increasingly aggressive French intervention in the borderlands.

Hence, searing critiques notwithstanding—including purported lies and arrogance—this French envoy was not wholly off base. He helped to bring French clerics to the region, who could act as informal lobbyists and agents, as they won friends by building churches, hospitals and schools.[41]

Since so many "Texans" were actually U.S. nationals and had fought against redcoats in 1812—or earlier—London was

38. Justin H. Smith, *The Annexation of Texas*, New York: Baker and Taylor, 1911, 76 (abbrev. J.H. Smith).

39. Edward Everett, ed., *The Writings and Speeches of Daniel Webster...*, *Volume VIII*, Boston: Little Brown, 1903, 292 (abbrev. Everett).

40. Monsieur de Saligny to Monsieur le Comte, 17 April 1839, in Saligny.

41. François Lagarde, "Diplomacy, Commerce and Colonization: Saligny and the Republic of Texas," in François Lagarde, ed., *The French in Texas: History, Migration, Culture*, Austin: U of Texas Press, 2003, 107-123, 113 (abbrev. Lagarde).

compromised in seeking to appeal like Paris to the Lone Star republic. Then there was the ascendancy of fire-breathing antislavery
advocates, buoyed by Caribbean abolition, at a time when slavery
was tolerated in the French Caribbean, and the ancient competition
between London and Paris had yet to dissipate. Thus, speaking from
London in 1839, John Scobie denounced the "robber state," which
had been recognized by Washington and "we grieve to say by France
also...." Texas vessels often transporting the enslaved had free rein
on the seas, while "interdicted...are Haitian ships at Jamaica...most
unwisely and unjustly...." Texas, he said, had a "deep stake in the
slave trade" and would scorn a treaty against it, he predicted (actually, on the ropes, Texas did ink a pact with London on this score in
1842). The existent law which declared the slave trade to be "piracy,"
he scoffed, "is scarcely better than waste paper." He was scornful of
"Texian perfidy...these monsters desecrated the soil of Texas by the reestablishment of slavery and the slave trade...." Santa Anna, the premier settler villain, was "well known to be friendly to Great Britain,"
representing an open invitation to spurn Texas and "check" Washington besides. Annexation, then in motion, would increase value of
the enslaved in the U.S. while weakening Mexico, hampering that
nation's ability to pay "our merchants." Scobie too saw secession as
"a war between slavery and emancipation," hinting at 1861. But this
"robber state" was "doomed to destruction or expatriation," likely
at the hands of "the Indians within its borders" or the "hordes of
characterless villains" that were gaining strength. This "multitude of
cutthroats, desperadoes and criminals (now seen as) Texian heroes
and statesmen"—"confessed enemies of the human race"—were
bound to bear poisoned fruit. In their anti-Indigenous fury, Texas
elites "have become more vile than their republican brethren." Texas
was bound to outweigh eastern Virginia where, he emphasized, the
enslaved, *constitute the entire available wealth.*" From Mississippi
arriving recently in Texas and Arkansas were "15,000 slaves," while
Washington was "watching like the eagle for her prey" to be gobbled since Texas was "dependent upon [the U.S.] for its emigrants,
for its slave population and for its defence...." The Africans, he
said, "on the first favourable opportunity presented to them, [will]
take vengeance for the deep injuries and wrongs which they have
suffered"—a prediction that proved to be prescient.[42]

Scobie's fellow Briton, William Kennedy, asked a question that
seemed to invite a positive response to the dismay of old and new

---

42. Scobie.

republics alike: "does any portion of the people of England," he asked, "desire...to liberate the negroes of the Southern States by the frightful process of a servile war[?]"[43]

* * *

Part of the problem for the control of the continent south of Canada was that former Spanish colonies continued to carry the stain of religious and anti-Protestant and anti-Jewish bigotry, while the more pragmatic had long since moved toward a synthetic "whiteness." It was in 1840 that the Philadelphia-based visitor to the borderlands, W.L. McCalla, sniffed, "it is not probable that the eight millions of Mexico have more than half a million of what we would call [a] white man"; in effect, there were "many Negroes,"[44] signposts of inferiority, it was thought.

Thus, Samuel Issacks, who happened to be Jewish, was among the 300 original settlers in Texas. Henri Castro, a prominent invader subsequently, was of a similar religious heritage. Even more arrived post-1865, helping to shift the balance of forces even more toward the settlers: by 1880 there were about 3000 Jewish Americans in Texas. Michael Seeligson arrived in Texas in 1829 but by the pivotal year of 1839 was in Houston, before settling in Galveston—where he became mayor by 1848 as Mexico was in the process of being further denuded of its territory. There was a fair amount of anti-Jewish bigotry in Texas, but unlike Mexico, the Lone Star republic did not have to deal to the same degree with the toxic aftermath of the Inquisition. The "whiteness" project proved effective to the degree that few of these migrants questioned slavery and quite a number were slaveholders, buttressing the system. This was especially the case in Galveston, the traditional epicenter of slave trading and slavery wherein the tendency to define oneself "racially" in juxtaposition with Africans, was most pronounced.[45]

---

43. Kennedy, 389.

44. W.L. McCalla, *Adventures in Texas Chiefly in the Spring and Summer of 1840...*, Philadelphia: Author, 1841, 80. See also *Laws and Decrees of the State of Coahuila and Texas...also the Colonization Law of Tamaulipas...*, Houston: Telegraph Power, 1839.

45. Bryan Edward Stone, "West of Center: Jews on the Real and Imagined Frontiers of Texas," Ph.D. dissertation, UT-A, 2003, 47, 58, 89, 103-104, 114. See also Jacob de Cordova, *Texas: Her Resources and Her Public Men, a Companion for J. de Cordova's New and Correct Map of the State of Texas*, Philadelphia: Crozet, 1858, 64: "As Texas is emphatically an agricultural [state],

In full flight from Europe, often cold, drizzly and miserable, many migrants to Texas were quite taken by what they saw. Texas seemed pleasant by comparison, despite the unwelcoming denizens and often fierce wildlife. John Leonard Riddell arrived in 1839—from similarly dismal Massachusetts in his case—and was dazzled by the "broad verdant valley" and "enchantment" of San Antonio. Of course, there were "fire and drought" and it was "surrounded by a country really held by the savages"[46]—but the death squad known as the Texas Rangers would soon systematically address this latter nagging matter. It was not coincidence that the bone chilling "rebel yell" which was deployed during the secessionist war of 1861, was said to have originated during the all-consuming wars with the Comanche in the 1840s.[47]

Still, he was drawn to the "trees and herbaceous plants like those in Louisiana," then marred by "a black bear come down from a distant hill...." However, even wild animals seemed to be part of the anti-colonial coalition since "we could not shoot the bear...to prevent our being discovered by the Indians...." Nonetheless, their impulse for mayhem meant "they...killed about two bears a day," rapidly reducing their once significant numbers. "Half of them are fat," he said with disgust, "and exceeding the eating" too—but the "bees are wonderfully abundant," though it was not evident that their then state could last long given settler barbarism.[48] This tendency backfired when a "fatal accident occurred...occasioned by carelessness in handling firearms,"[49] ubiquitous in most cases in light of the profusion of settler antagonists.

After that unnerving incident, "considerable alarm was provided" when the stillness was punctured by an "unusual howl...." Was it a "black howl" or was it a "signal" by a "Comanche Indian" for an assault? In that instant, there was hardly a difference, since the present "large white wolf indigenous to the San Saba Mountains," also

---

the immigration of the children of Israel has been very limited and as yet there are not synagogues established.... they have established two burial grounds and a benevolent institution...the oldest of these burial grounds is situated in Galveston...."

46. Notebook, 25 September 1839, Box 4, #27, John Leonard Riddell Manuscripts, Tulane U, New Orleans (abbrev. Riddell).

47. Megan Kate Nelson, *The Three-Cornered War: The Union, the Confederacy and Native Peoples in the Fight for the West*, New York: Scribner, 2020, 62 (abbrev. M.K. Nelson).

48. Riddell, 20 October 1839, Box 4, #27.

49. Ibid., 26 October 1839.

soon to be exterminated, was "twice the size of a large black wolf and sufficiently bold and strong to destroy a horse"[50]—or a settler for that matter.

Days later, the fear of the settlers exploded in the face of Indigenes. A settler "attack was boldly made," and "Indians were killed by rifles." Just as important was the plunder, the divvying of which could attract more settlers to the mayhem to come: "some 30 or 40 horses and mules, all the saddles...buffalo robes and blankets and most of the...arms of the Indians were among the booty...." The settlers had to be even more belligerent since, it was thought, "the fact is the Mexicans have an aversion to killing the Comanches...for by doing so there is a danger of murdering their relatives," an oblique reference to the often impermeable ethnic and color line in the slaveholders' republic. Hence, "the prisoner taken was the son of a Mexican woman by a negro father. He was born in Bexar," i.e., San Antonio. The mother had been "taken by the Comanches...when she was very young" and her offspring, the "Negro," was a "perfect Comanche in habits.... our prisoner was mortally wounded by a shot through the breast and back, yet he conversed in Spanish." As death approached, "he arose on his feet and chanted aloud his Indian death song for a minute or more, lay down and in ten or twelve silently expired...."

Pleased with the success in liquidating a trifecta—a man of African and Mexican origin with Comanche orientation—the settlers then pivoted quickly to "division of the plunder," but the "thievish Mexicans...concealed away the most valuable part of it...." The "Americans"—meaning settlers—"were so exasperated by their palpable trickery that they with one voice declare that in their next engagement they will not be very particular as to who is a Mexican or...and Indian"[51] when the bullets started flying. Then what should have been anticipated occurred: "the Americans and Mexicans of our party hate each other most cordially," he concluded.[52] Not unrelated was the next occurrence: "Frank the colored man whom I have engaged to serve me...left"[53]—before returning, perhaps unable to reach Mexico.

"Frank" may have left at least temporarily in the face of an even more deteriorating socio-political climate coincident with the inauguration of President Lamar in December 1838. It may have been

50. Ibid., 28 October 1839.

51. Ibid., ca. November 1839.

52. Ibid., ca. November 1839.

53. Ibid., 13 November 1839.

folklore, but stories about the mass suicide of the Indigenes known as the Biloxi—or the Pascagoula—who actually were sited east of Texas, was an indicator of a crisis that also afflicted the older republic that too may have been spreading from the Lone Star republic like a gushing oil spill. For by placing so much duress on East Texas, settlers were compelling Indigenes to move elsewhere: to Louisiana or Indian Territory, for example. The victims were the Cherokee, Delaware, Shawnee, Caddo, Kickapoo, Biloxi, Creek, even some Seminoles. Scholar Kenneth Wiggins Porter argues that by 1839 all of these groupings were "hostile" to a degree—including the Choctaw and Alabama--and were open to allying with Mexico.[54]

The Briton William Kennedy concurred, noting that "irruptions and outrages of the Indians, both on the north-eastern and north-western frontiers of Texas, were frequent during the winter and spring of 1839."[55]

John Reagan, a stellar figure among Texas colonists and a leading secessionist by 1861, earlier corroborated the scholar's handiwork and also denounced the Cherokee for collaborating with Mexico against the settlers, as well as the "Shawnees, Delawares, Kickapoos and most of the wild tribes...."[56] The literate Reagan should have also acknowledged that he and his cohort administered the knockout blow to Cherokees that Spaniards began to undermine in the 1700s; thus, when this ethnic group was finally driven out of Smith and Van Zandt counties in 1839, the Spaniards could have claimed partial credit.[57]

Welcoming Lamar in 1838 was a joint revolt of Mexicans and Indigenes in Shelby County in eastern Texas, adjacent to Nacogdoches. Mexicans and Indigenes, according to a pro-settler account, "came to an understanding in 1838 and rebelled...." Then, "in the summer of 1839," said John Middleton, "the Cherokees became hostile and resolved to fight" and settlers strained to "prevent the Cherokees from being supplied with arms and ammunition by other Indians and Mexicans...." Yet the ultimate defeat of these Indigenous combatants and their allies only whetted the appetite of settlers, who then began to battle each other—"Regulators" versus "Moderators"—for the booty: land, stocked with the enslaved.[58]

---

54. Kenneth Wiggins Porter, "A Legend of the Biloxi', *Journal of American Folklore*, April-June 1946, Box 28, Porter Papers.

55. Kennedy, 340-341.

56. John A. Reagan, *Memoirs*, New York: Neale, 1906, 29, 35.

57. Barbee.

58. John W. Middleton, *History of the Regulators and Moderators and the Shelby County War in 1841 and 1842 in the Republic of Texas*, Fort Worth: Loving, 1883, 9, 14.

John Hamilton was in eastern Texas in 1839 and was in a position to provide his "dear mother" with "horrid accounts" of "the Indian wars." He pointed the finger of accusation at "all the rascals that leave the United States" and "come right to Texas"; thus, "we have a good many rascals here," he added ruefully. "Sam Houston has had several challenges,"[59] he said obliquely, an understatement given the anti-Indigenous ruckus that helped to sully his reputation among settlers. Fellow founder David Burnet—who like many settlers seemed to bear an intense grudge toward Cherokee—charged that Houston was "half Indian," a serious charge given his previous associations and intimate ties with them and the warm friendship he was said to maintain.[60]

John Day Andrew may not have been a "rascal" but that did not prevent him from inquiring about moving from Virginia to Texas in a message to Texas leader Anson Jones (who too was to die of suicide). Therein he reminded that Texas could not survive without slavery and its expansion, a point that barely needed reiteration to Jones.[61]

Because of this slavery obsession, between 1835 and 1847 Texas's population of the enslaved increased tenfold, from about 4000 to almost 40,000 and flourishing on the foundation of their unpaid labor, the number of settlers quadrupled.[62] This was a bonanza for this particular category of commodity fetishists in that an enslaved African in the 1830s cost purchasers $1500—and a "mere" $400 in Cuba.[63] Hence, a steady stream of slave ships snaked through the Gulf of Mexico from Cuba to Galveston.[64]

Britain's William Kennedy blamed "Cuba speculators" for "smuggling a number of negroes into Texas," and the latter republic for "encouraging the African slave trade...."[65] The notorious slave trader Monroe Edwards confirmed to President Lamar that Africans were being shipped into Texas via Havana.[66]

---

59. John Hamilton to "Dear Mother," 21 December 1839, John and William Hamilton Correspondence, Library of Congress, Washington, D.C. (abbrev. Hamilton Correspondence).

60. Chambless, 181, 219, 22.

61. John Day Andrews to Anson Jones, 20 October 1838, Texas Legation.

62. Shelton,75.

63. M.R. Moore, 90.

64. *Telegraph & Texas Register*, 1 May 1839.

65. Kennedy, 385, 387.

66. Monroe Edwards, New Orleans, to President Lamar, in Michael R. Green, ed., *Calendar of the Papers of Mirabeau Buonaparte Lamar*, Austin: Texas State Library, 1982, 296 (abbrev. Green, *Calendar*).

And although northern cities like Philadelphia were within decades to find themselves in mortal combat with Texans, it was in May 1839 that President Lamar was assured of the "present and daily increasing intercourse between this city [Philadelphia]" and his rump republic.[67]

Life was rough then for settlers, including anxiety propelled by rebellious Indigenes. "We liv[e] in what is generally termed the barracks," said Hamilton, "it is a log house about 80 ft. long[,] about 40 ft. wide with holes in it"; this primitive architecture was "uncomfortable," an adaptation to the hostile surroundings. There were "no white women," their presence deemed inappropriate for the surroundings. There were "2 nig[g]ers [and] they do all the cooking and washing and mending," reducing the need for "white women," though the "corn bread and bacon all the time" was monotonous.[68]

"This beautiful country was misrepresented," Hamilton said oddly, as he alluded to the "good many troubles and trials since I have landed in Texas,"[69] capped by his August 1839 revelation: "we all expect that we will be invaded by Mexico this fall...."[70]

The ferocity of the Indigenes, the fierce refusal to accept secession embodied in both Mexico and many Tejanos, and the rebelliousness of the enslaved, all provided a stiff challenge to settlers virtually unique in North America—which, in response, generated a mind-numbing savagery on their part. A self-described emigrant arriving in the newest slaveholders' republic in 1840 placidly depicted an act of barbarity that should have shocked. Describing an Indigene shot for allegedly seeking to steal a horse, he observed calmly that "the body was dragged some distance and hung upon a tree, as a warning to other Indian depredators, where it remained for several months and until eaten up piecemeal by the wolves and vultures...." Such vile tactics fed dismissive attitudes toward those being fought: Mexicans, he said, were "superior" to Comanches but "less effective by far than the Cherokees," and even the latter had purported defects with their mastery of Spanish compared to the English of the enslaved. He was well aware of the "fugitives" with little to lose and "cutthroats" who

---

67. Letter to President Lamar, 1 May 1839, Box 2-9/2, Texas Republic SoS.

68. John Hamilton to Mother, 22 January 1839, Hamilton Correspondence. See also Jo Ella Powell Exley, ed., *Texas Tears and Texas Sunshine: Voices of Frontier Women*, College Station: TA&MU Press, 1985, 31: In the 1830s Ann Raney Thomas Coleman commented, "The country was full of bachelors but very few ladies."

69. John Hamilton to Brother, ca. 1839, Hamilton Correspondence.

70. Ibid., John Hamilton to Brother, 8 August 1839.

were then pouring into Texas, since he seemed to be one of them and knew of what he spoke. Perhaps prematurely, he spoke of the defeat of the Caddo, leaving only the Comanche and Cherokee to be feared, a sign of occluded vision that allowed him to ignore crude cruelty.[71]

Thus, when in 1840 Comanches came within miles of Durango, Texas, the authorities placed a price of $100 for every male scalp, $50 for a female. With this enticement, footloose foreigners and even some Indigenes friendly to the republic began a kind of Comanche hunt, organizing scalping festivals. The scandalous James Kirker, appropriately with roots in ever stormy Northern Ireland, abandoned his Apache "friends" and planned to snatch their scalps—who could tell the difference? His band of desperados came to include random Shawnees and even some Mexicans.[72]

The utter brutality of early Texas seeped into the marrow of the republic, then U.S. state. One of Texas's early leaders, Louis Wigfall, after fighting the Seminoles in Florida—he was renowned for his marksmanship—arrived in Texas by 1840 and in less than half a year, was involved in a fist fight, two actual duels, three near-duels and one shooting, leaving in his wake one fatality and two wounded, including the "stormy petrel," Wigfall himself.[73]

Growingly, settlers were beginning to see Mexicans and Tejanos as more of a threat than certain Indigenes. President Lamar was introduced to Pierre Juzan, a Choctaw leader in search of his enslaved Africans, evidently enticed to flee by Mexicans.[74] Also reaching Lamar's attention was a demand from Silvanus Hatch of Jackson County for the return of one of his runaways[75] and a similar plaint from Henry J. Jewett in Austin, who further condemned the purported bad influence on the enslaved of "Mexicans and renegade whites."[76] According to scholar Arnoldo De León, "Mexicanos took the audacious step of sabotaging chattel racial slavery by rescuing Negroes from bondage and transporting them to freedom.... Mexican American resistance to slavery persisted until the eve of the Civil War."[77]

---

71. An Emigrant, *Texas in 1840, or the Emigrant's Guide to the New Republic*, New York: Arno, 1973 [originally published 1840], 42, 227.

72. Memorandum, n.d., File on James Kirker, Box 11, Stoes Papers.

73. King, 25, 35, 49.

74. W.M. Williams, Red River County, to President Lamar, 1 April 1840, in Green, *Calendar*, 203.

75. Ibid., Silvanus Hatch to President Lamar, 5 May 1840, 208.

76. Ibid., Henry J. Jewett to President Lamar, 21 June 1840, 211.

77. De León, 28.

Africans were fleeing because of the flux and chaos in Texas combining with the harshness unleashed by the Lamar regime. "Mexicanos" often were penalized for aiding Africans in doing so.

So, despite palpable barriers and a concomitant draining treasury, Texas was growing, especially because of the unpaid labor that continued to arrive. "Our country is populating very fast," said the settler John Hamilton in August 1840; "property and money," as ever were linked. "What I mean by property," he explained, "are Negroes, at the crossing of the Sabine about fifty miles from where I live there has been about 600 Negroes run into Texas within the last 2 months and it has been in proportion throughout the rest of the Republic...."[78]

Free British subjects of African origin with roots in Barbados could have added texture to Hamilton's point. Du Bois de Saligny, the French envoy in Texas, recalled in 1840 that "an American by the name of Taylor in collusion with some free colored persons on this Caribbean island succeeded in abducting by trickery or force several Negro[es]" and "took them ashore at Sabine Bay on American territory," then to Texas "where he sold them...."[79] In essence, Texas with its voracious appetite for enslaved labor represented a clear and present danger to Africans globally.

This obvious downside encased the opposite as well in that Barbados was a British possession, which meant this abduction—unlike those from the coast of Africa, for example—would not go unchallenged. Months later there was signed a "Treaty Between the Republic of Texas and Great Britain for Suppression of the African Slave Trade" with a tart reference included pertaining to chained Africans "found on board of Texian vessels detained on the coast of Brazil"—which would be sent to "British settlements" on the coast of Africa, likely Sierra Leone.[80]

The pressure on the open seas from the Royal Navy may have further incentivized slave traders smuggling Africans from the older slaveholders' republic to the newest one. This is what Lord Palmerston was told weeks before signing of the anti-slave trade treaty. "Traffic in slaves," said his informant, was "carried on at this moment

---

78. John Hamilton to Brother, 6 August 1840, Hamilton Correspondence.

79. Du Bois de Saligny to Dalmatia, 9 February 1840, in Nancy Nichols Barker, ed., *The French Legation in Texas, Volume I: Recognition, Rupture and Reconciliation*, Austin: Texas State Historical Commission, 1971, 122.

80. "Treaty Between the Republic of Texas and Great Britain for Suppression of the African Slave Trade," 16 November 1840, Texas State Archives-Austin (abbrev. Texas Archives).

in the most barefaced manner between the southern states of America and the Republic of Texas"; there were "two voyages a month from the states to Texas" with "one hundred [on] each month per month...." Stern measures were needed, e.g., "seizure of the boats thus employed" especially "considering that Mexico the country which in the eyes of Great Britain still holds the sovereignty of Texas" and also considering that "was the first civilized [*sic*] nation that abolished slavery." Texas and its rival *cum* comrade in Washington were aiming at the "dismemberment" of Mexico, which would be "ruinous" and "repugnant...to British interests...."[81] Thus, bringing the enslaved to Texas by sea was barred but acceptable overland from the U.S.: seizing ships on the high seas only led to more continentally bound and enchained coffles.[82]

But London was receiving contrasting signals and had to walk a tightrope separating a growing abolitionist movement on the one hand and the "Lords of the Loom" on the other. For just before this upbraiding message about Texas, the Colonial Secretary reported that the "cotton lands of Texas...will yield 3 times as much cotton as the Carolinas or Georgia to the acre[,] twice as much as Alabama and from 40 percent more than the lands of Louisiana and Mississippi...." Galveston was "the best" of Texas's four ports. The population was then "estimated at 150,000 souls [and] are chiefly Americans, a few Germans and some English and Irish. These are principally bankrupt swindlers and felons from the United States," he harrumphed with more to come since Texas's "newspapers teem with invitations to the debtors of America to seek for safety in the New Republic...." Deadbeats from New Orleans were arriving steadily, and "murder and every other crime is of great frequency in Texas," making it "unsafe to walk through the streets of the principal towns without being armed...." The sharp dagger known as the "Bowie knife is the weapon most in vogue," but even here Britain had an interest since the "greater number of these weapons are manufactured in Sheffield and Birmingham...." Contrary to Lord Palmerston's previous correspondent, he demanded recognition be accorded the newest slaveholding republic. Yes, the objection to recognition was bondage; however, the "price of slaves in Texas is enormous owing to the great

---

81. N. Maillard to Lord Palmerston, 15 September 1840, Box 2-23/755, Texas Republic SoS. This letter is reprinted in Ephraim Douglas Adams, ed., *British Diplomatic Correspondence Concerning the Republic of Texas, 1838-1846*, Austin: Texas State Historical Association, ca, 1918, 27-29 (abbrev. E.D. Adams).

82. Ibid., James Hook to Lord Palmerston, 30 April 1841, 36.

demand for labour" with "1500 to 2000 dollars" and only "3 and 400 dollars in the Savannah market," one of the deepest and most liquid beyond New Orleans. This fed a "competition between the Spanish slaveholders," meaning Cuba, and "others, and those of the United States particularly those of Virginia, Carolinas, Georgia, Kentucky, Missouri and Tennessee"—indeed, the Slave South writ large. A few years before there had been a request for U.S. annexation but Washington "thought fit to decline," and this rebuff "engendered a feeling of hostility" to Washington, but as was to be the case so often in Texas, the elite attitude had been "inflated...with such sentiments or admiration at their own prowess as are only equated by their profound contempt for the Mexicans and Indians...."[83]

In sum, Texas's overblown ego had caused the republic to accumulate a growing array of antagonists, leaving it vulnerable to manipulation by the severest antagonist of all: London. For, as leading U.S. politico Daniel Webster recognized in responding to John C. Calhoun, the Slave South—including Texas—had numerous "competitors" in producing cotton, including "South America...India and Egypt."[84]

The Colonial Secretary in London may have overdetermined the age old competition with Paris in making his calculations, for France not only recognized the rump republic early on but had better contacts there as a result. Du Bois de Saligny chortled in early 1840 that "the recognition of the new republic by [Paris] has caused universal joy in this country...." Like a keen settler he kept a close eye on the Comanches, "the most belligerent and powerful of the Indian tribes of Texas," and cautioned to look askance at their "friendly overtures" to Lamar. "Many persons here," he said, "see only a trap of the part of the Comanches...." He suggested that "Lipans and the Tonkaways [sic], mortal enemies of the Comanches and three years allied with the Texians," should be somehow reenlisted. But even they, especially the Lipan Apaches, could hardly be trusted, since they had opted for a "war to the death" and "commenced their depredations."[85]

Texas's increase in the population of the enslaved may have occurred at neighboring Louisiana's expense. In the crucial year of 1840 marching forward, the Pelican State's percentage of Negroes declined from 55% to 50.7% by 1850, to 49.5% by 1860; this decline

---

83. Memorandum from Francis Sheridan, Colonial Secretary, 12 July 1840, Box 2-23/755, Texas Republic SoS.

84. Remarks, 3 March 1840, in Everett, Volume VIII, 267.

85. Alphonse Du Bois de Saligny to "M. the Marshall," 19 January 1840, Box 1, Saligny.

included the Free Negro population which left the state in considerable number—but would find no sanctuary in Texas.[86]

Barreling ahead heedlessly, taking on enemies with seeming insouciance, as Lord Palmerston's interlocutor indicated, Texas was also bent on dismembering Mexico. Secession created, if not worsened, strains throughout Mexico, the Yucatan not least, where the Indigenous continued to harbor unresolved grievances.[87] When they revolted in the early 1840s, Texas—its genocidal approach to Indigenes notwithstanding—rallied to their defense, though their victory could have led to a rear base for Indigenes to attack to the north. However, punishing and weakening Mexico was the overriding ambition then. The navy of Texas was sent to their shores to ally with their agent, George Fisher, yet another freebooter. He had fought the Ottoman Turks in Belgrade, then it was on to Austria and Italy and Hamburg, then Mexico—but now, said one who met him, "his feelings were all Texan."[88]

He may have encountered another of his kind, the future Texas Ranger Nelson Lee. Born in 1807, by 1831 he was enmeshed in the "Black Hawk War," then it was on to Brazil and São Tomé, West Africa, where he seemed shocked to meet "the black governor of the island...." Then it was on to Apalachicola where the Seminoles continued to seethe furiously. But he arrived in Galveston just in time to join the navy; he freely admitted that the "object of this expedition was to draw the Mexicans away from Texas...." Still, he questioned the "Indian policy of the United States" which "constantly exposed" the "frontier settlements" to "depredations"; lest that be misinterpreted, he added quickly that this oppressed group "cherish an inveterate and undying hatred of the white man whom they regard as usurpers."[89]

The embattled Yucantanese, nonetheless, were accused of an "attempt to exterminate white and mestizo Mexicans...[and] asked the American army for weapons"[90]—and, like Texas, were not promptly rebuffed because of the desire to dismember this troublesome neighbor.

Yet another observer found it relevant that near the town of Tizmin in Yucatan, there was a village where resided a "colony of negroes

---

86. McConnell, *Negro Troops*, 105.

87. Morrison, 106.

88. John Stephens, *Incidents of Travel in Yucatan, Volume I*, New York: Harper & Bros., 1843, 81, 82, 84-85.

89. Lee, 13, 14, 16, 19, 139, 177.

90. Guardino, 340.

from St. Domingo [Haiti] numbering about seventy males"; he "feared," therefore "ultimately a re-enactment of the bloody scenes of St. Domingo," still fresh in historical memory. Thus, there was a "danger that menaced the white race in Yucatan," as this group was "surrounded by an Indian population four times their number," i.e., a "large colored population far outnumbering the whites," i.e. "six" to "one." In Yucatan, "left to itself," he warned, "an insurrection would be productive of the most awful calamities...." He advised that it would not be "long" before "some 'Tecumseh' or 'Black Hawk' may rise up and the most disastrous, heart rending and bloody scenes will be re-enacted," which was "certainly fraught with danger to the white race...." Yet, it was the old adversary Santa Anna that "menace[d] Yucatan with an invasion," and it was he and his forces who had to be confronted. For the rebels there had "declared their independence of Mexico"; whatever was to emerge in independent Yucatan or Mexico, after the dust cleared, "the elective franchise" would "extend" to "all, not excepting the Indians or the blacks. The latter class is principally composed of runaway slaves from the neighboring islands," but Yucatan victory would mean "all religions are tolerated."[91] Perhaps that latter factor, along with the value of pulverizing Mexico overrode all else.

But the Yucatanese were also getting aid from neighboring British Honduras, despite London's stated aim of preventing the wrecking of Mexico. This was likely not official London, for the rebels were also receiving assistance from the neighboring Mexican region (and later state) of Quintana Roo, and it would be illogical to conclude that Mexico was conspiring against itself. But Washington feared something different—that London was eyeing the seizure of the Yucatan and, like a domino, that would mean the fall of Cuba into Britain's hands. Both Texas and Yucatan were impacted by the war in the former, insofar as it led to higher expenses for Mexico and the resultant republic, leaving both vulnerable. Washington and London stood to gain from an incapacitated Mexico, with Britain gaining more influence there and the slaveholder republic benefiting from chaos there.[92] And Texas benefited in that dealing with Yucatan

---

91. B.M. Norman, *Rambles in Yucatan: A Visit to the Remarkable Ruins*, New York: Langley, 1843, 226, 227, 233, 234, 65, 82.

92. Christopher Paetzold, "The British Participation in the Caste War of Yucatan," M.A. thesis, Dalhousie U, 1994, 15, 50, 51. See also Sophia Betsworth Hunt, "Grasping the Gulf: Conquest and Indigenous Power from Florida to Yucatan in the Age of Revolutions," Ph.D. dissertation, U of Michigan, 2017.

reduced the probability of Mexico seeking to reclaim its territory of the north lost to secession.[93]

Underscoring the throbbing interest in dismembering Mexico was the simultaneous support for the secessionist Republic of Rio Grande in the borderlands, with Laredo, Texas, being an epicenter of skullduggery.[94]

Ironically, a number of Indigenes in Texas in 1836 considered the war over Texas a "white man's war" while independent Texas weighed in about four years later by aiding Indigenes,[95] which could have led the latter to conclude—inaccurately—that they were pursuing a winning diplomatic strategy.

But Mexico too had contradictions that were difficult to resolve. It was in October 1840 that the U.S. emissary in Mazatlán noted that "the 'Apache' tribe...invaded the northeast...Sonora in a strong body"; and defeated the government troops; there were "fears...that the Yake [Yaqui] tribe in the neighborhood of Guaymas would rise and take possession of the port"; already there was a British ship "now on the coast taking treasure for England," forestalling the envoy's nation doing same.[96]

With a depleted treasury and a growing list of adversaries, Texas was in the throes of crisis, leaving limited alternatives, including annexation by the U.S. Yet this would only disrupt the sectional balance between the Slave States and those to the north, delivering civil war: 1836 was a civil war over slavery and, like a precursor of Typhoid Mary, Texas seemed to bring the virulent bacteria that was war to whatever jurisdiction it joined.

93. Haynes, Somervell, 132.

94. Wagner, 2.

95. Shuck, 140.

96. John Parrott to "Sir," 28 October 1840, Reel 1, Despatches from U.S. Consuls in Mazatlan, NARA.

Chapter 6

Annexation Nearer, 1841-1843

As the 1840s unfolded, sovereign Texas was a mess, hurtling toward untrammeled chaos, making annexation by its older slaveholding sibling virtually inexorable.

Subsequently, the virulently anti-Indigene historian J.W. Wilbarger admitted that "the spring of 1841 was rendered remarkable by the frequency of Indian raids."[1] By the end of the year in the nearby Cherokee Nation, a report emerged that "wild Indians" proclaimed "they were at war with the Texians," a conflict not unrelated to the "the most deadly hatred existing in the minds of the Comanches toward settlers," which "forbids all negociacion [sic]...." There was a suspicion that Indigenes were not only appropriating horses and mules from settlers but the enslaved too.[2] "Wild Comanches" were responsible for this latter "crime," it was said,[3] which—to be fair—was also a practice of certain Euro-Americans purloiners too.[4] The maddening frenzy toward Comanches was so intense that it was Sam Houston who accused "traders" of "packing poison...three hundred and fifty Comanches were poisoned and died" in one ghastly episode.[5] On the other hand, in 1843 two enslaved Africans poisoned a local family in the vicinity of Nacogdoches, placing seeds of "Jameson's [jimson] weed" in their coffee.[6]

---

1. Wilbarger, 289.

2. To Sir from Fort Gibson, Cherokee Nation, 14 November 1841, Richard Barnes Mason Correspondence Regarding Texas Indians, Huntington Library (abbrev. Mason Correspondence).

3. Ibid., Letter, 10 February 1842.

4. Ibid., Statement of James Edwards on slaves stolen by Mr. Robertson in Texas from Fort Holmes, Creek Nation, 10 February 1842: "James Edwards a white man, residing in the Creek Nation, having a Creek family."

5. Statement by Sam Houston, ca. 1838, in Amelia W. Williams and Eugene Barker, eds., *The Writings of Sam Houston, 1813-1863, Volume III...*, Austin: Pemberton, 1970, 451 (abbrev. Williams and Barker).

6. McReynolds, 195.

The incessant warfare was shaping the very fiber of settler identity to the point where one scholar argues that "Texian settlers based their identity on negative sentiment toward Native Americans,"[7] an unfortunate precondition for liquidation of them and the emergence of fascism subsequently. Notably troubling is the conclusion by scholar Brian DeLay that "political use of the term *Anglo-Saxon* in a strictly racial sense was unusual in the early 1830s but commonplace by the 1840s," which included a "steady increase in damning pr[o]scriptions of 'mongrel' Mexicans...."[8] The "worst" of these abuses of Africans, Indigenes and Mexicans, says scholar James McReynolds, occurred between "the years 1839 and 1841," including "eviction notices" of Tejanos.[9] At play was the accumulation of bigotry generated by genocidal thrusts against the Indigenous, "evictions" of Tejanos and pulverizing of Africans.

This runaway "Anglo-Saxonism" fused with a pre-existing "Negrophobia," creating a cyclonic hysteria that was generated further by the continuing repercussions of the Nat Turner revolt of the enslaved in 1831 in Virginia. This was reflected in the thinking of Senator Robert Walker of Mississippi, slaveholder and prominent U.S. leader, when he debated before the U.S. Supreme Court the notion of barring the interstate slave trade,[10] a measure which could have impacted Texas interests.

Making an already complex climate even more difficult for the settlers were the ever closer ties between the Caddo and Africans. This was discussed in the U.S. Congress in August 1842, though the descriptions may have been a ruse to further rationalize seizing Indigenous land by claiming what was at issue was actually a more palatable and relatable expropriation of Negroes. Still, these leaders—the "Grappes"—were designated as "colored people-griffs. The father passed for a Frenchman but [has] a brown skin," and the mother was also a "griff," often defined as one of mixed Indigenous and African ancestry. The attestant, Cesair Lafitte, carried a surname

---

7. Penelope Lea Jacobus, "The Scramble for Texas: European Diplomacy and Imperial Interest in the Republic of Texas, 1835-1846," Ph.D. dissertation, U of Texas-El Paso, 2020, 425 (abbrev. Jacobus), University of Texas-El Paso (abbrev. UT-EP).

8. DeLay, 246.

9. McReynolds, 266.

10. "Argument of Robert J. Walker, Esq. Before the Supreme Court of the United States on the Mississippi Slave Question at January Term 1841. Involving the Power of Congress and of the States to Prohibit the Interstate Slave Trade," Philadelphia: Clark, 1841, Huntington Library.

that at once inspired suspicion and confidence, since the family had been intimately involved in ousting Indigenes and enslaving Africans alike. So, doubtlessly, power-mongers listened when he attested that "François Grappe the father...stood high with the Indians and was their civil adviser in most important matters; was held in high esteem by the Indians to his death and understood the language better than themselves. The children of Grappe were not raised among the Indians but hunted with them," it was said. These offspring, Jacques and Balthazar, "spoke the Indian tongue about as well as he (deponent) did and Dominique about as well as the Creoles generally...." Grappe, the father, "was of mixed blood...of what nation he does not know but has heard an aunt of Grappe's say that he was of the Chittimiche tribe," while "John Pierre and Onezieme Grappe are the legitimate sons of John Baptist Grappe, who was the full brother of Francois Grappe...." These sons, including Honore, were "nearly black, their mother being a negress...." These Caddo apparently were seeking allies since they "came into this country to avoid the Osages of whom they stood in fear...." The Caddo became dependent upon the Grappes and were "in the habit of calling on Francois Grappe to assist and advise them in their intercourse and business transactions with the French and Spanish authorities and in their business transactions generally."[11]

This anxiety about the Caddo was accelerated further by the perception that Mexico was threatening Texas independence and collaborating with Indigenes to that end. More than any other current U.S. state, Texas was born in the brine not just of racism but a unique chauvinism suffused with bellicosity and warmongering. Thus, in the spring of 1842 a Galveston periodical was enthusiastic in reporting that Washington was "anxious for war with England," but went further to urge that next the older republic "should take Mexico in hand, provided Texas does not settle her hash in the meantime.... atonement is required and nothing but Mexican blood will wash out the disgrace...." The reporter was happy to note that the U.S. "is preparing [to] declare war against Mexico. This is too good news to be true...."[12]

A particular problem that Texas faced was that Washington had sited "Indian Territory" on its northern border, forming a kind of

---

11. U.S. Congress. House of Representatives. 27th Congress, 2nd Session. Rep. No. 1035. "The Caddo Indian Treaty," 20 August 1842, Huntington Library.

12. *Galveston Daily News*, 19 April 1842.

rear base for Indigenous raids southward. A visitor to the region in 1841, Ethan Allen Hitchcock, noticed that a "slave among wild Indians is almost as free as his owner."[13] The perception that this might be accurate fueled runaways northward to Indian Territory, as well as southward from Missouri but it also might have lubricated the path toward fleeing slaveholding republics altogether. For in the early 1840s a group of enslaved Africans perpetrated a significant uprising in Webbers Falls in today's Oklahoma; hundreds of them escaped and began to flee en masse toward Mexico.[14]

They were supplied with horses, rifles and ammunition, insuring that life would be difficult for any Texans who sought to block their passage. Cherokee and Choctaw were the prime victims of this capital flight.[15] The fact that Indigenes—even those who were slaveholders—were often besieged themselves, was a factor in facilitating the flight of their "property" and complicating life for Texas settlers. The ampler point was that turmoil in Indian Territory easily was exported to Texas, contributing to the overall disjointedness in the latter.

By early 1841, enslavers in Texas had had enough. They passed a law targeting "runaway slaves," providing a bounty to any who snagged them. Slaveholders were to be indemnified if one of their prized possessions was executed. Of course, it was promulgated that "no slave shall carry a gun" and, in fact, this weapon could "be seized and taken from said slave, by any white person...."[16] By 1 January 1842 Free Negroes had to depart the new republic—or become enslaved.[17]

Predictably, an early maroon colony materialized just across the border in Coahuila precisely in 1842, with one analyst pointing out that "the liberty of runaways and *Mexicanidad* would become intertwined...." These maroons, according to James David Nichols, were "comprised of African Americans who had likely accompanied the

---

13. Foreman, *Traveler*, 187.

14. Jimmie Lewis Franklin, *Journey Toward Hope: A History of Blacks in Oklahoma*, Norman: U of Oklahoma Press, 1982, 8 (abbrev. Franklin).

15. Celia E. Naylor, *African Cherokees in Indian Territory: From Chattel to Citizens*, Chapel Hill: U of North Carolina Press, 2008, 42, 44, 47 (abbrev. Naylor).

16. Statute, 5 February 1841, in Williamson S. Oldham and George W. White, compilers, *A Digest of the General Statute Laws of the State of Texas... which were in Force Before the Declaration of Independence...*, Austin: Marshall, 1859, 407 (abbrev. Oldham and White).

17. Caughfield, 151.

Mexican Cherokees when they first arrived four years ago.... [some] could even speak the Cherokee language...." Though he adds that Comanches were the "great adversaries to the runaways," suggesting that this potent group was willing to spare none in returning to an Edenic era before settler colonialism descended. It is not evident that this animus encompassed "Free Afro-Indians" or "Black migrants" from Indian Territory, who were the "largest" segment of this encampment. And, there were a "large number of Free Blacks too," reflective of their post-1841 expulsion from Texas. Many of these migrants were multilingual, speaking English Creek, Seminole—and Spanish.[18]

The fearsome Comanche, in sum, continued to solidify their martial reputation. In the spring of 1841 Secretary of State Daniel Webster was told by a consul in Matamoros that the Comanche had "become very troublesome.... they have nearly entire possession of the country lying between the Rio Grande and Nueces River"; their "robberies and assassinations" had "caused a considerable decline in the inland trade.... so formidable are these outlaws that they have recently defeated two separate detachments of troops in attempting to arrest them...."[19]

Subsequently, the Mexican government found that as of 1842, the population of the Comanche, Kiowa, Apache, Arapaho and Cheyenne was still a formidable 47,620—enough to cause havoc for settlers. Mexico also charged that sovereign Texas and Washington were playing a dangerous game, encouraging Comanches and other Indigenes to attack to the south: this was "tolerated, permitted [and] festered" by these slaveholders. They also "afforded them a market for bartering the spoils of their incursions into Mexico," not to mention Texas raiding inside Mexico and blaming Indigenes. "It was not in Zacatecas alone," said this official document, that "the Indians were guided in their work of murder and robbery by intelligent white men." Also complicating was the reality that the Spanish "language" was "more or less known by the prairie Indians...." Like other observers, Mexico saw the formation of Indian Territory as placing pressure on Texas, not necessarily for the best.[20]

A British visitor to Texas in 1843 confirmed that Texas settlers masqueraded as Indigenes and committed depredations against their fellow settlers in order to inflame the political climate, a harbinger of

18. Nichols 2018, 189, 194, 195.

19. D.W. Smith to Secretary of State Webster, 12 May 1841, Reel 2, Despatches from U.S. Consuls in Matamoros, NARA.

20. *Report of the Committee of Investigation 1873*, 246, 252, 284-285, 341.

the next century's notorious "false flag" operations. This was a "common practice for some time," he said. They would even cross the border to steal the enslaved from Arkansas and Louisiana and then resell in Texas. Plus, Texas cotton, he said, was becoming dependent upon mills controlled by Cherokee in Texas and Indian Territory, a practice that undermined these Indigenes ultimately. The pace of this devilment picked up in the wake of the post-1837 economic downturn with even slaveholders getting in on the action, selling their enslaved property from Mississippi and points eastward into Texas, raising the inference that they could make insurance claims after purported "theft." In words that continue to resonate, the author opined, "[the] democratic form of government is powerless when the nation is so utterly depraved."[21]

Thus, the settlers in and outside Texas sought aggressively not only to uproot Indigenes from their land but to blunt their development, push them back socio-economically, so they could continue to deride them as "underdeveloped." Thus, it was also in 1842 that the treaty brokered with the Sac and Fox, originally of the Great Lakes region before being deported to Indian Territory, mandated that "blacksmiths and gunsmiths' tools with the stock of iron and steel on hand" was "to be removed" forthwith.[22]

Hence, it was not only the Comanche presence that impelled the new slaveholders' republic to launch the ill-fated Mier Expedition in 1842, an attempt to hoist the Lone Star flag decisively over this contested realm of the borderlands. It was also a response to a continuing series of skirmishes with Mexico along the border, as Haiti's friend—with both seen as roughly equivalent to post-1959 Cuba in potential for subversion—was unreconciled to Texas sovereignty. (Intriguingly Sam Houston wanted to blockade Mexican ports, as was done to Cuba post-1959). After hearing of his republic's severe setback, Sam Houston beckoned an enslaved man who had not fled, requested a bottle of Madeira wine and intoxicated himself into insensibility. Mier demonstrated, like few other events, that Texas had wildly overestimated its capabilities and, if not careful, could be swallowed by Mexico. It helped to frighten Texas toward

---

21. Captain Marryat, *Narrative of the Travels and Adventures of Monsieur Violet in California, Sonora and Western Texas*, New York: Harper & Bros., 1843 (abbrev. Marryat). See also Stephen Robinson, *False Flags: Disguised German Raiders of World War II*, Wollombi, Australia: Exisle, 2016.

22. "Treaty Between United States and Sac and Fox Indians," 11 October 1842, Huntington Library.

annexation[23] and fed an ever more feverish campaign targeting the wider North American public, warning of the dire consequences of the "recent occupation of San Antonio by our Mexican foe."[24] Likewise, U.S. prisoners then held in Tepic, Mexico, for various reasons were highlighted.[25]

By February 1842 Sam Houston was advising that "the news direct from Mexico is that Santa Anna will soon have a strong force to invade Texas" and "harass our frontier towns...."[26] As early as March 1842 Sam Houston felt compelled to issue a broadside warning against an "invasion" of the "southwestern frontier," meaning "immediate preparation for defensive [sic] war...."[27] By April 1842 the Texas legation in Washington heard of the "startling news of the Mexican invasion," which came—surprisingly—as a surprise. The villainized Santa Anna was "firmly bent upon the establishment of a monarchy," though James Reilly found "untrue" the "rumor that Great Britain aids him with money [and] supplies...." Washington was another story in that this nation "held the Mexican government to a strict account for the many and frequent outrages committed upon American citizens & [the] American flag...." Enthusiastically, he reminded that "we have a great many powerful men and warm friends here who will never see Texas trodden down [and] if circumstances require it thousands would fly to the rescue" of the beleaguered regime. He was satisfied that London would not fly to the rescue of Mexico since already Lord Ashburton had arrived in Washington—"he is aged about 65 I should imagine from his appearance"—for the purpose of "settling the long political accounts": "I entertain not the least doubt that all will be amicably adjusted and war averted."[28]

By June 1842 Houston's correspondent was not as sanguine and informed him nervously that "the Indians have become very troublesome above Austin these three or four days past...such attempts

---

23. Haynes, Somervell, 22, 129, 140, 146. See also William Preston Stapp, *The Prisoners of Perote: A Journal Kept by the Author who was Captured by the Mexicans at Mier, December 25, 1842, and Released from Perote, May 16, 1844*, Philadelphia: Zieber, 1845.

24. Broadside from Edward Burleson, ca. 1842, Green Papers, UNC-CH.

25. List of 23 American Citizens Held Prisoner at Tepic, Mexico, 1840, Huntington Library.

26. Sam Houston to "Dear Sir," 15 February 1842, Box 1, Thomas William Ward Papers, APL (abbrev. Ward Papers).

27. Sam Houston Broadside, 10 May 1842, Box 1, Ward Papers.

28. James Reilly to Thomas W. Ward, 29 April 1842, Box 1, Ward Papers.

were made by Suckett and one of their negroes to shoot the Indians but unsuccessfully...."[29]

The correspondent identified as "Captain Marryat" writing in 1843 detailed how in the aftermath of these incursions, Tejanos fled, as the unrest in Yucatan caused the Mexican military to retreat there—justifying the Texas strategy of stoking unrest there to divert their Mexican neighbor—and taking their place in the vicinity of San Antonio were "drunkards, thieves and murderers. The same desertion has taken place in Goliad, Velasco, Nacogdoches...."[30]

Writing from Washington in the same year as Mier (1842), the polemicist known as "Probus" was utterly disrespectful to the settler class of the new republic, chiding them since "their Negroes" were "on the tiptoe of expectation and rejoicing that Mexicans were coming to free them...." He referenced a "colored man in Philadelphia, the acknowledged son of the late Hutchins G. Burton, formerly a representative in Congress and governor of North Carolina," who "gave his son a good education," leaving the inference to be drawn that he was somehow privy to the plot. The smelliness of Texas was reflected in the person of the former president who was Sam Houston's friend. Andrew Jackson, said "Probus," sought to annex Texas as early as 1835 and "offered the appointment of first governor of the new territory" to Burton, along with "forty thousand acres of land, one thousand of which and a gang of negroes to cultivate, he offered to bestow upon his son if he would emigrate...." Frankly, why Jackson would be so provocative seems to be inconsistent with reality, but "Probus" improved his credibility when he echoed matters on the record, e.g., Texas conducting the slave trade via Havana with "the protection and agency of the United States consul at Havana," a close relative of the sainted Thomas Jefferson. He detailed the attempt to circumvent antislavery laws by creating "indentures of apprenticeships for 99 years...." The number of U.S.-flagged slave ships detected by the Royal Navy, said Probus, went from 13 in 1838, to 32 by 1839, to 50 by 1840, with Texas the frequent port of call. Lewis Cass was crucial to the plot, "this worthy representative of slaveholders and slave breeders" who were seeking to place him in the White House. Like Sam Houston, he too was a toady for French interests. Also coming in for condemnation was Henry Wise, a favorite son of Virginia, who warned starkly that "the standard of insurrection" was now "raised" on the border by "a horde of slaves, Indians and Mexicans" bent on

---

29. Letter to Sam Houston, 22 June 1842, Box 1, Ward Papers.
30. Marryat, 53.

pushing the "boundary line of Arkansas and Louisiana" too northward. The ban on the foreign slave trade had backfired, driving up
the price of the enslaved, inspiring breeders, all for Texas's benefit
which was making slavery even more monstrous. "Fathers sell their
own children, brothers, their own sisters."[31]

And the unprincipled kidnapped strangers. Caleb Green was
among those who knew that unwitting Africans were shipped from
their home continent to Texas, then compelled to work there or supplied to markets eastward.[32]

A "confidential" message from Opelousas in 1842 reported the
ghastly "constant importation of slaves into this country from Texas!"
Apparently the smuggling of a Barbadian a few years earlier was
not unique since this messenger recalled how "at the mouth of the
Sabine I learned" that a "brig laden with Negroes from Barbados"
arrived during that same time. She "landed her cargo & departed
unmolested"; besides "slaves are habitually imported into that country [Texas] from Africa...." The correspondent had written Poinsett,
the prominent U.S. official, in protest, to no avail.[33]

This state of affairs was of growing concern in London and
not just because subjects of the Queen were being kidnapped. It
was also in 1842 that the British traveler James Silk Buckingham
detected an "increase[d] value of slaves" based on a "demand for
slaves to clear the new lands in Texas...." Worse, Texas and Louisiana were increasingly joined at the hip, hastening annexation and
the consolidation of slavery at a time when London was jousting
with Washington in the Oregon Territory, including today's British Columbia. This intrepid traveler was also aware of a matter
with national security implication for the slaveholding republics:
"Emancipation of all slaves in Mexico is known to them," speaking
of the enslaved in North America, while "the [abolitionist] example of England in the West India islands is fresh and recent...."[34]
He also noticed that the Choctaws north of Texas "have nearly 200
white men married to Indian females living among them as part of
their tribe and about 600 negro slaves."[35] This intermarriage trend

31. Probus.
32. Caleb Green, Jr. to Caleb Green, Sr., 19 April 1842, Caleb Green Letters,
Historic New Orleans.
33. Ibid., To "My Dear Brother," 19 April 1842.
34. James Silk Buckingham, *The Slave States of America, Volume I*, London:
Fisher, 1842, 235, 507-508 (abbrev. Buckingham).
35. Buckingham, Volume II, 100, 433.

seemed to be accelerating as the distress of Indigenes grew, as if it were part of a concerted effort.[36]

Worsening the deteriorating climate was the jingoism of President Lamar, who at the same time was boasting of claiming more Mexican territory and, according to Mexico's official journal, the slaveholding republic was triggering raids by hostile Indigenes south of the border in order to lay the groundwork for an invasion.[37] The insurgency in Yucatan was joined by others in today's Nuevo León and Tamaulipas, inflaming the border relentlessly, keeping Mexico off-balance and hampering dreams to recover the lost territory that was Texas.

Texas, as was to become the pattern, still maintained militant poses, despite its declension. Somehow in 1841 a private dispute between the French envoy in Austin, Texas, and a hotelier led to a break in diplomatic ties with this potent booster, encouraging the de facto abolitionist duo of Haiti and British abolitionists. Lamar and others continued to maintain their demented dream of expanding westward and challenging the U.S. in the race to the Pacific. Fellow U.S. jingoists did not seem to grasp that Texas's secession from Mexico formed precedent for a similar breakaway from the older slaveholding republic.[38]

Thus, by 1842 the older republic had raced to California—still Mexican soil. Secretary of State Daniel Wester was told then that "American settlers and trappers" were "daily coming into the northern part of [California]" armed "and in violation of the laws...." Real "fears were entertained that they would take possession of the country," and in response Mexican troops had arrived "with the effect of removing the settlers,"[39] unwilling to see a replay of pre-1836 Texas.

The first step in that long journey for Texas was conquering nearby New Mexico. This was the case although it was unclear if the new republic controlled the expansive territory abutting the "Land of Enchantment." A map of Texas published in 1841 featured only counties from the east, with the west bare, as if it were *terra incognita*.[40]

Nonetheless, the famed U.S. trader and invader Josiah Gregg was among his compatriots who denounced the "most glaring outrages

36. Cf. Anne de Courcy, *The Husband Hunters: American Heiresses who Married into the British Aristocracy*, New York: St. Martin's, 2017 (abbrev. de Courcy).

37. DeLay, 214.

38. Jacobus, 314, 356, 378, 379.

39. John Parrott to Secretary of State Webster, 25 April 1842, Reel 1, Despatches from U.S. Consuls in Oaxaca, NARA.

40. *First Settlers of the Republic of Texas, Headright Land Grants which were Reported as Genuine and Legal by the Traveling Commissioners, January 1840*, Austin: Cruger & Wing, 1841, Maryland Historical Society-Baltimore.

upon American citizens [that] were committed in 1841 upon the occasion of the Texan Santa Fe expedition." Irate, Gregg continued, "the greatest excitement raged in Santa Fe against Americans, whose lives appeared in imminent danger...."[41]

This ill-considered "expedition" ignited a firestorm of protest in Boston by an articulate spokesman, as it was dawning slowly that the problem child that was Texas and its parents in the Slave South were steadily dragging the older republic into one fracas after another. As George Allen put it: "The fierce war cry of the South against Mexico, after the capture of the scoundrel expedition against Santa Fe, to add that territory to Texas, that it might thereby become master of California...with the chain of slavery stretched over them all"—i.e., the unheeding slaveholders were challenging Washington as they relied on that same regime to bail it out when underwater. "What else but slavery prompted that scheme which, time and time again, sought by authority of Congress to push all these tribes beyond the Mississippi." But it was not just slavery: the "pretext for war with the Red Man is necessary," involving "war of expulsion or extermination" if this hellish scheme was to unfold.[42]

Daniel Webster was among those who knew that U.S. nationals were captured with Texans in Santa Fe, yet another assault on Mexico that paved the road to war in 1846.[43] Perhaps belatedly, Charles Elliot, the British emissary in the new republic, informed his capital of the "volunteer expedition...preparing in the South Western part of the Union, with the purpose to make another attempt to penetrate into the Northern Provinces of Mexico through Upper Texas" with a "simultaneous attempt...to be made on Matamoros by sea...." The plundering of Mexico was "highly popular" in both republics, he thought, while the "results in Yucatan" distracted their southern neighbor from focusing sufficiently on this danger. "War" was en route, in any event.[44]

41. Josiah Gregg, *Commerce of the Prairies or the Journal of a Santa Fe Trader During Eight Expeditions Across the Great Western Frontier and a Residence of Nearly Nine Years in Northern New Mexico, Volume I,* New York: Langley, 1845, 230 (abbrev. Gregg).

42. George Allen, *The Complaint of Mexico, and Conspiracy Against Liberty,* Boston: Aiden, 1843, Huntington Library.

43. Daniel Webster to Mr. Thompson, 5 April 1842, in *The Writings and Speeches of Daniel Webster...,* Boston: Little Brown, 1903, Volume XII, 101 (abbrev. *Daniel Webster*).

44. Charles Elliot to "My Lord," 28 January 1843, Box 2-23/755, Texas Republic SoS.

The Secretary of State was also informed when in May 1842 "excitement" was "created" in Matamoros "in consequence of a threatened invasion by the Texians," leading to "barricades on the streets."[45]

The implication was clear: Texas aggression against Mexican territory was not just putting U.S. nationals in jeopardy but, as well, the old and newer slaveholders' republics were in accord on the necessity to denude Mexico—either jointly or separately.

In any case, by the early 1840s Texas and its western neighbor were locked in a virtual war.[46] Even the French emissary in Texas seemed taken aback that a new republic with so many festering problems would be so audacious, not grasping the emerging U.S. axiom: if you have a problem, enlarge it, as that will be clarifying and introduce new dynamics changing the nature of the original matter. Du Bois Saligny thought that Texas envoys in France were negotiating directly with the authorities there, whereby in return for a "loan of [five] million dollars" they would conquer New Mexico and "share with us the products of all the mines of this province...which would be exploited by a [French] Company and by French engineers...." As this Frenchman saw things, "the Mexican republic...is doomed to perish" and "the day is not [that] far away," so picking over the carcass should commence right away. "The Spanish race," he predicted, "will have disappeared from Mexico as a nation, to make [room] for the Anglo-American race.... lately the United States has regarded all Mexico as a prize that was destined for them...." Russia too, he said, was lusting after Mexico's northernmost provinces, pointing to the "extraordinary development of Russia's possession in the North West...." He had conferred with Joel Poinsett about this in Washington "three years ago"—though he did not apparently share his viewpoint that "Texians are admirably placed to take this trade away from the Americans," i.e., trade to the west, placing Santa Fe in the crosshairs.[47]

Texas was well positioned to deflect these various challengers. By 1842 the new republic had legations in Calcutta, Le Havre, New Orleans, Natchez, Mobile, Bremen, Cincinnati, and Boston.[48] In late 1841, Sam Houston was told of a St. Louisan who wanted to be consul so

---

45. D.W. Smith to Secretary of State Webster, 30 May 1842, Reel 2, Despatches from U.S. Consuls in Matamoros, NARA.

46. Bill Platt and Moises Gonzales, *Slavery in the Southwest: Genizaro Identity, Dignity and the Law*, Durham: Carolina Academic Press, 2019, 30.

47. Du Bois de Saligny to "M. the Marshall," 4 May 1840, Box 1, Saligny.

48. Reports, ca. 1842, Box 2-9/1, Texas Republic SoS.

as to "give those necessary facilities to emigrants" who were needed in order to better occupy seized land.[49]

Paris was also well positioned to leap on the gravy train driven by Texas. By January 1841 a plan had developed to bring minimally 8000 new migrants—mostly French—to the new republic.[50] Vienna born George Erath, who became a leading settler, confirmed that "since our constitution granted the right of citizenship and of voting after six months' residence to any race [sic], European governments early sought to control through colonization...American institutions"; thus, Paris "proposed to settle eight thousand armed Frenchmen on the Brazos...," and even London devised a "scheme...to crowd into this country a foreign element to prevent with their vote our annexation to the United States...."[51]

London was disadvantaged in this context since—according to their emissary William Kennedy—Sam Houston himself was the "leading advocate of French interests in Texas...."[52] Houston was not alone. When France did not sign the so-called "Quintuple" treaty engineered by London in 1842 and designed to curb the African Slave Trade, abolitionist Charles Sumner of Massachusetts alleged that Paris was "under the influence" of Lewis Cass of Michigan, a U.S. potentate, and influential Boston jurist Henry Wheaton.[53]

Houston was the key Texas figure, Kennedy thought, since he was a "friend and protégé of General [Andrew] Jackson," the former president of a nation that was "actively intriguing" for "annexation."[54] In turn Kennedy was assailed for his unspecified "perfidy and ingratitude," along with engendering jealousy on the part of Houston.[55] Kennedy was hardly a favorite in Texas since the British nation he represented was, he said, "very properly prohibited from availing themselves of slave labour," meaning an "increase" in the "outlay on household servants,"[56] giving settlers a taste of the future dispensation. Kennedy felt that the U.S. press backed by Henry Clay,

---

49. Letter to Sam Houston, 28 October 1841, Box 2-9/2, Texas Republic SoS.

50. Lagarde, 107-123, 113.

51. Erath, 80.

52. William Kennedy to Earl of Aberdeen, 20 October 1841, Box 2-23/755, Texas Republic SoS.

53. Report by Sumner, 1842, in Pierce, Volume II, 191.

54. William Kennedy to Earl of Aberdeen, 9 November 1841, Box 2-23/755, Texas Republic SoS.

55. Ibid., J. Hamilton to Earl of Aberdeen, 25 March 1842.

56. Ibid., William Kennedy to Earl of Aberdeen, 8 June 1842.

quadrennial presidential aspirant from Kentucky, was circulating the "impression" that "Mexico was secretly prompted by England in her persevering hostility to Texas"—and not the brazen ripoff of her territory that was the cause of rancor. The wily Clay and others encouraged this notion feeling that it would eventually drive Texas into the willing embrace of Washington, knowing it could not stand up against Britain, Mexico—and Haiti too. "No falsehood is too rampant," he averred ruefully, "to serve the purpose of the hour...."[57]

Another emblem of the frayed tie between Texas and Britain was revealed in the words of Kennedy's comrade Charles Elliot, who scorned republic hero Sam Houston for his "career" which was "strange and wild," including "habitual drunkenness, a residence of several years among the Cherokees"—which contributed to the impression that he was too soft to manhandle Indigenes—and the "begetting of sons and daughters" that resulted.[58]

London was still caught between a burgeoning abolitionist movement and the "Lords of the Loom" who longed for more Texas cotton produced by enslavement. This yawning chasm helps to explain London's often flailing diplomacy, which eventuated in abject failure with annexation. Sam Houston sensed this flaw in London's armor when he asserted challengingly that Britain "knows very well that a slave population will develop the resources of a new country in one eighth of the time it would take by free labor"[59]; he realized that London's wallet outstripped its ethics.

There were other concerns too. Pressing Texas on the "right to search" its vessels because of slave trading suspicions did not go down well in Galveston; thus, bilateral ties had an "imperfect character," it was conceded understatedly in 1842. Texas was attracting to its shores "miserable paupers," not the "respectable class of British emigrants," but the former were more likely to staff the military and navy, creating sympathy within these two institutions that was difficult to ignore. Besides, said this London correspondent, "English papers have been filled for some time past by advertisements of the Mexican government warning people from obtaining land under the 'usurping Texian authorities,'" and this "would not be recognized" by Mexico upon its return. This "absurd notice has had considerable influence," was the conclusion. Annexation was viewed as giving

57. Ibid., William Kennedy to Earl of Aberdeen, 15 June 1842.

58. Ibid., Charles Elliot to "My Dear Sir," 15 November 1842.

59. Statement by Sam Houston, 8 November 1843, in Williams and Barker, Volume III, 448.

the U.S. "command of the Gulf and of strengthening Southern interests that the North might be tempted to seek a counterbalance in Canada"[60]—i.e., prompting a companion war of aggression.

Somehow London saw Texas as a buffer state which could shield Mexico from the rapacious neighbor in Washington, while the newer slaveholding republic could be manipulated like a marionette due to its many frailties. The idea was that abolition in Texas would weaken slavery in the U.S., naive artlessness at its most malignant.[61]

Texas's annexation to the U.S. was in part a result of a failure of British diplomacy. London's envoys continued to see Texas as not only a buffer but overplayed the new republic's role as a rival to Washington, failing to see that their commonalities—land grabs and enslavement—would drive them closer together, especially as Texas's finances plummeted. By mid-1843 the Earl of Aberdeen was told that "desperadoes from every part of the South, eager to penetrate into Mexico," were crowding into Texas: the desire to plunder this southern neighbor united both slaveholding republics and, besides, as the regime of President Jackson showed, the U.S. could well be described as a "Desperado Democracy" just as Texas was a "Rascal Republic," with "white" ruffians playing an outsized role. Thus, when Yucatan rebels were aided, Charles Elliot thought it was "much more of a United States...New Orleans expedition than a Texian...." Even Sam Houston was mistrusted—"very unpopular in the United States and here because of his moderate policy with regard to Mexico and...his determined opposition to these purposes of interference in the affairs of Yucatan"[62]—and this was the case on both sides of the Sabine.

London's emissaries continued to believe that Texas could be flipped to abolitionism and away from being a major slave trader, as facile as thinking that land grabs could be magically halted (absent massive force). The Earl of Aberdeen again was told that "the abolition of slavery in [Texas] would be agreeable in England," which was true but then came the misdirection: "it would be practicable to raise a loan there on the security of the lands in Texas in furtherance of that object,"[63] i.e., a leveraged buyout of the enslaved, and London would receive land in return, if matters evolved as predicted.

---

60. Statement from London, 15 March 1842, Box 2-9/1, Texas Republic SoS. In the same place see also Letter to Anson Jones, 14 April 1843.

61. Jacobus, 162, 200.

62. Charles Elliot to Earl of Aberdeen, 21 June 1843, Box 2-23/755, Texas Republic SoS.

63. Ibid., Charles Elliot to Earl of Aberdeen, 15 July 1843.

But why should Washington, let alone Paris, stand for this? Already Louisiana was claiming land westward—which London knew[64]—as if Washington were hedging against the possibility that Texas would become a sellout.

Undaunted, Britain was apparently lobbying Mexico to recognize Texas if slavery were to be banned—though the very possibility could, at least, cause the U.S. to overthrow the "Rascal Republic."[65]

In the spring of 1841 Lord Palmerston was reminded by an emissary, James Hook, that Paris had recognized Texas three years earlier, gaining a clear advantage over the cross-channel competitor. Hook sought to split the difference which was bound to be unrealistically ineffectual: recognize Texas but push for abolition—the latter was akin to demanding that the zebra rid itself of stripes.

Hook pressed on. Texas was "much larger than France," with a population of 220,000 and 40,000 Indigenous and 10,000 enslaved, he estimated. He marveled at the purported progress of the new republic: "there is not in the records of history," he gushed emphatically, "any instance of a nation rising as <u>rapidly as</u> the Republic of Texas…." The timber of Texas alone could undercut in price the "teak of Sierra Leone…." Thus, splitting hairs, engage Texas diplomatically but make abolition a "sine qua non," thereby "inflicting a mortal wound on the giant slavery existing" in the older republic too. Apparently, London's man was so bedazzled by the riches to be purloined from Texas via enslaved labor that he deluded himself into thinking that "friends of abolition are numerous and powerful" in the new republic[66]—though he was not seemingly including Africans and Indigenes. Still, the magnetic attraction of freedom due south in Mexico fueled a form of runaway abolition to the point where as of 1843 a subsequent analyst declared that losses were so great that the enslaved were "hardly…worth owning."[67]

Despite its epochal ambitions, the till was almost empty—or so said Sam Houston in July 1841. He emphasized, "there *is no money in Texas* but our depreciated notes…." He conceded he may have refracted the republic's own problems through his own narrow lens, since he was simultaneously bemoaning the problem afflicting so many enslavers: "two valuable negro boys for which I had paid in cash $2100 previous to my visit to Nashville, ran away last spring

64. Ibid., Charles Elliot to Earl of Aberdeen, 30 September 1843.

65. Ibid., Charles Elliot to Earl of Aberdeen, 10 October 1843.

66. Ibid., James Hook to Lord Palmerston, 30 April 1841. An 1842 estimate placed the number of the enslaved at 11,500: Maillard, 261.

67. J.H. Smith, 111.

to Mexico. Thus you can see I'm in bad luck!"[68]—and so was the republic he helped to found.

The situation was so dire that Texas felt compelled to go to London with its begging bowl, despite Britain's close relationship with Mexico.[69]

Texas could well be considered the "Rascal Republic," a magnet attracting the disreputable from far and wide. The surfeit of unscrupulousness merged with the spectacular violence visited upon the enslaved, the Indigenous and those of Mexican origin to create an overall culture of rampant violence, that has yet to dissipate essentially. This was the message to Irish-born Thomas W. Ward, whose migration to Texas brought him to critical battles during the Counter-Revolution of 1836. By 1841 he was informed that "to swindle someone is certain" in this land, meaning some foresaw "no remedy but the pistol and Bowie knife. What I mean is cool premeditated murder in such a way as to avoid suspicion"; more to the point, said Andrew Briscoe, a fellow counter-revolutionary and merchant besides, "if you will horsewhip him you will do a god's service and if you not, I will do it myself"—"I should have done it before,"[70] he said with convincing panache.

Fortunately for those who were being ravaged, doctors in search of paying patients knew that Texas was ideal. This list included D.C. Pinckney of South Carolina, who was seeking—said a colleague—"permanent settlement" and had the "reputation of being the first physician and surgeon in his county and is universally esteemed" in addition.[71]

John B. Denton was on the wrong end of this unleashed fury by 1841, just as Dr. Pinckney was arriving. Born in Tennessee, this Methodist arrived in Texas by 1837; described as "five feet ten inches high, very erect; had black, slightly black curly hair, a broad, high forehead, weighed one hundred and sixty pounds...." He was in murderous pursuit of Indigenes just after their defeat in Tarrant County, near today's Dallas, when he was shot in the breast—and died.[72]

---

68. Sam Houston to General W.G. Harding, 17 July 1841, in Williams and Barker, Volume III, 10.

69. "Convention Between Her Majesty and the Republick [*sic*] of Texas, Containing Agreements Relative to Publick [*sic*] Debt," London, 14 November 1840, London: Harrison, 1842, Huntington Library.

70. Andrew Briscoe to Thomas W. Ward, 19 December 1841, Box 1, Ward Papers.

71. L.B. Northrup to General A.S. Johnson, ca. 1840, CCSC.

72. William Allen, *Captain John B. Denton: Preacher, Lawyer and Soldier, His Life and Times in Tennessee, Arkansas, and Texas*, Chicago: Donnelly, 1905, 37, 39, 40, 34.

Yet the rewards in Texas were so grand—gigantic plots of land seized from Indigenes and a supple inflow of the enslaved to work same—that replacements for Denton in the "Rascal Republic" were not so difficult as might have been imagined. Among the arrivals was Oran Milo Roberts, born in South Carolina in 1815 and growing up in an enslaver family in Alabama. This man, described by his biographer as "certainly a believer in white supremacy," arrived in Texas in November 1841 and by 1857 owned seven slaves—a year that coincided with the suicide of fellow Carolinian, U.S. Senator Thomas Rusk, suggesting that self-inflicted violence was an unavoidable aspect of the culture too.[73]

James Pope Cole arrived in Galveston by 1839 from Beaufort, South Carolina, known to be a hotbed of African restiveness, and found no surcease in Texas since by 1842 he was organizing militia in case of Mexican invasion accompanied by simultaneous domestic uprisings.[74]

They were also arriving from across the Atlantic. This burgeoning list of migrants included Henri Castro, a Jewish man, who earlier had moved from Portugal to France. Swiss Catholics—17,000 all told—also desired to escape religious persecution and sought to move to Texas too. But Castro's Colony, as it was termed, proved essential to the new republic's fortunes. The grant to him and his confederates included the entire land between San Antonio and the Rio Grande, a so-called "no man's land" where there roamed Indigenes, rogues, and at times bands of Mexican soldiers; Castro's Colony for a time was the westernmost settlement and was designed to foil challengers to Texas sovereignty.[75]

Attracting European settlers increased revenue which the depleted coffers of Texas needed desperately. The energetic Castro recruited 2000 Europeans, including French, Germans, Belgians, Dutch, and Hungarians, to complement his Sephardic background and create an ever more serpentine "Anglo" identity, the Texas variation on "whiteness" which was designed to expel melanin deficient Mexicans from this hallowed category.[76]

---

73. William C. Yancey, "The Old Alcalde: Oran Milo Roberts, Texas' Forgotten Fire-Eater," Ph.D. dissertation, UNT, 2016, 10, 41, 98, 101, 104 (abbrev. Yancey).

74. Mary Cole Farrow Long, *Stranger in a Strange Land: From Beaufort, South Carolina to Galveston Island, Republic of Texas, A Biography of Judge James Pope Cole*, Belton, Texas: Bear Hollow, 1986, x (abbrev. M.C.F. Long).

75. Bobby Weaver, "Castro's Colony: Empresario Colonization in Texas, 1842-1865," Ph.d. dissertation, TTU, 1983, 24, 55, 114, 152.

76. Bobby D. Weaver, *Castro's Colony: Empresario Development in Texas, 1842-1865:* College Station: TA&MU Press, 1985.

Castro adapted enthusiastically to the unsettled clime, within a few years bringing scores of emigrants via New Orleans to Lavaca, while exclaiming bizarrely but appropriately, "God and the colony are my religion...."[77]

A major asset to sovereign Texas was granted in 1842 when thousands of German emigrants were primed to move en masse north of Mexico. A leading scholar of this trend concludes that few of these "German-Americans" defended slavery as a "positive good," as was the case broadly among settlers, but "not many actively campaigned against it," a view contrary to what some have concluded. Instead, scholar Mischa Honeck rebuts the "myth of a German Texas population unanimously opposed to slavery."[78]

The settler regime needed boots on the ground—men and women with rifles—to establish a credible claim to the land. It was in the spring of 1842 that Ashbel Smith, leading Texas diplomat, was informed anxiously that the "people of Texas and indeed of the Upper Colorado valley generally had for some days...been in the highest stage of commotion and excitement" fearing "abandonment of the seat of government and its occupation by the savages...." Thus, the "frontier would recede" creating untold suffering among settlers. "Watch Britain closely," this diplomat was told. "It is pretty extensively believed here that she is secretly [linked] with Mexico in her present enterprise against Texas...."[79]

This grave concern was echoed by Thomas Farrow Smith in Fannin County. He reached Anson Jones, to be known as the "Architect of Annexation" and the final president of sovereign Texas, and told him that "considerable excitement prevails in this county in consequence [of] Mexican emissaries" stirring up the "Wild Indians." They were "enlisting them in behalf of Mexico to wage a war of extermination against Northern Texas," and had "succeeded with the Kickapoo—Waco, Shawnee, Delaware, Keechi [K'itaish or Kichai] and a portion of the Cherokee and Creek...."[80]

---

77. Henri Castro to George Cupples, 25 April 1845, Henry [sic] Castro Collection, Huntington Library.

78. Mischa Honeck, 'We Are the Revolutionists': German Speaking Immigrants and American Abolitionists after 1848, Athens: U of Georgia Press, 2011, 29 (abbrev. Honeck).

79. Washington D. Miller to Ashbel Smith, 6 April 1842, in E.W. Winkler, ed., Manuscripts, Letters and Documents of Early Texians, 1821-1845, Austin: Steck, 1937, 258 (abbrev. Winkler).

80. Thomas Farrow Smith to Anson Jones, 22 April 1842, in Winfrey, 125-126.

Washington did not have to be reminded that if a loose coalition of Britain, Mexico and Haiti could repel Texas, the older slaveholding republic could be jeopardized. Of course, this raised the question as to why some Texans were still posing as a rival to the U.S., if it had to be bailed out by Washington. Logic was driving annexation. Ashbel Smith, a top Texas envoy in London, knew that there was a "considerable party in this country who desire the abolition of slavery in Texas, in order that it may become a refuge for fugitive slaves from the United States...becoming in the event of abolition a sort of continental Hayti, populated chiefly by blacks. This is not a recent project."[81]

This idea that Texas was en route to becoming a "Hayti" on the Gulf of Mexico was not singular to Smith's thinking. According to Charles Elliot, London's man, Sam Houston had told him that "unless" there was a "settlement of the difficulties with Mexico... getting rid of the mischief he foresaw that Texas would sooner or later become the 'impound' of the black and coloured population of the United States to the incalculable injury of its well understood interest and happiness...." Yes, this may have been the old "Black Scare" that often was used to forge an ersatz "white solidarity"; still, it reflected real apprehension.[82]

Smith may have heard of the sentiment expressed in the inquiries to the British consul in Galveston. "What is the number of whites and of coloured people," asked the Earl of Aberdeen in 1843; "what was the population...in...1832...any slaves imported...within the last ten years either direct from Africa or from other quarters...is there in the state in which you reside a party favourable to the abolition of slavery...."[83]

William Kennedy replied, detailing a "white population" of 80,000; "Indians at 12,000"; "slaves at 16 000"; 'free persons of colour are few....'" (All of these estimates seem somewhat low compared to other censuses.) In 1832, he said, there were 20,000 "whites," 2000 "Negroes and 15,000 Indians." The counter-revolution of 1836, he offered, had the "effect of breaking up settlements and dispersing slaves...attracting a crowd of military adventurers" and "speculators" from the older slaveholding republic. The Cherokee were

---

81. Ashbel Smith to Anson Jones, 2 July 1843, in George P. Garrison, *Diplomatic Correspondence of the Republic of Texas, Volume II, Part III*, Washington: Government Printing Office, 1911, 1102 (abbrev. Garrison).

82. Charles Eliot to Earl of Aberdeen, 8 June 1843, Box 2-23/755, Texas Republic SoS.

83. Ibid., Earl of Aberdeen to William Kennedy, 30 May 1843.

treated brusquely as "intruders" and many were "expelled" along with other Indigenes. Then there was the notorious Monroe Edwards (and his partner Christopher Dart), who purchased the enslaved in Havana and brought them to Texas before getting in a legal wrangle that caused him to flee to the U.S., then Britain, where he disruptively infiltrated abolitionist societies. Despite his subsequent jailing in New York, the enslaved from Cuba continued flowing into Texas. Bluntly, he asserted, "there are no means for...ascertaining the annual [number] of slaves imported from the United States," but he did know that "nearly all have been introduced by American immigrants...." Naturally, "manumission of slaves is of rare occurrence..." while "laws and regulations have become...less favorable to slaves since Texas obtained the position of independent state...." Dismissing abruptly past thinking, he acknowledged that "there is no professed or recognition section of citizens in Texas favourable to the abolition of slavery," at least "through open association, public meetings or the agency of the press...." Shockingly, "the difference in the eye of the law between a free white and a free coloured man is extreme," to the point where no Free Negro was allowed to reside in Texas on pain of being "arrested" and "sold into slavery."[84] The next day Kennedy reported that the local seditionist, Stephen Andrews of Houston, an attorney with the gumption to launch an abolitionist project from Galveston, was unceremoniously expelled from Texas.[85]

This seditious thinking from London may have occurred to Secretary of State Webster when the Texas legation complained to him in December 1842 about "predatory warfare" of Mexico spurred by "rancheros" of the Rio Grande Valley, along with "fragments of the Mexican army" and "Indians." Mexico, charged Isaac Van Zandt, a Texas leader of Dutch descent, was "inciting the numerous band of hostile Indians" for the "reconquest of Texas," and the U.S, as the "first" to recognize Texas diplomatically, was duty bound to intercede.[86] Or, thought some U.S. war hawks, the older sibling was duty bound to annex this problematic nation that could not stand on its own feet, while others thought that doing so would only import a troublesome hornet's nest into one's living-room.

---

84. Ibid., William Kennedy to Earl of Aberdeen, 5 September 1843.

85. Ibid., William Kennedy to Earl of Aberdeen, 6 September 1843.

86. Isaac Van Zandt to Secretary of State Webster, 14 December 1842, in U.S. Congress, House of Representatives, 28th Congress, 1st Session. Doc. No. 271, Texas. Message from the President of the United States...Rejected Treaty for the Annexation of the Republic of Texas to the United States...10 July 1844, Huntington Library.

Congressman Archibald Linn of upstate New York was one of the many objectors to annexation; in April 1842 he strode to the floor of the House of Representatives and excoriated his opponents. "Slavery was the very basis of the league formed between the northern speculator and southern slave-dealer," he thundered. "To the honor of the Hispano-American of Texas be it said, they had no part in the wicked design of these [counter-]revolutionists. They had seen too many of the indescribable horrors of the African slave trade...." He knew that "to introduce and perpetrate slavery in Texas was the original intention of many of the early emigrants," and as early as 1803 a "great dissatisfaction existed" at not including Texas in that cession. Then "during the agitation of the great Missouri question, the desire to annex Texas was very manifest...." Thus Senator Thomas Hart Benton was among "the first to advocate the annexation of Texas as a measure calculated to promote and extend slavery...." Since Texas, which in some iterations extended as far north as Wyoming, could be divided into "nine states as large as Kentucky," then enslavers "instead of looking to the shores of Africa for the supply of serviles," [sic] they could look to the existing slave states "where slave labor is unprofitable...." These new breeding grounds then "[diminish] the outlet for the Indians inhabiting the states of Georgia, Alabama, Mississippi and Tennessee...."

Linn was stunned when during the "presidential election in Texas last fall, the great and controlling question was annexation. The election of Houston, the candidate in favor of annexation, by a very large majority over Lamar, who was opposed to it" was quite telling. Annexation would mean war with London since "England will not behold the event with indifference...."[87]

Congressman Linn's intervention was part of a spirited debate that erupted in Congress in the spring of 1842 as Texas's decrepitude was thought by many to leave few alternatives beyond annexation. Congressman Henry Wise of Virginia—who was to preside as governor over John Brown's hanging in 1859 and was chief U.S. envoy in the 1840s as the U.S. role in the African Slave Trade to Brazil spiraled—warned darkly of the "possibility that Mexican arms might back the slaves of Texas beyond the Sabine upon Louisiana and Arkansas," with a possible domino effect spilling into Tennessee and Kentucky. "Shall we sit still," he cried, "while the standard of insurrection

---

87. "Speech of Mr. Linn of New York upon the Mission to Mexico and Annexation of Texas Delivered in the House of Representatives of the U.S.," 13 April 1842, NYHS.

is raised on our borders.... no," he answered, "it is our duty to at once to say to Mexico, 'If you strike Texas, you strike us,'" a de facto annexation. He threateningly warned the "abolition party" to "hide their diminished heads," for "very quickly" they could be "subject... to the law of tar and feathers," which was not empty verbiage. The winning ticket, he said, was for the U.S. to back Texas or run the risk of being overrun by the British, Mexicans, Indigenes and Africans.

Responding in kind, John Quincy Adams, the former president, acknowledged that "servile insurrection" was not unlikely but was skeptical of Texas—drowning in debt—seeking to seize New Mexico, while Santa Anna had "avowed" his determination "to drive slavery beyond the Sabine." Thus, he intoned, "if we shall go to war with Mexico and which necessarily follows, go to war with Great Britain, to annex Texas," disaster would logically follow. The Slave South and especially Texas were becoming an albatross around the neck of Washington, delivering external antagonists prolifically with potentially catastrophic results. This was a step toward civil war in North America. "The day is not remote," he counseled, "when in one of the slave states, an invading army from abroad may be combined with an insurrection of the slaves and with a civil war, and the danger still further heightened by an irruption of that whole body of Indians whom you have accumulated and compressed together as if for the very purpose of organizing them for a hostile movement upon our frontier...." Yet, recklessly, enslavers were demanding "all Mexico added to the United States," maybe the "Isthmus of Panama," perhaps "on to Cape Horn...."[88]

---

88. "Mr. Adams' Speech on War with Great Britain and Mexico with the Speeches of Messrs. Wise and Ingersoll to which it is in Reply...House of Representatives," ca. 14 April 1842, Huntington Library.

Chapter 7

Prelude to Annexation, 1844

As Texas hurtled toward its rendezvous with destiny—annexation to a budding superpower—an influential elite continued to dream of outfoxing Washington. But this was becoming more like a pipe-dream in light of a shrinking treasury, a neighbor in Mexico that was hardly reconciled to secession, obstreperous Africans difficult to contain as long as they could flee north to Indian Territory or to the southern neighbor—and looming menacingly were still formidable Indigenes.

Still, this fear of Texas becoming a real rival of Washington continued to inflame cockles in the older slaveholding republic. "Let Texas long be refused" by the U.S., counseled future president James Buchanan, "and she would go on to become a rival" and, more dangerously still, "must of necessity attach herself to some foreign nation," likely Britain. "Slavery is destined to exist in Texas," said the po faced Pennsylvanian, "whether we admit her into our Union or not."[1]

Thomas Jefferson Rusk, who was to serve Texas in the United States Senate by 1846, by 1843 was pessimistic: "Great apathy exists amongst the people here on all subjects," he said from Nacogdoches. This was "owing to the extreme hardness of the times. Crops are fine," he conceded "but cotton bears so low a price that the prospect of better times is rather dull...."[2]

Then there were the U.S. dissenters, principally above the Mason-Dixon Line, who thought annexation of this rump republic would be inheriting all of its manifold problems, besides incorporating a province that would strengthen the Slave South and tip the sectional balance even more. That was suggested by Judge William Jay, scion of a founding family in New York, who wailed in late 1843 that Texas

---

1. Speech, 14 February 1845, in J.B. Moore, Volume VI, 107, and Speech, 8 June 1844, 40.

2. Thomas Rusk to Thomas William Ward, 23 September 1843, Box 1, Ward Papers.

annexation would bid "farewell to every hope of freeing our country from the plague of slavery" since this peculiar institution "may in time be extended from Maine to Panama...." Just as some enslavers were also indicating that liquidating the union was an option, Judge Jay insisted annexation would mean "my voice, my efforts, will be for dissolution if Texas be annexed" since "we of the North will be become the serf of the slaveholders" otherwise.[3] John Quincy Adams was likewise apoplectic about the possibility of annexation; this was "the first step to the conquest of all Mexico, of the West India islands, of a maritime, colonizing slave tainted monarchy and of extinguished freedom."[4]

Elite Texans were fretting also, weighing carefully the correlation of global forces. By 1843, Ashbel Smith was convinced that one of the rump republic's chief boosters was slated to soften solidarity. "Abolition of slavery in the French Colonies," was "certain at no distant period" since the "abolition party in Europe is numerous, powerful and very active; and is determined ere long to attack the institutions of slavery in America by every means it can employ. The subject is fraught with much importance to Texas."[5]

This was accurate and prescient. France moved to abolition by 1848, at which point Texas was tucked safely into the Union with the backup needed to resist the mildest antislavery. It was also the case that as of August 1844 even Sam Houston had reason to believe that "if the Government of the United States does not act immediately and consummate the work of annexation, Texas is forever lost" since both Paris and London were united in opposition to a U.S. takeover.[6] Despite the wide differences between the two European powers, their common anti-annexation posture short-circuited the old strategy stretching back to 1776, allowing settlers to deftly deploy arbitrage between the two to their advantage.[7]

In his dotage in 1843, Andrew Jackson continued to "still view" the rump republic as being "of the utmost importance to the safety of the U. States and particularly to the safety of New Orleans," which was not inaccurate. The sad state of Texas and the ramifications for

---

3. Judge William Jay to Liberty Press, 21 October 1843, in Abel and Klingberg, 12-13.

4. Entry, June 1844, in C.F. Adams, Volume 12, 49.

5. Ashbel Smith to Anson Jones, 27 April 1843 in Garrison, Volume II, Part III, 1441-1442.

6. Sam Houston to General J.P. Henderson, 16 August 1844, Texas Collection, Missouri Historical Society-St. Louis (abbrev. MoHS).

7. Frederick Merk, *Slavery and the Annexation of Texas*, New York: Knopf, 1972, 110.

Washington left him suspicious. "I never could see," he averred skeptically, "why Texas was quietly surrendered to Spain by the negotiation at Washington unless it was the jealousy of the rising greatness of the south and west and the fear of losing the political ascendancy in the north...." The doomsday scenario he envisioned was a London-influenced Texas "declares war against us, marches through Louisiana and Arkansas, makes a lodgment on the Mississippi, excite[s] the Negroes to insurrection, the lower country fall[s] and with it New Orleans and a servile war rages all over the southern and western country...." Texas, he intoned gravely, "is altogether important to the safety of the northwest,"[8] leaving few alternatives beyond annexation as the rump republic could hardly survive independently, bluster aside.

Jackson, he of the rail-thin frame and shock of whitening hair, was also worried about France—but London, more than that. "I have no doubt but England is encouraging Mexico to invade Texas" and "if Texas will not yield to her wishes, she will secretly furnish the means to enable Mexico to march a formidable army into Texas, to drive the Texians east of the Sabine and then sell Texas to Great Britain for her national debt in ten days thereafter. I fear Texas is lost to the United States,"[9] he announced with wild prematurity.

He was not singular in misjudgment. By late December 1843, James Reilly from Texas's legation in Washington was to "consider the chance" of annexation "as utterly hopeless" and that joining the U.S. was as likely as "annexation to China"; unfortunately, he continued, "our statesmen have no other policy by which to preserve us from Mexico," except joining the U.S.[10]

Reflecting the difficult diplomatic posture of Texas, Thomas William Ward, the Irish-born leader of the "Rascal Republic," realized by late 1843 that the "permanent establishment of our peace rests now, not so much" in Mexico but in England. The fact that the "Texas crop [cotton] this year will be heavier than it has ever been before..." might not be sufficient to tip the scales in Manchester—or London.[11]

In his twilight Jackson did not cease, announcing in December 1844 that Texas "will be a province of England in less than six years and be involved in war with the United States. She will be inundated

---

8. Andrew Jackson to Aaron Brown, 9 February 1843, in Bassett, Volume VI, 201-202.

9. Ibid., Andrew Jackson to Major W.B. Lewis, 1 August 1844, 306-307.

10. James Reilly to Thomas William Ward, 31 December 1843, Box 1, Ward Papers.

11. Ibid., Thomas William Ward to James W. Byrne, 22 November 1843.

with emigrants from England" and "abolition of slavery the result," making it a London satrap *cum* rival rather than a sovereign rival of the U.S. "England wants Texas," he decried, "next Cuba and then Oregon," leaving the slaveholders' republic effectively encircled.[12] Louis Wigfall, a South Carolinian who was to become a chief Texas secessionist in 1861, also linked Texas and Oregon as "questions" to "bring us into war with Great Britain," which would be "the most unfortunate event that has ever befallen the South...."[13]

Mexico was working in concert with London, or so thought President John Tyler, who informed his predecessor, Jackson, in 1844 that Britain "urged Mexico to recognize Texas upon the condition that Texas would abolish slavery...."[14]

A Texas periodical agreed, asserting that Lord Brougham pushed for Texas abolition as a prod to Washington, and Mexico recognizing the "Rascal Republic" was part of his calculation.[15] This was no mangling of London's cogitations, for Lord Brougham told the House of Lords that "the importance of Texas could not be underrated" since a "large number of slaves were constantly being sent overland to that country...." With rising emphasis, he insisted that London must *"put a stop to the habit of breeding slaves for the Texas market,"* as was the custom in Virginia, making *"abolition of slavery in Texas"* a must, for he was *"convinced that it would ultimately end in the abolition of slavery throughout the whole of America...."*[16]

His stirring words were mirrored by those of Congressman Joshua Giddings of Ohio. With passion he assailed annexation's impending success as a victory for "slave breeders." Abel Upshur, John C. Calhoun and other premier enslavers argued that the "continuance of slavery in the South would be endangered by the abolition of that institution in Texas," but he said that Washington had "no constitutional right to interfere" with abolition. Annexation, he apprised, could mean dissolution of the union—a renewed republic, that was to emerge in 1865.[17]

---

12. Andrew Jackson to A.J. Donelson, 2 December 1844, in Bassett, Volume VI, 334-335.

13. Louis Wigfall to Armistead Burt, 7 April 1844, Box 2r300, Louis Wigfall Papers, UT-A (abbrev. Wigfall Papers).

14. President Tyler to Andrew Jackson, 18 April 1844, in Bassett, Volume VI, 279.

15. *Telegraph & Texas Register*, 11 October 1843.

16. Comment by Lord Brougham, 15 August 1843, in Richard K. Crallé, ed., *The Works of John C. Calhoun: Reports and Public Letters, Volume V*, New York: Appleton,1953-1955, 315.

17. Speech of Mr. J.R. Giddings of Ohio Upon the Annexation of Texas, Delivered in the House of Representatives..., May 1844, AAS.

Texas, said Jackson was a gaping security flaw in the security of the older slaveholders' republic. "Our slaves in the great valley of the Mississippi," he said with utter seriousness, were effectively "worth nothing because they would all run over into [London's] Texas, "liberated and lost to their owners...."[18] This also meant that since the investor class parlayed capital often on the basis of the impending future, as much as the roiling present, this was deflating the most critical sector of the economy: the enslaved. Texas as the key to overturning New Orleans—the emporium of the enslaved—was a repetitive theme of Jackson's.[19]

A historian surveying the scene in 1911 acknowledged that with the enslaved fleeing in droves southward from Texas and abolitionism rising, this unique species of property was increasingly "hardly to be worth owning"[20]—a de facto abolition, in short.

In a "confidential" message to the influential Francis P. Blair of Maryland, Jackson continued to hammer the point that "the greatest inducement of England is to get Texas ceded to her by Mexico, in payment of the great debt Mexico owes her. The situation of Texas is distressing, she is pressed down with debt, has no revenue, and cannot borrow" and therefore "will have to resign her negroes to England at $250 a head," leaving "Indians and Negroes, a [Canada] on our west as well as the north, servile war, an asylum for all runaway slaves...."[21] London's leverage over Mexico was taken seriously. Duff Green, the prominent Southerner, wrote Calhoun from Mexico in 1844, advising of Britain's "mortgage on the Californias," which could cause both to fall into London's waiting hands. "If the money [debt] is not paid," he asserted, "the creditors shall take possession."[22]

Green's movements in Mexico were monitored by the British envoy there, noting that "General...Green [wants to] renew vigorous offensive hostilities against Mexico...for the further acquisition of territory...." Thus, "schemes for the raising of men and funds, founded upon these acquisitions," were in motion. Yet somehow Charles Elliott found that "Texas will turn aside from any projects of that

---

18. Andrew Jackson to Major William Lewis, 8 April 1844, in Bassett, Volume VI, 277.

19. Andrew Jackson to F.P. Blair, 11 May 1844, in Bassett, Volume VI, 285-286.

20. J.H. Smith, 111.

21. Andrew Jackson to Francis P. Blair, 18 May 1844, in Bassett, Volume VI, 293-294.

22. Duff Green to John C. Calhoun, 28 October 1844, in Jameson, 975.

kind,"[23] a mind-boggling analytical blunder. Elliott who had a role in the Opium War that contributed to London taking Hong Kong in the early 1840s, seemingly had been sampling this intoxicating product.[24] (Interestingly, the U.S. consul also told the Texas leader Anson Jones about Green's movements, as if he were conspiring against the nation that employed him.)[25]

Continuing in that vein, when Elliott visited Washington-on-the-Brazos in December 1844 his conversation with President Anson Jones—the final leader of sovereign Texas—he found that the "most violent adherence to annexation here came from a rising sugar growing interest" so "they might enjoy the protection afforded to native grown sugar under the United States tariff...." Jones, he said, was opposed to war with Mexico since it would bring to Texas "a class of persons of a bad description, of whom they had now almost got rid,"[26] also a fierce overestimation. However, to their credit, British envoys continued from Galveston to surveil the "Rascal Republic's" adherence to relevant slave trade treaties, including from the Cape of Good Hope,[27] where Mozambicans increasingly were being enslaved and transported across the Atlantic.

Regrettably, misestimation was not unique to Elliott. When fellow envoy William Kennedy arrived in Texas, he spoke misleadingly about the "confidence reposed in me by the Government and people of Texas" that "materially contributed to allay the excitement in favour of immediate annexation...which prevailed at the [time] of my arrival...."[28]

To be fair, Elliott was sufficiently attuned to recognize by December 1844 that the arrival in Galveston of Duff Green was suspect. He was to be "consul...almost without duties," indicative of another purpose: "coupling General Green's family connexion with Mr. Calhoun"—his daughter was the mother of Calhoun's grandson—"and the fact of his own involvement in the annexation agitation" demonstrated that something else was at play. "His true position here is that of secret agent," planning for further aggression against

23. Charles Elliott to Earl of Aberdeen, 10 December 1844, Box 2-23/755, Texas Republic SoS.

24. Haynes, Somervell, 56.

25. U.S. Consul, Galveston to President Jones, 8 October 1844, Box 2-9/2, Texas Republic SoS.

26. Ibid., Charles Elliott to Earl of Aberdeen, 28 December 1844, Box 2-3/755.

27. Ibid., William Kennedy to Anson Jones, 21 October 1844, Box 2-9/2.

28. Ibid., William Kennedy to Earl of Aberdeen, 20 April 1842, Box 2-23/755.

Mexico. "Extended mischief against Mexico" was at stake, "for it is manifest that their objects are not limited to the annexation of Texas only"; no, a further land grab was in train. Sure, there was "an old feud between General Houston and [Green]" but it paled into insignificance given their shared aim. "The foundation of all [Green's] schemes is the incorporation of a land company…with powers not unlike those of the East India Company…." The "real object," he insisted, "is to transfer almost all the powers of the constituted authorities of this country, with the use of its flag, for the purposes of disturbance and spoilation of Mexico, to a confederacy of political speculators and capitalists in the United States…." That is, "conquests beyond the Rio Grande are to be parceled out and sold for the advantage of the company," and to that end they were to "foment the disorders and discontent in the Northern provinces of Mexico…." Green's inglorious record was recalled, e.g., "the nullification agitation," an early step toward rejecting Washington on the road to civil war. Like Quincy Adams, he foresaw "in this strange scheme some…preparing for the disruption of the South from the North…and ultimately for the establishment of a great confederacy extending from the Atlantic to the Pacific, with the possession of California…." This was no more than a "conspiracy against Mexico"; indeed, "one of General Green's schemes contemplated the removal of some of the Indian Nations now within the United States to the regions between their Western border and the Rio Grande, probably with the intention of dispossessing the tribes in actual occupation, and pressing upon Mexico in that way…."[29]

Such keen analysis sheds light on why future president James Buchanan upbraided Elliott, who "transcended all reasonable bounds" in his "hostile spirit towards the United States…."[30]

All the while, London was keeping a close eye on Paris's ministrations regionally, including a plan whereby "opponents of annexation" were to be backed by France, Sam Houston to be lured with "inducements," including "leadership of the American Democratic Party & the prospect of being candidate…for the presidency in the year 1848."[31]

The future Confederate Ambrose Dudley Mann, writing from Bremen, advised Calhoun of the ramified ties between Texas and the

---

29. Ibid., Charles Elliott to Earl of Aberdeen, 29 December 1844.

30. James Buchanan to Mr. Donelson, 15 June 1845, in J.B. Moore, Volume VI, 171, 174.

31. William Kennedy to Earl of Aberdeen, 18 June 1844, Box 2-23/755, Texas Republic SoS.

"Hanse-towns," which were displeasing to Mexico. However, as Mann saw it, the Hanseatic League was just another stalking horse for London. "Hamburgh [Hamburg] is an English city," he claimed, "almost as much under the control of the British Ministry as Washington is under the control of the Federal Government. Its merchants derive their chief benefits in trade from England."[32] Settlers would have been interested to hear the contemporaneous report from London's man, who reported that "among the European settlers, the Germans have the reputation of being the most successful. They are generally laborious, persevering and eager," and, perhaps, willing to collaborate with Britain.[33] This was bad news, thought Green, since "the British Ministry is openly supporting Santa Anna."[34]

Matters financial were also on the minds of the senatorial troika—Thomas Hart Benton of Missouri, Henry Clay of Kentucky, and Alexander Barrow of Louisiana. In a joint publication in 1844 they contended that holders of Texas debt—then at an estimated $13 million and rising by the day—owners of land and "speculators" generally desired annexation, which could increase their investment at the expense of Washington's treasury.[35]

It is unclear if that sum encompassed county debt, for in Travis County, where the eventual capital of Austin was sited, in 1844 the authorities found the debt to be a "large amount beyond the ability to pay" and consequently, they moved to "declare the County of Travis insolvent and unable to pay her public debt."[36]

By September 1844, a correspondent of Thomas William Ward was en route from Natchitoches to Clay's Kentucky. "Politics run very high here," he was told, as "Whigs & Democrats are struggling for ascendancy...." However, the "signs of the times are in favor of Mr. Clay. Texas between the two parties I fear is to be made a victim. The Democrats [are] promising annexation—the Whigs in the South are

---

32. Ambrose Dudley Mann to Calhoun, 31 October 1844, in Jameson, 982.

33. Galveston Consul to Earl of Aberdeen, 9 September 1844, Box 2-23/755, Texas Republic SoS.

34. Duff Green to Calhoun, 29 November 1844 in Jameson, 1000.

35. Letter of Henry Clay in "Letters of Messrs. Clay, Benton and Barrow on the Subject of the Annexation of Texas to the United States," 17 April 1844, Raleigh: Clay Letter, 1844, MoHS. See also "Texas Annexation Bill[,] Speech of Mr. Benton of Missouri in Reply to Mr. McDuffie, Delivered in the Senate of the United States, June 15, 1844," Washington, D.C.: Gideon's Office, 1844 (abbrev. Texas Annexation Bill), MoHS.

36. Minutes, 5 March 1844, Box 1, Travis County Commissioners Court Minutes, APL.

our friends" but "in the North, like the Democrats opposed,"[37] leaving Clay's Whigs destined for the dustbin of history.

Even some Whigs in Mississippi were generally opposed to annexation. This formation, however, described as the "party of property" with "[a] high correlation between Whig voting strength and [a] percentage of slaves," found unity on Texas difficult, as enslavers and non-enslavers split, portending the dissolution of the party with shards emerging in the next decade in the nascent Republican Party.[38] Arguably, a factor that served to wreck the Whigs was their inability to adopt a united and common view of annexation.[39]

Washington had to annex because an incautious Texas, pressed on all sides, seemed bent on a riverboat gamble by expanding rashly. Thomas Hart Benton, an architect of the older republic's expansionism, seemed to want annexation but balked in 1836 because of the war with Mexico. Senator Barrow was uneasy about the Upper South moving away from slavery and toward manufacturing—"increasing" as of 1844, he maintained—creating a de facto ally of the North. If Texas were to be annexed, the enslaved would be further drained from Virginia, further weakening the sectional balance.[40] Benton then feared that an unheeding Texas would spur "dissolution of the Union and the formation of the Southern Confederacy to include California,"[41] a premonition of 1861.

Blair concurred: "I did not believe [John C.] Calhoun wished the Texas annexation"; instead, "Calhoun and his old Junto of conspirators are more than ever anxious to separate the South from the North. They want Texas only as a bone of contention...." Thus, "Calhoun and his associates [are] for keeping Texas out of the Union to make it [a] means of separation between the slaveholding and non slaveholding states and part of a New Confederacy of the former,"[42]

---

37. Letter, 12 September 1844, Box 1, Ward Papers.

38. Laura Ellyn Smith, "Southerners Divided: The Opposition of Mississippi Whigs to Texas Annexation During the Presidential Election of 1844 as Portrayed by 'The Republican' of Woodville, Mississippi," *Journal of Mississippi History*, 80 (Nos. 3&4, Fall/Winter 2018): 133-153, 133, 137.

39. Haynes, Somervell, 232.

40. Letters of Benton and Barrow in "Annexation of Texas: Opinions of Messrs. Clay, Polk, Benton & Van Buren on the Immediate Annexation of Texas," Washington, D.C.?, 1844, MoHS (abbrev. Annexation of Texas: Opinions).

41. Thomas Hart Benton to Andrew Jackson, 28 May 1844, in Bassett, Volume VI, 296.

42. Ibid., Francis P. Blair to Andrew Jackson, 7 July 1844, 299.

another premonition of 1861. In sum, Texas was key to the enhanced fortunes of enslavers, and annexation encouraged them in their grotesque ambition—which was only defeated with the massive expenditure of blood and treasure by 1865.

Louis Wigfall, the fire-breathing Texan via South Carolina, retained a clipping detailing a "great Texas meeting" in the Palmetto State. "We shall not resist the separation from the union of such states as denounce slaveholding members of the confederacy as unworthy of connection with them" and "avow the purpose of not tolerating admission into the union of any new slaveholding state...." "Annexation," said this febrile report, was the "paramount question of the time" and essential to "securing [the] institution of slavery...."[43]

A more cautious Senator Benton then opposed the South Carolina initiative to just take Texas.[44] Yet since he was justifiably regarded as a "right good hater of the British,"[45] it would be difficult for him to resist the London-baiting that was an accoutrement of the reigning bellicosity in Washington.

Wigfall, as early as 1844, was apocalyptic about what the slaveholding republics were about to endure. If "Texas is not admitted to the Union," he emoted, "the day is not distant when we shall be forced to free our negroes and then fight them"; thus, "we must either fight for them now—or fight them before a quarter of a century elapses...."[46] As early as 1844, Wigfall was said to be an avid secessionist with Texas motivating his treason.[47]

But Wigfall was not the only enslaver who was distressed about what would befall his class if Texas were rebuffed—and how slavery could better survive if it were to be embraced. As the debate intensified in 1844, J.H. Hammond told Calhoun candidly that "I have not been for any length of time in close contact with my negroes until this year since 1839. I am astonished and shocked," he confessed unashamedly, "to find that some of them are aware of the opinions of the presidential candidates on the subject of slavery and doubtless what much of the abolitionists are doing...." The enslaved were buoyed by events: "there is a growing spirit of insubordination among the slaves," he cautioned; "in the lower part of this district

43. *Edgefield Advertiser*, 5 June 1844, Box 2r300, Wigfall Papers.

44. Texas Annexation Bill. At MoHS, see also "Speech of Mr. Benton...in Secret Session on the Treaty for the Annexation of Texas," Washington, D.C.: Globe, 1844.

45. Junius.

46. *Edgefield Advertiser*, 25 September 1844, Box 2r300, Wigfall Papers.

47. King, 49.

they have fired several houses recently. This is fearful-horrible," he exclaimed. Then with rising emphasis he argued, "A *quick* and *potent* remedy must be applied. *Disunion if needs be*," but annexation for certain to bolster the enslaver class.[48]

Visiting Texas in 1844, G.W. Featherstonhaugh initially dismissed the capabilities of the human property he espied—"the poor slaves I saw here did not appear to me to stand any higher in the scale of animal existence than the horse"—then with disquietude aflutter, thought they might very well be induced to stampede: "we may well look back with apprehension," he said with disconcertment unbound, "to a future time, when the negro race and its congeners, who already count by millions, may strive though it is to be hoped in vain, for the mastery of our own descendants...." Then they could move in an endangering direction: "'I will visit the sins of the father upon the children unto the third and fourth generations'" would "manifest apply" he declaimed. But what to do? Slavery was expiring in Maryland and Virginia, exhausting the soil along with it, and Texas was the prime option to continue the system.[49]

The uniqueness of Texas, which likely influenced Wigfall too, was also exhibited in 1844 when George Wilkins Kendall toured the "Rascal Republic" and met a settler victimized by scalping. He perpetually sported a hat in order to hide the disfigurement, and the visitor at first thought him to be "guilty" of "rudeness" or "forgetfulness"[50]—until he figured out reality. He was a living embodiment of the peril involved in settler colonialism, which reached its awful apex in Texas.

Yet another visitor, Matilda Charlotte Houstoun was similarly stunned by what she saw that same year, 1844. There was the "vast extent of crime," as "the whole of the population are described as dishonest and bloodthirsty; the very refuse of the vile" worsened the disarray, exacerbating the "almost non-existence of courts of law...." As was to be the case especially post-1865, "Lynch Law is the only description of retributive justice to be looked for here" since "the Texans almost without exception, carry their national weapon, the Bowie knife," the equivalent of a small sharpened sword. The "Lipan

---

48. J.H. Hammond to John C. Calhoun, 10 May 1844, in Jameson, 953, 955.

49. G.W. Featherstonhaugh, *Excursion Through the Slave States...*, New York: Harper & Brothers, 1844, 125.

50. George Wilkins Kendall, *Narrative of the Texan Santa Fe Expedition, Comprising a Description of a Tour Through Texas...*, *Volume I*, New York: Harper and Brothers, 1844, 26.

[Apache]...poor people...have no reason either to like or respect the whites," while enslaving makes the perpetrator "tyrannical... unmerciful...despotic," leaving the enslaved "vain, revengeful, cunning and indolent...." It was the "policy of the slaveholder to keep the negroes in a state of entire ignorance...." Like so many others, before and since, she admonished one and all that the "day of reckoning must come" and "civil war" was among the dire possibilities.[51]

It may have been worse considering the penumbra of the Battle of Walker's Creek, which one historian claims "changed the course of American history"; what happened was the unveiling of a new Colt revolver that allowed for the killing of more Comanche, a precursor to the morbidity induced by the "Military-Industrial Complex" of the 20th-century U.S. What happened also was the ferocious display of fighting mettle by the Texas Rangers, which enhanced their value, leading to more tax dollars allocated to those who could execute the oft stated cry for "extermination" of Indigenes.[52] The increased mortality of Comanche may have helped convince the Choctaw to continue executing the Treaty of Rabbit Creek, one of the more significant land cessions of the horrific Indian Removal Act.[53]

Thus the Tonkawa were not officially part of this treaty, but even signatories were subjected to what befell them: they suffered repeated displacements, including in 1844, 1855, 1859, then in 1863 at the hands of the so-called Confederates, then three or four times thereafter at the behest of Washington. This occurred, though they fought the Comanche on the settlers' behalf, and especially with Sam Houston's men toiling as spies and scouts against Mexico.[54] The tragedy of Native American history is that those who fought were often extinguished and those who collaborated frequently met a similar fate.

Fierce combat against Indigenes was a chapter in a saga by which the U.S. prepared to seize more Mexican land. Months before annexation

---

51. Matilda Charlotte Houstoun, *Texas and the Gulf of Mexico or Yachting in the New World, Volume II,* London: Murray, 1844, 98, 100, 101, 197, 220, 224, 225. See also *Sketches of Life in the United States of North America and Texas as Observed by Friedrich W. Von Werde,* compiled by Emil Drescher, Waco: Texian Press, 1970 [originally published 1844].

52. Swanson, 62.

53.   "Message from the President of the United States Transmitting in Relation to the Proceedings and Conduct of the Choctaw Commission Under the Treaty of Dancing Rabbit Creek," 30 January 1844, U.S. Congress, Senate, 28th Congress, 1st Session, Huntington Library.

54. Deborah Lamont Newlin, "The Tonkawa People: A Tribal History, From Earliest Times to 1893," M.A. thesis, TTU, 1981, 1, 22 (abbrev. Newlin).

was formalized in late December 1845, the U.S. Secretary of War was informing General Zachary Taylor—a future president—about plans for the army of "occupation in Texas" he commanded. What were the numbers of Mexican troops he detected, then at Matamoros and along other border posts: what was "their position, the conditions of them?"[55] Excessively boastful braggadocio aside, sovereign Texas was incapable of protecting itself in the face of strenuous opposition from Indigenes, Africans and Mexicans alike. Big Brother in Washington was compelled to ride to the rescue.

"Defend Texas from invasion and Indian hostilities," said Secretary of War William Marcy, "and should Mexico invade it you will employ all your forces to repulse the invaders...." He was authorized duly to invade to the south, if the urgency arrived.[56]

Yet another future president, James Buchanan, made it clear that "extinguishing the Indian title" to land was crucial to annexation, which gave Texan impetus to what had been unfolding: aggressive efforts to expropriate the original inhabitants. But his other admonition was brushed aside: "absolute and exclusive [federal] control over the Comanches and other fierce and warlike tribes which now roam over her territory...." Yet there was concord on the point that "war with these tribes" was "indispensable" and the further point that "our Indian policy should be extended over Texas" was to be the case: up to a point.[57]

Months after Buchanan's missive, another U.S. agent was to be found on the Arkansas River, traipsing through Indian Country, the land of the Kiowas, Comanches and Quapaw: Lieutenant J.W. Albert and the other soldiers "saw great numbers of blacks," he said, "wearing shawl-turbans, which seems well-suited to their pseudo Moorish character. These people are supposed to be superior in intelligence to the Indians," he advised, "who mostly have recourse to them in their intercourse with whites."[58]

---

55. William Marcy to General Taylor, 30 July 1845, Record Group 46, 29th Congress, President's Messages, Messages Suggesting Legislation or Submitting Specific Information, Box 33, NARA-DC.

56. Ibid., William Marcy to General Taylor, 30 August 1845.

57. Letter from James Buchanan, 10 March 1845, "Original Reports...State Department..., 29th Congress, 1st Session, 8 December 1845-7 August 1846, NARA-DC (abbrev. Original Reports)

58. Report from the Arkansas River, 17 October 1845, U.S. Congress. Senate. 29th Congress, 1st Session. Message to the President...Comanche Indians...1845," Huntington Library.

Buchanan, not necessarily in response, backed up his bold words with the proposal that thousands more troops be dispatched to the borderlands to confront "Mexican or Indian incursion."[59] Making it clear, Buchanan told Andrew Donelson, future Know-Nothing leader, that "our conduct shall be in perfect contrast to that pursued by the British,"[60] presumably meaning pro-slavery maximally.

Speaking for Mexico, General Juan Almonte was outraged and offended and irked by impending annexation. It was an "act of aggression," he proclaimed, "the most unjust which be recorded in the annals of modern history"; the "despoiling of a friendly nation… of [a] considerable portion of her territory" was beyond the pale; in fact, he promised, Mexico would eventually "invalidate" this land grab and reserved his nation's "right…to recover" Texas.[61]

The odyssey of Wigfall—and Lamar too—also suggests why Texas was critical to the emergence of contemporary fascism. For Waddy Thompson was also a South Carolinian and, said John Quincy Adams, was the "owner of one hundred slaves," but he was "against the annex-ation of Texas," unlike Wigfall. Yet as Adams would have it, Thompson who "opposes the annexation of Texas on Southern grounds as a Southern man" was bound to succumb to pressure in that Calhoun and others of that ilk once had a similar view but as of July 1844 were "all now rabid annexationists. Thompson will be converted like them."[62] At least Thompson had some knowledge of Spanish, which distin-guished him from many of his comrades tasked with understanding of Mexico.[63] The broader point was that annexation helped to form a template that was to separate hardcore conservatives (Thompson) from proto-fascists (Wigfall).

In sum, Wigfall was not for turning, he was not a "Louie-come-lately" to the cause but obstinate from the inception.

To a similar degree the same could be said about his fellow Texan and former governor Mirabeau Lamar, whose roots in France and Georgia gave him a double-barreled heritage conducive to the roots of fascism. He was of French Huguenot background, a group

---

59. James Buchanan to Andrew Donelson, 23 May 1845, in Original Reports.

60. James Buchanan to Andrew Donelson, 3 June 1845, in Record Group 46, NARA-DC.

61. Ibid., General Juan Almonte to Secretary of State John Calhoun, 6 March 1845.

62. Entry, July 1844, in C.F. Adams, 68.

63. Haynes, Somervell, 188. See Horne, *Confronting Black Jacobins* for more on Mirabeau Lamar.

that also played a pivotal role in the citadel of reaction in the older republic: Wigfall's South Carolina. Lamar opposed annexation initially and even after turning, continued to be the avatar of the now fading dream that Texas could rival the U.S. by continuing to move westward to California. Finally, after annexation, he served as U.S. envoy in Argentina, Costa Rica and Nicaragua, the latter in the 1850s emerging as a target for U.S. enslavers, in a replay of "Anglo"-Texas. By the 1870s he was touting the construction of a Texas-Pacific railway, the latest scheme for engulfing Indigenes.[64] His service abroad could be seen as an anticipation of a mature U.S. imperialism that was then blossoming, with Managua as an early target, following Mexico and countless Indigenous polities.

Yet it was in 1844, when addressing his erstwhile fellow Georgians, that Lamar admitted, "I was at one period opposed to the union of the two countries," speaking of the U.S. and Texas, but in light of London's "meddling deeply with Texian affairs," and Mexico-Texas "relations" too, he was rapidly reconsidering. For Britain had the "commanding" role in Mexico with the latter clamoring for abolition and no annexation, with annexation being the prime path to "strengthening [the] system of slavery...." Absent annexation, Texas could not withstand abolitionist pressure and London's "fanaticism." He feared that this pressure already had created the "consequent idea of insecurity to negro property [which] has arrested emigration...." from sites like Georgia, though the flow from Europe had yet to cease and was "continuous and great and is still increasing"—but the downside was the concomitant growth of "anti slavery" that was part of the baggage of some. This meant slavery was "precarious" in Texas and was bound to be more so without annexation. This could lead to the "tragedy of St. Domingo"—a "reign of terror," the enslaver's nightmare—but Texas, by way of contrast, could become the firewall bulking the entire system. He then estimated that "one fourth of the planters" in Georgia were then "contemplating" the idea of "tak[ing]...their Negroes in safety to Texas," which seems contrary to the continuing reality of neighboring abolitionist Mexico.[65] It remained true, however, that annexation could possibly depress land prices, harming speculators in the U.S. and Texas too, not to mention slave prices.

---

64. James Buford Lamar, "L.Q.C. Lamar: Pragmatic Patriot," Ph.D. dissertation, LSU, 1968, viii, 5, 214.

65. "Letter of General Mirabeau Lamar, ex-President of Texas on the Subject of Annexation, Addressed to Several Citizens of Macon...," 1844, Huntington Library.

The "Committee on Foreign Relations" of Thompson's South Carolina, which did not always concur with its U.S. Senate counterpart, said in 1843 that Texas should be "incorporated" into the U.S.[66] and this maneuver "should be promptly taken."[67] That was not all. By 1844 the hotheads in the Palmetto State demanded that their forces should "extend to the Republic of Texas pecuniary aid in case she should be attacked by any foreign power," presumably Mexico or Britain. Setting aside the Supremacy Clause of the Union, which affirmed that Washington should have primacy in foreign affairs, the war hawks argued that if a nation could send "aid" to "Greeks" fighting against the Ottomans, then surely assisting Texas was appropriate. "If the exigency should ever arise," it was said, "Texas will not stretch out her hands to us in vain. South Carolina identifies with her noble struggle and her nobler destiny" against "their indolent oppressor," meaning Mexico.[68]

In some sense an irrepressible conflict was emerging. New York contained numerous investors in slave-based cotton, but one of its leading politicos, William Seward—soon to become U.S. Secretary of State—during the heated election of 1844 spoke to Syracuse and wondered rhetorically, "what will Texas cost? It will cost a war with Mexico—an unjust war—a war to extend the slave trade and the slave piracy…." Worse, "in such a war the nations of Europe and of South America would decide against us,"[69] possibly destroying the fruits of 1836—and 1776.

Other New Yorkers joined Seward's plaint, while adding the twist that if Texas were annexed, then Canada should follow in order to retain the sectional balance.[70] Residents of Milford, Massachusetts,

---

66. Statement, 1843, #81, Committee on Foreign Relations, South Carolina Department of Archives and History-Columbia (abbrev. CFR).

67. Statement, 1843, #80, CFR.

68. Statement, 1844, #268, CFR.

69. William Seward, "The Election of 1844," 13 July 1844, in George E. Baker, ed., *The Works of William H. Seward, Volume III*, New York: Redfield, 1853, 25 (abbrev. Baker, Seward).

70. Petition, 15 January 1844, 2, 5, 10, 14, 15, Box No. N.A. of LC 136, 137, 138, RG 233, Records of the U.S. House of Representatives, 26th-28th Congress, 1840-1845, NARA-DC: "Your petitioners respectfully beg to repudiate the belief that this Government has any claim to the Canadas; yet they are persuaded that if the Mexican province of Texas can be constitutionally added [by] the South, the British possessions could and should be [by] the North…."

assayed that annexation would mean the "death knell of the present Federal Union...."[71]

Jackson sought to foil this plan of buttressing annexation by arguing that Texas actually already belonged to Washington: "we had obtained Texas as part of Louisiana by Treaty and why not restore Texas to her vested rights under the Treaty of 1803" to vitiate the "combined influence of England and Mexico."[72] As of 1844, James K. Polk, who was to preside over the defenestration of Mexico by 1846, echoed this jingoism disguised as legalism by stressing his demand of *"immediate re-annexation"* of Texas, since—supposedly—this land belonged to U.S. at least from 1803-1819.[73]

Indicative of the recklessness then emerging was the resonance of the latter idea. It was adopted by Robert Walker, a leading figure in Mississippi; he demanded a "re-annexation" of Texas and had opposed the treaty with Spain which "surrendered" this territory. He too was worried about abolitionist strength and the presumed threat of Free Negroes and the looming London threat. He was willing to entertain a plan whereby enfeebled Negroes could move south of the border.[74]

This latter point was absurd, said Boston's James Freeman Clarke. Realism meant that annexation would enhance the value of slaves and the commodities they produced too. "There are [many] southerners who own Texas lands to a large amount which would increase in value," he contended, if Texas were to be annexed, and this included Walker and the recently deceased Secretary of State Abel Upshur. This reflected the weight of slavery within the Union in that "no Northerner has ever served a second term," including Van Buren and Quincy Adams. "Every Southerner, save the present incumbent [Tyler] has. A majority of the judges of the Supreme

---

71. Ibid., Petition, 25 March 1844: "The territory of Texas rightfully belongs to...Mexico.... Texas with her lawless population of renegade ruffian adventurers, her mock Republican Constitution decreeing eternal slavery to the colored race and her desperate insolvency, is a sheer burlesque on the very name Republic" engineered by "selfish machinations of slaveholders" bent on "provoking a war with Mexico and perhaps England." Ironically, this would be "exposing the whole slaveholding region to the horrors of insurrection...."

72. Andrew Jackson to Francis P. Blair, 26 July 1844 in Bassett, Volume VI, 304.

73. Letter of James K. Polk 17 April 1844 in Annexation of Texas: Opinions.

74. Ibid., Letter of Mr. Walker of Mississippi Relative to the Annexation of Texas.

Court, of the Speakers of the House, of the Officers in the Army and Navy, have always been from the South."[75] What could not be said at this juncture is this: that is why the South so confidently and boldly launched secession in 1861.

This influence was weighing heavily on the mind of the man who called himself John Adams of Houston, Texas. The Slave South "must make common cause with Texas": there was "no alternative," he argued "for the danger" had arrived forcefully and soon "the scenes of Southampton [Nat Turner] and San Domingo will be renewed among them...." Moreover, the "tocsin has already been sounded in the British parliament"; the question was, put bluntly, whether U.S. nationals would stand with their homeland—or London. "Ever since the revolution," he said, apparently speaking of 1836, "agents from the abolition societies have been in the country" proselytizing, reflecting the "omnipotent influence of the British in the councils of Mexico...." His message in late 1843 was simple and sharp: "Prepare for a servile war," he announced portentously, for the dynamic duo of Britain and Mexico "may yet resort to...Black Colonization on the Rio Grande...."[76]

Given his hyperbolic alarm, Adams doubtlessly would have been even more concerned, had he been made aware of the rally in New York City of U.S. Negroes in May 1844 clamoring against annexation.[77]

The perhaps pseudonymous Adams was addressing the real John Quincy Adams, former president and by the 1840s a strident critic of Texas and annexation. Sam Houston was dismissed as little more than the "agent" of Andrew Jackson and his Tennessee minions, and the latter's envoy in Mexico, Anthony Butler, a "Mississippi land-jobber" in Texas[78]—who quickly compromised his Jacksonian diplomacy by dabbling as a "speculator in Texan lands"[79]: all of whom were "distrusted altogether" in London. He maintained the

---

75. "The Annexation of Texas[,] a Sermon Delivered in the Masonic Temple on Fast Day by James Freeman Clarke," Boston: Christian World, 1844, AAS. At the same site, see also "The Legion of Liberty. Remonstrance of Some Free Men, States and Presses to the Texas Rebellion Against the Laws of Nature and of Nations," Albany: Patriot Office, 1843.

76. John Adams of Houston to "The Hon. John Quincy Adams and the Other Twenty Members of Congress...Remonstrating Against the Annexation of Texas to the American Union...," 20 October 1843, VaHS-R.

77. Baumgartner, 109.

78. Entry, 1843, in C.F. Adams, Volume XI, 349.

79. Ibid., Entry, April 1843, 354.

then fashionable settler hostility to Britain, however, alleging that this power was not in "favor [of] abolition of slavery, either in our Southern States or in Texas" but would "readily acquiesce both in the annexation of Texas to this Union and to the perpetuation of slavery here, to weaken and to rule us."[80]

Mr. Adams of Houston, among others, should not have been taken aback by Quincy Adams's stern stance. As early as 1820, he was "disinclined to have either Texas or Florida"—today's epicenters of reaction—"without a restriction excluding slavery."[81] By 1837 he had sniffed the "germ" of secession, i.e., a "Southern Convention with South Carolina at its head, which is to divide this Union into a Northern, a Southern and a Western Confederacy, with Texas and a fourth part of Mexico annexed to the confederacy of the South. The movement of Calhoun in the Senate and of [Francis W.] Pickens in the House is obviously combined with this project, which is offensive as regards the North American Union and defensive against the progress of the abolition of slavery."[82]

By December 1844, said William Kennedy, the London emissary, Calhoun and those of his enslaving class "would prefer war with England" rather than walk away from annexation.[83] This reflected the adamant pressure to which Secretary of State Calhoun was subjected. Jabez Hammond told him that he agreed with the view that Texas rightfully belonged to Washington in any case, which was backed up by invoking the Monroe Doctrine to block London. Foremost was blunting the escape route of the enslaved to abolitionist Mexico.[84]

Quincy Adams's distinguished son, Charles Francis Adams, was similarly acerbic about Texas's pretensions, terming annexation as little more than a "'coup de main,'" recalling how earlier Texas separated from "Coahuila [Mexico]…making a new constitution for the former which omitted the clause abolishing slavery…."[85]

Carolina was one matter. New Orleans, arguably one of the most important cities in the slaveholders' republic, was quite another.

---

80. Ibid., Entry, May 1843, 374.

81. Ibid., Entry, March 1820, Volume V, 54.

82. Ibid., Entry, October 1837, Volume IX, 421.

83. William Kennedy to Earl of Aberdeen, 5 December 1844, Box 2-23/755, Texas Republic SoS.

84. "Letter to John C. Calhoun on the Annexation of Texas," Cooperstown: Phinney, 1844, AAS.

85. Charles Francis Adams, *Texas and the Massachusetts Resolutions*, Boston: Eastburn, 1844, 3, 17.

Texas in abolitionist hands could threaten the entire enslavement enterprise—or so thought S.W. Downs, a militia leader and future U.S. Senator in the Pelican State. At a New Orleans rally saluting annexation, he proclaimed that states' rights mandated his state's ability to "regulate...negro slavery" which "existed antecedent to the Constitution and still exists apart from it...." Opposition to annexation was "insulting" and "inconsistent with mutual respect...." Moreover, there were "frightful consequences which must result from now damming up the natural flow of the colored population to the Southwest...." This was simply "re-annexation," reverting to the line that Texas was already in the purview of Washington. Like Jackson, he thought if Texas were not annexed, it would be "thrown into the arms of England," heightening their campaign to claim California. There were real "dangers to New Orleans from British arms from Texas...." Texas in British hands would affix irreversibly a "strong iron hoop around our Union"; thus, Texas must be claimed: "this moment must not be lost..."[86]

This was also the argument of Andrew Jackson in 1844, i.e., annex Texas, otherwise "the safety of the south and west is put in jeopardy" while "endanger[ing] New Orleans...with all the horrors and a servile war and its consequences, aided as it will, by Great Britain and the...abolitionists...."[87]

This idea of a Mexican invasion northward was not entirely mythical. Still fresh in the minds of those like Houston's Adams was the spectacle of the failed "expedition" to Santa Fe. The spectator known as Madame Calderón de la Barca, speaking from her perch in Mexico, allowed that a "good deal of interest has been excited here lately about the Texian prisoners taken prisoner...the first detachment of whom have arrived, after a march of nearly two thousand miles... stripped of their hats and shoes"; it was "said to be the intention of Santa Anna to have them put in chains and sent out to sweep the streets...."[88]

New Orleans and the North were not the only sectional disputes that required resolution. By 1844 Joseph Smith with his followers in

---

86. Speech of S.W. Downs Before a Public Meeting of the People of the Parrish of Union on the Annexation of Texas. Delivered at Farmersville on the 19th June 1844, New Orleans: Noble, 1844, Historic New Orleans.

87. Andrew Jackson to Francis P. Blair, 5 March 1844 in Bassett, Volume VI, 271-272.

88. Madame Calderón de la Barca [Frances Erskine Inglis], *Life in Mexico During a Residence of Two Years in that Country, Volume II*, Boston: Little Brown, 1843, 388-389.

the relatively recent Church of Latter Day Saints or Mormons had fled for their lives from the Northeast to the Midwest, then to what was Mexican territory in today's Utah. Then he was recommending banning slavery and dispatching Negroes to the borderlands. Taking such a stance nationally was likely unwise, and as one subsequent scholar put it, he became "the first declared presidential candidate in American history to be assassinated." It did not help matters that he and his congregants were perceived as not maintaining the requisite hostility toward the Indigenous. For the longest time during the antebellum era, the matter of Mormons was a major domestic—and to a degree foreign—question, determining U.S. troop levels and the debate over slavery, indicating that it intersected with Texas.[89]

In the aftermath of the violence unleashed against Mormons in the 1840s, a number of them thought they could negotiate with sovereign Texas to settle in the borderlands themselves. Though denizens of the old republic often found the Mormons problematic, independent Texas gained leverage by acting as their informal ally as LDS leaders engaged in productive talks with Sam Houston himself. The active Mormons also dispatched envoys to Britain, Russia and France in search of their own leverage; the flexible LDS leaders were critical of both slavery and abolitionism and demanded reparations—for enslavers who freed their property, which may have eased their talks with Texans. If that rhetorical posture was insufficiently soothing, the fact that their armed fighters—the "Nauvoo Legion"—were in 1844 four times the size of the Texas military at the epochal battle of San Jacinto may have been convincing. However, though the Texans often allied with Indigenes—to fight another, especially the Comanches—even they were probably unsettled by LDS seeking an alliance with the Cherokee. Yet settlers in both regions—Texas, then Utah—were unhappy with Washington. Mormons had come to loathe Washington and were less dependent on slavery, meaning they were not forced to bend the knee and kowtow. Certainly, Washington as "'Satan's Kingdom,'" a phrase of Brigham Young's, was hardly uttered in Texas. Surely, the Mexican alliance that LDS contemplated was beyond the ken of Texas.[90]

Even the putative Mexican ally later admitted the "participation of the Mormons" in various schemes; they were "accused of sometimes instigating and at others leading the Indians on to warfare, as was discovered in the case of Chism, an American trader who furnished

89. Dirkmaat, 48, 73, 8, 14, 15.
90. Richards, 45, 287, 292, 302, 307, 324, 328.

arms and ammunition to the Indians...." They were emulating other U.S. nationals who acted as a fence for loot taken from Mexico by Indigenes.[91]

John Baylor, a Texas and Confederate hero and the epitome of genocide against the Indigenous, fought the Seminoles for three years, as well as the Navajos—and the Mormons. The idea was afloat that the Mormons were much too eager to oppose Washington, up to and including secessionist plots in Oregon and elsewhere, making them a wild card concerning Texas and Mexico. What the scholar Donald Shaw Frazier terms "Confederate Imperialists," given their thirst for various land grabs, become the foundation for U.S. imperialists in subsequent decades.[92]

91. *Report of the Committee of Investigation 1873*, 356.
92. Frazier, 96, 171.

Chapter *8*

Annexation Apocalypse, 1844-1845

In the waning days of 1845, the annexation of Texas was realized, a dream that was bruited virtually with the arrival of the first settlers in the 1820s.[1] This was a staggering blow to European powers that objected and to Indigenous polities who may have been the biggest losers of all, insofar as the expiring "Rascal Republic" retained control of "its" expansive public land, providing more baubles to dangle before and attract incoming ruffians and cutthroats so necessary to confront the original inhabitants and control the enslaved. In the larger scheme of things, it was generative of further war and enslavement and in that sense was no less than an apocalypse.

Texas settlers continued to stew and smart over the disastrous Mier Expedition, wherein they sought to control the land between the Rio Grande and the Nueces River, which they claimed was rightfully theirs. Mexico disagreed and administered a shellacking in the process. General Thomas Jefferson Green, who was present at the creation in 1836, was stunned when he espied "the tribe of Carancawa Indians who just previously...committed some depredations" along the border—"upon our coast"—and were carrying a "British flag." Perhaps worse, after the beatdown so ungenerously administered by Mexico, he and his forces saw in Matamoros a scene that was chilling: "among the populace were a large number of Negroes who [had] absconded from Texas: these were among the foremost in their abusive epithets and our men, without the power of punishing such insolence, would gnash their teeth in rage...." Though Matamoros was "the most defenceless city in Mexico," supposedly, they could only stare in barely suppressed raging bewilderment and comfort themselves with bitter philippics targeting abolitionism. For like his presidential namesake, it was this "writer's fortune to have

---

1. In 1829 the settler William Morris wrote a pamphlet on the "necessity of annexing" Texas to the U.S. See William Morris to Stephen F. Austin, 21 July 1830, in Winkler, 96.

been born a slave owner in one of the most densely populated slave districts of the Roanoke," in his native Virginia. Unashamedly, he confessed that he had been an "owner of slaves all my life"[2]—yet within a stone's throw was a refuge for this valuable property, which he saw as unforgivable.

By mid-1844 the U.S. State Department was told that as looming tensions rose between Mexico and Texas, "Comanche Indians have become very troublesome" in Matamoros; "they have nearly entire possession of the country lying between the Rio Grande and Nueces River" while "no effective measures have been adopted to check their depredations which they are committing with perfect impunity. The authorities have taken no notice of them," scoffed Consul Richard Bell, in his remarks to Secretary of State John C. Calhoun. Unsurprisingly, "importations have nearly ceased" as bilateral trade was frozen.[3]

It was also in 1844 that Calhoun was informed that if annexation of Texas did not occur then this rascal republic would become a portal for invasion of the federal union. A Texas in bad shape had become a threat of a unique sort, still willing to contest Washington for control of neighboring New Mexico, yet requiring an expensive rescue simultaneously. Still, it was possible that the costs could be offset, for in anticipation of annexation, the price of the enslaved had risen almost 30%. "In no country in America," said Jabez Delano Hammond, one of Calhoun's more affluent compatriots, "can slave labor be employed to greater advantage than Texas,"[4] which was fiendishly accurate.

Appropriately, there was a certain illegitimacy to annexation in that Texas entered the federal union not by treaty per the vaunted U.S. Constitution's strictures in dealing with a foreign nation but by a joint resolution of the dual Houses of Congress, after the former procedure requiring a super-majority was deemed untenable—a point noticed by Daniel Webster among others.[5]

Charles Sumner also noticed that Texas annexation failed as a treaty on 12 April 1844 and did not receive the requisite 2/3 vote but passed as a Joint Resolution of Congress.[6]

---

2. Thomas J. Green, Journal of the Texian Expedition Against Mier..., New York: Harper & Bros., 1845, 73, 124, 428, 431.

3. Richard Bell to Secretary Calhoun, 5 July 1844, Reel 2, Despatches from U.S. Consuls in Matamoros, NARA.

4. "Letter to the Hon. John C. Calhoun on the Annexation of Texas," Cooperstown: Phinney, 1844, Huntington Library.

5. Statement in *Daniel Webster*, Volume I, 140.

6. Pierce, Volume II, 310.

Annexation, he averred later, was "plotted during Jackson's administration, obstructed by Van Buren's and consummated by Tyler's"; it was little more than a "conspiracy of the aggressive and fanatical partisans of slavery to consolidate their power in the national government"[7]—which was accurate but eventuated as a catastrophic victory in that the enslavers overreached, ignited a civil war and forfeited their most valuable property.

This theme of annexation as improper legally, if not disastrous strategically, was sounded repeatedly, but pro-slavery forces just steamrollered ahead. It was all "unconstitutional," said Massachusetts residents, and "the constitution has made no provision for holding foreign territory, <u>still</u> less," it was announced emphatically, "<u>for incorporating foreign nations into our union....</u>"[8] One petition received by Congress in 1845 from Connecticut asserted that the entire Texas "project" was "unconstitutional" and thus was "tending to dissolution of the Union...."[9] A petition from Brandon, Vermont, also warned of "dissolution"—but presciently excoriated South Carolina and its doctrine of "nullification" of Washington decrees to which it objected and, as well, how they "imprisoned numerous... citizens" of the "free states" on spurious grounds.[10] A petition from the state of New York found annexation to be a "disgrace to our national character," not least because of its undermining of abolition: "the shameless prostration of the inalienable rights of man to life, liberty and the pursuit of happiness," it was declaimed, "in a land where, by the Mexican Constitution, human liberty had been permanently established, forbids the thought of such an amalgamation" with the federal union.[11]

Andrew Jackson was to expire by mid-1845, but appropriately this man so essential to land grabs chose the first day of the year to provide a kind of ideological testament. "How long the present

---

7. Statement of Sumner, ca. 1845, in Pierce, Volume III, 98.

8. Massachusetts Petition, 13 & 15 January 1845, Records of U.S. House of Representatives.

9. Petition, 25 January and 1 February 1845, Box no. N.A. of LC 136, 137, 138, Record Group 233, Records of the U.S. House of Representatives, 26th, 28th Congress, 1840-1845, NARA-DC.

10. Ibid., Petition from Brandon, Vermont, 18 January 1845. At the same site see yet another Vermont petition opposing annexation, dated 2 &3 & 12 December 1845, and from Maine, 12 January 1845, and Massachusetts, 30 January 1845. See also Petition from New York, 10 December 1845, HR 29 A-G21.1 to 21.4 HR 29A—G22.1, 22.2, NARA-DC.

11. Ibid., Petition from New York, 1845.

influence of England can be successfully resisted in Texas is becoming a very questionable matter," he sighed. "Unless Congress acts upon this subject speedily," he argued, "Texas will be beyond her grasp and lost to the United States forever, except regained by the sword." But it was the specter of London to which he kept returning: "What will be the situation in our country with British manufactories introduced duty free into Texas,"[12] he asked rhetorically as he reiterated his demand for annexation, not least since London's "influence" in the borderlands was "beginning to spread and gain strength in Texas."[13] If this trend persisted, he warned, a "strong iron hoop around the Union" would result, that could be strangling, threatening New Orleans and placing the prize that was California beyond Washington's grasp.[14]

Jackson, the ultimate land seizer, insisted that "since the establishment of the Federal Constitution no question has arisen of so great importance to the welfare and safety of the people of the United States" as annexing Texas. The latter republic had "labored for many years" to oust Indigenes but they remained on the western frontier where they could be susceptible to London's and Mexico's influence: a "foreign power acquir[ing] control over Texas" was too ghastly to consider.[15]

Days before he passed from the scene, virtually in his dying breath, Jackson in a "confidential" message to President James K. Polk—whose land grabs made his predecessor seem a piker by comparison—rebuked the "rattling of British drums" designed to "alarm us and to give life to their friends in the United States, such as the Hartford Convention men" who were thought to have raised secession from the republic decades earlier, i.e., the "federalists and abolitionists...."[16] The Earl of Aberdeen was told that Jackson asserted forcefully that "'we want Texas because we want California'"—"'and we want California

---

12. Andrew Jackson to Francis P. Blair, 1 January 1845, in Bassett, Volume VI, 350-351.

13. Ibid., Andrew Jackson to Major William B. Lewis, 1 January 1845, 352.

14. Letter from Andrew Jackson, 11 March 1844, in U.S. Congress, House of Representatives, 28th Congress, 1st Session, Doc. No. 271, Texas. Message from the President of the United States..., Rejected Treaty for the Annexation of the Republic of Texas to the United States..., [1844] (abbrev. Rejected Treaty), Huntington Library.

15. Andrew Jackson to Mr. Dawson of Alabama, 28 August 1844, Huntington Library.

16. Andrew Jackson to President Polk, 2 May 1845, in Bassett, Volume VI, 504-505.

because we desire to obtain maritime ascendancy in the Pacific, with the advantages consequent on an easy and comparatively speedy communication with India and China...."' London was also told that this was the gathering consensus in Washington.[17] Republican warmongers may have been chastened by the caution from U.S. agent Charles Wickliffe, who counseled that in case of a war waged against Mexico, the latter would cede California promptly to London.[18]

Yet just before annexation, the U.S. State Department was informed that Texas continued to see itself as the "nucleus" of future states stretching to the Pacific and "rivalling the United States."[19]

Meanwhile, the enslaved continued to flee to freedom in Mexico,[20] enraging the slaveholding class and generating intense velocity toward a war of punishment. Those who remained were similarly sullen: by September 1845, a few months before actual annexation, dire warnings of an insurrection of the enslaved in eastern Texas were bruited.[21]

Indirectly, this restiveness was confirmed by Charles Elliott, writing from Galveston in March 1845, when he recounted his most recent conversation with Ashbel Smith, who once more stressed the pro-annexation sentiments of sugar barons, heavily dependent upon enslaved labor, and to the extent these enslavers were left in an unattended sovereign state they could nonetheless challenge Louisiana's crop effectively. The sugar interest with its unsteady labor force requiring increased force to keep in line was the "party most favourable to annexation," it was said. All Elliott could do in response was to offer the unrealistic deal of Mexico recognizing Texas if the latter agreed not be annexed,[22] yet another manifestation of the abject failure of British diplomacy.

Revealingly, on the day before the July 4th holiday in 1845, Elliott, then in New Orleans, recounted the unanimous vote in the Texas Congress

17. William Kennedy to Earl of Aberdeen, 30 December 1845, Box 2-23/756, Texas Republic SoS.

18. Charles Wickliffe to James Buchanan, 3 April 1845, in William Manning, ed., Diplomatic Correspondence of the United States, Inter-American Affairs, 1831-1860, Volume II, Washington, D.C.: Carnegie Endowment, 1939, 421 (abbrev. Manning).

19. Andrew Donelson to Secretary Calhoun, 26 November 1844, Despatches from U.S. Ministers to Texas, Reel 2, NARA.

20. Ray, 11.

21. Newsome, 46. See also Telegraph & Texas Register, 15 September 1845.

22. Charles Elliott to Earl of Aberdeen, 6 March 1845, Box 2-23/755, Texas Republic SoS.

in favor of annexation. "Discussion" of this momentous measure "was considered dangerous" in the soon-to-evaporate "Rascal Republic"; there was the clear "apprehension of violence." Perceptively he recognized that "this measure is no doubt an immense triumph to the great slave trade interests of this country." In the prelude to this vote, "men, women and children...have risen in value at least 30 percent since this scheme was proposed by Mr. Tyler in 1844.... their avowed purpose is that the slaves are to be worked off in Texas till slavery can no longer be turned to profitable account and that the wreck of the race is to [be] driven forth into the Mexican provinces."[23]

Northern abolitionists often agreed with London's anti-annexation posture, reinforcing the misleading notion that they were no more than agents of the Crown, a point magnified when John Quincy Adams saluted British abolitionists for their activism stretching back to the 1770s, which could easily be interpreted as casting shadows on the otherwise sacred founding of the settler state.[24]

Adams repeatedly warned that his nation was entering perilous waters, raising the inauspicious specter of "servile war, complicated" by "an Indian war.... your Seminole war is already spreading to the Creeks," he advised in 1844, which could easily "sweep along with them your Negro slaves and put arms into their hands"; then there was the "Mexican invader," meaning "you have a Mexican, Indian and a Negro war upon your hands," a nightmare for the rapacious republicans.[25]

Congressman Joshua Giddings of Ohio also focused on slavery as a motive force for annexation, observing that it was "regarded by [Texas] cotton growers, as more profitable to drive their slaves so hard that the intensity of their labor shall produce death in seven years; and then to supply their places by fresh purchases, than it is to treat them leniently...." And "upon sugar plantations...slaves are worked still harder"—five instead of seven years. Attentive to the intersection of land and labor, he reminded that "for forty years scarcely a treaty was formed with our [sic] Southwestern...Indians that did not contain stipulations in favor of slavery...." He was well aware of the national security implications of the present course, recalling

23. Ibid., Charles Elliott to Earl of Aberdeen, 3 July 1845.

24. Report by John Quincy Adams, 4 April 1844, in U.S. Congress, House of Representatives, 28th Congress, 1st Session, Report No. 404, Huntington Library.

25. "The Anti-Texass Legion Protest of Some Free Men, States and Presses Against the Texass Rebellion Against the Laws of Nature and of Nations," Albany: Patriot Office, 1844, NYHS.

cogently that "we are less able to resist an invading foe with our present union, than the Free States would be if they composed a separate government, without any association with the Slave States...." For in "case of serious invasion [the latter section] would be unable to watch their own slaves" and "every addition of slave territory renders us weaker," with the ongoing "Florida war" simply confirming the obvious.[26]

On cue, the South Carolinian, Langdon Cheeves—a prominent member of the War Hawk faction targeting London and a former Speaker of the House—arrived in Texas with a plan, it was said, "for the purchase of cheap sugar and cotton lands in Texas...." He feared, it was said, "there might exist some prejudice against [him] for the course pursued in South Carolina towards Texas in 1836," when support was seen as lacking—but he need not have worried.[27]

Cheeves was an exemplar whose various interests—anti-London, land seizures, slavery—merged in his enthusiasm for adding Texas to the federal union. The rejection of annexation, he said, was an "egregious folly" since London "has already had her emissaries in Texas" with expansive ambitions. As he saw things, an unholy "union of Whigs, Manufacturers and Abolitionists" blocked annexation: "shall these brave and generous men perish under the hands of the mongrel breed of Mexico," he posed with rhetorical querulousness. Damn the federal union if it failed to act, since he also claimed "there is nothing in the Constitution of the Union to forbid the States loaning them [Texas] money," for this republic "must, sooner or later, become a part of our nation at whatever cost...."[28]

Yet another Carolinian, Louis Wigfall, arrived opportunistically in Marshall, Texas, in 1846; this town was sited in Harrison County, which contained more of the enslaved than any other county in what was becoming the Lone Star State. Indeed, the population defined as "white" was outnumbered by the enslaved, making his arrival even more desirable—to the settlers. This county was then the third most populous in Texas and one of the wealthiest by dint of unpaid labor.[29]

---

26. Speech of J.R. Giddings of Ohio on the Annexation of Texas, Delivered in the House of Representatives..., in Committee of Whole on the State of the Union, January 22, 1845, AAS.

27. *Journal of a Trip to Texas by David McCord*, 15 December 1844, Langdon Cheeves Papers, CCSC.

28. "Letter of the Hon. Langdon Cheeves to the 'Charleston Mercury' on Southern Wrongs," September 1844, Huntington Library.

29. King, 81-82.

For a kind of land rush was on, comparable to the forthcoming gold rush on the Pacific coast, and to confront numerous antagonists—Mexicans, Indigenes, Africans—those who could be defined as "white" were welcomed across class lines and past records aside. This lengthy list included August Buchel, born in Hesse in today's Germany, trained militarily in Paris, a combatant in the "Carlist Wars" of Spain—all before becoming an instructor in the Turkish military. So trained, he sailed to Texas in 1845 under the auspices of the "German Emigration Company," organized land grabbers.[30]

Yet his fellow settler, Congressman O.B. Fickler of Illinois, provided rationale for his arrival, contending that the "designs of Great Britain are upon Texas," a "selfish policy"—whereas "with Texas added to our Union, we can successfully compete with British India" in producing crops.[31] But Congressman Chesselden Ellis of New York broke ranks with Giddings too, noting that in 1839 Texas "consumed more than one-fourth in amount of all our domestic manufactures exported abroad." Hence, "confine the negro population within the limits of the present states and you inevitably fix it upon them forever [slave status] or in time convert it into a continental Hayti!"[32]

George Edward Ellis from Boston compiled the sentiments of his fellow Bay Staters, which were not friendly toward annexation. Of the land claims in Texas, "seven eighths are held by citizens of the United States," making statehood just another land grab. This was "equal to one hundred millions of acres," still staggering in retrospect. Then there was the currency play involved with "Texas Scrip," the conversion of which flowed to a certain presidential candidate: "James Polk owes his election" to this manipulation, and annexation meant inflation of land and property values.[33]

Congressman Ezra Dean, also of Ohio, reprimanded Polk too, who owed "his nomination and subsequent election in a great measure" to his pro-annexation view, just as Van Buren owed his setback in his quest "for the nomination of president by the Baltimore convention...entirely to the views he entertained on the [same] subject...."[34]

---

30. Robert W. Stephens, "August Buchel: Texan Soldier of Fortune," 1970, CCSC.

31. Speech of Mr. O.B. Ficklin of Illinois on the Annexation of Texas, Delivered in the House of Representatives, January 23, 1845, Washington, D.C.: Globe, 1845, AAS.

32. Speech of Mr. Chesselden Ellis of New York on the Annexation of Texas: Delivered in House of Representatives, January 24, 1845, AAS.

33. Ellis.

34. Speech by Mr. Ezra Dean of Ohio on the Annexation of Texas Delivered in the House of Representatives, January 10, 1845, AAS.

Even Sam Houston, a major beneficiary of annexation, confessed to the primacy of land—belonging to his purported Indigenous allies. "I own two leagues...two thirds lying on both sides of the [Trinity] River," stretching from the far north to the Gulf of Mexico, quite an asset. Yet even he was appalled by the greediness of some of his comrades in this respect, advising a leader of the potent General Land Office—with oversight of gargantuan amounts of territory—"not to issue patents" to them since "they are bad men," unlike himself of course.[35]

The denigration of Sam Houston in the prelude to annexation was breathtaking, anticipating the scorning he received when he opposed 1861 secession—as shall be seen, he had more ambitious goals—which drove him to a premature grave. Thomas Jefferson Green, a brigadier general for Texas in 1836 and a commander during the ill-fated Mier expedition, who then became a state legislator in early California, slammed Houston for "pandering to the intrigues of a French diplomatist who asked to make Texas a 'Franco Texian' dependency." Then there was his "nefarious attempt to put her under British vassalage" and his "correspondence with the bloodthirsty Santa Anna" and "his extravagant friendship to our Indian enemies." Above all, there were "his compound frauds to defeat annexation." Without referencing Houston's land deals, he termed him "the most corrupt man personally and politically I ever knew," a trait reflected in "his blubbering lamentations over his Cherokee connections...."[36]

Weeks before the final consummation of annexation, yet another former republican leader in Texas, David Burnet, emulating Houston, carped about his land grants. "I have written you MANY times," he of the heavy beard stressed to the man in charge, "and I am quite anxious to know something about my headright and...640 acre tract," and-he added coyly, "I have other business in which you only can aid me,"[37] as crass opportunism accelerated. Not to be left out, Anson Jones found the time before annexation was complete to "thank" Thomas W. Ward, of the "General Land Office," for "your careful attention to my land matters...."[38]

* * *

35. Sam Houston to Thomas William Ward, 28 October 1845, Box 1, Ward Papers.

36. Broadside, 25 October 1845, Green Papers.

37. David G. Burnet to Thomas William Ward, 19 November 1845, Box 1, Ward Papers.

38. Ibid., Anson Jones to Thomas William Ward, 11 October 1845.

Annexation of Texas led inexorably to war with Mexico and an even greater land grab from the latter. It was also evident that sovereign Texas was having difficulty in confronting the vast array of antagonists in its path. Due north the enslaved Africans in Indian Territory remained unsettled; in 1841 a hardy group of them executed a major uprising on the farms near Webbers Falls; as noted, 200 of them fled on a journey due south to Mexico, which unavoidably would bring them across Texas soil where their presence would be inspirational.[39] The escaping scores had horses, rifles and ammunition, problematizing any attempt to halt their progress. It was also in 1841 that those who remained engineered an uprising against their Cherokee and Choctaw masters. Though enslaved, they were hardly ciphers in light of their frequent role as interpreters, providing leverage in the critical field of communications, often serving as mediators in fractious bargaining with Euro-Americans. Since the enslaved in nearby jurisdictions—Texas and Arkansas included—often escaped to Indian Territory, this was an indication of the kind of arbitrage that Africans could wield.[40]

Fleeing enslavement aside, there was good reason for Africans to abscond from Indian Territory. Capturing runaways was a lucrative sideline for a number of Chickasaw,[41] and getting as far away as possible from them made good sense.

Thus, in 1843 Arkansas barred entrance to Free Negroes, a partial response to the resentment exuded at their presence by Euro-American members of the working class and middle class. As a direct result, the Razorback state contained the smallest Free Negro population of all slave states, an adjunct of the peculiarity of better options for this group in Indian Territory and the regional pressure exerted by draconian Texas, where—for example—Free Negroes, especially seafarers, were barred from Galveston. Also concentrating the minds of enslavers was the perception that as the 1840s unfolded, Mexico was dispatching envoys to incite insurrection among the enslaved.[42]

U.S. envoy to Mexico Waddy Thompson advised that "Mexico will not and cannot enter into any arrangement, except on the basis of re-annexation and the abolition of slavery"—and was backed up in this regard by London.[43]

---

39. Franklin, 8.

40. Naylor, 42, 44, 47, 97, 98.

41. Art Burton, "Cherokee Slave Revolt of 1842," in Ty Wilson and Karen Coody Cooper, eds., Oklahoma Black Cherokees, Charleston: History Press, 2017, 63-68, 64.

42. Lack,, 60, 108, 111, 135.

43. Waddy Thompson to W.S. Murphy, 25 November 1943, in Manning, 322.

Isaac van Zandt, a Mississippian who became a Texas legislator, floated the notion to Secretary of State Webster that Mexico was considering a "general invasion of Texas" but, as well, had launched a "clandestine approach" of inserting "small bands of rancheros from the Valley of the Rio Grande accompanied by Indians" into Texas; "elements of the Mexican army" were involved, he advised darkly. By way of "barbarous massacres and inhuman butcheries" Mexico was "inciting the numerous tribes of hostile Indians who reside along our northern frontier"[44]—a thinly veiled reference to both Indian Territory and the fearsome Comanches.[45]

Secretary of State John C. Calhoun was similarly explicit, asserting that Mexico was "instigating the Indian tribes on our southwestern frontier to acts of hostility against our citizens," which, he argued, was violative of bilateral treaty obligations:[46] a novel point for a representative of a serial violator of treaties. Texas was likewise accused by a U.S. official, charged with seeking to "excite the Choctaw and Chickasaw Indians in the United States to make war upon the Indians of Texas,"[47] likely Comanches. As long as Indigenes existed in non-negligible numbers, the conclusion was reached that settler colonialism was unsafe.

Sam Houston, who often saw farther than his comrades in the ruling elite, conceded that annexation was favored mostly because of fear of Mexican revanchism, a fear made even more real in light of the latter nation's desire for abolition in its former province; so he instructed London and Paris that if they could vouchsafe Texas security, independence would continue to the detriment of Washington. Yet London was being advised to go as far as aiding the Indigenes to combat Texas settlers, as one more way to weaken slavery. To hedge, Texas continued the policy of southward dismemberment by aiding the independence of Yucatan, apparent threats to white supremacy notwithstanding, and egging on the Republic of Rio Grande in northern Mexico. Still, given that even Hamburg in a nascent Germany was hostile to slavery, and even Prussia was willing to mediate between Mexico and the U.S., which did not bode well for Texas, it was apparent that the options for the latter republic were narrowing.[48]

---

44. Isaac van Zandt to Daniel Webster, 14 April 1842, in Rejected Treaty.

45. See also Abert.

46. Secretary Calhoun to Andrew Donelson, 17 September 1844, in Manning, 80.

47. Joseph Eve to Daniel Webster, 15 September 1842, Despatches from U.S. Ministers to Texas, Reel 2, NARA.

48. Jacobus, 399-400, 305, 306, 204. See also Mark Nackman, *A Nation within a Nation: The Rise of Texas Nationalism*, Port Washington: Kennikat, 1975.

As for Houston, he had reason to have insight into the larger implications of enslavement since he suffered the loss of two valuable Africans who had fled to Mexico.[49]

The real threat that abolitionist forces and/or antagonists of sovereign Texas would seek to undermine enslavers by bolstering the enslaved was a factor that caused the slaveholding class to gain backup by joining the federal union in Washington. In the prelude to annexation and war, Stephen Andrews—a singular species: a Euro-Texan abolitionist—was sending enslavers' hearts aflutter in London by simply showing up there. "He has seen Lord Aberdeen," groused U.S. Secretary of State Abel Upshur, and had been "deputed by the abolitionists of Texas" to work out an antislavery deal with the planet's reigning power. A leveraged buyout of Texas enslavers was said to be one option, part of a "general plan" of abolition for the "entire continent." This, warned Upshur, would "destroy all competition with…her colonies" and simultaneously would create a "refuge" for the enslaved fleeing Arkansas and Louisiana. Andrews's presumed plans, growled Upshur, were a "calamity so serious to every part of our country...."[50]

Andrews was being surveilled, as Upshur was told of his "family at Houston," given his role as "a lawyer" and a "man of some property."[51] Andrews was also being watched by a U.S. official when he arrived in Galveston. "A resident lawyer of Houston of some ability and an eloquent speaker" was how he was described, as startlingly "in a public speech" he intended to explain patiently "the necessity of an immediate call of a convention to form a new constitution to abolish slavery, the government paying for the slaves [and]that the British government would advance the money," imposing a "lien upon the landed property which would place Texas under the protection of England...." Predictably, he was "denied the privilege of making a speech," then, fed-up, "about thirty of the citizens put him in a boat and peaceably landed him at Virginia Point on the other side of the bay with orders never to return to Galveston...."[52]

49. Lewis Tappan to John Scobie, 13 May 1842, in Abel and Klingberg, 135.

50. Abel Upshur to W.S. Murphy, 8 August 1843, in Rejected Treaty. This correspondence can also be found in Manning, 44-49. For similar correspondence see "Proceedings of the Senate and Documents Relative to Texas, From Which the Injunction of Secrecy has been Removed..., 28th Congress, 1st Session...," 16 May 1844, NYHS.

51. W.S. Murphy to Abel Upshur, 24 September 1843, in Rejected Treaty.

52. Joseph Eve to Secretary Webster, 29 March 1843, Despatches from U.S. Ministers to Texas, Reel 2, NARA.

London, Upshur was informed, was "anxious to get rid of the constitution of Texas because it secures...the rights of the master to his slave"[53] and, it was thought, had the power to make its aspiration a reality. Secretary Upshur saw Texas as a kind of weak link in the chain that bound the enslaved in that this sprawling prison camp was uniquely vulnerable to pressure from London, which could then ricochet and implode next door in Louisiana and eastward. This "demands the serious attention" of Washington, he huffed.[54] To remove ambiguity, speaking officially, Richard Pakenham told Upshur directly that, yes, London desired the abolition of slavery in Texas.[55]

Waxing philosophically, Upshur ruminated that "from time immemorial the relation of master and slave could ever live together as equals in the same country and under the same government" was absurd. Thus, abolition must mean either expulsion of the newly freed—or "exterminate[ion]"; "this choice would be for the slaves," he advised grimly "because they are the weaker party." Yet he was also concerned about the impact of abolition on the overall U.S. economy, since three-fourths of his nation's exports, he claimed, were "due to slave labor"; thus, "we must cease to import when we cease to export," meaning ruining the textile industry and the U.S. generally. Enslavement could not survive in the U.S. if abolition seized Texas, and an enslaved Cuba would be next, allowing London to seize the island.[56]

Antislavery campaigners in Massachusetts concurred concerning Cuba, indicative of the "new epoch" the nation had entered with potentially catastrophic consequences. "These victors," it was said with asperity, "stand upon a volcano and they know it."[57]

President John Tyler, a slaveholder like most of his predecessors, worried that his nation was "almost surrounded" by the possession of European powers," e.g., "the Canadas, New Brunswick and Nova Scotia," along with unnamed "islands" and Cuba, and a weakened Texas "would complete the circle" or encirclement. Tyler was alarmist-in-chief as regards Texas. If annexation did not occur, this vast land would become a "smuggling power" draining his nation's economy. Then "numerous and warlike Indians" could ally with European powers with a like result.[58]

---

53. W.S. Murphy to Abel Upshur, 23 September 1843, in Rejected Treaty.

54. Ibid., Abel Upshur to Edward Everett, 28 September 1843.

55. Ibid., Richard Pakenham to Abel Upshur, 26 December 1843.

56. Ibid., Abel Upshur to Edward Everett, 28 September 1843.

57. "Report of the Massachusetts Committee to Prevent the Admission of Texas as a Slave State," 1845, NYHS.

58. Remarks by John Tyler, 22 April 1844, in Rejected Treaty.

The scholar Penelope Lea Jacobus argues that European powers were souring on both Washington and its sibling republic. These trans-Atlantic neighbors, she argues, saw Texas as little more than the U.S. distilled, sworn to the "perpetration of slavery and a thirst for conquest," imbued by "vanity, expansionism, political unreliability... dishonesty" and, above all, "anti-Europeanism."[59] During the 1812 war, London—with the aid of enslaved Africans in Washington—had come within a hair's breadth of reversing 1776 and now, it was thought widely, London could reverse 1836.

Despite these apparent reservations about Texas, European nations—Britain foremost—were not above seeking to manipulate the "Rascal Republic" against Washington. Daniel Webster, speaking at a convention of his soon-to-be-defunct Whig Party in Springfield, Mass., expressed the fear that barring annexation, there were those who suspected that leveraging Texas against the federal union would become ever more realizable. It was this apprehension that drove James K. Polk, a Democrat, into the White House: Polk, said Webster, was "nominated at Baltimore expressly for Texas.... Polk is the synonym of Texas...."[60] A vulnerable Texas—wracked by rebellious Africans and Indigenes, boosted by an angry neighbor in Mexico—was dangerous to itself and, perhaps, even more dangerous to its neighbor and soon-to-be partner in the federal union.

Annexation ended the life of sovereign Texas, while collateral damage too was inflicted upon the Whigs, exacerbating sectional tensions ripped asunder on the axis of slavery. It was "humbugging," said the Reverend George Allen of Massachusetts to claim that annexation would mean abolition since actually the opposite was the case: consider that "effecting a foreign policy" hostile to London, which annexation delivered, was "as dangerous as it is wicked," leading to "certain consequences of an insurrection of their slaves"—and heightening conflicts among Whigs to the benefit of pro-slavery Democrats.[61]

Actually, said one antislavery advocate, Texas annexation represented the "detestable conjunction of slaveholding Whigs and Free State Democrats." Stephen C. Phillips denounced the idea that slavery would expire on its own, lunacy which he blamed on "Free State Democrats" seeking to rationalize their perfidy. Texas, then a whopping 400,000 square miles (about 267, 000 today—it then

59. Jacobus, 413.

60. Speech, 9 August 1844, in *Daniel Webster*, Volume XIII, 245.

61. Reverend George Allen, "An Appeal to the People of Massachusetts on the Texas Question," Boston: Little and Brown, 1844, NYHS.

included vast territories that were incorporated into adjacent states) was equivalent to "fifty states of the size of Massachusetts...more than twice as large as England and all the Middle States taken collectively"; the next step, he alerted, was to bring "more than fifty" new members of the House to Washington and then "bring within the Union the whole remaining portion of the Mexican republic"— then Cuba, and these rampaging hordes also had a "design upon St. Domingo," meaning today's Dominican Republic and Haiti. The annexation scheme also would mean a surplus of cotton, driving down the price to manufacturers, not irrelevant in New England.[62]

This national and regional fissure was reflected in the person— and state—of Kentucky's Cassius Clay, an erstwhile Whig. Speaking from Boston in 1844, he zeroed in on Texas, charging that "if you enslave blacks" today, even he could be enslaved tomorrow,[63] a message not crafted for consumption by pro-slavery Whigs.

These speculations about London's motives were not altogether misplaced. Abolitionists there acknowledged that Texas cotton was competing with that commodity in Africa and, especially, British India. They knew that Texas was the recipient of a flood of the enslaved from Virginia and the Upper South, but there was "despair" before 1845 that Texas could be kept out of the federal union.[64]

More than this, said antislavery advocate Orville Dewey, annexation would inflate the fortunes of "slave breeding states," especially the home of presidents: Virginia. There, along with Maryland, Kentucky and Tennessee, said this New York cleric, "the business is breeding. They do not marry; they breed."[65]

London abolitionists were told apocalyptically that "our ultimate and entire triumph" would be flummoxed by annexation of Texas, contributing to similar trends in Mexico and "far beyond."[66] At the same time, hundreds of enslaved Africans continued to disembark in Galveston via Cuba, bolstering the peculiar institution as it debilitated abolitionism.[67]

---

62. Phillips.

63. Speech of the Honorable Cassius Clay, Boston, 1844, NYHS.

64. British and Foreign Anti-Slavery Reporter, 27 December 1843, in Abel and Klingberg, 12.

65. Orville Dewey, "Discourse on Slavery and the Annexation of Texas," New York: Francis, 1844, NYHS.

66. Simeon Jocelyn to British Foreign and Anti-Slavery Society, 1 April 1842 in Abel and Klingberg, 94-95.

67. Ibid., Lewis Tappan to John Scobie, 13 May 1842, 135.

But London, the armed guardian of abolitionism, along with Haiti and Mexico, was constrained by its growing global commitments, not only in India but due north in the Oregon Territory. Lewis Tappan, the U.S. abolitionist, thought that enslavers were willing to go to war with Britain in order to enforce annexation, and London was unwilling to test this hypothesis,[68] not least because of fear of losing what became British Columbia in the process.

This was understandable since the rascal republicans were breathing fire, issuing ever more virulent imprecations, threatening to bring down the temple around themselves (and others), which was credible insofar as the nation seemed to be crashing in any case. The prominent Texas historian Clarence Wharton warned threateningly that if London and Paris had sought to block annexation, "there would have been a world war."[69] This thought had also occurred to a congressional correspondent in early 1845. This citizen worried that "foreign powers" would not be "quiet looking on in the matter" of Texas, the annexation of which would indicate that "slavery has spread its minions far beyond its constitutional limits and threatens disunion...." The "British," it was reported, "would sooner acquire Texas and take to them Oregon and all west of the Rocky Mountains, than tamely submit to an augmentation especially of the Slave Power...."[70]

A Vermont petition bearing hundreds of signatures arrived at the doorstep of the U.S. Congress with a similar message.[71]

France, which had been so helpful to Washington's expansionism, blanched at the idea of annexation.[72] As it became clearer that Texas would join the federal union, certain European powers came to realize that instead of buttressing a potential prod against Washington, they actually had been buttressing the U.S. itself. In apparent response to the debility of Texas—leaving it up for grabs—in March 1844 more than 40 foreign vessels arrived in Galveston, including four from England and nine from Bremen.[73]

---

68. Ibid., Lewis Tappan to John Beaumont, 30 January 1844, 169.

69. Wharton, 238.

70. Letter, 3 February 1845, Box No. N.A. of LC 136, 137, 138, Record Group 233, Records of the U.S. House of Representatives, 26th and 28th Congress, 1840-1845, NARA-DC.

71. Ibid., Vermont Petition, January 1845.

72. Statement by France, 1845, in James D. Richardson, ed., *The Messages and Papers of Jefferson Davis and the Confederacy, Including Diplomatic Correspondence, 1861-1865*, New York: Chelsea House, 1966, 335-336 (abbrev. J.D. Richardson, *Messages and Papers of Jefferson Davis*).

73. Lagarde, 107-123, 117.

This direness attracted the riveted attention of Boston-based abolitionists. Stephen C. Phillips knew that the counter-revolution of 1836 was driven by "slaveholders belonging to the United States who were intent upon defeating the antislavery policy of the Mexican republic" but now felt compelled to denude this southern neighbor further, which was distorting the larger republic's security. "We have seen," he said, "the army and navy of the United States withdrawn from almost every station within the limits of our own country, or within the range of our commerce and concentrated upon the frontier and coasts or in the immediate vicinity of Texas...." Besides, these maneuvers were a "victory to the South" and an "injurious defeat" for their sectional opponent.[74]

Revealingly, just after ratifying annexation, Texas delegates turned almost instantaneously to requesting assistance in repulsing the Indigenous. Their resolution demanded that the U.S. immediately dispatch troops "for the security and tranquility of our frontier...." Conveniently for the import industry, no bars were erected against bringing enslaved Africans from elsewhere to Texas. Hailed was the hawkish Robert Walker, the Mississippian who occupied top posts in Washington. He was accorded "gratitude" by those assembled and was saluted as "one of [our] earliest, best and most efficient friends, in procuring the recognition of...independence...and...annexation...." Tellingly, this declaration was "unanimously adopted...."[75]

Just before this, Walker complained that abolition would render the enslaved "debased and miserable"; besides, either Washington or London would dominate Texas eventually and he assuredly preferred the former.[76] The scholar Ben Wynne asserts accurately that "in the United States Senate there was [no] greater champion of the Texas cause than Mississippian Robert Walker" and, along with his brother, Duncan Walker, both "were involved in land speculation in Texas."[77] National chauvinism merged with land greed and its complement, enslavement, to create a cyclonic effect that led to annexation, then war against Mexico.

---

74. Phillips.

75. *Journals of the Convention Assembled at the City of Austin on the Fourth of July 1845 for the Purpose of Framing a Constitution for the State of Texas,* Austin: Miner & Cruger, 1845, 12-16, 116, 117, NYHS.

76. "Letter of Mr. Robert Walker of Mississippi Relative to the Annexation in Reply to the Call of the People of Carroll County, Kentucky, His Views on that Subject," Washington: Globe, 1844, NYHS.

77. Ben Wynne, *The Man Who Punched Jefferson Davis: The Political Life of Henry Foote, Southern Unionist,* Baton Rouge: LSU Press, 2018, 57.

This was nothing new. After Andrew Jackson presided over the expulsion of Indigenes from Alabama, post-1816, it was found that the names of his relatives and his two closest business confederates somehow appeared on the titles of more than 45,000 acres of newly opened land. Texas was simply a land grab on a much larger scale.[78]

Texans further prepared to enter the federal union in November 1845 by—as was typical of broadening the base of settler colonialism in the English speaking world—promulgating a Bill of Rights that mandated "no religious test" and the "right to worship God." That said, the document speedily moved on to a paramount issue: "insurrection" of the enslaved could bring the death penalty; further, "the legislature shall have no power to pass laws for the emancipation of slaves without the consent of their owners"; and, yes, the authorities were allowed to bar the presence of the enslaved who had perpetrated "high crimes in other States or Territories."[79]

*   *   *

Sovereign Texas lusted ravenously after Mexican territory it had yet to swallow, especially neighboring New Mexico. But the federal union also had a hungry eye on this vast land, seen as a stepping-stone to the Pacific coast and the jackpot that was China and India. However, the appetite of Texas exceeded its digestive ability. It could hardly stave off obstreperous Indigenes, rebellious Africans and alienated Mexico and, as a result, would have to be bailed out by fellow rascal republicans in Washington.

As the clock wound down signaling the U.S. war on Mexico in 1846, conflicts between U.S. settlers in Santa Fe and the authorities continued to escalate. "Injuries suffered by the Americans resident at Santa Fe," said the U.S. Consul Manuel Alvarez, "and myself from the hands of the Mexican authorities," continued to occur.[80] Repetitively, Secretary of State Daniel Webster was told that "injuries and

78. Steve Inskeep, *Jacksonland: President Andrew Jackson, Cherokee Chief John Ross and a Great American Land Grab*, New York: Penguin, 2015, 91.

79. Texas State Constitution, 10 November 1845, Doc. No. 16, 29th Congress, 1st Session, U.S. House of Representatives, ARC/OPA/ID #595453, NARA-DC. See also Oldham and White, 13-31. See also "Correspondence Between Nathan Appleton and John G. Palfrey Intended as a Supplement to Mr. Palfrey's Pamphlet on the Slave Power," Boston: Eastburn, 1846, MoHS, also at NYHS (abbrev. Appleton and Palfrey).

80. Manuel Alvarez to Secretary of State Daniel Webster, 15 December 1841, Reel 1, Despatches from U.S. Consuls in Santa Fe, NARA.

injustice imposed on the American citizens" in New Mexico continued to be perpetrated as a result of the "evil dispositions of some
of the public officers...." The U.S. consul continued to bemoan "all
the wrongs that the citizens of the United States have endured,"
including murder of traders, U.S. nationals paying higher fees to
marry,[81] especially men marrying local women, which seemed to
be a property-grabbing strategy—romance aside. Around Taos, the
Indigenes—particularly the Yuta—were said to "have been in various houses of Americans to insult and threaten them.... American
citizens have a full right to the protection of the government," the
U.S. consul demanded.[82]

Sensing that this charge would be used as a pretext for an invasion,
Mexico's representative Dr. Guadalupe Miranda responded that his
government had sought to restrain the activity to which objection
was taken,[83] but the gears of invasion were already in motion.

Complaints to Mexico notwithstanding, it was also the case that
even before 1846, the U.S. consul was reporting that "the enemy (the
Texans) were at hand,"[84] i.e., citizens of the federal union sited in
Washington also needed protection from the next door neighbor.
Sensing that Alvarez's entreaties were being ignored, a group of U.S.
nationals in New Mexico described the "extreme excitement from
danger" they faced: "we are surrounded," they complained, as an
"invading expedition of about three hundred and twenty five men
from Texas is approaching," and this, combined with the seeming
lethargy of the local government in protecting foreigners—or even
the regime itself—provided a toxic brew. These petitioners found
that the authorities were "exasperated against all the foreigners here"
and thus "we consider our lives and properties in imminent danger...." The prospect was that soon "we shall all have been robbed
and probably murdered...." First, the authorities will have "vanquished the Texans," and then "would return with his troops and
destroy all us foreigners. This conduct," it was announced morosely,
"together with innumerable insults," were among the "injustices" of
an "unlawful" nature to which they were "daily subjected...."[85]

New Mexico illustrated that even as it was seeking a bailout in
Washington, Texas had not relinquished the dream of challenging
the older sibling. This was dangerous, could weaken both, leaving

81. Ibid., Consul to Secretary Webster, n.d., ca. 1842.
82. Ibid., Manuel Alvarez to Dr. Guadalupe Miranda, n.d.
83. Ibid., Dr. Guadalupe Miranda to Manuel Alvarez, 14 July 1841.
84. Ibid., Manuel Alvarez to Dr. Guadalupe Miranda, 14 September 1841.
85. Ibid., Petition by U.S. nationals, 16 September 1841.

the two more susceptible to being overrun by a lethal combination of Mexicans, British, Indigenes—and Africans.

This drumbeat continued incessantly with Alvarez then reporting to Secretary Webster the "rumor" that "considerable bodies of Texian forces were upon [the] march for New Mexico...." This "body of lawless men had banded together upon the head waters of the Arkansas and Platte River, calling themselves Texian but they were thought only to be a band of robbers"—a replay of 1836 in other words. "A Col. [Charles] Warfield said to be of the Texian army has assumed the command of this gang...with the view of plundering the caravan from Mexico to the United States," as the Texans, as was their custom, overreached. "Considerable excitement" prevailed and—also typically—"many of our citizens...leagued themselves with Warfield," as "spies in the country [were] holding constant communication with him...." Moreover, "large parties of Mexicans" were "daily selling...to the tribes within our borders," while "a number of Americans without any license whatever, have established a village on this side of the Arkansas [River]," which stretched in the territory just north of Mexico in today's Colorado and involved "traffic to the Indians...." With mounting woe, Alvarez instructed that "unless the predatory bands of Texians are restrained...," utter devastation was nigh. Also at issue was that "Gov. [Manuel] Armijo, a very large merchant has been struggling for some time to monopolize the commerce of the province,"[86] to the consternation of Texians and U.S. nationals alike.

Agreeing with Alvarez was Edward Everett Hale, who sought to answer the still relevant question "How to Conquer Texas Before Texas Conquers Us" he asked of the "unprincipled population of adventurers" who will "prove the Austria of the confederacy [and] overrule all opposition," though "its population is about that of the state of New Hampshire...."[87]

Simultaneously, Secretary Webster was told that Mexico was buying from Liverpool "two war steamers," an assertion that "produced some excitement in Galveston" as it would give this dissatisfied neighbor "command of the gulph and enable it to transport an army by sea [to] Galveston...the most important point and having more wealth than any other place in Texas...."[88]

---

86. Ibid., Manuel Alvarez to Secretary of State, 14 July 1843.

87. Hale.

88. Joseph Eve, consul to Secretary Webster, 11 June 1842, Despatches from U.S. Ministers to Texas, Reel 1, NARA.

The "gulph" was becoming crowded, as both London and Paris had each sent a "vessel of war" there, according to the U.S. consul in Galveston. "Two thousand men" were said to be "east of the Rio Grande" en route to Corpus Christi, while "five hundred volunteers in Texas from the United States" were on the march. A besieged Texas was "pledging its unappropriated land and its revenue" too in return for a "loan from a banking [house] in Paris...."[89]

Conflicts with "Texians" notwithstanding, Washington was determined to denude Mexico of territory, as the budding superpower lurched toward the Pacific coast. By 1845, Texas was exhausted, unable to resist its many foes and, in a real sense, was rescued by the federal union. The U.S. military was instructed that once annexation attached, Texas was "entitled...to defence and protection from foreign invasion and Indian incursions,"[90] which easily morphed into "invasion" of another sort—southward to Mexico.

* * *

The man known as the "architect of annexation," the fourth and final president of sovereign Texas—Anson Jones—by 1848 reflected on his handiwork. Annexation was proposed in Congress as early as 1837 but, he said, received "little favor or encouragement from the American government and General Jackson's administration closed without having done more for Texas than to accord a bare acknowledgment of her nationality...." Spurned, Texas itself was opposed to annexation, he said, but soon the young republic was "brought to the extremest point of depression—her means exhausted—her credit utterly prostrated—the loan sought all over the U. States and Europe, refused on any terms—pressed and oppressed with debts—her currency at a discount of 97½ per cent—the Navy had gone to Yucatan—the army to Santa Fe and captivity—the frontiers of a thousand miles assailed by hostile Indians—Mexico exasperated by the Executive menace that Texas would extend her boundaries as far south and west as the sword might mark the boundary, preparing and threatening to make predatory incursions or to invade the country...."

89. Ibid., Joseph Eve to Secretary Webster, 8 June 1842.

90. "Orders and Instructions to General Taylor," 28 May 1845, in "Message of the President of the United States with the Correspondence...on the Subject of the Mexican War," Washington: Wendell and Benthuysen, 1848, Huntington Library.

All the while, sovereign Texas "had neither arms or ammunition for an army and was destitute of munitions of war…the trade and business of the country prostrated…in some parts of the country the citizens in arms against each other and the laws—our foreign relations anything but favorable—no treaty or amity with the U. States—England hesitating about ratifying the one made with her—France estranged and about assuming a hostile attitude in consequence of the [discourteous] treatment Mr. Saligny [the French envoy] had received in Texas…government itself on the eve of apparent dissolution…."

For those who doubted his veracity, he added, "this is by no means an exaggerated account of the situation of affairs [as of] December '41…." Worse, Washington was opposed to annexation if it meant war with Mexico, but by 1841 "finances of the country had improved" somewhat and were "brightening" further by 1843; thus, "a jealousy and rivalry began to exist between the U. States and Great Britain and France on the other, in relation to Texas"—and to its benefit too.

Yet symptomatic of the rancorous politics, this "architect of annexation" felt compelled to deny strenuously that he was a "traitor" or otherwise "acting for the U. States…."[91]

Jones may have overestimated the condition of Texas's finances post-1843 but the dismal portrait he painted was generally accurate. The Republic of Texas was a danger to itself and to Washington, but even annexation proved to be a poisoned chalice insofar as it served to set the stage for a catastrophic civil war in which the valued property that had driven events—Africans—was lost and then remained on this territory with many unwilling to accede to whatever status quo was foisted upon them.

---

91. Anson Jones, "Letters Relating to the History of Annexation," Galveston: Civilian Office, 1848, APL.

Chapter 9

Annexing Texas Means War with Mexico and U.S. Civil War, 1845-1848

Looking back contentedly as Reconstruction was crumbling in the 1870s, Texas Founding Father Ashbel Smith reflected happily on his handiwork: "its influences will endure," he insisted, "as long as the white races shall live on the continent of North America...." After all, Texas—he contended—made James K. Polk president, who engineered the transformative 1846-1848 war which dismembered Mexico as it profoundly contributed to the accretion of Washington's reach; for it was Texas that was "the sole occasion of the war with Mexico." Then peering over the horizon, looking past the rubble of the Confederacy's similarly transformative loss in war, he asked, "will the future historian find in the annexation of Texas the first act of the mighty drama which culminated in secession and on which the curtain fell at Appomattox courthouse?"[1] And with more foresight, he could have asked, "was Texas the first act in the ultimate devolution of the rapacious republic into fascism?"

Perhaps not, given another trend that rose during this same tempestuous era: for by various means hundreds of Africans flocked to the Mexican military in order to combat the primary enslavers.[2] "Some of the negro servants," said one U.S. officer in deepest southern Texas, were "running away from camp, Gatlin has lost his boy and Major Rains' Sandy has gone too and several others. All they had to do," it was said wondrously, was "to get across the river." (Naturally, Richard Gatlin later threw in his lot with the so-called Confederate States of America.)[3] His comrade Corydon Donnavan,

---

1. A. Smith.

2. Baumgartner, 109. See also Lewis, 57.

3. Letter, 11 April 1846, in Robert Ferrell, ed., *Monterrey Is Ours! The Mexican War Letters of Lieutenant Dana, 1845-1847*, Lexington: U Press of Kentucky, 2014, 42 (abbrev. Ferrell). See also Gene M. Brack, *Mexico Views*

in his self-described "adventures in Mexico" in 1847, was stunned to ascertain that "negroes are allowed to vote" there.[4] Eventually they could do so due north also, which leavened the more retrograde impulses there.

However, given the enticements offered to various European emigrants, more of them continued to pour into Texas, buttressing primitivism. As early as 1840, one of this group—the self-described "Texas Emigrant" named Col. Edward Stiff—threatened Mexico about "hostility" to Texas: "she cannot regain" her, he maintained, and if this neighbor were not careful, "hostilities will not cease until under the walls of the Mexican capital, the victorious standard of the Anglo-Saxons will be raised...then the mingled forces of the United States and Texas will dictate the terms of peace with similar motives and objects in view to those entertained by Cortes," i.e., the genocidal conquistador.[5]

At first glance this was a gargantuan success for enslavers: protecting Texas from Indigenes, along with foreign and domestic abolitionists, while gobbling up even more territory with the potential for further bondage. It is estimated that a whopping half of Mexican territory was seized by the warmongers.[6] However, from a wider perspective, the 1846-1848 war was an overreach, upsetting the sectional balance as it energized abolitionism. But also from a wider perspective, the war oriented the U.S. toward Latin America and the Pacific, setting the stage within decades for a major push by U.S. imperialism toward Cuba and Puerto Rico, the Philippines and Hawaii.[7]

Significantly, when in immediate prelude to annexation Secretary of State Upshur met with Juan Almonte, Mexico's U.S. emissary, their "informal conversation," said the former, revolved around Texas. Upshur said bluntly that this former Mexican province "would

---

Manifest Destiny, 1821-1846: An Essay on the Origins of the Mexican War, Albuquerque: U of New Mexico Press, 1975.

4. Corydon Donnavan, *Adventures in Mexico...Sold Into Slavery*, Cincinnati: Robinson and Jones, 1847, 104.

5. Stiff, 183, 184: Prophetically, he added that "the abolition of slavery and other incidental questions will continue to be agitated in the United States.... more unlikely things have happened in the world, than a union between the Texans and the slave holding portions of the United States," a de facto result then in motion.

6. Pekka Hamalainen, *Lakota America: A New History of Indigenous Power*, New Haven: Yale U Press, 2019, 211 (abbrev. Hamalainen).

7. Connors and Muñoz, 498-516, 500.

never go back" to the state from which it had seceded since their "slave property was [now] larger & of course the sacrifice would be greater," because of "the liberation of the slaves under the Mexican Constitution...." According to Upshur, Almonte "acknowledged the force of my remarks...."[8] How could he not? For lurking blatantly in the shadow of annexation was war against Almonte's nation, a deadly couple not unlike murder and suicide. Or so said influential U.S. diplomat and former Secretary of the Treasury Albert Gallatin, who announced in 1848 that "there is not the slightest doubt that the annexation of Texas was tantamount to a declaration of war against Mexico...."[9]

The U.S. envoy sent to Mexico City to present the terms of capitulation, Nicholas Trist, acknowledged that "among the points which came under discussion was the exclusion of slavery from all territory which should pass from Mexico"; he knew that "if it were proposed to the people of the United States"—meaning Euro-Americans—"to part with a portion of their territory in order that the *Inquisition* should be therein established, the proposal could not excite stronger feelings of abhorrence than those awakened in Mexico by the prospect of the introduction of slavery in any territory parted with by her...." In fact, he emphasized further the "bare *mention* of the subject in any treaty to which the U.S. were a party was an absolute impossibility...." Yet in this case the irresistible force of the South overwhelmed the immovable object of the North since Trist also proclaimed that "if it were in their power to offer the whole territory... increased ten fold in value" and "covered a foot thick all over with pure gold, upon the single condition that slavery should be excluded therefrom, I could not entertain the offer for a moment...."[10]

The commonwealth of presidents—Virginia—in March 1847 promptly adopted a resolution expressing stern objection to barring slavery from newly seized Mexican land; this was little more than an "attack on the dearest rights of the South," it was added huffily.[11]

---

8. Memorandum of Conversation by Secretary Upshur, 16 February 1844, in Manning, 577.

9. Albert Gallatin, *Peace with Mexico*, Cincinnati: Daily Atlas, 1848, AAS.

10. Nicholas Trist, U.S. Commissioner to Mexico to Secretary of State James Buchanan, 4 September 1847 in Manning, 933. See also "Speech of Hon. David Kaufman of Texas on the Slavery Question, Delivered in the House of Representatives, February 10, 1847," Washington: Blair and Rives, 1847, NYHS.

11. "Resolutions of Virginia...adopted by the General Assembly...," 8 March 1847, VaHS-R.

James Freaner, who emerged from a slaveholding family, took credit for persuading Trist—whose experience included a stint alongside Andrew Jackson—to go beyond his presidential instructions and execute a cession that rivaled the Louisiana Purchase in adding to the rapacious republic's territory.[12] Shockingly, annexing all of Mexico was being contemplated.[13]

The prosecutor of this scandalous war, President James K. Polk, included in his circle a man whose draconian attitude neatly summarized a national attitude: "the way to treat an ugly or stubborn negro when you first got him," he announced knowingly, was to give him a "d-nd drubbing at the start and he would learn how to behave himself...."[14] As so often happened, this was the approach taken to Mexico as well. As the war was commencing, the president met with the "French Minister," as he noted then: "it was this person," he observed "who by his intervention with the Mexican government induced that government to agree to recognize the independence of Texas last year upon condition that Texas would agree not to annex herself to any other country," yet another corrupted bargain that was said to include Sam Houston.[15]

Officially, the U.S. war with Mexico began on 25 April 1846 and ended 2 February 1848, but as should be evident by now, in many ways this conflict was an extension of 1836 and/or the arrival of Stephen F. Austin and his comrades decades earlier. It was on Sunday, 29 March 1846, that Sam Houston came to the White House to confer. "I was much pleased to see him," said Polk, "have been with him in Congress twenty years ago and always his friend"; they shared

---

12. Alan D. Gaff and Donald H. Gaff, eds., *From the Halls of the Montezumas: Mexican War Dispatches from James L. Freaner, Writing Under the Name 'Mustang,'* Denton: UNT Press, 2019, 4, 33, 92 (abbrev. Gaff and Gaff). See also Albert Castel, "The Clerk who Defied a President: Nicholas Trist's Treaty with Mexico," *Virginia Calvacade*, 34 (No. 3, Winter 1985): 136-143. See also George P. Hammond, ed., *The Treaty of Guadalupe Hidalgo February Second 1848*, Berkeley: Friends of the Bancroft Library, 1949, Huntington Library.

13. Timothy Evans Buttram, "'Swallowing Mexico Without Any Grease': The Absence of Controversy over the Feasibility of Annexing all Mexico, 1847-1848," M.A. thesis, U of New Hampshire, 2008.

14. Note, 11 February 1846 in Milo Milton Quaife, ed., *The Diary of James K. Polk During His Presidency, 1845 to 1849, Volume I*, Chicago: McClurg, 1910, 217 (abbrev. Quaife).

15. Ibid., Entry, 24 April 1846, 350. See also Timothy Johnson and Nathaniel C. Hughes, Jr., eds., *A Fighter from Way Back: The Mexican War Diary of Lt. Daniel Harvey Hill, 4th Artillery, U.S.A.*, Kent: Kent State U Press, 2002.

Tennessee roots and Polk "found him...fully determined to support my administration," suggestive of how the war was to open new vistas for land speculators like Houston.[16] Polk also found time to meet with Alexander Atocha, yet another speculator with Spanish roots and U.S. nationality, who had run afoul of Mexico after a residence there. He was arrested there and ordered to depart. Yet he apparently had valuable intelligence to impart since he had communed with Santa Anna, the penultimate Mexican leader, in Havana, and Atocha was able to tell the president that the Mexican was "in constant communication with his friends in Mexico" after his own brief rupture with the authorities in his homeland. Santa Anna, Polk was told, was "received by every vessel that left Vera Cruz," leaving him with "hundreds of letters," redolent of a base of support.[17] Washington thought it had reason to believe that Santa Anna and other leading Mexicans were in thrall to London. By 1847 Washington was told with "regret" that a "British government vessel" was headed from Havana to Vera Cruz in order to bring to Mexico "distinguished Mexican officers," e.g., "General Paredes, who was secretly landed" in an "extraordinary transaction...."[18]

James Buchanan, a future president, and Secretary of State only since March 1845, declared after the war began that the U.S. "object was not to dismember Mexico or make conquests...in going to war we did not do so with a view to acquire either California or New Mexico or any other part of the Mexican territory...." Perhaps Polk misheard this then diplomat, perhaps his words require extreme parsing to comport with reality, perhaps this was yet another example of the self-deception of early imperialism—whatever the case, Buchanan's words were false. The less credulous president "told him that though we had not gone to war for conquest...it was clear that in making peace we would if practicable obtain California and such other portions of Mexican territory as would be sufficient to indemnify our claimants on Mexico and to defray the expenses of war," a bottomless well of claims. Buchanan's timorous words may have been shaped by what else he told Polk: "he thought it almost certain that both England and France would join with Mexico in the

16. Entry, 29 March 1846, in Quaife, 309.

17. Ibid., Entry, 13 February 1846, 222, 224.

18. Letter, 18 August 1847, in "Messages of the President of the United States with the Correspondence...on the Subject of the Mexican War..." Washington: Wendell and Van Benthuysen, 1848, Huntington Library.

war against us," which left the president "much astonished at the views expressed by Mr. Buchanan...."[19]

Anti-Catholicism lurked menacingly during this war with Mexico. One study finds this pestilence to be "the single most consistent characteristic exhibited by [Euro-]American travelers in Europe from 1750 through 1860," rivaled by "hatred toward England" which "was never far below the surface of early national culture."[20] The former helps explain why Polk was heartened by the enlistment of "Bishop Hughes" of New York, essential for "disabusing the minds of the Catholic priests & people of Mexico" and dismissing the "false impressions...of the hostile designs of this country on their religion" or "church property" for that matter—a "false idea" he assured. The president inquired "whether some of the priests of the U.S. who spoke the Spanish language could be induced to accompany our army as chaplains and others to visit Mexico in advance of the army...."[21]

The Presbyterian missionary Melinda Rankin envisioned Texas—and its spreading tentacles—"as an agent to operate upon the Papal power in Mexico" since "Romanism still lingers in the Rio Grande valley...."[22]

Polk was also ambivalent at best about General Winfield Scott leading his troops; he felt his "administration" was not "safe in [en] trusting the command of the army in the Mexican war" to him, given "his bitter hostility towards the administration...."[23] Scott, perhaps the most successful U.S. military figure between the secession from London in the late 18th century through the U.S. Civil War, also was a challenger for the White House on the Whig Party ticket in 1852[24]; he may have tipped his antislavery credentials which emerged during the civil war to the consternation of President Polk or his Secretary of the Treasury, Robert Walker of Mississippi, who boldly and rashly said "he would be fighting...the whole world" in order to reinstall slavery in Mexico.[25]

---

19. Entry, 13 May 1846, in Quaife, 395.

20. Kilbride, 115, 2.

21. Entry, 19 May 1846 in Quaife, 407.

22. Melinda Rankin, *Texas in 1850*, Boston: Damrell & Moore, 1850, 54.

23. Entry, 21 May 1846, in Quaife, 415.

24. Timothy Johnson, *Winfield Scott: The Quest for Military Glory*, Lawrence: U Press of Kansas, 1998. See also Joel Sibley, *Storm Over Texas: The Annexation Controversy and the Road to Civil War*, New York: Oxford U Press, 2005.

25. Entry, 30 June 1846, in Quaife, 495.

Walker's idea was not his alone, as the Texas legislature demanded the same, combined with the cession of the bulk of Mexico.[26] James Freaner, Trist's comrade, as of September 1847 was mulling the explosive notion that "if we did annex...states of Mexico, Puebla, Vera Cruz, San Luis, Guanajuato, Guadalajara...the North would never consent to the existence of slavery in any of them," so what would be the point? Would these potential new joiners to the federal union only serve to strengthen the sectional rival? He thought to "allow them all the rights and immunities which we as free [sic] citizens enjoy could bring about a state of affairs, which would endanger the existence of our own free [slaveholding] institutions...." What may have influenced Freaner's dour outlook was his receipt of "daily reports" from Mexico during the war "of the rising of the populace and assassination of our army...."[27]

This included "murder, poisoning" and "assaults." The future Mississippi governor, John Quitman, who gained experience as a Military Governor in Mexico, denounced the "rebellious and incendiary spirit" he found among the local press, which required a severe crackdown. "If we put our heads outside the gates of the city," he complained, "we get our throats cut"[28]—a deterrent to annexation. By September 1847 there was a raucous revolt in Mexico City targeting the invaders; gaining valuable experience soon to be deployed against Washington was the future Confederate leader, P.G.T. Beauregard, and a raft of future post-1861 secessionists. In Mexico they received a foretaste of what they were to receive a decade and a half later: On a daily basis U.S. soldiers were slated for assault and/ or assassination throughout their unwanted presence in Mexico City, while the invaders scorned and brutalized those they encountered.[29]

This jarring experience was shared by other future Confederates too. Robert E. Lee played a prominent part in this invasion, sharpening his martial skills. His older brother, Lieutenant Sidney Smith Lee,

---

26. "Resolutions of the Legislature of Texas, Protesting Against the Relinquishment by the United States of Conquered Mexican Provinces or States in their Possession without Indemnity; and Also Against Any Law Which Shall be intended to Prevent the Citizens of Slaveholding States from taking their Property with Them in Emigrating to Said Acquired Territory," 28 February 1848, 30th Congress, 1st Session, House of Representatives, Miscellaneous No. 27, Baylor U.

27. Freaner column, 17 September 1847 in Gaff and Gaff, 174.

28. Ibid., Freaner columns, 17 and 28 September 1847, 7 October 1847, 25 November 1847, 212, 215, 227, 285.

29. Cox, 173, 176., 198.

was involved in the bombardment of Vera Cruz, while the younger Lee was wounded during the storming of Chapultepec. Then so hardened, he along with yet another future rebel, Kirby Smith, was posted to Texas where he was involved in routing Indigenes and chasing Mexican hero Juan Cortina.[30] Mexico's resistance also proved to aid Washington too in that fierce pro-slavery fighters, e.g., Pierce Butler of South Carolina, were killed on the battlefield south of the border, thus sparing soldiers of the federal union from executing this task.[31]

There was not just a continuity between the war in Mexico and the U.S. Civil War. A number of the invaders had sharpened their military acumen by warring against Indigenes. John Abercrombie, for example, fought them in Florida before moving on to Mexico[32]—as did James Duncan[33] and a number of others. For U.S. and rebel officers during the Civil War, Mexico—along with analogous conflicts in Florida and the Midwest (Black Hawk War)—served as a training ground.[34]

By late 1847, as the conflict in Mexico seemed to be winding down, President Polk's annual message continued to scorn this southern neighbor for "not appreciating our forbearance" as the "Mexican people generally became hostile to the United States [and] availed themselves of every opportunity to commit the most savage excesses upon our troops. Large numbers of the population took up...arms and engaging in guerrilla warfare, robbed and murdered in the most cruel manner individual soldiers, or small parties...bands of guerilleros [sic] and robbers infested the roads, harassed our trains...." He found this all hard to fathom though he acknowledged that the invading U.S. military continued to "draw supplies...from the enemy without paying for them...."[35]

Walker's unsurprising démarche, calling for overturning abolition in Mexico, met with pushback, perhaps because of Buchanan's fear that it would bring bloody conflict with European powers. "Fierce and violent discussion" erupted, said the president, along

---

30. A.L. Long, ed.,with the assistance of Marcus J. Wright, *Memoirs of Robert E. Lee, His Military and Personal History...*, New York: Stoddart, 1886, 47, 53, 77.

31. Note in Gaff and Gaff, 143.

32. Ibid., Column, 25 November 1847, 304.

33. Ibid., Note, 135.

34. Lewis, 57.

35. President Polk's Annual Message, 7 December 1847, in J.B. Moore, Volume VII, 466.

with "mischievous & wicked agitation" when discussion emerged concerning the fraught point that "slavery shall never exist in any territory which we may acquire from Mexico...."[36] Tempers were not quelled when a bill was introduced into the House of Representatives "on the subject of slavery, which had produced much sensation in the body" said Polk. "The Slavery Question," said the president, "is assuming a fearful & most important aspect" that could "ultimately threaten the Union itself...." In a naïve attempt at misdirection, Polk advised Olympically that slavery "has and can have no legitimate connection with the war with Mexico or the terms of peace...."[37]

President Polk also had to execute some fancy footwork to keep the Church of Latter Day Saints of today's Utah at bay, where they were busily building a kind of theocracy. He formed a LDS battalion to help foil an anti-Washington revolt that could have led to London's intervention on the side of the rebels. There was also a fear that LDS would use the cover of war as a cover for revenge against their many real and imagined foes. Their movement away from abolitionism certainly helped their image in Washington—though it complicated their image among the nascent Republican Party—founder Joseph Smith's prophesies of a civil war arising out of the horror of slavery and their own premature secessionism set aside.[38]

*   *   *

The Comanches, the "Lords of the Plains," may have been seduced by their mid-1846 meeting with President Polk, who told his diary that he conferred with "between 40 and 50 chiefs and braves of the Comanche and other bands and tribes of wild Indians from the prairies in the north of Texas" and he was at pains in "assuring them that they might rely upon the friendship and protection of the U.S."[39]— yet another unkept pledge.

Comanche leadership should have recognized that the land hunger that drove war endangered their very existence, mandating urgent consultations in London, perhaps St. Petersburg. For equally indicative is the point that the U.S. Congress voted overwhelmingly

36. Entry, 16 January 1846, in Quaife, Volume II, 330.

37. Ibid., Entry, 4 January 1847, 304.

38. Dirkmaat, 99, 140, 292, 355, 393. See also Heman Hale Smith, "The Lyman Wight Colony in Texas, 1846-1858," Huntington Library.

39. Entry, 1 July 1846 in Quaife, Volume II, 1. See also U.S. Congress, Senate. 29th Congress, 1st Session, Message to the President...Comanche Indians..., 1845.

for war with Mexico—40 to 2 in the Senate with a similar proportion in the House assenting.[40]

As war against Mexico was unfolding in June 1846, Congressman John Hale took to the floor of the House of Representatives and provocatively waved the words of the pro-slavery bloc. The recently deceased Secretary of State Abel Upshur was cited for the proposition that "the greatest calamities the United State could experience are…1st, 'the establishment of a predominating British influence'" in Texas and the companion of same: "'the abolition of domestic slavery in Texas….'" Mississippi's Robert Walker as early as 1844 had threatened disunion unless annexation was placed on the fast track and went further by emphatically threatening a rival bloc in its stead to challenge a debilitated Washington, i.e., "'*separation of the South and Southwest from the North and their re-union with Texas,*'" which was to occur by 1861. In the face of strictures against slave trading, he promised virtually in any case "a system of unbounded smuggling through Texas into the West and Southwest." As he was then serving in Washington as Secretary of the Treasury, his threat to undermine the influence of the government he was serving at the highest level could not be ignored easily.[41]

The ubiquitous presence of Mississippians and Carolinians like Wigfall, along with the salience of the matter of slavery and dispossession, preordained the turbo-charging of racism, a constituent element of U.S.-Texas formation in any event. The scholar Brian DeLay asserts accurately that "race could never have the same discourse potency for Mexicans that it did for Tex[ans] and Americans [meaning Euro-Americans], for the simple reason that Mexico was a republic comprised mostly of Indians and Mestizos…." [42] In a war driven by racism, Mexico then was disadvantaged.

George Gordon Meade, a premier U.S. military leader who earned his spurs fighting Indigenes in Florida, then Mexicans, was

40. Grandin, 88. See also "Messages of the President of the United States: with the Correspondence, Therewith Communicated Between the Secretary of War and Other Officers of the Government Upon the Subject of the Mexican War: 30th Congress, 1st Session: Executive Document No. 56, House of Representatives, 1845-1849," Washington: Wendell and Benthuysen, 1848, Huntington Library (abbrev. Messages of the President, 1848).

41. "Speech of John P. Hale Upon the Slavery Resolutions in the House of Representatives, June 25th, 1846," NYHS. See also "Letter from John P. Hale of New Hampshire to His Constituents on the Proposed Annexation of Texas," Washington, D.C.: Blair & Rives, 1845, AAS.

42. DeLay, 206.

contemptuous of the denizens of Monterrey, Mexico, and "their mixture with the Indian and negro race and the effect of climate" which
was—supposedly—"enervating them, render[ing] them a listless
race, destitute of the energy necessary for a war which is solely one
of enterprise."[43] The columnist James Freaner said with confidence
in late 1847 that the "Anglo Saxon race will eventually possess and
govern" Mexico and in the process "sweep from existence the degenerate race which now cumbers the land."[44] In short, annexation then
war against Mexico was a spectacular setback for Africans and the
Indigenous.

Nonetheless, a number of U.S. nationals asserted that it was they
who were the targets of bias. That was the audacious claim of E.J.
Harrison of New Orleans, who wrote at length about being taken by
Mexicans during the epochal battle of Goliad in 1835; he denounced
the "dark browned swarthy Mexican[s]" who presided over his "captivity during which period I had been sold—actually sold as a slave,"
he said with bewilderment; it was not just him, he was "in company
with half a dozen others," i.e., "Americans," who were designated to
work in mines "seven hundred feet below the surface of the earth...."
The ultimate indignity, he intimated, was when his captors "called me
a slave," for then, said Harrison, "I felt my blood boil.... I should have
beat his brains out with my hammer"; during the turmoil of war, he
managed to escape to New Orleans by September 1847—though his
profound resentment of "inhuman Mexicans" remained intact.[45] This
waspish viewpoint was shared by H.H. McConnell, who argued that
Mexicans "like all mixed races" were "more or less degraded...."[46]

These rancid attitudes were imbibed readily, as exemplified by the
1846 arrival in the borderlands of F.A. Wislizenus who announced
beamingly, "I am a German by birth and an American by choice"; yet
he was there long enough to find a "deep rancour of the Indian race
against the white has continued to the present time" and, yes, "the
principal ingredient in the Mexican race is Indian blood," implicating

---

43. George Meade, *The Life and Letters of George Gordon Meade, Major General United States Army, Volume I*, Scribner's, 1913, 120 (abbrev. Meade).

44. Column, October 1847 in Gaff and Gaff, 271.

45. *The Thrilling, Startling and Wonderful Narrative of Lieutenant Harrison
who was Taken Prisoner at Goliad in 1835...by the Inhuman Mexicans...*, Cincinnati: Author, 1848, Huntington Library.

46. H.H. McConnell, Five Years a Cavalryman, *or Sketches of Regular
Army on the Texas Frontier, 1866-1871*, Norman: U of Oklahoma Press, 1996,
[originally published Jacksboro, Texas: Rogers, 1889], Huntington Library
(abbrev. H.H. McConnell).

this southern neighbor in the presumed dislike. However, like other invaders, he praised the women he encountered and denounced the men. He was pleased with his arrival in Monterrey since "most of the stores at least belonged to the Americans...." He also had an expansive view in that starting from Independence, Missouri, he spotted signposts pointing to Oregon—though, he added cogently, "Japan, China, the East Indies, etc. might have been added...."[47]

Likewise, the roving columnist James Freaner, when he alighted in Mexico City, lusted longingly in pursuit of the "ladies of Mexico." This was part of a larger strategy, he considered: do not just annex Mexico, he asserted but "annex her daughters,"[48] or marry them, which would deliver the added "benefit" of being in position to have a firmer hold on the nation's resources and land. To that end, a fellow journalist declared, "'I would not be surprised if our army was to remain in the country for a few years, to see this republic inhabited by a white population,'"[49] in a kind of conquest by rape and prevaricated marriage.

Protestations notwithstanding, Mexicans had a more plausible expectation that it was they who were on the verge of enslavement by the invaders. After all, the invaders had fetishized enslavement and exterminated Indigenes. Alternatively, there were those Mexicans who felt that those victimized by barbarity north of the border would take advantage of the bloody war by rebelling, providing a breather to those then being invaded. When some U.S. soldiers defected to the Mexican side, it underlay the idea that somehow, some way, the war of aggression would backfire.[50]

Certainly the backlash against years of U.S. maltreatment of Mexicans was felt intensely by some Euro-Americans. Stephen Smith was released from prison in Mexico just before the invasion and was endlessly irked about the "worst of bad treatment" he endured; his goal then was to "embark for California," still under Mexican rule, however, where—presumably—he could exact revenge upon the "cruel and unjust conduct" to which he had been subjected. "The account of damages will be very great," he assured, as he promised to inform "my friend the Hon. John C. Calhoun," who would undoubtedly

47. F.A. Wislizenus, *Memoir of a Tour to Northern Mexico Connected with Colonel Doniphan's Expedition in 1846 and 1847*, Washington: Tipping & Streeper, 1848.

48. Column, 20 May 1848, in Gaff and Gaff, 417. See also Caughfield.

49. Column, 21 June 1848, in Gaff and Gaff, 418.

50. Guardino, 219.

be sympathetic.[51] William G. Dryden was among the U.S. nationals who was roughed up in Mexico; he was spotted by a compatriot with "iron bars round his legs weighing about 30 pounds," this after disputes involving his contracting to do engineering work in Chihuahua.[52] The swirling controversy surrounding alleged misdeeds of Mexicans served to justify atrocities against these purported victimizers.[53]

In order to generate the requisite bloodlust, the invaders had to convince themselves they were the party being wronged. Writing in 1846, Waddy Thompson, longtime U.S. diplomat, was upset when he saw Santa Anna, the Mexican leader, ensconced in "a very splendid barouche drawn by four American horses and I am ashamed to say driven by an American. I can never become reconciled," he sputtered, "to seeing a native American performing the offices of a menial servant," i.e., labor for Negroes: "no decent Southern American could be induced to drive anybody's coach or clean his shoes," and it was possible if the war had gone in a different direction, his dystopia would have become reality.[54]

Somehow the enslavers honed a pervasive sense of grievance, as if they were the victims. This approach was summarized by the South Carolina legislature's Committee on Federal Relations in 1847 when it contended that the war was "commenced by an invasion of our soil & the slaughter of our countrymen"; thus, "the United States were not only bound by their national honor to repel the invaders but were justifiable on every principle of public policy in carrying the war into the Enemy's own country."[55]

Inexorably, the racism and chauvinism of the invaders bled into a centuries-long anti-Catholicism, and likely spurred the anti-immigrant Know Nothing movement that soon was to arise. Naturally, Robert Walker was among those who deployed harsh and scalding religiosity to generate bellicosity. Henry Wise, who was to preside over the execution of the heroic John Brown in the following decade, wanted to plunder church wealth in Mexico and throughout

---

51. Stephen Smith to Consul John Black, 10 June 1845, Despatches of U.S. Consuls in Mexico City, Reel 4, NARA.

52. "Claims Against Mexico...Commission of 1848...Undocketed Claim No. 8...," Huntington Library.

53. Isaac George, *Heroes and Incidents of the Mexican War Containing Doniphan's Expedition...*, Greensburg, Pa.: Review, 1903, 31, 135.

54. Waddy Thompson, *Recollections of Mexico*: New York: Wiley and Putnam, 1846, 216 (abbrev. Thompson).

55. CFR, 1847, #82.

the hemisphere. Waddy Thompson provided dazzling visions of the wealth to be gleaned by seizing gold and silver crucifixes, gem-imbued statues and gilded altars. As had been the case for centuries, invidiously comparing the skin color and intelligence of Mexicans to Africans was deemed a suitable rationale for pillaging. Such horrid attitudes underpinned atrocities perpetrated by the invaders that generally went unpunished, along with desecration of churches. Cession of all of Mexico was an insistent demand.[56]

It was Thompson who noticed "a good many Negroes in Vera Cruz, probably more than in any other part of Mexico...." In that regard he viewed Santa Anna warily as a possible vector of abolitionism: "five feet ten inches high," his "complexion"—suspiciously—was "of an olive cast but" thankfully "not indicating any mixture of blood...."[57]

Inevitably, the dislocation and profit-seeking of war meant more enslaved Africans began to flow into Texas, along with disputes about this valuable property,[58] which was not conducive to enslaver unity in the face of showdowns with abolitionist and antislavery forces. Expectedly, the former Free Negro kidnapped into slavery, Solomon Northrup, recalled the sorrow in slave quarters as Mexico lost the war, perhaps recognizing that a sanctuary for the enslaved had been breached.[59]

The rigidity of pro-slavery forces reflected the profundity and magnitude of their immense victory with annexation, followed swiftly by the conquest of a good deal of Mexican territory. At the same time, it is likely that the setback to their cause served to radicalize abolitionists, making them more susceptible to the conclusion that only a shattering confrontation would bring delivery from slavery.[60]

"There never was a period," claimed Mississippi's Robert Walker in 1844, "when the South was in so much danger as at this moment...," mandating extreme measures of violence. He unleashed a brutal

---

56. John Christopher Pinheiro, "Crusade and Conquest: Anti-Catholicism, Manifest Destiny and the United States-Mexican War of 1846-1848," U of Tennessee-Knoxville, 2001, 3, 28, 31,123, 135, 140, 148, 192, 230.

57. Thompson, 5.

58. "In the Supreme Court of the State of Texas...January Term 1851..., Fowler, Clepper, et al., Appellants vs. George Stoneum, Appellee...." KF 220, T49, 1847, n. 7, NYHS.

59. Gassner, 27.

60. Appleton and Palfrey. See also "Speech of Hon. S.A. Douglas, of Illinois on the War with Mexico and the Boundary of the Rio Grande Delivered in the Senate of the United States, Tuesday, February 1, 1848," Washington: Congressional Globe, 1848, Huntington Library.

assault on Whigs hostile to his views, especially Joshua Giddings of Ohio[61]; such attacks helped to push this Congressman toward "Free Soil" forces, then the ultimately triumphant anti-slavery Republican Party. In other words, the extremism of enslavers ultimately backfired in pushing their antagonists toward more forceful measures that eventuated in expropriation of their most prized possession: Africans.

The Whig Party was not the only victim of the enhanced federal union. Independent Texas was reeling in the runup to 1845, then the war with Indigenes flexing their muscles against settlers. But now able to call upon the bulked-up union, while dangling land grants before mesmerized settlers, attracting them in droves, the literal ground beneath the feet of the original inhabitants of Texas began to recede— as did they. Thus, in 1842 Anson Jones received the anxious message from Fannin County that "considerable excitement prevails…in consequence" of "Mexican emissaries…among the Wild Indians… enlisting them in behalf of Mexico to wage a war of extermination against Northern Texas." The southern neighbor had "succeeded with the Kickapoos—Waco, Shawnee, Delaware, Coushatta and a portion of the Cherokee and Creek"—but, alas, annexation followed by war sounded the tocsin on the heyday of Indigenes, and instead, "extermination" was visited upon them.[62]

A participant in this carnival of blood was John Joel Glanton of Texas, a prominent scalper in Sonora who, like many, could not tell the difference between Mexicans and Indigenes so—says scholar Joseph Allen Stout—"soon became the scourge of both." He was prominent among those who thought the U.S. should have annexed Sonora and Baja California during or after the war.[63] Annexing more Mexican soil would presumably blunt the ongoing problem of sanctuaries being provided for fleeing Africans or raiding Indigenes:

61. Robert Walker, "The South In Danger; being a Document Published by the Democratic Association of Washington, D.C. for the Circulation in the South and Showing the Designs of the Annexation of Texas to be the Security and Perpetuation of Slavery," 1844, NYHS.

62. Thomas Farrow Smith to Anson Jones, 22 April 1842, in Winfrey, 125-126. See also Reverend L.L. Allen, *A Thrilling Sketch of the Life of the Distinguished Chief Okah Tubbee, Alias William Chubbee, Son of the Head Chief, Mosholeh Tubbee, of the Choctaw Nation of Indians*, New York: publisher not Identified, 1848, Huntington Library.

63. Joseph Allen Stout, "The Last Years of Manifest Destiny: Filibustering in Northwestern Mexico, 1848-1862," Ph.D. dissertation, Oklahoma State U, 1971, 30, 42 (abbrev. Joseph Allen Stout, Last Years).

moving westward to the Pacific allayed part of the problem but how far south would Washington have to expand in order to resolve the entire problem? Tierra del Fuego?

Undaunted, John Hamilton joined the Texas Rangers, rapidly developing a bloodstained reputation. As the war was jutting to a close in early 1848 he informed his mother that he had enlisted for a year-long term in order to patrol the Rio Grande border "to keep Indians and Mexicans from committing depredations on the Americans and friendly Mexican traders," with the Mexicans generally being a "miserable set of beings...." Somehow he managed to think that "Americans are doing them a service to over run their country and enlighten and give [them] some idea of freedom...." He accorded these denizens the ultimate insult from his group's standpoint in proclaiming that the "poorer classes are not a particle better than our Southern Negroes...."[64]

Strikingly, when the settler George F. Ruxton arrived on the upper Arkansas River he noticed that among the "hunters" he saw were "four Delaware Indians," and "Big Nigger," who "had married a squaw from the Taos pueblo and happening to be in New Mexico with his spouse at the time of the late rising against the Americans [and] he very naturally took part with the people by whom he had been adopted. In the attack on the Indian pueblo it was said that Big Nigger particularly distinguished himself" in that "the Delaware killed nearly all who fell on the side of the Americans, his squaw loading his rifle and encouraging him in the fight...." The two "managed to escape "after the capture of the pueblo and made [their] way to the mountains on the Arkansas" and "retired" there notwithstanding "a price was put upon his head...." He was not singular in that an "Indian trader, who had just returned from the Cheyenne village at the 'Big Timber' on the Arkansas had purchased from some Koways [sic]...an American Negro...."[65]

As the war was concluding, Senator Thomas Rusk of Texas took to the floor of the chambers and unleashed a tirade, declaring that his state had been "surrounded by hostile Indians" who "settled among us" and "greatly exceeded our own population in point of numbers.... Mexican agents had been among them urging them to take

64. John Hamilton to Mother, 25 January 1848, Hamilton Correspondence.

65. George F. Ruxton, *Adventures in Mexico and the Rocky Mountains*, Glorieta, N.M.: Rio Grande Press, 1973 [originally published 1847], 284, 285. See also James Madison Cutts, *The Conquest of California and New Mexico, by the Forces of the United States in the Years 1846 & 1847*, Albuquerque: Horn & Wallace, 1965 [originally published 1847] (abbrev. Cutts).

up the tomahawk and scalping knife and exterminate the Texans...."[66] The scholar Thomas Richards, Jr., has observed that "frontier whites in both Arkansas and Texas had long warned of an Indian-Mexican alliance," and Senator Rusk would have concurred.[67]

The war itself was devastating for Indigenes in the borderlands: unbridled was a pre-existing fury against the original inhabitants of the land. Samuel Reid described Carankawas "gathering oysters to put an end to seashore and fishing" and, pressed by Texas settlers, they "resolved to put an [end to] their name forever. Murdering their women and children, the warriors sought for some uninhabited island where they could wait patiently for that death which was forever to destroy all [t]races...," this tragedy occurring in Padre Island, Texas.[68]

Other Indigenes were bent on homicide, not suicide. Weeks after the war was launched, H.L. Kinney of the U.S. noted that all U.S. troops led by General Zachary Taylor were now near Matamoros, thus the "whole western frontier is now far more exposed to the depredations of the Indians," as the "call for volunteers is...draining this whole frontier of effective men...." Understandably, a "well grounded alarm" was sounded: this was a "sober fact" and "may become the subject of historical regret...."[69] Thus, in the midst of war with Mexico in July 1846, one U.S. military officer noticed a "quite strong force of Comanches in the country somewhere on this side of the Rio Grande. They have been committing depredations on the inhabitants and they [the latter] are all scared to death."[70]

By 1850 with the bone and sinew of the federal union added to Texas's flabbiness, a treaty was brokered between Washington on the one hand and "the Comanche, Caddo, Lipan, Quapaw, Tawakoni and Waco tribes of Indians" on the other; *inter alia*, it was agreed that the latter grouping would "deliver" to the U.S. authorities "all white persons or negroes who are now among the Indians of Texas

---

66. "Speech of Mr. T.J. Rusk of Texas on the Mexican War, Delivered in the Senate of the United States, February 17, 1848," Washington: Towers, 1848, Huntington Library.

67. Richards, 269.

68. Samuel C. Reid, Jr., *The Scouting Expeditions of McCulloch's Texas Rangers or the Summer and Fall Campaign of the Army of the United States in Mexico-1846; including Skirmishes with the Mexicans..., Storming of Monterrey...*, Philadelphia: Zieber, 1848, 40.

69. H.L. Kinney to D.S. Kaufman, 14 May 1846, in Messages of the President, 1848.

70. Letter, 29 July 1846, in Ferrell, 103. See also Abert.

as prisoners or runaways," and, yes, the U.S. could use "force" in this regard. As if that were not enough, a separate article articulated that Indigenes did "agree to deliver as soon as found all runaway negroes...and not knowingly to allow [any] negro or negroes to pass through the Indian country into Mexico, without arresting him or them."[71]

In sum, a blow was administered against both the enslaved and Indigenes simultaneously. The same could be said of the Treaty of Tehuacana Creek with the Comanches and Lipan, and other such pacts which sought to undercut sanctuaries provided by Indigenes.[72]

The foregoing notwithstanding, London's delegate in Texas, writing from New Orleans, by the Spring of 1846 thought he had detected a "strange and dangerous plot against Mexico...to induce the removed Indians on the western frontier of the United States (Cherokee and other tribes) by bribes of land in then outlying Mexican regions legislatively appropriated by Texas, to press on into New Mexico and thence into California; following up that movement with other emigration...." In addition, "Comanche and kindred tribes" were being enticed too, "guaranteeing to them large tracts of these Mexican regions...." As matters evolved, this proposal proved as null and void as other pacts negotiated with Indigenes.[73] Why should settlers relinquish land to Indigenes they were busily liquidating? This was part of the ham-fisted analysis that allowed London's revolting spawn to grow and flourish.

Before the apocalypse of annexation and war, potential settlers organized via the "German Emigration Company," founded in 1842 ("mostly composed of princes and noblemen," it was announced with brio). But even then it was known that "hostile Indians" were a stumbling block and they "had to be conquered by force or by treaty"; these "dangerous tribes of hostile savages" were notably active near New Braunfels and Indianola and Fredericksburg, which necessitated the recruitment of "Colonel Jack Hays, the celebrated Indian fighter."[74]

---

71. Treaty, 10 December 1850, in Winfrey and James M. Day, compilers, *The Indian Papers of Texas and the Southwest, 1825-1916*, Austin: Texas State Historical Association, 1995, 130-136, 132.

72. Hampton, 81.

73. Charles Eliot to Earl of Aberdeen, 21 April 1846, Box 2-23/756, Texas Republic SoS.

74. "Answer to Interrogatories in Case No. 396, Mary O. Paschal, et al. vs. Theodore Evans, District Court of McCulloch County, Texas, November Term, 1893," Austin: Pemberton, 1894, reprinted 1964, Huntington Library.

Yet this U.S. victory did not sate the nation's voracious appetite but whetted its churning gastric juices for further conquests, emboldening the confrontation with London over the Oregon Territory.[75] As the war was being launched in February 1846, the U.S. consul in Mexico City, John Black, reported nervously the "rumor" that the "English minister had officially made application to [Mexico] asking...to land...twenty thousand foreign troops said to be destined for Oregon...." A former member of the cabinet there confided to Black that this eventuality was "very probable," which was part of London's devious plan to form a "monarchy" south of Texas.[76]

Significantly, London may have had an unacknowledged advantage in dealing with its former colony. As the war was being launched in 1846, Waddy Thompson of the U.S. marveled, "I never met an Englishman there that I did not feel the full force of 'the white skin and the English language,'" supposed chief advantages of Washington in Mexico.[77] W.S. Murphy, a U.S. diplomat in the region, thought it went deeper. "There is a British party in Galveston," he charged, that was "overbearing, impudent and ferocious...." Just as there was a "paper of the Americans," the "'Galveston Evening News,'" there was likewise an "organ of the British party here," the "'Galveston Civilian.'" Anticipating charges by the 1950s that the U.S. diplomatic corps had been penetrated by Moscow, then Murphy saw "Consul [A.M.] Green" of the U.S. as "the near relation by marriage of the Editor of 'Civilian' and his constant [companion]" besides.[78]

When it appeared that there was a failure of the annexation treaty with Texas, Murphy maintained to John C. Calhoun, no less, that the "the British party in Galveston are elated."[79] When the moment arrived for serious discussion of how Mexico in 1848 should be parceled and divvied up, even right-wing patriots were accused of being British agents if they were not perceived as being aggressive

---

75. Speech of Mr. E.D. Culver of New York on the Texas and Oregon Question. Delivered in the House of Representatives...January 30th, 1846, AAS. At the same site, see also Speech of Mr. Jacob Brinkerhoff of Ohio on the Annexation of Texas. Delivered in the House of Representatives. January 13th, 1845.

76. John Black to Secretary of State James Buchanan, 27 February 1846, Reel 5, Despatches from U.S. Consuls in Mexico City, NARA.

77. Thompson, 157.

78. Consul W.S. Murphy to Sir, 24 May 1844, Despatches from U.S. Ministers to Texas, 1836-1845, Reel 2, NARA.

79. Ibid., W.S. Murphy to Secretary Calhoun, 9 June 1844.

land grabbers,[80] just as in the 1950s, those insufficiently anti-Moscow were accused of being equivalent to traitors.[81]

It was not just Galveston or Vera Cruz where London's tentacles were thought to reach. In Chihuahua, Mexico, U.S. officialdom found the "British Consul" to be "offensively officious," giving "aid and comfort to the Mexicans in furnishing them to some extent, with the sinews and munitions of war...."[82] In New Mexico Josiah Gregg discovered the "notorious fact that while the English are universally treated with considerable consideration and respect..., the Americans residing in the southern parts of the republic are frequently taunted with the effeminacy of their government...."[83]

Weeks after maundering about "monarchy," Black counseled that London was planning an "addition to their force in the Pacific of four...steamers and a fifty gun ship" setup that demanded a countervailing response from the U.S.[84] By May 1846 Consul Black was verging on hysteria, as he was fed the notion that a "'larger English line of battleship [was] anchored off San Blas [Mexico] having on board a large [number] of troops and said to be bound for San Diego, Upper California," and, maybe, headed to the "'Columbia River.'"[85]

Ever devious, the U.S. strategist George Gordon Meade thought London's demonstrated interest in Oregon could be leveraged against this power. He thought that Mexico would take advantage by "prolonging the negotiations" with Washington, then "breaking them off in the hopes of assistance from England. On the other hand, England will exert all her influence with Mexico...in order to embarrass us and render us more ready to compromise upon...Oregon"—but as matters evolved, both Mexico and Britain were outmaneuvered.[86]

This amounted to payback for the 1812 war and the torching of Washington, D.C., by the redcoats in league with the enslaved, and could also lead down the road to snatching Canada, which Northern hawks long had thought could balance sectionally the annexation of

80. Column, 28 March 1848, in Gaff and Gaff, 354.

81. See e.g., Gerald Horne, *Communist Front? The Civil Rights Congress, 1946-1956*, New York: International, 2021 (abbrev. Horne, *Communist*).

82. *The Conquest of Santa Fe and Subjugation of New Mexico by the Military Forces of the United States...*, Philadelphia: H. Packer, 1847, Huntington Library (abbrev. *Conquest of Santa Fe*).

83. Gregg, 227.

84. John Black to Secretary Buchanan, 19 March 1846, Reel 5, Despatches from U.S. Consuls in Mexico City, NARA.

85. Ibid., John Black to Secretary Buchanan, 16 May 1846.

86. Meade, Volume I, 44.

Texas. President Tyler had charged London with hypocrisy in light of the "annexation" of Ireland and Scotland.[87] Lord Palmerston in London was informed by a colleague in Paris to expect an assault on Canada, for example, following the dismemberment of Mexico.[88]

There was a pecking order in the borderlands, in other words. For Mexico, Indigenes and Africans, London was seen—relatively— as an ally (France less so), while U.S. nationals were viewed more favorably (relatively) than the "Texians." (By late 1847 the journalist James Freaner anticipated what occurred during the U.S. Civil War, when France maneuvered to place a puppet on the throne in Mexico City: at this early date, he said, Paris was seeking "to place a prince [in Mexico] to govern and rule."[89]) For example, Kiowa were not alone in seeing Texians as enemies and, according to one study, were "friendly toward Americans."[90]

Events were proceeding apace with President Polk proclaiming by November 1846 that "inhabitants of the Northern Provinces of Mexico were ready to revolt & establish an independent republic & would do so if they could have a guaranty from the U.S." Secretary of State Buchanan "gave in substance the guarantees required...except- ing New Mexico and the Californias from the guaranty," already reserved for Washington.[91]

With the encouragement of Texas, Yucatan had declared indepen- dence in 1840, rejoined the nation in 1843, seceded again in 1845, then sought to reunite in 1848 while in the throes of what has been described as a "bloody race war," a gruesomeness to which "Texians" seemed oblivious in terms of "blowback" to their homesteads.[92] By early 1847 Buchanan was conferring with Don José Rovera, recorded as "commissioner [of] the Provisional Government of Yucatan," with the "purpose of re-establishing friendly and commercial rela- tions between that state and the United States" as this restive region "continued to maintain her neutrality...in the existing war between Mexico and the United States" per the "decree of the Extraordinary Congress of Yucatan...." Soon, Buchanan worried that his Mexican interlocutors "changed this neutrality into a state of hostility against the United States" as he feared that "Yucatanese are carrying on a

---

87. Rejected Treaty, June 11, 1844.

88. "Private" message to Lord Palmerston from Paris, 27 March 1847, Box 2-23/755, Texas Republic SoS.

89. Column, 13 October 1847, in Gaff and Gaff, 233.

90. Newcomb, 356.

91. Entry, 28 November 1846, in Quaife, Volume II, 253.

92. Note in Joseph and Henderson, 225.

contraband trade and furnishing Mexico with arms and ammunition of war...."[93]

By 1848, hawkish Jefferson Davis, future paramount Confederate leader, wounded Yucatan severely when he suggested an occupation of this rich territory.[94]

Sorting through the fallout and rubble in 1848 while in Marshfield, Mass., Daniel Webster concluded that it was his erstwhile comrades north of the Mason-Dixon line who "let Texas in" the federal union: "ten Senators from slaveholding states of the Whig Party, resisted Texas...but the southern Whig votes against Texas were overpowered by the Democratic votes from free states and from New England among the rest. Yes," he asserted wearily, "if there had not been votes from New England in favor of Texas, Texas would have [stayed] out of the Union to this day" in that there were "four votes in the Senate from New England in favor of the admission of Texas.... Van Buren by the wave of his hand, could have kept out Texas" but chose not to do so: "he was silent..." And why not? The illicit slave trade was dominated by Northerners who stood to benefit as Texas began to import by means mostly foul an enslaved labor force. Indeed, with annexation and the war, Galveston began to compete seriously with New Orleans as a chief distribution center for dispersing enslaved Africans.[95] Another analyst charged that Van Buren was "for abolition and against it," which was typical of the ambivalence of certain northerners about the peculiar institution and the annexation that it produced.[96]

During the war with Mexico, the settler Susan Shelby Magoffin received a glimpse of the growing strength of the Indigenous when she bumped into an "Indian chief," a "Comanche" who spoke "quite good English and some Spanish" though his intimidating presence spoke louder than words. Also speaking Spanish was another man she encountered: General Pedro Ampudia, was Cuban by birth, joined the Mexican military in 1842, and fought courageously against invaders from the north: his presence too was an emblem of a growing challenge to the invaders that would not be suppressed easily. Also in Ampudia's camp was Nicholas Pino who was implicated in

93. John Buchanan to John Mason, 22 February 1847, in J.B. Moore, Volume VII, 222.

94. Note, Rowland, Volume I, xv.

95. See also Webster Speech, 1 September 1848, Yale University. Tyler and Murphy, xxv.

96. *Colonel Crockett's Exploits and Adventures in Texas...Written by Himself*, New York: Graham, 1848, Huntington Library.

the Mexican effort to drive out U.S. officials from New Mexico and was arrested by the incoming authorities by December 1846. Perhaps more daunting for Ms. Magoffin was the report she received in January 1847: "news that the Taos people have risen and murdered every American citizen in Taos including the Governor (then on a visit there)"; his body was chopped into small bits. Ampudia was not the only soldier on the battlefield with experience beyond the immediate borders. Henry Smith Turner of the U.S. attended cavalry school in France, then participated in the invasion of California, which brought the biggest prize of the war and was wounded in the process. He was accompanied by Antoine Robidou, né Roubidoux, who served as an interpreter for the top honcho of the U.S. side, Stephen Kearny.[97]

So, annexation led to war which led to the dismembering of Mexico and the enrichment of Washington. Inexpert European diplomacy too was a causative factor explaining this debacle. But in the end this was a catastrophic victory for the slaveholders' republic in that it served to hasten the showdown that was civil war.

---

97. Drum, 112, 125, 136, 170, 184, 190.

Chapter 10

Texas, California and the Golden Aftermath of War, 1848-1851

Part of Washington's problem was that the land they wanted to swallow was already inhabited, especially by those not defined as "white"— with ousting and/or liquidating the mass as far south as Guatemala likely beyond their ken. There was an "All Mexico Movement" in the U.S. pushing for a gigantic annexation; but just like annexing Canada—yet another huge task—this garnered more support north of the Mason-Dixon Line. As for the entire seizing of Mexico: Southerners blanched at the idea of incorporating so much so-called "racial mixing," though that did not stop their hunger for Cuba, along with other targeted seizures, e.g., Nicaragua and pieces of Mexico.[1]

A big piece of the puzzle was New Mexico. For it was clear that drivers impelling both annexation and war were further enslavement and its complement, massive land grabs due west, with Santa Fe a way station on the road to the Pacific. As had been the case before 1846, afterward the state of Texas demanded more territory that belonged to Mexico, with increased enslavement of Africans in the offing. Congressman Giddings analogized what was intended for New Mexico to the earlier partition of "prostrate Poland" since "people of New Mexico loathe and abhor the Texans," and the "slave power" that predominated there.[2] Undaunted, Texas was accused by a congressman of "taking possession of four counties, said to be a part of New Mexico, by force" as more stage whispers about "disunion" and "civil war" and "secession" began to be heard.[3]

---

1. Caughfield, 135.

2. "Speech of Hon. J.R. Giddings of Ohio in the House of Representatives, Monday August 13, 1850 on the Bill Establishing the Bill Between Texas and New Mexico…," NYHS.

3. "Speech of Hon. C.H. Williams of Tennessee on the Texas and New Mexico Question Delivered in the House of Representatives, Friday August 9, 1850," NYHS.

Predictably, future Confederate leaders played a prominent role in the attack on New Mexico. Sterling Price, a future traitorous leader, was among those who scorned the "attempt to excite the people of this territory against the American government," especially the leaders there, Thomas Ortiz and Diego Archuleta. "Many of the most influential persons in the northern part of this territory," it was reported tremulously, "were engaged in the rebellion," and the "object of the insurrectionists " was "to put to death every American and every Mexican who had accepted office under the American government...."[4]

Yet another U.S. national confirmed the above, describing an "attempt to produce a revolution" that was "concerted at the house of Thomas Ortiz" designed to "take bloody possession of Santa Fe...." As with revolts of the enslaved in previous centuries, the "attempt was to have been made on Christmas night," said the analyst James Madison Cutts. However, "the whole plot was disclosed to Americans by Mexican women...." Other Mexicans, said Cutts, were "very haughty—they would jostle the Americans in the streets [and] refuse to speak with them...."[5]

This was not the first occasion when residents of New Mexico revolted against incipient U.S. and/or Texas rule. It was in 1837 when Josiah Gregg noticed that "Indians...joined the Mexican insurgents in another bloody conspiracy.... the truth is, the Pueblos in every part of Mexico have always been ripe for insurrection," although "the immediate cause of the present outbreak in the north, however, had its origin among the Hispano Mexican population...." Again, a butchering unfolded. "American traders were particularly uneasy, expecting every instant that their lives and property would fall [in] sacrifice to the ferocity of the rabble," and since the "first step of the revolutionists was to seize all the property of their proscribed or murdered victims," their uneasiness was comprehensible. "Americans were everywhere accused of being the instigators of this insurrection, which was openly pronounced another Texas affair...." Then there were "most glaring outrages upon American citizens [that] were committed in 1841" with a similar result: "the greatest excitement raged in Santa Fe against Americans, whose lives... appeared in imminent danger...."[6]

The invaders thought they had good reason to crack down on New Mexicans. In early 1847 they found that "all the Americans, without

---

4. *Conquest of Santa Fe.*
5. Cutts.
6. Gregg, Volume I, 129, 132, 133, 134, 227, 230.

distinction, throughout the state and such New Mexicans as had favored the American government...were to be massacred or driven from the country...." It seemed, it was reported, that a "mulatto girl...had married one of the conspirators," then squealed, but then a second conspiracy emerged involving "officers of the State and the priests," leading to a "rebellion" that "broke out in every part of the state simultaneously...." The result? "[T]he governor and his retinue were murdered in the most cruel and inhuman manner by the Pueblos and Mexicans...."[7]

Given their role in inciting mayhem, Daniel Webster continued to rail against Texas, which even then was threatening disunion unless her maximum demands were met: "she was ready to maintain her claim by force of arms" while "six or seven of the largest states had already taken measures looking toward secession.... troops were enlisted by her [Texas] and many thousand persons in the South disaffected toward the Union or desiring of breaking it up, were ready to make common cause with Texas; to join her ranks and see what they could make in a war to establish the right of Texas to New Mexico."[8]

Ostensibly weak, Texas was still able to drive a hard bargain because of the backup provided by her fellow enslavers in Congress and elsewhere. The so-called "Compromise of 1850" caused the state to abandon her unwarranted claims in return for the federal union assuming her massive debt,[9] an issue more complicated than it appeared at first blush,[10] involving as it did the enriching of some at the expense of others.

Congressman Charles Clarke of New York State found it difficult to accept that the alleged "compromise" provided the former rascal republic with "at least seventy thousand square miles of territory, now free, to Texas [enslavers]"; slavery was now deemed licit in a land "nine times as large as the state of Massachusetts" with the

7. John T. Hughes, *Doniphan's Expedition Containing an Account of the Conquest of New Mexico...*, Cincinnati: James, 1848, 391-393.

8. Speech, 22 May 1851, in *Daniel Webster*, Volume IV, 242.

9. Frazier, 9. On the Compromise see also Horace Mann, *Horace Mann's Letters on the Extension of Slavery into California and New Mexico: And on the Duty of the Congress to Provide the Trial by Jury for Fugitive Slaves*, Washington, D.C.: Buell and Blanchard, 1850, Huntington Library [reprinted Yellow Springs: Antioch Press, 1935] (abbrev. Mann).

10. "Petition of Citizens of New Orleans, Creditors of New Orleans of the Late Republic of Texas to the Thirty Second Congress," New Orleans: Hinton, 1852, AAS.

further "intention to make…Indian Territory into a slave state…." Ominously, "Texas passed a law extending her boundaries to the Pacific" and "she is about to pass laws to raise an army to go and seize…New Mexico," which was little more than "treason"—that was to flower by 1861.[11] There was a suspicion that Texas inside the union was more dangerous than the Lone Star state being denied representation in Washington, for now it could push aggressively for more concessions to enslavers with the support of powers from Richmond to Baton Rouge.

Congressman Giddings was livid about this deal, especially since the "people of New Mexico loath[e] and abhor the Texans," as he asked irritably, "why are we called on to consign this large portion of New Mexico…to slavery" as a compromise? "Of what possible benefit can Texas be to the Union," he asked quizzically, "since she professed to belong to it, we have been at constant and heavy expense to protect her against the miserable hordes of savages,"[12] his dismissive descriptor of the proud Indigenes.

Even as Congressman Giddings was preparing his well wrought remarks, Robert Neighbors on behalf of Texas was en route to Santa Fe with a kind of annexation in mind.[13]

The sad destiny of the Tigua ethnic group is reflective of what befell those who found themselves under Texas's jurisdiction, after losing the Mexican aegis. Early on Texas sought to bar Indigenes from federal jurisdiction, which was admittedly harsh but was mild compared to the new regime in Austin. Promptly initiated was a genocidal campaign against the Tigua; that many Euro-Texans viewed them as being actually Mexican did not bode well for either

---

11. "Speech of Hon. Charles E. Clarke of New York on the Bill Establishing the Boundary Between Texas and New Mexico Delivered in the House of Representatives, August 30, 1850," Washington, D.C.: Buell & Blanchard, 1850, NYHS. At the same site, see "Speech of D.S. Kaufman of Texas on the Slavery Question and its Adjustment Delivered in the House of Representatives, Monday, June 10, 1850," Washington: Congressional Globe, 1850. Also at this site, see "Speech of Hon. Timothy Pillsbury of Texas in the House of Representatives, August 8, 1848, On the Boundary of Texas, Slavery…."

12. "Speech of J.R. Giddings of Ohio in the House of Representatives, Monday, August 13, 1850, on the Bill Establishing the Boundaries between Texas and New Mexico," AAS.

13. "Remarks of Mr. Rusk of Texas on the Motion to Strike out the Thirty-Ninth Section of the 'Compromise Bill' being the Proposition of Texas Delivered in the Senate of the United States, June 14, 1850," Huntington Library. See also J.C. Duval, *Early Times in Texas*, Austin: Gammel, 1892.

group. The Tigua were hardly as culpable for what befell Indigenes as others, e.g., Apaches and Comanches, who found it necessary to fight Mexico fiercely, which paved the way for the 1848 disaster by draining this republic's resources, while overextending them over an expansive territory. So heartened was a giddy Texas that post-1848 it claimed not just the eastern half of New Mexico but land stretching as far north as Cheyenne, Wyoming.[14]

Texas and its U.S. partner gained even more clout in that the former declared previous pacts with Indigenes void, putting the latter in a difficult bargaining position, especially since the republicans were willing to deploy all manner of coercive violence. Simultaneously, bands of Kickapoos, Shawnees, and Delawares and a significant portion of Waco, Wichita and Tawakonies had established a lucrative trade in Indian Territory, land already being eyed hungrily by the colonizers—especially since it was thought that this trade was based on loot from Texas settlers. By 1850 Tawakonies, Caddo, and Quapaws were compelled to sign a pact binding them to return runaway Africans, yet another priority beyond taking land.[15]

Near that same time, the Cherokee ousted from their homeland years earlier in the southeastern quadrant in North America, found their new homeland in Indian Territory unsettling. "Human life in the Cherokee country is in danger—great danger," said Chief John Ross, as there was a "desperate gang of banditti—half breeds," was his descriptor, who were "notorious in this nation as wanton murderers, house burners and horse stealers," among other "bloody deeds."[16]

Comanches remained adamant. By the 1850s there were an estimated 20,000 in the vicinity and as one interloper pointed out, "they entertain an inherent dislike for the whites"; indeed, he stressed, they feel "*the whites were such great rascals*" they could not "trust" them, that there were "few, if any, *honest*, white men; showing that," he said of one leader encountered, "he entertained bitter hostility towards us."[17]

14. Scott C. Comar, "The Tigua Indians of Ysleta Del Sur: A Borderland's Community," Ph.D. dissertation, UT-EP, 2015, 3, 165, 172, 177-178 (abbrev. Comar).

15. Earl Henry Elam, "Anglo American Relations with the Wichita Indians in Texas, 1822-1859," M.A. thesis, TTU, 1967, 93, 98, 115-116 (abbrev. Elam).

16. Letter, 4 February 1846, in "Memorial of John Ross and Others...on the Subject of the Existing Difficulties in...the Cherokee Nation...and their Relations with the United States...", U.S. Congress, Senate, 29th Congress, 1st Session...: 1846," Princeton U.

17. W.B. Parker, *Notes Taken During the Expedition Commanded by Captain R.B. Marcy, USA, Through Unexplored Texas in the Summer and Fall of 1854*, Philadelphia: Hayes & Zell, 1856, 231 (abbrev. Parker, *Notes*).

Understandably. For as unsanitary settlers began traipsing across the continent toward the goldfields of California they left in their wake a cholera epidemic that devastated Comanches. In response this pulverized group began migrating southward—but this brought them into conflict with the similarly militant Apaches, a contradiction that settlers began to manipulate. The two became unreconstructed antagonists for a good deal of the period leading to Reconstruction's 1876 demise. Per previous praxis, Comanches often prevailed on the plains but were often outmatched in the hills where Apaches were the true lords.[18]

Tragically, more illuminative of the disastrous impact of the settler victory over Mexico and the weakening of the ability of this state to back Indigenes across the border was the sharp decline in the strength of Texas's Tonkawa, who by the 1850s were on a slippery slope of misery from a heyday of renown for creating warriors. Sadly, they began allying with settlers in battling Comanches, who in turn looked upon so-called "reservation Indians" as enemies and raided them—and settlers too. The next step on the road of decline for the Tonkawa was their alignment with secessionist rebels. Of course, they found it difficult to be neutral or even support the federal union when leaders of this formation often espoused liquidation of all Indigenes and, to that end, allowed Texas to retain "control" of public lands, unlike other states, which empowered the most murderous impulses of settlers.[19]

Arguably, a strategic blunder was committed by the Tonkawa when they allied with settlers generally—even before joining the secessionists. Their leader, Placido, fought against the Cherokees in 1839 and against Comanches at the Battle of Plum Creek in 1840 (though his mother was allegedly a Comanche captive). He served as a scout for settlers before the instrumental Battle of Antelope Hills of the 1850s and led assaults against famed Comanche chiefs, including Iron Jacket and Peta Nocona. Yet Placido and his compatriots, who had done so much for settlers, were still expelled during the 1850s and placed on a reservation in Indian Territory. Even then he refused to cooperate with Washington during the U.S. Civil War and retained allegiance to the Lone Star State. His Negro counterpart might be Britton (Brit) Johnson, born enslaved but winning freedom, and by 1860 he was an orderly for officers at Fort Belknap, Texas, established to repel Kiowa and Comanche alike. Yet he too settled

18. Wallace and Hoebel, 149, 288.
19. Newlin, 57, 60, 73, 80, 104, 106.

with the settlers, becoming a noted scout and Indian fighter before he was killed by Indigenes in 1871. It would be proper to infer that Indigenes and Negroes, at least individually, often thought they could not overcome the potency of settlers and thus had to cut deals with them instead, despite their unreliability and violent venality.[20]

A telling sign postwar was the rapid exodus southward to Mexico by numerous Indigenes. Mexico argued that a good deal of this southward migration was involuntary. Such was the case with the remnants of the Karankawa [Carancahua], pulverized by the rascal republicans, then driven post-1848 into Mexico.[21] The Seminole leader known as "Wild Cat" was born in Florida and became a ferocious battler against settlers, before leading an evacuation westward. By 1849, like a latter-day Tecumseh, he was conferring with Caddo, Comanche and Waco, urging that they join him and his people in Mexico. Reputedly he pledged to avoid warring against those deemed to be "Wild Indians," reassurance to the Comanche often labeled with this intended insult but, instead, would unite with them. The Seminoles were known to incorporate runaway Africans, and it was estimated that in their northern Mexico redoubt there were "three thousand colored men…." Finally, Texas settlers had had enough: by 1855, led by J.H. Callahan, they crossed the border with the supposed intent of punishing antagonistic Lipan Apache but actually to retrieve the valuable commodity that was enslaved Africans. Soon Negroes themselves retaliated, as an insurrection was plotted in Colorado County with guns, pistols and ammunition found and 200 plotters detained. Three were hanged. Two were whipped to death. The rest were severely flogged. The entire Mexican population was expelled, for it was thought they were unindicted co-conspirators.[22] Since the enslaved intended to fight their way to Mexico, this contributed to the draconian decision.[23] Moreover, taken seriously by the rapacious republicans were the stories about Santa Anna seeking to foment a rebellion of the enslaved in the U.S., which one student of the period states was "not impossible."[24]

---

20. Thomas Cutrer, "'My Wild Hunt Indians': The Journal of Willis L. Lang, First Lieutenant, Waco Rangers, 23 April-7 September," n.d., UOk-N (abbrev. Cutrer).

21. *Report of the Committee of Investigation 1873.* See also R.N. Richardson, 77.

22. Manuscript on 1849-1850, Box 23, Porter Papers. For more on "Wild Cat" see James M. Smallwood, "Black Texans During Reconstruction, 1865-1874," Ph.D. dissertation, TTU, 1974, 62 (abbrev. Smallwood).

23. Smallwood, 66.

24. Baumgartner, 209.

Callahan's crew were among the professional slave hunters stationed along the border, who at times wandered into Mexico and sought to kidnap Free Negroes and drag them into Texas slavery. In response Mexico often sought to move this targeted group deeper into the interior.[25] Among those who made it to the interior was Alex Washington, described as a "black man"; unfortunately he suffered an "inflammation of the bowels," said the U.S. envoy in Acapulco, and was "accidentally left" behind by a departing steamer and expired; he "was a seaman and left no effects whatever."[26]

Texas extremists often berated the purported pusillanimity of Washington that curbed a more aggressive approach to battling along the border—and this became a rationale for secession in 1861. This attitude was captured in extraordinary remarks of Senator Rusk of Texas. In 1850 he took to the floor of this chamber and proclaimed that "when Texas with less than thirty thousand inhabitants...was struggling against a nation of eight millions of people that were overrunning the country and threatening extermination," it survived, though "Indians belonging to the United States, who had been driven to our borders, were in our territory...warring upon our wives and children. On the day that I was engaged in the Battle of San Jacinto, my wife and children had to take refuge with the late gallant Gen. Gaines on this side of the Sabine, to avoid being scalped by the Indians of the United States, from whom this Government was bound by solemn treaty to protect them...." Senator Houston then interjected, "and whose annuities were paid in ammunition in arms...." Continuing, Senator Rusk said, "with one tribe of Indians [Caddo] the United States made a treaty requiring them to go into the territory of Texas and never return within the limits of the United States and under that treaty they were supplied with $10,000 worth of powder, lead and arms which were used in war upon our defenceless wives and children. When pursued they would retreat into the territory of the United States" and "this state of things has not ceased even now...." Speaking as if he were still representing a separate regime and not as an elected representative of same, he exhorted, "four or five hundred of your Indians, driven out of Florida and other states, are upon the soil of Texas and engaged...in hostilities and depredations";

---

25. James David Nichols, "The Limits of Liberty: African Americans, Indians and Peons in the Texas-Mexico Borderlands, 1820-1860," Ph.D. dissertation, State U of New York-Stony Brook, 2012, 213, 223 (abbrev. Nichols 2012).

26. A.A. McClure to Secretary of State Daniel Webster, 19 May 1851, Reel 1, Despatches from U.S. Consuls in Acapulco, NARA.

"such wrong and degradation," he said with a flourish, should end forthwith.[27]

But Texans—even those at the pinnacle of power, like Rusk—were often blithely unaware of the calculations of global policy, which meant taking account of London and, at times, Paris, when contemplating encroachments in Mexico. Yet Mexico did not perceive restraint from Washington; by early 1850 their envoy Luis de la Rosa was outraged by the presence of alien troops from their neighbor lolling in Piedras Negras near Aguila; they "introduced themselves into the Mexican territory in the state of Coahuila," he added, then "beat and outraged two or three citizens…in order to carry away by force…a coloured man who was there, a fugitive from Texas."[28] The reality was that as late as 1851 and beyond, the states of Coahuila, Tamaulipas and Nuevo León were—according to Washington's Major General John Wool—"as much under the authority of the United States, as any state of the American union,"[29] in a kind of creeping annexation.

In 1850 Secretary of State John Clayton was told of the presence of a U.S. national in Chihuahua, born auspiciously in soon-to-be-secessionist South Carolina, who resided in Mexico 21 years and was "well-known to General Taylor" who spearheaded the invasion of Mexico in the first instance. He was said to be a "true American you have only to command,"[30] as if annexation had not ended with Texas. In 1851 the news from Mazatlán was about "rumors that parties of Americans were organizing in the state of California and the Rio Grande…for the purpose of invading Lower California…," in the vicinity of today's Mexican metropolis that is Tijuana. As a result, the U.S. consul, R.R. Galton, found a "strong prejudice here against American citizens…caused by the large number of unprincipaled [sic] and lawless Americans" who were "committing robberies and depredations of various kinds…."[31]

27. "Speech of Mr. Rusk of Texas in Reply to Mr. Benton in Relation to the Boundaries of the State of Texas, Delivered in the Senate of the United States, July 16, 1850," Washington: Towers, 1850, Huntington Library.

28. Luis de la Rosa to Secretary of State John Clayton, 15 March 1850, in Manning, Volume IX, Mexico, Washington, D.C.: Carnegie, 1938, 350.

29. *A Narrative of Major General [John] Wool's Campaign in Mexico in the Years 1846, 1847 & 1848*, Albany: Little, 1851, 56.

30. Consul to Secretary Clayton, 27 August 1850, Reel 1, Despatches from U.S. Consuls in Chihuahua, NARA.

31. R.R. Galton, Consul to Secretary of State Webster, 2 July 1851, Reel 2, Despatches from U.S. Consuls in Mazatlan, NARA.

This brigandage ironically contributed to unrivaled animus toward "Wild Cat" on the part of settlers, as he was accused credibly of conspiring repeatedly against them.[32] The perception was that he and his people were less hostile to Africans than settlers. Mexicans added to the volatility since they were thought to be more willing to welcome this "mixed" body into their homes and churches.[33] Today, there is a sizable community of Indigenous-African descendants in Brackettville, Texas, adjacent to San Antonio, and the offspring of the postwar sojourners.[34]

Yet also attracting the animosity of settlers were the Kickapoo, forced from the Great Lakes region to Indian Territory (and Kansas) and Texas, then Mexico, where they allied with the military and became feared by settlers as a result.[35] Although settlers often were able to repress pre-existing tensions between Protestants and Catholics and Christians and Jews, one explanation for the far-reaching defeat of Indigenes was their seeming inability to act similarly. Thus, Kickapoo often despised Pawnee, who in return frequently harassed the former. Then after 1836, as the victorious settlers sought to compel all Indigenes in the eastern section of the new republic to remove to Indian Territory, Kickapoo objected and were encouraged by Mexican comrades, and thus began their repeated attacks that lasted until the 1880s—although one of their many victories was a stinging defeat of Confederates at the Battle of Dove Creek in Texas in January 1865.[36] Ironically, numerous Indigenes and Africans rescued Washington during the Civil War—and were repaid insultingly with further dispossession.

This led to a grassroots settler crusade to exterminate Indigenes, with governments threatened with mayhem and overthrow if they failed to comply—the nucleus of fascism, in other words. Washington was establishing reservations instead, intensifying hostility to federal union and, presumably, paving the way for Texas secession. A December 1850 treaty brokered with the Comanche was indicative of allied interests of settlers insofar as they were not allowed to let Negroes pass through their land into Mexico but were pledged to transport them to settler hands instead. Besides Comanche, Caddo, Lipan, Tawakoni (related to the Wichita) and Waco were also induced

---

32. J.D. Riley, 71.

33. Smallwood, 63.

34. "The Hawkins' Negroes go to Mexico: A Footnote from Tradition," Box 28, Porter Papers.

35. Koch, 223-234, 229, 230.

36. Unclear author, "The Southern Kickapoos: A Study in Nineteenth Century Cultural Persistence," ca. 1983, UOk-N.

to ink such an agreement. Like finagling lawyers, the settlers none-theless refused to recognize any Indigenous claims to the land, treaty language aside. Also magnifying settler anger was the inability of Washington, which assumed ultimate jurisdiction in Texas—via the Supremacy Clause of the vaunted U.S. Constitution—by 1845. Texas, sitting alongside a Mexico with little incentive to cooperate with its former province, was an attractive site for Indigenes pressed else-where and in search of wherewithal. This appeared to be the case for the Cherokee and Choctaw displaced to Indian Territory years earlier—though the Kickapoos, according to one pro-settler analysis, were "the worst," all of which increased the frequency and decibel level of the repetitive cries for "extermination."[37]

The critique of Washington persisted, though by 1850 the regime was spending about $200 million on various conflicts with Indigenes, billions in contemporary terms.[38] Comanche were a prime victim of this process, though they too had allied with settlers, including in battling Mormons in the 1850s.[39]

There was a kind of perverse "domino theory" generated by U.S. expansionism: since Mexico was thought to provide sanctuary to fleeing and valuable Negroes and raiding Indigenes as well, the impulse was created to grab more territory southward. Furthermore, by 1852 Washington was informed about events in Tehuantepec, the shortest distance between the Gulf of Mexico and the Pacific Ocean and, thus, a possible shortcut to the recently seized California. The U.S. envoy kept tabs on the "number of troops, about six hundred" there that "has not been increased, although the country is full of rumors of the designs and intentions of the Americans to possess themselves of the Isthmus."[40]

It was not just the isthmus. By the Spring of 1851 up to 5000 U.S. nationals were visiting Acapulco but, said their envoy there, they were subject to "abuses." He wanted battleships "stationed" there,[41] yet another reason for annexation.

---

37. Koch, 259-286, 265, 266, 272, 279, 281, 282, 283.

38. Howard Lackman, "The Howard-Neighbors Controversy: A Cross-Section in West Texas Indian Affairs," *Panhandle Plains Historical Review*, unclear provenance, UOk-N.

39. Brad Agnew, "The 1858 War Against the Comanches," *Chronicles of Oklahoma*, 211-229, 219, UOk-N.

40. Charles Webster to State Department, 8 May 1852, Reel 1, Despatches from U.S. Consuls in Tehuantepec, NARA.

41. A.A. McClure to Daniel Webster, 19 May 1851, Reel 1, Despatches from U.S. Consuls in Acapulco, NARA.

A further impediment to seizing more Mexican territory was the abject resistance that U.S. nationals received there whenever they showed their pasty faces, a resistance backed adamantly by London. Reporting from Mazatlán, Mexico, just before hostilities erupted in 1846, Consul John Parrott urged that naval forces be sent to the future Golden State: "not a moment should be lost," he advised, "in taking possession of that important country," though he knew that "our flag may be waving over California this very moment...." Inevitably, British vessels continued to "throw obstacles in the way and endeavor to prevent our taking possession of California"—"they will not do so," he pledged. While in Mazatlán there was "much excitement" and it was "unsafe to appear in the streets," local fortitude was bolstered since the "Mexican government confidentially expects that England will espouse her cause...." This was an emblem of the point that "Mexico may be said to be completely in the hands of the English"; still, he thought it "advisable our troops should march at once against Monterrey and Saltillo and occupy the former place if not the latter"—although "taking possession of California" was the priority since "San Francisco can be fortified at very little expense...."[42]

As was to be expected in this inflamed context, Sam Houston, who had served Texas in Washington and still bore the purported stain of being soft on Indigenes, was pelted with invective. As extermination accelerated in the 1850s, the Texan—and future California enslaver—Thomas Jefferson Green castigated Houston for the "proof of his many crimes" and "his abolitionist treason"; he was the "presidential candidate of the abolitionists" and was little more than a "Benedict Arnold, black with that treason to that section which gave him birth—in comparison to which the treason of [Aaron] Burr is exalted patriotism—the betrayal by Judas of the Son of Peace" was puny relatively. Perhaps worse, said Green, was "his praises of the faithless Indian" or, maybe, "his dirty polygamy and desertion of his former wives," or possibly it was his "opium eating" or how he "lay drunk for months" at critical moments, then "swearing that he would hang...General Austin as a traitor...." What of the "dastardly flight of Gen. Houston before an inferior force of Mexicans?" "Does the Senator deny," he posed querulously, that "[he]...abused Mr. [John C.] Calhoun for more than thirty years," referring to the hero

---

42. John Parrott to Secretary Buchanan, 4 January 1846, Reel 1, Despatches from U.S. Consuls in Mazatlan, NARA.

of slavocracy. Or what of Houston's attempt to "vilify and calumni-ate the lamented Henry Clay?"[43]

Galveston, just south of the future metropolis that took Houston's name, was easily accessible by sea, making it an attractive port of call for those fleeing soil exhaustion and stagnation in the Carolinas and thereabouts, delivering even more emigrants not unwilling to embrace an incipient fascism—or willing to join the crusade of "Gen-eral" Green. As was to become the case during the Civil War, this town was becoming a bellwether of slavery, as suggested by the 1846 election of Galveston's largest slaveholder (and Baptist deacon)—James Sydnor—as mayor. He was simply the symbol of a wider trend: during the decade or so following the end of the war against Mexico, the number of enslaved skyrocketed in Texas from about 58,000 to a staggering 182,000 with illicitly seized Free Negroes being part of the remix. Unavoidably this also meant engrossing enrichment for some and an enhanced desire for more land of the Indigenous to replicate the dastardly pattern.[44]

Before the war with Mexico, Charles Sumner, soon to gather renown as an abolitionist solon, had declared that a "respectable number" in his republic were "in favor of dissolution of the Union in the event of annexation of Texas."[45] By 1850, as he examined the mot-tled landscape of politics, Sumner averred that "the Slavery Question has become paramount here at last." The worm had turned, however, and it was now the "Slave States" that "threaten to dissolve the Union if slavery is prohibited by Congress in the new territories or abolished in the District of Columbia," yet even he seemed oddly blasé about the "Canadian Question" which "promises to help antislavery. The annexation of that colony to the United States would 'redress the bal-ance' which has been turned in favor of slavery by the annexation of Texas."[46]

Many of these horribly maltreated Africans wound up in the tor-turous sugar plantations of Brazoria County, not far from Galveston or Houston. The industry commenced in the 1820s with the first per-manent mill constructed in 1834 by a Louisianan, William Stafford. The mythology arose that Negroes multiplied faster and lived lon-ger in the cane region, perhaps a reason to work them harder and

---

43. "Reply of Gen. Thomas J. Green to the Speech of General Sam Hous-ton in the Senate of the United States," 1 August 1854, Green Papers.

44. M.C.F. Long, x, 8, 33, 18.

45. Charles Sumner to Judge Story, 5 February 1845 in Pierce, Volume III, 98.

46. Ibid., Charles Sumner to Lee Morpeth, 8 January 1850, 211.

import more of them. By 1849 the industry was on firmer footing as the county was leading the state in producing the still popular sweetener. But soon inclement weather was harming the crop, which could lead to breakup of families as mothers were sold eastward and daughters northward.[47]

Still, if enslavers were paying attention they would have taken closer note of worrisome trends. By 1849 a U.S. Negro, James Pennington, received an honorary degree from the University of Heidelberg, betokening a growing revulsion toward slavery in a land that had supplied a significant number of emigrants to Texas. Already few Germans defended slavery as a "positive good" becoming normative in the renewed rascal republic. Some of them even pressed for a free state in west Texas in the 1850s. The 1850s visitor Frederick Law Olmsted—to be esteemed as the landscape architect of Manhattan's Central Park—was suitably impressed by the German settlers he met in Texas, which may have buoyed him sufficiently to the point where he donated a howitzer to abolitionist crusaders in Lawrence, Kansas. Not unrelated is the remarkable occurrence in 1850s Ohio where Negroes encouraged teaching of the German language in their schools, just as the revolutionary poet Gottfried Kinkel received donations from this otherwise impecunious community.[48]

Indigenes and Africans were not the only ones making a run for the border. Shortly after the war ended, Washington's emissary reporting from Matamoros gushed about the "attention of large capitalists" that had "turned" to this region; "no doubt," said Thomas Slemons, "but that the commerce of all the Mexican states on this side of the Sierra Madre can be made subservient to the interests of American commerce," which "opens to our commerce and agriculture a valley almost equal to that of the Mississippi," referring to the banks of the Rio Grande.[49]

Among those heading to fabled wealth along the Pacific—with Hawaii, then China and Japan next in the crosshairs—was Texas's Thomas Jefferson Green; blatantly contravening Mexico's previous legal regime and indicating a prime reason for the war in the first instance, he was accompanied by 15 enslaved Africans. He was joined by another Texan, Thomas Thorn, who arrived in California

---

47. Sandra Lee Watts, "A History of the Sugar Cane Industry with Special Reference to Brazoria County," M.A. thesis, Rice U, 1969, 6, 9, 16, 16, 42 (abbrev. S.L. Watts).

48. Honeck, 1, 29, 39, 42, 64, 65, 80.

49. Thomas Slemons, Consul to Secretary Buchanan, 12 November 1848, Reel 2, Despatches from U.S. Consuls in Matamoros, NARA.

with 30 enslaved Africans. The future Confederate leader Judah Benjamin indicated further that he thought the optimal railway route to the Pacific led through Mexico rather than Texas, suggesting further interference in the internal affairs of the former. Intoxicated with their successes, settler leaders began to discuss dreamily introducing slavery into Hawaii. Green, uppermost among these chauvinists, quickly became a potent force in California, along with other Texans; he sat in the first legislature and pushed the legislation establishing the University of California. James Gadsden, who gave his name to yet another land cession ripped from Mexico, conspired with Green to implant slavery in California. Gadsden's southern route to California facilitated migration to Los Angeles along the nearby Gila River Trail, converting this then sleepy Mexican outpost into a hotbed of proslavery sentiment. Also headed from Texas to California was David Terry—albeit with roots in Mississippi—who wound up killing David Broderick, a sitting U.S. Senator, in a duel (the last such senator killed before Huey Long in 1936, then Robert F. Kennedy in 1968) before being killed himself after assaulting a member of the California Supreme Court. He was the embodiment of the worst excesses of the "Wild West" and the "Old South," for he had become an engine of the "Know Nothing" movement and backed the reopening of the ignominious African Slave Trade.

Utah too was en route to the wealth of California, and there the Church of Latter Day Saints reeled back and forth like a yoyo on supporting abolitionism, then slavery, likely influenced by the prevailing political winds. By the 1850s some among this group were actually backing the international slave trade.[50]

It seemed that abolitionists were fighting a losing battle in seeking to bar enslavement from former Mexican soil. In March 1849 President Polk confided to his diary his own reservations about applying pre-1848 Mexican law on slavery in California and New Mexico particularly, especially since "many of the Southern members of Congress of both Houses came into my room in great excitement" in high dudgeon about these "very obnoxious laws."[51]

But it was California—not New Mexico nor Utah—that faced the vaunted riches of Asia, and leading the way there was the Mississippian William Gwin. The historian Kevin Waite has underlined the point that Gwin, who represented the Golden State in the U.S. Senate for a good deal of the 1850s, owned 200 enslaved Africans in

---

50. Waite, 60, 104, 117, 134, 138, 148, 162, 180, 191.
51. Entry, 3 March 1849 in Quaife, Volume IV, 362.

the Magnolia State, his California ties notwithstanding. He shed no tears when his fellow senator, the anti-slavery David Broderick, was gunned down by Terry, the former Texas Ranger.[52] Proudly representing the Golden State, it was Senator Gwin who in the 1850s said, "I will state…that California year after year, has passed a fugitive slave law—a local law."[53]

Tragically, California also renewed a trend that had beset Indigenes from the inception of European invasion of the continent centuries earlier: in the immediate aftermath of the 1848 takeover, a recent report estimated that as many as 20,000 Indigenes were enslaved.[54] This does not include the numerous darker-skinned Mexicans who were said to be enslaved by U.S. tyrants in the 1850s.[55] Even the proto-imperialist U.S. analyst Cora Montgomery proclaimed in 1852 that "our Indian policy is a blot on the very name of Christianity."[56]

On the verge of the consolidation of the U.S. takeover of California in 1848, a U.S. official recalled that he had "visited Upper California… during the summer of 1845" and estimated that the "white population was then estimated at 15,000 souls" and the "domesticated Indian population living with whites 4000"; and there was also an "Indian population living on the borders of the whites in detached villages…." But "since 1845 a considerable augmentation has taken place in the white population of Upper California, growing out of immigration from this country and Oregon,"[57] as the settler invasion escalated.

Also performing yeoman service for enslavers, this time in New Mexico and Arizona, were the Texans Lewis Owings and the Territorial Secretary James Lucas—who shaped a slave code with the former becoming a Confederate leader. They were joined by Miguel Otero, who married into a prominent pro-slavery Charleston family.[58]

In previous years, Texas republicans had seemed to cater to Indigenes in faraway Yucatan as a tool to foment discord in Mexico,

---

52. *Los Angeles Times*, 10 September 2021.

53. "Invasion of Harper's Ferry—Dangers and Duties of the South, Remarks of Senators Clay of Alabama, Gwin of California and Others, Delivered in the Senate of the United States, December 13, 1859," Huntington Library.

54. *New York Times*, 28 October 2021.

55. Baumgartner, 221.

56. Cora Montgomery, *Eagle Pass: Or, Life on the Border*, New York: Putnam, 1852, v.

57. "Late Consul" John Parrott to Secretary Buchanan, 13 July 1848, Reel 1, Despatches from U.S. Consuls in Mazatlan, NARA.

58. Waite, 221,204.

making the nation more vulnerable to dismemberment. But as the war was expiring in 1848, and Washington was waltzing away with a colossal prize of land, President Polk had begun to issue harried alerts about the "Indians of Yucatan" who were "waging a war of extermination against the white race," sparing "neither age nor sex"; he then sought to "defend the white inhabitants against the incursion of the Indians, in the same way that we have employed our troops in other states of the Mexican republic in our possession...."[59] In sum, trans-border defense of white supremacy was exalted en route to the blossoming of U.S. imperialism.

Weeks after the formal conclusion of the war with Mexico, Secretary of State James Buchanan noted casually that his nation had taken the "port of Laguna and the island of Carmen" in Yucatan, the apparent purpose to provide a "refuge" for racial comrades "from the fury of the Indians"; he opined in a self-serving manner that "if peace were concluded," Mexico "would not be able to afford the white inhabitants of Yucatan the prompt and efficient aid necessary to save them from destruction," an evident priority of U.S. foreign policy. Self-righteously, said the future president, this was a "voluntary sacrifice made by the United States in the cause of their brethren of Spanish origin...." After years of stirring unrest, he allowed that a "primary cause of the war will be found in the inveterate hostility of the Indians against the Spanish race. Its avowed object is the extermination or expulsion of this race," a process with which he was intimately familiar, "and the re-acquisition of Indian sovereignty over Yucatan. The Indians must have known that the government of Mexico neither could nor would afford assistance to the Spanish race...." Conveniently, he found it "impossible" to determine the "number of whites" the U.S. was seeking to protect, though Indigenes, he said, "greatly preponderate in Yucatan"; already a "great number of whites have been killed by the Indians" and "more than fifty thousand of them have been compelled to emigrate to neighboring countries...."[60]

But just as during the 1950s Washington demonized challenges to the status quo as being motivated by Moscow, a century earlier, the enemy *du jour* was London. Hence, not far distant from Yucatan was the land known as British Honduras, later Belize. By 1850 Buchanan was complaining that "British authorities" there were "furnishing

---

59. Message of President Polk, 29 April 1848, in J.B. Moore, Volume VIII, 54-55.

60. Ibid., Secretary Buchanan to Henry Hilliard, Chairman Pro Tem of House Committee on Foreign Affairs, 3 May 1848, 56.

the savages with arms" with the "eventual object...to establish a protectorate over the Indians," meaning Washington had to crush Indigenes.[61] By 1854, Buchanan was reporting from London about the "*Morning Post* believed to be his organ [Lord Palmerston's]," which was "incessant in its abuse of the United States," and quite "disparaging." Still eyeing Canada insatiably, he told Washington that London was "withdrawing troops" from this giant territory "for the purpose of reinforcing the army of the Crimea," as he condemned the "dishonesty" of a parliamentarian who cautioned about U.S. plans for "'annexation'" of this territory that included such prizes as Ontario and Quebec.[62]

Secretary Buchanan and his comrades then pivoted and rang ever louder alarms about "a war of races" that had "arisen between the Indians and the Spanish in Guatemala and the Yucatan" and, like an oil spill was now manifesting in "the civil war now raging in Venezuela," which too "partakes of this character."[63] As Buchanan saw things, part of the problem with his negotiating with his Mexican counterparts was their "entire ignorance of the English language" (he was silent about his knowledge of Spanish).[64]

Finally, Secretary Buchanan snapped. Months after the formal termination of the war in Mexico, he requested "three or four thousand troops" be deployed "against the Indians of Yucatan and, if need be, against the Indians of other portions of Mexico."[65]

Nonetheless, Waddy Thompson, an old Mexico hand, in the febrile postwar climate spun the incursions into the Yucatan as a way to prevent an attack on Galveston by Mexico. For he was "informed by an officer of high rank in the Mexican army" who was "in the entire confidence of General Santa Anna that the ultimate destination of the Mexican army sent into Yucatan was an attack on Texas"; that is, "pacification would take place without a blow being struck and that an attack was then immediately to be made on Galveston." Fortunately, he said with a sigh of satisfaction, "the plan was defeated by [the] expedition to Yucatan."[66]

---

61. Ibid., Secretary Buchanan to Mr. Grund, 13 April 1850, 377.

62. Ibid., James Buchanan to Secretary of State William Marcy, 21 November 1854, Volume IX, 275.

63. Ibid., Secretary Buchanan to Mr. Appleton, 1 June 1848, Volume VIII, 74.

64. Ibid., Secretary Buchanan to Mr. Clifford, 2 March 1849, 350.

65. Ibid., Secretary Buchanan to Mr. Clifford, 7 August 1848, 154.

66. Waddy Thompson to "My Dear Sir...," 2 August 1848, Green Papers.

This was designed to quell the "savage and cruel war...against the white race" and "save them from destruction," as Washington's Pan-Europeanism was internationalized, a policy that would pay rich dividends on the old continent and beyond for decades to come. Recommended was the immediate sending of "10,000 lbs. of powder to enable the white race to defend themselves against the Indians"—though President Polk fretted that this huge cache could find its way into the hands of Mexicans fueling further resistance against U.S. forces. Secretary Buchanan objected strenuously to this demurrer; Polk was taken aback when this subordinate "removed his seat to one of the windows of my office and with his back turned toward me appeared for some time to be looking out of the window" in a "petulant" and disrespectful display of arrogance. But the president knew what was popular—and what was not—so he acceded to send the powder "so it would be used by the white race to repel the attacks of the Indians...."[67]

In a manner that had marked the early stages of the Texas takeover, "certain citizens" of the rapacious republic were unwilling to wait for troop deployments and, said Buchanan, were "now engaged in preparing a military expedition for the invasion of Mexico"—this, after the formal war had ended officially. "Their object...is to revolutionize the Northern States of that republic and to establish what they denominate the Republic of Sierra Madre...."[68]

The pre-eminent land grabber President Polk also had noticed with a dearth of surprise what was transpiring in August 1848 with the "contemplated movement or expedition of citizens of the U.S. of hostile character towards Mexico, the object of which was said to be to revolutionize the Northern provinces of Mexico and to establish the Republic of Sierra Madre...."[69]

With promptitude sent to Washington was a curiously worded document in English, proclaiming the "Declaration of Independence" of this rump republic purporting to represent the "unanimous" viewpoint of those assembled on 16 June 1849, i.e., "the seven northern states" of Mexico. Conspicuously, the document began with an echo of 1776: "When in the course of human events," though they were infinitely more honest than their forebears, observing candidly that they were "tired of the National Declaration that Slavery shall not

67. Entry, 7 March 1848, in Quaife, Volume III, 372.

68. Secretary Buchanan to Mr. Durant, 30 August 1848, in J.B. Moore, Volume VIII, 192.

69. Entry, 29 August 1848, in Quaife, Volume IV, 103.

exist in our Land, when peonage a system hideous and cruel, unrestricted and unnoticed," prevailed; here Matamoros was a stand-in for Philadelphia.[70]

Typically opportunistic, the assault on peonage was a mere device to rationalize and extend enslavement. Still, a kind of debt peonage was imbedded in the western borderlands, and the post-1865 dispensation came to resemble it; however, as the Pueblo and other Indigenes often sympathized with the enslaved, it became even more difficult to install this horrid system of labor there.[71]

By 1851, the U.S. consul there, J.F. Waddell, was willing to recognize the obvious, if only obliquely; he referred to "rumors" that this "movement" had "received material assistance in men, arms and money from the Left Bank of the Rio Grande" and that the "present leader [José] Carbajal" was amply aided by "insurgents…joined by a considerable body of foreigners"; candidly he asserted that "their entire success is attributable to the fact that they have received such assistance" from those to the north.[72]

Consul Waddell further exposed the secessionist pretensions by unmasking the point that the "insurgents" had as their "real object…a mere smuggling" scheme, spearheaded by "a few misguided Americans," à la 1836, who were now mired in "quarreling" over the real and imagined spoils.[73]

However, the riches seemed so unimaginable that "many Americans [had] joined the insurgent forces" and were "reinforced by a well organized body of men from the interior of Texas," all embodying the "reckless spirit of adventure among our countrymen"; even the "majority of the inhabitants of Brownsville" tended to "concur in condemning the part taken by Americans in the recent fight at Camargo," site of a tumultuous battle. "A narrow stream," he said in referring to the Rio Grande, "is the only obstacle to be encountered in effecting a junction with the insurgents and a wild and inhabited region afford a thousand securities against discovery," guaranteeing the "presence of so many Americans with the insurgents." The good news was how the "zeal of Carvajal's adherents" had been "very

---

70. "Declaration of Independence," 16 June 1849, Reel 2, Despatches from U.S. Consuls in Matamoros, NARA.

71. William S. Kiser, *Borderlands of Slavery: The Struggle Over Captivity and Peonage in the American Southwest*, Philadelphia: U of Pennsylvania, 2017, 55, 39, 40.

72. Consul J.F. Waddell to Secretary of State Webster, 25 September 1851, Reel 2, Despatches from U.S. Consuls in Matamoros, NARA.

73. Ibid., Consul J.F. Waddell to "Sir," 1 October 1851.

considerably diminished" due to the stiff resistance encountered[74]: for days on end Carvajal and his comrades had been besieged.[75]

The Texas-born, Virginia-educated Carvajal was suited uniquely for this odious mission. He was backed in this ignominiousness by Texas luminaries, e.g., Charles Stillman and John Salmon"Rip" Ford, who promised and delivered armed aid. In return they demanded that northern Mexico should no longer provide a refuge for runaway Africans numbering in the thousands, who had fled oppression in Texas. Carvajal agreed with this devil's bargain that also implicated the similarly devilish brother-in-law of Jefferson Davis, Joseph Howell, yet another Mississippian though he headed the "New Orleans Volunteers," who mimicked in their bloodthirstiness the malevolence of the Texas Rangers. However, Ford was among those who did not endorse wholeheartedly the idea of using Mexican labor in conjunction with enslaved African labor, since the former created alienation among the latter, encouraging them to flee—often a few miles to freedom.[76]

The gallantry of Mexico's forces repulsed the secessionists successfully. Even the U.S. envoy was outraged by the rebels' "most cowardly nature" and the "atrocious barbarity" they exhibited, "which shock humanity and have stained with everlasting infamy the misguided men who have been lured from their quiet homes to rally around the standard of a rebel...." This "miserable scheme of heartless speculators" was worthy of rebuke, he said. Waddell was so moved since they "set fire to a large building (in the same block with my office)," shedding light on his insight. There was "killing and wounding some few persons among the latter myself!" said the chagrined envoy. The invaders, he said accusingly, were taking advantage of the treaty between Mexico and the U.S. which said nationals of the former then on the latter's land could travel southward "without the payment of any tax or contribution. This was the foundation of the revolutionary invasion," he emphasized in explicating his "uncompromising opposition to this nefarious scheme."[77]

He was referring to the secessionists' invasion of Camargo, Mexico, where they were "entirely dispersed" and vanquished to the point where, he opined, "they cannot again disturb the peace of this

---

74. Ibid., Consul Waddell to Secretary Webster, 7 October 1851.

75. Ibid., Consul Waddell to Secretary Webster, November 1851.

76. W.J. Hughes, 139, 141, 155.

77. Consul Waddell to Secretary Webster, November 1851, Reel 2, Despatches from U.S. Consuls in Matamoros, NARA.

frontier."[78] Secretary of State Webster conceded that a "body of men from the state of Texas had joined the insurgents in the neighboring Mexican state" and that "insurrection adverted to has been...instigated by those who have been thwarted in attempting to carry on illicit trade with the Mexican Republic...."[79]

If he had been more candid, Consul Waddell would have spent more time limning the various misdeeds of bigwigs Richard King and Charles Stillman, the latter given credit for the founding of Brownsville, Texas, in 1849. Both became uncommonly wealthy in the postwar climate, yet another outgrowth of the dismemberment of Mexico—though they failed in attaining further encroachments of land in Tamaulipas.[80]

Sensing the unfolding of yet another piratical venture, U.S. settlers were flocking to Texas and points southward. As matters had evolved, Tennessee—often associated with the early life of Sam Houston—supplied more of this group than any other state, followed by Alabama, rapidly gaining a merited reputation as the Lone Star State's fraternal twin.[81]

Drunk with success, U.S. settlers' roaming eyes began to alight on other quarry. Once again, the Mississippian Robert Walker was in the vanguard; "he called to see me," said President Polk shortly after the end of the war in Mexico, and opened a discussion "in relation to the purchase of the island of Cuba from Spain." The president admitted that this was "of consideration in the Cabinet lately...." Little was done to discourage "volunteers in Mexico" who "after their discharge" sought to "go to Cuba" in order to "engage with the Cubans in an attempt to revolutionize that island"—though the Washington consensus was avoiding the turning over the island to its inhabitants at all cost.[82]

Polk was in a position to recognize that postwar, pumped up by the success in unraveling Mexico, filibustering expeditions southward by U.S. nationals increased. Not only Cuba but Nicaragua was in the crosshairs. Similarly, since the cost of a field hand was approaching a still hefty $1500, the idea was not just to seize territory but cheaper humans too, along with reopening the African Slave Trade. Thus in July 1850, as debate over New Mexico escalated, 250 armed Texans

---

78. Ibid., Consul Waddell to Secretary Webster, 2 March 1852.

79. Secretary of State Webster to Luis de la Rosa, 4 November 1851, in Manning, Volume IX, 98.

80. James Robert Crews, "Reconstruction in Brownsville, Texas," M.A. thesis, TTU, 1969, 8, 33 (abbrev. Crews).

81. Buenger, x.

82. Entry, 9 June 1848, in Quaife, Volume III, 485.

departed Corpus Christi to join Narciso López in Cuba in order to wrest the island away from Madrid.[83]

An issue inimical to the seizure of northern Mexico, perhaps, was the evident inhospitable attitude in southern Texas with regard to enslavement. As of 1850 there were a reported 53 slaves in Cameron County, where Brownsville was sited. However, a reason for this paucity was the easy escape to Mexico and freedom, which an Anschluss would have obviated.[84]

Resisting the original inhabitants at all costs was the credo of yet another Mississippian, Willis Lang, who became a prominent Texas Ranger, then a Confederate leader—a familiarly practiced path. In the Lone Star State he was vocal in threatening violence against Austin unless the authorities acted with more vigor in attacking the Indigenous raiders emerging from the southwestern quarter of Indian Territory, then attacking Texas. He was joined in this monstrous quest by Middleton Tate Johnson, born in South Carolina in 1810, elected to office in Alabama by 1832, then arrived in his pro-slavery journey in Texas by 1840; by 1844 he was elected to office there before fighting to preserve and extend his gains in Mexico by 1846 and joining the Texas Rangers. He too became a leading secessionist. Yet another familiarly practiced path was taken by William Fitzhugh, born in Kentucky by 1818, then it was on to the enslaving state of Missouri, then to Florida to combat Indigenes, then to Texas by the pivotal year of 1845. He too fought in Mexico before joining the secessionists, bringing valuable military experience.[85]

The 1850s were to bring more attempts to seize more territory, Nicaragua in one telling instance. Yet the settler regime in Texas had yet to extirpate both Indigenous and African resistance, and as long as that was the case, their entire project was in jeopardy.

---

83. See also Horne, *Race to Revolution*, 82-87.
84. Crews, 8.
85. Cutrer.

Chapter **11**

Toward Civil War with Texas in the Vanguard, 1851-1857

Recall that France in the prelude to 1845, then 1848, had been complicit in providing aid and comfort to rapacious republicans, bombarding Mexico and seeking to outfox London by maneuvering to their right on abolitionism. Intentional or not, Paris wound up being a useful tool of Washington, an ironic position for a major power. Yet during this same era, France was returning to the abolitionism that had been declared in the empire during the early stages of the Haitian Revolution, which was bound to deliver tensions with Washington. Emblematically, Charles Sumner, the future firebrand senatorial abolitionist, found himself in France in December 1849, and was struck by the fact that "at the School of Law in Paris I have sat for weeks on the same benches with colored pupils, listening like myself to the learned lectures," which he interpreted as an argument against Jim Crow schools in his own Massachusetts.[1]

As tensions between London and Washington showed few signs of abating, the strategic posture of the rascal republicans was deteriorating, though attempts to seize more territory in Cuba and Nicaragua among other sites in the 1850s had hardly abated in response.

* * *

Just as U.S. clamps in Mexico were being affixed in 1847, U.S. diplomat John Parrott reported from Havana that "during my residence here I have discovered that the sympathies of all nations, English, French and Spanish are entirely against us and in favor of the Mexicans, the same appears to be the case on the Pacific side also...every article which appears in the journals of the United States favorable to Mexico is faithfully translated...."[2]

---

1. Letter from Charles Sumner, 4 December 1849, in Pierce, Volume I, 297.
2. John Parrott to Secretary Buchanan, 6 February 1847, Reel 1, Despatches from U.S. Consuls in Mazatlan, NARA.

At this juncture and quite tellingly, residing in Mexico were about 1000 "Germans"—mostly from the Hanse towns—and about 1000 Englishmen and about 2000 Frenchmen.[3] There was a widespread view north of the border that the U.S. should seize more Mexican territory, even after 1848, but with the souring of Paris joining London's already similar view toward the U.S., this would not be simple to execute, not least since there were so many Europeans in Mexico City. In fact between 1848 and up to 1861, many more thousands of Frenchmen journeyed to Mexico and California in search of fortune. By 1851 there were an estimated 20,000 French emigrants out west where U.S. nationals' attitude toward them was symbolized by their dismissive reference to them using the epithet generally reserved for Mexicans: they called them "greasers."[4]

Hence, from their perch in Galveston, French emissaries beginning in 1848 filed report after report lamenting what was occurring due south, especially the prospect of further dismemberment, e.g., the erstwhile Republic of Sierra Madre. Tampico, which was to become a Confederate headquarters, was viewed suspiciously in this regard, as was the racial conflict in Yucatan which—it was thought—could easily spread throughout the nation.[5] However—if the French emissary's view was to be taken as representative of his nation— Paris was hamstrung by excess admiration of the U.S., in terms of respect for private property and the ability of sects, e.g., the Mormons to flourish, while circumscribing them at the same time: unlike Europe, it was said.[6]

Even before it was reported by U.S. envoys, their French counterparts had noticed the rise of the Republic of Sierra Madre, along with the increased U.S. migration to Tampico bringing speculative capital with them.[7] Again, more than their U.S. counterparts, French diplomats sensed that demobilized soldiers from the U.S. were in

---

3. Jacobus, 73. See also Frederick Law Olmsted, *A Journey Through Texas; or a Saddle Trip on the Southwestern Frontier with a Statistical Appendix*, New York: Dix, Edwards, 1857, 329 (abbrev. Olmsted, *Journey*). He found "Jew Germans in Texas and in Texas the Jews, as everywhere else, speculate in everything—in popular sympathies, prejudices and bigotries, in politics, in slavery. Some of them own slaves, other sell them on commission."

4. Joseph Allen Stout, *The Liberators: Filibustering Expeditions into Mexico, 1848-1852 and the Last Thrust of Manifest Destiny*, Los Angeles: Westernlore, 1973, 13, 50 (abbrev. Joseph Allen Stout, *Liberators*).

5. Report, 4 July 1848, Galveston Consulate.

6. Ibid., Report, 3 August 1848.

7. Ibid., Report, 23 August 1848.

the vanguard of the continuing attempt to dismember Mexico. They were among those heading southward since life and land were cheaper. Some had been living on the streets of New Orleans but were then pouring into Corpus Christi with mayhem in mind. Inferentially signaling the trans-colonial power of "Anglo-Saxonism" as a lubricant for expansion, even Paris's man—who was a presumed targeted victim of this philosophy—subscribed to it, as he disparaged Mexicans, who were described contemptuously.[8]

This diplomat was also quite critical of certain French emigrants to the borderlands, those who were involved in a Utopian Socialist project, Icaria, with roots in Le Havre. He was hostile to their alleged communism and compared them invidiously to German peers.[9] He may have had in mind the man known as "Colonel Sangberg...a German by birth" according to a U.S. observer in Chihuahua where both were sited; he was an officer in the "Mexican army, a favorite of [the] president" and bent on "protecting the frontier from Indian depredations" ostensibly, but actually he was "solely calculated to annoy and molest our American commerce of this frontier...." Coincidentally, since this German visited El Paso "desertion from our army appear[s] to me," said the U.S. consul, "to be almost alarming and the govt. must be losing a considerable amount of the property brought away with them in every case...."[10] Or he may have had in mind Adolf Luderitz, who in the 1850s lived and traveled in Mexico and the U.S. before decamping to Southern Africa where, like Austin and Houston, he bequeathed his name to a city in Namibia that continues to carry his name.[11]

This Frenchman may have been disdainful of his countrymen arriving in droves, but their arrival in North America was taken quite seriously in Washington. Speaking from San Blas, Mexico, in April 1852, Consul William Forbes noted nervously the "emigration from California into Sonora of a considerable number of Frenchmen...."[12] By then there were an estimated 6000 French nationals in San Francisco, making Paris a real threat to continued U.S.

---

8. Ibid., Report, 1 November 1848.

9. Ibid., Report, 1 December 1848.

10. U.S. Consul to "Sir," 8 June 1852, Reel 1, Despatches from U.S. Consuls in Chihuahua, NARA.

11. David Olusoga and Casper W. Erichsen, *The Kaiser's Holocaust: Germany's Forgotten Genocide*, London: Faber and Faber, 30.

12. Consul William Forbes to Secretary Webster, 23 April 1852, Despatches from U.S. Consuls in San Blas, NARA.

hegemony, as the subsequent 1860s seizure of Mexico under Maximilian demonstrated.[13]

As was to be the case by the onset of the U.S. Civil War, there was quite a bit of cross-pollination between Paris and the North American enslavers. William Gwin, often described as California's "First [U.S.] Senator," was among this group and was a comrade of Sam Houston besides. He spent a good deal of the Civil War ensconced comfortably in Paris, where rebels outnumbered U.S. patriots. His home there, says his biographer, was "headquarters of the Southern colony"; before that, during the 1850s, he was all too familiar with the proliferating band of gold hunters from the north invading Sonora, for the ubiquitous thinking then was that the rapacious republicans would eventually swallow Mexico in any case, so why not get started, just as it had gobbled Texas, Arizona, New Mexico and California, among other vast lands. And, as shall be seen, when opportunist Frenchmen seized Mexico during the Civil War, secessionists stood to profit.[14] Interestingly, John C. Fremont, an early leader of the Republican Party and likewise anti-slavery, was also a primary territorial aggrandizer in California—and happened to be of French descent.[15] Similarly, it was in 1856 that the military man of French ancestry, P.G.T. Beauregard, tried to join the notorious filibusterer William Walker in seizing Nicaragua, a warmup for his becoming a leading Confederate. He not only spoke French and English but Spanish too, making him a natural vector for hemispheric expansionism.[16]

Still, unwilling to be outflanked by this de facto Southern U.S.-French alliance, Washington seemed to think that any attempts to seize Sonora should be left to U.S. compatriots; by 1853 even James Gadsden had detected a "filibustering expedition" that was "unlawful" headed to Sonora, comprised of his countrymen.[17] That same

13. Scott Martelle, *William Walker's Wars: How One Man's Private American Army Tried to Conquer Mexico, Nicaragua and Honduras*, Chicago: Chicago Review Press, 2019, 55 (abbrev. Martelle).

14. Lately Thomas, *Between Two Empires: The Life Story of California's First Senator, William McKendree Gwin*, Boston: Houghton Mifflin, 1969, 286, 287 (abbrev. L. Thomas).

15. Virginia H. Taylor, *The Franco-Texan Land Company*, Austin: U of Texas Press, 1969, xiv. See also Leonard Richards, *The California Gold Rush and the Coming of the Civil War*, New York: Vintage, 2007.

16. T. Harry Williams, ed., *With Beauregard in Mexico: The Mexican War Reminiscences of P.G.T. Beauregard*, Baton Rouge: LSU Press, 1956, 39, 106.

17. James Gadsden to William Forbes, 19 November 1853, Reel 1, Despatches from U.S. Consuls in San Blas, NARA.

year the U.S. pirate William Walker had dug his sharp talons into Baja California and a few weeks later sought to seize Sonora too. Gadsden, who affixed his name to yet another Mexican cession, knew that the growing hatred of the neighbor to the north hampered execution of the piratical "purchase" from Mexico that was to carry his name.[18]

Like Sam Houston, whom in a sense he was emulating, Walker too had roots in Tennessee.[19] As with the early invasion of Texas in the prelude to 1836, Walker attracted a criminal gang of Texas Rangers, who began to freelance soon after arriving in Nicaragua, venturing to the rich mining region of Chontales, then plundered various estates and villages, while executing those with the gumption to resist— before being killed in response by a group of Nicaraguans and, revealingly, French miners. For whatever reason, Walker's cutthroats did attract some Negro support.[20] Trenchantly, the barriers enslavers confronted in "Bleeding Kansas" may have convinced some to head south—or so Walker suggested—accompanied by his trusty Texas companion Samuel Lockridge.[21] Alternatively, the point has been made that by Summer 1855, U.S. cavalry had been sent to Kansas, allowing more Texans to waltz southward.[22] Lockridge arrived in Nicaragua to bolster Walker backed with 235 soldiers-of-fortune, ready, willing and able to pillage.[23]

Walker's uncle, Lipscomb Norvell, Jr., was an early invader of what became the "Lone Star State," and was part of a family that included Lipscomb Norvell, Sr., who fought the British in the 1776 war, making this the First Family of Secession, Adventurism and Filibustering. It was not evident that the Norvells were as "anti-Catholic" as their relative, Walker, but were surely as aggrandizing. Imitating Austin and Houston, Walker declared himself president of Baja California, and since his parents owned slave property, this did not augur well for U.S. Negroes; the same held true for his so-called "Republic of Sonora" that countenanced slavery. Also like his Texas predecessors, he thought he could play on the contradictions between London

---

18. Joseph Allen Stout, Last Years, 85. 94, 135.

19. Robert E. May, "Manifest Destiny's Filibusters," in Sam W. Haynes and Christopher Morris, eds., *Manifest Destiny and Empire: American Antebellum Expansionism*, College Station: TA&MU Press, 1997, 146-179, 154.

20. Michael Gobat, *Empire by Invitation: William Walker and Manifest Destiny in Central America*, Cambridge: Harvard U Press, 2018, 108, 115.

21. William Walker, *The War in Nicaragua*, Mobile: Goetzel, 1860.

22. Hampton, 125.

23. Martelle, 210.

and Washington in order to prevail. To pander to the latter by 1856 he reversed promptly Nicaragua's 1838 edict barring enslavement. Paris was not neglected either, since by 1856 the French-born and premier Louisiana politician Pierre Soulé visited him in Nicaragua.[24]

Nonetheless, as Gadsden's purchase—or theft—of land from Mexico was being executed, a U.S. comrade was unsated and demanded insistently, "'We must have Sonora and Chihuahua...[for with both] we gain [Lower] California and by railroad to Guayamas [sic] render our state of Texas the great highway of nations....'"[25]

According to the U.S. consul in the city that became Ciudad Juárez, Chihuahua was "in a state of revolution," a buzzword that often presaged a U.S. takeover.[26] There was a "great deal of excitement in this place, among both Americans and Mexicans," with the latter fearing reasonably yet another assault at the hands of the former; "much ill feeling exists against our countrymen," said the U.S. consul, as yet another territorial dispute raged.[27] In nearby New Mexico, wrestling with the U.S. takeover still in 1852, Congressman Richard H. Weightman from the "Land of Enchantment" was disenchanted with what he was seeing—or so he told his colleagues in Washington. His opponents, he said, were "fomenting disorder among the mixed portion of the inhabitants" and "pandering to the passions of the Mexican portion of the population and directing them against the American born citizens" and, perilously, they were "gathering around...a corrupt Catholic Priesthood,"[28] adding a layer of religious conflict on top of already overwrought matters of "race" and. nationality.

Guaymas, Mexico, was occupying considerable mental energy among U.S. settlers. It was also in 1854 that the U.S. consul there found that "great excitement exists...on account of the filibustering expedition against Lower California and Sonora," a subject he knew well since the "governor" there "publicly expresses his opinion" as to the consul himself "being one of the principal instigators...." The local authorities "ordered" the "prefect" to his door with the design to "have" this consul "banished to a remote place in the interior...."

24. Ibid., 13, 17, 54, 55, 68, 95, 117, 199, 201, 210.

25. Hahn, 235.

26. Consul David R. Diffenderrfer to Secretary of State Edward Everett, 18 January 1853, Reel 1, Despatches from U.S. Consuls in Paso del Norte [Ciudad Juárez].

27. Ibid., Consul David R. Diffenderrfer to Secretary of State Edward Everett, 23 March 1853.

28. "Speech of Hon. Richard H. Weightman of New Mexico Delivered in the House of Representatives, March 15, 1852," Huntington Library.

Viewed suspiciously was that a "British subject" was in "actual command of the Mexican naval forces at Guaymas" who was slated "to supersede" local authorities.[29]

It was as if another kind of gold rush was taking place, this one a scramble to see who could become the next Stephen F. Austin and, *inter alia*, egotistically impose one's name on purloined land. By the Summer of 1854 the U.S. envoy in Tampico, soon to be a Confederate citadel, was speaking of a "powerful expedition of American filibusterers" that were "preparing to leave New Orleans" for the "purpose of capturing this place," a scandal so notorious that it had been reported in local headlines.[30]

Similar to their U.S. peers, these French emigrants often had military experience—Algeria in their case—and arrived with an "armed force," meaning they could possibly duplicate Texas 1836 out west.[31] There were U.S. nationals too in San Blas, Mexico—a reported 200 as of mid-1852—but a considerable portion of these would-be "Anglo-Saxons" were "destitute," which could either inspire them into remunerative brigandage or indicate they did not have the stamina for the task.[32]

Farther south in Acapulco, the news delivered to Washington was similarly discouraging. Secretary of State Daniel Webster was told in April 1852 that "outrages" were "daily committed against American citizens and American property...." The consulate was so desperate that it even moved to protest what had befallen an "American negro named George Boon" who had "been two weeks confined in the castle at this place on the most baseless charge of murder without trial...."[33] Boon's demise was an example of the point that as repression against U.S. Negroes rose, more were fleeing southward. By 1854 Davis Blake, a man described as a "colored seaman" of "New York died in the harbor," referring to Vera Cruz, according to the U.S. envoy there.[34] By 1856 yet another U.S. Negro, the "aged...Wiliam

29. Consul Juan Robinson to John Cripps, U.S. envoy in Mexico, 22 February 1854, Reel 1, Despatches from U.S. Consuls in Guaymas, NARA.

30. Consul Franklin Chase to Secretary of State William Marcy, 8 September 1854, Reel 1, Despatches from U.S. Consuls in Tampico, NARA. See also *El Comercio* [Mexico], ca. September 1854 [date blotted].

31. Consul William Forbes to Secretary Marcy, 18 May 1853, Reel 1, Despatches from U.S. Consuls in San Blas, NARA.

32. Ibid., R.P. Letcher to William Forbes, 17 July 1852.

33. Consul Francis Rice to Secretary Webster, 13 April 1852, Reel 1, Despatches from U.S. Consuls in Acapulco, NARA.

34. John T. Pickett to Secretary Marcy, 21 August 1854, Reel 6, Despatches from U.S. Consuls in Vera Cruz, NARA.

Bailey reared at Annapolis," who had "served" his "country faithfully as a gunner on an American ship of war in the last war with England," according to a U.S. observer in Matamoros, was slain by a "deserter from Fort Brown," Texas, though the deceased had become "a soldier under the Mexican government...." It was unclear if the "murder" in Matamoros took place precisely because of his defection to the Mexican military.[35]

The arrival of the sable "citizenry" on these shores was igniting angst at the U.S. consulate. "American vessels are occasionally wrecked upon the coasts of Mexico," Washington was told after Blake's expiration and "usually have colored seamen," described as "citizens"; rather than facilitating their return northward, Consul John T. Pickett seemed to prefer that they become Mexican nationals,[36] only creating one more potential antagonist to Washington beyond its immediate jurisdiction.

The confounded consul contacted the U.S. Attorney General with a still profound inquiry, "are persons of...African race citizens of the United States or not...[?]" He thought he knew the answer: "I entertain the negative view," he offered since Washington was "essentially a 'white government.'"[37] His opinion was endorsed by the U.S. Supreme Court in 1857 in the infamous *Dred Scott* decision, which was hailed by Texas Lieutenant Governor Francis Richard Lubbock, who bequeathed his name to a major West Texas metropolis.[38]

Complementarily, Pickett reached Don Juan de Dios Arzamendi of Vera Cruz officialdom, who apparently had inquired about the presence there of U.S. nationals of "'seditious'" or "'dangerous'" character. Pickett responded, "there are here a number of refugiated [sic] negro slaves from the states of Louisiana [and] Texas...[who] are worthy and peaceful Mexican citizens" and, he added, there were also "deserters from the American army."[39]

By 1853 the Texas legislature had become exasperated by the increasing influx of "refugiated" Africans into Mexico and demanded

---

35. Consul to "Sir," 25 October 1856, Reel 2, Despatches from U.S. Consuls in Matamoros, NARA.

36. Letter from John T. Pickett, 10 July 1854, Reel 6, Despatches from U.S. Consuls in Vera Cruz, NARA.

37. Ibid., John T. Pickett to Attorney General Caleb Cushing, 25 January 1855.

38. Raymond Paul Flusche, "Francis Richard Lubbock," M.A. thesis, TTU, 1947, 24 (abbrev. Flusche).

39. John T. Pickett to General Don Juan de Dios Arzamendi, 12 August 1855, Reel 6, Despatches from U.S. Consuls in Vera Cruz, NARA.

that Washington negotiate a new treaty that would in effect extend southward "Fugitive Slave Laws"—that mandated that states north of the Mason-Dixon Line be complicit in return of runaways. The lawmakers mused that a "thief" could arrive in Texas, seize Africans, take them to Mexico and even sell them back to the original owners. The seeming inability of Washington to negotiate such a pact was just one more factor alienating Texas settlers from Washington serving to rationalize secession.[40] But it was worse than seeming inability since in 1857 Mexico, in Article II, Section I of its Constitution, boldly reaffirmed abolitionism.[41] As a further slap in the face of their enslaving neighbor, it was in 1856 that Mexico's president, Ignacio Comonfort, offered to bring 100 U.S. Negro families to Vera Cruz, where they would receive 2500 acres to develop[42]—and perhaps, some might speculate, form a base of opposition to enslavers.

Reporting from nearby El Paso, Texas, a U.S. agent pointed to the obvious, that the "Rio Grande being fordable nine months in the year...persons pass and repass freely," while a "passport" (generally barred from U.S. Negroes) was available for a "fee of two dollars...." Militarizing the border to prevent de facto Negro prisoners from leaving likely had a downside in that "commerce" in the neighborhood "has decreased since 1851," said David R. Diffenderrfer. "Hardly a day passes but what some act is considered and the criminal escapes across the river and is safe...."[43] When Mexico sought to impose tariffs on imports, commerce was suppressed further and, anger in El Paso rose.[44]

For through the years of the 1850s, the number of runaways heading to Mexico seemed to be increasing. The sojourning Frederick Law Olmsted noticed this in 1857. Across the border in Mexico he encountered "runaway slaves," including a man born in Virginia but sold to Texas before fleeing circa 1852. He spoke Spanish fluently. Those like him, said Olmsted, were arriving regularly, "forty" in the "last three months," all "excited with being free" and bent on exercising newly found rights "after they had learned the language,

---

40. Pridgen. See also Oran Lonnie Sinclair, "Crossroads of Conviction: A Study of the Texas Political Mind, 1856-1861," Ph.D. dissertation, Rice U, 1975.

41. Hammack, 27. For more on this potent point, see also Gassner, 34.

42. Fatima Shaik, *Economy Hall: The Hidden History of a Free Black Brotherhood*, Historic New Orleans, 2021, 166.

43. Consul Diffenderrfer to Sir, 1 March 1854, Reel 1, Despatches from U.S. Consuls in Paso del Norte, NARA.

44. Ibid., Consul Diffenderrfer to Sir, 1 October 1855.

which did not generally take them long...." The "government was very just to them," which only hardened their allegiance, making them even more of a threat to their former homeland, especially after "several" of them "had acquired wealth and positions of honor," virtually impossible back home. A "colored man," said Olmsted, "if he could behave himself decently, had rather an advantage over a white American" for "people generally liked them better...."[45]

The hawkish settler John Salmon "Rip" Ford said that at one point in the 1850s about 10% of the entire enslaved population had fled, likely an exaggeration but indication of the state of mind of rattled enslavers, a conundrum not aided when Mexicans continually opposed returning this species of property. (Reputedly, the percentage of lighter-skinned Negroes heading southward amongst the runaways seemed markedly high, perhaps an indication of how they could more easily blend in and even "pass" for Mexican or inspire more *simpático* treatment on the part of the latter.)

As aforementioned, by 1856 there was a plot by the enslaved, purportedly assisted by local Mexicans in Texas, to rebel and flee to Mexico. The rebels were prepared to fight the entire way there. Consonant with the growing statewide practice, they adopted secret signs and passwords; one of the principal instigators was a Free Negro or one perceived as such.[46] There was a wider panic about slave rebelliousness, apparently inspired by the Fremont anti-slavery campaign for the White House, which in turn infuriated enslavers.[47] The enslaved in Texas were understandably igniting panic in that some were armed, willing to fight, and reportedly had held a secret convention to that end, which was said to include liquidating those defined as "white." In this society drowning in arms, the rebels had managed to accumulate their share, along with sharpened objects that could be deadly when used properly. Arguably the perception that Mexican peons in the vicinity were aiding their enslaved comrades may have weakened both systems of exploitation—or, possibly, the ruthlessness required to implant these harsh labor systems created a police state conducive for the ultimate flourishing of fascism.[48]

45. Olmsted, *Journey*, 323, 324, 325.

46. *Galveston News*, ca. September 1856, Texas State Laws Collection, UT-A.

47. Harvey Wish, "The Slave Insurrection Panic of 1856," *Journal of Southern History*, 5 (No. 2, May 1939): 206-222, 207. For source for previous paragraph, see Nichols 2012, 41, 44.

48. Nichols 2012, 32, 41, 52, 57.

The outrage over slave revolts led to plans to attack the settlements along the border formed by Wild Cat, John Horse and others who were perceived as Negro. This was especially the case after the abortive rebellion of 3 September 1856 and three more plots that were uncovered soon thereafter.[49]

For despite the battering that Mexico had received during the war, this Haitian comrade continued to be a burr under the saddle of Texas. By mid-1852 the U.S. man in Matamoros was dyspeptic in informing Secretary of State Webster that "within a few leagues of this place an armed and organized band of Mexicans and savages are permitted to exist," perpetrating "outrageous depredations" with the authorities exercising "no _visible_ disposition to arrest their work of destruction...[emphasis-original]."[50]

Denizens of Matamoros may have thought that they were the ones in jeopardy for by 1855 José Santiago Vidaurri, who was to serve as governor of Nuevo León and Coahuila, was enmeshed in a bloody battle at Saltillo due west. With 2000 men under his command, he mimicked the so-called Republic of Sierra Madre that was to lead him to an association withU.S. secessionists. He imposed a defeat on his opponents who included Wild Cat—whom the U.S. consul called the "famous Seminole"—and "about 200 of his followers," who "committed the principal damage...with their unerring rifles."[51] In Tampico a U.S. agent was saddened to find that "no pains are spared to stigmatize...Vidaurri," painted accurately as Washington's man.[52]

He was such a placeman for the U.S. that he was analogized to Governor Lamar of the Texas Republic, a proponent of Indigenous genocide, opponent of Indigenous citizenship who sought the extermination of "'sanguinary savages [and] wild cannibals....'" Vidaurri villainized the Lipan, among others—though like the flexibility of his patrons, he deployed them against Comanches, Mexicans and Cherokees, while inviting Seminoles and Kickapoo to combat Lipan. His scorched earth policies resembled those of Texas republicans.[53]

---

49. Carrigan, 41-69, 57. See also Barbara E. Ledbetter, "Black and Mexican Slaves in Young County, Texas, 1856-1865," in Bruce A. Glasrud, et al., eds., _Slavery to Integration: Black Americans in West Texas_, Abilene: State House Press, 27-30.

50. J.F. Waddell, Consul to Secretary Webster, 15 June 1852, Reel 2, Despatches from U.S. Consuls in Matamoros, NARA.

51. Ibid., Consul Thomas Dirgan to Secretary Marcy, 8 August 1855.

52. Consul Franklin Chase to Secretary Marcy, 31 August 1855, Reel 2, Despatches from U.S. Consuls in Tampico, NARA.

53. Hampton, 6, 8, 58, 119, 123.

Vidaurri was embraced in Washington since there was much at stake. For there were considerable U.S. investments in Tampico specifically, and Mexico generally, to the point where war vessels were requested to protect this booty.[54] By 1856 Vidaurri was enjoying success—as Consul James Armstrong put it—"in establishing his government over the country bounded on this frontier as certain and inevitable...like that of our General [William] Harney towards the Indians,"[55] referring to a future Confederate who, not coincidentally, was a major liquidator of Indigenes. As Vidaurri gained strength in this portion of the borderlands, by 1857 the reality was—according to officialdom—that "direct American trade to this frontier in domestic and foreign goods is estimated at more value than the American imports at all the other Mexican ports"; "commerce on the Rio Grande," the message conveyed to future Confederate John Slidell, "is in a pecuniary and commercial point of view the most important in the republic" and "the trade is increasing." Those of Slidell's ilk, who had been exerting inordinate pressure on Mexico, up to and including spearheading the 1840s war, stood to benefit from this pummeling when they seceded in 1861.[56]

It was also in 1857 that the visitor from the U.S. Northeast, Frederick Law Olmsted, wandered into Texas like a stranger in a strange land. He had been a landscape architect and as he surveyed the vexed moonscape of the borderlands, one could easily imagine his conducting a redesign in his mind's eye. Unlike many analysts today, he realized instinctively the parlous position of Texas, having to maneuver among the major powers, along with Indigenous nations, Mexicans and often angry Africans. For he perceived an "interest taken in foreign affairs" that was palpable. One "gentleman of property in eastern Texas" was anticipating a "general war in Europe," which would leave him in a "pretty fix, with cotton down to four cents a pound. Curse those Turks!"—a reference to the war in the Crimea, yet another step downward for the once mighty Ottomans. "If he thought there would be a general war, he would take every [damned] nigger he'd go...right down to New Orleans and sell them for what they'd bring. They'd never be so high again as they were now and if there should come a general war they wouldn't be worth

54. Consul Franklin Chase to Secretary Marcy, 9 January 1857, Reel 2, Despatches from U.S. Consuls in Tampico, NARA.

55. Consul James Armstrong to Secretary Marcy, 11 November 1856, Reel 2, Despatches from U.S. Consuls in Matamoros, NARA.

56. Ibid., Consul to John Slidell, 27 November 1857.

half so much next year. There were some infernal rascals somewhere in the world," recognizing that it took one to know one. Aghast, he continued, "Turks and Russians and Prussians and Dutchmen and Frenchmen—just be put in a bag together and slung into hell." As for Olmsted, he peremptorily dismissed the still resonant notion of a German exception as to slavery, for as soon as these Hanse men and others "acquired property, they followed the customs of the country and purchased slaves, like other white people...." Tellingly, a day or two after arriving in West Texas, "there was the hanging of a Mexican. The whole population left the town to see," as "the Mexicans looked on imperturbable...." The rascal republicans "in speaking of them," meaning Mexicans, "constantly distinguish themselves as 'white folks,'" the ruling race, in short. This racializing proceeded though there were "a few of old Spanish blood" who had "purchased negro servants but most of them regard slavery with abhorrence," yet another reason for the rascals to seek their ouster. "Runaways were *constantly* arriving here," he stressed with wonder, which was feeding the persistent "scheme of separating the Rio Grande" and "erecting the 'Republic of Sierra Madre' by American aid, given under the promise of the immediate passage of a law for the rendition of slaves...a favorite [proposal] with the slave proprietors of the Southwest...." This proposal could also flummox what was in motion: in Eagle Pass, Texas, Mexicans and Indigenes were uniting to repel potential annexations.[57]

This Texas slaveowner was not the only Euro-American who was seeking to gauge the correlation of forces globally in order to map his nation's next move. By 1857, James Buchanan, an architect of Mexico's dismemberment, was now in the White House and he was taken by the fact that "England and France were engaged in a war against China and urged the United States to become a party to it," which provided leverage in ducking abolitionist pressure or even repulsing fellow filibusterers due south. Still, this war was "undertaken to accomplish objects in which we had a common interest with themselves. This was the fact," was his sober assessment.[58]

The logic of "extermination"—as adumbrated by Olmsted—did not necessarily halt at the Rio Grande, in short. Ironically, there was an influential school of thought in Washington that sought to expel—or "diffuse"—U.S. Negroes southward, up to and including, as one man put it, dispatching "'ten thousand Negroes to Mexico more

---

57. Olmsted, *Journey*, 118, 133, 159, 163, 324, 333.
58. Remarks, 1857 in J.B. Moore, Volume XII, 241.

readily than a single hundred to Africa'"—but the porous southern border, allowing for a capital flight that was to their dismay harming the pocketbooks of enslavers, was attaining a similar object. It was the savvy Negro journalist and editor Mary Ann Shadd who advocated migration of her people to Mexico in league with London's pressure to unify that republic with a Negro-dominated territory of the U.S. itself.[59]

Thus, while Washington was seeking to endorse pro-slavery stances inside and outside the republic, likewise the republic was boosting advocates of same. In January 1847 President Polk accorded Jefferson Davis—premier enslaver—an honor and military experience that would soon prove to be invaluable in promoting his secessionist scheme. He was granted a "commission as Brigadier General of the [U.S.] Army...to serve during the war with Mexico," a sign of his purported "distinguished gallantry and military skill...especially in the battles of *Monterey* and *Buena Vista*," with the "severe wound you received in the latter place" as indicative of his willingness to engage in fierce combat.[60] By 1850 Senator Davis had strode into the chambers and uttered a stemwinding denunciation of Mexico's 1824 act mandating "the prohibition of the traffic in slaves," fanning sectional flames by adding that "this was a prohibition against slaves into California and New Mexico from the United States, while those territories belonged to the Mexican Republic...." This was "clearly inoperative" in light of the recent seizure of this land, he claimed, though he could not resist a jab at Mexico's similar "decree of 1829," little more than "the decree of a usurper," he sniffed.[61] Pounding on an open door, he demanded the legalization of slavery in California since gold mining was "better adapted to slave labor than...any other species of labor," and the same held true, he said, for work in New Mexico. Consonant with the temper of the times in elevated precincts in Washington, he assayed that Mexico "since the abolition of slavery" had "become so impoverished that, to derive money for her support, she sold territory to the United States...."[62] This latter claim did not sate his appetite for more Mexican land. By late 1851 he instructed the "people of Mississippi," meaning those defined as "white," that the war with Mexico could have led to "total

59. Sebastian Page, *Black Resettlement and the American Civil War*, New York: Cambridge U Press, 2021, 148 (abbrev. S. Page).

60. President Polk to Jefferson Davis, 19 May 1847, in Rowland, Volume I, 73.

61. Ibid., Speech of Jefferson Davis, 13-14 February 1850, 263-308, 272.

62. Ibid., Remarks by Jefferson Davis, 14 February 1850, 289.

destruction of the Mexican government" and "to the swallowing up of the whole of Mexico by the United States. There was a large party who desired this true," which was true, "and Southern men of the highest stations were of it," similarly accurate.[63]

Though the escalation of Indigenous resistance postwar in the Lone Star State was among the factors alienating settlers from the federal headquarters in Washington, they had little reason to carp since it was Davis—a "Southern man" of the "highest station"—who was Secretary of War in 1853 and able to draw upon tax revenues generated by enslaved labor and Free Negroes alike in order to foment suppression. It was then that the future ersatz president candidly recognized that "repressing hostilities among the Indian tribes and of protecting frontier settlements from their depredations is the most difficult on which the Army has now to perform and nowhere has it been found more difficult [than] on the western frontier of Texas." Marking him as a squishy "liberal" in then ascendant Texas terms, he posited that "if...the Indians were limited to a defined territory... set aside [on] a tract of land...gathered and concentrated there," it could reduce the problem (settlers made of sterner stuff were moving toward "extermination").[64] By 1854 public meetings in Texas were proliferating, focused on ever more hyperventilating about purported Indigenous depredations, which served to accelerate the drive toward "extermination."[65]

However, a desperate Davis was moving toward extraordinary remedies. Like others in Washington, he was a student of French colonialism as a pattern setter. He was conversant, for example, with French tobacco and cotton cultivation in Algeria and the Caribbean[66] and turned to North Africa again for pointers on subjugation of Indigenes.

He told President Franklin Pierce in December 1853 that "by the annexation of Texas and the acquisition of New Mexico and California, our Indian population has been increased from 240,000 to more than 400,000" of "predatory and war-like" groups; thus, based on colonialism in Algeria, he wanted to deploy a military force on

---

63. Ibid., Jefferson Davis in the *Mississippi Free Trader*, 8 October 1851, Volume II, 88.

64. Ibid., Secretary Davis to Governor P.H. Bell, 19 September 1853, 265.

65. Proceedings of Public Meeting, 24 May 1854, Box 301-2, Governor Elisha M. Pease Papers, Texas Archives.

66. E.B. Buchanan to Jefferson Davis, 1 August 1854, in Rowland, Volume II, 372.

camels.[67] As matters evolved—and foreseeably—by 1858 camels were shipped to Galveston, but the cargo also was said to include a disguised landing of 200 Africans destined for slavery.[68]

President Pierce, who was deeply influenced by his Secretary of War, was prone to endorse his most far-fetched schemes,[69] especially since by many accounts, Indigenous resistance was rising by 1853.[70] Intriguingly, it was in nearby Indian Territory also in 1853 that a revolt was hatched by Free Negroes near the headwaters of the "Muddy" Boggy River.[71] Coincidentally enough, it was also in 1853 that the abolitionist Lewis Tappan chortled in New York City that the "whole world" was "talking or reading" about U.S. enslavement, especially inspired by the novel by Harriet Beecher Stowe: *Uncle Tom's Cabin*.[72]

Visiting Mexico in 1855, the territorial finagler James Gadsden found the novel "translated into Spanish" and "found in almost every domicile," which continued to "impress" Mexicans "with Anglo-American designs to enslave them," not a reliable basis for fruitful bilateral ties. In fact, one of the Mexican "Minister[s]" he interacted with had "recently been very prolific in his commentaries on the institution of African slavery, as it exists in the United States." But, as Gadsden saw it, he was not wholly responsible since "his condemnation of the abuses and practices" northward "seem to have emanated from… London…."[73] Perhaps. But this was small solace to the family of California politico Henry A. Crabb, former Whig then pro-slavery Know Nothing, who wound up beheaded after filibustering in Sonora.[74]

While Davis, a prominent Washingtonian, was on a path leading to rupture, with Texas and Mexico being a *casus belli*, there were others moving in an opposing direction. By 1861 William Seward was part of an elite class in Washington, serving as U.S. Secretary of State

67. Ibid., Secretary Davis to President Pierce, 1 December 1853, 292-333, 304.

68. *Confederate Military History…written by Distinguished Men of the South and Edited by General Clement E. Evans of Georgia and Colonel O.M. Roberts, Volume XI*, Atlanta: Confederate Publishing, 1899, 10.

69. Joseph Allen Stout, Last Years, 135.

70. Elam, 125. See also "Treaty Between the United States and the Chasta [*sic*] and Other Tribes of Indians," 18 November 1854, Huntington Library.

71. Franklin, 9.

72. Remarks by Lewis Tappan, 15 February 1853, in Abel and Klingberg, 319.

73. James Gadsden to Secretary Marcy, 3 April 1855, in Manning, Volume IX, 750.

74. Joseph Allen Stout, Last Years, 146.

and protecting the republic's flanks against the repetitive gnawing of Confederates led by Davis. In 1849 a debate was unfolding
in Congress about abrogating Mexican abolitionist laws in recently
seized territories, backed avidly by Davis's comrade Robert Walker.
There was significant support for this measure in the U.S. Senate,
but Governor Seward of New York flexed his sinewy muscles in
seeking to defeat it.[75] Before then, at a mass meeting of the Whigs
in Yates County, N.Y., in October 1844, this future Republican Party
leader groused about how the "American Empire" was "engrafting
Texas," turbocharging the "domestic slave trade": "it exposes us
to danger from abroad," said this future chief diplomat accurately.
"The democracy of the Texas party," he said with similar perceptive-
ness, "is aristocracy for the white race and bondage for the black."
By 1853, on the verge of the founding of the anti-slavery Republican
Party, he was singing from the same hymnbook as the nation slid
irrevocably toward civil war.[76]

U.S. nationals were arriving in the vicinity of Acapulco in significant number then, since, as Webster was informed, the consulate
was not far from "the whole of the Panama area" and "Nicaragua...
as well as...Vera Cruz," all future and ongoing targets for piratical
adventurism. "Things are going...from bad to worse here," said
Consul Francis Rice, since "in no part of the world do so many Americans land as in this [area]" and those observing were all too aware of
what they were capable of executing.[77] As if they were seeding the
entire hemisphere for slavery's extension or even eventual secession,
Southerners—especially Texans—managed to be appointed to critical diplomatic posts in the Americas. This included the Irish-born
military man Thomas W. Ward, who bloodily served the Republic
of Texas, receiving thousands of acres of land in the bargain; but by
1854 he was U.S. consul in Panama, the crucial chokepoint between
two continents.[78]

In the meantime, matters deteriorated further when Rice himself
was "arrested...imprisoned in a hold 6-1/2 by 12 feet and only 6 or
7 to the ceiling" for reasons he thought spurious, and in the ultimate
indignity, it was "occupied by five or six of the lowest dregs of the

75. Note, ca. 1849 in Baker, Seward, Volume I, lxxxiv.

76. Ibid., Speech, 29 October 1844, Volume III, 260, 268, 269, 272.

77. Francis Rice to Secretary Webster, 8 June 1852, Reel 1, Despatches
from U.S. Consuls in Acapulco, NARA.

78. Thomas W. Ward to "My Dear Wife," Box 1, Ward Papers. In the same
collection see also the letter from Ward to "His Excellency José María Unutia
Anino, Governor of the Province of Panama," 26 January 1854.

negroes of Acapulco...."[79] Even President Millard Fillmore shook himself out of his usual administrative slumber and felt compelled to make an official statement about what had happened to Rice.[80]

By 1854 the problem of U.S. settlers crossing Mexican territory in order to reach the lucrative goldfields of California was manifesting once more, especially in Tehuantepec. There were "vexatious" matters, said Consul Charles Webster, since "sailing vessels from Panama to San Francisco are frequently longer in making the voyage than the clippers from New York & the same port." And because of tricky currents, "ships [were] becalmed on this coast fourteen days at a time," and since "at least nine tenths of the population is composed of Pueblo Indians," the stranded settlers were not necessarily embraced. Nevertheless, he emphasized, "mails can be carried between New Orleans and San Francisco by this isthmus [of Tehuantepec] in <u>fourteen days....</u>"

This unease with foreign visitors was notably the case for a sector of "Pueblo El Barrio" that was "composed almost entirely of Samboes, descendants of the slaves...." The "Zapotecas" were the "most numerous" and "most intelligent race of Indians in the country," said this amateur anthropologist but they were hardly more embracing of these alien visitors, though they were both "docile" and "industrious." "The whites form a very insignificant portion of the population," he added with a hint of sadness, "not being more than one hundred or one hundred and fifty on the whole isthmus," and "of this number one third are French and Spaniards," not necessarily pro-U.S., in sum. Still, he was heartened that the "system pursued by the Spanish [sic] government" there "suggests the adoption of a like or similar policy among the wandering "tribes" existing in the territories of the United States. To provide a sense of comparability of danger, he declared that the "number of wild or uncivilized Indians in the United States, is estimated at about five hundred thousands, occupying an immense territory, continually waging war," while the "number of Pueblo Indians in this state alone...amounts to nearly or quite the whole indigenous population of the United States...."

This exposed the frailty of previous efforts by the Republic of Texas to create problems for Mexico by aligning with Indigenes in

---

79. Francis Rice to R.P. Letcher, 14 June 1852, Reel 1, Despatches from U.S. Consuls in Acapulco, NARA.

80. Ibid., "Message from the President...in Relation to the Imprisonment of the United States Consuls and other American Citizens in [the] castle of Acapulco...January 17, 1853."

Yucatan that later led to Washington's attempt to tamp down the resultant fires.

Yet qualms about Indigenes aside, what had attracted the consul's riveting attention was the "considerable mahogany" all about, much of it "sent to New Orleans," not to mention "silver mines" in Oaxaca, gold too. Then there was Soconusco—subject of a territorial dispute with Guatemala—which created possibilities for destabilization.[81]

In part what was happening in Mexico was that the U.S. war of aggression had been terribly dislocating and disruptive, which not only attracted the greedy intention of major powers but also spurred on domestic militancy that complicated the ability of Paris and Washington to capitalize on the situation. Thus, by August 1852 the U.S. press was up in arms about Mexico in that "Indians are creating great alarm in the city of Mexico" and "have come down in the country far below Chihuahua and in the neighborhood of San Louis [sic] Potosi. In the state of Zacatecas, which is only two hundred miles to the north of the city of Mexico, they have in numbers of three hundred at a time attacked many haciendas…. several combats have taken place between the savages and the Mexicans, in which the latter have been invariably defeated…."[82] Would this spreading revolt spread northward to the border?

Still, there may have been hurdles to surmount in order for invaders to conquer Acapulco, for as Washington was told, there was "continual overpowering heat and sickness and earthquakes of daily occurrence," along with "yellow fever…." By 1853 the "great rush of emigration to California" via this Pacific Coast port was slowing[83]—although yellow fever was not necessarily receding. It was during that same year that David Terry, a prominent Texan who became a leader in California too, was made aware that "we are surrounded by sickness and death, that awful scourge of yellow fever is slaying [and] preying upon the Europeans and strangers at a fearful rate. None of the old citizens have been attacked" but "Galveston is suffering worse than New Orleans has" and was "much worse than it was in forty-nine…."[84]

---

81. Consul Charles Webster to the U.S. State Department, 10 March 1854, Reel 1, Despatches from U.S. Consuls in Tehuantepec, NARA.

82. Clipping, 13 August 1852, Reel 1, Despatches from U.S. Consuls in Acapulco, NARA.

83. Ibid., Consul Charles Denman to Secretary of State William Marcy, 29 September 1853.

84. C. Tucker to Cornelia Runnels, 14 September 1853, Box 1, David Terry Papers, Huntington Library. See also E.P. Hunt vs. A.S. Johnston, et al., in the Supreme Court of Texas at Galveston, 1855, NYHS.

This cascade of U.S. settlers into Mexico, combined with the headiness and exhilaration delivered by the continuing seizure of lands, may have influenced the founding in 1854 of the Knights of the Golden Circle, which sought to extend slavery within the hemisphere,[85] putatively grasping the nettle of finding a safe boundary for slavery—that obviously Mexico did not provide—by making the institution boundless. KGC had a disproportionate number of members in Texas, but this did not preclude the founding of "The Lone Star of the West," a so-called "secret society" with similar aims with the noted buccaneer John "Rip" Ford as pre-eminent leader: taking Cuba, also on the KGC agenda, was their primary goal. Like the Ku Klux Klan, which emerged post-Civil War and carried the seeds of fascism, LSW too was highly ritualistic.[86] It was also in 1854 that Texas witnessed the introduction of yet another organization described as "secret," the so-called "Know Nothing or American Party," which for a time included Sam Houston who was reportedly tied to KGC too.[87]

Ford's desire to seize Cuba was not his impulse alone. His fellow Texan, Congressman Volney Howard, made it clear that taking the island was a priority. Otherwise a "second St. Domingo with a view of striking a blow in the United States" was inevitable, an event that he and his comrades "cannot permit...so near [our] shores...." London was the evil genius masterminding unrest, he thought, since this power wanted to "bring about a revolution in Cuba" by way of erecting the horror of horrors—a "Black Military Republic under British protection"—making Cuba, he insisted, "far more necessary to us than Gibraltar or Malta to England...."[88]

It was Ford who backed the formation in Mexico of what one analyst termed a "revolutionary movement...with the proviso that a newly formed junta would cooperate in returning escaped blacks.... fire-eater considered the problem troublesome enough to warrant

---

85. Naylor, 137.

86. W.J. Hughes, 169. See also Stephen B. Oates, ed., *Rip Ford's Texas*, Austin: U of Texas Press, 1963, xxx. Purportedly, Ford was also part of the Knights of the Golden Circle.

87. Helen Marie Pease, "Elisha Marshall Pease (A Biography)," B.A. thesis, Incarnate Word College, May 1937, Box 112, (abbrev. H.M. Pease), Pease, Graham and Nile Families Papers-APL (abbrev. Pease, Graham, Nile Papers).

88. Hon. Volney Howard of Texas on the Acquisition of Cuba Delivered in the House of Representatives, January 6, 1853, Washington, D.C.: Globe, 1853, Huntington Library.

either war with Mexico or secession from the union...." As the 1850s unspooled, it did seem that the enslaved were devising ever more elaborate plots to organize, what the analyst Paul Dean Lack called "massive escapes to Mexico"; dangerously, the plotters, he added, "usually possessed arms of all kind."[89] By 1855, according to one estimate, 4000 enslaved Africans had fled Texas, principally to Mexico, with a value of $3.2 million.[90]

More extravagantly, some pro-slavery forces alleged that 200,000 of the enslaved had escaped to Mexico, which was more of a reflection of their increasingly inflamed and hysterical mindset than anything else. Bounty hunters determined to retrieve this property by any means necessary flourished, including not only Ford but Santos Benavides of Mexican origin (though Tejanos were said collectively to own only about 60 slaves during this era): he went on to become a Confederate military man. The reward for capture of those who had fled could amount to a handsome $600 per slave.

Illustrative of the theme that repression in Texas was so severe in part because of the resistance encountered—abolitionist Mexico, rebellious Comanches and other Indigenes particularly—not only was there a busy depot of the fabled "Underground Railroad" in McAllen, Texas, on the border, in the form of Nathaniel Jackson's ranch, but also residing in the Rio Grande Valley in the 1850s was John Ferdinand Webber, patriarch of a so-called "mixed race" family; he had engaged in an affair with Silvia Hector, a neighbor's property, that led to a brood of 11 children. But also illustrative was that he could not tolerate the cruel racism endured by his family and relocated to Mexico, where he became Juan Fernando Webber—and likely emulated Jackson, who too had married an enslaved woman, Matilda Hicks.[91]

With the short memories that routinely afflicted rapacious republicans, elite Texans failed to recall how desperate they were on the verge of annexation in 1845 and how Washington bailed them out; but in the succeeding decade they increasingly viewed the federal union as being dangerously infested with abolitionists and incapable of defending enslaving interests—especially vis-à-vis Mexico—which

89. Lack, 249, 250, 259.

90. Audain, 127.

91. Roseann Bacha-Garza, "Race and Ethnicity Along the Antebellum Rio Grande," in Roseann Bacha-Garza, et.al., eds., *The Civil War on the Rio Grande, 1846-1876*, College Station: TA&MU Press, 2019, 82-106, 83, 84, 89, 92, 93, 94, 95 (abbrev. Bacha-Garza, *Civil War*).

mandated yet another secession, along with more land grabs en route to this cherished goal.

By 1861 there were some among these groups, but especially KGC, who thought simply fighting a sectional war was misguided and this energy should have been directed southward. In the preceding decade, the 1850s, the slavery lobby was pushing for carving at least three slave states out of territory then claimed by Texas, as an offset to California which—despite the presence of slavery—was technically not deemed a slave state. Horace Mann, the leading educator, was choleric in consideration of this measure: "Admit slavery there," he roared, "and the power of government will be invoked to exterminate these Indians, as it was before to exterminate the Cherokees and Seminoles...."[92] As things evolved, "extermination" proceeded in coming years, both after 1861 and irrespective of whether Texas was carved up or not.

Yet another restraint shackling the Knights was the uncertainty of settlers, filibusterers and invaders being able to overcome Indigenes, who—in light of the disastrous experience of European powers in Texas—may have been aided by London in a replay of Tecumseh and the 1812 war. This thought had occurred to Randolph Marcy, a military man who had fought in the Blackhawk War, the war in Mexico, then battled the Mormons in Utah, before providing a guide to pioneers crossing the continent. Although his roots were in the U.S. Northeast, he spoke like a Texas settler when in 1854 he derided the Comanches: "most of them having never even seen a white man" were more dangerous, possibly less able to be seduced by racial legerdemain: they were "the most powerful nation in existence," he said.

But for those wishing to align with them, there was a downside, according to Marcy, in that "within the past few years the Comanches have (for whatever reason I could not learn) taken an inveterate dislike to the Negroes and have massacred several small parties of those who attempted to escape from the Seminoles and cross the plains for the purpose of joining Wild Cat upon the Rio Grande. Upon inquiring of them the cause of their hostility to the blacks, they replied that it was because they were slaves to the whites, that they were sorry for them" and thus, felt the urge to send them to "another world" beyond. This was a tactical and strategic blunder not only in that it disrupted the anti-settler coalition, for even Marcy

---

92. Mann. See also "Slavery in California and New Mexico...Speech of Mr. Orin Fowler of Massachusetts in the House of Representatives, March 11, 1850...," Washington, D.C.: Buell and Blanchard.

knew that if they joined Wild Cat they would "augment to such a degree…their marauding operations along the Mexican border…." The Comanches, he told his readers, "have also been hostile toward the Delawares and Shawnees," also easily manipulable. But perpetuating a trend worthy of more scrutiny, he noticed that Comanches were "so extremely jealous of their own freedom that they will often commit suicide rather than be taken prisoners"—and, ironically, "are the more prone to enslave others…." Also potentially manipulable was the allegation that "hardships imposed upon the females are most severe and cruel"—"every degrading office that is imposed upon the black by the most tyrannical master," he said, "falls among the Comanches, to the lot of the wretched female…."[93]

Marcy also traveled through what was termed "unexplored Texas" in 1854. There he saw "two Negroes chained together by the neck and driven along the road, by several men," while the "Free Negro was undergoing the infliction of sixty lashes laid on with an unmerciful hand," eliciting anguished "groans and cries…." Along the way, he noticed that "most of the Choctaws hold slaves…. they look upon them as mere beasts of burden and treat them accordingly…." Nonetheless, "our quondam host," said this observer, "was…fullblooded" and "served in the Creek War with General Jackson and like all of his tribe, was very proud of the fact that they have always been allies of the United States"[94]: yet one more reason for their ultimate defeat.

---

93. Randolph Marcy, "Exploration of the Red River of Louisiana in the Year 1852…33rd Congress, 1st Session, Senate Executive Document," Washington, D.C.: Beverly Tucker, 1854, 108, 111, Historic New Orleans.

94. Parker, *Notes*, 17.

Chapter 12

Civil War Approaches, Texas at Issue, 1857-1859

By 1857 and the year of the *Dred Scott* decision placing a legal imprimatur on the non-citizenship of U.S. Negroes, the political situation in Texas, the borderlands and nationally was spinning out of control. Settlers were demanding the liquidation of Indigenes (moderates thought they should be placed on reservations); the enslaved were skedaddling to freedom in Mexico to the consternation of enslavers; to the northwest of Texas in Utah, religious dissidents in the Church of Latter Day Saints were on the warpath, drawing the attention of the U.S. military, meaning fewer to patrol the borderlands. Secession was in the air as many in the Slave South were convinced that Washington was incapable of bringing Mexico to accept a treaty forcing the return of fleeing Africans, nor was the federal union capable of liquidating Indigenes in the manner demanded.

Texas chauvinists, such as "Rip" Ford, backed secession since Washington was seen as incapable of protecting settlers against the Indigenous; as he saw it, Texas was alone in facing this knotty problem—so, as early as June 1858, he demanded secession. It was near that time that the soon-to-be Confederate Secretary of State, Robert Toombs, arrived in Houston, then Austin, speaking to packed houses. The companion of this blinkered thinking was that sectional animosities should be diverted into the unifying channel of foreign conquest, e.g., swallowing the entire Rio Grande valley as a first step.[1]

Foreign conquest, genocide, escalating enslavement: all told, Texas was continuing to plant the seeds of a unique fascism that began to bloom in the 21st century.

* * *

---

1. W.J. Hughes, 254, 265, 177.

By 1931 Texas was a bastion of Jim Crow and, thus, an analyst then did not seem to be entirely upset about what he noticed in 1857: "the cry was heard everywhere," said J. Marvin Hunter, "'run the Indians out of Texas.'" By then Texans directed by the future Confederate leader John Baylor were confronting venomously U.S. forces who they thought were overly protective of Indigenes, i.e., the pro-reservation settlers were seen as sellouts or worse by the pro-genocide settlers (perversely post-Civil War, the victors seemed to emulate Baylor at his worst). The Baylor legions were explicit in dehumanizing Indigenes as "'Creatures [and] least useful of all the creatures who ever lived upon the earth,'" but somehow were "'securely wrapped in the American flag,'" now worthy of being supplanted. As Baylor saw things, these intended victims were "being aided by the United States troops," making them abettors susceptible to liquidation too. Their stronghold was Jacksboro, Texas, where their appropriately named scandal sheet, *The White Man*, was published, whose specialty was the almost anarchic venting of spleen against Robert Neighbors, a U.S. agent who ultimately was murdered by Baylor's forces in an anticipation of civil war. The triggerman, Ed Cornett, shot him in the back with a double-barreled shotgun loaded with twelve buckshot in both barrels.[2]

A ticklish issue driving secession—at least in Texas—was the perception, as put by scholar Earl Henry Elam, "[federal] agents talked peace" regarding Indigenes, and "the settlers made war," once again illustrating that it is folly to focus wholly on elites in explicating the strength of proto-fascism: there was bottom-up support too, as the grassroots defined as "white" did not want to miss out on the fruits of plunder. But the annexation deal, as noted, delivered a lush plum to Texas settlers in the form of control over public lands, providing them with propulsion in their felt desire to expel—or liquidate—Indigenes, and undermined any effort by Washington toward the supposed moderation of construction of reservations.[3]

Thus, the Karankawa were pushed toward extinction during this cruel epoch.[4]

Twistedly, Caddo became a major victim of this turn: along with Comanche, Cherokee and Kickapoo they were derided subsequently as "most obnoxious," though they had aided settlers in combating

---

2. J. Martin Hunter, *The Bloody Trail in Texas: Sketches and Narratives of the Indian Raids and Atrocities On Our Frontier*, Bandera, Texas: JMH, 1932. For more on Neighbors, see also Tanner, 87.

3. Elam, 150.

4. Newcomb, 343.

Comanches. But in an outburst of racial chauvinism, endemic in settler colonialism, the bulk of Euro-Texans turned against all Indigenes and, as Neighbors was being slaughtered, fixed a date for the massacre of what was termed "the reservation Indians," Caddo especially.[5] As late as 1858, Tonkawa were still assisting settlers in fighting Comanches, but this did not halt their own liquidation.[6] By 1859 Tonkawa were expelled formally from Texas.[7] In their version of benignity, other settlers forced Indigenes from Texas to Indian Territory instead of slaughtering them.[8]

By February 1858, Jefferson Davis, in sizing up the situation then and shortly, recalled how once "Indians...lived upon fertile valleys with abundance of game," but "the people of Texas [settlers] has now driven the Indians from the fertile plains into the arid region where but little game is to be found; and now by necessity, they commit forays for plunder in order that they may obtain food,"[9] and in a vicious cycle this led to murderous attacks upon them.

Davis's assessment seems overly sympathetic to Indigenes—"by necessity they commit forays"—but as matters evolved, it was his comrades who rebelled against Washington in part because the central power was seen as lethargic in repulsing Indigenes. After the Civil War, a Mexican delegation pointed out that in 1858 Kiowa leaders "in whose behalf the general government intervened when they had been arrested, tried and condemned by the Texan courts, gave rise to an acrimonious debate in which the Indian policy of that government was bitterly denounced.... the policy of the federal government...required the liberation of the Kiowa chiefs...."[10]

By December 1858, like night following day, disturbing reports emerged from Brownsville: "tribe of Indians exterminated...to the last warrior," was the gleeful headline, with "women and children" included—though charitably, like livestock, they were "distributed among the different ranches...." With an absence of elegy, it was announced: "this ends the once powerful tribe of Tampacaus..." with more "tribes" on the hit list.[11] Also by 1858 a reign of terror unleashed

5. Gleason, 62.

6. Newlin, 80.

7. Himmel, 10.

8. David La Vere, ed., *Life Among Texas Indians: The WPA Narratives*, College Station: TA&MU Press, 1998, 40.

9. Speech, 10 February 1858 in Rowland, Volume III, 175.

10. *Report of the Committee of Investigation 1873*, 443.

11. *Southern Intelligencer*, 1 December 1858, AAS.

against Indigenes had driven many from the state, the lucky ones who were not simply killed.[12]

Even Washington, no neophyte in the bloody realm of genocide, was taken aback by Austin's depredations, to the alienating dismay of Texas land grabbers and enslavers. Nonplussed, the Secretary of the Interior admitted that "it gives me great pain to refer to the treatment which the Texas Reserve Indians and their Superintendent and Agents have received," an oblique reference to mass murder. "Removal of the Indians was demanded under a threat of extermination," it was said, so the decision was made to abandon reservations. But settlers demanded "immediate removal," not some elongated process so "Reserve Indians lived in daily fear of being murdered" and their exit was insufficient: "threats were then made that the Indians should not depart unmolested...." Washington was reduced to deploying the "army to protect them in their exodus...." They fled to Indian Territory, some straggling into Mexico, but Texas settlers remained dissatisfied. Thus, Neighbors was "wantonly attacked and murdered...."[13]

Some Cherokees there may have welcomed the displaced for by 1859 in Tahlequah a census revealed the presence of 21,000 Cherokees; 4000 Africans; and 1000 defined as "white"[14]—and the newcomers could have bolstered opposition to the latter. This was a dire necessity since in Texas the population had grown by a staggering 325% between 1847 and 1860, from 212,295 to 604,215.[15]

Texas settlers were unimpressed with the uproar over their misdeeds. C.B. Underhill in Bosque County instead accused Indigenes of murder, referring to them to with curious contempt as "rascally black throats...." The "immense sums of money lavished and misappropriated on Indian agencies by the United States government and in feeding and arming our savage enemies," he sputtered, was the real crime; Washington "gave to three tribes—the Comanches, Kioways [sic] and Apaches—eight hundred fine-made American rifles and shotguns," and the recipients said they "intended to wipe out

12. de Wit, 74.

13. "Annual Report of the Secretary of the Interior to Congress, of December 1, 1859," Box 1, Heflin Papers (abbrev. Annual Report of the Secretary of the Interior, 1859).

14. Ibid., George Butler to "Sir," 10 September 1859. See also Sedgwick, 356. Census figures above are confirmed here.

15. Miguel Ángel González-Quiroga, *War and Peace on the Rio Grande Frontier, 1830-1880*, Norman: U of Oklahoma Press, 2020, 91 (abbrev. González-Quiroga).

the white people on the Texas border!" That is, there was an "exterminating war" unfolding, but it was "against the white race"; and then he lurched toward relative moderation by demanding "they will have to be removed...."[16]

The early pro-genocide historian J.W. Wilbarger concurred with Underhill, observing that "from 1858 to 1875 Indian raids were frequent," taking advantage of Civil War and Reconstruction dislocation, "and they scarcely ever visited the settlement without carrying with them a large number of horses and generally a few scalps of the settlers ornamented their belts...." It was in 1859, he spluttered, that these diabolical "red devils...commenced their depredations in Parker County...and so it was in Jack County," too, leaving settlers few options besides genocide—in his opinion.[17] In a precursor of fascist atrocities in Europe,[18] settlers themselves organized in posses to rout Indigenes.[19]

Settlers too were upset by the failure of Mexicans and Mexican Americans to respond to the colonial diktat. Again, in 1857 there was a scrap involving those of Mexican origin and their carting goods from the coast to San Antonio; on one occasion a body of mounted men, disguised and armed, fired upon the carters, killing one and gravely wounding three others, all of which occurred in Goliad County, whose very name evoked shrieks from those with longer memories. Although there were those of Mexican origin on both sides of the battle, the Mexican legation was sufficiently distraught that it protested to Secretary of State Lewis Cass. Evidently they were distressed by the reports concerning "committees of armed men" with the "exclusive purpose of hunting down Mexicans...spoiling them of their property and putting them to death," along with the stories of how "residents of Mexican origins [were] expelled" to Mexico.[20]

But what noticeably riled settlers was the credible accusation that the carters or "*carreteros*" were aiding absconding Africans, assisting their escape southward and instigating insurrections of the

---

16. C.B. Underhill to "Editors," January 1859, in Annual Report of the Secretary of the Interior, 1859.

17. Wilbarger, 508, 534.

18. Jan Gross, *Neighbors: The Destruction of the Jewish Community in Jedwabne, Poland*, Princeton: Princeton U Press, 2012.

19. Thomas H. Espy to Sam Houston, 20 February 1860, Box 2, Governor Sam Houston Papers, Texas Archives (abbrev. Sam Houston Papers).

20. "Executive Office, Austin, 11 November 1857, Message [to] Gentlemen of the Senate and of the House of Representatives...in the Month of September Last...," Box 46, Pease, Graham, Nile Papers.

enslaved.[21] The visitor Frederick Law Olmsted during his visit to Texas reported "stories we had heard of the danger to slavery in the West by the fraternizing of the blacks with Mexicans," and the "Cart War" seemed to confirm the most palpable fears: supposedly, the Mexicans "helped them in all their habits," speaking of Africans, "married them [and] ran them off every day to Mexico."[22]

At once this entire episode, ostensibly involving just carts, revealed the problem involved in seeking to maltreat routinely Mexicans in a way that was akin to the confronting of Indigenes and Negroes—for this "Cart War" exposed that the victimized had the advantage of being backed up by state power with the potential to recruit allies in London and other influential capitals. This also made secessionists more favorable to the French takeover of Mexico during the Civil War, in that it would disrupt the natural alliance between and among Mexicans on both sides of the border.

Moreover, by the 1850s Yucatan was unraveling to the point that the Mexican periodical *El Siglo Diez y Nueve* was reporting more extensively on "*vender* [selling]" of "*esclavos* [slaves]"—meaning "*los indios*"[23]—but if history was a guide, strident voices, even in Washington, would object to this kind of labor supply. Even Frederick Douglass, the vaunted Negro abolitionist who staunchly opposed the 1840s war, was discussing a bill in Congress in early 1859 calling for the appropriation of "$50,000 to establish in Yucatan or Central America a Free Negro Nation."[24] Even if the locals and Mexico City had concurred, there was realistic apprehension that U.S. Negroes would amount to a Trojan Horse for Washington, if they were allowed to arrive.[25]

Moreover, as of 1859 the report emanated from Mérida in Yucatan about "outrages against various American citizens," along with "seizures" of their assets,[26] calling into question receptivity to an influx

---

21. David Urbano, "When the Smoke Lifted: The 1857-1858 'Cart War' of South Texas," Ph.D. dissertation, U of Houston, 2009, 119.

22. Frederick Law Olmsted, *The Cotton Kingdom: A Traveler's Observations on Cotton and Slavery in the American Slave States...*, *Volume I*, New York: Mason, 1861, 372 (abbrev. Olmsted, *Cotton*).

23. *El Siglo Diez y Nueve*, 12 August 1855, Reel 6, Despatches from U.S. Consuls in Vera Cruz, NARA.

24. *Frederick Douglass' Paper*, 18 February 1859.

25. Matthew D. Harris, "*Struggle for Sovereignty: An African American Colonization Attempt and Delicate Independence in Mid-Nineteenth Century Central America*," Ph.D. dissertation, West Virginia U, 2020.

26. Consul R. Juanes y Patrullo to Secretary of State, 31 March 1859, Reel 1, Despatches from U.S. Consuls in Mérida, 1843-1897, NARA.

of U.S. Negroes—sponsored by Washington, as opposed to arriving on their own—in any case.

An article of faith in the rapacious republic was that unrest in Mexico of whatever stripe was ultimately beneficial. Thus, the War of Reform in Mexico, 1857-1860, was viewed like manna from heaven in Austin, to the point that weapons were purchased from rascal republicans.[27] This conflict was utterly destructive, stripping Mexico of firm defenses it could have maintained against intervention. Secretary of State Lewis Cass was told by his informant in Vera Cruz that "even the invasion and conquest of Mexico by the American armies of 1847 had nothing like the destructive effects upon agriculture, manufacturing" and the economy as the conflict at hand.[28]

By 1859 the so-called "McLane-Ocampo" pact was signed, which would have made Mexico a protectorate of the U.S., allowing the latter to intervene willy nilly while opening the door to annexation and even extradition of fleeing property.[29] However, Washington might have argued that the attempt to establish a "protectorate" was defensive in nature. Or so thought Consul John Black in Mexico City. Even before the takeover by France during the U.S. Civil War, he was complaining in late 1858 that the "French Minister is managing this government like a puppet" and "spends the greater part of his time between the [presidential] Palace and the Archbishop and he is ever seen either going in or coming out of the Palace...." War vessels with the French flag fluttering were crowding into Vera Cruz and were "expected...to make a large demand on the Mexican government for a large amount due to French subjects, the government of course are unable to pay," auguring seizure of assets. Yet instead of cozying up to the U.S. in response, the regime was "doing all they can to drive foreigners from the country," more specifically, "they hate Americans above all others [and] would not hesitate to send them all away...."[30]

Instead, the government was cozying up to other powers in order to repel their northern neighbor, said Black. As London and Paris were ratcheting up pressure on Mexican City for repayment of debts, the "French Minister" decided "to send orders to the commander of

27. González-Quiroga, 167.

28. R.B.J. Twyman to Secretary Cass, 30 September 1859, Reel 7, Despatches from U.S. Consuls in Vera Cruz, NARA.

29. Michael Allen Ridge, Jr., "A Country in Need of American Instruction: The U.S. Mission to Shape and Transform Mexico, 1848-1911," Ph.D. dissertation, U of Iowa, 2012, 50-51.

30. Consul John Black to Secretary of State Lewis Cass, 18 November 1858, Reel 5, Despatches from U.S. Consuls in Mexico City. NARA.

the French naval forces at Vera Cruz to stop the landing of Americans…at all hazards…."[31]

A continuing problem for those in Austin with such ambitious dreams was not only the stiff objection from London but, unlike Texas 1836, in great swaths of Mexico there were not enough U.S. nationals on the ground to bring about concrete steps toward annexation. The report from Tehuantepec in 1858 was that "in the whole state of Chiapas…there is but one American residing…. I do not know of any Americans residing in the state of Oaxaca beyond the Isthmus," said Consul Charles Webster.[32] Besides, U.S. visitors were being treated ungraciously, portending bitter struggles if a replay of 1846 were contemplated. In Oaxaca, said Webster, these sojourners were subjected to "gross and flagrant…insult," including "pelting…with stones…. this is entirely an Indian country district," he said; "prejudices are strong and foreigners generally here are called in derision heretics, Jews and Yankees…shouted out to them as they pass along…."[33]

Those on the road to secession in Texas, especially those with short memories, were wondering if marriage to Washington had delivered a net gain. Many saw abolitionism growing throughout North America and actually believed that these elements were little more than London's puppets, not unlike advocates of desegregation a century later were seen as Moscow's puppets. Yet, even ostensibly "antislavery" forces in the U.S. were displeased with Britain; for example, the constitution of Oregon in 1858 was "anti-slavery" in that it sought to bar slavery, while circumscribing the rights of others: "No negro, Chinaman or Mulatto shall have the right of suffrage," was among the provisions that countless London abolitionists would find distasteful.[34]

Still, this unholy alliance captained by London—it was thought—compromised not only efforts to crack down on Mexican abolitionism but even to exterminate Indigenes in that Washington was seemingly falling short in delivering frontier protection.[35]

By 1857 an official body in Austin made it clear that abolitionism was the equivalent of being a front for London. For it was London, it

---

31. Ibid., Consul John Black to Secretary of State Lewis Cass, 18 February 1859.

32. Consul Charles Webster to Secretary of State Lewis Cass, 20 December 1858, Reel 1, Despatches from U.S. Consuls in Tehuantepec, NARA.

33. Ibid., Charles Webster to John Forsyth, 7 December 1857.

34. Constitution of Oregon, 5 April 1858 in U.S. Senate, 35th Congress, 1st Session, Misc. Doc., Huntington Library.

35. H.M. Pease.

was stated with assurance, that "conceived the idea of supplanting the United States in the production of cotton by a system of conquest and forced labor in the eastern world," and thereby chose to destroy enslavement of Africans "in this country...."[36] London was seen as the Enemy Incarnate.

But not far behind was a Caribbean outpost of abolitionism. It was soon-to-be president James Buchanan who in 1856 was astonished when he appeared at the opening of Parliament: "what struck me most forcibly," he said with astoundment, "was the appearance in the Diplomatic Box of a full blooded black negro as the Representative of His Imperial Majesty of Hayti."[37]

And attempts to extend the frontier by expanding southward at Mexico's—and Spanish Cuba's—expense from the standpoint of Southern war hawks were stymied by the weak-kneed abolitionists, backed by London, not keen on seeing a strengthening of the Slave South. By 1857 yet another expedition was launched from Texas soil—San Antonio in this case—and headed for Nicaragua under the telling banner of "Alamo Rangers." This attracted nervous attention in Mexico, which surmised that its lands—or its watery boundaries—would have to be traversed in the process.[38] Weeks later in Acapulco charges were filed against Dr. Joseph Smith because of his role in a filibustering expedition involving "[William] Walker in Lower California."[39]

But even European powers that were not abolitionist—e.g., Spain—joined with Britain and France in standing against a U.S. seizure in Central America. Regarding further taking of Mexican land, even there, as noted, the Slave South had to compete with France, and as of 1857 worry was expressed to Washington about a "Spanish invasion" of Mexico. This traffic jam of potential pirates likely stymied each of them in the short term. Washington's man in Vera Cruz was getting frustrated. John T. Pickett denounced "this imbecile people," speaking of Mexicans, while observing that a "well appointed Spanish army could penetrate to the capital without a Winfield Scott to lead it,"[40]

---

36. "Report of the Committee on Slaves and Slavery in Relation to the Importation of African Slaves," Austin: Marshall, 1857, AAS.

37. James Buchanan to Harriet Lane, 1 February 1856, in J.B. Moore, Volume X, 28-29.

38. *Mexican Extraordinary* [Mexican journal], 24 March 1857, Reel 6, Despatches from U.S. Consuls in Vera Cruz, NARA.

39. Charles L. Denman to John Black, 27 May 1857, Reel 5, Despatches from U.S. Consuls in Mexico City, NARA.

40. John T. Pickett to Secretary of State Lewis Cass, 20 May 1857, Reel 6, Despatches from U.S. Consuls in Vera Cruz, NARA.

a lure for the U.S. to replay the 1846 intervention before some other power did so. But, again, given the explosiveness of dissent directed at this earlier war, was it not likely that this would recur in the 1850s and would it be easier for the Slave South to maneuver absent the perceived strangulating albatross of abolitionist fellow-citizens?

Yet with all these snarled matters, there were others of similar import. Maybe enslavers were so driven by the euphoria provided by the filthy lucre that unpaid labor provided that, like a strung-out addict, they could not help but cry out for more Africans. In the haze of euphoria they evaded the downside risk of slave revolts, along with capital flight across the border with resultant diplomatic bruising. A legislator from Galveston, the major port of entry for the enslaved, called in November 1857 for legalizing the African Slave Trade—which had hardly stopped in any case since 1836. Hedging bets, it was also thought that William Walker and his lumpen comrades in Nicaragua could form a base for this illicit commerce on the Caribbean coast, within hailing distance of Texas. This unsavory scheme had proceeded to the point where in Managua the terms "Texan" and "plunder" were seen as coterminous. By 1859 legalizing the African Slave Trade had become the major issue among the elite of Texas voters. But this nettlesome matter just added to sectional friction, leading inescapably to war. Yet with their penchant for creating "facts on the ground," then allowing law to catch up, by 1859 presidential candidate Stephen Douglas contended that more Africans had been imported into the U.S. in 1859 "'than had ever been imported during any one year before even when the trade was legal.'" Swaggering with blustering self-regard, some Texans contemplated simply seizing thousands of Free Negroes and enslaving them. Others thought that Texas would have more flexibility outside of the federal union, perhaps even returning to independence.[41] While politicians were debating whether the slave trade should be reopened, Richard Drake, the self-confessed "slave smuggler," bragged, perhaps excessively, that in the era leading up to 1857, he transported about "half a million blacks from African coasts to America," with a goodly number winding up in Cuba and/or Galveston.[42]

Of course, there was another alternative to increasing the slave supply that had not been unreliable. But here the *Southern Intelligencer* advised against pursuing this path: "we admonish our

---

41. Fornell, 266, 273, 276, 294, 302, 357-358.

42. Richard Drake, *Revelations of a Slave Smuggler...*, New York: De Witt, 1860, *passim*.

contemporaries," it was said rebukingly, "not to waste their 'affections' upon the sable daughters of Ham. It is a dangerous business."[43]

This latter revelation would not have surprised the intrepid reporter Henry Morton Stanley, who was to encounter Dr. Livingston famously in Central Africa. However, in the 1850s he was spending time in New Orleans and traveling upriver to other sites where he noticed "gross familiarities with female slaves." His father was then in Havana providing him with further insight to this inhumane system.[44]

Despite the established prominence of Galveston as a slaving port, even the Texas Supreme Court in 1856 in bowing deference acquiesced to "Louisiana decisions," which "are entitled to peculiar weight on this subject [of slavery]," as "New Orleans is [the] great commercial emporium of the South West."[45]

This was not the only form of "affections" that raised eyebrows and temperatures alike. Bastrop, Texas, was visited by "respectable citizens of Austin" in Summer 1859 and the latter wandered into a "Mexican camp" populated by a "large number of peons, Mexican women and slaves" with one of the latter "with his arm around a señora" and "another señora laying a shawl over a slave while he was reclining on the ground." Outraged, the interlopers wanted to arrest them all but were persuaded otherwise by the reporter.[46]

By April 1859 the agenda of Texas enslavers was articulate: "annexation of Cuba, the reopening of the African Slave Trade and... and Act of Congress conferring upon Texas the right to enter into an extradition treaty with Mexico...for the reclamation of fugitive slaves"[47]—all of which would be difficult to attain in the obtaining federal union. Anticipating their anti-government descendants of the early 21st century, the motto adopted increasingly by these forces was that "the world is too much governed,"[48] i.e., it was the central government that was seen as blocking expansion of slavery and normalizing the African Slave Trade.

And it was the federal government that was seemingly incapable of compelling Mexico to extradite the formerly enslaved, a point that became exceedingly relevant in the late 1850s when the burghers of

---

43. *Southern Intelligencer*, 8 June 1859.

44. D. Stanley, 125, 127, 146, 153, 161.

45. "Robert Mills v. A.S. Johnston, et al.," "Supreme Court of Texas at Galveston," 1856, NYHS.

46. *Southern Intelligencer*, 7 July 1859.

47. Ibid., 27 April 1859.

48. Ibid., 27 July 1859.

Corpus Christi journeyed to South Carolina to buy the enslaved in order to grow cotton—and many fled promptly to Mexico.[49] Thus, by 1859 a company of 100 men formed an armed posse to invade Mexico to recover fugitive property, the kind of operation designed exquisitely to alienate already disaffected neighbors and encourage them to welcome a countervailing power to their shores.[50]

The voice of this belligerence was the *Southern Intelligencer*, initiated in Austin in 1856. By 1857 it was gaining its stride and cheered as "four more cargoes of Negroes from Africa, numbering 1783 [souls]" had "landed on the Cuban coast" a short sail from Galveston. This dark cargo had been "obtained on the African coast at very little cost" and was "worth an aggregate of $1,069,800," a spectacular rate of return sure to incentivize even the most fainthearted. The observant reporter realized that "the enormous profits of the slave trade embolden the traders to run all risk" and, assuredly, the Royal Navy "cannot stop the trade," it was said triumphantly.[51]

More confident voices thought there was no need to lobby for legalizing the African Slave Trade since natural increase was sufficient to create a steady supply. "In 1890," it was stated confidently, the "slave population will be 9,700,000" and "in 1930 it will swell to 30,000,000...."[52] But how could they be so confident? Was this not like boasting of the longevity of the 1000-year Reich—in 1944?

In these same pages was a typical story in March 1859: two Negroes belonging to W.K. Hamblen of Milam County were apprehended near Fredericksburg as they were "making for Mexico...."[53] Hedging further, enslavers were ecstatic when in neighboring New Mexico a bill was passed in 1859 protecting slave property,[54] accompanied by a slave code.[55] An indicator of the utter seriousness of Austin legislators was their deciding to print a whopping 10,000 copies of a document demanding the "repeal of all treaties prohibiting the importation of African slaves into the slaveholding states...."[56] That was in 1857. By

49. González-Quiroga, 91.

50. Resolution to form a Company, 3 February 1859, Box 308-21, Governor Hardin Runnels Papers, Texas Archives.

51. *Southern Intelligencer*, 7 October 1857.

52. Ibid., 28 April 1858.

53. Ibid., 2 March 1859.

54. Ibid., 6 April 1859.

55. Frazier, 57.

56. "A Report and Treatise on Slavery and the Slavery Agitation...printed by Order of the House of Representatives of Texas, December 1857," Austin: Marshall, 1857, Huntington Library (abbrev. A Report and Treatise).

the next year serious debates erupted about enslaving Free Negroes; complimenting this audacity was that a rich commerce in so-called "Stolen Negroes" developed in Galveston and Houston.[57] Those "stolen" could have come from anywhere—making these two cities dangerous to the health of Africans globally.

It was also in 1857, the year that the crisis of slavery reached such a fever pitch, that Austin legislators produced the noted report contending that the examples of Jamaica and Haiti demonstrated that abolition did not work, while Brazil and Texas showed that slavery did work. Again, reopening the African Slave Trade officially was the primary demand, while depicting abolitionism as a British plot was a primary rationale: "the principal moves on the chessboard of American abolitionism," it was said, "have been dictated by Exeter Hall [London] by English minds," which had delivered a "spirit of political madness" now at a "climax."[58]

By 1858 the conclusion of enslavers was crystal clear; as one grouping put it, "suitable guarantees for the protection of slavery," were demanded, and "failing in that then to pursue such course as will tend to form a new Union of all the Slave States...." A signatory was James Throckmorton,[59] who was to serve as governor by 1866 when bloodiness was the order of the day. Echoing him was the convention of the Texas Democratic Party in 1859, where filibustering in the Caribbean was promulgated, along with formally reopening the African Slave Trade to Cuba as a complement. William Walker, viewed as a hero by many delegates, was also backed by Hamilton Stuart, influential editor of a local periodical and Collector of Customs too.[60]

But, alas, there was no unanimity among settlers about reopening the slave trade globally. A minority report from the U.S. Congress in 1859 thought that such a measure would be "ruinous in the extreme to the best interest of the slaveholding states themselves." There were already "wild Africans in great numbers," indeed the region was "overstocked with wild Africans...." Even John C. Calhoun, it was purported, said suppress this commerce. "We have four millions now" of Africans "and they are increasing at a much more rapid rate than the whites"—so, why bring more? Besides, there was a "high price of negroes now" that importations could alter and, no,

---

57. Lack, 142-143, 233.

58. A Report and Treatise.

59. Report by "Union Association," ca. 1858, Box 39, Pease, Graham, Niles Papers.

60. Jimmie Eugene Hicks, "The Texas Secession Convention, 1860-1861," M.A. thesis, 1962, U of Southern California, 1962, 20, 21.

this deflation would not benefit the "'poor man,'" since arrival of more of the enslaved would undermine their position in the market-place and drive them away, although he had "always shown himself ready to take up arms when the tocsin of war has been sounded...." Even now, "emigrants of the rural class from Europe seldom settle at the South, because they do not like to live in near proximity to many slaves...." More Africans "would produce fear and dread," the "apprehension of danger," amounting to a "suicidal policy," both "demoralizing and injurious." New arrivals were likely to be alienated and have a baneful impact "upon our present civilized and happy negro population," tending to "render them unhappy, discon-tented and insubordinate," fomenting the "spirit of insurrection and revenge...." Then with a final point crafted to clinch the argument, it was announced triumphantly that "by the year 1920" there would be "upwards of thirty one millions of negroes," so why import more?[61]

Since Free Negroes were often blamed—wrongly—for unrest among the enslaved, detaining or enslaving them was an objective in any case, reducing the need for imports. By the year of *Dred Scott,* 1857, hysteria was spreading about arson perpetrated by the enslaved. Mansions, buggies, warehouses, jails, this attack on property was engendering the fear of an attack on the foundations of society, includ-ing property relations—which encompassed bondage itself, meaning revolutionary rupture, which soon was to come. A Galveston edito-rialist advised that "'our city seems to be infested with incendiaries, who are ready with torches to set fire to our buildings whenever a norther occurs to spread the flames.'"[62]

From the viewpoint of Texas enslavers, it seemed that a noose was tightening around their collective neck. Arson-besotted Africans were on the march. Once friendly Frenchmen seemed poised to sup-plant their erstwhile comrades in Austin as the chief marauders in Mexico. Comanches and other Indigenes had yet to surrender. And abolitionism was said to have infected the ascending Republican Party.

Due north in Indian Territory the news may have appeared enchanting at first blush, however. In Tishomingo City, headquar-ters of the Chickasaws, the legislature was accorded "no power to pass laws for the emancipation of slaves without the consent of

---

61. Minority Report of the Committee on Federal Relations of the House of Representatives Relative to the Repeal of the Laws of the United States Against the African Slave Trade," Baton Rouge: Taylor, 1859, Tulane U.

62. Lack, 259, 265.

their owners" and "without paying their owners previous to such emancipation a full equivalent in money...." Similarly, "harboring runaway Negroes" was circumscribed: violation of this measure meant a fine "not less than one hundred nor more than five hundred dollars, one half of which shall go to the informer...." Negroes were barred from "holding property" including "any horse, mule, cow, hog, sheep, gun, pistol or knife over four inches long in the blade...." Likewise, "all white persons known to be abolitionists... shall be deemed unfriendly and dangerous...." Negroes were barred from voting and to "all persons other than a negro [it] is hereby prohibited from cohabiting with a negro or negroes...."[63]

All this could be seen as being in sync with the Austin ethos. Yet read against the grain, it could be seen otherwise. For example, these measures all emerged from 1856-1858 as the aforementioned pressures on rascal republicans began to mount. A knife with a three inch blade could cause mayhem. A rifle was not included on this list either. Why bar harboring runaways unless it was contemplated or happening? Why the necessity to outlaw abolitionist "whites?"

During the same time similar measures were enacted among Cherokees, Creeks and Seminoles (those who had not fled to Mexico, in other words). Those defined as being "Free Negro" were "order[ed] off the limits of their respective counties" and those who refused to depart were to be sold "to the highest bidder for cash...." These Indigenes were "expressly prohibited from trading with any negro or negroes, slaves without a permit from their owners...."[64]

Reasoning akin to the Chickasaws is applicable here. Why bar trading unless it were contemplated or happening? Why oust Free Negroes unless their presence was troublesome or about to become so? Or at least Austin could have thought so.

Actually, Austin's—and Washington's—policy of stirring unrest in Mexico may have been backfiring, weakening state structures and combining with pre-existing antipathy to the northern neighbor. Rampant abolitionism facilitated the arrival of runaways from Texas. One visitor in the 1850s wandered to Fort Clark, "the most remote military station of the United States," he opined, and not far from where Seminoles had decamped, near Brackettville, Texas, and

---

63. "Constitution, Law and Treaties of the Chickasaws," Tishomingo City: Foster, 1860 [including Constitution and Statutes], Huntington Library.

64. "An Act Authorizing the Appointment of Commissioners to Meet the Cherokees, Creeks and Seminoles, to Make International Laws...approved October 22, 1858...," Huntington Library. See also Joshua R. Giddings, *The Exiles of Florida*, Columbus, Ohio: Follett, Foster, 1858 (abbrev. Giddings).

there he found "runaway Negroes from Texas" who "had concealed themselves...."[65]

This visitor may have known what was then outraging settlers in the borderlands. The Republic of Sierra Madre, the attempt by Carvajal and Texas bounty hunters to forge Mexican secession on the basis of slavery (and facilitate extradition of fleeing property) ran aground in the 1850s: in the words of scholar Miguel Ángel González-Quiroga, they were vanquished by a "large body of Seminoles and Maroons... that had recently settled in Coahuila...." Similarly throttled was Vidaurri, who in this scholar's words, wanted to populate Nuevo León and Coahuila with "docile Indians, [captured] runaway slaves and German colonists from Texas...."[66] Another scholar, William John Hughes, noted that Vidaurri, then in control of Nuevo León, was offered aid in men and money by Texas authorities to return fugitive Negroes, along with collaborating in anti-Seminole maneuvers along the border.[67]

Despite the thwarting of Vidaurri and his comrades, they inflicted considerable damage, softening up the nation for a foreign takeover, i.e., by France. In the city that became Ciudad Juárez, adjacent to El Paso, Texas, by 1858 "import and export of goods" had been "entirely stopped," said the U.S. envoy. Yes, Vidaurri "[and] the wealthier portion of the people" were "in favor of a United States protectorate" and yet "another party" were "in favor of annexation" altogether, à la Texas 1845. But these forces, he admitted, were "quite small" and at best were "composed of some of the middle class..." Indeed, there was "bitter hostility to annexation or the sale of territory to the United States among all classes...." But, typically, he blamed ignorance for this state of affairs since "not more than one person in twenty is able to read and write," along with the pervasive influence of "bigoted priests,"[68] the all purpose target of the growing Know Nothing movement in the U.S. itself.

Actually, by 1858 U.S. authorities were squirreling away broadsides that trumpeted "*Viva la Independencia y Soberanía* [sovereignty] *de Tamaulipas*," along with "*los estados de Nuevo León y Coahuila, San Luis, Querétaro, Zacatecas, Guanajuato, Jalisco, Oaxaca, Michoacán y*

65. Julius Froebel, *Seven Years' Travel in Central America, Northern Mexico and the Far West of the United States*, London: Bentley, 1869, 422 (abbrev. Froebel).

66. González-Quiroga,, 99, 107.

67. W.J. Hughes, 168.

68. Consul David R. Diffenderrfer to Secretary Cass, 10 April 1858, Reel 1, Despatches from U.S. Consuls in Paso del Norte, NARA.

Otros...."[69] With eagerness Secretary of State Lewis Cass was told that same year that "should the revolution continue in this country, large quantities of foreign and domestic goods will no doubt be imported here," likely a shot of adrenalin to the bloodstream of the U.S. economy; "states north of the Sierra Madre may eventually occasion a complete separation from the Mother Country and lead to a declaration of independence," was the hopeful conclusion. Importantly, "Col. [Samuel] Lockridge," a Texan and "second in command under Gen. [William] Walker of Nicaragua...recently arrived at Brownsville"[70]— and where he ventured, fireworks were sure to follow.

However, it is probable that the likes of Walker received a rude welcome from quite a number in the vicinity. For by 1858 one analyst had detected a trend that had long since been prevalent: across the border in Matamoros, "among the population were a number of Negroes who had absconded from Texas; these were among the foremost in their abusive epithets" aimed at northern invaders not least.[71]

When secession in Mexico was throttled, the probability of same due north became more likely in that the demands of Texas for extradition of the formerly enslaved became less likely. This was profoundly crucial in that, plausibly, as shall be seen, Texas was the most important seceding state. Anti-secession in Mexico was seen as a token of abolitionist strength: Texas's bête noire.

For the constitutional bar in Mexico against extraditing runaways infuriated settlers, leading hundreds in 1858 to forward a resolution to Senator James Pinckney Henderson of Texas, objecting irritably to these legal measures.[72] Mexico was unrepentant, even after the Civil War, continuing to denounce enslavers invading to seize Africans that had fled Texas, turning Matamoros, Reynosa and Laredo in particular into a kind of wasteland. "Kidnapping of free men of color," it was said bitingly, "has also been among the crimes planned on the Texas side, to be executed in Mexico.... the Mexican frontier has been the constant victim of invasion organized in or departing from the United States...." When Piedras Negras was invaded in the 1850s, the planning was done in San Antonio on the "pretext" of chasing

---

69. Broadside, 4 January 1858, Reel 3, Despatches from U.S. Consuls in Matamoros, NARA.

70. Ibid., Consul Peter Seuzeneau to Secretary Cass, 21 March 1858.

71. Henry Howe, *Adventures and Achievements of Americans: A Series of Narratives Illustrating their Heroism, Self-Reliance, Genius and Enterprise*, New York: Tuttle, 1858, 389.

72. Appendix, 24 March 1858, in Pridgen.

"Lipan Indians" but with the intention of effectuating the "capture of fugitive slaves, a great number of which had taken refuge on the frontier of Coahuila," then going further and executing the "occupation of the country...."[73] So argued an official Mexican body with barely concealed fury.

Even when enslaved Africans stayed on within the confines of the U.S., they could still foment problems: in July 1858 a youthful enslaved African owned by U.S. military leader William T.H. Brooks was slain by a Navajo in the borderlands. Given the value of enslaved property, this was a major loss and, thus, led to another war against Indigenes. Of course, the U.S. authorities there, according to scholar David Lanehart, "sanctioned slave raids against the Navajos," along with "encouraging volunteer punitive expeditions against the Indians,"[74] diminishing their ranks and making enslaved Africans all the more valuable.

Still, more ideological flexibility on the part of the northern republic where—it was thought—pragmatism reigned, might have been helpful. That is, despite the obvious fact that Mexicans like Carvajal and Vidaurri were more than willing to collaborate with the U.S., as they were doing so, certain U.S. officials led a vendetta against Juan Robinson of the U.S. diplomatic corps. He was "intimately connected with Mexican interests[,] his son being prefect of the city of Guaymas," while "he is also married to a Mexican woman"; he was "not an American citizen," said W.D. Porter, commander of a U.S. naval vessel, and had "sworn allegiance to the government of Mexico during the late war...."[75] He was allowed to serve Washington, though the harassment he absorbed was a deterrent to doing so.

Robinson was not the only worry. Secretary of State Cass, as Mexican secession was being strangled, was told worriedly of "alarm as regards the future" of this neighbor and informed that "the Democratic Party" in the Slave South "will seek aid from the filibusters of the South," e.g., Walker and his gang. "Noble occupation of the U.S. Navy is gone as regards Nicaragua," was the dejected inference of the Vera Cruz consul. Already, there was fretting about what was to shortly occur: the "Monroe Doctrine [has been] violated by an attempt to seat a European and Catholic Prince upon the throne of Montezuma

---

73. *Report of the Committee of Investigation 1873*, 178, 191.

74. David T. Lanehart, "The Navajos and the Peace Commission of 1867," M.A. thesis, TTU, 1981, 18, 15 (abbrev. Lanehart).

75. W.D. Porter to Farrelly Alden, Vice Consul, 18 November 1859, Reel 1, Despatches from U.S. Consuls in Guaymas, NARA.

and Iturbide,"[76] although Walker's emulation of same hardly received condemnation.

As ever, Washington was angling to militarize Mexico. Also in 1858, President Buchanan was apprised by "American merchants" in Vera Cruz of the "fear" they felt daily, which was "imperiling…lives and property to a degree never known before"; the "request," per usual, was to insure that "some man-of-war be ordered here…."[77]

However, Washington saw itself—minimally—as a paranoid with real fears. For as their agent sailed from Vera Cruz to Mobile, his instructions for Washington were sufficiently sensitive that the Secretary Cass was told that "everything" would be "communicate[d]… [of] importance to you in person…." The subtext was that Spain was "preparing to commence hostilities against Mexico," underlining the "importance of there being an efficient United States vessel of war stationed at this port…." The correspondent, R.B.J. Twyman, like many envoys of the U.S. in the hemisphere, had roots in the Slave South, Kentucky in his case,[78] which raised searching queries about their pre-Civil War motives: was this just a bald attempt to sneakily seize more of Mexico to augment Texas or to damage the U.S. military in conflict with Mexico, France and Spain before Fort Sumter assault in 1861? And it was not just Vera Cruz that was at issue. By February 1858 in Acapulco, a U.S. observer had spotted "vessels of war" from France and Britain approaching not so stealthily.[79] But with the U.S. diplomatic corps festooned with future traitors, who could know for sure?

Yet it was hard to discount all of these reports since shortly Paris was to conquer Mexico. By December 1858, correspondingly, Twyman's hair was figuratively on fire as he spotted the arrival in Vera Cruz "of a very formidable French fleet…. there are now five French vessels of war…two large steamers, two brigs and one frigate" lurking nearby. He dismissed the usual excuse for this gunboat diplomacy, that it was just an aggressive way to impose a creditor's rights. For also offshore were "four Spanish war vessels" and "three or more British vessels" en route.[80]

---

76. John Pickett to Secretary Cass, 20 February 1858, Reel 7, Despatches from U.S. Consuls in Vera Cruz, NARA.

77. Ibid., Consul to President Buchanan, 23 October 1858.

78. Ibid., Consul R.B. J. Twyman to Secretary Cass, 7 November 1858.

79. Vice Consul William Denman, 12 February 1858, Reel 2, Despatches from U.S. Consuls in Acapulco, NARA.

80. R.B.J. Twyman to Secretary Cass, 2 December 1858, Reel 7, Despatches from U.S. Consuls in Vera Cruz, NARA.

But by sponsoring the dismemberment of Mexico in the first instance, Washington should have realized that major powers would not stand idly by without seeking to get a piece of the action, with possible untoward consequences for the rapacious republic itself. Official Mexico agreed that the so-called Republic of Sierra Madre was sponsored by Washington, aided by Texas, and was the first step toward further conquest of this neighbor's soil. To that end, Austin and Washington were willing to conduct what today would be termed "false flag" operations, i.e., "Disguised whites or Bogus Indians" would attack Texas in order to defame Indigenes and inflame settlers, the latter being collateral damage. This brigandage was possible, said the Mexican authorities since "in the county of Dimmit... on the Rio Grande, north of Webb and south of Maverick, the inhabitants are for the greater part thieves and murderers.... they hire escaped prisoners from the jails in Mexico and employ them in stealing horses from Mexico"—and "murder the Mexican travelers."[81]

Yet the rascal republic saw no alternative beyond pursuing its destructive course, motivated in no small part by the ignition of settler colonialism in the first place: land seizures. Thus, it was also in 1858 that the U.S. was eyeing Sonora more hungrily than ever, specifically Guaymas, about 400 miles from the border. By December the State Department was told of a plan to "develop the immense riches of this state in minerals and in agriculture," since "all here know that under the American government it would be certain and easy of accomplishment...." Overcoming the stumbling block was a U.S. specialty: "mines in a majority of the richest districts," said the U.S. delegate there, "cannot be worked because small bands of Apaches drive out the miners. Cattle cannot be raised on the superb grazing lands even near the towns, because the Apaches drive them off...." A single option remained: "[the] only means of saving this state from a return to almost barbarism will be found to be its annexation to the United States...." Apparently, Secretary of State Cass, a Michigander who served both presidents Jackson and Buchanan faithfully, was bent on "obtaining in a proper manner the territory of Sonora and Lower California." Though the real estate was left unspecified, its "striking advantages" were not: "soil unrivalled in fertility by that of any state in the union," with bountiful crops of sugar, "mines of silver...mines of gold, copper and lead," along with bismuth and a "superb harbour...which can be made the terminus of a railroad from El Paso...." Like many in Washington peering over the western

---

81. *Report of the Committee of Investigation 1873*, 379, 392.

horizon, "transit for the China trade" was paramount, and Guaymas was ideal in that regard. This port would also "furnish an outlet to the sea of easy access for the territory of Arizona," while Lower California "is ready and anxious to come under the American government"—or so it was thought.[82]

The consul, Charles Pomeroy Stone, a key depredator in Mexico during the U.S. war who later served as a top military officer in Egypt,[83] advised in late 1858 that the presumed fecklessness in Mexico meant that the government "abandons the state to Apaches permitting them to roam over the land killing and carrying into captivity inhabitants"; anticipating and impelling the genocidal impulse inhering in settler colonialism, he railed against the "great scourge," i.e., the Apaches. Yet, he argued, instead of pulverizing these Indigenes, Mexico "resorted to the use of exciting the people of this state by supposed hatred of Americans and known hatred of filibusters...." Sure, there was "approach by sea and by land of large parties of Americans [and] filibusters," but Stone wanted the searchlight of concern on Indigenes, not invaders from the north. Instead, the regime there was determined on "repelling the American barbarians," a cynical way to deflect irritation of the masses northward, though this populace "preferred American rule which would protect them from Apaches" by dint of the iron fist. He knew this since the mere sight of the "American flag" was "received by rejoicing and gratitude," though he also knew that the "whole state will be united as one man against filibusters." But, he did not note, that this hated group was often seen as inseparable from the U.S. itself. Still, in the final analysis, he thought that the "only means of saving this state from a return to almost barbarism will be found in its annexation to the U. States."[84] Indeed, this approach did pave the way to a foreign takeover: France's.

Like clockwork, a few weeks later Cass was informed that "occupation by U.S. forces of this state and Chihuahua" was rumored, though "fury" would ensue. Just in case, Consul Charles P. Stone requested "ships of war" and "troops" be sent "immediately" since "one day would be sufficient to change the government quietly." Yes, he conceded "some little bloodshed may become necessary" and this "will cause a bitter feeling which it would be advisable to

82. Acting Consul to Secretary Cass, 23 December 1858, Reel 1, Despatches from U.S. Consuls in Guaymas, NARA.

83. William B. Hesseltine and Hazel C. Wolf, *The Blue and the Gray on the Nile*, Chicago: U of Chicago Press, 1961.

84. Consul Charles P. Stone to Secretary Cass, 23 December 1858, Reel 1, Despatches from U.S. Consuls in Guaymas, NARA.

avoid"[85]—but this was a small price to pay in light of the pot of gold at rainbow's end.

Later that year in a foretold development, the U.S. consulate there was invaded by Mexican soldiers who roughly took down the flag, then dragged it through the streets as it was being stomped. Scores of soldiers were shouting "'Muert[e] a Los American[o]s,'" i.e., "death" to their neighbors.[86]

At the same time in Guaymas, President Buchanan was informed anxiously, "neither the French or Spanish vice consuls have been insulted."[87] This tellingly signaled that it would be easier to effectuate a French takeover of Mexico than one by the U.S., with Washington setting in motion this doomsday scenario.

But like a compulsive obsessive, Washington could not resist seeking to intimidate its neighbor, though by weakening Mexico for the benefit of European powers, this wrongheaded policy was ultimately jeopardizing U.S. national security and—in light of secession—territorial integrity. By early 1859 the U.S. consul in Acapulco—who like many of his peers had roots in the Slave South, Texas in his case, which raised questions about his counsel so close to secession—watched the arrival of a U.S. Navy vessel, which was welcome, he offered, since "the quietness and security of this port is most important to the United States from the fact that here the passengers streamed from Panama, Nicaragua and Tehuantepec for California and Oregon...." Their "depot of supplies" was there and, he continued, "we have on average not less than four thousand Americans passing through monthly, spending from six hours to as many days in [this] place...." For their—and U.S. security—it was "well to have vessels of war call here as frequently as possible"[88]—though Paris, Madrid and London may have thought along parallel lines. Minimally, said Consul Isaac McMickens, a "coal depot" was needed in Acapulco since "there is no coal [in] private hands for sale on the coast from Panama to San Francisco,"[89] i.e., either local state entities had to be weakened or local private entities had to be strengthened, either of which was not necessarily positive for a strong regime in

---

85. Ibid., Charles P. Stone to Secretary Cass, 26 January 1859.

86. Ibid., Farrelly Alden, Vice Consul to Captain W.D. Porter, 18 November 1859.

87. Ibid., Farrelly Alden to President Buchanan, 19 November 1859.

88. Consul Isaac McMickens to U.S. State Department, 26 December 1859, Reel 2, Despatches from U.S. Consuls in Acapulco, NARA.

89. Ibid., Isaac McMickens to Secretary Cass, 12 February 1859.

Mexico City, which was not good news for Washington as French rule approached.

Awakening belatedly to the vexing reality, Consul Twyman in Vera Cruz wanted his nation to cut a deal with anti-intervention forces in Mexico, led by President Benito Juárez, to save Mexico from European powers—but for the intended victim, that would be akin to cutting a deal with the jackal to avoid the lion. The addled Twyman, instead, was thinking that this maneuver "would throw open the doors of Mexico to immigration and the Anglo Saxon race (Americans)," he clarified, "would pour in" and "would give the United States a controlling influence," to the point that "in twenty years the two Republics would stand together, as one nation and one people...." Thus, he dissented from the White House consensus—"the president's message...of occupying Chihuahua and Sonora," meaning "another war between United States and Mexico would...result," with those very same European powers joining the latter to Washington's clear detriment.[90]

Twyman's view was hard to accept, for simultaneously from Chihuahua emerged a frantic plea: "Indians murder the inhabitants at the city gates, every day it is getting worse" and a "proper thinking portion of the inhabitants are desirous for the United States to take the state and keep it...."[91]

U.S. elites could not decide if Mexico should be kept in a state of turmoil so as to weaken it for conquest—or run the risk of another beneficiary scooping up the bounty: European powers. Given the "revolutionary state of the country," said the U.S. envoy in Chihuahua, "I consider it unsafe to longer remain," the "revolution here which had the conservative or Church Party been successful would have cost the foreign residents of this place," meaning U.S. nationals, "their property and perhaps their lives...." The idea was to "sack the stores of all the Mexican merchants that are 'liberals' and of all the foreign merchants"; worryingly, "the rabble readily join any such enterprise" and "immediately bellow 'Death to the Gringos'...."[92] The further danger was that the state of turmoil would mean the "rabble" would aid a French intervention to the dismay of Washington's security.

Still, Twyman had cards to play. For it was also in 1859 that self-proclaimed "Citizens of the Hanseatic & Other Cities of Germany"

90. Consul Twyman to Secretary Cass, 21 January 1859, Reel 7, Despatches from U.S. Consuls in Vera Cruz, NARA.

91. Consul to Secretary Cass, 28 January 1859, Reel 1, Despatches from U.S. Consuls in Chihuahua, NARA.

92. Ibid., Consul George MacManus to Secretary Cass, 12 July 1859.

requested his consular services, for they were "without efficient protection from their own governments."[93] Secretary Cass agreed,[94] not only opening the door to migration across the ocean of more "whites" armoring against rebellious Indigenes and Africans but besides, this would create an ally in the heart of the "old continent" that could prove useful against those same European powers.

93. "Citizens of the Hanseatic...." to Consul Twyman, early 1859, Reel 7, Despatches from U.S. Consuls in Vera Cruz, NARA.

94. Ibid., Secretary Cass to Albert Schumaker, 2 August 1858.

Chapter *13*

Texas and the Onset of the U.S. Civil War, 1860-1861

As the moment for the attack on Fort Sumter in 1861 approached, it was evident that Texas would either join secession with South Carolina and the rest—or return to its pre-1845 status of independence. Lone Star settlers were exasperated with voices from Washington seeming to rein in genocide against Indigenes, or blocking the formal reopening of the African Slave Trade, or tending to align with London in abolitionist appeals, or failing to muscle Mexico toward extraditing runaway Africans.

Austin felt that Washington was unable to provide the backup envisioned in 1845 in terms of confronting Indigenes, Mexicans and Africans, and ditching the older republic was in order. Texas had been only one of two states in Dixie to submit secession to a [mostly white male] popular vote, and, the toll was 46,129 to 14,796 for disunion; in Webb and Zapata counties not a single vote was registered against secession, while in Starr County, only two votes were opposed. In Cameron County, the vote was 600 to 37 in favor of secession. Santo Benavides, the highest ranking Tejano in rebel military ranks, even raised his own regiment, though—to be fair—a hero of the Mexican secessionist venture was Colonel Antonio Zapata, defined as "mulatto."[1] By way of comparison, Fort Bend County near Houston voted for secession by 486 to 0, making it one of six Texas counties that voted unanimously for disunion.[2]

Texas was that rare Confederate state that actually voted for secession (as opposed to holding a convention), the vote occurring in February 1861 on the basis of gender and "race" limitations of the

---

1. Jerry Thompson and Lawrence T. Jones III, *Civil War and Revolution on the Rio Grande Frontier: A Narrative...History*, Austin: Texas State Historical Association, 2004, 3, 31, 77, 35 (abbrev. Thompson and Jones).

2. Adrien D. Ivan, "Masters No More: Abolition and Texas Planters, 1860-1890," Ph.D. dissertation, UNT, 2010, 146 (abbrev. A.D. Ivan).

electorate. Still, many had in mind reverting to pre-1845 independence and not simply following South Carolina into a new entity.
Their sentiments were embedded in the Knights of the Golden Circle,
whose base was in Texas, a state with wider hemispheric ambitions.[3]

The Lincoln emissary Elisha Oscar Crosby, whose fluency in
Spanish gave him insight into wider matters, during the winter of
1860-1861 "heard the same idea expressed myself by Southern men
in Washington," i.e., "making the Gulf of Mexico a great inland sea
surrounded by a Slave Empire,"[4] reflecting the ideological perva-
siveness of KGC. Secession followed by independence was more of
an option in Texas than elsewhere in the Confederacy.[5]

It was also in February 1861 when political leaders convening in
Austin resolved in their proclaimed "No. 1" ordinance that "whereas
the Federal Government has failed to accomplish the purposes of the
compact of union...in giving protection either to the persons of our
people upon an exposed frontier or the property,"[6] that the union
was broken.

In the prelude to this crucial gathering, Governor Houston in
dissenting on secession took time to denounce John Brown "and
his miserable associates" who conducted the "raid upon Harper's
Ferry" but also reminded that "Indians ravage a portion of [our]
frontier. Mexico renders insecure [our] entire western boundary. The
slaves are liable to escape and no fugitive slave law is pledged for
their recovery," all of which were "causes which have induced these
[secession] resolutions" and none of which Washington had been
able to resolve.[7]

But Texas was different from Carolina, Houston contended, since
the latter had a cordon of slave states cocooning it, while the Lone
Star State had Indian Territory—and Mexico—making secession

---

3. Linda Sybert Hudson, "Military Knights of the Golden Circle in Texas,
1854-1861," M.A. thesis, Stephen F. Austin U, 1990, 111 (abbrev. L.S. Hudson).

4. Charles Albro Booker, ed., *Memoirs of Elisha Oscar Crosby, Reminiscences
of California and Guatemala from 1849 to 1864*, San Marino: Huntington, 1945,
94 (abbrev. Booker).

5. Clayton E. Jewett, "On Its Own: Texas in the Confederacy," Ph.D. dissertation, Catholic U, 1998, 51 (abbrev. Jewett).

6. "Ordinances passed by the State Convention," 2 February 1861 in "The
constitution of the State of Texas in 1861. The Constitution of the Confederate States of America, the Ordinances of the Texas Convention and Address
to the People of Texas," Austin: Marshall, 1861, Huntington Library.

7. Message of Gov. Houston of Texas on Secession, 1860, Huntington
Library.

more problematic.[8] More than many rebelling states, Washington's inability to corral then liquidate Indigenes was central to Texas's 1861 revolt.[9]

Thumbs down on secession did not mean satisfaction with Washington, in that the governor was thought to be close to the Knights of the Golden Circle and its vast hemispheric ambitions targeting Mexico and Cuba in the first instance. Speaking in San Antonio in 1860, political leader Charles Anderson said "the next step for our state" could be to "re-establish her separate independence under the 'Lone Star government.'"[10]

Looking back, the Texas rebel William Watson acknowledged that his state "had been undecided on secession" and "had been more inclined to fall back on her former independence."[11]

Veteran Indian fighter and 1836 counter-revolutionary George Erath said that 1845 annexation had been a gross error, an opinion not unique to him. Further, he saw secession as simply the first step toward reestablishing Texas sovereignty; for Washington by annexation had also "gained through Texas nearly one half of her territory including the golden California." Yet the man who gave his surname to Erath County, Texas, also maintained, "I believed in our right to secede but was not in favor of making use of the right," adding to the complexity of 1861 attitudes.[12]

By 1860 there was at least a three-way split in Texas—there were pro-Washington sentiments that were to bloom, especially among Africans; then there was a Confederate faction, i.e., secede with the Slave South; then there was a KGC faction, i.e., secede and resume the pre-1845 status which could (but not necessarily) lead to further ties with the emergent Confederate States.[13] Texas at the head of a flock of enslaving vultures was the idea, fulfilling the long-term

---

8. Message from Gov. Houston of Texas on Secession, 24 January 1861, Huntington Library.

9. Jewett, 48.

10. Speech of Charles Anderson, Esq., On the State of the Country, at a Meeting of the People of Bexar County, at San Antonio, 24 November 1860, Huntington Library.

11. William Watson, *Life in the Confederate Army…*, New York: Scribner's, 1888, 119.

12. Erath, 83, 90, 94.

13. William H. Bell, "Knights of the Golden Circle, Its Organization and Activities in Texas Prior to the Civil War," M.A. thesis, Texas College of Arts and Industries, 1965, 164 (abbrev. Bell).

ambition of challenging Washington. Or, to put it another way, the other enslaving states would be the Supremes to Texas's Diana Ross.

The complication was that Texas had an unquenchable appetite for more unpaid labor, though the arrival of more Africans tended to deepen the already raging fear and anxiety that afflicted settlers. Between 1835 and 1846 the population of the enslaved had more than quadrupled from 4000 to 39,000—but by 1860 there were 182,566 officially, with the next few years delivering even more,[14] as enslavers fled with their property to what appeared to be a safe harbor as New Orleans fell and Vicksburg was squeezed. More granularly, the enslaved population in 1850 was more than 50% of the total population in 6 Texas eastern counties. By 1860 13 eastern counties had more than 50% population of the enslaved, and even in certain western counties, the enslaved population amounted to 25% of the total, a real challenge for domestic security.[15]

Thus, on the eve of civil war, Bastrop, Texas, was a hotbed of insurrectionary activity by the enslaved, and runaways from all points of the azimuth could be found there. "The year of 1860," says scholar James David Nichols, "witnessed plots and rumors of slave rebellion all over the South,"[16] though Texas's peculiar geography, bordered by abolitionist Mexico to the south and often disgruntled Indian Territory to the north, made it a unique source of contagion. The appropriately named periodical *The White Man*, sited in Weatherford, Texas, coincidentally in 1860, worriedly fretted about "the late excitement about negro insurrections and incendiarism which frightened all our women and children and kept thousands of true conservative men from the polls...." Nearby in their bloodstained pages was a companion story about yet another "abolition plot," referring to Selma, Ala.: a "servile insurrection" of the "well armed." Much hysteria flowed about further Negro plans, along with sniping at Sam Houston and others seen as not in accord with their frequently radical remedies.[17]

The Slave South had an advantage in being in the vanguard of supplying military officers against Black Hawk, the Seminoles and the Mexicans, accumulating military experience that would prove invaluable in the early stages of the Civil War. Robert E. Lee himself spent three years in Texas: 1846-1847, 1856-1857, and 1860-1861. A good deal of his time was spent chasing the Mexican folk hero Juan

---

14. Shelton, 75-76.

15. Andrew T. Fede, *Homicide Justified: The Legality of Killing Slaves in the U.S. and the Atlantic World*, Athens: U of Georgia Press, 2019, 220.

16. Nichols 2012, 44.

17. *The White Man*, 13 September 1860.

Cortina, who was feared and despised by Texas settlers because of his staunch opposition to land grabbing. By 1859 this swashbuckling raider had captured virtually Brownsville and audaciously occupied U.S. military barracks, though it was suspected that official Mexico had aided him. War was feared and might have intervened but for the advent of sectional flaring. Still, the point is that Lee was garnering battlefield nous that extended the shelf life of civil war.[18]

The same held true for his comrade and fellow traitor J.E.B. Stuart, who arrived in what he called "Comanche Land" as early as 1855.[19] As with Lee, his encounters in "Comanche Land" were unpleasant, but did prepare him for more bloodiness in the southeast quadrant of North America.[20] On the other hand, leading Civil War fighters on both sides—Sherman, Sheridan, Grant, et al.—had all earned their spurs as Indian fighters before unleashing bloodshed on their erstwhile fellow citizens.[21]

Clearly, the unrest did not leave Mexico unaffected. By early 1860 the report from Chihuahua was that residents were fleeing: "all the stores are closed," said the U.S. observer, George Macmanus, "as all the merchants that could have moved...cross[ed] into Texas...."[22]

But Mexico was punching back, for it was then that Juan Cortina, a national hero, became more prominent. By early 1860 he was being denounced by a U.S. official as a "bandit" who was "recruiting...on the Mexican side of the Rio Grande," near Matamoros. His band was amply "armed" thanks to "rifles bought in the United States...." His plan, it was thought, was "to annihilate the 'gringos'" or "white men," as the term was then defined. Secretary of State Cass was instructed sternly that the "Rio Grande cannot continue to be [the] line between Mexico and the United States much longer for the hatred of Mexicans for everything American will be an everlasting barrier...either the Mexicans must move further back or the American; the two never can live in peace together."[23]

---

18. John H. Jenkins, ed., *Robert E. Lee on the Rio Grande: The Correspondence of Robert E. Lee on the Texas Border, 1860*, Austin: Jenkins, 1988, 5, 7, 12-13.

19. J.E.B. Stuart to "My Dear Jack," 1 March 1855, Box 1, Hairston Wilson Family Papers, UNC-CH.

20. Rupert Richardson, "The Comanche Reservation in Texas," *West Texas Historical Association Yearbook*, 5 (June 1929): 47-71, 47, UOk-N.

21. W. Johnson, 55.

22. George Macmanus to Secretary Cass, 3 February 1860 Reel 1, Despatches from U.S. Consuls in Chihuahua, NARA.

23. Consul Richard Fitzpatrick to Secretary Cass, 4 January 1860, Reel 3, Despatches from U.S. Consuls in Matamoros, NARA.

By the Summer of 1860, Matamoros remained in chaotic turmoil—
or so said the U.S. consul. "The cry was 'down with Carvajal,' down
with the Gringos"—now defined as "white men foreigners"—and
"'death to the Yankees,'" more pointedly. Carvajal was the local quis-
ling and embodiment of pro-U.S. secession in Mexico. Behind the
unrest was Cortina, especially his "friends and sympathizers" who
were "most active." As they peered across the border, they decided
quite reasonably that they did not want to be "slaves to the Yankees,"
but as the U.S. consul saw it, "these people are, and always have been
deadly hostile to every American (unless he is a negro or mulatto)...."
They were not afflicted with amnesia either in that "they never will
forget the occurrences of our late war with Mexico and if our government intends to protect the lives and property of our citizens in this
country it must be done by force," and certainly it "cannot be done by
treaty stipulations,"[24] seen as tools of the wimps and the weak.

This reference to the "negro or mulatto" was hardly happenstance,
for as reality had demonstrated and a recent scholar has confirmed,
U.S. Negroes "experienced far less racism in Mexico than in the United
States, especially from Mexican officials well-versed in the value of
anti-'Yanqui' centralism.... race was a secondary concern in the lives
of most African-Americans in Mexico," contrary to their homeland.
Their allegiance was cemented further when the government sought
to facilitate their movement farther south into the interior so as to
foil kidnappers and bounty hunters. Still, U.S. Negroes were said
to have joined Cortina's band, sending settler vehemence hurtling
wildly into the ionosphere.[25] Around Brownsville, said one resident
there, Cortina "has the sympathy of the whole race & makes it a
war of races. He proclaims the knife & no quarter to Americans"; on
the other hand, said this knowing informant, "they say we are drift-
ing into a war, which will enable us to reclaim our slaves," many of
whom were a stone's throw away in Matamoros.[26]

At once this bound these migrants to their new homeland, making
them among the most militant in confronting Texas, and it simultaneously infuriated settlers in the borderlands, fueling the felt desire
to push the boundaries of the Lone Star State farther southward. The

---

24. Ibid., Consul Fitzpatrick to Secretary Cass, 6 July 1860. See also Florence Johnson Scott, *"Old Rough and Ready" on the Rio Grande*: San Antonio:
Naylor, 1935, 66 (abbrev. F.J. Scott). The term "gringos," says the author,
stems from the 1840s war as the invaders would often sing the lyric "green
grows the grass" loudly and repeatedly.

25. Nichols 2012, 13, 229, 292.

26. Letter, 25 November 1859, Gilbert Kingsbury Papers, UT-A.

U.S. consul may have known that the staunchest opponents of secession in Mexico as embodied by Carvajal were those like Francisco Avalos, who was defined as "Afro-Mestizo," making him an object of vicious ridicule by Texas settlers. Those like Avalos were seen as the intestinal foes of the northern neighbors, for he and those like him were less capable of being bribed and more reliable and fierce on the battlefield, especially since losing could mean enslavement.[27]

Coincidentally enough, the best that West Point had to offer were to be found in the borderlands for the same reason that Stuart had arrived: Comanches were on the march, and as one retrospective analyst put it, by the "Fall of 1860 Indian depredations had been more frequent than usual and had been characterized by an unusual ferocity on the part of the Indians."[28] Eastern New Mexico was not immune; according to a subsequent analysis, matters had "remained calm until March 1858 when the Comanches suddenly unleashed their pent-up fury" to the dismay of many settlers while fueling the genocidal fury of others.[29]

By 1859 Corporal James Pike, a Texas Ranger, was encountering Caddo as he neared a "stream named after Jim Ned, a Caddo Warrior.... his father was a very black negro, while the mother was a full blooded Indian woman," yet he added quizzically, "Jim Ned is very white and would pass for a white man in almost any crowd,"[30] creating espionage opportunity and more opportunity for marauding. For at least in Hood County, Texas, Caddo were seen "as much a terror" as the fearsome Comanche—or so said 19th-century historian Thomas T. Ewell. Shortly before the Civil War commenced, the genocidal John Baylor led a brutal campaign against Indigenes, including Caddo, "intending to destroy them or drive them from the reservation [near] Fort Belknap.... he was joined by frontier people" but was "foiled by the intervention of the United States authorities and Indian depredations continued for many years"[31] thereafter—and providing more impetus for "frontier people" to join Confederates.

---

27. Nichols 2012, 133, 124.

28. H.H. McConnell, 122.

29. Charles Leroy Kenner, "A History of Mexican Plains Indian Relations," Ph.d. dissertation, TTU, 1966, 191.

30. Corporal James Pike, *The Scout and Ranger: Being the Personal Adventures...as a Texas Ranger in the Indian Wars...*, Cincinnati: Hawley, 1865, 77 (abbrev. Pike).

31. Thomas T. Ewell, *A History of Hood County, Texas...also a Sketch of the History of Somervell County*, Granbury, Texas: Granbury News, 1895, 4, 5, 81.

By 1860 neighboring New Mexico remained aflame. Their delegate, M.A. Otero, informed Congress that aid was needed desperately "for the suppression of Indian hostilities," spearheaded by Indigenes "opposing the advances of Christianity...." This conflict had been raging since the U.S. takeover, and matters were spiraling out of control "even more than [when] we lived under the government of Mexico," though then there was "a war existing and which had existed for many years between the Mexicans and Navajos...." In one recent year alone there had been "more murders and robberies" than "during any one year" under Mexico; besides Navajo, "the Utah... and Southern Apaches" were discontented. Imbibing the spirit of Texas, he suggested that "mounted volunteers" should "raise a regiment or two...and let them kill every Indian they met"—"that is my plan," he assured. "It is a Jacksonian plan," which was accurate: "I would treat them as your fathers treated the Indians in Ohio,"[32] was his salutation, as the demand for genocide escalated, which was not assuaged by civil war and, indeed, might have exacerbated it.

In turn, such perceptions fueled more vigilante mobs and posses by settlers, which also bound them together in a cyclonic tunnel of genocidal ire. Somewhat appropriately, one of the critical petitions seeking to organize a posse to hunt down Indigenes came from Comanche County.[33]

Settlers were becoming more desperate with every passing day. In 1859 the visitor Julius Froebel declared with certainty, "it is a fact that the whites have attempted to poison whole tribes of Indians and I have myself often heard the question discussed how this could be effected in the best manner...." With malevolence aforethought, settlers had "designed introduction of the smallpox amongst a remote Indian tribe"—he had "heard it related with every particular...."[34]

As ever, land grabs were at issue, and the plunder was so lush that it unavoidably ignited conflict between and among settlers,[35] unhealthy for unity so desperately needed on the cusp of civil war.

---

32. "Speech of Hon. M.A. Otero of New Mexico in the House of Representatives, April 18, 1860," Huntington Library.

33. Petition from Comanche County, 1860, Box 2, Sam Houston Papers. In the same vein and collection see also Frank M. Collier to Governor Houston, 3 March 1860, and Petition from Charles Adams, 5 December 1860.

34. Froebel, 272.

35. "Speech of Hon. Sam Houston of Texas Exposing the Malfeasance and Corruption of John Charles Watrous Judge of the Federal Court in Texas and of His Confederates Delivered in the Senate of the United States, February 3, 1859," New York: Russell, 1860, Huntington Library.

However, an epoxy that forged unity was the identity politics of common racial and ethnic heritage of the elite and their base, who could credibly paint a picture of being besieged by Indigenes, Mexicans and Africans. The census for 1860 revealed, in the words of scholar James M. McReynolds, "Anglos dominated slave ownership.... only three families with Spanish surnames...owned slaves," the major source of wealth.[36]

While settlers were squabbling over divvying up the booty, it was not only Comanches who were on the march. Runaways were becoming more common. The insurrection of the enslaved in 1856 seemed to be a harbinger of more to come, which appeared to eventuate when mass fires erupted in 1860. John Reagan, who was soon to serve in Jefferson Davis's Cabinet, thought it was all an abolitionist plot.[37] By December 1860, Kentucky Governor Beriah Magoffin was told that "during the past summer the abolition incendiary has lit up the prairies of Texas, fired the dwellings of the inhabitants, burned down whole towns and [administered] poison for her citizens, thus literally executing the terrible denunciations of fanaticism against the slaveholder," meaning "'alarm to their sleep, fire to their dwellings and poison to their food.'"[38]

With futility, Austin busied itself in the prelude to Fort Sumter by passing even more lengthy and detailed laws seeking to restrain runaways, as if their pronouncements would be sufficient to stanch the ceaseless flow southward.[39] One bill declared that "any person who shall in the presence or hearing of any slave, utter words calculated and with the intent to render such slave discontented with his state of slavery" and "to render said slave discontented" could face up to five years of imprisonment. A similar penalty was to be accorded those who "produce in slaves a spirit of insubordination with the intent to...incite negroes in this state to rebel or make insurrection...." [40] On the cusp of secession, Texas crafters mandated bluntly

---

36. James M. Reynolds, "Family Life in a Borderland Community: Nacogdoches, Texas, 1779-1861," Ph.D. dissertation, TTU, 1978, 191.

37. Newsome, 72, 74, 75.

38. S.F. Hale, Commissioner of Alabama to Governor Magoffin, 27 December 1860, in *The War of the Rebellion, A Compilation of the Official Records of the Union and Confederate Armies,* Series IV, Volume I, Section 1, Washington, D.C.: Department of War, 1900, 4 (abbrev. *War of the Rebellion*).

39. "Laws of the Eighth Legislature of the State of Texas: Extra Session...," Austin: Marshall, 1861, UNC-CH.

40. "General Laws of the Eighth Legislature of the State of Texas," Austin: Marshall, 1860, Duke U.

that "the legislature shall have no power to pass laws for the emancipation of slaves," and—in a note of caution—ruled that no enslaved could arrive who may have perpetrated felonies elsewhere.[41]

Understandably, Reagan and legislators were worried: there was a six-week-long rolling wave of unrest by the enslaved, involving attacks on towns among other macro-aggressions.[42] In July 1860 a fire in Dallas utterly destroyed a good deal of the town square. Under relentless questioning, an enslaved boy who had reported the fire implicated every enslaved person in the county; on the threat of death he claimed that the plot had been devised by two abolitionist preachers, which led to mass whippings of the enslaved and three designated as ringleaders—and hanged.[43]

A few decades after these conflagrations, an analyst in North Texas recalled that "in the summer of 1860 Dallas was burned and the people were expecting a negro insurrection...." A number of the suspected plotters were executed and "a great many in the county were whipped...." Simultaneously, Indigenes were on the warpath, causing the writer, George Jackson, to state, "never before have we seen so much anguish. Men, women and children lie mangled in corpses...." Yet, the carnage all around notwithstanding, he still contended—as was the settler consensus—"slavery has been a great blessing to the negro...."[44]

Hysteria spread like wildfires as enslavers in neighboring Arkansas panicked and launched a round of lynchings that served to inflame Africans further.[45] Due west in Indian Territory, Africans among the Choctaws revolted,[46] seemingly inspired by Texas.

Events unwinding due north in Indian Territory were bound to induce agita among Texas settlers. By 1860, the missionary James Anderson Slover posited that "full blooded Indians began to get their eyes open on the doings of the Northern Board of Missions" in that previously "for many years the Board forbid its Missionary to baptize or receive any slaveholder into the churches...unless

41. "The Constitution of the State of Texas as Amended in 1861...of the Confederate States of America...," Austin: Marshall, 1861, CCSC (abbrev. Texas Constitution 1861).

42. James Walvin, *Freedom: The Overthrowing of the Slave Empires*, New York: Pegasus, 2019, 152.

43. James T. Matthews, "Major's Confederate Cavalry Brigade," M.A. thesis, TTU, 1991, 31.

44. George Jackson, *Sixty Years in Texas*, Dallas: Wilkinson, 1908, 86, 152.

45. K.H. Jones, 69.

46. Naylor, 155.

such person would emancipate their slaves...."[47] At that juncture in Hawaii, the epigram had arisen that when the missionaries arrived, they had the Bible and the Indigenes had the land, but shortly there-after the situation had reversed and the Euro-American comrades of the missionaries had the land and the Indigenes had the Bible.[48]

In other words, the presumed advantage delivered to settlers by religious conversion was undermined by a lunge toward abolition, with untoward consequence for the peculiar institution.

With what appeared to be formulaic precision, by October 1860, ram-pant fears of insurrections of the enslaved in Indian Territory arose, contributing to anxieties due south in Texas, a syndrome unalleviated by the ongoing genocide and expulsion of Indigenes.[49] Those who sought to incite the enslaved had quite a bit of clay to mold. By 1860 there were 2511 of the enslaved in the Cherokee Nation; 2349 amongst the Choctaw, 14% of the total population; 1532 among the Creek, 10% of the population; 975 among Chickasaw or 18% of the total.[50]

Passing through this vicinity in the Fall of 1860, the perambulating settler W.E.H. Gramp noticed that "on our route we passed through four Indian tribes—the Quapaws, the Cherokees, the Chickasaws and the Creeks...." What struck him was "a good deal of wealth and culture among many of the families of the half breeds. Some of them had plantations and owned property and slaves," though, alterna-tively, some of them may have continued to resent the usurpers who had invaded and seized the land. Intriguingly, there was "silly talk about northern incendiaries coming South and inciting insurrection among the negroes.... the town had been burned (much of it) a few weeks before our arrival and this burning...was attributed to the Northern incendiaries."[51]

* * *

Befitting a state where advocates of placing Indigenes in precursors of 20th-century Bantustans in apartheid South Africa were designated

---

47. "Autobiography of James Anderson Slover...," 1860, UOk-N (abbrev. J.A. Slover).

48. See e.g., Gerald Horne, *The White Pacific: U.S. Imperialism and Black Slav-ery in the South Seas After the Civil War*, Honolulu: U of Hawaii Press, 2007.

49. de Wit, 66, 74.

50. Alaina E. Roberts, *I've Been Here All the While: Black Freedom on Native Land*, Philadelphia: U of Pennsylvania Press, 2021, 24 (abbrev. A.E. Roberts).

51. W.E.H.Gramp, *The Journal of a Grandfather*, St. Louis: W.E. Hughes, 1912, 43, 45 (abbrev. W.E.H. Gramp).

as "moderate," as against proponents of extermination or genocide, there was no unanimity of opinion in elite circles regarding seceding from the grip of Washington. There were those who wished to return to the status quo ante of pre-1845 independence, and there were others who saw secession as a diversion from more ambitious goals, e.g., annexing more of Mexico before moving on to Cuba, perhaps à la Walker, making another run at seizure of Central America.

This latter force was embodied in the aforementioned Knights of the Golden Circle, which had earmarks of the pre-existing Know Nothing movement and the subsequent Ku Klux Klan in its penchant for covert action and clandestineness. The titular leader of the KGC, George Bickley, admitted that his group received the bulk of its support from Texas,[52] ironically the bulwark of the emerging Confederate States of America. Bickley claimed there were 8000 Knights in Texas, the largest complement nationally. As with the Civil War, and settler colonialism generally and 20th-century fascism, the KGC involved class collaboration between and among financial and economic elites and poorer and working-class elements who aspired to climb the greasy pole of success by dint of pillage.[53]

By the fall of 1860 Bickley arrived in Galveston seized with the notion of seizing Mexico; he received a "cordial welcome in Texas" generally and an "enthusiastic reception" in Houston, according to a subsequent observer. What drove him and his comrades was the febrile idea of forming a huge slavery empire with Texas at the center and including Mexico, the Caribbean and—to begin—the northern portion of South America, where enslavement was not unknown.[54]

Bickley was quite confident, referring to the "powerful military organization" he headed. It was primed to "go to Mexico" to form a "DEFENSIVE COLONY," he stressed modestly, so it could "become a centre, drawing to itself every good citizen who desires relief from the anarchy and civil wars which have so devastated the country since 1824," a reference to the Mexican Constitution which so outraged Texas settlers. "We would settle and Americanize Mexico," he insisted, continuing the 1840s war, which enslavers had sponsored and Texas consolidated, but the failure to entrench enslavement in

---

52. Ernest Laner, "Knights of the Golden Circle," in Amy Louise Wood, ed., *The New Encyclopedia of Southern Culture, Volume XIX*, Chapel Hill: U of North Carolina Press, 2011, 243-244.

53. L.S. Hudson, 91.

54. Jimmie Hicks, "Some Letters Concerning the Knights of the Golden Circle in Texas, 1860-1861," *Southwestern Historical Quarterly*, 65 (No. 1, July 1961): 80-86, 80.

California, New Mexico and Arizona had compromised. He was seething about Mexico since "there is scarcely any form of injury which has not been suffered by our citizens [there] during the last few years." The times demanded that the "Gulf of Mexico must be commanded which can only be done by owning Mexico and the West Indies," London and Madrid be damned. He was more dismissive of Mexicans, comparing those who were "ambitious" to "imitative monkeys," though luringly "no portion of the world rivals Mexico in all the elements of wealth and comfort...." There was one gigantic missing factor, however: "why should not slave institutions equally elevate Mexico" as in Brazil, he asked querulously. The KGC at least would guarantee 25 new slave states to enhance a "Southern Confederacy...as in the case of Texas." The surety was to "protect by law all Africans landed" in this renewed empire.[55]

Because of the clandestineness of the KGC it is not easy to confirm one of the more explosive allegations about it, that Sam Houston himself and his lack of enthusiasm about secession were grounded in his alleged role as the kingpin of the KGC. Supposedly, he had a "Grand Plan" that involved annexing more of Mexico—which was certainly in motion as the Spring of 1861 approached—settling somehow the sectional controversy which would allow for more freedom of movement for annexationists, then somehow leapfrogging into the White House. One scholar terms this thesis "apparently untrue," though the preceding adverb dilutes the descriptor.[56] Congressman S.S. Cox of Ohio believed it was true, pointing out on the floor of the House in 1860 that the Texas governor had demanded federal aid, and if it was not forthcoming "he threatens to conquer a peace on Mexican soil,"[57] consonant with KGC.

What is true is that speaking from Huntsville, Texas, in November 1860, he admitted that he did "hesitate to plunge into revolution now," meaning secession, though he quickly added and provocatively, "it is not because I am ready to submit to Black Republican Rule...." But he then undermined a prop of secessionists by asserting that "Mr. Lincoln has been constitutionally elected"—before giving more comfort to this opponents by noting that "I deprecate his success...." But a man who had fought a war 25 years earlier for counter-revolution was reluctant to traverse this same path due to the "horrors" involved. "If

55. George Bickley, "Address to the People of the Southern States," Richmond, 1860, Huntington Library.

56. Crenshaw, 23-50, 42.

57. "Speech of Hon. S.S. Cox Delivered in the House of Representatives, March 19, 1860," Oberlin College.

the Union be dissolved now, will we have additional security for slavery?" He knew that "our treasury is nearly empty, we have near half a million of dollars in the treasury of the United States; a million of our School Fund is invested in U.S. Bonds; we have an extensive frontier to defend," along with "fanaticism in the North...." Sentimentally, he averred in words veritably tear-stained, "I am now an aged man. My locks have become white," and he was unready for fighting fellow citizens.[58]

Like many of his compatriots, however, Houston was more than ready to combat Indigenes, Africans and Mexicans. The KGC, to which he was sympathetic, saw Mexico as the first domino to fall, and to that end, styled itself as a kind of British East India Company—a devilish mix of investment and arms. Cuba too was eyed, but was hard to pull off given staunch opposition not only from the then occupying force of Spain, but Britain was not supportive of this takeover either. Walker in Nicaragua was an exemplar of the mode envisioned—and, coincidentally, former leader of sovereign Texas, Mirabeau Lamar, was envoy there in the 1850s—yet another example of how enslavers were manipulating foreign policy to their advantage in the prelude to 1861. An animating notion was to disperse the enslaved over a larger territory on the premise that they were much too concentrated as matters then stood and needed to be diffused in order to reduce their ability to revolt. Land and construction of railways, a proven boondoggle, was also part of their fever dreams.[59]

Thus, as the time for civil war approached, many Texas settlers were concentrating on another looming conflict. During the Spring of 1860, the Knights of the Golden Circle—the outfit that sought to expand enslavement beyond the confines of North America, especially to Cuba—also sought to raise a force of 12,000 men to invade Mexico under the reputed command of Sam Houston himself. According to an observant Texas Ranger, they were to be paid by "English capitalists at the rate of eighteen dollars per month," and all the plunder one could scoop up. In the crosshairs were Nuevo León, Chihuahua, Coahuila and Tamaulipas, all slated for annexation to the rascal republic. Houston was said to keep a low profile, though he was promised a "fabulous sum" or perhaps a rich "annuity" to his spouse. "Nearly all the Texas Rangers were induced" to join, said

---

58. "Letter from General Houston," 14 November 1860, Huntsville, Box 39, Pease, Graham, Niles Papers.

59. L.S. Hudson, 22, 24, 29, 58. See also Nancy Boothe Parker, "Mirabeau B. Lamar's Texas Journal," M.A. thesis, Rice U, 1979, xiii. Lamar was also U.S. envoy in Costa Rica.

the Ranger James Pike. "All the great estates in Mexico were to be confiscated," and "mines in Sonora were to be parceled out." But these grandiose plans were intercepted by civil war—though like others sympathetic to KGC, Pike was hostile to secession, seeing it as a diversion from further hemispheric looting.[60]

Certainly, anti-Mexican psychosis served to propel the KGC in Texas. The same could be said for anti-German sentiment, which often was imbued too with anti-Catholicism, all of which undergirded the Know Nothing movement that also had a base in the Lone Star State. Like secessionists, they too were frustrated by the federal union, finding it overly constraining, though their option favored pre-1845 sovereignty. One Texan felt that his state should stand against both the federal union and the Confederacy, via a KGC companion, the "Lone Star Association."[61]

Another ideological companion was the Order of the Lone Star, also known as the Lone Star of the West. These forces attained a popularity and scale in Texas dwarfing other regions. "In no locale did it reach such amazing proportions," said one staggered historian, referring to Texas. It was not just the Comanches and Kickapoo and Caddo and Lipan Apache and next door Navajo, it was also, says this historian, William H. Bell, the Seminole, whose raids were "exasperating" and forcing extremism: repression bred resistance then further repression in a seemingly endless cycle. Recall that "Wild Cat" and his compatriots had left Indian Territory, he then received a commission in the Mexican army and in addition ten acres of land for each family, then "made himself especially obnoxious by assisting slaves to flee to Mexico," according to an acerbic critic—and may have had a hand in insuring this enslaved property in Texas was gifted "strychnine and firearms…"[62] for unpleasant ends.

After decades of warfare and their expulsion from Florida, Washington had exported the problem of the Seminoles to Texas's borders, which settlers there could understandably see as yet another example of fecklessness justifying divorce.[63] As civil war crept closer, credible stories emerged that the authorities in Coahuila actually supported materially and morally Seminole assaults on Texas. U.S. officials in Eagle Pass were told as much with the allegation made that Wild Cat himself had boasted of such. During the so-called

60. Pike, 137, 138, 139.
61. Fornell, 365, 369, 389, 390.
62. Bell, 25, 29, 44, 45, 48, 70, 104.
63. Giddings.

"Revolution of Ayutla" in Mexico designed to undermine Santa Anna, this leader was said to have been backed by Seminoles and, in return, were backed against Texas settlers.[64]

The singular challenge to Texas sovereignty presented by the triple threat of Africans, Indigenes and Mexicans led to a fierce counter-reaction personified by KGC.

No better—or worse—example of the KGC and Texas perfidy is the case of David Twiggs, who commanded a significant percentage of U.S. forces, who happened to be stationed along the border in light of persistent conflict there, and promptly turned over to the traitors a sizable arsenal of cannon, horses, artillery and other weaponry. This weakened Washington, as it strengthened the rebels. He too was said to be part of the KGC,[65] suggesting that despising Washington was the common currency of secessionists and the KGC alike. Twiggs was born in Georgia, underscoring that Texas roots were not the sole qualification for KGC sympathies. At the time of secession there were an estimated 2500 U.S. troops along the border and stretching to San Antonio and points west, all of whom were jeopardized by Twiggs's peremptoriness.[66]

Twiggs's treachery, surrendering a great portion of federal materiel, had placed in the hands of traitors a significant percentage of Texas's arms, made all the more alarming as it was executed in a clandestine fashion combined with repression of foes.[67]

Twiggs's perfidy was saluted in Texas. On the eve of civil war, Senator John Hemphill of Texas reminded his colleagues that "freely and without price, Texas brought an empire to the United States" in land and treasure in 1845, yet Washington, he charged, "has constructed no forts, no courthouses, finished no arsenals, no custom houses and stored but a very limited supply of arms...." While Washington was fiddling, Texas was burning: "frontiers have been desolated by the savage," he said hotly. Texas bolted from Mexico and can bolt from

---

64. J.D. Riley, 71.

65. David Siklenat, *Raising the White Flag: How Surrender Defined the Civil War*, Chapel Hill: U of North Carolina Press, 2019. See also G. Nelson, 88.

66. W.J. Hughes, 272.

67. Horace Greeley in pamphlet, "Origins and Objects of the Slaveholders' Conspiracy Against Democratic Principles as well as Against the National Union—Illustrated in the Speeches of Andrew Jackson Hamilton, in the Statements of Lorenzo Sherwood, Ex-Member of the Texas Legislature and the Publications," New York: Baker & Godwin, 1862, Huntington Library (abbrev. Origins and Objects).

the U.S.,[68] and in any case, said the legislator and his comrades, like Twiggs they were simply reclaiming what was rightfully Confederate property. Hemphill was a force to reckon with and a prototypical Texan: a native of South Carolina, he arrived in Texas in 1838 after fighting Seminoles in Florida, then became the "John Marshall" of the state as Chief Justice, formulating legal opinions sanctifying enslavement and dispossession.[69]

The stormy petrel Louis Wigfall concurred. This Texas Congressman averred that when Texas entered the U.S. it relinquished military and diplomatic armor, so reclaiming same was just. In any case, he said in September 1860, "slaveholding states greatly sympathized with" Texas since "she had been populated chiefly with their citizens," which was true.[70]

In retrospect it is difficult to ascertain if those like Twiggs—Southerners in the (temporary) employ of Washington—had wormed their way into influential posts in order to benefit secessionists, or was it simply incompetence on the part of the federal union that had allowed it. Washington naively acquiesced to placing potential secessionists in sensitive posts, pre-1861. Thus, in 1861, John T. Pickett, who had been the U.S. representative in Vera Cruz, moved inland to become the Confederate envoy in Mexico City.[71] In March 1861 in Chihuahua, U.S. envoy George Macmanus submitted his "resignation": in a mastery of overstatement, he concluded that his move was mandatory "as the United States no longer exists...."[72] Prior to this prematurity, he had spent a "few months" in California, likely stirring up anti-Washington stances.[73]

In Indian Territory, so vital to Texas security, Washington's placemen stepped aside as secessionists took over and—per capitalist opportunism—often conspired in the pilfering of tens of thousands of Indigenous-owned livestock, a factor in driving a number of Indigenes into the waiting embrace of secessionists,[74] which was to

---

68. "Speech of John Hemphill of Texas on the State of the Union Delivered in the Senate of the United States, January 28, 1861," AAS.

69. J.P. Hart, "John Hemphill—Chief Justice of Texas," *Case and Comment*, 55 (No. 5, September-October 1950): 12-19, 12, 18, CCSC.

70. Speech of Louis Wigfall, 3 September 1860, CCSC.

71. Vice Consul Charles Rieken to Secretary of State William Seward, 2 July 1861, Reel 8, Despatches from U.S. Consuls in Vera Cruz, NARA.

72. George Macmanus to Secretary of State Seward, 24 March 1861, Reel 1, Despatches from U.S. Consuls in Chihuahua, NARA.

73. Ibid., George Macmanus to Secretary Cass, 20 December 1859.

74. Annie Heloise Abel, *The American Indian and the End of the Confederacy, 1863-1866*, Lincoln, Neb.: Bison Books, 1993 (abbrev. Abel 1993).

bedevil the war effort for years to come. But although Indigenes had a hard time swallowing the point that land grabbers in Washington were the "good guys" in this conflict, secessionists were to find that it would not be easy for those who advocated genocide to maintain a steady alliance with intended victims. Still, it was in early 1861 that Texas dispatched envoys to the Choctaw, Chickasaw, Creek and other Cherokee nations to aid in preparing them for alliance with the Confederacy.[75] Yet it is fair to say that there was no unanimity of opinion on the Civil War in Indian Territory, for surging in importance during this era were the anti-slavery militants of the Keetoowah Society.[76]

The Texas patriot George Erath may have had KS in mind when the asserted that "the Indians held to their old idea that the people of Texas were a different tribe from those of the United States and that they could make war on the one without the other having a right to interfere...." Or he may have contemplated Kickapoo, who fought Confederates vigorously,[77] just as Choctaws generally pursued an opposing path, with the fading Tonkawa acting similarly (though their leadership was close to the slain Robert Neighbors).[78] In any event, KS, which tended to be comprised of "full blood" or Cherokee not subject to unions with settlers (these were "half bloods"), were seen as akin to the Kickapoo. Or so said Henry Henderson, born in 1840 near what is now Muskogee, Oklahoma. His mother had been enslaved and his father was Cherokee: "I fought with the Cherokee Pin Indians," or KS, he said, while "half bloods [were] going into the Confederate Army and the full bloods into the Union Army, thus causing much discord and strife...."[79]

Despite their noteworthy genocidal faction, the rebels had an advantage in the person of Albert Pike, who had negotiated land claims pre-1861 on behalf of Cherokee, Choctaw and Chickasaw. Nevertheless, it took quite a leap of faith for Indigenes to accept these rebels as allies when their ranks included Earl Van Dorn, a West Point graduate and Texan from Mississippi, whose bona fides were questioned by one scholar because of his "less than honorable dealings...with already married women," but who as a U.S. officer led a detachment under a flag of truce to Comanche lines—then slaughtered them all.

---

75. Texas Constitution 1861.

76. A.E. Roberts, 28.

77. Erath, 98.

78. Jason Cannon Abbott, "A History of the Tonkawa Indians to 1867," M.A. thesis, Tarleton State U, 1996, 63, 59.

79. Oral History, Henry Henderson, 26 November 1937, IPP.

Nonetheless, some of the most effective fighters against Lincoln's military were Indigenes armed by Pike.[80]

On the other hand, the 1860 census revealed the presence of only 14 enslaved Africans in the three southernmost Texas counties, heavily populated by those of Mexican and Indigenous origin. In Zapata County, Mexican Americans often opposed openly aligning with the rebels, with some understandably fearing the end result would be their own enslavement. This helped to buoy folk hero Juan Cortina, who was said to be heading toward Brownsville.[81] If accompanied by a competent legal advisor, he could have argued that the goal of retaking Texas was justifiable on the grounds that it rightfully belonged to Mexico and no longer had Washington's imprimatur and protection, vitiating the 1848 treaty that ended the war of aggression. An astute legal eagle in Washington could have concurred insofar as it weakened the bulwark of the traitors: Texas.

Perhaps because Washington had been so assiduous in capitulating to the ideological whims of enslavers, it was not just Indigenes who had a hard time taking this capital seriously as an avatar of freedom. This was particularly the case during the early stages of the war, when the Lincoln line was that saving the union—not necessarily abolition—was the issue. Thus, says one analyst, the "individual who most influenced president [Jefferson] Davis...was José Agustín Quintero," a Cuban born in Havana in 1829.[82] His origins notwithstanding, he was well known among Know Nothing circles in Texas, contributing to their Tejano journals.[83] There were Mexican Americans who enlisted on the rebel side though they "proved utterly unreliable" as fighters, according to one source, with a number fleeing to Mexico in order to evade conscription.[84]

There was substantial pro-U.S. sympathy among Mexican-Americans, though like Indigenes, many had a hard time accepting the headquarters

---

80. Paul Thomas Fisher, "Confederate Empire and the Indian Treaties: Pike, McCulloch and the Five Civilized Tribes, 1861-1862," M.A. thesis, Baylor U, 2011, 30-31, 75, 96-97.

81. Ronald N. Gray, "Edmund J. Davis: Radical Republican and Reconstruction Governor of Texas" Ph.D. dissertation, TTU, 1976, 14 (abbrev. Gray, Davis).

82. James William Daddysman, "The Matamoros Trade, 1861-1865," Ph.D. dissertation, West Virginia U, 1976, 48, 103, 105, 106, 107 (abbrev. Daddysman 1976).

83. De León, 187.

84. Ella Lonn, *Foreigners in the Confederacy*, Chapel Hill: U of North Carolina Press, 1940, 234.

of land grabbing as champions of liberty. Thus, their sentiment was more anti-Texas than pro-Washington, with this group expressing little loyalty to either side.[85]

Why should Washington be trusted, especially in the early stages when its maneuvers were so misguided? One of the first foreign policy decisions of the incoming Lincoln regime was to send an emissary to Central America with "'secret instructions'" to find a "Liberia" for U.S. Negroes in the region. Perhaps fearing this would be the receipt of a Trojan Horse, Guatemalan leaders objected stridently as did other regional leaders.[86]

KGC influence in Texas notwithstanding, when Fort Sumter was bombarded in the Spring of 1861 signaling civil war, Lone Star leader Louis Wigfall was on the scene as cheerleader and strategist.[87] In the latter capacity he was on a vessel in Charleston's harbor and was the first to issue terms of surrender to the federal forces.[88]

In the months before secession, abolitionist stalwart Charles Sumner found Texas's Wigfall to be "the most offensive figure of all,"[89] a crowning distinction for the Lone Star State. When Horace Greeley, influential newspaperman and Republican, "was assaulted in Washington," Sumner found it necessary to mention that it was "by a Texas member,"[90] though not Wigfall—apparently.

Wigfall clashed repeatedly with Sam Houston. His fervent desire to reopen the African Slave Trade formally meant that Sumner and his colleagues despised him. Though he wanted more Africans in his sight, he also feared a replay of the perceived horrors of the Haitian Revolution. The audacious Wigfall plotted—reputedly—to kidnap a presidential contender in 1860 so that his preferred candidate could prevail. The disputatious Wigfall also quarreled often with Jefferson Davis and thought that this leader should be executed. In some ways, he was a typical Texas gunslinger.[91]

And benefiting a man who considered himself in the first instance a Texas patriot—and not a devotee of Washington—he was quite hostile to this capital. One of his peers told him in March 1861 in

85. Crews, 45.

86. Booker, xvii, 87, 88.

87. Louise Wigfall Wright, "Memories of the Beginning and End of the Southern Confederacy," *McClure's*, 23 (No. 5, September 1904): 451-464, 462, Huntington Library.

88. Grear, 106-107.

89. Note, ca. 1860, in Pierce, Volume III, 610.

90. Ibid., note, ca. 1860, 495.

91. King, 92, 118, 173, 231, 304.

words that resonated with the recipient that "if certain contingencies came about he would go away from this country and join some other nation; even the Comanches he would prefer...." But again these were not isolated views, as Wigfall was told also that Texas's "Harrison County has gone for secession by a vote of 868 to 44," while "four or five of the adjoining counties have gone almost unanimously for secession...."[92]

This was precisely his base of electoral support: as the saying goes, it was not just the pastor but the people in the pews who preached enslavement and genocide. Wigfall, an enslaver, recognized the value of this commodity; as early as 1846 facing insolvency, he sold Africans to satisfy debts and 15 years later was championing war so if need be, he could do it again.[93]

Wigfall, who was an exemplar of the "fire-eater" of enslavement and secession, the hardest of hardliners, had a mass base, a sine qua non for an emerging fascism. That men born abroad and those of African descent comprised more than half of the U.S. army during the war was also an emblem of the mass support for the rebels, though arguably this suggests that foreigners and Negroes won the war, not necessarily subject of applause in various precincts nationally.[94]

*   *   *

By March 1861, Texas propagandists were crowing that "reliable information showed" that voting for secession were "32,000...more than half of the largest poll ever given at an election in this State. In opposition there were comparatively few votes...." Whereas secession was perpetrated in most states, led by South Carolina, by way of convention involving scores, Texans were bold enough to sustain this measure by a vote of thousands of Euro-American men. Defended adamantly was the "propriety of secession before the commencement of the Abolition administration," meaning Lincoln.[95] Elite Texans demonized the incoming president, as they vociferously defended enslavement of Africans. Though the Texas Republic drew heavily from U.S. coffers to stay afloat during its existence, this reliance was forgotten by 1861, and was substituted by demonizing Washington amid enthusiastic defense of slavery as a boon to Africans not

---

92. Halsey to "Dear Louly," 30 March 1861, Box 2R299, Wigfall Papers.
93. *Edgefield Advertiser*, 1846, Box 2R300, Wigfall Papers.
94. Hahn, *292*.
95. Texas Constitution 1861.

least, and full-throated denunciations of Lincoln.[96] En route to Central Africa in search of Dr. Livingston, Henry Morton Stanley found that slaveholders thought Lincoln's election meant "pure robbery," an opinion validated, it was thought, when slavery was abolished without compensation.[97]

At the apex of Wigfall's mass base was Robert Mills, known as the "Duke of Brazoria," this feudal nickname appropriate in that he was not just one of the wealthiest men in Texas and the nation in 1861, with a net worth of about $5 million, a king's ransom. He also owned more Africans than any person in the state, freeing an astonishing 800 by 1865, a powerful whack at his fortunes, serving to illuminate why terrorism emerged that same year. Born in Kentucky, he helped finance the 1836 revolt to preserve slavery before attempting a replay in 1861. He was not alone. Alongside him was William Moody, born in 1828 in Virginia, who owned a "mere" two dozen Africans by 1860 and argued passionately, as a result, for secession and even served in the Confederate military. Like feudal barons of the past, Moody's daughter wed Mills's grand-nephew.[98]

Yet marital alliances aside, Mills and Moody in their advocacy of secession—first from Mexico, then from the U.S.—represented a tradition stretching back to 1688 when enslaving interests clipped the wings of the monarch in order to elbow their way into the heart of this odious commerce.[99] Mills was present at the creation in 1836 of the next stage of this painfully grotesque drama, the dress rehearsal for the final act, which commenced in 1861.[100] Students of history, secessionists in 1861 sought to time their historic move with the 25th anniversary of the previous secession: 2 March 1836.[101]

Continuing the historical analogy, Jefferson Davis cited the precedent of the Declaration of Independence in his own April 1861 formulation and slated his inauguration on George Washington's birthday, as the founder on horseback was portrayed on the "Great Seal of the Confederacy." Feebly and inaccurately, Charles Sumner responded by claiming that this founder was an "'abolitionist,'" emblematic of the contradictions ensnaring the older republic. Credibly, Robert Toombs,

96. John Nathan Cravens, *James Harper Starr: Financier of the Republic of Texas*, Austin: Daughters of the Republic of Texas, 1950, 63-64, 122.

97. D. Stanley, 163.

98. Shelton, 66.

99. Gerald Horne, *Counter-Revolution of 1776*.

100. Torget, *Cotton*, 22.

101. Jewett, 47.

who became Secretary of State for the rebels, assayed that "'African slavery existed in [the] then colonies at the commencement of the American Revolution...[and] was inextricably interwoven with the framework of society....'" Fellow rebels analogized the U.S. to London in 1776 and depicted this nation as enemies of the founders.[102] "Ever and anon," began a Galveston cleric in 1860, "secession has become a necessity from the days of Abraham to the days of Washington and Garibaldi," especially the former since "two or more nations were born at once on the 4th of July 1776...." Amid arcane references to a "Jew store," the Reverend J.E. Carnes reminded that "people of the North are hostile to the Negro and to slavery," which was not far wrong and did not bode well for Africans.[103]

The initial ideologist of the "Lost Cause," Edward A. Pollard, contended that secession was nothing new in the republic and definitely not in the North: "The right of it had been reserved by the State of New York, on her adoption of the Federal Constitution" and was "threatened on four separate occasions by the state of Massachusetts"; and, he said, at the time of annexation, Texas had not renounced secession altogether—like saying "I do" at your wedding, with a caveat.[104]

In this context, Texas—which seceded not once but twice—was, per Wigfall, an ideological leader of the rebels. The eastern two-thirds of Texas, the heart of slavery, was as large as Alabama and Mississippi combined. With over 590 slave narratives materializing in the Lone Star State, Texas produced more of these valuable documents than any state, meaning a good deal of what we think we know about slavery is in fact what we know about slavery just north of Mexico.[105]

Thus, Texas slavery was renowned for its harshness, perhaps a product of resistance buoyed by Mexicans and Indigenes. As enslaved began to pour into the state during the war, fear was instilled in the

---

102. Jonathan B. Crider, "The Memory of the American Revolution in the Politics of the Civil War," M.A. thesis, TTU, 2008, 21, 66, 69, 75, 77, 79, 90.

103. Reverend J.E. Carnes, "Address on the Duty of the Slave States in the Present Crisis Delivered in Galveston, December 12th, 1860," Galveston: 'News' Book and Job Office, 1860, Huntington Library.

104. Pollard, 85.

105. Andrew Waters, ed., *I Was Born in Slavery: Personal Accounts of Slavery in Texas*, Winston-Salem: Blair, 2003, xviii (abbrev. A. Waters).

Africans' very marrow at the thought of taking this "Overland Middle Passage," then arriving in a living hell.[106]

Texas was also a military leader of the rebels, with John Bell Hood's Texas Brigade becoming one of the most courageous units in Robert E. Lee's entire force.[107] Thus, as Lee's forces were collapsing in April 1865, many in Texas resolved to carry on, seeking to ally with France's Mexico, a possibility since the Lone Star State had suffered less than other sections of the war and, because of exports from Matamoros and Tampico throughout, was well-positioned. More Texans had fought for the rebels than from any other state except Lee's Virginia.[108]

Previously independent Texas, which contained a portion of the citizenry that continued to yearn for this status, was also more prone than other states to entertain overtures of foreign powers, e.g., when Paris, which had seized Mexico, sought to detach the Lone Star State from the Confederacy.[109] As if in preparation, by 1861 France had 17 consulates in the Slave South, with Galveston being among the most important (as of 1861, 39 powers had consulates in this same region).[110] By the Summer of 1861 there were 11 French warships cruising the coasts of the U.S. and 110,000 nationals from France on these shores.[111] By way of contrast, Russia, which was to become a major antagonist of Washington in coming decades and for years to come, backed Washington because of fear that otherwise London would gain an advantage.[112]

As for Mexico, before the French takeover, José Marcos Mugarrieta, an official of this neighbor, was made aware early on in April 1861

---

106. Jacqueline Jones, *Goddess of Anarchy: The Life and Times of Lucy Parsons, American Radical*, New York: Basic, 2017, 10.

107. L. Wright, 74.

108. Elsye Drennan Andress, "The Gubernatorial Career of Andrew Jackson Hamilton," M.A. thesis, TTU, 1955, 52, 53 (abbrev. Andress).

109. Edwin De Leon, *Secret History of Confederate Diplomacy Abroad*, Lawrence: U Press of Kansas, 2005, 163-164.

110. Milledge Bonham, "The French Consuls in the Confederate States," in *Studies in Southern History and Politics*, New York: Columbia U Press, 1914, 83-106, 84, 85 (abbrev. Bonham).

111. Steve Sainlaude, *France and the American Civil War: A Diplomatic History*, Chapel Hill: U of North Carolina Press, 8, 15 (abbrev. Sainlaude).

112. Alexander Noonan, "'A New Expression of that Entente Cordiale'? Russian American Relations and the 'Fleet Episode' of 1863," in David T. Gleeson and Simon Lewis, eds., *The Civil War as Global Conflict: Transnational Meanings of the American Civil War*, Columbia: U of South Carolina Press, 2014, 116-145, 124. See also Russell H. Bartley, *Imperial Russia and the Struggle for Latin American Independence, 1808-1828*, Austin: U of Texas Press, 1978.

that the rebels were headed to Washington bent on "taking captive the president" and "seizing the national archives...." It was thought that the U.S. was becoming as unstable as Mexico: "according to my reading of Mexican history," he said, "there never has been one presidential term from the time of the revolution in 1820 down to the present day when the candidate elected by the people ever served his four years...are we to inaugurate this Mexican system into the [U.S.],"[113] he asked with some mocking. Unfortunately, as I write in 2022, the answer remains unclear.

---

113. Report, 25 April 1861, Box 6, Mugarrieta Papers.

Chapter **14**

Texas as Rebel Bulwark during the Early Civil War, 1861-1862

After the assault on Fort Sumter, the rebels bolted out of the chutes with all guns blazing. Texas was well-positioned to inflict pulverizing damage on the Lincoln forces: the Lone Star State had more than its share of martial experience, having fought the Mexicans in their own secession, skirmished repeatedly with what was likely the most skilled of Indigenous fighters—Comanche—while seeking to contain an ever growing African population not averse to aligning with settler foes. Indeed, far from the Mississippi River and the crucial Virginia-Washington-Gettysburg theater alike, while having backup from friends in Mexico, Texas emerged in 1865 less damaged than its peers and with an enhanced African population as enslavers fled to their soil, insuring that it would then become a major battleground for Reconstruction. Thus, Texas could spare troops to send eastward and by April 1865 was willing to continue fighting and, to a degree, did so as enslavers fled en masse to Mexico, Brazil and Cuba.[1]

In the latter case, migration by enslavers was eased by, e.g., the presence in Louisiana of the Yznaga family, of Cuban origin, which controlled a plantation with 300 enslaved Africans.[2]

Even Robert E. Lee acknowledged his reliance on the mettle of Texas's fighting men.[3] And as late as May 1865 John "Rip" Ford and his men continued to slaughter scores of U.S. soldiers at Palmito Ranch in southern Texas, giving rebels confidence that surrender was wildly premature.[4]

Typical Texas braggadocio set aside, at first blush the state was more vulnerable than it appeared. As early as November 1861

---

1. M.R. Moore, 168.

2. de Courcy, 107.

3. Mrs. D. Giraud Wright, *A Southern Girl in '61: The War-Time Memories of a Confederate Senator's Daughter*, New York: Doubleday, Page, 1905, 94 (abbrev. D.G. Wright).

4. L.S. Hudson, 86.

Governor John Andrew of Massachusetts, from the comforts of Boston, like a football coach, thought the rebels should be attacked at its strongest point. The Lone Star State, he counseled, was "the state easiest to take and hold," which should be pursued immediately, then "proclaim martial law...free all the slaves, compensating loyal owners if necessary," and thus "demonstrate to foreign powers that this war is to stop the spread of slavery,"[5] failure to proclaim such being a stumbling block to creating a global coalition for the federals. In sum, Texas's strength—being able to ship troops eastward to other battlefields—may have boomeranged. One scholar says that two-thirds of all military companies raised in Texas fought east of the Mississippi River—but this may have eroded strength at home.[6]

Almost predictably, the bluster balloon of Texas was punctured in October 1862, when Galveston surrendered, and though it was retaken a few months later, it was inevitable that the Austin bullies lost some of their swagger—and confidence. For the vessels and sailors there were an important aspect of the rebels' navy.[7]

Supplied via Tampico, Texas was still able to bluster about fighting on—at least as long as France controlled Mexico. As early as July 1861 Secretary of State Seward was told that Vera Cruz, was a key link in this chain: "from this port by way of Texas" arrived arms to the rebels generally[8]. By August 1861 more bad news arrived on Seward's desk in the form of a missive from Mazatlán informing him that present there were "some six or seven Americans" with "traitorous and rebellious sentiments" with "violent feelings of hostility to the United States...." Although they had the temerity to "display the secession flag in their houses," they continued to seek the diplomatic protection of U.S. Consul Edward Conner.[9]

By early 1862 President Lincoln was told that Mazatlán was "the most important" port on the Pacific, next to San Francisco, being "situated at the mouth of the Gulf of California" and "within a few days of the ports of Upper California," thereby potentially placing Northern California in jeopardy. It was also a "port of disembarkation of the disloyal citizens" providing rebels with unparalleled reach in the

5. Governor Andrew to Assistant Secretary of the Navy, Gustavus Fox, 27 November 1861, in *War of the Rebellion*, Series I, Volume XV, 412.

6. Grear, 100.

7. Fornell, 406.

8. Charles Rieken, Vice Consul to Secretary Seward, 25 July 1861, Reel 8, Despatches from U.S. Consuls in Vera Cruz, NARA.

9. Edward Conner to Secretary Seward, 28 August 1861, Reel 2, Despatches from U.S. Consuls in Mazatlan, NARA.

hemisphere and easing travel by rambunctious Texans to the Golden State "and other southwestern states" too.[10]

Mazatlán was challenged as an important Pacific port by Acapulco, and by early 1862 secessionists were bold and confident of success. It was then that Secretary Seward was informed that "persons residing here who claim to be American citizens" were seeking consular "protection" though they were "contending...for the supremacy of the rebellious states and rejoice in the reverse of the federal arms."[11]

By October 1862 the struggle continued, this time in Monterrey as Secretary Seward was notified that a "great amount of goods" were "sent from here across the Rio Grande," including "goods and ammunition," principally to Texas. In recent months "the trade [had] grown to be of such magnitude" that Vice Consul M.M. Kimmey despaired: "it was increasing every day," he moaned, involving "enormous quantities of cotton, belonging to" Texas and its neighbors. In fact, he groaned, "enough goods go from and through this place to supply the whole rebel army," facilitated since their "agents are here" in profusion: "agents are scattered through this country contracting for all the flour and corn that can be had.... large trains are daily leaving for the different points on the Rio Grande...most of them go to Eagle Pass, loaded with blankets, shoes, leather, cloth, cotton goods of kinds, coffee, rice, sugar, powder, saltpeter, sulphur, medicines and, in fact, almost everything needed to supply the wants of the rebels...."[12]

Though a good deal of this profit was skimmed by rebels, much of it remained in the pockets of Mexicans too, providing a rationale for backing secession—or even the French takeover of Mexico, which too was pro-secession for that matter. By September 1862 Washington knew well of the "American capital employed here," speaking of Mexico City; however, there was "no American commercial house here. The entire commerce is in the hands of Germans, English, Frenchmen and Spaniards," a factor that underlined why a foreign takeover ensued that same year. The "American population here," it was reported, "numbers about one hundred," though "over one half of the same are naturalized" and a "great many of the latter have

10. Ibid., Consul Richard Robertson to President Lincoln, 22 January 1862, Reel 1.

11. Consul Lewis Ely to Secretary Seward, 25 February 1862, Reel 2, Despatches from U.S. Consuls in Acapulco, NARA.

12. M.M. Kimmey, Vice Consul to Secretary Seward, 29 October 1862, in *War of the Rebellion*, Series III, Volume II, 949.

become so out of speculation," suggesting they were not exactly fervent patriots who could be relied upon.[13]

Tampico became one of the most important nodes of rebel support, as Secretary of State Seward well knew. By November 1861 he was informed that "secessionists in Texas have lately found their way to this city" and though "in distressed circumstances" they were worthy of surveillance.[14] Washington thought that rebel vessels were flying the Mexican flag and sending arms just north of Tamaulipas.[15] When a British vessel was captured by U.S. forces in Matamoros in early 1862, the worst fears about international aid to the rebels was confirmed.[16]

Yet by early 1862 there was an attack on this city, but the "besiegers," according to a U.S. observer, were "badly beaten" and "retired to Brownsville," carting "two cannons to Fort Brown, there is no doubt that they were aided by soldiers from the southern army." The problem for the rebels in this heavily Mexican town in Texas was that "most of the citizens of Brownsville being really Union men" was complexifying—though "Confederates occupy both the Texan and Mexican side of the Rio Grande at its mouth," making Matamoros "the great thoroughfare to the Southern States,"[17] a veritable lifeline for secession. At the same time, Brownsville being substantially "loyal" meant that the U.S. legation in Matamoros was—said the envoy—"continually besieged with refugees and deserters...."[18]

Also in early 1862, a force was being organized in Brownsville and the vicinity to seize Matamoros and, said the U.S. emissary, "many Texans were joining...." Purportedly the "real object" was "the capture of all the Americans on this side," meaning Mexico. Indicative of the turmoil that did not terminate with Appomattox, Secretary Seward was informed that "Texas troops are becoming demoralized

13. Consul Marcus Otterbourg to State Department, 28 September 1862, Reel 6, Despatches from U.S. Consuls in Mexico City, NARA.

14. Consul Franklin Chase to Secretary Seward, 26 November 1861, Reel 3, Despatches from U.S. Consuls in Tampico, NARA.

15. Ibid., Franklin Chase to Governor of Tamaulipas, 24 December 1861.

16. Earl Russell to Mr. Adams, 19 April 1862, in "Correspondence with Mr. Adams Respecting Neutral Rights and Duties, Presented to Both Houses of Parliament by Command of Her Majesty," North American No. 6, London: Harrison and Sons, 1862, Huntington Library.

17. Consul Leonard Price to "Sir," 1 March 1862, Reel 3, Despatches from U.S. Consuls in Matamoros, NARA.

18. Ibid., Consul Pierce to Secretary Seward, 21 March 1862.

and disorderly in the extreme, declaring that they will burn and destroy everything of both friend and foe."[19]

Not only "deserters" and "refugees" but traitors and loyalists too continued to cross the border to Matamoros to the point that the U.S. emissary said, "today [it] presents the appearance of an American town," and Monterrey too.[20] By April 1862 Washington knew that "several rebel officers" had arrived in Matamoros; in league with the "police force" they were "arresting all the Americans [loyalists] that were obvious to them and were about to take them over to Texas...." Audaciously, they were "bursting doors open and walking in with pistols presented" and though "many of the Mexican officers and citizens earnestly protested,"[21] it was mostly for naught. Thus, when the leading loyalist Texas politician A.J. Hamilton arrived there, "with fifteen men" accompanying him, "he having escaped from Austin on horseback," five times as many men—"seventy five"— were "sent down the river on the Texas side to capture him."[22]

By October 1862 the fugitive had arrived in Brooklyn, where he addressed an enthusiastic audience. He was introduced as an "eminent Union refugee," as the stage was crowded with various eminences, providing an idea of why he was pursued across borders.[23] Rebels desperately wanted Hamilton to pay a steep price since he had roots in Alabama, was raised to be a slaveholder, and his defection sent a signal about the ultimate fortunes of secession. Texas had been a sanctuary for these types, including a previous governor, Hardin Runnels of Mississippi—who had the distinction of earlier defeating Sam Houston at the polls.[24]

However, Texas loyalists too had weaknesses that were revealed when one of them—Lorenzo Sherwood, a former member of the legislature in Austin—spoke in upstate New York in October 1862. He opposed the rebels, he said, since their purpose was—allegedly— to "Mexicanize the American people," a concept difficult to parse decades later. He too had "grown wearied and disgusted with the mawkish sensibility over the negro, when there is so much higher and more available ground to take in favor of the white man...." Unashamedly he added with emphasis, "My sympathies are enlisted

19. Ibid., Consul Pierce to Secretary Seward, 24 March 1862.
20. Ibid., Consul Pierce to Secretary Seward, 30 April 1862.
21. Ibid., Consul Pierce to Secretary Seward, 26 April 1862.
22. Ibid., Consul Pierce to Secretary Seward, 26 August 1862.
23. Origins and Objects.
24. Ibid., Horace Greeley on A.J. Hamilton.

in the great cause of *white humanity in its shirt sleeves,*" presumably meaning that enslaved labor was unfair competition.[25]

Texas, which had been battered because of its proximity to Mexico, was now keeping secession afloat not least because of this same proximity—but this opportunity also contained danger.

Moreover, these lengthy supply lines—from Matamoros to the north, east and west—may have overextended the capacity of the Lone Star State. For by November 1862 Governor Lubbock –born in the future cockpit of conflict that was Charleston in 1817[26]—was telling Jefferson Davis to "require no more men to leave Texas," since this rebel bulwark was "almost denuded of her best fighting men. We have over sixty regiments in the Confederate service, very few of which are in the state"; moreover, "our men took with them the best arms they could control" and "our people are really uneasy," surrounded as they were by combative Indigenes, resentful Mexicans and unsettled Africans. Then there were the "Jayhawkers,"[27] the fighting federal force in Kansas, not too far away.

The "Jayhawkers" may have been gazing southward to Texas because as early as August 1862 the news was that "Texans in large numbers are coming to [neighboring] Missouri armed" and "without discipline...."[28]

Armies fight on their stomachs. With supply lines overextended, by August 1862 not only Texas troops but those of Arkansas and Louisiana too were "assembling in large numbers in northwestern Arkansas for the purpose of invading Missouri." It was not just military goals that motivated this since, said Brigadier General J.M. Schofield of the rebels, "this they are compelled to do for subsistence."[29]

Texans were also fighting Michiganders in Tennessee. "The First Regiment Texas Rangers," said Colonel John Parkhurst of the Ninth

---

25. "The Slaveholders' Rebellion Against the Democratic Institutions as well as Against the National Union, As set Forth in the Speech of the Hon. Lorenzo Sherwood, Ex-Member of the Texan Legislature, Delivered at Champlain in Northern New York, October 1862..., New York: Westcott, 1862," AAS (abbrev. Slaveholders' Rebellion).

26. Grear, 114.

27. Governor Lubbock to President Davis, 13 November 1862, in *War of the Rebellion*, Series I, Volume LIII, 833.

28. Ibid., Clark Wright, Springfield, Missouri, to Brigadier General Schofield, 9 August 1862, Series I, Volume XIII, 221.

29. Ibid., Brigadier General Schofield to Major General Halleck, 30 August 1862, Series I, Volume XIII, 606.

Michigan Infantry, were in Murfreesboro. Many of their opponents "had recently taken the oath of allegiance" to Washington, and shockingly, he said, "there were also quite a number of negroes attached to the Texas and Georgia troops, who were armed and equipped."[30]

Weeks later General P.O. Hebert of the rebel force concluded gloomily that the "position of the State of Texas is an anomalous one. A portion of its citizens and inhabitants are disaffected; the German element, which is very considerable, nearly entirely so," to the point where "martial law more necessary today than ever in Texas...." Startlingly, "Governor Lubbock...fully concur[s]...."[31]

As the above suggests, railways were rediscovered as, *inter alia*, a force of war, a fact exemplified in December 1861 when there was consideration of dispatching 1000 U.S. Negroes southward to build a rail line from Vera Cruz to Mexico City.[32] By 1862, the authorities in New Orleans, soon to be overwhelmed by federal forces, worriedly underscored that "without this [rail]road Texas is entirely isolated from the balance of the Confederacy. With it she will be closely annexed to it and add vastly to its strength" and provide "the means of furnishing us with very considerable war munitions which are being received through Mexico and Texas ports...."[33]

The impulse toward independence in Texas was not squelched during the war. France, a major player in the region, especially after seizing Mexico in 1862, that same year sought to detach the Lone Star State from the rebels, leading to an expulsion of their diplomats from Galveston and Richmond.[34] Besides aforementioned warships cruising in adjacent waters, France had multiple assets in North America, including priests—the "Oblate Fathers" in this case—who ministered on the Texas frontier and were sited in Brownsville and were quite sympathetic to the rebels.[35]

---

30. Ibid., Report of Colonel John G. Parkhurst, 13 July 1862, Series I, Volume XVI, Part I, 803.

31. Ibid., General P.O. Hebert to General S. Cooper, 11 October 1862, Series I, Volume LIII, 828.

32. S. Page, 150.

33. Resolution Passed by Common Council, New Orleans, 22 March 1862, in *War of the Rebellion*, Series IV, Volume III, Section II, 1013-1014.

34. Secretary of State Judah Benjamin to John Slidell in Paris, 17 October 1862, in James Richardson, ed., *A Compilation of the Messages and Papers of the Confederacy, Including the Diplomatic Correspondence, 1861-1865, Volume II*, Nashville: U.S. Publishing Company, 1906, 334-337, 334.

35. F.J. Scott, 106.

Despite this ouster, Paris continued to hold advantages, given the tens of thousands of French origin among the disloyal, especially in Louisiana. One rebel leader was referred to benevolently as "Prince Charles Polignac, a French gentleman of ancient lineage and a brigadier in the Confederate army...."[36] Louis Wigfall's daughter referred to him appreciatively as a "fiery little man; erect in figure with a keen black eye" and "dark waxed moustache...."[37]

This so-called "Lafayette of the South" had fought in the Crimea, bringing to the rebels extensive martial experience. He had traveled to Nicaragua, bringing expeditionary experience as well. He could—if need be—confer with top rebel officials who were fluent in French, e.g., John Slidell and Secretary of State Judah Benjamin. The late U.S. president Zachary Taylor had encouraged his children to learn this language, evidentiary of the close alliance between these partners. Since U.S. military manuals were fundamentally translations from French, Polignac brought yet another credential. His mother was British, giving him entrée in London as well. His insight there was that London was playing the Civil War combatants off against each other to the detriment of both. He was an undisputed rebel hero.[38] The same could be said for the Prussian consul at New Orleans, August Reichard, who became a brigadier general for the rebels.[39]

There were other rebels too of a similar "lineage," e.g., those denoted as "French Texans," who routinely celebrated Bastille Day or the anniversary of the anti-monarchial revolt.[40] Paris's envoy in New Orleans allowed nationals of his regime to join militias, not negligible since they were estimated to be 5% of the population. Paris was hedging in any case, first mandating that their nationals there execute emancipation in 1848 or within three years—then extending it to a decade.[41] James Buchanan, the outgoing president, was no rebel—at least not officially—but he remained in touch with those who had ties to France and Algeria after the war had commenced.[42]

---

36. Richard Taylor, *Destruction and Reconstruction: Personal Experiences of the Late War*, New York: Appleton, 1879, 153 (abbrev. R. Taylor).

37. D.G. Wright, 92.

38. Jeff Kinard, *Lafayette of the South: Prince Camille de Polignac and the American Civil War*, College Station: TA&MU Press, 2001, xiii, 8, 11, 16, 86, 113, 148, 169 (abbrev. Kinard).

39. Bonham, 84.

40. De León, 182.

41. Sainlaude, 82.

42. Mr. Cobden to James Buchanan, 5 September 1861, in J.B. Moore, Volume XI, 218.

Certainly the rebels were dickering madly, flailing about. John Bigelow, a federal man in Paris, thought that the secessionists were able to cut a deal for "restoration of British supremacy in the insurgent states" in return for aid to "overthrow of the government at Washington...." There was "construction in the dockyards of France of several vessels of war for the Confederate navy," while their agent, John Slidell, was huddling with the Emperor. Supposedly, the idea was to fake building vessels for Italy, before shipping same to the rebels. To buttress the rebel case he mentioned that "one half of the privates" of the federals "were foreigners, especially Germans and Irish...while our troops were almost exclusively born of our soil," suggesting that his cause had more domestic backing—at least among the all important Euro-American community. Moreover, Slidell cited with likely accuracy "my own family where French was habitually spoken. He asked me whether we anticipated no difficulty from our slaves...this was the only allusion made to slavery during the interview," though telling nonetheless. "The Confederate government had no objection to his seizing St. Domingo," meaning Haiti, no surprise there. The Emperor "had no scruple in declaring that his sympathies were entirely with the South...." He also confided that fellow royal, King Leopold of Belgium, was visited recently by Queen Victoria, both— he said—bearing rebel sympathies. Slidell sought to send his own son to St. Cyr, France's West Point, for training, as a testament to his loyalties.[43]

Paris was crawling with rebels then, and conceivably Bigelow could have bumped into James Morris Morgan there in 1862, who conceded proudly that "We Confederates in Europe were very secretive and mysterious...."[44] Or he could have encountered the Mississippi enslaver who became a U.S. Senator from California, William Gwin, who also happened to be in Paris.[45] The "coincidence" of so many rebels decamping to Paris in the midst of a life-or-death war gave resonance to the claim that France was seeking to cut fissiparous deals with secessionists, for example, enticing Texas into the fold, away from Richmond.[46]

---

43. John Bigelow, *France and the Confederate Navy, 1862-1868*, New York: Harper & Bros., 1888, iii, 116, 117, 118, 126, 127, 130, 133, 139 (abbrev. Bigelow).

44. James Morris Morgan, *Recollections of a Rebel Reefer*, Boston: Houghton Mifflin, 1917, 110 (abbrev. J.M. Morgan).

45. Joseph Allen Stout, *Liberators*, 171.

46. Message from Judah P. Benjamin, in J.D. Richardson, *Messages and Papers of Jefferson Davis*, 334-337, 334.

Ultimately this would lead to a fissure between the disloyal and France, but before this rupture, Paris's envoy in Galveston acted in accord with this conversation. He was cooperating hand-in-glove with rebel General E.B. Nichols, using the latter's son as a go-between—though he professed strict neutrality. He wanted more French vessels nearby, however.[47] Nevertheless, the arrogant rebels could not resist overstepping, as the French consul by mid-1862 complained continually about insults to his nation's flag, along with verbal aggressions. Some rebels were upset that a number of Frenchmen would not renounce U.S. naturalization, with rising tensions leading to the familiar: a request for the arrival in the Gulf of Mexico of French vessels.[48] Rebels were also upset when Paris sought to block conscription of French nationals.[49]

Yet there was considerable sympathy overseas for the federals, albeit on false pretenses. By September 1861 Secretary of State Seward received a newsflash from Alexandria, Egypt, about resident Italians—"refugees from revolutionary troubles at home"—who exuded "strong sympathy with our government," though "their enthusiasm…[was] founded…to some extent on the mistaken supposition that the abolition of slavery was one of the objects" of Washington. They "offered their military services" as a result of this mistaken supposition. Plus, the local Greeks, "estimated at 10,000" strong, with "many of the wealthiest and most influential residents," were likewise "friendly" to the federals. Even "French inhabitants" were "for the most part with us. But the English, who are comparatively few, are much less sympathetic…."[50]

Even the local authorities offered to sell the federals "Minié Rifles" of the "latest style and first quality," about "forty thousand, half entirely unused, the other half very little used" at "eleven dollars apiece," that had acquitted themselves well during the recent "Crimean War."[51] This was useful intelligence since this latter 1850s conflict resonated in Texas—or so thought the intrepid visitor, Frederick Olmsted.[52]

Perhaps coincidentally arrived news from Egypt that production of cotton was growing by leaps and bounds, which could undercut

47. Report, 2 August 1862, Galveston Consulate.

48. Ibid., Report, 25 June 1862.

49. Ibid., Report, 23 May 1862. See also at the same site, Report of 5 June 1862.

50. Consul William Thayer to Secretary Seward, 30 September 1861, Reel 3, Despatches from U.S. Consuls in Alexandria, Egypt, NARA.

51. Ibid., Mr. Thayer to Secretary Seward, 19 November 1861.

52. Olmsted, *Cotton*, Volume II, 11.

the presumed King Cotton of Dixie, especially in gaining leverage in Manchester. By November 1862 Seward was informed that the crop in this African giant was "two thirds greater than in any previous season" and "could supply a million bales a year," a potential blow to Texas insofar as it was a lodestar of production of this commodity too. Since the "governor (mayor) of Alexandria" was a "large cotton planter," it suggests that this policy was not coincidence, just as Richmond's "order to facilitate the export of cotton from New Orleans caused an immediate fall in the Egyptian article," according to the U.S. consul, William Thayer.

Though the U.S. war had been "calamitous," it "has not been without its compensation" in Africa, especially in auguring a cessation of the centuries' long African Slave Trade. Still, there was unease in the minds of some with the Emancipation Proclamation as it could spell the demise of the rebels, halting the flow of gold via cotton to Egypt. It could also mean a "sudden influx of wealth" via the forthcoming Suez Canal, meaning shipping cotton from India, avoiding the Cape of Good Hope, saving 5000 miles and challenging Egyptian cotton. Egypt also worried about future ties to the U.S. which stretched back to mutual conflicts decades earlier with Tripoli.[53]

*   *   *

Texas held the key to the future: the push toward the Pacific, a point well understood in Austin. "Texas and Texans wore the mantel of imperialism comfortably," was one accurately pithy summary. However, Austin also knew—at least intermittently—that Texas needed support in order to confront adequately their vast array of antagonists, led by Indigenes, Mexicans and Africans. Thus Lone Star advocates were loath to align with John C. Calhoun and other premature secessionists at their convention in Nashville in 1850,[54] an important "secret" gathering that anti-rebel forces continued to rebuke.[55]

On the other hand, Texas confronted challenges beyond the conjuring of its peers, including antagonistic Mexicans on the south and recalcitrant Indigenes on the north. Yes, the rebels had solid support among Indians, Stand Watie in the first place—described as a "half breed"—and reputedly leader of the final detachment to surrender

53. Mr. Thayer to Secretary Seward, 12 November 1862, Reel 3, Despatches from U.S. Consuls in Alexandria, NARA.

54. Frazier, 35, 36.

55. Slaveholders' Rebellion.

well after Appomattox. Still, when General Albert Pike of the rebels arrived in the Cherokee Nation in May 1861—Watie notwithstanding—he was threatened by a band of what was called the "Pin Cherokee" or the "Keetowah" (described as "full blood"), who were opposed to Watie's entanglement. Reportedly Chief John Ross, the titular leader, who owned scores of Africans, was said to be opposed to Watie's stance too. "He was between two fires," said a local missionary, "the South and the North." He was trapped by his own neighbors, not only Texas but also Arkansas and Missouri. But in the chaotic dislocation of war and despite being trapped behind enemy lines, Chief Ross noticed that "the Negroes turned themselves loose in wild confusion, got some guns, some pistols and those of them that could not get a gun or pistol got clubs and took horses"—and took off. This was near Cherokee headquarters at Tahlequah, where the news quickly emerged that the (formerly) enslaved "intended to kill every white man living" there, then "burn the town." Soon many of these intended victims were fleeing themselves, to the presumed sanctuary that was Arkansas.[56]

It is not clear if those fleeing included missionaries, though by early 1862 the rebel regime had appointed a Presbyterian cleric to attend to the spiritual "needs" of the Cherokee.[57] A few weeks later, it was not angry Africans on the march but there was a "great deal of excitement," said Stephen Foreman, the cleric in question, because the "Yankees" are "advancing on us...."[58] Foreman, of Cherokee ancestry, followed a key battle at Bentonville, Ark., "by our forces," speaking of the rebels, and, he added, "relatives I have in Col. Watie's regiment...."[59] Foreman did not seem pleased when he found that "several Indians are said to be with the Feds acting as guides—assisting them and committing various depredations...."[60]

This notion of "half breed" did often coincide with willing to compromise with enslavers, as represented by the career of the missionary—Foreman—appointed by rebel officialdom, who confessed openly, "being a half breed, I naturally fell on the Watie side...."[61] Going further, he cried, "I am a southern man from principle" and "for some years," he stressed, had "been fighting the principles and

---

56. J.A. Slover.

57. Entry, 10 February 1862, in Diary, Stephen Foreman Collection, UOk-N (abbrev. Stephen Foreman Collection).

58. Ibid., Entry, 1 March 1862.

59. Ibid., Entry, 10 March 1862.

60. Ibid., Entry, 4 July 1862.

61. Ibid., Entry, 16 July 1862.

<u>practices</u> of the abolitionists...."[62] Too often to note, he was repetitive in describing himself as "being a strong Southern man...."[63]

Watie sought to escape the fire from the north, being the only Indigene commissioned as a brigadier general by the rebels. He had signed the sellout 1835 treaty sending his people to Indian Territory; his cousin, John Ridge, was assassinated as a direct result, and Watie himself barely escaped this dire fate.[64]

As suggested by the foregoing, the Cherokees were split on the axis of secession. The Nation was truly trapped "between two fires": General Pike was persuasive, but his comrades included maniacal proponents of genocidal anti-Indigenous marauding, while Washington had a weak case given a demonstrated record of land grabbing. Nevertheless, a contemporary reporter found that the "Loyal League" of the Nation "embraced the great mass of the men of the Cherokee Nation, especially the full-blooded Indians." In Watie's crew, said this observer, the "majority of the men were white men and the majority of these white men were not citizens of the Cherokee Nation.... Choctaws and Chickasaws and many of the Creeks... had already joined the rebellion," assisted by "Indian agents" who were "traitors, even those appointed by Mr. Lincoln...." Under a certain duress, the Cherokee Nation in sizable number backed the rebels and, it was stressed, *"this convention was held and this action was taken only as a means of escaping extermination.* A band of Stand Watie's rebels had already concealed arms in a hotel," and were waiting to pounce. "In case the convention had determined on a contrary course," said this Washingtonian, "this band was prepared then and there to open a war of extermination on the loyal Cherokees...." They were surrounded. "On the South was Texas—in the East were Missouri—*all hostile*—to the North." Already anti-rebel Creeks, Seminoles and Cherokees had fled to Kansas. Thus, it took until February 1863 for the Cherokee Nation to revoke the duress-soaked treaty with the rebels and then abrogate slavery "unconditionally and forever" with three-fourths of able bodied men of the loyal Cherokee fighting in the federal army, a substantially larger proportion of men than from any state, according to one source.[65]

---

62. Ibid., Entry, 18 July 1862.

63. Ibid., Entry, 20 July 1862.

64. Clipping, *Tulsa Daily World*, 3 June 1956, Box 6, Division of Manuscripts Collection, UOk-N.

65. "Memorial of the Delegates of the Cherokee Nation to the President of the United States and the Senate and House of Representatives in Congress," including "Washington Chronicle, "1866, Box 4, Paul Biebell Papers, UOk-N.

Nevertheless, the road to February 1863 was unsmooth. By August 1861, 4000 Cherokee, almost all adult men, were convening in Tahlequah. Chief Ross told those assembled that this was a "conflict between the whites." "Our situation is peculiar," he maintained, and to "remain neutral" should be the goal, though he acknowledged the other conflict: "the full blood against the white and mixed blood citizens," which could rip Cherokee asunder. Yet, he stormed on insisting "whether you are faithful to the Constitution and laws of our country...particularly that of slavery," the "time has come...for an alliance" with the rebels.[66]

By October 1861, Chief Ross was sounding a similar note, finding that the federal union was "dissolve[d]" with "success almost uninterrupted" by the rebels, "marked by brilliant victories"; with prematurity he announced, "of its final result there seems no grounds for a reasonable doubt" of their triumph. Initially, the Cherokees chose to hedge, be "quiet," but now with a rebel conquest in sight, there was "no cause to hesitate," especially since "our geographical position and domestic institutions allied us to the South." Referencing the ubiquitous General Pike and his recent deals with Comanche and other Indigenes, which had created "ten full companies, with two reserve companies," he sought to join the bandwagon, since this "will show that the Cherokee people are ready to do all in their power in defense of the Confederate cause which has now become our own...." Thus, the treaty he inked with the rebels was deemed by him to be the "most important ever negotiated on behalf of the Cherokee Nation" and "will mark a new era.... it gives us a delegate in Congress," a breakthrough even now: "our citizens will no longer be dragged upon flimsy pretexts to be imprisoned and tried before distant tribunals."[67] Actually, Washington's victory in 1865 provided a further rationale to punish unreservedly Indigenes, be they Cherokee or others.

For the treaty with the rebels was one of the more important inked by either party. It was an "alliance offensive and defensive" between the two, encompassing "country west of Arkansas and Missouri." Mutual "rendition of slaves" was brokered. "Institution of slavery" was deemed "legal and has existed from time immemorial." The Cherokee Nation agreed that "it will raise and furnish a regiment

---

66. Chief Ross to Chief Headmen and Warriors of Seminoles, 21 August 1861, Box 1, Ross Collection. See also Minnie Moore Wilson, *The Seminoles of Florida*, Philadelphia: American Printing House, 1896.

67. John Ross to National Committee and Council, 9 October 1861, Box 1, Ross Collection.

of ten companies of mounted men" and "the men shall be armed by the Confederate States" and "not be moved beyond the limits of the Indian Country west of Arkansas without their consent...." Their youth were to be trained at a rebel military school and Choctaw, Chickasaw, Creek and Seminole had a similar privilege.[68]

Tonkawa, who had suffered grievously under the Washington regime, were unmentioned but they too allied with the rebels in the earliest stage of the war.[69]

These troubling alliances emerged partly because Washington had discredited itself with its blatant anti-Indigene psychosis, and for many Indigenes this was the devil they knew. Retrospectively, it is complicated to explain Indigenes who joined either side though one can salute the Pequot who joined the Colored Troops, and it is equally understandable why the Catawba of the Carolinas joined Robert E. Lee's forces. West of the Mississippi River there was a fear that Indigenes would take advantage of the split among settlers and wreak havoc, which existed in Indian Territory in any case.[70]

Yet whatever illusions may have been held concerning the rebels particularly soon began to dissipate. Soon after assuming office in 1861, Governor Lubbock of Texas told his legislature that "our Indian troubles should occupy your attention," referring brusquely to "our Indian enemies" and "their numerous atrocities." Despite not being a major site of federal military maneuvers, he pledged that his state "can and will double the number of her men in the field" and pointed ominously to the "foundries in the state," capable of producing "iron of a quality well adapted" for "manufacture of these weapons"; many of the latter were already "in the hands of private parties," who possessed a "large number of firearms,"[71] boding ill for Indigenes.

Ignoring the strategic objective of the rebels to at least neutralize Indigenes, Governor Lubbock continued to castigate policies that veered toward reservations and away from genocide[72]

Perhaps sensing an outcome when rebels, including genocide advocates, faced off against a regime bent on dispossession, Kickapoo in 1861 began to flee Kansas for Mexico—but had to pass through battle-strewn Texas. Reputedly, this group of Indigenes gained the name

---

68. "Treaty with the Cherokees, October 7th, 1861...Congress...Confederate States of America...," Historic New Orleans.

69. Newlin, 106.

70. de Wit, 19, 21.

71. Governor Lubbock to Senate and House, 15 November 1861 in *War of the Rebellion*, Series IV, Volume I, Section II, 725.

72. Flusche, 61.

for which they are now known when they would run to attacking settlers shouting "'Kickapoos! Kickapoos!'" interpreted as meaning "'White Man's Friends.'"[73] But, like the Cherokees, they should have come to realize that when it came to Indigenes, the settlers' as "friends" were wholly unreliable. And given that Kickapoo were denounced by a settler advocate as "this vicious tribe [that] particularly hated Texans,"[74] they may ultimately have realized what was going on. Still, by mid-1862 the Kickapoo were forced to sign a treaty with Washington ceding territory, especially for the purpose of all-important railways.[75]

By way of contrast, the wily Cochise and his Apache comrades chose 1861 to unleash a war—heading from Texas westward—that startled setters with the vehemence of their ferocity. This conflict was shaped indelibly by the genocidal thrust by the rebel leader, John Baylor, who explicitly demanded "extermination." His forces also gobbled several thousand square miles of Mexico, after they expelled the federals from Arizona. His rebel colleague, Henry Sibley, sought a takeover of California, then Northern Mexico, with veterans of William Walker's adventurism in Nicaragua joining him, along with the potent John Samuel Shropshire of Kentucky, a member of the slaveholding aristocracy. Naturally, he moved west with the enslaved in tow. According to one study, about 10% of Baylor's forces was "Hispanic," meaning of Mexican origin.[76] One source contends that 9900 men of Mexican origin fought alongside the rebels, with half from New Mexico, with Texas next—though those with roots in San Antonio were overrepresented among the latter. Charles David Grear argues further that three times as many men of Mexican origin fought alongside the enslavers, as opposed to federal forces.[77]

This was the seeming case, though the visitor to Texas, Frederick Olmsted, found that "Mexicans were regarded in a somewhat unchristian tone, not as heretics or heathens, to be converted with flannel and tracts, but rather as vermin, to be exterminated...."[78] Such attitudes serve to explicate why an official Mexican body averred that "the great majority of the Mexicans" in Texas "presented an absolute resistance and it was only a small number who joined the Confederates"; those

---

73. "The Flight of the Kickapoos," *Chronicles of Oklahoma*, 1 (No. 2, October 1921): 150-156.

74. J.D. Riley, 248.

75. "Treaty Between the United States of America and the Kickapoo Tribe of Indians," 28 June 1862, Huntington Library.

76. Frazier, 107, 117, 122, 137, 143, 146, 156, 173, 349.

77. Grear, 191, 192.

78. Olmsted, *Cotton*, Volume II, 19.

of Mexican origin, it was said, "found themselves persecuted and… oppressed" under rebel rule, providing more reason to flee. "Several inoffensive inhabitants were assassinated," giving this group more reason for "abandoning their interests and property" in rebel jurisdictions and collaborating with the U.S. forces.[79]

Retrospectively, pro-rebel enlistments by those of Mexican origin seem like an inflated figure—however, it remains true that secessionist trends emanated from both sides of the border, and those of Mexican origin were not unaffected. Recall Santos Benavides, for example, who was akin to Stand Watie in that he attained the highest rank of any man of Mexican origin who served with the rebels. Born in 1823, he lived under five different flags—Mexico, Texas, the so-called Republic of the Rio Grande, U.S., and the so-called Confederate States of America— and if he had been around in 1821 he would have been under the Spanish flag. He too was a vaunted Indian fighter, which may have predisposed him to favor the rebels, thought to maintain the hardest of the hardlines. Even Benito Juárez, the Mexican leader of Indigenous (Zapotec) origin thought to be his staunchest opponent, was said by a Benavides biographer to be a "wily constitutional lawyer" who "continued to play both sides in the American Civil War and allowed the Confederate trade to continue without interruption" where he wielded influence. Like Indigenes, Mexicans had to think long and hard before opposing the most avid supporters of enslavement in North America. "Rip" Ford, a Texas chauvinist, found more anti-rebel sentiment in Mexico, as opposed to among Mexican-Americans.[80]

Yet a number of key New Mexican leaders of "Hispanic" origin were not so friendly to the rebels. Addressing the legislature in early 1862, Facundo Pino and Speaker J.M. Gallegos initially agreed with settlers of whatever stripe that "savage tribes of Indians [are a foe]," then swerved sharply: "but we have now another enemy…. this enemy is Texas and the Texans. With their hostile armed regiments, [these] rebels to the Government of the United States…are without money or credit," making them prime candidates to become pillagers and plunderers. "They are our ancient enemies," said these two men; "twenty years ago they came with intents like they now come…. we are a free people and our fathers ever abhorred negro slavery and slavery," unlike these arrogant rebels: "we have condemned and put slavery from among our laws. It is not congenial with our history…."[81]

---

79. *Report of the Committee of Investigation 1873*, 49, 66.

80. J.D. Riley, 208.

81. Address [to] the Legislative Assembly of New Mexico, 29 January 1862, Huntington Library.

These were brave words in light of the force then faced. Texas rebels controlled Fort Bliss, a hop, skip and jump from New Mexico, seen as a pushover as they stampeded toward the Pacific. Those of Mexican origin were split, with General Sibley reportedly controlling four regiments of Mexican volunteers. As early as July 1861 Baylor felt sufficiently confident to demand the surrender of Fort Fillmore, a critical waystation en route to the Pacific.[82]

But it was also in March 1862 that the rebel ruler of Arizona, John Baylor, issued his notorious "extermination" order, which even Jefferson Davis thought a bit much, but it illuminated how Texans were the hardest of the hardliners and were primed to provide examples for a subsequent fascism.[83] Texans also participated in the slaying of captured Negro troops as Lone Star residents were implicated in some of the more gruesome adventures of the war.[84]

Cagily, when considering secession, the Texas leadership thought that "hesitation on the part of Texas would tend to produce similar hesitation in Arizona and New Mexico as to their connection with the Confederacy" and "would operate unfavorably on the neighboring government and people of Mexico," to the detriment of the overall enslavement project, meaning to the detriment of Texas too. Thus, "prompt and permanent connection of Texas with the Confederacy could not fail to have a favorable influence on the Border States,"[85] to the overall benefit of the enslavement project.

This dampened the Knights of the Golden Circle idea of Texas independence, then expansion in the hemisphere—but, obviously, did not forestall it altogether. In fact, by 1862 the KGC was not only— as ever—eyeing Cuba and Mexico but Canada too; they had been joined by a knockoff: Order of the Lone Star.[86] That same year the KGC in Texas was said to have "severely punished" German abolitionists there; headquartered in San Antonio, it reportedly contained

---

82. Stevens T. Norvell, "New Mexico in the Civil War: Military Order of the Loyal Legion of the United States," Commandery of the District of New Mexico, 7 January 1903, Huntington Library.

83. George Wythe Baylor, *John Robert Baylor: Confederate Governor of Arizona*, Tucson: Arizona Pioneers' Historical Society, 1966, 13.

84. Grear, 23.

85. Address to the People of Texas, 30 March 1861, in *War of the Rebellion*, Series IV, Volume I, 195.

86. "KGC an Authentic Exposition of the Origin Objects and Secret Work of the Organization Known as the Golden Circle...," February 1862, Huntington Library.

"eight thousand men" and continued to "hold in subjection the sentiments and conduct of the entire state,"[87] said a scalding critic.

Austin also realized that just as joining the U.S. could bolster efforts to combat local Indigenes and Mexicans, a similar outlook was at play in 1861 with secession. By August 1861 Secretary of State Seward was told of the "design of the Southern Confederation...to seize all of these," meaning New Mexico and Chihuahua alike, to "possess itself of the entire Tierra Caliente of New Mexico, that being well adapted to slave labor."[88] Reputedly, the governor of Chihuahua provided the rebels' initial de facto diplomatic recognition,[89] as the authorities there capitulated—once more—to rebel proposals for a joint mission against Indigenes, leaving them "subjugated or exterminated."[90] Texas would be the ultimate beneficiary while the entire rebel treasury would subsidize same.

By December 1861 Secretary of State Seward had more reason to shed tears as he was told of the "gloomy...accounts from Arizona" involving "robbery and murder of our citizens by the Indians," while "our miners have been driven from their mines" and "numerous assemblages of disloyal citizens" proliferated.[91] That same month the warmongers in Richmond celebrated upon hearing that Lieutenant Colonel John Baylor and his band of cutthroats had taken Arizona, "thus opening a pathway to the Pacific," they cackled, "and guaranteeing Western Texas from the dangers incident to allowing the Indian tribes in that extensive territory, to remain under foreign influence...."[92]

"Emigration from California is steadily on the increase" to Sonora bordering Arizona. Such was the news by December 1862: "the

---

87. Major J.T. Sprague, *The Treachery in Texas, and the Secession of Texas and the Arrest of the United States Officers and Soldiers, Serving in Texas, Read Before the New York Historical Society, June 25, 1861*, New York: Press of the Rebellion Record, 1862, NYHS.

88. Legation in Mexico to Secretary Seward, 28 August 1861, in *War of the Rebellion*, Series I, Volume L, Part I, 626.

89. Waite, 268.

90. Henry Hopkins Sibley to Governor of Chihuahua, 12 December 1861, in John P. Wilson and Jerry Thompson, eds., *The Civil War in West Texas and New Mexico: The Lost Letterbook of Brigadier General Henry Hopkins Sibley*, El Paso: Texas Western Press, 2001, 86-88, 88 (abbrev. Wilson and Thompson).

91. William L. Baker to Secretary Seward, 28 December 1861, Reel 1, Despatches from U.S. Consuls in Guaymas, NARA.

92. "Report of the Secretary of War," 14 December 1861, War Department of Confederate States of America, Huntington Library.

largest share...being secessionist...."[93] Among the latter was Colonel James Riley of the rebel forces, who conferred auspiciously with local leaders.[94] General Sibley, his superior, barking orders from Fort Bliss, wanted Sonora leaders to cooperate in suppressing Indigenes and demanded the right of his forces to engage in hot pursuit across the border: the "market of Sonora," he enthused, provided "immense advantages" for mutual benefit.[95]

Indigenes as a whole were trapped "between two fires," North and South, be it Arizona or Indian Territory. Ross—reportedly more fluent in English than Cherokee, with a Euro-American wife besides—executed a pivoting reversal that was symptomatic. "Comancheria," or the Comanche nation, stretched from Texas to Kansas and was a force to be reckoned with; like the Cherokee, they fought on both sides. Choctaw, which included major slaveholders, tended to be pro-rebel. Opothleyahyola and his Creeks were pro-Washington. Yet Indian Territory was the only federal land to be overrun by rebels, indicative of their strength there and the dearth of confidence in Washington. Just as Africans in Indian Territory seized the time to rebel and flee, Comanche sought to roll back settlements in Texas as far south as Fort Worth, while Kansas endured Comanche, Kiowa and Cheyenne—especially the militant Dog Soldiers—raids and attacks on settlers. The mighty Comanche, who as ever were the most determined warriors, faced the mightiest blows after 1865, dampening any celebratory impact of this sanguinary conflict.[96]

At any rate, whatever Confederate-Comanche entente that existed had collapsed by 1862.[97] Cheyenne had good reason to combat the federals, for one of the early acts of the incoming Lincoln regime was compelling their massive cession of land, along with that of Arapahoe.[98]

---

93. William L. Baker to Secretary Seward, 1 December 1862, Reel 1, Despatches from U.S. Consuls in Guaymas, NARA.

94. Ibid., William L. Baker to Secretary Seward, 21 March 1862.

95. Ibid., General Sibley to Sonora governor, 16 December 1861. See also Jerry Thompson, *Henry Hopkins Sibley: Confederate General of the West*, Natchitoches: Northwestern State U Press, 1987.

96. de Wit, 69, 74, 75, 82. For more on pro-rebel Cheyenne, see George E. Hyde, *A Life of George Bent, Written from His Letters*, Norman: U of Oklahoma Press, 1968.

97. Wallace and Hoebel, 305.

98. "Treaty Between the United States of America and the Arapahoe and Cheyenne Indians of the Upper Arkansas River, Concluded February 18, 1861...Proclaimed December 5, 1861," Huntington Library.

There had been a constant, and often feverish civil war among a number of Indigenous groupings in the decades leading up to the U.S. Civil War, a product of the strains engendered by dispossession and the pressure to conform, especially enslave. The era from 1861-1865 witnessed an efflorescence of hostility as certain Cherokees rebuked "uncivilized and ignorant full-bloods" seen as pro-U.S.— or at least, anti-slavery—versus, generally speaking, purported "intelligent half breeds and slave owners." The former, embedded in the Keetowah Society, was said to have sought the "destruction of half breeds and white men living in the Nation...." The latter's seriousness was ratified when some among them aligned with the bloodthirsty terrorist rebels surrounding William Quantrill. In December 1861, in Pea Ridge, Ark., squaring off, among others, were pro-rebel Cherokees versus Creeks, Seminoles, Wichita, Kickapoos and Delaware. With the rebels were the Choctaw, who supposedly did not furnish a single warrior to the federals throughout the war, as they contributed two full regiments of 1600 and 1800 respectively to the men in gray. Chickasaws furnished them with one battalion of 1200, while the split Creeks delivered two regiments of 1500 men to the enslavers.[99]

In some ways, Cherokee were the most important fighting force since they were akin to "swing voters" who could be swayed in either direction, meaning they were more likely to be lobbied. Ever since the compromises that caused them to evacuate their ancestral homeland for Indian Territory, the Keetowah seemed to be on the upswing but, alas, the dilemma of Indigenes was exposed when it came to pass that even those on the "winning" side ultimately lost miserably.[100]

This saddening result is all the more remarkable given the Keetowah allegiance to the ultimate victors of the Civil War. Despite internal rifts, by July 1862 an observer noticed that the "Confederate flag could not be hoisted anywhere in the [Cherokee] Nation without danger of personal violence to those attempting it. The strong feeling of the full blooded Indians in behalf of the Union and against the rebels," said a Kansas observer, "was further strengthened by what is known as the 'Pin' [Keetowah] order," who resisted "the encroachments and exactions of the half breeds who were rapidly absorbing all the wealth of the Nation," aided by those defined as "white."[101]

99. "The Reporter," 29 May 1903, Box 2, Ross Collection.

100. Ibid., "The Reporter," 12 June 1903.

101. "The Weekly Conservative," Leavenworth, Kansas, 24 July 1862, Box 6, Division of Manuscripts Collection, UOk-N.

However, the "Pin" had internal adversaries. Indian Territory served as a buffer for rebel Texas, protecting it from lancing attacks from Kansas, and hence it was a strategic coup when Cherokee and other Indigenes threw in their lot with Austin.[102]

Though Texas, the linchpin of the rebels, likely suffered less than its peers from the ravages of war, positioning its unique brand of politics to gain more sway post-1865, Indian Territory was battered as much or more than any other section of North America. This was particularly so for Cherokee Nation, which may have been riven by more ideological fissures. This was layered on top of a de facto civil war that had been raging since 1835. The fact that Cherokee (and Choctaw) were represented at the rebel Congress in Richmond did not help their case with the victors, postwar. Yet the fact that the Osage, who were mostly pro-Washington, hardly fared better, illustrated the inescapable pitfalls Indigenes had to confront. Still, Watie soared far beyond whatever call of duty he heard, since he and his Indigenous brigade marched more miles, took part in more battles, likely engaged in more skirmishes, captured more wagons and horses and mules than possibly any other brigade west of the Mississippi. Indigenes lost more men in action in proportion to those enlisted than any other demographic among the rebels, including any other Southern state. Watie was the last leader to surrender formally—23 June 1865. Unlike other slaveholders, they were forced to disgorge more property to the newly freed, who also gained suffrage rights. "Citizens of no other Southern State were forced to divide their inheritance with their former slaves," says one analyst. Even the Choctaw and Chickasaw obtained somewhat better terms. Perhaps the victors took to heart the point that one of Watie's sons was named Saladin, the warrior renowned for defeating Crusaders centuries earlier.[103]

It was not just Indian Territory that suffered grievously during the war; it is likely that the orgy of violence unleashed in North America accelerated pre-existing trends already afflicting Indigenes. Seeing their settler antagonists at each other's throats, Indigenes—Cheyenne's "Dog Soldiers," Cochise, and others—seized the opportunity to reclaim lost territory and defend themselves with added vigor. In turn, another trend accelerated: settlers not waiting upon defense provided by armed forces formed militia and posses and went on a rampage in Oregon and northern California among other

---

102. "The War No One Wanted," n.d., Julia A. 'Julee' Short Collection, UOk-N.

103. "Life of General Stand Watie," n.d., John Jordan Collection, UOk-N.

sites, igniting slaughter that continued postwar, a nasty habit difficult to extirpate.[104]

This vortex of violence meant that Indian Territory most noticeably was bound to descend into chaos. By the Summer of 1862 in the Cherokee Nation, amid stories of chaotic raiding to snatch enslaved property, the missionary Stephen Foreman reproved Chief Ross for "trying to be a northern and southern man both at the same time,"[105] a classic hedge as battlefield winds were shifting chaotically.

*   *   *

Despite the advantage delivered by the menacing presence of Texas, a mortal blow to the rebels' cause was struck in 1862 when New Orleans—the largest city in the South as of 1861 and commercially the most important—fell into the hands of the federals in 1862. It was reportedly the world's largest exporting port and had a complement of French speakers, including rebel hero P.G.T. Beauregard, who died there.[106]

The Louisiana setback, coupled with the companion (temporary) seizure of Galveston, was devastating for rebel chances. And the Emancipation Proclamation—effectively—was the turning point in the conflict insofar as it brought the federals a sable arm, while encouraging the rebels' slave labor force to flee. Sensing that it was easier to duck bondage the farther one fled from the South, passing through Indian Territory and the vicinity were a passel of Africans presumably headed to Mexico, adding to their numbers in Texas especially. Thomas Cole escaped enslavement in Tennessee and by 1861 had aligned with the federal military and wound up in the Lone Star State.[107]

In Weatherford, Texas, a crucible of enslavement and genocide, it was during the Summer of 1861 that a "colored man named Dick" was "found under the bed" and "taken out and whipped," this after a "dirk knife" was found on him. Under duress he "confessed that he and three others had determined to kill all the white men and children of the town and take the white women for the colored race,"

---

104. A.J. Bledsoe, *Indian Wars of the Northwest: A California Sketch*, Oakland: Bio Books, 1956, 225.

105. Entry, Diary, 9 July 1862, Stephen Foreman Collection.

106. Bielski, xi, xvii, 10.

107. Nicholas Guyatt, "'The Future Empire of Our Freedmen: Republican Colonization Schemes in Texas and Mexico," in Adam Arenson and Andrew R. Graybill, eds., *Civil War Wests: Testing the Limits of the United States*, Berkeley: U of California Press, 2015, 31.

along with "threatening acts [that] terrorized the citizens," of which he was not deemed to be one: he was executed, said an analysis penned decades after the fact.[108]

However, the rebels had their own advantages, especially the French seizure of Mexico by 1862, which enslavers had prepared by their repetitive weakening of this neighbor beginning with Texas secession of 1836.

108. J.S. Grace and R.B. Jones, *A New History of Parker County*, Weatherford, Texas: Taylor/Parker County Historical Association, 1987, 136, 137.

Chapter 15

Texas, Iron Fist of Treason, 1862-1864

For decades Washington had pursued a hidebound policy toward Mexico, involving capitulations to enslavers, especially in Texas in 1836, then 1845. By early 1862 a debilitated Mexico was besieged by putative creditors led by France, whose ties in the Gulf of Mexico extended at least to the early 18th century and the founding of New Orleans. "Liberals" led by Juárez had emerged triumphant over their conservative foes by this juncture, but Paris felt correctly he was undesigned to play the role of French puppet. Although the heroic Juárez and his forces repulsed the French at Puebla on Cinco de Mayo 1862 (5 May), they could not prevent the ascension of the so-called Emperor Maximilian and his spouse Carlota, daughter of Belgium's monarch. Washington objected, but was bogged down fighting secessionists. After Appomattox, however, the course of conflict in Mexico changed, and Juárez's forces surged—leading to one of the earliest renditions of "Juneteenth," which came to be the guarantor of 19 June 1865, today's holiday marking an official end of enslavement in Texas and in the U.S. itself. Two years later to the day, on 19 June 1867, Maximilian was executed summarily, barring a rearguard rebel war launched against Washington from south of the border that could have led to a more disguised form of enslavement.[1]

However, there were other complexities of this struggle that made life more complicated for secessionists. Ironically, days after the Emancipation Proclamation went into effect, Washington's man in Alexandria, Egypt, was startled by a matter of "grave importance" that "produces much excitement...four hundred and fifty black soldiers were...taken by railway" and "shipped on board the French transport steamer...[to] Mexico with the object of aiding the...emperor...." These "Negroes, with others" were "dressed in Zouave uniform and

---

1. Edward Shawcross, *The Last Emperor of Mexico*, New York: Basic, 2021 (abbrev. Shawcross).

fully armed," a sight constructed to instill horror in settlers of whatever stripe, but particularly those of neighboring Texas. It may have unduly alarmed Consul William Thayer, for midway before his urgent alert to Secretary of State Seward, their number had grown to "1000." He concluded uneasily that perhaps the "attempt of the Emperor of the French [in Paris] to introduce a regiment of free black troops into a country contiguous to our slaveholding states" could be intimidating there and "may be a subject of curiosity to ourselves...."[2]

Assuredly, the French dispatch of African troops rationalized the similar U.S. maneuver, and placed more pressure on the secessionists to violate first principles and do the same: but once Africans were bearing weapons on one side, how could enslavement of Africans be long maintained?

The sight of this dark-skinned African brigade was disconcerting to some in northern Egypt too. There was "public disapproval" that "demanded official explanations" of why these "Darfour and Nubian" soldiers were deployed. Uneasy police officers were "seizing a number of black men, some of them known as porters on the wharf" in retaliation, as if they thought they were in Galveston. This "produced a visible terror in the black population...amid a great outcry of women and children,"[3] a message to Texas that would resonate post-1865.

For although these armed Africans had been sent to Mexico ostensibly to fortify Paris's developing alliance with the rebels in light of Washington's backing of Juárez, the men in gray were hardly prepared—racially or politically—for this intervention. They were revolted at the very idea of fighting armed Africans in blue, as if this were beneath them: arms in sable hands were leveling, "reducing" the "ruling race" to the level of mudsill, while raising the possibility of being vanquished altogether with implications too fantastical to consider.[4]

If the thinking of Lincoln's envoy to Central America is representative of a cross-section of opinion in Washington, then the federals were nervous too. For they now had to wonder if France would stop with Mexico and, once again, exploit the weaknesses of other southern neighbors and establish a beachhead within hailing distance of the U.S.—assuming the rebels were defeated—with grave implications for national security.[5] A troubling sign emerged in early 1863

2. Consul Thayer to Secretary Seward, 9 January 1863, Reel 3, Despatches from U.S. Consuls in Alexandria, NARA.

3. Ibid., Consul Thayer to Secretary Seward, 18 January 1863.

4. Kinard, 148.

5. Booker, 88, 93.

when word arrived from Matamoros that a rebel passport would be required for entry, which was "aiding the rebels directly,"[6] according to a U.S. official. By mid-1863 the message from Matamoros was that "Texas and Arizona are to be included in the price paid the French" for their aid to rebels.[7]

By late 1863 Jefferson Davis was receiving detailed reports from France, not necessarily at odds with the above. Pierre Adolphe Rost was born in France but rose to the commanding heights of society in Louisiana before, back in his homeland, receiving a commission from Davis. There he enjoyed the "warm sympathy of all my neighbors for us and our cause...," he said gushingly. He thought, "of late we had been losing ground in France," an "unfavorable change." Yes, the "Emperor...is probably still favorably inclined towards us but as he says himself sentiment cannot be the basis of political action. When the French army was marching on Mexico and the northern press threatened war, he felt all the importance of consolidating our nationality and was ready to recognize us if England would join him," which was not in the cards and may have been an excuse for a Parisian evasion in any case. Then rebel leader Alexander Stephens was sent to France "entrusted...to cede to France Texas and perhaps a part of Louisiana in consideration of which that power was to recognize the Confederate States...." The analogy was how Paris had gained Nice and Savoy from what is now Italy. Paris was angling for the biggest enchilada, i.e., the "surrender of Texas to France would remove all obstacles to our recognition...." The problem was that the prime rebel envoy, John Slidell, "had neither authority nor desire to negotiate...." Paris was dangling Texas as a bargaining chip, telling the federals if they did not "meddle with Mexican affairs, France will not *at present* interfere between the North and the South...[emphasis-author]." Rost articulated the Austin consensus at least that "the surrender of Texas for re-annexation to Mexico I do not consider possible under any circumstances"—though it was clear that Washington had bungled things catastrophically by weakening Mexico to the point that it could be seized and used as a launching pad to seize (previous) federal territory.[8]

---

6. Consul Leonard Pierce to Secretary Seward, 4 March 1863, Reel 3, Despatches from U.S. Consuls in Matamoros, NARA.

7. Consul Leonard Pierce to Secretary Seward, 6 June 1863, in *War of the Rebellion*, Series III, Volume III, Additions and Corrections, 521.

8. Pierre [Peter] Adolphe Rost to Jefferson Davis, 24 December 1863, Box 1, Jefferson Davis Papers, Emory U, Atlanta (abbrev. Jefferson Davis Papers).

And it was not just "previous" territory. By 1863, Senator J.A. McDougall of California was discussing with his colleagues in Washington if France would seek to reclaim his state on behalf of their Mexican satrap.[9]

Not only had Washington's boneheaded policies maneuvered the rascal republic into this enervating position but the rebels had contributed to the strategic cul de sac too. Jefferson Davis told a Parisian agent that he would accept any deal—"'anything...except reunion with that nation of miscreants. We should prefer to be governed by the King of Dahomey himself,'" which almost transpired in the broadest sense. Or, he was reputed to have said, "'even...becoming a province in the Mexican empire under French protection'" was an option, "'pure and simple.'"[10] And while Davis negotiated with Paris, the man who joined him in flight from the federals in 1865, Governor Lubbock of Texas, was poring over a message from the French consul in Galveston concerning an alliance with France which included material support—but the Lone Star State would have to resume independence, not necessarily an onerous status.[11]

France was negotiating from a position of strength, the seizure of Mexico aside. For the French consul in New Orleans reminded General Benjamin Butler, in charge since the 1862 takeover, that there were "thousands of French citizens here," meaning Paris's posture could not be ignored easily.[12] Still, French nationals in New Orleans were at times uncooperative with the new regime—as if they were a bloc of rebel agents—causing General Butler to rebuke their "objectionable expressions...."[13] At times it seemed that the major resistance in this river port was from French nationals. General Butler sent Secretary Seward a "digest of the laws of France upon the subject of slavery," that indicated that every owner of slaves forfeited his or her nationality by owning them, though it would take more

---

9. Speech by Hon. J.A. McDougall of California...on Tuesday, February 3, 1863,...[on] French Interference in Mexico...," Baltimore: Murphy, 1863, Huntington Library.

10. Charles Girard, *A Visit to the Confederate States of America in 1863*, Tuscaloosa: Confederate Publishing Company, 1863, 92.

11. Flusche, 56.

12. Acting French Consul to General Butler, 16 September 1862, in *Private and Official Correspondence of General Benjamin F. Butler, During the Period of the Civil War, Volume I*, Norwood, Mass.: Plimpton, 1917, 298 (abbrev. Butler Correspondence).

13. Ibid., General Butler to Count Mejan, French Consul, 1 November 1862, 433.

than smart legalisms to alter a crucial property relation, especially since the Paris envoy interpreted this to mean losing only "the right to vote in France" not "loss...of nationality...." Still, he was correct to think that this was "a most vital question here where every man of any property is an owner of slaves and every other man claims to be a French citizen...."[14] Of course, the French consul was handing out "certificates" granting citizenship like it was confetti, as if he were planning on a revanchist overturn. This was "strange," thought a Butler interlocutor, particularly since this document was provided to "Creoles born here, who have been on the police," and others "who have been members of military companies and have shown their rights as citizens at the election polls with knives and revolvers in hand...." Among these militarized men was the "Vice Consul of Italy" who had "been a private in the Garibaldi company...."[15]

Why should Paris "settle" for seizing Mexico when the latter's former province, Texas, had proven to be so bumptiously cantankerous in recent decades, opening the door for it being swallowed too if Paris maneuvered properly? It was also in 1863 that the French consul in Richmond was beyond furious after hearing of the "injustice and oppression" visited upon his compatriots in San Antonio and thereabouts with a number being conscripted forcibly—including a French diplomat.[16] Assuming that France continued ruling great swaths of Mexico, what would Texas do if not burdened by war? It made sense for Paris to look ahead and take Texas too.

Already in New Orleans under federal control, Frenchmen were flexing their muscles as if the clock had turned back to 1802. "Very few of the French subjects here have taken the oath of neutrality," complained General Benjamin Butler; this contrasted with "officers of the French Legion" who "had with your knowledge and assent," he told Paris's man, "taken the oath to support the [rebel] constitution...." Plus, this envoy seemed overly concerned about the "disquiet which you say there are signs manifesting themselves among the black population" and their "desire to break their bonds...." Archly, he added, this "disquiet" was "natural when their masters had set them the example of rebellion against constituted authorities, that the negroes, being an imitative race, should do likewise.... surely, the representative of the Emperor, who does not tolerate slavery in

---

14. Ibid., General Butler to Secretary Seward, 14 November 1862, 467.

15. Ibid., Anonymous to General Butler, n.d., ca. November 1862, 479.

16. J.A. Campbell, Assistant Secretary of War-Richmond to Major General Magruder, 22 January 1863, in *War of the Rebellion*, Series IV, Volume II, 1900, 366.

France, does not desire his countrymen to be armed for the purpose of preventing the negroes from breaking their bonds"[17]—maybe.

For the French emissary haughtily—and falsely—claimed that "prejudice of race and color certainly does not exist in France," the threadbare Parisian line still touted to the naïve, then pivoted to assail the "fear" purportedly instilled by the emancipated. He feared those "who were slaves, and are now at once elevated to the rank of free men and citizens and will abuse their freedom...." With sang-froid he demanded that his compatriots "ought to be excused if they fear the social revolution which is going on now and of which a terrible example has been seen" at a local French plantation.[18]

Paris's man was not just issuing verbal rebukes. General Butler recalled that when the men in blue first landed, "nearly the entire foreign population of the city enrolled itself" in military contingents; "they were armed, uniformed and equipped, drilled and maneuvered"—and "reported for service to the Confederate Generals," and "many of the foreign officers took the oath of allegiance to the Confederate States. The Brigadier General in command of the European brigade, Paul Juge, a naturalized citizen of the United States but born in France, renounced his citizenship and applied to the French government to be restored to his former citizenship," as if he were betting on the ultimate rule of France.[19]

Moreover, the French in New Orleans were turning against emancipation, as if they did not expect this new regime to endure. The French envoy was "making large claims...for negroes and other property," said Butler; instead of "neutrality," he saw "bitter hostility."[20]

Count Méjan of Paris thought he had reason to object to developing trends, for "every night" a close countryman experienced emancipated Africans who sought to "take away...fruits...even...household utensils..." He confronted them, and they replied abruptly that "they were the masters and would do as they liked.... one of the negroes fired a shot at him, upon his full breast.... the same negro then wounded him badly on his face with his musket, wounding his face [again] cruelly...." He was irate about these "armed negroes" and the "fears which resulted from the disarming of the white people...."[21]

---

17. General Butler to Count Mejan, 14 August 1862, in Butler Correspondence, 188.

18. Ibid., Acting French Consul to General Butler, 13 October 1862, 376.

19. Ibid., General Butler to Secretary of War Edwin Stanton, 12 October 1862, 361.

20. Ibid., General Butler to Secretary Seward, 24 October 1862, 398.

21. Ibid., Count Mejan to General Butler, 7 November 1862, 459.

However, the envoy's compatriots were hardly pacifists, and soon General Butler carped about "outrage...on my colored soldiers...," reminding French interlopers that these men were "of the same hue and blood as those of your celebrated compatriots and author, Alexander Dumas...."[22]

*   *   *

The ascension of Maximilian was even more evident in Tampico. By early 1863 French vessels, which habitually had been prowling in the Gulf of Mexico, were now a virtual fixture in this critical port and were quite active in buzzing U.S. ships on behalf of the rebels, diverting Washington resources. It was "hazardous to allow our merchant vessels to trade with the Mexican ports during the existence of this French war without a convoy," the consul there pointedly messaged Seward.[23]

Of similar concern was Don José Miguel Arroyo, for this Mexican consul in New Orleans was seen in Washington as an "active partisan of the monarchial party" and was busily organizing an "expedition composed of secessionists on the frontiers of Mexico and Texas" with the goal of subduing Juárez's forces. He was sponsored by General J.B. Magruder, formerly of West Point and a veteran of war in Mexico, and now a leading light among secessionists. As early as September 1863, Washington was aware that in the event of a "defeat of the rebel troops," Magruder already had plans to "take shelter in Tamaulipas and aid in establishing an imperial government in this country" in league with the self-styled emperor, whose French sponsor was seeking to "inflict incalculable injury upon the government of the United States."[24]

But it was not just Paris and their minions. The idea in London seemed to be that they enjoyed rascal republics so immensely that they would like to see two of them—one in Washington, the other in Richmond; thus, by October 1863, arriving in Tampico laden with cotton from Galveston, was a British flagged ship—a common trend.[25]

A similar report arrived in Washington from London, describing "steamers under the English flag...preparing to carry on trade through Matamoros and Texas...."[26]

---

22. Ibid., General Butler to "Fauconnet," 14 October 1862, 360.

23. Consul Franklin Chase to Secretary Seward, 12 February 1863, Reel 4, Despatches from U.S. Consuls in Tampico, NARA.

24. Ibid., Consul Chase to Secretary Seward, 17 September 1863.

25. Ibid., Consul Chase to Secretary Seward, 13 October 1863.

26. F.H. Morse to Secretary Seward, 28 November 1863, in *War of the Rebellion*, Series III, Volume II, 948.

Still, whatever certain Londoners may have desired, the animus toward slavery was so strong that it would be difficult for Whitehall to implement a so-called two-state solution on the west bank of the Atlantic. It was also in 1863 that an English emancipationist charged that the "greatest example of buccaneering known to the present generation is the seizure of Texas" by "American colonists," as "they schemed to subject the country to the curse of slavery...brigandage and then war...." Then "the Mexican war which followed politically was [no] worse than our Asiatic wars," an oblique reference to India, "but about as bad...." Then the escapade of folly continued with "buccaneering attacks on Cuba and Nicaragua," with the Ostend Manifesto designed to snatch the former island just another demerit on the record of these "avowed defenders of the African Slave Trade...."[27]

William Walker's adventure in Nicaragua continued to resonate even after it seemed to disappear. Walker was ousted in Central America not least because of internal opposition, as evidenced by the fact that the militant U.S. Negro, Martin Delany, had been elected as mayor of San Juan del Norte (Greytown) as the invasion was unfolding.[28] By late 1863 the report emerged from Vera Cruz that one "Bruno Natzmer," one of Walker's comrades, was collaborating with French occupiers in Mexico, and after the feisty buccaneer got into a tiff with an opponent, Natzmer "threatened to send [him] to Martinique,"[29] i.e., to an uncertain fate in the Caribbean.

By January 1863 as a kind of rebuke of the Emancipation Proclamation, Major General John Bankhead Magruder—speaking from Galveston—reported with glee to "My Dear Mr. President," referring to Jefferson Davis: "I have taken & destroyed a considerable portion of the enemy's fleet and dispersed the remainder." He "already sent two cargoes of cotton to sea [and] will send another tomorrow," while the strategically critical "Sabine Pass is also clear [and] will clear the whole coast I think...."[30]

---

27. F.W. Newman, "Character of the Southern States of America," Letter to a friend who had joined the Southern Independence Association, London, Manchester: Union and Emancipation Society's Deport, 1863, Oberlin College.

28. S. Page, 173.

29. Wallace Smith to Consul D.L. Lane, 17 December 1863, Reel 9, Despatches from U.S. Consuls in Vera Cruz, NARA.

30. General Bankhead to Jefferson Davis, 6 January 1863, Box 1, Jefferson Davis Papers.

This was a major triumph for the rebels, reversing a temporary setback and extending the shelf life of the war. Tellingly, at the war's close in 1865, Galveston and Charleston were the only unconquered ports still held by rebels.[31]

Magruder understandably was ecstatic about his triumph: "our boats pursued the enemy thirty miles to sea," he said, and "captured thirteen heavy guns, one hundred and twenty nine prisoners and one million dollars worth of stores...."[32] The "enemy's ship proved to be a splendid ironclad steamer built in the Clyde," he enthused. He "anticipated an easy conquest" nonetheless, and was not disappointed with this triumph of "great political importance," for this vessel "contained almost all the Texans out of the state, who had proved recreant to their duty to the Confederacy and to Texas," and now would pay. Thus, "Smith, the deserter was tried regularly the next day by a general court martial" and promptly was "publicly shot in Galveston." There were mop-up operations, i.e., "insurrection among the Germans in Colorado, Fayette and Austin counties, eight hundred being reported in arms to resist the conscript law and the state draft." He also "declared martial [law] in these three counties," suspending the already frail reed of civil liberties, "and had the ringleaders lodged in jail"; they were to be "turned over to the civil authorities for trial," so that now "the whole coast and island are now in our possession and that the Rio Grande is strongly occupied...."[33]

The unforgiving response to the "Germans" was an overreaction to what had been happening; thus in October 1862 German refugees from Texas were circulating near Matamoros and were then being organized into a federal military detachment to attack the men in gray.[34] Weeks later they were among the men who were said to be "bitterly disappointed that they cannot invade Texas at once."[35] General Butler took seriously what he was told—that the rebels "can be subjugated but not conciliated," and there were "but two classes of

31. Robert Morris Franklin, "Battle of Galveston, 1 January 1863," Speech at Magruder Camp of United Confederate Veterans, Galveston, 2 April 1911, Galveston: San Luis Press, 1975, Huntington Library.

32. Report of Major General Magruder, 24 January 1863, in *Official Reports of Battles*, Richmond: Smith, 1864, 503-504 (abbrev. Official Reports of Battles).

33. Ibid., Report of Major General Magruder, 26 February 1863, 505.

34. George S. Denison to Salmon P. Chase, 27 October 1862, in Butler Correspondence, 412.

35. Ibid., George S. Denison to Salmon P. Chase, 25 December 1862, 550.

people here faithful to the United States, they are the Germans and colored population...."[36]

Back in occupied New Orleans, from where this assault was launched, gloominess reigned. That was not the case a few months earlier when a federal leader spoke optimistically of the "departure of the fleet to attack and capture Galveston. They accomplished the object without loss," he said prematurely, and a detachment was en route to "occupy the town and island...."[37] Then in a head-snapping maneuver, news was received in a gloating occupied New Orleans of the "daring and successful attack on Galveston...by the Confederates...."[38] The naval authorities in Washington seeking a knockout blow had encouraged the "occupation of Texas," deemed "imperative."[39] General Butler agreed that "any expedition to Texas could start from here"[40]—but this proved to be a classic overreach.

For soon federal leader George Denison had recognized the "disaster" that Magruder was marking. That drove him to an inescapable truth: "the government can finish the war in twelve months in one way and in only one. Arm the negroes"—but, he thought, only General Butler, who he "wished" was "president," was thinking along these profound lines.[41]

Yet even within Lincoln's ranks, there was ambivalence—at best— about this transformative move. Shortly after the Emancipation Proclamation took effect, Congressman William H. Wadsworth of hotly contested Kentucky said that enlisting Negro soldiers showed that the rascal republic was now a "failed" state, little more than a "drowning man," grasping for straws.[42]

*   *   *

"I will take Texas," said Butler to Washington, "if you will send any men."[43] "With 5000 more men" he could "cut off...Texas," and

36. Ibid., "JPM" to General Butler, 18 July 1862, Volume II, 84.

37. Ibid., George Denison to Secretary Chase, 27 October 1862, Volume II, 412.

38. Ibid., L.C. Turner to General Butler, 15 January 1863, Volume III, 10.

39. Ibid., U.S. Navy Department to General Butler, 17 November 1862, Volume I, 349.

40. Ibid., General Butler to Secretary Stanton, 16 August 1862, Volume I, 194.

41. Ibid., George S. Denison to Secretary Chase, 8 January 1863, Volume I, 571.

42. Speech of Hon. William H. Wadsworth of Kentucky on the Enlistment of Negro Soldiers Delivered in the House of Representatives, January 30, 1863, Washington, D.C., 1863, Huntington Library.

43. General Butler to Secretary Chase, 14 November 1862, Butler Correspondence, Volume II, 426.

with "7000 men, I will take and hold Mobile."[44] The "Texas men" in New Orleans wanted to "invade" their homeland "at once"; "fifty thousand men," was the word to Washington "together with the Union forces now in Arkansas and at El Paso...would be fully able to accomplish this in two or three months after the opening of the river."[45] General Butler was made aware of the "great cotton mart of Texas,"[46] so essential to rebel fortunes and their pursuance of war.

But Corpus Christi also delivered dispiriting news to the federals: "the enemy" was "retreating in double quick" was the Summer 1862 report. "They left in their retreat, their ammunition box, hatchet, rat-tail files...rifle cartridges," as, said the rebel reporter, "we chased them to their gunboats...."[47]

Rebel celebration may have been premature in that at the same time federals were mulling an "expedition" to Texas, for "when the rebel army retreats from Vicksburg and Port Hudson, they may go to Texas," opening the possibility of "crush[ing] of Gen. Banks' forces." Within shouting distance of Galveston was the city of Houston, and its "capture" should be "the first object": such was the message to Secretary of the Treasury Salmon Chase. For "this is the center of railroads" and therefore critical to moving troops and materiel alike. This city held "the controlling position (in the military sense) of the state." Importantly, "the slave population is large in that part of the state and if *properly* employed would prove a great source of weakness to the rebels [emphasis-original]."[48]

Five railroads converged in Houston, while a trunk road went to Galveston, making the latter the only point on the Texas coast where all rebel forces within 150 miles could be amassed within hours.[49] Railways, mostly built by enslaved labor, which a pre-war journalist called "'the greatest creative agent in rapidly germinating the elements of a series of slave states...,'" a reality that Houston undergirded.[50]

Rebels too remained active in Chihuahua and points westward too. By early 1863 a former U.S. consul, sensing the direction of prevailing

---

44. Ibid., General Butler to Henry Wilson, 12 November 1862, 466.

45. Ibid., George S. Denison to Secretary Chase, 25 December 1862, 550.

46. Ibid., Charles Bartles to General Butler, 15 December 1862, 535.

47. Report of Major A.M. Hobly, 18 August 1862, in *Official Reports of Battles*, 493.

48. Report to Salmon P. Chase, 28 November 1862, in Butler Correspondence, Volume II, 504.

49. Ibid., William Alexander to Hon. P.M. Blair, 13 January 1863, 577.

50. Daddysman 1976, 167.

winds, had begun to display decided "secession proclivities," or so said the current envoy there. This defector, George Macmanus, may have been overly influenced by the rumored advance of Texans toward Arizona with the wider aim of garnering a port on the Gulf of California.[51] Macmanus had joined a prominent mercantile house there and likely had begun to count his profits from a secessionist victory.[52] But it was more than just a former consul who had become a turncoat; there was also the Texan Daniel Murphy, who was beavering away, purchasing arms, powder and saltpeter for rebels in San Antonio.[53]

The rebels had reason to think that Chihuahua was simply another version of Tampico in that even the U.S. emissary there thought that "Juárez is president of this republic but he does not command in Chihuahua [emphasis-original]."[54] When the consul there was compelled to lower the U.S. flag over the consulate because local rebels objected,[55] a sign of the balance of forces in Mexico was rendered.

As if he were contemplating a blue-gray battle to unfold in Chihuahua, the new U.S. consul—Reuben Creel of Kentucky, who had resided there for 16 years—provided Washington with a detailed description of the topography: "in many places a man can travel fifty or sixty miles without seeing a drop of water," and then there would be "three months of the rainy season" when "roads become heavy," i.e., impassable. The city had a population of "one hundred and forty thousand," of "which Indians (Tauramaras [Tarahumara]) of pure race form one eighth...." Fierce campaigns "which the Mexicans undertake against the Apaches" were continuously weakening the state. Creel nonetheless trafficked in the insulting albeit "prevalent idea in the United States and Europe that the Mexicans are a cowardly people...." Continuing his soldierly assessment, he outlined that the government there "has about eight hundred guns of all sorts and sizes, twelve pieces of artillery badly mounted, six thousand rounds of American rifle powder and equipment for one thousand men," i.e., the "people and the state are very badly armed"—with the militia being "useless"—though prospectively he found that "lead is

---

51. Consul James Carleton to Secretary Seward, 20 February 1863, Reel 1, Despatches from U.S. Consuls in Chihuahua, NARA.

52. Ibid., Major David Fergusson to Consul Carleton, 14 February 1863.

53. Ibid., Reuben Creel to Secretary Seward, 28 November 1863.

54. Ibid., Reuben Creel to Secretary Seward, 10 December 1863.

55. Ibid., Affidavit of Frank Mollman of the Kingdom of Hanover, 12 December 1863.

plentiful being extracted in abundance from Mexican mines...."[56] But Seward had to be wary, since by his own admission most of Creel's relatives back home were rebels.[57]

Washington would have been justified in suspecting that he was little more than a double agent. However, unless an elaborate ruse was at play, this suspicion may have been disabused when a rebel agent in Chihuahua witnessed Creel's arrest by the authorities,[58] an extraordinary diplomatic faux pas.

Actually, this diplomatic overreach may have been driven by weakness more than strength, for as of August 1863, the federal governor of New Mexico was of the view that the "states of Chihuahua and Sonora have been and are now anxious to be incorporated into the government of the United States"; moreover, he added, "there is no part of Mexico that would be of more importance to our country at the present and all future time than these two states." As if further annexation was on order, he wrote: "purchase of these states at this time might save much difficulty and embarrassment hereafter." In the midst of a deadly conflict with rebels, the governor continued to prosecute what he called the "Navajo War" with the federals fielding 1200 men, "well equipped and supplied," he said. He had no alternative, he believed, since "depredations daily committed are astonishing," occurring amid "discovery of very rich and extensive gold fields" in neighboring Arizona, and it was known that Indigenes "will doubtless make resistance to its occupancy by the miners...." With sobriety, he concluded, "many lives will be lost unless a strong military force should be stationed" there—so, instead, "many lives" of Indigenes were sacrificed.[59]

Monterrey was little different. Just before the dawning of 1863, more cotton was arriving from Texas "than ever," said one source, along with "all kinds of army goods," and "enormous quantities of blankets" were headed northward "daily intended for the rebel army."[60] By October 1863 Seward was alert to a "very unfortunate" trend as one "vessel" after another was "loaded with arms" headed

56. Ibid., Reuben Creel to Secretary Seward, 30 November 1863.

57. Ibid., Reuben Creel to James Carleton, 9 November 1863.

58. Ibid., Affidavit of George Macmanus, 12 December 1863.

59. Governor Connelly to Secretary Seward, 23 August 1863, in *War of the Rebellion*, Series III, Volume III, Additions and Corrections, 797. See also Wilson and Thompson.

60. Consul Kimmey to Secretary Seward, 21 November 1862, Reel 1, Despatches from U.S. Consuls in Monterrey, NARA.

due north with "enough guns to arm every man in Texas."[61] It was also in 1863 that Jefferson Davis learned that "between 600 and 700 mules have already been purchased in Texas for the Cis-Mississippi Department," and it was deemed "advisable to increase the number from Mexico and possibly California." But since "unbroken Mexican horses [were] entirely useless" and "to obtain horses from Europe is certainly impracticable," the importance of Texas was underscored further.[62]

This critical linkage was magnified after Vicksburg 1863, for at that point Texas found it difficult to ship across the Mississippi River—especially cattle—further hampering Austin and the rebels generally.[63] Vicksburg became important again to Texas rebels when soldiers "were steamed" there, as was recounted subsequently, "and here disembarked under the auspices of a negro guard. This was the most humiliating experience of the whole period of captivity." Like the loss of billions of dollars in enslaved property, it was devastating psychologically and politically for the "ruling race" to find themselves staring down the barrel of a rifle administered by their former property.[64]

Soon rebels were to exact revenge, as recounted by George Mays then of Oklahoma. He recounted a battle at the insultingly named "Nigger Creek," where the rebels "came upon the federal negro soldiers who were making hay. The Confederates surrounded them and opened fire and the negroes caught unaware were slaughtered," one of many such instances. "There are not any negroes living anywhere close to Nigger Creek now," he continued, as "they seem to have a great horror of the creek...."[65]

In the spring of 1863 commerce between Mazatlán and San Francisco was increasing, but given the pre-existing strength of rebels and Frenchmen and the influence of William Gwin, an enslaver in that U.S. city, it was not clear if this was good news for the federals. "Years ago we had in this port," speaking of Mazatlán, "a more numerous American population than any of the other cities of Mexico or than that of any other city on the Pacific coast south of Upper California," and the city was still a magnet for migrants, given

---

61. Ibid., Consul Kimmey to Secretary Seward, 5 October 1863.

62. A.C. Myers to Jefferson Davis, 4 March 1863 in *War of the Rebellion*, Series IV, Volume II, 417.

63. M.K. Nelson, 219.

64. Victor M. Rose, *Ross' Texas Brigade...*, Louisville: Courier-Journal, 1882, 183 (abbrev. V.M. Rose).

65. Oral History, George Mays, 25 February 1938, IPP.

investments in silver:[66] this was the message to Seward. Unlike Tampico and Acapulco, U.S.-flagged steamers were "constantly stopping here for coal," noticeably from the "Atlantic states," en route to "Upper California" and hampering its defection to the rebels: this was the message to Navy Secretary Gideon Welles.[67] However, soon a French flotilla arrived en route to Mazatlán to place more pressure on the Pacific coast.[68]

Yet the most magnetic Mexican port of all was likely Tampico; it was yoked to secessionists umbilically, and their treason would have collapsed much earlier but for its steady aid to traitors. By early 1864 blockade runners between Texas and this port were operating brazenly under "the British, Hanoverian and Russian flags," according to a perceptive spectator, delivering cargoes of cotton to Mexico to be shipped mostly to Europe and returning northward with "munitions of war...."[69]

Tampico had become a hideaway for notorious rebels, including Charles Gayarré of Louisiana. His mission was to ship arms and munitions northward. The U.S. envoy described him as a "native of New Orleans and although of light complexion he is of the colored race" and "may pass for a white person,"[70] which was not inaccurate. Educated in Paris, it was likely that he was fluent in French. His specialty was shipping arms to Galveston.[71] Washington sought mightily to detain him since—according to an official report, profound in implication—"our country has not in any part of the world a more insidious, active & vengeful enemy...."[72]

Then in April 1864 a crimp was put in this smooth operation when the engineer of it all—Charles Gayarré of Louisiana, described as a "merchant of Tampico"—was detained in New York. Interestingly, the appeal for his release was sent via the French consul in New Orleans.[73]

---

66. Consul Richard Robertson to Secretary Seward, 24 May 1863, Reel 2, Despatches from U.S. Consuls in Mazatlan, NARA.

67. Charles Bell, Flag Officer to Secretary Welles, 3 February 1862, Reel 2, Despatches from U.S. Consuls in Acapulco, NARA.

68. Ibid., Consul Lewis Ely to Secretary Seward, 14 January 1863.

69. Franklin Chase to Frederick W. Seward, Assistant Secretary of State, 2 March 1864, Reel 4, Despatches from U.S. Consuls in Tampico, NARA.

70. Ibid., Consul Chase to Secretary Seward, 23 February 1863.

71. Ibid., Affidavit from Silvanus W. Aldrich, 20 February 1863.

72. Ibid., Report, 30 June 1863.

73. Ibid., E Marc to Secretary Seward, 9 April 1864.

Described as a "mulatto" in his hometown, Gayarré was arrested at the urgent behest of the U.S. War Department—indicative of his importance—who depicted him as a "arms smuggler to Texas" and "exceedingly adroit"; he had perpetrated "incalculable injuries on our country" and "openly and insolently avowed himself an enemy to the Union...."[74]

Yet by the time of this timely detention, the machine he had constructed was operating with hardly a hitch. By the summer of 1864 vessels groaning with cotton bales continued to arrive in Tampico. "French and reactionary Mexican forces are operating with great energy,"[75] was the understated message to Washington. By the early fall of 1864, the elusive Gayarré had managed to return to Tampico, arriving on a German bark, and—said the worried U.S. consul— "already" had begun to "employ threats of vengeance against me and my government." This envoy was flabbergasted by his release especially after this revenge seeker "attempted to get up a mob against my house."[76]

With the chief engineer back at the controls, blockade runners continued to arrive steadily in Tampico, especially from Galveston. The confounded consul found it hard to believe in the humongous "aid" that "our countrymen" provide to treason, though by then secessionists did not consider themselves to be categorized with Washington's compatriots. Still, they did "feign to be loyal" as they "bought up all the small vessels they could find here, loaded [them] and despatched them to Texas"; their next move was on a "British packet" headed to "Havana."[77] Despite the strength of London abolitionism, "British agents and blockade runners," often aided by "Germans," were "always the boldest of the blockade traffickers," said Consul Franklin Chase in Tampico.[78]

The "forced trade in cotton," he bellowed, represented an "astounding degree of success between this port and Galveston...."[79] By Christmas 1864 blockade runners were as busy as ever, cruising to the "coast of Texas" unremittingly. In Tampico, the beleaguered consul lamented, rebel agents "purchased all the percussion, caps, powder and firearms they could find," all designed to create more

---

74. Ibid., Memorandum, 29 March 1863 and Report from R.J. Chew of U.S. Consular Bureau, 23 April 1864.

75. Ibid., Franklin Chase to Assistant Secretary Seward, 27 July 1864.

76. Ibid., Consul Chase to Assistant Secretary Seward, 26 September 1864.

77. Ibid.

78. Ibid., Consul Chase to Assistant Secretary Seward, 15 November 1864.

79. Ibid.

loyal corpses. "Aid" from "British consuls" continued "uninterruptedly" and, he concluded, was "far more efficient and beneficial than could be afforded by...consuls from the so-called [Confederate states]...."[80]

Texas as the supplier of secession, with its physical plant largely escaping unscathed, was positioned advantageously for postwar advantage. It also created enormous opportunities for wartime profiteering. By mid 1863 Brigadier General William Steele of Fort Smith, Ark., found it to be a "fact of common notoriety that fortunes have been made during this war, not only by speculators but by some of the disbursing officers too"; this was a "cause for distrust" particularly in the Lone Star State, where certain men had "been too intimate with certain speculators," notably in "Northern Texas... these speculators control large sums of money and have some political influence"[81] as well. By the spring of 1863, Indian Territory, continuously ravaged, was being supplied by what a Cherokee missionary termed "twelve hundred pounds of flour from Texas" at an unrevealed price.[82]

Matamoros continued to plague the federals too. For a good deal of the war, it was said to be the only port through which unrestricted commerce existed with rebel domains.[83] By mid-1863 Benavides, the Mexican secessionist, was cooperating with Spanish agents, and what were described as "the church party or *reaccionarios* [reactionaries]" had descended on Brownsville, where they actually hoisted the Mexican flag—then crossed the border to seek to occupy Matamoros,[84] perceived as containing a complement of Juárez supporters.

The same held true for nearby Zapata County, where many of Mexican origin were openly hostile to the rebels. John Webber, a settler who presided over an inter-racial family in the borderlands, was likely an agent of Washington operating against the rebels. The borderlands folk hero Juan Cortina was accused of intermittently being friendly to the rebels but mostly operated against the interests of the secessionists. "'He hates Americans; particularly Texans,'" was the considered opinion of traitor "Rip" Ford, who had reason to know that Cortina possessed "'an old and deep-seated grudge against

---

80. Ibid., Consul Chase to Assistant Secretary Seward, 25 December 1864.

81. Brigadier General William Steele to Lieutenant General Smith, 24 June 1863 in *War of the Rebellion*, Series I, Volume XXII, Part II, 883.

82. Entry, 10 April 1863, Diary, Stephen Foreman Collection.

83. Crews, 49.

84. Consul Pierce to Secretary Seward, 6 June 1863, in *War of the Rebellion*, Additions and Corrections, Series III, Volume III, 521-522.

Brownsville'" too.[85] Cortina, a relatively small man with a red beard and gray eyes, struck fear in the hearts of rebels in southern Texas,[86] especially because he was seen as welcoming fugitive slaves in his ranks who had a special animus toward enslavers.[87]

Although rebels had won the secession vote at the staggering rate of 20-1 in Cameron County, by late 1863 the men in blue had taken Brownsville, the chief urban node, and held it until 1864, which hindered the use of neighboring Matamoros as a Confederate port. According to the scholar James Robert Crews, there was "considerable Unionist sentiment among the Mexican-Americans" there that "may well have grown from anti-Texas feeling;" but in sum they "felt little loyalty to either side...."[88]

Moreover, the Unionist Benjamin F. McIntyre, while serving militarily in the region, noticed that "a large number of negroes who had been sent by their masters to Mexico previous to our coming into Brownsville...have been coming over and joining" his forces in the "Corps d'Afrique," mostly from Louisiana.[89] Their intimidating presence may have inspired Lincoln's comrade Major General John Palmer to offer to lead an expedition of African-Americans into Mexico at a time when the French had yet to be vanquished.[90]

However, many in Brownville-Matamoros were hostile to the French occupiers and favorable to Juárez—and ultimately Cortina—and their contest with Vidaurri and Benavides and Quintero and other "Hispanic" quislings. This compromised the ability of the rebels to maintain their grip there; for example, there was a plan to place more enslaved there as teamsters, but this would have been the equivalent of providing a free pass for them to cross the border to freedom. It also compromised the ability of Texas to continue to ship troops eastward.[91]

However, squeezing Matamoros may have contributed to a boom in other Mexican ports. In December 1863 Manzanillo was found by

---

85. James Arthur Irby, "Line of the Rio Grande: War and Trade on the Confederate Pioneer, 1861-1865," Ph.D. dissertation, U of Georgia, 1969, 31, 77, 159, 174, 178 (abbrev. Irby).

86. Charles William Goldfinch, "Juan N. Cortina, 1824-1892: A Reappraisal," Ph.D. dissertation, U of Chicago, 1949.

87. Gassner, 68.

88. Crews, 41, 45.

89. Entry, 11 November 1863, in Nannie F. Tilley, ed., *Federals on the Frontier: The Diary of Benjamin F. McIntyre, 1862-1864*, Austin: U of Texas Press, 1963, 254 (abbrev. Tilley, *McIntyre*).

90. S. Page, 154.

91. Daddysman 1976, 124,125, 136.

a U.S. spectator to be enjoying a "very large trade now," as "flows here arising from the blockade of the gulf ports and the occupation of San Blas by the French" was impactful.[92] However, being on the Pacific coast, Manzanillo was not as available for cotton exports from Texas, which was crucial for the rebels' fortunes.[93]

Predictably, by August 1863, M.C. Meigs, quartermaster of the U.S. military, announced forbiddingly that "the only Slave State in which we have not a firm foothold is Texas," a reality augmented by an "alarming immigration of blacks," the enslaved, from eastward, Alabama and Georgia, as enslavers were contemplating a last stand akin to the Alamo roughly a quarter of a century earlier.[94]

Texas was ensnared by a violent storm of swirling currents of racism. As the Emancipation Proclamation began to bite, more Africans were arriving at a time when Indigenes had seized the opportunity to reverse previous losses, while Mexico was seized with conflict between French interlopers and the Juárez forces. By February 1863, Governor Lubbock was seething publicly, while addressing legislators. The "studied purpose on the part of Mr. Lincoln's government," he said contemptuously, was "to Africanize the Southern Confederacy" by dint of emancipation. Arming Africans was akin to a war crime: Lincoln was "fighting us under blackest and most damning of all flags" and was determined "to incite to servile war," leaving few options beyond executing summarily prisoners-of-war, which needed little prompting in any case. Stunningly, he asserted that the men in blue were an "enemy more barbarous than the Indian...." Yet desertion remained a problem worsening the strategic environment. Meeting in Marshall, Texas, months before these pained remarks, rebel governors west of the Mississippi dug in their heels, demanding that the confederal constitution should be amended to exclude any state from membership that disallowed enslavement of Africans—in case any backsliding on this bedrock matter was being contemplated. But this was like the Vatican reaffirming Catholicism: the fact that it was done was indicative of a fundamental weakness.[95]

---

92. W.H. Blake to Secretary Seward, 31 December 1863, Reel 1, Despatches from U.S. Consuls in Manzanillo, NARA.

93. Stephen Andrew Townsend, "The Rio Grande Expedition, 1863-1865," Ph.D. dissertation, UNT, 2001, 1.

94. Report from M.C. Meigs, ca. August 1863, in *War of the Rebellion*, Series III, Volume III, Additions and Corrections, 599.

95. Message of Governor F.R. Lubbock to the Extra Session of the Ninth Legislature of the State of Texas Delivered February 5th, 1863, Austin: State

Clearly, the declaration of emancipation shook Texas enslavers to their core, for they returned to this distressing matter repeatedly. The legislature echoed Lubbock's distraught mien when it charged angrily that "our enemies are seeking to bring upon us a servile war by arming our slaves and placing them in the ranks of their armies"; they were "inciting insurrection and insubordination"—and worse.[96] Hurriedly—and worriedly—passed was "an act to provide against hostile invasion of the state of Texas by persons of color"; if this were to occur "he shall be deemed to have forfeited his freedom," if not his life.[97] Yet when another law was passed circumscribing draft dodging,[98] it was redolent of the crisis that even the strongest rebel state—treason's iron fist—was enduring.

Even before the formalizing of emancipation, Africans had been heading toward federal lines, and this trend escalated after 1 January 1863. But even before this exalted date, Africans had been engaging the rebels militarily. For the embodiment of genocide, John Baylor, reported almost casually that he "sent out a party to rob and plunder the Choctaw Indians, attacked them, took all their wagons and killed three hundred of them, mostly negroes"—and "captured their artillery."[99] Then the vaunted "Ross Brigade," one of Texas's most battle-hardened forces, was faced with the specter of their scouts retreating frenetically as an observer referred to their being "hotly pursued by about two hundred negro cavalry...." Nonplussed General Ross, for whom a number of entities in the state continue to be named, despite his enslaving credentials, mounted his steed and cried, "'Charge them,'" referring to the "'black apes' as the boys called the negro soldiers...."[100]

Yet what infuriated Austin most notably was the action of General Benjamin Butler, the man in blue presiding over the prize that was New Orleans after its seizure in 1862, who did not hesitate to threaten

Gazette, 1863. This document includes material on rebel governors' confab, 9 August 1862, Duke U, Durham, N.C.

96. General Laws of the Extra Session of the Ninth Legislature of the State of Texas, Austin: Texas Almanac, 1863, Duke. At the same site, see also Special Laws of the Extra Session of the Ninth Legislature of the State of Texas, Austin: Texas Almanac, 1863.

97. Act to Provide Against the Hostile Invasion of the State of Texas by Persons of Color...approved March 6th, 1863, Texas Archives.

98. See Law on Conscription, 6 March 1863, Texas Archives.

99. John Baylor to "Darling Emy," 22 April 1862?, Box 1, John Robert Baylor Papers, UT-A.

100. V.M. Rose, 105.

that he would "call on Africa" to attack westward and elsewhere, "and I do not think I shall call in vain. I have determined to use the services of the free colored men," he added threateningly.[101] His fellow federal, George S. Denison, added that the "Free Negroes of Louisiana are certainly superior as a class to the Creoles (descendants of French and Spanish settlers). They are intelligent, energetic and industrious, as is evident from the fact (as stated to me) that they own one seventh of the real estate in this city.... these men will be good soldiers,"[102] not good news for neighboring Texas, a likely site where they would be able to display their martial talents. It was in late November 1862 that President Lincoln was informed of the linkage between New Orleans and a proposed assault on Texas: "any expedition" to this neighbor had to have New Orleans as a "base of supplies...."[103] Not waiting to be punched, as early as September 1862 General Butler found that "Partisan Texas Rangers...ambushed" some of his men not far from the Algiers neighborhood of New Orleans.[104]

However, it would be a gross error to overstate the Texas predicament; surely there was suffering, but likely not as horrible as what was transpiring eastward. By mid-1863 refugees continued to arrive in Monterrey—some "nearly naked"—bearing the intelligence that "several guerrilla companies are being organized" in the Lone Star State "to operate on the frontiers of Kansas and Missouri," where the terrorist William Quantrill spread disorder.[105]

Promulgating a declaration of emancipation placed the rebels in the snapping jaws of a cruel dilemma that even Quantrill could not resolve: angry armed Africans were bearing down on Galveston, yet there was a felt desire to continue the importation of even more Africans—the essence of the labor supply and the source of immense wealth. It was also in 1863 that opponents of the rebels claimed they had purloined secret instructions of the latter's top diplomat—Judah P. Benjamin detailing a plan to resuscitate formally the African Slave Trade, though this could compromise relations with London and likely Paris too. Undaunted, Benjamin was said to be unequivocal about "authorizing the importation of slaves from

---

101. General Butler to Secretary of War Edwin Stanton, 14 August 1862, in Butler Correspondence, Volume II, 191.

102. Ibid., George S. Denison to Secretary Chase, 26 August 1862, 228.

103. Ibid., General Butler to President Lincoln, 29 November 1862, 512.

104. Ibid., General Butler to Major General Halleck, 10 September 1862, 278.

105. Consul Kimmey to Secretary Seward, 4 June 1863, Reel 1, Despatches from U.S. Consuls in Monterrey, NARA.

Africa," which critics asserted was a plan "prefigured at the outbreak of the rebellion...."[106]

An adjunct of these cruel plans was the continual fleeing of Africans south of the border, albeit into a war zone, but one where enslavement was forbidden. By April 1863 a U.S. official in Monterrey encountered a "Negro man born in the state of Louisiana"; this veteran was making "enquiries respecting a pension due him as a soldier...at the Battle of New Orleans January 8th 1815," the gaining of which would provide a financial cushion.[107] There were bound to be more following his footsteps southward for it was in 1863 that Texas called on Free Negroes to depart forthwith—or be enslaved.[108]

Africans escaping from a chaotic Indian Territory to Mexico often had to traverse Texas at a time when enslavers from Arkansas thought the Lone Star State was a refuge, bringing more Africans to the state, adding to the disarray. During the course of the war, an estimated 150,000 enslaved Africans crossed the Red River, including at least half of those controlled by Arkansas's largest enslaver, Elisha Worthington, who wound up in Tarrant County. Again, this attempt to salvage enslavement was not just a product of those like Worthington; it is estimated that a relative handful of men of European ancestry from the Razorback State joined the federal military, while some of the most enthusiastic backers of reopening formally the African Slave Trade came from this neighbor of Texas.[109]

Worthington was escaping to Texas from Arkansas since the latter state was under siege. By late 1862 and early 1863 the northwest section of the state, along with the adjoining Cherokee Nation, was overrun by those described as "Jayhawkers, Tories and hostile Indians," the latter including an "unknown number of Indian cavalry estimated at about three thousand armed men...."[110]

While this rout was occurring, it was unclear where the Cherokee Christian missionary—and rebel sympathizer—Stephen Foreman was presiding. Routinely, he preached submission in the Cherokee language—Matthew 6:19-21, encouraging the dispossessed to

---

106. "The African Slave Trade, the Secret Purpose of the Insurgents to Revive It. No Treaty Stipulations Against the Slave Trade..., Philadelphia: Sherman, 1863, Pennsylvania State U.

107. Consul Kimmey to Secretary Seward, 10 April 1863, Reel 1, Despatches from U.S. Consuls in Monterrey, NARA.

108. Nancy Head Bowen, "A Political Labyrinth: Texas in the Civil War—Questions in Continuity," Rice U, Ph.D. dissertation, 1974, 105.

109. K.H. Jones, 179, 187, 189, 178.

110. Report of General Hindman in *Official Reports of Battles*, 211.

continue disgorging "treasures on earth"[111]—while complaining about "wild Indians."[112]

Contrastingly, deemed "hostile" to the rebels were the Osage. A subsequent scholar found their "sympathies" to be with the "Unionists," while "numerous half-breeds joined the Union army" on the Kansas-Oklahoma border. However, when a "general uprising of the Indians" occurred there, it was "attributed to the machinations of the Confederates,"[113] which redounded to the detriment of the Osage. Rebels were noticeably hostile to anti-secessionists in Indian Territory and the vicinity since the enslaved there generally attained free status well before other sites, e.g., by mid-June 1863.[114] Increasingly, Indigenes—Watie notwithstanding—were perceived by rebels as being "hostile"; their seizing the split among settlers to seek to regain lost territory was seen in New Mexico, West Texas and Arizona as a threat to the secessionists.[115]

But the ultimate "threat" to the secessionists came from their very own wrongheaded policies: enslaving Africans while armed Africans were on the way to prop up their French ally in Mexico made little strategic sense. Articulating genocide against some Indigenes while seeking to ally with others was hypocrisy too breathtaking to stand. Inexorably, the rebels were headed for the dung heap of history.

111. Entry, 23 January 1863, Diary, Stephen Foreman Collection.

112. Ibid., Entry, 31 January 1863.

113. W.L. Bartles, "Massacre of Confederates by Osage Indians in 1863," "Before the 27th Annual Meeting of the Kansas Historical Society," 2 December 1902, Huntington Library.

114. Naylor, 152.

115. Hugh Edward Killin, "The Texans and the California Column," M.A. thesis, TTU, 1931, 79.

Chapter 16

Twilight of Texas Treason, 1864-1865

By 1864 it seemed that the civil wars were merging. That was the import of what Secretary of State Seward was told. "The Mexicans believe their destiny is tied up in the future of the U.S. government," was the word from Chihuahua, meaning the ongoing war between Washington and Richmond "exercises the most unfavorable influence" on this southern neighbor,[1] to the advantage of French occupiers over their legions of domestic opponents.

A civil war was erupting in Indian Territory too, and not just among the Cherokee. Sarah Odom was born enslaved in 1850 and was of partial Creek ancestry. By 1861, she recalled later, the Creeks split, as some thought a better deal could be gained from the secessionists. She also recalled when rebel negotiator Albert Pike showed up "to meet the head men of the Creeks, Choctaws and Chickasaws.... the whole village talked of nothing [else] for days.... Creeks really had a civil war among themselves and the northern Creeks won at first and then finally the southern whipped the northern Creeks and they headed for Kansas.... Creeks wanted no railroads, sensing it meant white people would invade...."[2]

As it seemed that North America was being carved up like a Thanksgiving turkey, it was not only France that wanted a piece. Looking back, it is easy to conclude that the ongoing effort to dismember Mexico had led to the companion idea of dismembering its northern neighbor too—both projects driven by narrowing mercenary dreams. Once the virus of real estate speculation was loosed, ripping nations apart for profit, which had propelled Texas 1836, why not do the same with the biggest enchilada of all: the U.S.? The Knights of the Golden Circle can be viewed in this context: "everyone knows," said one of their detractors, "how great an influence was exercised" by them "in preparing and organizing the Southern

---

1. Reuben Creel to Secretary Seward, 10 October 1864, Reel 1, Despatches from U.S. Consuls in Chihuahua, NARA.

2. Oral History, Sarah Odom, 17 December 1937, IPP.

Rebellion,"[3] then moving on to Cuba and other tempting targets—though other more virulent detractors saw the KGC as anti-civil war until the hemisphere was subjugated. The infamous KGC retained significant support in Texas and continued to engage in what one excitable critic termed "the most gigantic treasonable conspiracy the world has ever known."[4]

Traitors continued to plot with foreign powers too. By 1864 the enslaver and prominent Missourian Sterling Price had devised murky plans with Belgium's consul in St. Louis that did not bode well for the federals.[5]

Mexico was roiled tempestuously by the conflict between the French occupiers and the Juárez forces but, as if that were not enough, this land was being deluged by sojourners from the north, who were escaping their own civil war. Secretary of State Seward knew that "deserters" and rebel "sympathizers" were flowing ceaselessly into Manzanillo, placing them within striking distance of Arizona and San Francisco, if need be.[6] Due north along the ocean coast in Mazatlán, Seward was provided with a contrasting message in January 1864: "many loyal American citizens are constantly arriving at this place from Texas, many of them with families and all in a destitute condition...."[7]

However, by October "many" described as "rebel Americans...from San Francisco" were arriving in droves, accompanied by "rumors" of "outrages to be committed" by them. The balance may have been in favor of loyalists, however, since "the most riotous" were "constantly departing" for Texas to shore up sagging defenses there. "Last month

---

3. "The Great Northern Conspiracy of the 'O.S.L...,'" 1864, UVa-C. At the same site, see also Southern Chivalry, "The Adventures of G. Whillikens, CSA, Knight of the Golden Circle and of Guinea Pete, His Negro Squire. An Epic Doggerel in Six Books. By a Citizen of the Cotton Country, Philadelphia, 1861. See also at the same site, Edmund Wright, pseud., "The Narrative of Edmund Wright: His Adventures with and Escape from the Knights of the Golden Circle," Cincinnati: Hawley, 1864.

4. Felix Stidger, "Treason History of the Order of Sons of Liberty, Formerly Circle of Honor, Succeeded by the Knights of the Golden Circle, Afterward Order of American Knights: The Most Gigantic Treasonable Conspiracy the World Has Ever Known," U of Wisconsin-Madison.

5. "Report of the Judge Advocate General on the 'Order of African Knights' or 'The Sons of Liberty' a Western Conspiracy in aid of the Southern Rebellion," Washington, D.C.: Government Printing Office, 1864, Harvard U.

6. Consul W. H. Blake to Secretary Seward, 10 January 1864, Reel 1, Despatches from U.S. Consuls in Manzanillo, NARA.

7. Vice Consul B.R. Carman to Secretary Seward, 30 January 1864, Reel 3, Despatches from U.S. Consuls in Mazatlan, NARA.

some thirty left in a body well armed and were expecting to add more to their number en route. This morning," Secretary Seward was told, "fifteen others departed for the same destination...." Still, Mazatlán was slated to be a port for rebel piracy, according to U.S. officialdom: It was a "very modern town and is little known but undoubtedly is the most important point on the western coast of Mexico," and was "far preferable" to Acapulco "and even to Guaymas...." The cotton crop was delivering "great results," not good news for "King Cotton." It had "yielded from 400 to 500 pounds of clean cotton to the great acre," bringing "handsome profit...."[8]

As early as the fall of 1863, as the Emancipation Proclamation was unfolding, Seward ascertained that in Acapulco "the soil...is well adapted to growth of cotton,"[9] as if Dixie were already in the rearview mirror. By January 1865 Seward was informed that as for Mazatlán, the "cotton is ready to pick and there are no men to do the work," raising searching questions about the future labor force.

However, the appearance of ill-famed rebels in Mazatlán may have been part of an organized retreat, as the countdown to Appomattox heightened. In early January 1865, the brother of secessionist military leader P.G.T. Beauregard arrived from Mexico City en route to Guaymas; he was expected to shore up the French military. Expected soon was William Gwin, the Mississippi enslaver by way of California who had been spending quality time in France. "He comes on behalf of the French government," Secretary of State Seward was told, a strange assignment for a former U.S. Senator. Supposedly, he was "connected with these N.W. states of Mexico, Sonora, Durango, Sinaloa & Lower California," suggesting more secession shenanigans.[10] After this brief conferral in Vera Cruz, Gwin departed swiftly for France to meet with the emperor, with plotting against Washington unavoidably on the agenda.[11] By March 1865, the so-called "Lafayette of the South," Camille de Polignac, rebel military leader, had arrived in Matamoros, as plans proceeded for an orderly rebel retreat into Mexico by secessionists.[12]

---

8. Ibid., Consul B.R. Carman to Secretary Seward, 22 October 1864.

9. Consul Lewis Ely to Secretary Seward, 30 September 1863, Reel 2, Despatches from U.S. Consuls in Acapulco, NARA.

10. Consul Carman to Secretary Seward, 12 January 1865, Reel 3, Despatches from U.S. Consuls in Mazatlan, NARA. (This missive contains the quotation concluding the previous paragraph.)

11. Joseph Allen Stout, Last Years, 174.

12. Vera Cruz Herald, 2 March 1865, Reel 3, Despatches from U.S. Consuls in Vera Cruz, NARA.

In short, rebels and loyalists clashed along the Pacific and Caribbean coasts of Mexico, exporting their rancorous conflict southward and contributing mercilessly to the ongoing war in this neighbor.

If the battle with the secessionists had erupted on Mexican soil, it was more likely to have occurred with most intensity in Mazatlán, especially because it was closer to the northern neighbor. "American interests have increased...here...during the past year greatly by the numerous arrivals from California," said a U.S. emissary. With the war to conclude by the following year, U.S. "interests" were "daily becoming more important. Cotton has been cultivated" by "some American companies," and "mines here have attracted many from California," as "each steamer brings new emigration...."[13]

It was well that a stream of presumed loyalists continued to arrive, since by 1864 the news surfaced that scheming rebels in Markleeville, "Upper" California, in league, said one plotter, with "the Mormons and Indians on our east...aided by the French in Mexico... by a bold stroke [desired] to take the state out of the Union and to erect a Pacific Republic...."[14]

Paris emulated the federal union: expand or wither. With the Hampton Roads confab of loyalists and rebels in 1864, the fear arose that these combatants would reconcile, invoke the archaic Monroe Doctrine, and united drive European powers from the hemisphere, starting with France, then—perhaps---moving on to Spain, then Britain. Hampton Roads underscored that Richmond and Paris were an unlikely pairing, for as early as February 1861, Jefferson Davis had envisioned enlarging his rump republic by way of seizing a good deal of northern Mexico, especially the territory bordering Texas.[15] On the same wavelength, before the traitors' surrender in April 1865, Union General Ulysses S. Grant reportedly wanted a joint loyalist-rebel force to invade Mexico to oust the occupiers.[16]

---

13. Vice Consul B.R. Carman to Thomas Corwin, 18 March 1864, Reel 3, Despatches from U.S. Consuls in Mazatlan, NARA.

14. Captain Mitchell, Alpine Rifles, et.al. to Major General McDowell, 31 August 1864, in *War of the Rebellion*, Volume L, Series I, Part II, 961.

15. Sainlaude, 116, 119.

16. B.C. Curtis, 44. See also Julian Carr, "The Hampton Roads Conference...Refutation of the Statement by Mr. Lincoln Said if Union was Written at the Top of the Southern Commissioners Might Fill in the Balance," 1917, Huntington Library. As the high-level rebel-loyal delegations met, "no other person entered the room, except that once a Negro servant came in and was promptly sent out...."

Thus, despite the U.S. weakening of Mexico that had allowed France to swoop in and challenge Washington from the south, the idea of further encroachment had not dissipated either. Reporting from Acapulco, Consul Lewis Ely announced with misplaced confidence that the "Liberal Party" or Juárez forces "would be glad to see Mexico [as] an integral part of one great Republican Government under the shadow of the wings of one eagle, one aegis"—meaning Washington. The idea was that a victorious U.S. would contribute to the ouster of the French occupiers—then take their place, i.e., "admission of Mexico to the American union at no distant day...." Contextualizing the influx into Mazatlán and Manzanillo, Ely pointed out that "states bordering on the Pacific, viz. Guerrero, Sinaloa and Sonora are more alive to the importance of the 'kindly offices' of the U. States than are, perhaps, other states in the interior." The latter two—supposedly—"agitating" for "their independence with a view to ask admission into our union," the "governors are said to be at the head of the movement," seeing the "wisdom of acquiring this country [emphasis-original]."[17]

Nevertheless, this speculation about the future was premature in light of the formidably continuing French presence on both sides of the border. Rebels in Texas continued to clash with the French envoy about conscription,[18] who demanded more warships to be dispatched for punctuation of his claims. He was seeking to rally British and Spanish emissaries there to bolster his claim and he too began to speculate about Texas becoming independent, making it more susceptible to Parisian influence. He noticed Texas's out-sized contribution to rebel forces, which—it was thought—harmed the local economy, especially the cotton harvest. This was the case though the blockade of Galveston was seen as unserious in terms of the few federal vessels there, allowing rebel cargo to reach Havana, Jamaica—and Mexico—easily and receive imports from there and Europe too. On the one hand, Texas had autonomy in production of corn, wheat, beef, pork and poultry; on the other hand, despite the arrival of enslaved labor from other rebel states, costs of production remained elevated because of the stressors of war. And trade with loyal states continued despite war, which may have been more of a boon to Washington than Richmond.[19]

17. Consul Ely to Secretary Seward, 19 September 1863, Reel 2, Despatches from U.S. Consuls in Acapulco, NARA.

18. Report, 7 June 1862, Galveston Consulate. See more protests about this in Reports, 7-8-9 June 1862, at the same site.

19. Ibid., Report, 22 July 1862.

The idea of "King Cotton" may have been a chimera, but the point remained that this commodity wielded significant influence globally. "Cotton is in great excess of former years," was the report from Egypt by early 1864; it was "about two fifths that of the crop of the United States in former years," feeding a "rumor" that "France was about to recognize the Confederacy" but pulled back because of the Egyptian crop, which "caused a problem in price and bargains were made...." That is, it seemed that Paris was whipsawing Egyptian cotton versus its Dixie counterpart, which "resulted in very heavy losses" in Africa.[20]

Yet it is possible that the increased traffic between Alexandria and North America may have opened doors of opportunity for some U.S. Negroes, for by November 1864 a "colored man named John Johnson died here," said the U.S. consul. He was "without passport or papers" but had been "coming to Alexandria" for about "three years" from his home in Dover, Del., a continuing site of enslavement; he "had served as a seaman" and received his final resting place "in the Protestant burying ground"[21]—which likely would have been denied him back home, illuminating the yawning contrast between overseas and the homeland.

Nonetheless, as the U.S. Civil War waxed, proposing to Washington a takeover of Mexico was untimely at best. There was something about the rapacious republic—likely inbred as it dauntlessly moved westward across the continent—that drove it to gobble up more territory.

Despite the U.S. attempt to blockade rebel ports, war materiel continued to arrive—and not just via the reliable Tampico-Galveston route. In the spring of 1864 the authorities in Havana were shipping to the secessionists "100 Enfield rifles and 120 English tower muskets"—the "former are splendid," enthused Major General Magruder, while the "latter" were merely "strong and serviceable," with both capable of creating more casualties on the battlefield.[22]

Moreover, it was presumptuous of Washington to even consider more assaulting of Mexico when it had yet to squash a fearsome internal revolt. All this begs the question of the resistance the rapacious rascals would have encountered—and were encountering—from the likes of Cortina, who seemed to be gaining strength and assurance as

20. Consul William Thayer to Secretary Seward, 23 January 1864, Reel 3, Despatches from U.S. Consuls in Alexandria, NARA.

21. Ibid., Consul Charles Hale to Secretary Seward, 24 November 1864.

22. Major General J.B. Magruder to C.J. Helm, Havana, 2 April 1864, in *War of the Rebellion*, Volume XXXIV, Series I, Part III, 727.

the French occupation deepened. In January 1864 Matamoros was in a "complete uproar" since Cortina and his band had arrived. Given the proximity to rebel Texas, unsurprisingly there was pro-Paris sentiment there but with hardly blinking an eye, Cortina ordered these traitors to be shot. Others aligned with him then headed to Tampico to fight the French and in the process weaken this secessionist fortress. As a result, more Mexicans surged into Brownsville. Juárez's men were then in Saltillo but they too were headed to Matamoros—not good news for traitors of any kind—especially since he intended to establish a headquarters there. With a typical class insouciance, the U.S. representative there found that the "better class of Mexicans" were "anti-French," and it remained true that "all the French with but a few exceptions that reside here are secessionists and [rebel] sympathizers"[23]—though even this was not necessarily good news for Washington or Richmond since Paris had its own plans for this land.

Expectedly, the rebels did not flinch in embracing the possibility that their rump republic would become a toady for Paris. Rebel military leader John S. "Rip" Ford, based in Laredo, acknowledged that the pro-Confederate Mexican leader Santiago Vidaurri "and the French party would be our allies and I have never viewed the fact that we might be placed side by side with the French in Mexico as portending evil to our cause."[24]

Vidaurri attained the highest rank of any Mexican American who served alongside the traitors, though he also served as the military governor of Nuevo León and Coahuila, indicative of rebels' creeping annexation of more Mexican land. As the rebels appeared to be on the cusp of collapse, he led them to victory in the Battle of Laredo in March 1864.[25]

In the long run, the fact that Cortina was willing to recruit into his forces large numbers of African Americans, mostly from Texas, with unresolved grievances against Austin, was an ill omen for Austin.[26] This fed ongoing hysteria generated by Judah P. Benjamin's notion that their opponents were "exciting slaves to the murder of their masters."[27]

---

23. Consul Leonard Pierce to Secretary Seward, 16 January 1864, Reel 3, Despatches from U.S. Consuls in Matamoros, NARA.

24. Colonel Ford to Captain E.P. Turner, 17 April 1864, in *War of the Rebellion*, Volume XXXIV, Series I, Part II, 776.

25. J.D. Riley, 176, 191.

26. González-Quiroga, 234.

27. Bigelow, 171. See also James Dunwoody Bulloch, *The Secret Service of the Confederate States in Europe...*, London: Bentley, 1883.

With Africans arriving unwaveringly in the borderlands—often unaccompanied by their (former) masters—the scales were tipping further against the rebels. Thus, as the French occupiers were making their move there, U.S. Senator J.H. Lane devised a plan to "set apart a portion of the State of Texas for the use of Persons of African Descent...." He found that the 1860 census had revealed that there were 182,566 enslaved in the Lone Star State, but since the commencement of the war—he claimed—60% of the enslaved of Louisiana, 75% of those of Arkansas had decamped to Texas, and "at least one hundred thousand...have been transferred to the west side of the river from Mississippi and the other states making in all about 600,000...now in eastern Texas," as the press of war was forcing new thinking.[28]

Thus, by September 1864 as the rebel revolt began to limp badly, 400 French sailors landed and claimed Bagdad, Texas, theretofore home to a goodly number of traitorous profiteers. The problem for these mariners was that Cortina was nearby with a force three times as large, along with a reported 18 "pieces of cannon." Then he was collaborating with the men in blue, but his ultimate allegiance did not rest with them. The U.S. delegate surmised that some of his forces were headed to Brownsville, while others were intending to "fight their way to Brazos Santiago [Texas]...."[29]

When Brownsville fell to loyalist forces, a loud signal was emitted that the end was nigh for secession. For this simultaneously debilitated the crucial role of Matamoros as a de facto rebel port. It is likely that Judah P. Benjamin cringed, perhaps shed copious tears, when he read his mail in March 1864. The "surrender at Brownsville was one of the most cowardly and scandalous affairs which has happened in any country," the letter summarized. "Without seeing the enemy and forty eight hours before he [arrived] the general set fire to the town and a large quantity of cotton and other property, both public and private was destroyed and the general and his troops fled in terror."[30]

---

28. "Speech of Hon. J.H. Lane of Kansas in the Senate of the United States, February 16, 1864...to Set Apart a Portion of the State of Texas for the Use of Persons of African Descent," Washington, D.C.: Gibson Bros., 1864, Baylor U.

29. Consul Pierce to Secretary Seward, 1 September 1864, Reel 3, Despatches from U.S. Consuls in Matamoros, NARA.

30. R. Fitzpatrick, Commercial Agency of the Confederate States of America to Secretary of State Judah P. Benjamin, 8 March 1864, in *War of the Rebellion*, Volume XXXIV, Series I, Part II, 1030.

This surrender was all the more remarkable since about a year earlier Major General Magruder was informed that "an expedition is fitting out in New York of 20,000 men to take possession" of this strategically sited town,[31] but the defenders remained unprepared. Some may have fled to Laredo, where rebel commerce shifted after the fall of Brownsville.[32] By the summer of 1864, the visiting loyalist officer, Benjamin F. McIntyre, found the "constant movement of families from this side of the river into Mexico. Brownsville is—will soon be—deserted and its buildings closed…most of the white inhabitants will go to N.O. [New Orleans]—and the Mexicans to Mexico. Yet there is a class of wealthy citizens who will remain"[33]: this was accurate for there was more profiteering yet to take place. Among the opportunists was Charles Stillman, born in Connecticut, who arrived in Durango by 1827 at the tender age of 17 and went on to join the traitors—but sensing the direction of prevailing winds by the fall of 1863, he defected to the loyalists, becoming fabulously wealthy.[34]

Cortina had been accused of hedging, feeling understandably that enslavers in the rapacious republic would prevail. The crafty leader was also said to have backed the French—for a while.[35] However, by 1864 the fall of Brownsville demonstrated that a rebel—even an occupier—victory was a disintegrating possibility, a perception concretized in Matamoros when Cortina and the loyalist Texan A.J. Hamilton "walked arm in arm through the streets," according to an aghast rebel observer. Then solidifying the alliance, said Major General Magruder, "ten pieces of artillery were formally and officially presented to Governor Cortina by the federal authorities of Brownsville…."[36]

This was a crucial sign of aid to the anti-French occupation forces. In mid-June 1863 as the French attacked Puebla, Mexico, the U.S. emissary Morris Tausig was "proud to say that the American citizens

---

31. Ibid., H. Bee to Major General Magruder, 22 May 1863, Volume V, Series III, 870.

32. Crews, 55.

33. Entry, 14 July 1864, in Tilley, *McIntyre,* 372.

34. Daddysman 1976, 239.

35. Jerry Thompson, "Colonel José de los Santos Benavides and General Juan Nepomuceno Cortina: Two Astounding Civil War Tejanos," (abbrev. Thompson, "…Santos Benavides and…Cortina," in Bacha-Garza, *Civil War,* 138-158, 153.

36. Major General Magruder to Commissioner Slidell, 27 April 1864, in *War of the Rebellion,* Volume XXXIV, Series III, Part II, 796. The reference to "Governor Cortina" was not accidental for by then he was the de facto leader of Tamaulipas.

under command of Mr. James Lohse, although very few in numbers, have greatly insured that" the Juárez forces would be bolstered.[37] More than this, there were a considerable number of U.S. nationals fighting alongside Juárez,[38] 3000 by one estimate, compared to 2000 of their erstwhile compatriots with the occupiers.[39]

When the emperor and his spouse arrived in Mexico City by mid-June 1864, flags were hoisted at every consulate in town—except that of the U.S. Consul Charles Arnoux, who also received a ticket to a ball in honor of the royal couple, and pointedly declined the invitation.[40]

Another concerning sign for secessionists was the embrace of Andrew Hamilton above the Mason-Dixon line. He was an "eloquent Union refugee from Texas," according to a New Yorker: following in the footsteps of President Lincoln, he too was invited to speak at Cooper Union in Manhattan, where "the hall was densely filled." He did not disappoint as he regaled those assembled with tales of those "in Mexico...now 500 men who left as I left" and were then "hunted like wolves...."[41]

At the same time Secretary of State Seward assured fellow cabinet member, Secretary of War Stanton, that a "large number of citizens of the loyal states" in Mexico "have entered into the service of Cortina at Matamoros, who has also received a supply of arms and munitions of war from this country."[42]

Troublingly, even some loyalists were becoming critical of "Governor Cortina," whom one officer termed a "desperado" and "renegade outlaw and murderer of American citizens," who generated a "deep feeling of hatred and revenge against him upon this side of the river," i.e., Texas.[43]

---

37. Vice Consul Morris Tausig to "Sir," 15 June 1863, Reel 6, Despatches from U.S. Consuls in Mexico City, NARA.

38. Robert Benaway Brown, "Guns Over the Border: American Aid to the Juárez Government During the French Intervention," Ph.D. dissertation, U of Michigan, 1951, 86.

39. B.C. Curtis, 51.

40. Consul Arnoux to Secretary Seward, 29 June 1864, Reel 6, Despatches from U.S. Consuls in Mexico City, NARA.

41. Union Campaign Documents, Number 3: The Aristocratic Arm of the Rebellion, Col. Hamilton of Texas in New York, Albany: Weed, Parsons, 1864, AAS.

42. Secretary Seward to Secretary Stanton, 29 August 1864, in *War of the Rebellion*, Volume XLI, Series I, Part II, 916.

43. Entry, 5 April 1864 in Tilley, *McIntyre*, 324.

Simultaneously, Cortina had launched what amounted to a declaration of war against the rebels, which made sense since the secessionists were backing his enemy: French occupiers. This precarious state of affairs for the traitors brought "admiration and gratitude" from the men in blue.[44] The message from U.S. headquarters in Brownsville was depressing for the rebels: "Cortina informs me that he will do anything we want," though it remained accurate to "look upon Matamoros as an unsafe place."[45]

That is, even as late as September 1864 the rebels and occupiers had been wounded but not defeated. It was then that U.S. Brigadier General James Carleton of New Mexico was instructed that "the cotton trade between Texas and Mexico is very active and the rebels are now supplied with money and arms far more plentifully than at any past period. The avidity with which cotton is sought by speculators from all parts of Europe and from the interior of Mexico furnishes the Texans an opportunity which they do not neglect," especially since the French occupiers had made a comeback and "now occupy the cities of Monterrey and Matamoros." This was likely to last for a while since the people of "Chihuahua are politically dead...our war in the States has had a very potent influence (the wrong way) in Northern Mexico," meaning that it had solidified the cross-border right-wing, which was potent in both regions.[46]

The rebels were exasperated with Cortina at this juncture. He had "Rip" Ford's men on the run, and the mandate issued was not to treat him as a "prisoner of war" if apprehended "but as a robber and murderer and executed immediately"—which did not happen, as he survived until the 1890s. Besides, the rebels should have considered executing some of the men on their own side, as profiteers and speculators "exported...cotton illegally," which by the admission of leadership was having "so disastrous an effect upon the value of our currency," meaning a "frightful depreciation of confederate notes...."[47]

---

44. Major General John A. McClernand to Major General N.P. Banks, 8 April 1864, in *War of the Rebellion*, Volume XXXIV, Series I, Part III, 87.

45. Ibid., Report from U.S. Headquarters, Brownsville to Brigadier General Charles P. Stone, 16 January 1864, Volume XXXIV, Series I, Part II, 92.

46. Ibid., Reuben Creel of U.S. Consulate, Chihuahua, to Brigadier General James Carleton, Commanding Department of Santa Fe, New Mexico, 18 September 1864, Volume XLI, Series I, Part III, 245.

47. Ibid., J.G. Walker, Major General Commanding to Brigadier General J.E. Slaughter of Brownsville, 1 October 1864, Volume XLI, Series I, Part III, 743.

Currency depreciation was a sign of the decline of the entire rebel project. More precisely, the cotton and beef trade with Mexico was declining as the Confederacy did so vertiginously. This also fed a "lukewarmness and distressing apathy of the people," said Brigadier General W.R. Boggs; then "the most patriotic and reliable men are in the army, leaving at home to mold public opinion and to prey" those remaining, an "army of speculators and extortioners...."[48]

Matamoros by 1864 was yo-yoing back and forth between the French occupiers and their opponents, with the former surging back by September.[49] There was a similar checkered pattern in Vera Cruz. Pierre Soulé, a former U.S. Senator from Louisiana, born in France, arrived there from Havana,[50] a disturbing sign of secessionist pretensions. Blockade runners from Dixie continued to arrive from Texas, bulging with cotton to be conveyed via the Prussian consul.[51] Blithefully unaware that the secession project would be buried within months, on the last day of 1864, yet another blockade runner arrived with "334 bales of cotton," again for the Prussian consul; but this time the vessel hailed from Nassau. Nonetheless, local merchants in Vera Cruz were complaining that the ordinary stream of goods from Louisiana was drying up,[52] suggesting that the blockade might be working effectively. There were other mixed signals. A "great number of American citizens came to this country from New Orleans to be employed in construction of a railroad between this place and Orizaba" was the communication to Secretary Seward; but soon they were "in distress in a country where they cannot speak the language," so "necessity has compelled them to enlist as soldiers" in the French army,"[53] the equivalent of joining secession.

Southern Texas had been a rebel stronghold, but by 1864 it had been breached. It was then that Governor Pendleton Murrah of the Lone Star State was told bluntly of the "general demoralization" which "extended in some degree" to the entirety of "Texas confederate troops"; matters were desperate in the "Northern District of

48. Ibid., Major General J.G. Walker to Brigadier General W.R. Boggs, 10 October 1864, Volume XLI, Series I, Part III, 994.

49. Sainlaude, 114.

50. Consul A.S. Calderon to Secretary Seward, 30 September 1864, Reel 9, Despatches from U.S. Consuls in Vera Cruz, NARA.

51. Ibid., D.L. Lane to Secretary Seward, 22 November 1864.

52. Ibid., D.L. Lane to Secretary Seward, 31 December 1864.

53. Ibid., Consul A.S. Calderon to Secretary Seward, 1 September 1864.

Texas"—"a most deplorable and most dangerous state"[54]—hard by Indian Territory, then being plundered and pillaged.

Squire Hall was born in Indian Territory in 1863 and early on was informed of a "Negro uprising" there, wherein "male members" of the enslaved community were "practically exterminated...." His mother told him that "Yankee propagandists" fomented this and other revolts there that led to a "complete abandonment of the plantations" well before the close of the war, leaving utter devastation.[55]

Texas draft dodgers of various loyalties were detained by Mexican forces and escorted across the border,[56] as they often were perceived as troublemakers or, as in the past, an excuse for a kind of "squatter sovereignty." However, deserters from the Lone Star State were bound to be more hurtful to the rebels—but not altogether. Captain James A. Ware of the First Texas Cavalry was appalled by this "act of open hostility" as those "formerly residing" in his state had "taken refuge" across the border and were now "organized to invade this state."[57]

In short, the secessionists' insatiable appetite for unpaid African labor was backfiring and jeopardizing what had become the mainstay of treason: Texas. Scrambling to avoid being overtaken by events, the Lone Star firebrand, Louis Wigfall, countered by proposing to "substitute slaves for all soldiers employed" as "cooks, engineers, laborers," about "1000 men" in other words. "Impressment of Negroes has been practiced ever since the war commenced," he contended, but, alas, even this "stormy petrel" knew the downside: "we have never been able to keep the impressed negroes with an army near the enemy." Sighingly, he asserted the obvious: "They desert...."[58]

Things had gotten so bad for the rebels that Wigfall was feuding with Judah P. Benjamin over the latter's plan to free and arm the enslaved,[59] while the former thought they should only be deployed

54. Major General Magruder to Governor Murrah, 31 March 1864, in *War of the Rebellion*, Volume XXXIV, Series I, Part II, 1103.

55. Oral History, Squire Hall, ca. 1937-1938, IPP.

56. Consul Emmanuel Etchison to Secretary Seward, 15 January 1864, Reel 3, Despatches from U.S. Consuls in Matamoros, NARA.

57. Captain James A. Ware, Fort Duncan, Texas, to Commanding Officer, Piedras Negras, 23 April 1864, in *War of the Rebellion*, Volume XXXIV, Series I, Part II, 790.

58. Louis Wigfall to J.E. Johnston, 4 January 1864, Box 2R299, Wigfall Papers.

59. King, 340. See also Philip D. Dillard, *Jefferson Davis's Final Campaign: Confederate Nationalism and the Fight to Arm Slaves*, Macon: Mercer U Press, 2017.

as laborers and the like—although both recognized that the Confederacy was doomed unless they could carve out a new role for the Africans. Wigfall, a true believer, would rather destroy the Confederacy than end slavery. Inexorably, "compromises" were floated; one was for the rebels to deploy Negro soldiers but with a key caveat: "let the negroes fight negroes...[as] opposed to white men," meaning the "institution of slavery would still be maintained," then after the traitors' triumph, "the negroes...might be colonized—say to Mexico...or Central America...."[60]

Benjamin had veered well beyond the enslavers' consensus, even enlisting "General [Robert E.] Lee," said to be "strongly in favor [of] our using the Negroes for defense and emancipating them, if necessary for that purpose...." Pragmatically, but unrealistically, he asked querulously, "is it better for the negroes to fight for us or against us." He was also correct in asserting that his plan "will be of more value to us abroad than any diplomacy or treaty"[61]—but it was asking too much for a secession based on perpetual enslavement to conclude with compelled emancipation.

However, Benjamin may well have been more aware of hemispheric trends, for as he was embroiled in this rancorous debate, a loyalist diplomat in Mazatlán was "dreading the approach of Losada (an Indian chief) who came by land from Tepic with two thousand men Indians & Mexicans to cooperate with the French fleet"—along with "Algerine troops."[62] So, the French ally of the rebels was fighting alongside Africans, as the rebels themselves objected to same. All sides found it necessary to align with "non-whites" in defense of white supremacy!

While some rebels were still captivated by the receding nightmare of eternal enslavement of Africans, by February 1865 in Vera Cruz, the news arose about a "fight" that "took place about 6 leagues from this city...between Egyptians"—perhaps Algerians or Nubians or Sudanese—and "400 liberals" aligned with Juárez, "in which the former were defeated with considerable loss.... two thousand more Austrians and Belgians arrived here last week," said a U.S. observer,

60. "Native Georgian" to "Seddon," 29 September 1864, in *War of the Rebellion*, Volume III, Series IV, 693.

61. Ibid., Judah Benjamin to Fred A. Porcher, 21 December 1864, Volume III, Series IV, Section II, 959.

62. B.R. Carman to Secretary Seward, 31 December 1864, Reel 3, Despatches from U.S. Consuls in Mazatlan, NARA.

"making in all about 12,000 that have landed,"[63] as civil war in Mexico escalated, the same was spinning to a close due north.

While Wigfall and Benjamin were quarreling—perversely—about what role Africans would play in rescuing a slaveholders' republic, the Fifth Texas Cavalry Brigade was fighting in Poison Spring, Ark. There they participated in the slaughtering of Negro soldiers in blue—after the men surrendered—instead of taking them prisoner. Indigenes were also active in the massacre with some mutilating the bodies of the dead, as the waters ran red with the blood of the victimized.[64]

It was also in 1864 that this murderous brigade was saluted—"with pride and pleasure"—by the rebel leadership in Indian Territory, just across the border. This was merely one among the "brilliant victories" executed by these "gallant and chivalrous" cutthroats; singled out was the "noble old hero Stand Watie," Cherokee warrior. Again accidentally exposing what concerned them, the leadership "rejoiced to say perfect harmony and goodwill prevailed between the white and Indian troops"—after all, both were fighting to continue enslavement of Africans: thus, their mutual bloodthirstiness "increased good will of the Indian and white troops toward each other"—i.e., bonding over racist slaughter. Actually, this triumph was one among many by these marauders whose "gallantry, energy, enterprise, dash and judgment and completeness of success...has not been surpassed during the war...." Yes, it was concluded with ecstasy, "for the troops of the Indian Territory this has been a year of brilliant success...."[65]

Yet just before this ritualistic back-patting, Stand Waite himself, speaking on behalf of the "Executive Department" of the Cherokee Nation, reported tremblingly that "our own people, en masse with Creeks and the population of Northern Choctaw counties, were driven to take temporary refuge on Red River in Texas, where they at present abide"[66]—i.e., they were driven from Indian Territory as

---

63. D.L. Lane to Secretary Seward, 1 February 1865, Reel 9, Despatches from U.S. Consuls in Vera Cruz, NARA. See also Oral History, Julius Caesar Hill, 12 April 1937, IPP. Reportedly, this U.S. Negro traced his ancestry to northern Sudan, raising the tantalizing possibility that he may have descended from troops dispatched to the continent by Paris in the 1860s.

64. Charles David Grear, "Gano's Brigade: A History of the Fifth Texas Cavalry Brigade, 1863-1864," M.A. thesis, TTU, 2001, 3, 58, 92.

65. Confederate States of America District of Indian Territory, Circulars..., 7 October 1864, Huntington Library.

66. Stand Watie to National Committee, 11 July 1864, in *War of the Rebellion*, Volume XLI, Series I, Part II, 1046.

they were providing service to the rebel state. Lipan and Tonkawa, being perceived as pro-rebel, suffered massacres at the hands of pro-federal Indigenes[67]—though in the end, both were dispossessed further. Indian Territory was torn apart during the Civil War, as Africans became more restive, armed Negro troops abounded in the vicinity, and anti-rebel Indigenes too were up in arms.[68]

One point is worth repeating: Unfortunately—though not altogether surprisingly—there appeared to be a correlation between Indigenes with partial European ancestry (so-called "half breeds") and alignment with rebels and enslavement. Edmond Flint, born in 1852, was enslaved in the Choctaw Nation and found bondage there "not different" from the South as a whole; however, he added, "as a rule, the slave owning Indians were of mixed blood, tho' there were also a few full bloods who owned slaves." Irrespective of ancestry, the "largest slave owners settled along [the] Red River,"[69] close by Texas and gaining strength from there.

Texas sharpshooters, gunslingers and bare-knuckled brawlers had a well-merited reputation for unparalleled skill in slaughter: they had much experience after years of battling Mexicans, Comanches and a growing number of Africans, making them unique in the luridly grotesque art of shedding the blood of opponents. They were sent to headquarters in Richmond, perhaps the most important rebel site, and were stationed along the Potomac, key if Washington were to be taken. They stood alongside Wade Hampton in Virginia, one of the rebels' most celebrated leaders. They were to be found in Yorktown, the 18th-century site of a slaveholders' victory that set the Civil War in motion.[70]

The downside for the rebels was that the overconfidence in holding Texas led to these deployments eastward, which then weakened the defense of Galveston, then Brownsville, to the overall detriment of enslavement.

* * *

The travails of Negro soldiers, which began full bore during the Civil War, did not end there. After loyalists began to occupy part

---

67. Lahti, 114.

68. W.C. Gaines, 24, 25, 32.

69. Oral History, Edmond Flint, 29 November 1937, IPP.

70. Nicholas A. Davis, "The Campaign from Texas to Maryland," Richmond: Presbyterian Committee of Publications of the Confederate States, 1863, Huntington Library.

of Texas, the unscrupulous began to sell back into slavery men who had fled instantly to Union lines[71]—just one more reason why some in Galveston awaited the arrival of a largely African contingent of soldiers by 19 June 1865 before they decided that emancipation was nigh.

At the same time, other loyalists were welcoming Africans who fled to their lines: "they are the laborers of the Army," said one officer, and "work of a very disagreeable character" was "done by them... they are a fine looking set of men—all fair specimen of their native Africa...."[72]

Wigfall could have added that they not only deserted Texas but then donned a blue uniform and returned with rifle in hand. But the walls were closing in on the once grand rebels, and options were limited. In January 1864 Major General Magruder, who presided over a sprawling region stretching from Houston through enchanting New Mexico to the sagebrush of Arizona, confessed, "I called upon the planters of Fort Bend, Matagorda and Brazoria counties for their Negroes to do this work promptly," speaking of war duties; "a number of negroes had been exempted by the Cotton Bureau from impressment," but this ukase was countermanded, as the once sturdy rebel edifice continued to collapse.[73]

And at times they returned in blue with the crimson red of blood in their eyes, bent on retaliation. By early 1864 a federal officer in Texas said, "I have two regiments of colored troops, the first Engineers and Sixteenth Infantry Corps d'Afrique, stationed at Point Isabel and on Brazos Island."[74] It was this realistic phantasm of retaliatory violence that may have induced Major General J.B. Magruder, who was able to retrieve Galveston for the rebels in early 1863 when it seemed to be lost indefinitely, to remark a little more than a year later that those like himself could easily become the "slaves of slaves,"[75] the specter that had haunted enslavers since the institution had arisen in North America.

---

71. J. Holt, Judge Advocate General to President Lincoln, 24 May 1862, in *War of the Rebellion*, Volume VII, Series II, 159.

72. Entry, 9 April 1864, Tilley, *McIntyre*, 326.

73. Major General Magruder to Brigadier General W.R. Boggs, 6 January 1864, in *War of the Rebellion*, Volume XXXIV, Series I, Part II, 830.

74. Ibid., Major General F.J. Herron to Major General E.O.C. Ord, 11 February 1864, Volume XXXIV, Series I, Part II, 295.

75. Ibid., Major General J.B. Magruder to John Slidell, Commissioner to France, 27 April 1864, Volume XXXIV, Series I, Part II, 796.

The actual slaves continued to be a problem for the rebels in the borderlands, however; in early April 1864, the latest complaint in Eagle Pass was that an "officer" of the rebel army had been "robbed" of one of his most valuable possessions: "one negro"[76]—who could just as easily be transformed into an able avenging angel, determined to turn society upside down.

Rebels were panicking as the enslaved began to flee and augment the loyal military. Richmond accused Washington of seeking to "abduct" their unpaid labor force "or to incite them to insurrection or to employ Negroes in war or to overthrow the institution of African slavery and bring on a servile war...." This was akin to a war crime, said the bellowing retort, inconceivable "among civilized nations...."[77]

This hysteria about Negro soldiers infected Austin too. Shortly after Richmond's debate, the same occurred in the Lone Star State. This deployment was "without precedent in its atrocity and unchristian character," was the baleful conclusion. Effortlessly exuding nervousness, the legislators said that the "comparative exemption of our dear State from many of the more dire concomitants of war may have been construed as a cause for our unanimity in sustaining our government." But this was not true, it was noted unconvincingly, as they went a step further to "record our full confidence in the patriotism and ability of President Davis,"[78] the expression of which led to the obvious inference that the opposite was bubbling to the surface and that their leader had just received a kiss of death.

Past misdeeds were haunting Texas at an inopportune moment. In early 1864 a bulletin was received from Kansas about the arrival of "Caddo...about 300 in number. They are partially civilized," said the anthropologically inclined U.S. officer, "and were driven by the rebels from...Texas in consequence of their adherence to the government of the United States," and now were "in a destitute and starving

---

76. Ibid., Francisco Garcia, Piedras Negras to Commander, Eagle Pass, 5 April 1864, Volume XXXIV, Series I, Part III, 738. See also Captain John Ellis, *Indian Fighting on the Texas Frontier*, Amarillo: Russell & Cockrell, 1929, 41. "While I was away, the Indians attacked the ranch owned by Mrs. Twiggs a widow," this in 1864, "and after killing her daughter they captured Mrs. Twiggs, her grandchild and a colored woman, wife of an old Negro called 'Old Brit.'"

77. House of Representatives, Joint Resolution in Reference to the Treatment of Colored Troops, 15 February 1864, Huntington Library.

78. "Joint Resolutions of the State of Texas House of Representatives, May 4, 1864," Huntington Library.

condition."[79] Yet some were doubtlessly capable of retaliation against their tormentors. The tragedy of Indigenes was that no matter who prevailed in this titanic conflict, they were bound to be denuded of resources, perhaps their very lives—unless they engaged in urgent consultations with a foreign power in London, perhaps St. Petersburg/Moscow or even Tokyo then rising, cutting a deal allowing for a rescue.

The dilemma of the Indigenes was exposed in the Choctaw Nation. They were irked that treaties had not been observed by Washington, including the payment of an annuity. Hence, they were prone to deal with a new regime—the rebels—yet by the time of this full realization in 1864, the men in gray were on the verge of subjugation.[80]

Thus by December 1864, as the rebels tipped toward bankruptcy, a node in the Choctaw Nation was designated as the depot for any enslaved "recaptured within the Indian Territory," with the now manacled "turned over to Captain S.V. Smith, battalion [of the] 20th Texas Dismounted Cavalry,"[81] according to a local official. Yes, many of the troops in Indian Territory—especially within the Choctaw Nation—were Texans.[82]

By February 1864 currency speculators should have begun to dump their rebel currency for the report had emerged from the Cherokee Nation that "so far as the rebel Creek, Seminole and Chickasaw nations are concerned, the war is over. They have been destroyed or driven from their country. Those who are not seeking peace are fleeing to Mexico...."[83]

Also fleeing were Navajos in New Mexico, for a movement had arisen to enslave them with loyalist Kit Carson, claiming that this was actually beneficial to them—compared to being cast as prisoners.[84] The Battle of Adobe Walls, where he earned his spurs, was the

---

79. H.N.F. Read, Headquarters, Fort Larned, Kansas to Acting Assistant Adjutant General, Kansas City, Missouri, 10 January 1864, in *War of the Rebellion*, Volume XXXIV, Series I, Part II, 54.

80. Ibid., Brigadier General S.B.Maxey to Lieutenant General E. Kirby Smith, 26 January 1864, Volume XXXIV, Series I, Part II, 994.

81. "Doaksville Choctaw Nation...District Indian Territory," 20 December 1864, Huntington Library.

82. Circular, District Indian Territory, Fort Towson, Choctaw Nation, 25 December 1864, Huntington Library.

83. William A. Phillips, Fort Gibson, Cherokee Nation to "Sir," 24 February 1864, in *War of the Rebellion*, Additions and Corrections, Volume XXXIV, Series I, 108.

84. Lanehart, 33, 34.

second-largest single battle ever fought between the U.S. military and Indigenes on the plains (second to the Little Big Horn in 1876, which it prefigured) as they squared off against the ubiquitous Comanche and their Kiowa comrades. Typical of federal priorities was the bitter reality that by war's end Carson and company had seen far more action against Indigenes than secessionists. He had his hands full since the above Indigenous comrades were joined by Apaches, Arapahos, Cheyenne and Sioux in a broad anti-settler alliance; their raids had increased sharply by 1864. Comanches, per usual, were in the vanguard, pillaging settlers in Texas and delivering the booty next door in New Mexico, validating the term for them derived from the Ute word for "enemy." But sadly, over the decades Comanches had accumulated a full complement of baggage in that their enemies included Pawnees, Osages, Tonkawa, Navajos, Jicarilla Apaches—and more.[85]

Carson, forced into retreat during this epochal battle, was in accord with the rebel officer, Henry Sibley, who thought Indigenes should be enslaved—contrary to John Baylor who favored extermination. Generally, in southern New Mexico—abutting El Paso—these reactionary attitudes prevailed among so-called "Anglo" settlers who generally favored secession.[86] Thus, by October 1864 loyal leaders found themselves in an "exposed condition...I have but a handful of men all told," moaned Brigadier General James Carleton, and "New Mexico troops, except against Indians cannot be relied upon...to fight against Texans...." In sum, settlers had not lost sight of the settler colonial project in the midst of civil war; even Carleton insisted that "no peace should be made with them," meaning the Indigenous, "until they are soundly whipped...they should at once be soundly flogged"[87]—even at the expense of surrendering to invading Texans.

In the topsy-turvy world of early 1864 the loyal army was mulling the point that "our colored troops...are especially qualified for fighting guerrillas [and] could be usefully employed in guarding the entire line of this road from Vicksburg to Galveston.... Texas is said to be full of blacks who will be a valuable auxiliary in our operations," meaning "results of this campaign will be very great. As long

---

85. David A. Pafford, "Kit Carson's Last Fight: The Adobe Walls Campaign of 1864," Ph.D. dissertation, U of New Mexico, 2017, 4, 11, 13, 70, 80, 131, 133.

86. M.K. Nelson, 121, 7. See also Neil B. Carmony, ed., *The Civil War in Apacheland: Sergeant George Hand's Diary, California, Arizona, West Texas, New Mexico, 1861-1864*, Silver City, N.M.: High-Lonesome, 1996.

87. Brigadier General Carleton to Brigadier General Lorenzo Thomas, 9 October 1864, in *War of the Rebellion*, Volume XLI, Series I, Part III, 743.

as we are able to keep the enemy engaged in Texas," Major General Nathaniel Banks was told, "Louisiana and Arkansas will be safe and process of reconstruction can be carried on without interruption...." Already, his forces held "the harbor of Matagorda, the best on the coast, next to Galveston...."[88]

Such was the dilemma faced by the rebels, as their once seemingly invincible project headed toward a crash, with the enslaved being at the heart of the matter. By the spring of 1864 Washington again was considering the "occupation of Galveston," which if attained would have been a veritable death blow to secession's pretensions. "Whoever occupies Galveston in force," it was said accurately by an officer in blue, "holds the state of Texas. All the railroads of the state terminate there. All the inland navigable streams empty into the Gulf at easy striking distance from that point...."[89]

Ironically, Governor Lubbock of Texas concurred. Obsequiously addressing "His Excellency President Davis," he portrayed his state as the key to secession's fortunes, reinforcing the presumed belief of the Richmond resident that he did "not underrate the importance of Texas," since "were it be overrun its loss would draw after it Louisiana and Arkansas"—and he could have added adjoining states falling like dominoes, reaching to Virginia—"for Texas is the granary which nourishes the armies of the trans-Mississippi department...." The message? Send arms west right away. He too endorsed reliance more on African labor since if "controlled by a sufficiency of white wagon masters and overseers"—questionable since the Africans were prone to desert and their "controllers" were needed to fight—"they make most excellent teamsters and stock drivers. The Confederate government can control their services," he assured dubiously.[90]

There may be none more deluded or as immersed in self-deception than leaders on the brink of a catastrophic military defeat, especially one that destroys an entire system of production. For by February 1865 even the U.S. consul in Matamoros had noticed that Texas was "filled to overflowing with Negroes held as slaves, who have been sent hither from the states of Louisiana, Mississippi, Georgia, South Carolina and even Virginia in order to place them beyond the reach of

---

88. Ibid., D.C. Houston, Office of the Chief Engineer-New Orleans to Major General Banks, 22 January 1864, Volume XXXIV, Series I, Part I, 125.

89. Ibid., Brigadier General T.W. Sherman, New Orleans to Washington, D.C., 9 May 1864, Volume XXXIV, Series I, Part II, 516.

90. Ibid., Governor Lubbock to Jefferson Davis, 13 July 1864, Volume XLI, Series I, Part II, 1005.

the national arms."[91] This was more bad news for Africans and Indigenes, says scholar Jesse Dorsett: "It was a cliché among Negroes in Texas to say that these slave owners, newly arrived...on the eve of the collapse of the Confederacy were among the meanest of the human species,"[92] overfulfilling Texas's overflowing quota of bile and vitriol.

Sonny Greer was born enslaved in 1850 in Arkansas but recalled later that his "master" fled during the war to Texas with his unique property in tow; they settled near the Red River in Clarksville, where he found "refugees from all parts of the Indian Territory and Arkansas" who "came into Texas along [the] Red River during the war...."[93] William Lee Starr too was born enslaved, in Indian Territory in his case, but he too recalled his "master" escaping to a Rusk County, Texas, "plantation" during the war.[94] Other slicker enslavers, sensing the direction of emancipation winds, began a fire sale of the enslaved; that was the recollection of the enslaved man William Pierson, who wound up in Muskogee, Okla., though born in Virginia. "They tried to dispose of them, most any way they could," purveying them to obliviously unobservant settlers in Indian Territory.[95]

Morris Sheppard was born enslaved in Webbers Falls, in what is now Oklahoma, in 1847, but as the institution writhed in its death throes, his mother and two sisters were sold to more optimistic enslavers in Texas: "I never did see them any more," he cried.[96] In scenes reminiscent of the horrid "Trail of Tears," which propelled Indigenes to Indian Territory in the first place, the Negro Jordan D. Folsom recalled later how his grandmother and others were sold to slave dealers from Alabama to "wealthy Indians" who "tied the slaves together and drove them along the road just like cattle" until they reached the Kiamichi River, a tributary of the better known Red River, in adjacent Texas.[97]

That is, even as rebels were descending into a morass of defeat, they were creating a morass of new problems for the future. Texas, with an expanding Negro population, became a target-rich environment

---

91. Consul Etchison to Major General Hurlbut, Commander-Department of the Gulf, 27 February 1865, Reel 3, Despatches from U.S. Consuls in Matamoros, NARA.

92. Jesse Dorsett, "Blacks in Reconstruction Texas, 1865-1877," Ph.D. dissertation, TCU, 1981, 84 (abbrev. Dorsett).

93. Oral History, Sonny Greer, 18 August 1937, IPP.

94. Ibid., Oral History, William Lee Starr, ca. 1937-1938.

95. Ibid., Oral History, William Pierson, ca. 1937-1938.

96. Ibid., Oral History, Morris Sheppard, 22 February 1937.

97. Ibid. Oral History, Jordan D. Folsom, 17 February 1938.

for revenge-seeking white supremacists, complicating an effective postwar dispensation. Texas was also being filled to the brim with enslavers—soon to be defrocked—who would willingly join the revenge seekers, creating a hurricane of terror in the Lone Star State. This tragic state of affairs also sheds light on why federal troops had to show up in Galveston to compel emancipation—not because the Africans were unaware but because they still faced a bevy of brutalizers bent on barring the disintegration of a highly profitable system of production.

* * *

The rebels had aligned with the French occupiers, at a time when the forces of Cortina and Juárez were increasingly gaining momentum in the borderlands. In the spring of 1864 Texas secessionists were in a state of panic, especially out west near Eagle Pass, a stone's throw from Mexico. "Depredations committed by Yankees and renegades" were escalating, said Captain J.B. Weyman of the rebels. "If the course pursued by the Mexican authorities at present is continued," he wailed, "this whole frontier will be broken up...." Frighteningly, this was "tolerated, if not protected, by the Mexican authorities," who would "not deliver these thieves up when we identify them."[98]

As the rebel roof was caving in, stress intensified, meaning fervent squabbling between and among the once proud secessionists. It was also in 1864 that Santiago Vidaurri, the Confederate of Mexican origin, was furious at the blockage barring export of cotton southward which in turn meant—according to a military man—"no goods or merchandise" were allowed "to pass into Texas....." This led to the vituperative claim that "those Christ killing Jews" were "sucking the heart's blood out of the Confederates in Texas.... I will not under any circumstances leave here until I get revenge of the thieving Jews of this place," said T.P. McManus speaking from Piedras Negras. He was vociferous since "my expressman was waylaid" and "shot three times before he could get out his pistol. He was surrounded by 4 Mexicans, who, I presume were hired for that purpose by Jew cotton speculators" and "shot through the head."[99]

98. Captain Weyman, Commanding Post-Eagle Pass to Captain E.P. Turner, Houston, 5 April 1864, in *War of the Rebellion*, Volume XXXIV, Series I, Part III, 736.

99. Ibid., T.P. McManus to Major General N.J.T. Dana, 13 February 1864, Volume XXXIV, Series I, Part II, 316. See also General Benjamin Butler to

Unavoidably, the bigotry that propelled enslavement of Africans was spreading like an out-of-control virus infecting nearby communities. This too was not only another sign of the imminent collapse of the rebel project but, as well, how loyalists were not immune from this pestilence too. Yet another loyal military man spoke warmly of John Webber, patriarch of a racially integrated family in the borderlands, who was characterized as "'a very loyal friend of ours,'" meaning federals. He was essential in the important project "'to make the roads in his neighborhood difficult and hazardous for rebels and the Jews and speculators who are furnishing them....'"[100]

Loyalists were collapsing morally too—boding ill for Reconstruction—paying a stiff price for countenancing enslavement within the republic, as rebels were collapsing politically and economically. In an undated report, likely from late 1863 or early 1864, rebel leaders moaned that the "whole line of our seacoast from Virginia to Texas" was in jeopardy, because of the U.S. Navy, while "escape of our slaves" proceeded apace, as some made it "out to the vessels of the enemy seaward," making the "drain...immense...." The "low estimate" of the "number of slaves absconded" was "at 20,000"—much too low retrospectively—meaning "demoralization of the negroes that remain...." The absconders were, bizarrely, termed "traitors," presupposing they were citizens with reciprocal allegiances. Yet they continued to "go over to the enemy and afford him aid and comfort": all true. "Negroes occupy the position of spies": all true and the case for some time. They were "employed in secret expeditions for obtaining information by transmission of newspapers" and continued to "act as guides," which "proved of great value...." Worse, there was now the "threat of an army of trained Africans for the coming fall and winter campaigns," driven by "a lawless set of runaways...."[101]

Also true. For they were running away, far and wide.

Salmon P. Chase, Treasury Secretary, 22 October 1862, in Butler Correspondence, Volume I, 394.

100. Irby, 159.

101. Report from R.Q. Mallard, P.W. Fleming and E. Stacy, Liberty County, Georgia, n.d., in *War of the Rebellion*, Volume IV, Series III, 36.

Chapter *17*

Treason's End in Texas? 1865

By August 1865, well after the rebels had surrendered—formally—at Appomattox, Washington was so concerned about a deployment of armed Africans just south of Texas, that the victorious republic was now considering sending U.S. Negroes to the source of this potential problem: Egypt.[1]

This was an aspect of the untidily disordered climate rendered by the ongoing effort to dismember Mexico, which reached a crescendo in 1836, then descended thereafter until France seized upon the chaos, intervened militarily and began deploying contingents of armed Africans to fortify their occupation, challenging U.S. security. An architect of 1836, Ashbel Smith asked portentously on the 40th anniversary of this adventure—and the centenary of the similarly inclined 1776—if in the future annexation would be seen as generative of secession in 1861—then defeat in 1865.[2] Yes, after Texas joined the rapacious republic in 1845, its example helped to replicate its original secession in 1836 but, unfortunately, as I write, the final act of this drama has yet to reveal itself.

In essence, the ceremonial closure of the U.S. Civil War did not necessarily bring "peace," not only because diehards in Texas particularly refused to capitulate, but instead retreated to Mexico and fueled the war there. Supposedly, there were 50% more soldiers in Texas in late 1865 than had served in the entire U.S. army in 1860, a sign of how the flames of conflict continued to leap upward dangerously. As noted, slavery had expanded in Texas during the war, making it all the more difficult to uproot—hence, the massive deployment of armed men, including thousands of newly freed Africans, which served to infuriate those who had thought this bondage was normalized and inevitable.[3]

---

1. Charles Hale to Secretary Seward, 26 August 1865, Reel 4, Despatches from U.S. Consuls in Alexandria, NARA.

2. A. Smith, 13 August 1876.

3. Gregory Downs, *After Appomattox: Military Occupation and the Ends of War*, Cambridge: Harvard U Press, 2015, 27, 99.

Hunt County in Texas was not unusual. By 1860 fears of insurrections by the enslaved gripped the imaginations of Euro-Americans.
After the Civil War, the other war—that between Africans and those
who sought to keep them in chains—accelerated with agents of Washington attacked, Negro children assaulted and their schoolhouses
torched. Negro churches were treated likewise, while preachers and
teachers were subject to murder. Whatever possessions the emancipated had often were plundered.[4]

Edward A. Pollard, responsible for the still poisonous "Lost Cause"
coinage of the rebels, whitewashing their treason and enslaving, in
the early postwar riotous climate looked longingly to Texas as the
"last hope of the Confederacy," which remains true. He dismissed
Appomattox as the final act of treason and instead pointed to a
"skirmish near Brazos.... with the surrender of Gen. Smith the war
ended...." Much too late, he dismissed the very idea of "King Cotton"
as "silly...." But like many of the conquered, he barked he "would
sooner be under the government of England or France than under a
Union with men who have shown that they cannot keep good faith
and are the most barbarous and inhuman as well as treacherous of
mankind...." France may have been placed on this list unthinkingly
since Pollard conceded that a "few weeks before Richmond fell...a
messenger from France had arrived on the coast of North Carolina
and was making his way overland to Richmond with the news of the
recognition of the Southern Confederacy by the Emperor Napoleon!"[5]
Instead, this abortive recognition plan was executed post-April 1865
with the rebels regrouping in Mexico.

According to General Philip H. Sheridan of the loyalists, his superior, General Ulysses S. Grant, "looked upon the invasion of Mexico
by Maximilian as a part of the rebellion itself, because of the encouragement that invasion had received from the confederacy and that
our success in putting down secession would never be complete
until the French and Austrian invaders were compelled to quit the
territory of our sister republic...." But Secretary Seward was nervous, fearing being drawn into a "war with European powers...."
Grant won the strategic fracas.[6]

As noted, Indian Territory was broken by the war: this appalling
situation was complicated further when the enslaved there were

---

4. James A. Hathcock, "The Role of Violence in Hunt County, Texas
During Reconstruction," M.S. thesis, UNT, 2004, 18, 20, 53.

5. Pollard, 725-726, 363.

6. *Personal Memoirs of* Philip *Henry Sheridan, General United States Army,
Volume II*, New York: Appleton, 1904, 210 (abbrev. Sheridan, *Memoirs*).

freed. However, many Indigenous leaders thought that incorporating Africans into their ranks was preposterous: how could Washington ask Indigenous to do what it had yet to do? Worse, a reign of terror was unleashed against this former property as they were largely blamed for the post-April 1865 instability and upheaval. Many Indigenes blamed both Washington and the so-called "half breeds" who backed secession, while Africans were being victimized.[7]

Still, Indigenes were pushed further down the road of reparations than Dixie, so some Africans received land on which oil was discovered, creating riches to the point where an early Negro scholar said drily, "This wealth had a great influence on many of these people"[8]—and also many Euro-Americans too, who in 1921 in the so-called "Tulsa Massacre" struck back with venom and plundered these Africans.[9]

It was not just oil that attracted greedy settlers. R.L. Nichols of Pauls Valley, Okla., recalled later that after the war ended, "many of the slave negroes became wealthy by raising cattle and horses as they [had] free access to as fine a range as there ever was in any country...."[10]

Yet well before 1921 Negroes were confronting controversy because of the peculiarities of Indian Territory and its singular Reconstruction. Many Negroes far and wide moved there post-April 1865 and, as W.L. Allen recalled, "intermarried with the Cherokee Freedmen," gaining a foothold in property ownership, then leasing same to Euro-Americans—who, inexorably, sought to take advantage. He had to employ his "Winchester rifle" to settle one raging dispute.[11]

In sum, Indian Territory was upended by the time the war concluded. "There was never any nation of the people divided against each other like the Civil War divided the Cherokees," for "many of the Indians were wealthy slave owners," said Annie Elize Hendrix, a Cherokee born in 1852. There were "assassinations, robbing and burning of homes," while "Confederate factions moved their families south to the Choctaw Nation and those [who] supported the Union cause moved north into Kansas"[12]—then returned post-April 1865 baying for blood. Likely targeted was Robert Jones, reputed

---

7. Abel, 211, 273, 295. See also Annie Heloise Abel, *The American Indian as Slaveholder and Secessionist*, Lincoln: U of Nebraska Press, 1992.

8. Memoirs of W. Sherman Savage, 1979, Huntington Library.

9. Randy Krehbiel, *Tulsa, 1921: Reporting a Massacre*, Norman: U of Oklahoma Press, 2019 (abbrev. Krehbiel).

10. Oral History, R.L. Nichols, 22 December 1937, IPP.

11. Ibid., Oral History, W.L. Allen, 22 September 1937.

12. Ibid., Oral History, Annie Elize Hendrix, 3 March 1938.

to be the largest slaveholder in Indian Territory; he represented the Choctaw Nation at the rebel Congress in Richmond.[13]

According to Henry and Ida Falconer of Indian Territory, those like Jones "promised more liberal agreements to take the place of [Washington's] treaties," and "these promises...actuated most... Choctaw people to cast their lot with the cause of the South...." But Appomattox commenced the onslaught of outlaws in Indian Territory, including the Choctaw Nation, as disorder reigned supreme, vitiating pacts of all sorts; "lawlessness...intruded" was their prim formulation.[14]

And if not Jones, there were Creeks, the family of M. Yargee Ross, born in 1844, who acknowledged that "my grandfather...was one of the largest slave owners among the Muskogee.... he became the largest slave owner among his tribe." Tellingly, "the only English words she heard her father speak were 'Damn Nigger.'"[15]

Ineluctably, Indians were targeted in Indian Territory. Ben Williams worked as a Texas Ranger during the war—he had a father who was half-Cherokee—as he sought "to aid in the quelling of the Mexicans and Comanches...."[16] For according to John Criner, born in 1850, speaking later from Ardmore, Okla., of his rebel father, he recollected that "their greatest trouble during the war was with the Comanche Indians...."[17]

*   *   *

It was not just Mexico that received refugees from Dixie. Brazil and Cuba too accepted rebels in what one scholar has termed the "largest emigrant movement in United States history, rivaled only by African American 'Back to Africa'" campaigns. Rebel Rear Admiral John Tucker fled to Peru, obtained a plantation which he dubbed Manassas in honor of his beloved South, just as his comrade, Henry Price, wound up in Venezuela, while others wound up in Egypt and elsewhere in what amounted to an expanded version of "Manifest Destiny."[18] An estimated 5000 Negroes and "whites" moved to

---

13. Ibid., Oral History, Victor Locke, 25 October 1937.

14. Ibid., Oral History, Henry and Ida Falconer, ca. 1837-1838.

15. Ibid., Oral History, Muskogee Yargee Ross, ca. 1938.

16. Ibid., Oral History, Ben Williams, 12 July 1937.

17. Ibid., Oral History, John Criner, ca. 1937-1938.

18. Justin Horton, "The Second Lost Cause: Post-National Confederate Imperialism in the Americas," M.A. thesis, East Tennessee State U, 2007, 5, 9, 12, 51.

Mexico between 1865 and 1870, disproportionately from Texas; their scraps with Cortina forces as they crossed the border, something with which they were familiar, provided a reason why Virginians and Carolinians were less prone to do so—though Governor Isham Harris of Tennessee joined this perverse hegira with his unique property. Eliza McHatton, an enslaver from Louisiana, first moved to Texas, then to Mexico by 1864—where these Africans promptly fled from her control. Texas also provided 103 of the 154 families that moved to Brazil from 1865 to 1875.[19]

The traitors had not relinquished their idea of overthrowing the government in Washington and extending bondage of U.S. Negroes, this time from Mexico and Cuba and, least of all, faraway Brazil. It is the most perverse of ironies today that those who preen as the most patriotic are the lineal descendants of those who sought to rule in league with a foreign power.

Texans were hardly unfamiliar with this South American Empire under the rule of Dom Pedro II. Thomas J. Morgan, was secretary of the legation there from 1847-1850 and prior to that had raised a company of fighters for war in Texas in 1836.[20]

Among these migrating families was that of slaveholding A. Thomas Oliver in Austin County, who owned 100 humans—but post-April 1865 this wealth dwindled to evanescence, so he and his brood moved to Brazil, where abolition did not occur until 1888 and where he continued to wallow in human slavery. Leonard Groce planned to follow him; before 1865 his plantation if stretched out in a single line, would be a mile wide and 100 miles long.[21] Lu Lee was slated to follow them both, but from the other side of the class chasm. "I went back to Master Henry's house," said this former slave much later, "and he said he was going to take me and my sister to the free state of Brazil where they could keep slaves."[22] William Stewart, a Negro born in Mississippi in 1855, had a different remembrance speaking from Tulsa in 1937: he had been sold to the prominent Longstreet family of Georgia but after the war observed, "slave owners took

19. Todd W. Wahlstrom, *The Southern Exodus to Mexico: Migration Across the Borderlands after the American Civil War*, Lincoln: U of Nebraska Press, 2015, iv, xix-xx, 2, 34, 38, 40 (abbrev. Wahlstrom).

20. Note in Tom Chaffin and Michael David Cohen, eds., *Correspondence of James Polk, Volume XII, January-July 1847*, Knoxville: U of Tennessee Press, 2013, 297.

21. A.D. Ivan, 55.

22. Account of Lu Lee in A. Waters, 9-19, 18.

their slaves to Cuba and other southern islands. I remember seeing them leave."[23]

Thus, by late June 1865 it was like old times in Tampico. The "feeling in this place," said the message to Washington, "is still too much in favor of the late southern insurrection"; hence, "vessels of war" were requested urgently.[24] Governor Pendleton Murrah of Texas considered Brazil before galloping to Mexico, guided by a "mulatto Negro named George...," Like others of that ilk, the runaway executive was quite worried about being intercepted by Cortina's men. His comrade Magruder was among those who found irony in the flight of rebels to Mexico, after so many of them had seceded from same in 1836, then further dismembered this nation by 1848.[25]

They may have gone but largely had not been forgotten. Alexander Watkins Terrell, former rebel military leader, also exited to Mexico from Texas, where he joined—he said—the "army of occupation" at the "rank of colonel...in the imperial army." However, this was instrumental insofar as he insisted that if "an effort was made by [Washington] to drive the French troops out of Mexico, the struggle in the South would be renewed for France would become the ally of the Southern States," reigniting secession. "We had long been dreaming of French intervention" on the premise that the "Confederacy might rise again under foreign aid...." Terrell and the like were profoundly serious about subverting Washington. But Paris may also have been aware that Texas traitors had not ruled out the possibility as late as May 1865 of invading Mexico, ousting France and taking over, making these men the most unreliable of partners.[26]

Rebel military hero Jubal Early was also not the most resolute of partners. He too tried to settle there but decided—appropriately— early on that Mexico was "'an infernal humbug,'" with no chance of waging war with Washington as he had hoped. For he confessed openly "'my hatred for the infernal Yankees is increasing daily, if possible,'" said after stopping by Havana. For, typically, Texas was wracked with tumult, complicating his intended "'route over the Rio

23. Oral History, William Stewart, 20 October 1937, IPP.

24. Consul Franklin Chase to Acting Secretary of State William Hunter, 27 June 1865, Reel 4, Despatches from U.S. Consuls in Tampico, NARA.

25. Alexander Watkins Terrell, *From Texas to Mexico and the Court of Maximilian in 1865*, Dallas: Book Club of Texas, 1933, 7-8, 16, 20 (abbrev. A.W. Terrell).

26. A.W. Terrell, vii, 53, 54. See also Benn Pitman, ed., *The Trials for Treason at Indianapolis, Disclosing the Plans for Establishing a Northwestern Confederacy*, Cincinnati: Stach & Baldwin, 1865.

Grande [which] had become impracticable, on account of robbers and guerrillas...."'" Yet he made it to Mexico "'hoping there might be war with the U.S.,'" adding with presumed finality, "'I shall never return to the States unless I can come back under the Confederate flag.'"[27]

Early was an unusual fellow, a confirmed bachelor who—says his empathetic biographer—was attended to by a Negro retainer assiduously. Yet, the attendee "had such an antipathy for Negroes that he would not allow Charles [the enslaved attender] to drink in saloons kept by Negroes or in which other Negroes were allowed to drink"— and, of course, "not a Negro was in attendance" at this retainer's funeral.[28]

Also adding to the turmoil in Texas was the ongoing influx of foreigners of various stripes. There were tens of thousands of French combatants during the Civil War, not including those in Mexico; likewise for Germans and Irish, many of them winding up in the borderlands after the war formalistically ended.[29]

In sum, Texas was enduring a wrenching transition as enslaved and emancipated Africans arrived, along with Europeans who were being absorbed in an overall "white" community that had distinguished itself over the centuries precisely with its antipathy to those defined as "black." This was bound to be a combustible recipe for violent messiness.

Although many settlers in the borderlands were hotly opposed to the Juárez forces combating the French occupiers, General Philip Sheridan—a stellar fighter—was sent to this same region with a veteran Negro detachment under his command. He was accompanied by a still staggering 52,000 men, mostly African and battle-tested, with 30,000 sent to the Rio Grande where their presence was intimidating.[30]

---

27. William D. Hoyt, Jr., "New Light on General Jubal A. Early after Appomattox," *Journal of Southern History*, 9 (No. 1, February 1943): 113-116, 113, 114, 116.

28. William Parker Snow, *Southern Generals, Their Lives and Campaigns, Volume II*, New York: Richardson, 1866, [clipping pasted inside cover], Huntington Library (abbrev. W.P. Snow). See also Jubal Early, *A Memoir of the Last Year for Independence in the Confederate States of America Containing an Account of the Operations of His Commands in the Year 1864 and 1865*, Lynchburg: Button, 1867.

29. Sainlaude, 185. See also Howard Jones, *Blue and Gray Diplomacy: A History of Union and Confederate Foreign Relations*, Chapel Hill: U of North Carolina Press, 2010.

30. González-Quiroga, 233.

Sensing the state of play, many of these men defected to the Juárez forces—this lengthening list included the pioneer Negro historian George Washington Williams, who announced in his epochal text about Negro soldiers that he served as "officer of the Republican forces of the Mexican army...."[31] For a number of years Negro soldiers outnumbered other federal forces in Texas at a rate of three to one. Black enlisted men sold weapons illicitly to Juárez's forces and encouraged desertions from those of Maximilian. Other Negroes followed Washington Williams into Juárez's ranks. The census of 1900 showed Cameron and Hidalgo counties as possessing the highest rates of interracial marriage involving at least one Negro spouse in the U.S. at that time, mostly of Black men wedding women of Mexican origin. The problem with this deployment was that the strategic objective of Washington upon vanquishing the rebels was to administer the same to Indigenes and, tragically, many Negroes considered it to be an index of citizenship to cooperate in this crime against humanity.[32]

However, such Negro gallivanting further alienated settlers banking on a French victory so as to extend their treason and bondage. Robert E. Lee, the maestro of treason, considered the Texan brigades as his primary shock troops, many of whom were returning home after the ignominious defeat formalized in April 1865. The resultant raging turbulence in Texas induced General Sheridan to utter his now telling remark that if he owned both the Lone Star State and hell—he would rent out the former and reside in the latter.[33]

31. George Washington Williams, *A History of the Negro Troops in the War of the Rebellion, 1861-1865*, New York: Harper & Brothers, 1888, ix. See also Commission for United States Colored Troops, U.S. War Department, 1864-1865, Huntington Library. This document concerns the Negro cavalry and artillery men denoted as the "Corps d'Afrique." See also W. Stephen McBride, "From the Bluegrass to the Rio Grande: Kentucky's Colored Troops on the Border, 1866-1867," in Bacha-Garza, *Civil War*, 197-221.

32. James Leiker, "The Black Military Experience in the Rio Grande Valley," in Bacha-Garza, *Civil War*, 249-268, 256, 265. See also Michelle M. Mears, *And Grace Will Lead Me Home: African American Freedmen Communities of Austin, Texas, 1865-1928*, Lubbock: TTU Press, 2009.

33. William Lee Richter, "The Army in Texas During Reconstruction, 1865-1870," Ph.D. dissertation, LSU and Agricultural and Mechanical College, 1970, 14, 63, 70, 212 (abbrev. W.L. Richter). See also Judge J.W. Stevens, *Reminiscences of the Civil War: A Soldier in Hood's Texas Brigade, Army of Northern Virginia*, Hillsboro, Texas: Hillsboro Mirror Print, 1902. See also John C. West, *A Texan in Search of a Fight: Being the Diary and Letters of a Private Soldier in Hood's Texas Brigade*, Waco: Texian, 1969.

And so began the torturous path from war to Reconstruction to a new status quo: Jim Crow.

General Sheridan had been posted opposite Piedras Negras in Fort Duncan by mid-1853. He also had served in Indian Territory and knew Lieutenant Jerome Napoleon Bonaparte, who resigned in 1854 to accept service in Paris. He shared the genocidal impulses toward Indigenes, reflecting in Laredo on the "predatory incursions of these savages" (referring to "Lipan and Comanche Indians"), and he also knew a "smattering" of Spanish. The latter came in handy when he and his troops crossed the border in hot pursuit, "but the Mexicans quickly closed in around the Indians," he said dolefully, and "they escaped...." A factor in his evaluation was that "inhabitants of this frontier of Mexico were strongly marked with Indian characteristics, particularly with those of the Comanche type," as "few of the physical traits of the Spaniard remained...."[34]

*   *   *

By January 1865 secession was reeling, but that did not mean that war in the borderlands would end anytime soon. General U.S. Grant knew that William Gwin, a former U.S. Senator but then "a rebel of the most virulent order," had got himself appointed "governor" of Sonora. This was a "great danger," he said: "watch this matter closely."[35] Also worthy of watching was Edmund Kirby Smith, rebel leader, who early in 1865 sent a delegation to France led by the so-called "Lafayette of the South," Major General Polignac, with a clear brief: enhanced French intervention to salvage secession.[36]

But Polignac was affected by the bigotry that inhered in enslavement of Africans and massive dispossession. For despite being described as a "French gentleman of ancient lineage and brigadier in the Confederate army," mossback "Texans swore that a Frenchman, whose very name they could not pronounce should never command them and mutiny was threatened...."[37]

Despite these signals of impending collapse, rebel Senator W.S. Oldham, speaking from Richmond, rather arrogantly and unrealistically in January 1865 rejected a proposal from certain federals to

34. Sheridan, *Memoirs,* Volume I, 15, 18, 20, 25, 30, 33.

35. General Grant to Major General McDowell, 8 January 1865, in *War of the Rebellion, Volume L, Series I, Part II,* 1118.

36. Daddysman 1976, 287. See also Alwyn Barr, *Polignac's Texas Brigade,* College Station: TA&MU Press, 1998.

37. R. Taylor, 153.

"reform the Constitution" and "forever guarantee the institution of African slavery," a proposal aimed at the bulwark of secession: his own Lone Star State. He denounced this "insidious policy" to "divide and rule," though his sensitivity to the "appeal...made to our love of property..." was a recognition that the proposal was hardly far-fetched. But what tipped the scales was that his interlocutors were part of a team that had "armed our own slaves," an unforgivable sin and, secondarily had "recruited from the scum of Europe" to prevail, presumably failing in galvanizing compatriots.[38]

That is, by early 1865 it did not appear that secessionists—at least in Texas—were on the verge of surrender. Indeed, by late February Secretary of State Seward was enlightened about the "great many Americans here" in Mexico City and, to his consternation, "very few of these that lately came to this city can be classified as loyal citizens." Foremost among them was Pierre Soulé, of French extraction, who had served in the U.S. Senate before defecting to treason and still spoke English with a strong French accent.[39] However, there was a sign of retreat—in order to advance. Soulé's mission then was "to form a Louisiana colony near Puebla,"[40] as rebels were in the process of forming a beachhead of resistance to continue the struggle from due south. Countering this arrival was the presence in Mexico City of a trickle of U.S. Negroes, Kenny Barnes being the latest,[41] just as Soulé had decamped there.

At the same time, eastward in Tampico, the historic bastion of solidarity with the rebels, bales of cotton continued to arrive from Matamoros—"daily" was the sad refrain in February 1865.[42] However, "King Cotton," Dixie's presumed trump card, was steadily being demoted—"Princeling Cotton" may have been more apt—and not just on the coast of Mexico. That same month the message from Alexandria, Egypt, was that this commodity "overshadows everything else; even the production of breadstuffs, heretofore a principal article...has largely declined" as cotton seized the fields. The "export of cotton has increased in prodigious proportions," said the awestruck

38. Speech of Hon. W.S. Oldham of Texas, On the Resolutions of the State of Texas, Concerning Peace, Reconstruction and Independence in the Confederate States Senate, January 30, 1865, AAS.

39. J.M. Morgan, 76.

40. Consul Marcus Otterbourg to Secretary Seward, 27 February 1865, Reel 6, Despatches from U.S. Consuls in Mexico City, NARA.

41. Ibid., E. Thulle to Consul, 22 February 1865.

42. W. Wakefield, New Orleans to Secretary Seward, 17 February 1865, Reel 4, Despatches from U.S. Consuls in Tampico, NARA.

U.S. emissary; in 1861 the estimate was 60 million pounds produced, but by 1864 the figure had leapt skyward to 173 million pounds. Exponential growth would continue, it was thought, since European immigration had increased—"two or three thousand" weekly—while "gold and silver have poured into the country...." At that moment dockside in this Mediterranean port were a mere three U.S.-flagged ships, but there were 17 vessels there built in the republic[43]—with the former figure set to increase as cotton exports increased.

By late March 1865, days before Appomattox, immigrants also continued to arrive in Mexico City—the U.S. envoy counted them "at the rate of two to three hundred a month, most of them are French"—a bad omen for those who wanted a total cessation of the war in the U.S. or its southern neighbor. "Belgian and Austrian soldiers" were a constant presence too, he said, though some wanted to "take service in the United States," which may have been a poisoned chalice.

Furthermore, Texans were also settling, evidently for the long haul. They were among those who had "invested capital in church property,"[44] which was considerable. Also considerable was the growing presence of immigrants from the neighbor due north in Vera Cruz, a "large number" were "already employed" at the local English-language publication,[45] said a spectator.

The last gasp for the traitors seemed to arise at the same time, March 1865—appropriately—with John Baylor in New Mexico,[46] the most resolute proponent of genocide, though this was accurate only in the most orthodox sense. Even Jefferson Davis found Baylor's draconian policies reprehensible,[47] a kind of disunity on a fundamental matter that did not augur well for the rebels. This was the kind of incoherence that often afflicts an elite class wracked with conflict: contradictorily, both policies are pursued. Thus, as Baylor was seeking to liquidate every Indigene in sight, Davis by early 1865 found it "certainly desirable to secure friendly relations with all the tribes on the borders of...Texas," including those being hammered by Baylor, "and to make them auxiliary to operations against the enemy on the

---

43. Charles Hale to Secretary Seward, 24 February 1865, Reel 3, Despatches from U.S. Consuls in Alexandria, NARA.

44. Consul Marcus Otterbourg to "Sir," Reel 5, Despatches from U.S. Consuls in Mexico City, NARA.

45. Report, 2 March 1865, Reel 9, Despatches from U.S. Consuls in Vera Cruz, NARA.

46. Waite, 292.

47. B.C. Curtis, 81-82.

plains might best relieve" his forces; an "employment of a battalion of the Creeks or the Cherokees" was his desired option.[48]

In Anderson County, Texas, that same month there was little sign of imminent surrender. The federals captured mail from there that revealed a "great abundance of corn in Texas"; in fact "corn crops" were "better last year than they have been for years past and there has been more rain in Texas since the 1st of January than during the other portions of time I have been in Texas," according to this target of surveillance.[49] It was possible, per a subsequent investigation, that a German postmaster assisted in gaining access to this peculation.[50]

However, the federals did not pilfer what may have been their most significant intervention from the rebels: it was in March 1865 that the Freedmen's Bureau was authorized, arguably the republic's first social welfare organization and the beginning of a more muscular role for Washington that still receives sharp rebuke from secession's heirs.[51]

Appomattox was 9 April 1865, but Texas, which had escaped severe damage during the war, where the key ports of Galveston and Brownsville switched back and forth from rebel to loyal control, where Africans armed and otherwise continued to arrive—Texas remained enmeshed in battle. Days later Cortina with 600 men was up to the usual: besieging Matamoros, while his frequent sparring partner, Carbajal was busily organizing a force of Texans on the frontier to unite with likeminded Mexican forces.[52]

Yet the latter group found Appomattox "alarming in the extreme," as they wallowed in "insecurity," according to an observer, while their opponents led by Juárez "could not conceal their emotions of joy...."[53] But insecurity of a kind conjoined the two sides as both intended to soldier on.

By 15 April 1865 even a self-described Texas "private" thought "the war would be continued west of the [Mississippi] river and his state

---

48. Jefferson Davis to Secretary of War, 5 January 1865, in *War of the Rebellion*, Volume III, Series IV, 961-962.

49. A. Rumple to Dear Friends, 3 March 1865, Captured Mail Collection, VaHS-R.

50. Report from Caleb G. Forshey, 28 March 1866 in U.S. Congress. Joint Commission on Reconstruction. Report: Florida, Louisiana, Texas, Washington, D.C.: Government Printing Office, 1866,UT-A.

51. B.C. Curtis, 117.

52. Consul Franklin Chase to Assistant Secretary F.W. Seward, 18 April 1865, Despatches from U.S. Consuls in Tampico, NARA.

53. Ibid., Consul Chase to Assistant Secretary Seward, 26 April 1865.

could be "reinforced" thereby; the "patriotism" of himself and his comrades was "irreproachable, notwithstanding they had heard that the armies of Generals Lee, Johnston and Taylor had surrendered." But not surrendering was General E. Kirby Smith, who insisted "'you possess the means of long resisting invasion. You have hopes of succor from abroad,'" Mexico and France, perhaps others. General Magruder, the stalwart of Galveston, reminded them that "'six hundred Frenchmen under the first Napoleon, recaptured France from her enemies,'" whereas the "'army of the Trans-Mississippi Department is larger, in finer order.'" There was mass support for this campaign since "'our armies can…be supplied in almost any part of Texas…,'" and at any rate, as Major General John Forney contended, reports of a rebel surrender were a precursor of what came to be called "fake news." Presumably he was convinced when E. Kirby Smith and his men surrendered in New Orleans by May 1865,[54] especially since just before this bold maneuver, Smith reputedly was negotiating an even bolder move: transferring his forces to the self-styled Mexican emperor.[55]

Joseph Shelby was among the resolute Texans who refused to surrender. His sympathetic chronicler said that Shelby was repulsed by a "wave of Negro troops" that were about to "inundate" Texas, and he was buoyed by the reality of "soldiers breaking away from the iron bands of a rigid discipline" to hold "meetings, pleading against surrender. They knew Jefferson Davis was a fugitive, westward bound and they knew Texas was filled to overflowing with all kinds of supplies and war munitions," guaranteeing that war would continue. Said Shelby, "'Mr. Davis is on his way here,'" and "'our intercourse with the French is perfect…. fifty thousand men with arms in their hands have overthrown, ere now, a dynasty and established a kingdom…. we will march into Mexico,'" he declaimed. Key leaders from Texas were embraced by the French authorities in Mexico; likely they were impressed that "Texas was a vast arsenal" as "magnificent batteries of French artillery stood abandoned…. imported muskets were in all the towns and to fixed ammunition there was no limit," while at "Houston, Texas there was a vast depot of supplies filled with all kinds of quartermaster and commissary stores…." The rebels had a "sub-treasury in Austin, in the vaults of which were three hundred thousand dollars in gold and silver…." Even before Appomattox,

54. Joseph Palmer Blessington, *A Private Soldier: The Campaigns of Walker's Texas Division…*, New York: Lange, Little, 1875, 299, 303, 305.

55. W.P. Snow, Volume II, 468.

Texas rebels were retreating headlong into Mexico, though their "dreams" of "Cortez," the original plunderer and occupier, were hardly reassuring. Still, the rebel governor of Missouri—Thomas Reynolds, who spoke French—was on board. General Pierre Jeannin-gros, leading occupier, held Monterrey with a force of 5000 Mexican and French soldiers, along with erstwhile U.S. citizens, English, Irish, Arab, Turkish, German and African troops. The latter were in Coa-huila, within range of Texas and the U.S. generally. Leading rebels, e.g., Magruder, E. Kirby Smith, former Senator from Missouri Trusten Polk, John B. Clark, and many others remained ready to fight from Mexico, as the air was filled with stories of past glories in Algeria and Crimea. Shelby thought that instead of focusing on Tampico or Vera Cruz "surer results would have followed from a French landing at Mobile" and "better battles could have been fought on the Poto-mac than on the Rio Grande...." Shelby was pleading beseechingly to Paris, "give me a port as a basis of operations and I can organize an American force capable of keeping Maximilian upon his throne," for "without foreign aid he is lost...." His goal was to assemble a force of 40,000 troops, but since only one of his crew spoke French and a sim-ilar number knew Spanish, he may have overestimated the efficacy of his forces.[56]

With similar ambition, Maximilian purportedly tasked rebel leader General Sterling Price with raising a cavalry of 30,000[57]—and an estimated "20 to 25,000 traitors," said a recent scholar, actually joined his doomed side.[58]

Jefferson Davis began his retreat from Richmond, accompanied by Francis Lubbock, the slaveowner who had served as Texas governor. They retreated initially to Charlotte and were headed to Texas, the final rebel encampment, but were seized and jailed in Georgia.[59] The idea was to get to Texas, then coordinate with French-occupied Mex-ico to destabilize further the older republic. Despite their eminence, their detention was hardly fatal to rebel dreams of a comeback.

---

56. John Edwards, *Shelby's Expedition to Mexico: An Unwritten Leaf of the War*, Kansas City, Mo.: Kansas City Times Steam Book and Job Printing, 1872, 5-8, 10-12, 14, 23-24, 34-35, 38-39, 41-42, 51, 54 (abbrev. J. Edwards).

57. L. Thomas, 361.

58. Mary Margaret McAllen Amberson, "The Politics of Commerce: Mer-chants' and Military Officials' Machinations to Prolong Civil War Turmoil along the Lower Rio Grande, 1865-1867," M.A. thesis, UT-San Antonio, 2007, v, 7. See also Robert Warren Glover, "The West Gulf Blockade, 1861-1865: An Evaluation," Ph.D. dissertation, UNT, 1974.

59. Flusche, 58.

Routinely, rebels misestimated their strength, possibly because defense of enslavement was so natural, as in both 1776 and 1836—so why not 1861 too? Thus, one Dixie stalwart confessed, "to say that I was surprised at General Lee's surrender is to put it mildly. I was literally astounded," and revealingly his instant instinct was to per-ambulate with his "command straight to Maximilian and Mexico" to continue the struggle. Like the Knights of the Golden Circle, he too thought that "with five thousand such men as nucleus, it would have been no difficult matter for Maximilian to change the map of Mexico and of all the Latin republics...." This rebel, W.E.H. Gramp, "knew the Emperor Maximilian's chief aide in Mexico. This was General R.E. Gunner," giving him confidence that a deal could be cut. "I have known Mexico and the Latin Republics for more than half a cen-tury," he boasted in 1912. "Half a dozen fighters could always start a revolution there. I knew some of General [William] Walker's men," he said, referring to the mastermind of the abortive takeover of Nica-ragua in the 1850s. "One of his officers, Major Morey, after his return from General Walker's Nicaragua expedition, died in my house in Texas," providing faith that Mexico too could be conquered.[60]

For E. Kirby Smith, one of the more important rebels, was very much alive and rallying the still mobilized troops for a Mexican venture—at least before he too gave up in May 1865. Days after Appomattox he was to be found in Shreveport, a mere 20 miles from the Texas border, i.e., paydirt. "The crisis of our revolution is at hand," he confessed to a rally of Confederate soldiers, "great disasters have overtaken us," also true. "With you," he exhorted passionately, "rests the hopes of our nation and upon you depends the fate of our people.... show that you are worthy of your position in history...." He advised, not nec-essarily with inaccuracy, "protract the struggle and you will receive the aid of nations who already deeply sympathize with you," partic-ularly France. "Maintain your discipline" and pursue "securing the final success of our cause,"[61] he implored beseechingly in a far cry from surrender.

Like Governor Murrah of Texas, Governor Henry Watkins Allen of Louisiana—and rebel brigadier general as well—also headed south

60. W.E.H. Gramp, 114, 118, 121.

61. E. Kirby Smith's Last Appeal to the Soldiers of the Trans-Mississippi Army, Shreveport, 21 April 1865, Box 12 , Simon Bolivar Buckner Collection, Huntington Library. See also Theo Noel, *A Campaign from Santa Fe to the Mis-sissippi; Being a History of the Old Sibley Brigade from Its First Organization to the Present Time; Its Campaigns in New Mexico, Arizona, Texas, Louisiana and Arkansas in the Years, 1861-1864*, Shreveport: Shreveport News Printing, 1865.

of the border. Traveling via Texas to get there, he recollected receiving a "complete ovation" from those he encountered: "everybody rich and poor," said his amanuensis, "vied with each other in offering him attention and the most eager hospitality. The roof was deemed honored that sheltered his head for the night." For "at San Antonio he was feted" as "people did everything they could to express their admiration and grateful love toward him...." There he planned to connect with General Shelby and his entourage headed south. "I am perfectly willing to remain in exile the rest of life," he assured shakily. But he had to divert to Eagle Pass to cross the border, "having heard at San Antonio that the federals were in possession of Brownsville" once more. The train he boarded was bulging with importance, containing himself, his predecessor in Louisiana, Governor Thomas Moore; three friends of General Kirby Smith; Magruder; former Missouri Governor Sterling Price; General Shelby; and various other rebel governors and generals. By 22 June they reached Eagle Pass and by 3 July were ensconced in Monterrey.[62]

It was understandable why Governor Allen was hastening to the borderlands. For during the war, his most valuable property abandoned the plantation and burned his home to a crisp before doing so. Still, Governor Allen was no tyro, having journeyed to Europe alongside Judah P. Benjamin during the summer of 1859; and his familiarity with former Mexican leader Ignacio Comonfort was bound to be of assistance during his sojourn south of Texas.[63]

In sync with Smith was William Marshall Anderson—related to both the late Chief Justice John Marshall and the freebooter William Clark of Lewis & Clark infamy. He arrived in Coahuila on 13 April 1865 determined to construct "Colonization by the Confederates," though "speaking little Spanish" would circumscribe his ambition. "I pray God that Negro slavery may be re-established all through tropical America," was his opinion, which reflected the "Knights of the Golden Circle" of wartime yore. His experience in his new homeland with those who had been property had been limited, as he was stunned when he bumped into a Negro: "he speaks French, Spanish and English...with equal fluency and elegance," though this did not shake his narrow preconceptions. Maximilian permitted importation of the enslaved under the guise of peonage, while the definer of

62. Sarah A. Dorsey, *Recollections of Henry Watkins Allen, Brigadier-General Confederate States Army, Ex-Governor of Louisiana*, New York: Doolady, 1866, 307, 310, 325, 326, 327 (abbrev. S. Dorsey).

63. Luther Edward Chandler, "The Career of Henry Watkins Allen," Ph.D. dissertation, LSU, 1940, 35, 52-53.

this project—Matthew Fontaine Maury—encouraged Dixie families to bring their enslaved property with them.[64] To his dismay, his former property Domingo promptly departed from Anderson's control upon arriving in Mexico.[65]

Maury was among the many who envisioned peonage of the Negroes evolving into a kind of semi-slavery, congruent with antebellum Dixie.[66] By late May 1865, Maury, a leader of the forays into both Mexico and Brazil, was grousing about the depreciation of rebel currency, leaving him with mere pieces of paper hardly valuable, which caused him—as he noted dolorously—to embark on a "walk of thirty six miles" through the then dystopian wilds of war-strewn Georgia.[67] This certainly boosted his ongoing attempt to degrade Africans further for his own benefit.

Understandably, rebels in Texas were optimistic that the struggle would continue with Mexico as a rear base, not unlike how anti-apartheid fighters deployed to the newly independent post-1975 Mozambique until the Pretoria regime crumbled by 1994.[68] However, the tempestuous turmoil in Texas post-Appomattox offered grim prospects, as Comanche remained unreconciled, robbery was rampant, and in Guadalupe County, not far from San Antonio, still enslaved Africans were being urged to break the chains, arm themselves—and fight until freedom.[69]

As the latter suggests, just as Appomattox did not mean that hostilities ended instantaneously, neither did it signal automatically—as the hoopla nowadays concerning "Juneteenth" suggests—that enslavement ended with the treasonous rebels' formal surrender.

*   *   *

The rebel sojourner James Morris Morgan cavorted in Brazil, Cherbourg, Cape Town and Morocco (where he was attacked by "Moors"

64. Entries, 13 April 1865 and 6 May 1865, in R.E. Ruiz, xv.

65. Wahlstrom, 40-41.

66. Sharon Hartman and Frederick Stirton Weaver, eds., *Confederates in the Tropics: Charles Swett's Travelogue of 1868*, Jackson: U Press of Mississippi, 2011, 24.

67. Matthew Maury to "My Dear Aunt," 25 May 1865, UVa-C.

68. Gerald Horne, *White Supremacy Confronted: U.S. Imperialism and Anticommunism vs. the Liberation of Southern Africa, from Rhodes to Mandela*, New York: International, 2019 (abbrev. Horne, *White Supremacy*).

69. See Correspondence, 10-18 April 1865, Box 4, Governor Pendleton Murrah Papers, Texas Archives.

and fretted about being enslaved), and fraternized with Jefferson Davis and his spouse in Richmond—"dear friends," he said. He married into the family of George Trenholm, Davis's Secretary of the Treasury, who "owned steamships, railroads, hotels, city houses, cotton presses, wharves, plantations and thousands of slaves." He spoke French fluently and recalled his tarrying in Montgomery, Ala., where during the war he was comforted when "from every house containing a piano the soul stirring strains of the 'Marseillaise' [French anthem] floated out of the open windows." His uncle fought Seminoles in Florida, while Morgan himself was—naturally— contemptuous of Mexicans since "some of the highest aristocrats have a touch of the tar brush in their veins," while the masses were "notoriously lazy." Yet he could not quite comprehend why "there is no race on earth that the Mexicans, high or low, hate as they do the Americans." And although a U.S. Negro taught him horsemanship to the point where he "succeeded in astonishing the Bedouins in Egypt with some of my feats," he harbored pervasive "uncertainty" and "anxiety" about emancipation—like most of his class and hue. When post-Appomattox he was seeking to bury valuable silver for later reclamation, he admitted, "we were afraid to take any negroes into our confidence"—while a freedman "calmly watched," probably for his own reclamation. Then a "brutal negro soldier" detained him and the Trenholm patriarch as they were hiding gold. The armed man "struck me a fearful blow to my stomach," and quickly he "vomited blood." It was an "intentional humiliation," he wailed, to place Trenholm under "negro guard," when a Euro-American counterpart was readily available for the task.[70]

These real and imagined indignities suffused with class and "race" anxieties were endemic post-April 1865 and were shaped indelibly by what remains one of the largest uncompensated expropriations in world history—billions of dollars in slave property. These anxieties fed a terrorist insurgency and contributed to an ongoing hostility to the federal government that propels politics even today, paving the way for a unique brand of U.S. fascism. As social and class relations in Dixie were seemingly inverted, turned upside down, a painful explosion in a place like Texas was unavoidable.

"The Old Southward was moving westward" read the chilling conclusion of novelist Walter Taylor, suggesting doom and gloom for Indigenes, Mexicans and Africans alike, augmenting the already formidable ranks of both racists and dispossessors. "Train after

70. J.M. Morgan, 3, 6, 127, 135, 165, 173, 202, 220, 239, 246.

train of canvas covered wagons from Georgia, Alabama and Mississippi were following the new made trails to the unclaimed forests of Texas," he said. Animating their peregrinations, he said, was "resenting the loss of their slaves." Thus, "his hatred for the military officers and negro soldiers was now more intense than it had ever been," driving him to a ghastly resolution: "he resolves to kill every negro soldier" he encountered and was "just as determined to shoot the military leaders...."[71]

What was driving rebels into frenzied rage was what the 19th-century analyst Richard Taylor noticed: "loss of slaves destroyed the value of lands," and "bank stocks, bonds, all personal property, all accumulated wealth had disappeared," as "there fell upon the South a calamity surpassing any recorded in the annals or traditions of man."[72]

Looking back, the untrammeled rage that gripped all too many Euro-Texans at the prospect of their most valuable investment vanishing into thin air is hard to overestimate. Silas C. Turnbo hailed from adjacent Arkansas and served in neighboring Indian Territory, but his unvarnished sentiments mirrored those of the Lone Star State, where he also patrolled. "I have heard men say," he asseverated, "that they would die before the negroes should be freed...." He was not exaggerating. "Our uniforms were worn to rags and tatters," but their minds were armored against reason. It was in Princeton, Texas, in the north of the state, that they encountered a "lot of negro soldiers.... cavalrymen went into this house one day and shot 9 of these negroes dead with revolvers," who were "lying on their bunks when they were shot," a potential war crime. A fellow rebel announced dramatically, "'I am out to keep the negro from being free,'" the articulated strategic objective of the entire bloody war and, arguably, the republic's rationale from its inception. Turnbo estimated that the number of wolves and panthers increased during the war—perhaps because slaughtering humans, perhaps those of the Negro variety, was the priority.[73]

The non-fiction examples are legion of rebels having manifest difficulty in adjusting to the new order, which too was leading to repulsion and, at times, fleeing to Mexico—or terrorism. H.W. Graber had been a proud Texas Ranger, though he was born in Bremen and his father

---

71. Walter A. Taylor, *The Knights of the Dixie Wilds*, Boston: Meador, 1929, 85, 145, 146.

72. R. Taylor, 236.

73. *Journal of Silas C. Turnbo*, ca. 1865, UOk-N. See also Account of Lu Lee in A. Waters, 9-19, 12: "Animals like the way Indians smell better than any other people. Panthers would jump on white folks and niggers but not Indians."

was a manufacturer. The unrest of 1848 forced his move to Houston, then Waxahachie. Perhaps because of his newness in the region, unlike others he acknowledged that the slaying of Robert Neighbors in 1859 because of his purported friendliness to Indigenes "created quite an excitement...." He joined the traitors and wound up imprisoned in Kentucky, where he bumped heads with a "negro official called 'Captain Black'" who would "curse" him repeatedly, and instruct him to "'hike out, you d—n rebel' and sometimes push [him] along...." In a turnabout from earlier times, "this made me fear this negro to the extent that I always avoided him...." Finally they grappled with Graber unwisely "grabbing at his pistol," leaving the prisoner handcuffed which he proudly called "Yankee bracelets and I consider it an honor to wear them...." He began bonding with French-speaking rebel inmates and learned their language, but there was still "more trouble with negro guards...." Finally, he was freed and headed straight to war-torn Memphis "to see General [Nathan Bedford] Forrest, with whom I was well acquainted, having served under him in the early part of his career," renowned as founder of the bloodstained terroristic Ku Klux Klan, the premier organization of postbellum Dixie.[74]

Matthew Fontaine Maury was just one of many secessionists who happened to be of French ancestry. Also in this pecking order was Admiral Raphael Semmes, who served alongside Robert E. Lee during the war in Mexico and was better known as the swashbuckling rebel corsair whose telling ports of call during the war included Yucatan, racist South Africa, and France by Spring 1864. But for whatever reason he was notably taken with what he termed rhapsodically "glorious Texas!.... in a single generation," he rhapsodized, "thou hast changed the political condition four times," an example for Dixie, though he rejected 1845 annexation in that "in an evil hour you were beguiled into accepting the fatal embrace of the Yankee." But "bide thy time!" he advised, years after the war, for "thou wilt soon become an empire in thyself," though it was unclear if he were predicting a fascist U.S. dominated by Austin. In any case, his curiously and futuristically named son, O.J. Semmes, followed in his father's footsteps in military adventurism.[75]

---

74. H.W. Graber, *The Life Record of H.W. Graber, a Terry Texas Ranger, 1861-1865, Sixty Two Years in Texas*, Dallas?: HWG, 1916, 9, 10, 14, 18, 34, 103, 104, 105, 123, 127. See also U.S. Congress, House of Representatives, 38th Congress, 1st Session, Report on Fort Pillow Massacre, 6 May 1864, Report No. 65.

75. Admiral Raphael Semmes, *Service Afloat; or the Remarkable Career of the Confederate Cruisers Sumter and Alabama During the War Between the States*, Baltimore: Baltimore Publishing, 1887, 233, 537, 540, 791, 793, 794, 795, 801.

Semmes was not present during the final land battle of the war in May 1865, the Battle of Palmito Ranch, just east of Brownsville and consistent with this site's up-and-down wartime journey: the rebels prevailed.[76] Revealingly, at Palmito Ranch the 87th and 62nd Colored Infantry regiments were present.[77]

In light of the fact that reportedly 4000 Spanish-surnamed Tejanos served alongside the rebels and 950 with the federals in the Lower Rio Grande Valley during the height of the war, Palmito Ranch was hardly a shock, even after Appomattox.[78] But it was a foretaste of things to come that even after a formal surrender, rebel Texans fought on—and won.

Actually, the results of Appomattox may not have reached far-flung areas of Texas until well into May 1865, though as early as 27 April, Governor Pendleton Murrah communicated the news. But fundamentally, and befitting a once independent republic, he thought that his constituency should fight on, announcing predictively that "'it may yet be the privilege of Texas the youngest of the confederate sisters to redeem the cause of the confederacy from its present perils.'" That same day, the brigade commanded by General W.P. Hardeman encamped—appropriately—in Washington County, held a meeting, and resolved that Appomattox notwithstanding, they would not surrender until the so-called right of self-government was established, and declared their readiness to continue fighting. Partially at issue was the grand lifestyle some rebel officers had enjoyed and were unready to relinquish. General Magruder in Houston, according to a subsequent observer, was "living in a style not of strict Spartan simplicity" and was a "central figure of gay society." Fortunately, San Antonio was likely more important strategically, being a base of supplies; thus, when General E. Kirby Smith ventured to Houston from Shreveport in May 1865, it was not as threatening as it appeared at first glance. When Murrah, Smith, Magruder, Hardeman and others headed to Mexico, it was not only with the intent to continue the war, but they were fleeing helter-skelter certain localities where Africans—newly freed and otherwise—outnumbered others at times by a rate of ten to one. "If chaos ever reigned in any land," said this same observer, "it did in Texas from May to August 1865," and

76. Thompson and Jones, 3, 31, 77, 35.

77. Nichols 2012, 294.

78. Thompson, "...Santos Benavides and...Cortina," in Bacha-Garza, *Civil War*, 138-158, 138, 153. See also Jerry Thompson, *Cortina: Defending the Mexican Name in Texas*, College Station: TA&MU Press, 2007.

thereafter, "following the news of Lee's surrender, which fell like a thunderbolt upon the army and the people...."[79]

When Major General Philip H. Sheridan was assigned the command of all the territory west of the Mississippi River and south of the Arkansas River on 17 May 1865, the only "organized" rebel force was under the command of General E. Kirby Smith in Shreveport. Yes, twelve days later Smith ostensibly surrendered but, said Sheridan, this was "double dealing...as the Texas troops declined to surrender.... General Smith proceeded to Galveston and from thence escaped to Mexico, in violation of the agreement he had bound to observe.... knowing full well that the Texas troops did not intend to surrender...it was their constant boast that they were not conquered and that they would renew the fight at some future day," a more prescient prediction than then realized. Their plan was hampered when Jefferson Davis and Lubbock were snagged, hampering the design of forming a column of about 15,000 at Marshall, Texas—as thousands continued to cross the border into Mexico.[80]

---

79. John Walker on Reconstruction, before Texas Historical Society, 10 November 1896, Box 1, Morel Family Papers-Tulane U.

80. "Report of Operations of the United States Forces and General Information on the Condition of Affairs in the Military Division of the Southwest and Gulf and Department of the Gulf...from May 29, 1865...Major General Philip H. Sheridan...," Huntington Library (abbrev. Report of Operations). At the same site, see also "Fourteen Hundred and 91 Days in the Confederate Army, a Journal Kept by W.W. Heartsill for Four Years, One Month and One Day or Camp Life: Day by Day of the W.P. Lane Rangers, from April 19th 1861 to May 20th 1865," 1876.

Chapter 18

Juneteenth Emancipation? 1865-1866

The African known as Lu Lee was once enslaved in Texas. Subsequently he recalled that "Master [Wash] Ingram had 350 slaves when the war was over, but he didn't turn us loose, 'til a year after Surrender."[1] This experience was not unique. The scholar Robert Walter Shook wrote that by late 1865 "Negroes were reportedly in virtual slavery in the region between the Neches and Sabine as far north as Henderson...." By the summer of 1866, Brevet Major General C.C. Andrews held the "opinion that the reestablishment of slavery was imminent," while John T. Allen asserted that "secessionists still held negroes in bondage hoping for compensation...." The notorious Bob Lee gang were among what Shook termed the "organized companies of brigands that roamed Texas in the late 1860s" and were "wanted for holding negroes in bondage until July 1866," suggesting an updated version of the human trafficking that characterized the unlamented African Slave Trade.[2]

Eleven months after the enslaved in Harrison County were said to be emancipated, those in neighboring Rusk County labored at gunpoint for free, and slaveholders hanged or shot any who sought to escape bondage. In any case, the "Black Codes" of 1866 were said to have ignited "race war"—or "class war"—insofar as maintaining the horrid working conditions of Africans, a kind of "neo-slavery," was at the crux of the matter. Plantations became what were described as "sadistic death camps."[3]

The invoking of laboring at "gunpoint" should be taken seriously. For slaveholders reputedly killed scores of Africans as they sought to escape from bondage post-Appomattox. Through late 1865—at least—some slaveholders in Texas hoped that this form of property could be rescued. Their strained legalistic thinking was that General Lee's April 1865 edict did not apply to Texas, and slavery remained legal. Even in December 1865 many of this class held onto hope that

---

1. Lu Lee in A. Waters, 150-152.
2. Shook, 194, 197. 426-427.
3. Sitton and Conrad, 11.

they would be compensated for their expropriated property. Anderson Edwards remained a slave on a Rusk County plantation for one full year after the official termination on 19 June 1865. One slaveholding madam kept an African woman chained to her loom to bar her escape and continued to enslave her well after this official date of slavery's end. Some Africans remained enslaved for years, since this relationship depended not just on a change of the law but the balance of forces, domestically and globally. Other foul characters reenslaved those who been freed and shipped them to Cuba and Brazil for a hefty price. But even in Texas slavery persisted as late as 1868 and, again, Negroes were at times compelled to sign work "contracts" and killed if they refused.[4]

It was also in December 1865 that Brigadier General E.M. Gregory, a man in blue based in Galveston, found that "in some portions of the state...where our troops have not been quartered, freedmen are restrained from their freedom and slavery as virtually exists the same as though the old system of oppression was still in force...."[5]

Texas was not peculiar. Van Cockran, speaking years later from Wynnewood, Okla., recalled a time when he—born in 1850—was one of 115 enslaved persons in early 1865 in Indian Territory. After Appomattox, "everything went on just like it did before the war," he said, "except that Master John laid down his whip."[6] William Nail was born in 1860 in the Choctaw Nation, though his mother arrived there from Mississippi earlier. Speaking later from Poteau, Okla., he found that the "Chickasaw...[were] reluctant in recognizing the emancipation of the slaves and continued to hold them in slavery for some time after the close of the war...." Just before this slaveholders' fiasco, some in this class began to sell this unique property at a "very low price" in anticipation of abolition, as this asset assumed the perilous plateau of profound "risk" in that "making the purchase in the face of the national liberation of the slaves" was a chancy investment at best.[7]

The foregoing should be kept firmly in mind when considering the traditional story of "Juneteenth," or 19 June 1865, when—we are

4. Smallwood, 88, 99, 103, 159, 167.

5. Report of Brigadier General Gregory, 9 December 1865, Reel 1, FBR.

6. Oral History, Van Cockran, ca. 1937-1938, IPP. In the same collection, see also Oral History, Adeline Collins Wynnewood, 16 July 1937: This enslaved woman was born in the Chickasaw Nation and wound up with the Choctaws. "I was a big girl at the close of the Civil War," she recounted, and "a big negro man...did the whipping" with a "long black snake whip.... all the slaves sit down around this whipping post and watch...."

7. Ibid., Oral History, William Nail, ca. 1937-1938.

told—General Gordon Granger and his bevy of troops rode into Galveston to instruct the Africans that they were free.[8] This decree officially barring enslavement was potently important, immediate and short term impact set aside. For some unionists then knew, as one put it, "men who are strong rebels against the government, are almost invariably strong opponents of free labor" for these "enemies of free labor claim that slave labor is superior."[9] But with the banning of the latter, the former accelerated, not being dragged down by enchained competition, with resultant stronger "free labor" organization and resultant higher wages.[10]

"Free labor" was reinforced further because of the high expectations of the formerly enslaved, providing their efforts with intensified impetus. For many of them believed that when the soldiers in blue arrived, their mission included dividing the slaveholders' property amongst them,[11] a fervent wish that proved difficult to dissolve. As had been the tendency in Texas, at least since 1836 the ferocity of resistance was countervailed with often overwhelming force. By October 1865 the recently inaugurated Freedmen's Bureau reported from Galveston, where a few months earlier on 19 June Africans were supposedly freed, that planters "do not pay what the labor is worth" and substituted "the lash and corporal punishment" in lieu of adequate wages. This "imprudence of the white people" predictably meant "fears expressed of insurrection during the coming holiday...."[12]

For just as Appomattox did not instantaneously cause hostilities to cease but only marked a new stage in the struggle, the same can be said for "Juneteenth," especially because—as is well-known—the Emancipation Proclamation of 1863 did not necessarily free the enslaved in loyal states and did not necessarily reach those in disloyal states. In any case, before "Juneteenth," Willard Richardson, editor of the *Galveston News*, discussed these matters to the point where one scholar of this town points out that "Blacks in Galveston

---

8. Annette Gordon Reed, *On Juneteenth*, New York: Liveright, 2021.

9. Thomas W. Conway, General Superintendent of Freedmen, "The Freedmen of Louisiana. Final Report of the Bureau of Free Labor, Department of the Gulf to Major General E.R.S. Canby, Commanding," New Orleans: Times Book and Job Office, 1865, Huntington Library.

10. See e.g., Leon Fink, *Workingmen's Democracy: The Knights of Labor and American Democracy*, Urbana: U of Illinois Press, 1983.

11. Andress, 98.

12. Brigadier General E.M. Gregory, Galveston to O.O. Howard, Washington, D.C., 31 October 1865, Reel 1, FBR.

and Texas probably knew about the Emancipation Proclamation"; the problem was not lack of knowledge, the problem was mobilizing forces compelling slaveholders to abandon a highly profitable system of property without compensation.[13]

Texas Africans were hardly secure even by the "next Juneteenth," i.e., the execution of Maximilian on 19 June 1867, which was a severe setback to plans by the disloyal in the U.S. to construct a "neo-slavery" south of the border. At any rate, there are other striking aspects of the "original Juneteenth" in 1865 that are worthy of note. For it was on that impactful day that General Grant told recently installed President Andrew Johnson that if Maximilian continued in power, "I see nothing before us but a long expensive and bloody war, one in which the enemies of this country will be joined by tens of thousands of disciplined soldiers, embittered against their government...." Already, "French soldiers have fired on our men from the south side of the river in aid of the rebellion...." Already, "contract has been entered into with Doctor [William] Gwin, a traitor" and former slaveholder and pioneer Californian. The plot to "invite into Mexico armed immigrants" was well underway, jeopardizing—*inter alia*—abolition in Texas.[14]

Even the vaunted General Granger, on the very date he has been celebrated, was exceedingly nervous about "extensive robberies" that "are taking place in Texas, the property being conveyed into Mexico. The movement is supposed to be in the interests of the Imperialists."[15] Thus, the contemporaneous news from Mexico City was discouraging. Less than a fortnight after "Juneteenth," the report was that "quite a number of Americans arrived here during this month, a great many from the South,"[16] and likely accompanied by Negroes involuntarily. By 11 September 1865 there were reported about 350 rebels in Mexico City, with more arriving daily. The message to the State Department was that

---

13. Merri Jane Scheibe, "Galveston's First Reconstruction, 1865-1874," M.A. thesis, U of Houston-Clear Lake, 1992, 16, 91.

14. General Grant to President Johnson, 19 June 1865, in *War of the Rebellion, Volume XLVIII, Series I, Part II*, 923-924. See also Testimony of a Survivor, Private Justus Brooks, in A.W. Barber, compiler, *The Benevolent Raid of General Lew Wallace...how Mexico was Saved in 1864...the Monroe Doctrine in Action*, Washington, D.C.: Beresford, 1914. According to this source, it was Grant unbeknownst to Seward who began to collaborate with Juárez's forces, sending weapons that turned the tide against Maximilian.

15. General Granger to Major General F. Steele, 19 June 1865, in *War of the Rebellion, Volume XLVIII, Series I, Part II*, 930.

16. Consul Marcus Otterbourg to Acting Secretary of State Hunter, 28 June 1865, Reel 6, Despatches from U.S. Consuls in Mexico City, NARA.

the "influence of the so-called 'Confederates' has had much to do with the colonization scheme." Leading Texans were in the vanguard of this delegation.[17] By 30 September the same source reported that "about 500 Americans mostly southerners have come to this city during the last twelve months," and that the "whole number of emigrants to this city may be…approximately between five and six thousand (reliable statistics cannot be obtained)…." Leading traitors were "already engaged in making a reconnaissance of the land around Cordova and Orizaba as best adapted to the labor of negroes, whom it is proposed to employ under a system somewhat similar to that…in Louisiana…." The rebels were also engaged in "importations…of French goods," which had been "greatly increased" to the consternation of "English and German houses" miffed with the enhanced competition.[18]

Slavery was forsworn (formally), but as one recent study concluded—echoing W.E.B. Du Bois—the post-1865 slave trade continued "to a later date in Texas than anywhere else in the United States,"[19] with a number headed further south ultimately.

What was attempted in Mexico by migrating rebels provided a glimpse of what to come in Texas. Matthew Fontaine Maury, the renowned oceanographer of French ancestry who was a major interlocutor with the French-sponsored Maximilian, envisioned Negroes under the age of 21 apprenticing for two decades and those above this age, consigned to a decade; naturally, the traitors could arrive with their "property" who, once in a strange land, could be traduced into neo-slavery. One comrade of Juárez denounced the entire scheme as a subterfuge for reincorporating slavery in Mexico, seeking to form a "'New Virginia'" south of the border.[20]

To the contrary, Maury of Huguenot ancestry wailed that "never since the Revocation of the Edict of Nantes has such a class of people been found willing to expatriate themselves," speaking of traitors and their escape. Evidence to the contrary notwithstanding, he found charges that he sought to revive enslavement in Mexico to be "absurd."[21] Buttressing his claim was a September 1865 regulation

---

17. Ibid., Consul Otterbourg to Secretary Seward, 11 September 1865.

18. Ibid., Consul Otterbourg to Secretary Seward, 30 September 1865.

19. Govenar, 210.

20. A.J. Hanna, "The Role of Matthew Fontaine Maury in the Mexican Empire," *Virginia Magazine of History and Biography*, 55 (No. 2, 17 January 1947): no pagination, VaHS-R.

21. Matthew Fontaine Maury to "My Dear Friend," 8 August 1865, in Jacqueline Ambler Caskie, ed., *Life and Letters of Matthew Fontaine Maury*, Richmond: Richmond Press, 1928, 152-155, 153, 154.

under Maximilian's imprimatur mandating that "all persons of color are free by the mere act of touching Mexican soil"[22]—but, of course, there was a similar "regulation" in Texas then too, though it did not necessarily extirpate enslavement. Moreover, as Secretary Seward was informed, there was a proviso that if any of these new arrivals chose "desertion the working man apprehended shall be employed without any pay on the public works until he shall be reclaimed by his patron...."[23]

However, a desperate Maximilian was unwilling to turn away Maury and his comrades as long as tens of thousands of armed federals lurked on Mexico's northern border, poised—it seemed—to invade. By late July 1865 Henry Watkins Allen, erstwhile governor of Louisiana, was in Monterrey and found to his satisfaction that "Confederate exiles were most kindly treated," as he was "invited to breakfast with the French Commandant," then other "civil and military authorities"; that he knew little of the French or Spanish languages did not detain him. He was accompanied by two other governors, giving the delegation real heft. "It is my intention to settle permanently" was his preliminary conclusion; it was the "garden spot of this continent"— not far wrong—then he added what had beguiled northern neighbors for decades, "and in the hands of the Americans or the French," Mexico "will make a most delightful country in which to live," with the "great many very pretty women" attracting his dedicated attention. But soon his temper shifted, as he was reduced to "giving English lessons" since he added mournfully: "I am poor and penniless yet I am a free man; not shut up in a dreary prison." However, if he had conducted a more comprehensive analysis, he could have ascertained that the rebels had been defeated militarily but not politically in that the anti-African ethos that had driven the war was still resonant with roots stretching back to 1607, then deepened in 1776—and not easily uprooted in 1865.

But soon his fortunes took a turn for the better since he was "to be presented to the Emperor and Empress," as "Commander Maury" began to exert more influence: "he is in high favor at court" and "has become a citizen of Mexico...." During his conversation with Her Majesty in August 1865 he was delighted to ascertain that she "speaks the English language very well" and "assured us that we

22. Office of Colonization, "Decrees for the Encouragement of Immigration and Colonization," Mexico: Ignacio Cumplido, November 1865, Huntington Library.

23. Decree by Maximilian, 5 September 1865, Reel 5, Despatches from U.S. Consuls in Mexico City, NARA.

poor Confederate exiles had her heartfelt sympathy and that we were welcome in Mexico," indicating support for a rear base to raid northward and keep Washington's forces off balance. So heartened, soon Allen was "reading a Spanish paper every morning" and had made "arrangements to publish a newspaper in English...."[24]

This periodical, *Mexican Times*, reflected and projected this latest invasion of Mexico with a huge demand for bilingual dictionaries being the most visible symbol.[25] News from "home" was *de rigueur*, e.g., when P.G.T. Beauregard was arrested in his home in New Orleans, as it was feared that E. Kirby Smith—then in Mexico—was hidden there.[26]

Also communing in Mexico was the former rebel leader from Texas, Alexander Watkins Terrell. By early July 1865 he was in Eagle Pass,[27] carrying a letter from the similarly escaping Governor Murrah, a "personal friend" of Maximilian. Like other soon-to-be refugees, he denounced the prospect of being "herded between the bayonets of negro soldiers"—to be avoided at all costs; there was the fond "hope that France might aid the shattered Confederacy to arise."[28] To that end, in late July 1865 he was settled in Monterrey and was ecstatic to find that "the French general" he met "was profuse in his expression of praise for the long and heroic struggle made by the South...." Revealingly, he was conferring with the son of Mary Surratt as she was being executed for her role in the assassination of President Lincoln. He went on to confer with a high-level French general married to an "American lady," then met with former U.S. Senator William Gwin, a confirmed traitor—as was Terrell, perhaps more so since he disagreed firmly with the proposed fruits of Appomattox, objecting strenuously to "revolutionists against Spain after the fall of Iturbide" who "committed a great error in giving universal suffrage...." Befitting his eminence, Terrell—a future U.S. envoy to the Ottoman Empire—too conversed with the Emperor in English, after being introduced by Maury. He paid him the highest Dixie compliment by comparing him favorably to Polignac, the rebel leader of French ancestry, and could have paired him with Soulé, with whom he also held discussions.

---

24. S. Dorsey, 327, 329, 330, 331, 332.

25. *Mexican Times*, 16 September 1865.

26. Ibid., 30 September 1865.

27. Undated Clipping, Scrapbook, Box 2h22, Alexander Watkins Terrell Papers, UT-A (abbrev. Terrell Papers).

28. Ibid., *Houston Chronicle*, 14 February 1911, in Scrapbook, Box 2h23.

After these various meetings, his conclusion was firm and clear: "if an effort was made by [Washington] to drive the French troops out of Mexico, the struggle in the South would be renewed for France would become an ally of the Southern States," which meant in effect that Appomattox was simply a pause before reloading. "We had long been dreaming of French intervention," he said happily, since more than most he realized that the "Confederacy might rise again under foreign aid..." Of course, there was the none too niggling matter of the "antagonism of the Mexican population" toward the "invader," which put paid to Terrell's ambitions by the "next Juneteenth"—1867—when Maximilian was executed summarily. He was not taken aback by this turn as he recalled well the 1840s war with Mexico when this same population displayed "ferocity" toward other invaders as "American officers" were "cruelly butchered," this at a time when of the "general officers, everyone of whom was a southern man...."[29]

Terrell and Maury aside, one of the more influential rebel sojourners in Mexico was E. Kirby Smith, scion of a slaveholding family. He had visited Europe by 1858 and, appropriately, despised London as he embraced Paris. With roots in war-torn St. Augustine, Florida, he also received adroit military training at West Point in New York. But soon he was in Texas and after a failed Polish uprising against Russia, he sought to recruit the defeated for the Lone Star State. He was enthusiastic to find that there were thousands of enslaved Africans in Indian Territory, finding it "remarkable" and, likely, sensing allyship. During the war, General Smith's machinations were important in Matamoros, which the U.S. consul there then thought was a city as important to the Trans-Mississippi Confederacy as New York was to the U.S. The cold-blooded Smith also presided over the executions of various Negro troopers, though routinely he counseled simply selling enlisted men into slavery—and executing their Euro-American officers. He believed in "'giving no quarter to armed negroes,'" boilerplate among rebels—but like some of his peers, by 1864 he was willing to entertain emancipation in pursuit of rebel survival. By June 1865 he too was in Mexico where his knowledge of French and Spanish proved useful, though this marked a downfall

---

29. A.W. Terrell, 16, 24-25, 41, 43, 52, 53, 54, 55, 56, 61. See also Consul Charles Hale to Secretary of State Seward, 4 December 1866, Reel 4, Despatches from U.S. Consuls in Alexandria, NARA: "John Harrison Surratt was transferred under a sufficient guard from the quarantine grounds to the government prison where he remains.... he maintains his demeanor of reticence...."

for a man who once was seen as the defender of about one-third of the Confederacy from his perch in Shreveport. But soon he surrendered again, winding up back in Lynchburg by November 1865.[30] Still, by July 1865 Smith was among the reputed 4000 rebels, many being prominent leaders, who had gathered in Mexico as they plotted a comeback.[31]

Maury was not the only rebel who had organic ties to Mexico, albeit via France. Pierre Soulé and Judah P. Benjamin both had ties to Louisiana and spoke French, while John Slidell served as rebel envoy in Paris. Before the Civil War, all three were backing a venture to build a canal or railway across the Isthmus of Tehuantepec, a shortcut from the Caribbean Sea to the Pacific Ocean, a precursor of the Panama Canal.[32]

In the meantime, rebels had found a "workaround" in supplying the French and themselves, absent a canal. As early as 1 July 1865 the State Department was told that as for Mazatlán on Mexico's Pacific coast, the "only commerce of any consequence is that carried on with San Francisco for the supplying of the French forces," though the "trade with the interior" was "very limited...."[33] Late that next month, according to the U.S. emissary, "ninety more rebels from Texas" arrived in Mazatlán, "under the command of the well known and notorious 'Dan Showalter.'" Once more, San Francisco was their destination, although a "hundred more of the same gang have gone to Sonora under the command of Judge and Mrs. [David]Terry."[34]

Despite the fact that Guaymas was closer to the U.S.—or, perhaps, because of this factor—this city by late September 1865 had

30. Cyril Methodius Lagvanec, "Chevalier Bayard of the Confederacy: The Life and Career of Edmund Kirby Smith," Ph.D. dissertation, TA&MU, 1999, 367, 381, 439, 440, 502, 503, 504, 573-574, 592, 594.

31. Michael G. Webster, "Texan Manifest Destiny and the Mexican Border Conflict, 1865-1880," Ph.D. dissertation, Indiana U, 1972, 39 (abbrev. M.G. Webster).

32. T. W. Wahlstrom, "A Vision for Colonization: The Southern Migration Movement to Mexico after the Civil War," *Southern Historian*, 30 (Spring 2009): 50-66, 63. For yet another account of a rebel—this time from Texas—with French roots see Max Lale, ed., *The Civil War Letters of David R. Garrett...6th Texas Cavalry, 1861-1865*, Marshall, Texas: Port Caddo Press, 1963?

33. Consul B.R. Carman to Secretary Seward, 1 July 1865, Reel 3, Despatches from U.S. Consuls in Mazatlan, NARA.

34. Ibid., Consul Carman to Charles James, Collector of Customs, San Francisco, 21 August 1865.

witnessed "no arrival in this state of any of the prominent rebel leaders," except for a "son of the late Com. William D. Porter, recently executive officer of the pirate 'Florida' being the only person of this character at present in the city or state," said the U.S. envoy there.[35]

On the opposite coast in Tampico, rebels were up to their old tricks. A vessel had docked from New Orleans with "Mexican protection" and "under the imperial flag...."[36] Weeks later, in mid-August 1865, a vessel in Tampico was "preparing for sea under the command of the notorious rebel and blockade runner Captain Wilson"; it was "painted black and her crew is composed of rebel offenders," said the U.S. delegate, and was slated to "proceed to Havana" with suspect ends.[37] Tampico was also a switching point between the U.S. and points farther south, for as Maury instructed fellow rebels, "'there is water communication from New Orleans and New York direct to Vera Cruz or Tampico,'" and then farther, i.e., "migration to Brazil," since "there are many in the Southern States who are looking out for homes in foreign lands."[38]

Maury and J.B. Magruder were in charge of migration to Mexico from Dixie and by mid-October 1865 provided a helpful tip "to those who wish[,] come by land through Texas, the road is open at all times," and "to our friends from the Southern States we recommend especially the country around Tampico, Tuxpan and Vera Cruz," historic bastions of foreign influence. But it was not just Dixie, since one exile asserted that New York was "full of Confederates, many just out of prison," who "dined and supped by the very men they fought against,"[39] unnecessary south of the border.

Business was booming—or so it was averred. By November 1865 hosannas were tossed at the "Mexican authorities" since they "have been very kind to the Confederate exiles," though "emigration to Brazil" was also accelerating; "our correspondent estimates that upwards of fifty thousand of our Southern countrymen are now ready [to] emigrate thither." However, the message was why go all the way to Brazil when the borderlands held similar advantage? A close comrade of Kirby Smith had "just returned to Texas" from Virginia and thought the latter was an "uninterrupted scene of ruin and

---

35. Consul Edward Conner to Secretary Seward, 25 September 1865, Reel 1, Despatches from U.S. Consuls in Guaymas, NARA.

36. Consul Franklin Chase to Secretary Seward, 28 July 1865, Reel 4, Despatches from U.S. Consuls in Tampico, NARA.

37. Ibid., Consul Chase to Secretary Seward, 26 September 1865.

38. *Mexican Times*, 7 October 1865.

39. Ibid., 14 October 1865.

desperation," while the Lone Star State was a "paradise of prosperity in comparison with all other portions of the Confederacy," to the extent that the "very best classes of the people of Virginia contemplate emigrating to Texas as soon as possible," though Mexico and Brazil had not been ruled out either. Similarly, "foreigners," including "Swedes," were en route to the "Upper James River" to settle, and a "Polish colony is also to be established in Virginia," bolstering those defined as "white,"[40] with some of these too willing to entertain moving southwest.

This rebel journal in Mexico trumpeted migration from Dixie to this neighbor—and not returning—stressing that "every Confederate of note who has returned to any Southern State from Mexico, has been arrested...." They were compared heroically to "the Irish patriots and Kossuth and his companions [who] fly to the United States...."[41]

However, Tampico was not exactly free of conflict. By November 1865 the U.S. agent there abruptly renounced his earlier claim that a "war of extermination" was erupting[42]—though closer observers may have disagreed.

Just as rebels had infiltrated Tampico during the war, Frenchmen were at the helm there postwar. Or so argued the self-described "Blockade Runner," William Watson. Though Appomattox had been "disastrous...to the Southern cause," he conceded, "it did not, as a consequence, involve the overthrow of the Confederacy" since the "greater part of Lee's army would be transferred" to yet another officer and "with reinforcements...would be able to strike a fatal and decisive blow, which would at once turn the whole fortune of the war in favour of the South"; i.e., "they would claim for Texas, as a part of Mexico, the same right to sever her connection with the United States and again become independent or annex to Mexico," meaning "an alliance with Maximilian."[43]

In July 1865 Seward was informed anxiously about the fact that "notorious murderers" from due north were "daily arriving in Monterrey"; the U.S. consul wanted to see them "arrested" and added, "I have been called upon to do so by Union men from Texas,"[44] who

---

40. Ibid., 4 November 1865.

41. Ibid., 11 November 1865.

42. Consul Franklin Chase to Secretary Seward, 26 September 1865, Reel 4, Despatches from U.S. Consuls in Tampico, NARA.

43. William Watson, *The Adventures of a Blockade Runner or Trade in Times of War*, London: Unwin, 1898, 319 (abbrev. W. Watson, *Adventures*).

44. Consul Marcus Otterbourg to Secretary Seward, 11 July 1865, Reel 5, Despatches from U.S. Consuls in Mexico City, NARA.

knew many of the accused. Loyalists were unready to play nice with traitors. This attitude permeated and propelled the early "radical" thrust of Reconstruction and dissipated in the aftermath of the "Second Juneteenth," the slaying of Maximilian and the dissipation of the rebel threat to Washington. Thus, by August 1865 the recommendation from leading U.S. military men was that "deserters from the army [should] be remorselessly arrested, tried...and, if guilty, be forthwith shot to death...."[45] This harsh stance was a reflection of what one rebel mariner had detected: "many of the keenest blockade runners were Yankees," he said of those supplying rebels during and after the formal end to the war: they "professed sympathy with the South," said William Watson.[46]

Premier rebel leader Joseph Shelby had noticed a similar phenomenon, speaking of "quite a large concentration of Americans" that "had taken place in the City of Mexico. Many of these were penniless—all of them were soldiers"—and embittered. Matthew Fontaine Maury, who had attained notoriety earlier with his designs on Brazilian land, had garnered a plot of Mexican land—"Cordova" or "Carlota"—for their resettlement. But this was a difficult assignment, and many had barely alighted south of the border before they took off for—presumably—brighter horizons in China, Hawaii, Japan and elsewhere. Yet the burning fury toward Washington that motivated this mass migration was captured by the experience of "Colonel" John Perkins of Louisiana, a jurist of some fame and the preferred lawyer for the resident rich—and a slaveholder. He torched his dwelling, his cotton presses, his stables, barns and outhouses in an attempt to make a desert—then darted to Mexico, seeking to cripple Reconstruction, not altogether unsuccessfully.[47]

Perkins had reason to believe he was in good hands with Maury at the helm. By late June 1865 the illustrious oceanographer had navigated his way into a promising discussion with Maximilian. The "reception was all that I could wish," gushed Maury; "the Emperor is anxious to have our people come to him," and indicative of the monarch's ambitious plans, he was "going straight away to commence again the studies of the English language...." Extraordinarily important was that "he goes in strong and heartily for the idea of our

---

45. Brevet Brigadier General James Oakes to Brigadier General James Fry, 9 August 1865, in *War of the Rebellion, Volume V, Series III,* 803.

46. W. Watson, *Adventures,* 318.

47. J. Edwards, 78, 95, 105. Cf., Christina Regelski, "Strangers in a Strange Land: Voluntary Exile in the Civil War South," Ph.D. dissertation, Rice U, 2019.

people bring with them their negroes as apprentices,"[48] a nakedly bold circumvention of abolition.

Robert E. Lee, a close comrade of Maury's, had mixed feelings about his latest adventure. "I have a great admiration for Mexico," he said in early September 1865, referencing his earlier time along the border. "The salubrity of its climate, the fertility of its soil and the magnificence of its scenery, possess for me great charms...." But perceptively, he suspected that Washington would object to a "system of apprenticeship," while there would be abject "difficulty in persuading the freedmen to emigrate,"[49] a prescient concern.

Though he was commanding tens of thousands of troops along the border, including—pivotally—a goodly number of armed Africans, General Sheridan did not sound optimistic.

"All our military projects during the war, against Texas, had been failures and that on this account the Union people there had come to look upon the Government as weak," and hardly capable of enforcing an abolition decree. So, he was "determined to throw a large force into that state and along the Rio Grande border," which was "successfully achieved," though doubts lingered, especially since many in his ranks were homesick and longed to depart. But this was unlikely since "we found the line of that river and all northern Mexico in the hands of Imperialism...." This created an epic confrontation since "the appearance of our troops and the knowledge that friends were on the border, went like electricity to the homes and hearts of the Mexican people"—but if this were sufficient to tip the scales in Sheridan's favor was another matter altogether. Like his comrade General Grant, Sheridan too "always believed that the occupation of Mexico was a part of the rebellion...." Still, in Mexico "rebels who had escaped from our country received no sympathy," while in Texas and thereabouts "nearly every newspaper in the rebellious states was [in] sympathy for Maximilian and the sentiment of a large population of a large portion of the population was likewise...." Hence, the so-called "Cordova emigration scheme was gotten up, which had for its object the formation of a Maximilian-Americans party, composed [primarily] of Confederates...." By blocking departures from U.S. ports southward—"within the limits of my command"—Sheridan disrupted this venture.

---

48. Letter from M.F. Maury, 27 June 1865, in Lee Headquarter Papers, 624-631, VaHS-R.

49. Robert E. Lee to M.F. Maury, 8 September 1865, Letterbook of Robert E. Lee, VaHS-R.

Yet that did not stay the hand of the rebels who in Texas remained armed. "Civil affairs" there, said Sheridan realistically, were "unsatisfactory," for the motto of the supposed vanquished forces was "'pride in rebellion'; that it was a righteous but lost cause, being overpowered by the federal forces...." This meant that any "trial of a white man for the murder of a freedman in Texas," the latter being a common occurrence was bound to fail.

What Sheridan did not note but which proved to be of monumentally strategic importance was that both sides were united against what he termed "Indian depredations" and, to that end—and in a strategic blunder—armed Africans joined this crusade to their own detriment, as an insignia of their newly announced citizenship. Sheridan found it "strange" that the "greatest excitement" ensued "over a white man killed by Indians on an extensive frontier but over the killing of many freedmen in the settlements, nothing is done."[50]

The foregoing and his lengthy record illustrated that despite his lofty rank, he understood neither of the dual cruel logics of settler colonialism and white supremacy, essential to his overall mission—and, tragically, neither did U.S. Negroes.

For some in Washington found the construction of "reservations" for Indigenes as a precedent for building the same for the recently emancipated, a process which—arguably—has yet to cease. The fervent Republican Senator James Doolittle of Wisconsin, thought that Indian Territory could make room for the Negroes, and the antislavery advocate Francis P. Blair conceived a deal with Texas, whereby it would be readmitted to the Union on the premise that its vast public lands would be ceded to Black colonists, that could lead to many of them disappearing into Mexico.[51]

Retrospectively, it is not easy to discern if there was an actual ideological weakness among Negro leadership making it difficult for them to plot in the midst of a revolutionary situation—or even if they recognized same. Like Indigenes, they were bound to be overwhelmed, irrespective of whether rebels or loyalists prevailed, in the absence of international support.

*   *   *

One Hartford-based chronicler, when touring the region back then, observed that "Confederates made better treaties with the Indians

50. Report of Operations.
51. S. Page, 263, 269.

than ever the United States had made and even paid them one annuity in Confederate money,"[52] receipt of which was an earnest of how
Indigenes thought the war would eventuate.

Thus—officially—the last rebel general to surrender was the Cherokee leader Stand Watie: he relinquished his sword in what is now
Choctaw County, Oklahoma, just north of the Texas border. Baptized
as a Christian with the name Isaac, he had difficulty communicating
in the English language. He emerged from an ethnic group whereby
some of the richest slaveholders were Cherokee, who presided over a
system whereby Euro-Americans could join a clan through marriage,
but Negroes would be accorded one hundred lashes if they tried to do
the same. Watie, a brigadier general, also collaborated with William
Quantrill and Jesse James, who set the sub-region aflame both during
and after the war. It was true that the war was a catastrophe for the
Cherokee, insofar as a third of all wives were left widowed as a result,
along with a quarter of all children left orphaned. Yet Indigenes who
opposed secession hardly fared better, placing in clarifying perspective the missteps of Negro leadership during this difficult era.[53]

---

52. Edward King, *The Great South...*, Baton Rouge: LSU Press, 1972 [orig-
inally published in 1874; this version edited by W.M. Drake and R.R. Jones],
200 (abbrev. E. King, *Great South*).

53. Sedgwick, 151, 357. See also Frank Cunningham, *General Stand Watie's
Confederate Indians*, San Antonio: Naylor, 1959, and Walter Lee Brown, *A Life of
Albert Pike*, Fayetteville: U of Arkansas Press, 1997. See also Oral History, Lucy
Cherry, 26 November 1937, IPP: Described as "Choctaw half-breed," she was
born in Choctaw Nation in 1869 to a Negro mother, born in Alabama, who
was sold in a slave market in New Orleans to a man in Texas who dragged
here there. She moved to what is now Oklahoma after the Civil War. Cherry's
mother spoke Choctaw: "we observed the customs of the Indians," she said,
"and talked both the Choctaw language," i.e., the "native tongue of our father
and the English tongue of our mother...." Relevant to the above is that "the fees
for a white man to marry a Choctaw girl ranged from $60.00 to $100.00. This
fee was made high to prevent marriage with the white race. This also applied
to the negro race...." See also Oral History, J.G. Jennings, 18 February 1937,
IPP: Speaking from Muskogee, Okla., years later, this man born in 1876 spent
considerable time in Coffeyville, Ks., not far from Indian Territory: "on the reservation," he said, "as a general rule the white people were regarded as trash
with disrespect." They would travel to Kansas for alcoholic beverages then on
returning "every time they met a white man they would pull their six shooters
and make the white man get off his horse...would make the white man walk,
at the same time firing guns at his feet." Cf., Oral History, Louis Dorchester,
20 January 1938, IPP. In a home he knew well, "his negro wife kept one clean

Speaking from Bernice, Okla., years later, Arthur Beck of Chero-kee ancestry spoke fondly of the "great" Watie as "our neighbor" and spoke well of his intriguingly named son Saladin, bearing the name of the centuries-old vanquisher of the Crusaders. As Beck saw things, Watie's surrender—four days after "Juneteenth"—was abor-tive in that he was in the midst of "preparing to raise an army of ten thousand men, with the intention of invading Kansas...."[54]

The postwar Constitution and treaties brokered by the Choc-taw Nation were much more punitive to slaveholders than those imposed on Dixie. Reparations were mandated: "pay such persons of African descent" an amount, with the telling amendment that "all said persons of African descent" were "entitled to forty acres each of the lands of the nation...upon the same term as the Choctaws [and] shall be entitled to hold any office of trust or profit in this nation."[55]

Washington exacted a more stringent justice against Indigenous slave-holders, as compared to their Euro-American peers. The bilateral treaty between the Cherokees and the rebels was viewed as more favorable to the former than any pact signed by them with Washington, pre-1865. Then the 1866 treaty sought to disrupt common land ownership, a pri-ority then, by allocating 160 acres to the formerly enslaved, which Watie blasted as a "'dark treaty'" because it also gave the "freedmen" citizen-ship and suffrage, though wrangling over same continues even today.[56]

Such pacts were signed under duress in that 1865 also marked an acceleration of a centuries-long battle to oust Indigenes from the land, and Washington now had the added advantage of being able to enlist tens of thousands of battle-tested—and enormously grateful—U.S. Negroes, along with a steady stream of European migrants, some of whom had fought previously in Florida in the 1830s and Mexico in the 1840s. According to one study, wars against Indigenes commencing in 1865 were a "drain on the U.S. Treasury...double what it spent in 1864...over 20 million...."[57]

---

bedroom as guest room for Indian or white travelers. No negroes were to use that room for lodging."

54. Ibid., Oral History, Arthur Beck, 25 October 1937.

55. Treaty of 1866, 28 April 1866, and Treaty of 1883, 21 May 1883, in *Con-stitution and Laws of the Choctaw Nation, Together with the Treaties of 1837 1855, 1865...1866* , Dallas: Worley, 1894, 49, 335. Cf., Fay A. Yarbrough, *Choctaw Confederates: The American Civil War in Indian Country*, Chapel Hill: U of North Carolina Press, 2021.

56. Kievit, 65, 86.

57. John D. McDermott, *Circle of Fire: The Indian War of 1865*, Guilford, Conn.: Stackpole, 2003. 38, 48, 55, 166.

For shortly after Watie held aloft the white flag of surrender, U.S. Negro troops were descending in southern Texas but, according to one spectator, "the people [Euro-Americans] are very anxious to have our forces occupy the state but are much afraid of the negro troops & don't want to see them"; this was true not just in Galveston, which was "rather broken down" with war damage though "the state" as a whole "has not suffered from the war...."[58] By early July this spectator, Edward W. Bacon, was in Brownsville-Matamoros and had "spent yesterday afternoon in that place & was much pleased with the French troops whom I do not desire to fight with our wretched negroes, who as soldiers under the present system are almost a failure...."[59] Meanwhile, what Bacon may well have described as other "wretched Negroes," laborers due north in Houston were at the same time being "set free...[by] former owners," unlike others in this category, who "let them know that they were free," and the Africans "took all their [sur]names & added to their given names and have since gone by that name...."[60]

As for Cortina, still bedeviling borderland settlers, Bacon characterized him as "that prince of cutthroats and outlaws," but what was occupying Bacon then was "great deal of sickness & some suffering" he witnessed; there was "scurvy and broken bone fever": even "horses are on half rations...."[61] With every passing week, this U.S. national—like so many of his neighbors—was becoming more hostile to the presence of U.S. troops. Their presence, he huffed from Brownsville, "I am convinced, is not advantageous in any point of view, either that of health, of improvement in military knowledge, nor in the influence of respectable society...."[62]

Like other similarly situated Euro-Texans, Bacon found "nothing pleasurable and no news" along the border: "here there is absolutely nothing," he said with disgust, after a trip to Matamoros. Even the sight of an armadillo, "the oddest animal I think I ever saw," did not dent his fixed attitude. The "largest mortality" was "yet to come," along with "total sinful incompetency" of the military.[63] When he

---

58. Letter from Edward W. Bacon, 25 June 1865, Box 1, Edward W. Bacon Papers, AAS (abbrev. Bacon Papers).

59. Ibid., Letter from Edward W. Bacon, 5 July 1865.

60. Entry, 10 July 1865, John Augustus Ansley Journal, UT-A (abbrev. Ansley Journal).

61. Letter from Edward W. Bacon, 18 July 1865, Box 1, Bacon Papers.

62. Ibid., Letter from Edward W. Bacon, 5 August 1865.

63. Ibid., Letter from Edward W. Bacon, 10 August 1865.

denounced "this wretched country,"[64] he could have been referring to Mexico—or his homeland.

As for his compatriot James H. Rickard, his initial complaint was about a regional perennial, especially in Brownsville: "mosquitoes are very thick," he complained.[65] But by October he too was fixated on "the most exciting of anything about here now," meaning "the fighting across the river. Last Wednesday the liberals made an attack upon the city of Matamoros."[66] He saw what was occurring as the muscular enforcement of the Monroe Doctrine—the purported U.S. strictures against hemispheric intervention by other powers: i.e., driving Maximilian from power.[67]

It was not just mosquitoes that harassed the unwary. "Brazos is the most dismal and barren place in the world," said Levi Graybill, "not a drop of fresh water," but plenty of "lizards and scorpions" and "all kinds of venomous insects are found here," as if they were as prolific as "rabbits or hares"; then there were "geese, alligators" grouped curiously and revealingly, with "niggers and muskeetos." Mosquitoes were "of every variety and description, large & small, green, black & white, some with claws well sharpened...." Certain inhabitants were similarly inhospitable, he thought, as he "entered [a] house to see how the people live," and strangely "could not understand one word uttered by them as they were pure genuine Mexicans...." Matamoros was little better as he was struck by "natives here of a very dark color...."[68] Soon Graybill offered his "unconditional resignation" from the U.S. military,[69] his absence and the resignation of others similarly inclined perhaps igniting more reliance on the African troops he described with an offensive racist epithet.

Borderland settlers of various ideological stripes were not enthused when espying thousands of armed Africans in Texas. The wider question was how did they respond to armed Africans in Mexico with the aim of restoring the Confederacy? For by August 1865 the U.S. emissary in Alexandria, Egypt, was ringing an alarm bell about "nine hundred negroes from the Soudan or Upper Country of Egypt...to be embarked in French transports for Mexico...." There was "nothing

64. Ibid., Letter from Edward W. Bacon, 8 September 1865.

65. James H. Rickard to Sister, 21 September 1865, Box 1, James Helme Rickard Papers, AAS (abbrev. Rickard Papers).

66. Ibid., James H. Rickard to "Dear Sister," 29 October 1865.

67. Ibid., James H. Rickard to Dear Sister, 21 November 1865.

68. Levi Graybill to "Cousin Frank," 9 July 1865, Box 1, Levi Graybill Papers, Huntington Library (abbrev. Graybill Papers).

69. Ibid., Levi Graybill to Assistant Adjutant General, 7 July 1865.

clandestine about this proceeding" though there were "assurances that it is not proposed to increase this number...." Instead, the Egyptian leadership saw this deployment "as a necessary act of humanity to the Egyptian negroes who are now in Mexico," requiring backup in light of the scourge of yellow fever—though "only one...had died" from this epidemic. That Paris was subsidizing this adventure made it more palatable. The countermove proposed was placing "more than one hundred thousand" armed U.S. Negroes in Mexico along the border, which could have been transformative and revolutionary too. That was not all. Consul Charles Hale stressed that "what the Pasha [North African leader] has done in Mexico...the United States might do in Egypt at the request of some friendly power," i.e., send armed U.S. Negroes to North Africa and "provoke an intervention of the United States against himself," with similar transformative impact.[70]

Egypt continued to be wracked by enslavement of Africans, which these newly christened "African Americans" would likely oppose. The "superb position which our country at this moment occupies in the face of the world with reference to slavery and the negro race," said Hale, should be leveraged akin to London's crusading against slavery, which had delivered plaudits and acclaim.[71]

Still, Washington had good reason to seek to improve its global image splattered with the stain of slavery, for this could aid in defeating a formidable French force. By October 1865, just across the border from Brownsville, a key U.S. official was complaining that "French officers act in a very arbitrary and despotic manner toward all Americans imprisoning them without any just cause...rendering them very insecure both as regards life and property."[72] A few days later in Matamoros the same official found the "city...again in a state of siege..." as the French were confronted by a "liberal party... variously estimated at from 1800 to 3500 men, among whom are... several companies of negroes, made up of deserters and discharged soldiers from the United States army...."[73] The latter point was not a fluke, claimed the journal of traitors published in Mexico: "Negroes are, pro forma, discharged almost every hour, immediately after which they are enrolled by the so-called Liberals," and "receive a

---

70. Consul Charles Hale to Secretary Seward, 26 August 1865, Reel 4, Despatches from U.S. Consuls in Alexandria, NARA.

71. Ibid., Consul Hale to Secretary Seward, 9 September 1865.

72. Vice Consul Lucius Avery to Secretary of State, 9 October 1865, Reel 3, Despatches from U.S. Consuls in Matamoros, NARA.

73. Ibid., Vice Consul Avery to Sir, 26 October 1865.

handsome bounty...." The journal was further infuriated to report that a close relative of Kirby Smith "has been murdered by his Negro employees at Hempstead,"[74] Texas, yet another reason to remain in Mexico. On the other hand, these Negroes sensed that a French victory could mean a resurgence of neo-slavery to their detriment.

Down the road in nearby Bagdad, French officialdom was detained by November, as Cortina's men began to flex, and U.S. deserters continued to descend on Brownsville.[75] But a modicum of U.S. Negroes remained in General Sheridan's detachment with strict orders given, for example, to "obey" the commands of Captain Joseph W. Chamberlain, the "10th U.S. Colored Artillery Chief."[76]

Appomattox signaled a shift on the battlefield, not a total cessation of hostilities, for by mid-July 1865 General Grant was told alarmingly by General Sheridan about the "arrival of French and Austrian troops at Vera Cruz in considerable numbers"; a "considerable body of troops is being organized in France and Austria for Mexico" and "are to be sent to Matamoros in about two weeks."[77]

As the tumultuous year of 1865 began to fade into history, it was ever more clear that Appomattox may have promised more than it delivered. By December French officialdom that had been detained earlier in Matamoros was released; there was no vessel to return them home so the consul there requested an "American gunboat" be dispatched forthwith. For the French were far from surrendering, as a huge arsenal was just shipped to them from Havana. Roughly the same could be said of their Confederate comrades—Appomattox notwithstanding: "every steamer brings more" of them, was the news in Vera Cruz. "The Southerners," said Consul D.L. Lane, were "on their way to join the colony" being constructed with verve and "were very bitter in their feelings against our government"; they were "hoping a war will grow out of the Mexican Question between France and the United States," allowing the Confederacy to ascend. "In such an event they can bring to this country one hundred thousand men to help the French, that the whole South will rise again and fight for their independence," and "the French are anticipating

---

74. *Mexican Times*, 25 November 1865.

75. Consul D.L. Lane to Secretary Seward, 21 November 1865, Reel 9, Despatches from U.S. Consuls in Vera Cruz, NARA.

76. By Command of Major General Wright, 4 December 1865, "Index of General Orders, Department of Texas, 1865," Galveston, 31 January 1866, Huntington Library (abbrev. Index of General Orders).

77. General Sheridan to General Grant, 18 July 1865, in *War of the Rebellion, Volume XLVIII, Series I, Part II*, 1092.

the same"; they were "preparing for it" and "intend to fight to the last...." With a bravado mirroring that of the rebels, they insisted that "one Frenchman can whip ten Yankees!" Thus, there was "arrival of troops and munitions of war almost daily...."[78]

A few days later a U.S. military detachment made a 700-mile trip mostly in Texas's cotton growing areas. The "former masters," said Brigadier General E.M. Gregory of Galveston, harbored "hostility to everything pertaining to freedom," even those who recognized the advantages of "free labor." On this journey he spoke to an astonishing "25,000 freedmen and planters" and "found but few contracts made between employers and employees, such as had been made were verbal ones"—unworthy of the paper they were not written on. Still, conflict was brewing since "freedmen are well informed as to the value of their labor," and congruent with past praxis, yet another "Christmas insurrection" was being contemplated. "If however one does occur it will be brought about by the action of the white man and not the freedman...." For whatever reason, General Gregory commented that "freedmen are as a general thing strongly impressed with religious sentiments," subject to manipulation. Fortunately, they were "constantly inquiring for books" but "their rights are not properly acknowledged and guarded by the judiciary...."[79]

Thus, as had been the case since 1836 at least, U.S. Negroes continued to cross the border in search of freedom. This was not just those who wished to fight with arms in hand against the French occupiers but ordinary civilians seeking a better life. Many were greeted with something less than equanimity by U.S. officials. Thus, in late December 1865 in Matamoros, a U.S. agent determined that the "principal source of difficulty" of late "has been the large number of negroes who have come here during or since the rebellion and who being a proscribed race, <u>even here</u>," he underscored, "their rights were often trampled on and it was after repeated remonstrances that they were allowed to enjoy the privileges of white American citizens...."[80]

It was unclear how other Africans were faring civilly in Mexico, speaking of the troops dispatched from Alexandria, Egypt. More were scheduled to arrive by late 1865, but the plan had to be abandoned, the reason being—said the U.S. delegate there—"the trouble in the Soudan...caused...by the detestation entertained

---

78. Consul Lane to Secretary Seward, 6 December 1865, Reel 9, Despatches from U.S. Consuls in Vera Cruz, NARA.

79. Report of Brigadier General Gregory, 9 December 1865, Reel 1, FBR.

80. Vice Consul Avery to Secretary of State, 20 December 1865, Reel 3, Despatches from U.S. Consuls in Matamoros, NARA.

by the people and especially among the men enrolled for military duty, for the distant service...to which it was feared they were to be sent...."[81] As was their wont, the Egyptian authorities on behalf of their Parisian patrons, sought to repress this reluctance, which "surprised" the U.S. agent there, speaking of the "proposed expedition of negroes to Mexico...." One concession was that the soldiers would not be "slaves," an institution yet to be repressed in Sudan or Egypt for that matter. Their reluctance was not new and was present as early as 1863 when they were first deployed. Likewise shrouding this expedition was an additional factor, that the ostensible authority in Egypt, Ottoman Turkey, was not supportive.[82]

Thus, this deployment designed to bail out Maximilian faced insuperable obstacles, the "insurrection" in Sudan in the first instance. Even after it was "suppressed" in the words of Cherif Pasha, Minister of Foreign Affairs in Cairo, the "home sickness" of troops continued to fester in Mexico. "Slavery no longer exists in Egypt," he said stiffly, while adding a tad inconsistently that "all slaves enrolled under the flag become free in full right" anyway.[83]

Ironically, the distinct possibility arose of enslaved soldiers from Africa being dispatched to North America to confront the formerly enslaved—and now United States soldiers.

---

81. Consul Charles Hale to Secretary Seward, 13 November 1865, Reel 4, Despatches from U.S. Consuls in Alexandria, NARA.

82. Ibid., Consul Hale to Secretary Seward, 18 November 1865.

83. Ibid., Minister Pasha to Consul Hale, 16 November 1865.

Chapter *19*

Race War? 1865-1866

The travels of former rebel General Jubal Early in late 1865 were indicative of the unsteadiness of peace in the fractured U.S. By October he was in Galveston and picked up $500 dollars in gold from a Confederate cache, suggestive of their continued potency. By December he was in Cuba, where the authorities continued to view Washington suspiciously, well aware of its long-time desire to snatch the island from Spain's clutches. Early's ears were ringing with rumors about an impending war between Paris and Washington that could easily revive treasonous dreams in Dixie. "If war resulted," said his empathetic biographer, "Old Jube was determined to take up arms once more against the United States. With high hopes he left Havana for Mexico" but became angrily frustrated with a dearth of success. He was so determined to overthrow the federal regime, he was willing to upend a central tenet of settler colonialism and advocated rebels joining "'20,000 or 30,000 Comanches and Apaches'" to fight the U.S. and "'fight until they would be exterminated.'"[1] Still, as of early 1866 he was settled in Mexico, after a critical stopover in Texas: "we welcome him in our midst," said the still secessionist *Mexican Times*.[2]

"Old Jube" was then in Vera Cruz and spoke within earshot of the U.S. envoy, who recounted with emphasis how he "gave a thrilling account of his escape from the United States," allegedly on "horseback from Virginia to Galveston," then to the Bahamas, Havana—then Mexico.[3]

By April 1866 he was still in Vera Cruz, though "entirely disguised" he was headed back to Havana on a British vessel. The U.S. envoy monitoring his every move said disparagingly that "three or four weeks here makes good loyal citizens" of the most inveterate rebels,

---

1. Millard Kessler Bushing, *Old Jube: A Biography of General Jubal A. Early*, Boyce, Va.: Carr, 1961, 285, 290.

2. *Mexican Times*, 6 January 1866.

3. Consul D.L. Lane to Secretary Seward, 7 January 1866, Reel 9, Despatches from U.S. Consuls in Vera Cruz, NARA.

given the language difficulties and related problems. Rebel generals, said Consul D.L. Lane, "are cussed long, loud and deep for the glowing letters they sent home," as some of these prevaricators "bought lands near Cordova," the exile colony "for the purpose of speculation." Their "glowing letters" were designed to attract unwary homebuyers: one of these speculators confided that "if he was sure of a pardon he should return home...." As for the French, cluelessly they "make no distinction, all are Yankees that hail from the United States...."[4]

A rebel exile in Mexico City advised that "you can take a steamer from New Orleans for Vera Cruz," not that far, and from there to "Paso del Macho on the imperial railroad and then on to this city," not logistically difficult. But why leave home and hearth? "I see only trouble ahead for the South," said John Edwards. "[President] Johnson is certainly to go to the wall, and the Confederate States must either appeal again to the sword or go to the wall too"—and "the first will never be and the latter is only a question of time."[5]

From the other shore, General Sheridan was tracking Early's movements, not least since Maximilian's forces seemed to be gaining strength throughout the early stages of the post-Appomattox era, threatening to plunge the republic back into the maw of civil war. However, the French occupiers were strapped, as evidenced by their having to rely upon Sudanese soldiers in no mood to cross the Atlantic for combat. During the U.S. Civil War, it seemed that the rebels were highly motivated early on—until they met their match when the formerly enslaved Africans joined the men in blue providing an amplified motivation. When "Old Jube" considered a marriage of convenience with Comanches and Apaches, it was at a time in 1867 when Maximilian was in precipitous decline on the verge of abandoning northern Mexico as far south as Monterrey. Sheridan was arming Maximilian's opponents—as many as "30,000 muskets" at one juncture—and U.S. Negroes continued to defect to Juárez's ranks. But even then the good news from Mexico was in stark juxtaposition to troubling trends in Texas. Rebels proved "almost uncontrollable" as the Lone Star State headed toward "race war," as intended primary victims—Africans, Indigenous and their allies—seemed unprepared for the horror, though presumably having the backing of the federal regime. Although "detachments of troops were stationed in nearly

---

4. Ibid., Consul D.L. Lane to Secretary Seward, 6 April 1866.
5. John Edwards to "My Dear Tom," 18 September 1866, Mrs. L.N. Morgan Collection, UOk-N (abbrev. Morgan Collection).

every county of the state," said Sheridan, as early as 1866 pro-treason Governor James Throckmorton demanded their removal—and remained so disruptive that it was he who was removed by Sheridan in 1867. Sheridan lamented the "gross injustice toward the colored people," who already were undermining their perilous position by enlisting in droves to press a brutal offensive against those who could have been allies: the Indigenous. Thus, a "reign of lawlessness and disorder" prevailed, continuing until—and after—the pivotal 1876 presidential election, which formalized the collapse of Reconstruction. As for General Sheridan, who was despised by President Johnson, he went on to become a murderous Indian fighter, further eroding whatever allyship that Negroes could have pursued with the continent's original inhabitants.

* * *

By early January 1866, Matamoros remained a battleground—a "heroic city of a hundred sieges" was the pithy analysis heard in Washington. There were "gross outrages and murders" with defecting U.S. soldiers blamed, some of them African, according to Vice Consul Lucius Avery. "I was frequently obliged to directly interfere to rescue colored men (American citizens) from the imperial [Maximilian] ranks," as apparently the calculation had been made by the rescued that the French occupiers could not be beaten.[6] That said, Avery's major concern was the erstwhile men in gray, led by Brigadier General James Slaughter, who had drawn loyalist blood more than once. He contributed "his entire command to resist the republican forces" in Mexico and aid Maximilian. "Had it not been for the threatened active interference of confederate troops," said Avery, it was "probable that the republican forces would have been reestablished in Matamoros."[7]

By December 1865 filibusters from Texas were streaming into Mexico with the idea—said their chronicler—that their activity there "will hasten hostilities between the U.S. and France, which has been brewing for some months past...." N.C. Kendall of Texas also opined that "with the help of ten thousand Yankees the republican cause in that country would triumph," spelling disaster for rebel exiles.[8]

---

6. Vice Consul Avery to State Department, 10 January 1866, Reel 3, Despatches from U.S. Consuls in Matamoros, NARA. For source of previous paragraph, Sheridan, 233.

7. Ibid., Vice Consul Avery to State Department, 24 January 1866.

8. Sergeant N.C. Kendall, *Reminiscences of the Closing Scenes of the Great American Rebellion*, 1866, TTU (abbrev. N.C. Kendall).

Contemporaneously, the Texan James H. Rickard had heard "all sorts of rumors here about war with France," perhaps backed by London, as an "expedition" proceeded "from this side into Mexico...." "We have an ally in Russia," he reassured. Juárez's forces, amply endowed, he thought, were "offering $50 per month in gold for volunteers & expenses," backed by "regular troops...."[9] That was days before Christmas, while days after the arrival of the new year, Rickard remarked, "[U.S.] Grant is expected here soon so I hear," while Bagdad seemed up for grabs.[10]

The French emissary in Galveston too was struck by events in Bagdad and zeroed in on items supposedly stolen by those they called "*nègres*" [Negroes], which were said to be restituted to Euro-Americans. "Merchants and residents" of Matamoros were similarly upset.[11]

The idea that London might join in fortifying the occupation was not Rickard's alone. As Bagdad was contested, Secretary Seward was instructed that John Bull was also conferring with Spain on this same matter, i.e., "sustaining the Empire against the interference of the United States." But since arms for Maximilian were bought not just in Havana but New York City too, this indicated the broadening base of the occupation. Indeed, arms from Havana for Maximilian were delivered by U.S. vessels. Such vessels often had other baggage aboard in the form of high ranking rebels, one of whom upon arriving immediately pledged fealty to Maximilian and pledged to capture Cortina.[12]

On the opposite coast in Mazatlán, rebels were still arriving by January 1866. Correspondingly, Seward was told that the occupiers "look upon the Americans as enemies," meaning a man-o-war should be sent.[13]

In March 1866 rebels were flooding into Vera Cruz too—in "vessels and steamers in considerable numbers to join the Confederate Colony at Cordova," said a spectator. Maury, their sponsor, was en route to London in search of backing, while 9000 more French and Austrian

---

9. James H. Rickard to Sister, 22 December 1865, Rickard Papers.

10. Ibid., Letter from James H. Rickard, 14 January 1866.

11. Report, 8 February 1866, Galveston Consulate. Attached and similarly dated is a protest signed by the "Merchants and Residents" of Matamoros.

12. Consul D.L. Lane to Secretary Seward, 13 January 1866, Reel 9, Despatches from U.S. Consuls in Vera Cruz, NARA.

13. Consul B.R. Carman to Secretary Seward, 1 January 1866, Reel 3, Despatches from U.S. Consuls in Mazatlan, NARA.

troops were about to dock.[14] As May 1866 loomed, 1100 French troops landed and headed for the interior of Mexico, while a key Mexican supporter of the Emperor was of the view that the "only obstacle of the Empire was the United States," but these sly anti-Washington forces well "knew how to deal with the U.S. Congress…with plenty of money judiciously distributed among the Congressmen recognition would soon be brought about…." Meanwhile, rebel leader and premier diplomat Beverly Tucker of Virginia and his family arrived, thought to be headed straight to the Cordova Colony.[15]

For quite a while after Appomattox, the exiles were optimistic, perhaps unduly so: "the colony at Carlota grew apace and was prosperous," said one observer. This was at a moment when 40,000 rebels were expected to decamp to Mexico, providing an ongoing threat to U.S. security. France's maximum leader, Louis Napoleon, "believed religiously in the success of the Southern Confederacy," and this enthusiasm was exported to the colony. He may have been overly influenced by the stories that pointed to a rebel sub-treasury in Austin containing $300,000 in gold and silver, a hefty subsidy for subversion.[16]

As of March 1866 there was a French vessel sailing between New Orleans, Galveston and Mexican ports transporting, according to a U.S. analysis, "disaffected countrymen" so as to "enter the military service of the empire" and "augment the number of colonists at Cordoba [or Cordova] under the auspices of the notorious rebel M.F. Maury, imperial commissioner of colonization." Only recently "about fifty officers from the late rebel army" were delivered in Tampico—"all of whom are armed with a pair of revolvers and other weapons" and the "hope of seeing fresh troubles springing up in the southern states."[17]

France's consulate at Galveston kept a curious eye on U.S. troop movements and instructed Paris that the garrisons in Texas were strong. Federal troops were portrayed as disciplined and capable. "*Nègres*" were working well, it was thought. Cotton was being planted in profusion, and as of February 1866, it appeared that the harvest would be as significant.[18] Careful attention was paid by the consulate to wagons heading from San Antonio to Mexico with

---

14. Consul D.L. Lane to Secretary Seward, 9 March 1866, Reel 9, Despatches from U.S. Consuls in Vera Cruz, NARA.

15. Ibid., Consul Lane to Secretary Seward, 30 April 1866.

16. J. Edwards, 104, 78, 86, 13.

17. Consul Franklin Chase to Assistant Secretary F.W. Seward, 10 March 1866, Reel 4, Despatches from U.S. Consuls in Tampico, NARA.

18. Report, 13 February 1866, Galveston Consulate.

all manner of goods, though it was unclear if this cargo included ammunition for Juárez's forces—or the emperor's.[19]

When in early March 1866 a large number of U.S. forces, almost all cavalry, departed Galveston by sea for Mexico, they were described by Paris's man as not of African ancestry but of sizable stature and impressive.[20] The U.S. was adjudged by the consulate to be more competent than either the French or British in moving forces from one side of the nation to the other, and although harmony was detected between the soldiers of various ancestries, their analysis suggested that they did not view this as eternal.[21]

However, that was not the only issue there that was of concern in Washington. By February Hippolyte Lenoir in Bagdad "saw several drunken negroes in the uniform of U.S. soldiers breaking stones and driving the citizens out.... my door...was broken open by some of the band" and "they demanded my money" and "threatened to kill me and my wife." Then they "commenced breaking the furniture in the house" and "we had to leave." Returning home later, he found his home "completely gutted, everything...either destroyed or carried away...."[22]

A report in Spanish confirmed events akin to the above occurring in Matamoros with merchants there charging U.S. backing for anti-French forces along with "pillage of Bagdad by the negro forces"; this was a "robbery without parallel in modern history," little more than a "freebooting expedition" and "an armed invasion of the filibusters...."[23] Ironically, if the U.S. had moved to desegregate their armed forces, which was to require many more decades to effectuate, they could have disrupted—possibly—any retributive or redistributive tendencies among Negro troops. Instead, it was promulgated by January 1866 that "in the District of the Rio Grande, all the colored troops will constitute a Separate Brigade.... the Brigade of white troops in that District will remain a Separate Brigade as already constituted."[24]

Interestingly, French operatives surveilled the differences between these "separate brigades" and were much more critical of the Negroes.

19. Ibid., Report, 26 February 1866.

20. Ibid., Report, 4 March 1866.

21. Ibid., Report, 14 March 1866.

22. Hippolyte Lenoir to Consul Avery, 7 February 1866, Reel 3, Despatches from U.S. Consuls in Matamoros, NARA.

23. Translated Report, 16 January 1866, Reel 4, Despatches from U.S. Consuls in Tampico, NARA.

24. Index of General Orders.

Like certain Euro-Texans, their feeling was that Africans in the borderlands were doomed.[25]

Contrastingly, in Washington testimony piled up about a regime
of terror inflicted upon the emancipated. "There is a fearful state of
things," said Brigadier General W.E. Strong in early 1866: "the freedmen are in a worse condition than they ever were as slaves," as the
planters and their allies "take every opportunity to vent their rage
and hatred upon the blacks. They are frequently beaten unmerci-
fully and shot down like wild beasts...maltreated in every possible
way." It was the "same old story of cruelty only there is more of it
in Texas than any southern state I have visited," perhaps because of
the exponential growth of Africans in the state from 275,000 ca. 1861,
with 125,000 more arriving during the war, complicating what was
antiseptically called "race relations." The oppressors pleaded that
"there is no hope for a better condition of affairs unless they can be
permitted to resort to the overseer, whip and hounds...." Although
"Juneteenth" was said to declare enslavement extinct, according to
this military man, "two-thirds of the freedmen in the section of country which I travelled over have never received one cent of wages
since they were declared free...." He actually "saw freedmen east of
the Trinity River who did not know that they were free until I told
them...." This was the case in a good deal of East Texas: "the freedmen are still held in a state of slavery and are being treated with the
most intense cruelty by their former masters...." Others thought the
entire war was "to free the negroes and that if the [planters] were
beaten, all the lands and property would be taken from them and
given to the blacks and the poor white and rich people alike would
be enslaved...." Responsively, "very many of the ex-Confederate
officers and soldiers wear their old uniforms, with buttons, insignia of rank and nearly every [rebel] we met in travelling was armed
with a knife, seven shooter and double-barreled shotgun...." While
all this was occurring, "Comanches committed depredations in
November [1865] within fifteen or twenty miles of Waco," diverting
the attention of the blue suited army.[26]

About a month later Major General David Stanley reported on the
Lone Star State in similarly disturbing terms. There was a "widespread feeling" that Texas "had not been surrendered by [General]

---

25. Report, 26 February 1866, Galveston Consulate.

26. Report by Brigadier General W.E. Strong, 1 January 1866, in "U.S.
Congress, Joint Commission on Reconstruction, Report: Florida, Lou-
isiana, Texas," Washington, D.C., 1866 (abbrev. Joint Commission on
Reconstruction).

Lee," was not "conquered by the United States," and "slavery was still worth holding on to…." "I consider Texas in a worse condition than any other state," he announced, "for the reason that they were never whipped there…." Absent external pressure, these diehards "would hold them in a bondage more galling than they were ever held before and they would be in a worse condition. I have no hesitation in making that statement…." The notion of compensation for enslaved property, in any case, was "almost [a] universal feeling," i.e., "that the government was bound to pay for the negroes…." The Texas rebels were noticeably "insolent and overbearing," compared to those back east, possibly because they did not feel defeated. He saluted residents of German origin who were "even radical," but in light of the conflict with France, he observed, "if we become involved in a foreign war almost the entire American population of Texas would go over to our enemies," barring Negroes. "The [Euro-American] women were universally rebels, contemptuous" and "insolent." As for businessmen, they were "generally rascals," having "made more money there during the war" than they could count. Also there was "more solid money…in circulation in Texas than in any other state," improving their fortunes commensurately. Among these "leading men" was the chilling notion that the "negro was a doomed race" and, alas, they were willing to hasten the purportedly inevitable. Treasonous "leading men" were overrepresented among newspaper publishers: "I can safely say that four newspapers out of something like a hundred are the only ones that may be regarded as loyal…." But there were armed Negro soldiers, a formidable stumbling block, who encouraged the idea that "all the lands were to be divided among them…." Per the mythology of Negroes being unaware of emancipation before "Juneteenth," he commented that a "negro community is very much like a system of telegraph wires; what one knows the whole state knows in a very short time…." And with a final complicating flourish, he added, their supposed ally, Governor A.J. Hamilton, "drinks too much whiskey,"[27] rendering him unreliable, if not incoherent.

Governor Hamilton may have taken one nip too many from his flask in February 1866 when he said, "it is a favorite phrase of many that 'this is a white man's government.'" Well, he continued, "I thank God that this is a white man's government and I humbly trust that

---

27. Report by Major General David Stanley, 7 February 1866, in Joint Commission on Reconstruction. See also T.S. Bowers, Assistant Adjutant General to Major General H.G. Wright, 17 February 1866, in Index of General Orders, 1867. Here concern is expressed about newspapers with "sentiments of disloyalty and hostility to the Government."

the time will never come when it shall cease to be so...." Perhaps under pressure, he retreated a bit, seeming to praise emancipation—though also unfirm on the "right of suffrage too."[28] And this was an ally?

Lieutenant Colonel H.S. Hall also addressed the legislators. First he explained, "I lost my arm" in battle, then reaffirmed what had been bruited: "Christmas and New Year's holiday [just past] there was a general cry that there would be a negro insurrection...." But what grabbed attention was his conclusion that if the Freedmen's Bureau were withdrawn, then the newly emancipated would be "forced to labor without any compensation under some system of compulsion nearly the same as formerly" and "liable to worse treatment than ever before...."[29] General William Strong of the Bureau was in shock to find slavery existing in eastern Texas in the fall of 1865 and, again, by February 1866.[30]

Another witness in Washington of unclear identification confirmed the distressing news that if France and the U.S. moved toward war, this would lead to a "general declaration" of sovereignty in Texas, i.e., "securing the separate independence of Texas," for "that was the dominant idea in Texas during the late war—to separate from the Confederate States," again aided by Paris. Already, rebels then in Mexico had transferred detailed maps of Texas to "imperial authorities... for the forces of the French in the event of a war between the United States and France and Texas became the theatre of operations...." But this testifier too found it troubling that "since the surrender freedmen have been tried under the old slave code of Texas, convicted under that code and sentenced to the penitentiary,"[31] well on its way to supplanting the plantation as the site of oppression.

Meanwhile, the rebel migration to Mexico had not ceased—or so thought Charles Talcott, who had arrived only recently. The "number of Confederates here is now large," he said—before acknowledging that "many are disappointed that they have not been able to get into employment that pays handsomely...." On the one hand, he was

---

28. "Message of Governor A.J. Hamilton to the Texas State Convention... delivered February 10, 1866," Austin: State Gazette Book and Job Office, 1866, NYHS. Cf., Andrew Jackson Hamilton, "An Address on 'Suffrage and Reconstruction': The Duty of the People, the President and Congress," Boston: Impartial-Suffrage, 1866, AAS.

29. Report by Lieutenant Colonel H.S. Hall, 20 February 1866, in Joint Commission on Reconstruction.

30. W.L. Richter, 86.

31. Witness, February 1866, in Joint Committee on Reconstruction.

employed "as an engineer at $600 per [year]," but this was at the behest of a "wealthy Mexican...." Yes, he was "living pleasantly and comfortably," yet he confessed tearily, that he tended to "often long for dear old Virginia as it was & our old kind friends as they are." Besides, "the Confederates here in the city are not very interesting," and even "the children learn Spanish slowly," for "acquiring an entirely new language I find quite a task...."[32]

The French consulate in Galveston too was quite concerned with the activities of Negro troops in the borderlands, who were conflated with outlaws then rampaging—and whom the occupiers should have hanged.[33] However, since the occupiers were worried that European troops posted along the border might defect to the U.S.— which made Paris even more dependent upon disgruntled Sudanese and compromised Mexicans—this signaled that Maximilian's future was cloudy indeed.[34] One Euro-Texan bumped into some of these deserters who had crossed the border. Although in a separate note this man, N.C. Kendall, pointed out that "the planters of Louisiana are mostly of French or Spanish descent and the negroes speak the French almost altogether" in many areas of the state, "it is not uncommon to meet a shade that cannot either speak or understand a word of English." However, Juárez's forces, according to Kendall, were busily recruiting in Texas.[35]

For the *Mexican Times*, the rebel propaganda sheet, the incoming news was like blessed gifts from heaven, justifying their exile and plans to resume war. Back in Virginia, near Hampton Roads, their observer reported breathlessly about "serious trouble among the negroes," who were "provided with weapons of all kinds, muskets, carabines, pistols," making them "armed and dangerous. Many of them have been in the service and are able to use their weapons with effect," making "white people feel very insecure," leaving them "at the mercy" of the formerly enslaved.[36]

In truth, it was quite a turnabout when the formerly enslaved, forced into obsequiousness, were converted into gun-toting enforcers of order. "Negro troops are to garrison all but three of the Southern seacoast forts," blared the *Mexican Times*. "Whenever the white and colored soldiers are brought together," chided this journal, "the

---

32. Charles Talcott to "My Dear [Hill] Kean," 9 February 1866, Letters to Robert Garlick, UVa-C.

33. Report, 20 January 1866, Galveston Consulate.

34. Ibid., Report, 29 January 1866.

35. N.C. Kendall.

36. *Mexican Times*, 4 November 1865.

irrepressible conflict develops itself...." Accompanying this story was another depicting a kind of normalized slavery in Cuba.[37] Then there was another story about the perils of emancipation in Jamaica and the consequent "atrocities" inflicted by "infuriated negroes."[38] These exiles knew from harsh experience that their project would be sunk if it could be shown decisively and unequivocally that their patron, Maximilian, favored slavery. So this was denied vigorously by the traitorous expatriates, citing his 1860 journey to Brazil as evidence.[39]

Jamaica aside, the "diabolical acts of negro soldiers" in the U.S. were what got the blood boiling among these treasonous exiles in Mexico,[40] aided and abetted by the Freedmen's Bureau, that "brutal juggernaut of cruelty and oppression...." [41] The FB was a hated symbol of a new era among many settlers, akin to the manner in which white supremacists a century later looked upon "affirmative action." Former rebel leader N.C. Kendall called it the "biggest humbug that has ever been forced upon the American people...."[42]

Nor were such concerns assuaged when credible stories emerged about what scholar John McGraw termed "general dread throughout...East Texas" about a "negro insurrection" by December 1865. Frantic settlers then, he said, "took everything in the way of arms from the negroes" and sought to "disabuse the negroes'" minds of the idea that "forty acres and a mule" would be accorded to them in a grand Christmas present. Yet the apprehensions of the settlers surged nonetheless, as they "hourly expected a knife at their throats or flames over [their] heads."[43] This tumult was preceded by a so-called "Soldier-negro riot in Houston," unignored by the local press.[44]

A strategic objective of the planter class was to reduce sharply the number of Negro troops, perceived as a deterrent to maltreatment of Negro workers. "During the month of March" 1866, said General Gregory of the Freedmen's Bureau, "instances of maltreatment and violent abuse have perceptibly increased," which can be "readily traced to the very considerable reduction of the military

37. Ibid., 25 November 1865.

38. Ibid., 28 November 1865.

39. Ibid., 25 April 1866.

40. Ibid., 17 March 1866.

41. Ibid., 31 March 1866.

42. N.C. Kendall.

43. John McGraw, "The Texas Constitution of 1866," Ph.D. dissertation, TTU, 1959, 52, 54.

44. *Houston Telegraph*, 3 December 1865.

forces…. cruelties will increase in a ratio proportionate to the army reduction…."[45]

*   *   *

The inflamed rhetoric may have become more impassioned as the rebels' prospects for prevailing diminished, not just because of balking by Sudanese soldiers reluctant to be deployed thousands of miles from home, thereby imperiling Maximilian's shaky tenure and treasonous expatriation along with it. Alexander Watkins Terrell, the Texas rebel who went on to become a premier U.S. envoy, sensed as early as November 1865 that an entente was developing between Paris and Washington.[46]

Although the exiles may have forgotten, Paris was stung by the continuing effort from 1861-1865 by the secessionists to conscript French nationals for their flailing revolt.[47] Paris had to wonder if housing dead-enders in Mexico was worth it, particularly when lurking on Mexico's northern border were tens of thousands of soldiers in blue, a number with itchy trigger fingers, a reality monitored relentlessly from the Galveston consulate. Paris knew of their roots in the U.S. Midwest and were sufficiently close to describe a number of them as being tall and broad shouldered and that their equipment was imperfect but deadly; these troops being uninclined to drinking seemed troubling to this envoy. Besides their force could be easily reinforced from the Mississippi River or the Gulf of Mexico.[48]

Strikingly, the reports from France's man in Galveston echoed and shaped postwar Texas and U.S. conservatism. He thought that the problem with the newly emancipated was their own purported slothfulness, and that they would fare worse than during slavery, to the point where they could disappear.[49]

The persistent whining of the French envoy in Galveston illustrated the shakiness of the mission to Mexico. U.S. nationals simply did not comprehend that Paris was seeking to help Mexico to reconstitute itself, which was not easy since—it was thought—the nation was comprised not only of Spaniards and pirates from

---

45. General E.M. Gregory to O.O. Howard, 18 April 1866, Reel 1, FBR.

46. A.W. Terrell, 72.

47. On this dispute see Reports by Consul and responses by rebels, 10 June 1862; 11 June 1862; 14 June 1862; 15 June 1862; 23 June 1862; 24 June 1862; 25 June 1862; 27 June 1862, Galveston Consulate.

48. Ibid., Report, 15 December 1865.

49. Ibid., Report, 4 April 1866.

the Pan-European world but Africans and Indigenous too. He did not seem to think that ethnic diversity was a plus. Thus by late December 1865 the conclusion was reached that France's blood and treasure was being wasted in Mexico, at a time when Germany and Italy were consolidating. There was no need to overthrow Maximilian, as his regime would collapse from its own corpulent weight. The occupation, quite dangerously, was eroding anti-U.S. sentiment in Mexico, important for France's future hemispheric ambitions: unusually, French travelers in Mexico had to pretend they were from the U.S. in order to avoid harassment—or worse.[50] Yet one former rebel sergeant was speaking hopefully that the occupation would "hasten hostilities between the U.S. and France, which has been brewing for some months past...."[51]

Nevertheless, Paris thought that the Catholicism that prevailed in Mexico and the borderlands was an asset worthy of tapping. Priests had been building schools, winning friends and influencing more. Careful note was taken of a recent Democratic Party convention in New Orleans that declared that religiosity should be expelled from politics—though the inference was not drawn that this was simply a step toward settler unity, boding ill for Africans and Indigenes. Much attention was focused on conflicts between state and federal constitutions, as if Paris intended to engage in judicial arbitrage.[52] Subsequently, when Maximilian encountered difficulty in recruiting troops in Europe, the point was raised to recruit among Irish Catholics in the U.S. and elsewhere.[53]

Also not boding well for Maximilian was the point—which even Paris recognized—that the Emperor had difficulty in recruiting to his side anti-Juárez Mexicans. Instead, many of them were flocking to San Antonio, including Jesús Ortega, a leading jurist.[54]

The Emperor's difficulty in recruiting may have been influenced by the odious reputation of his allies. Alexander Watkins Terrell, the Texas luminary in exile, critiqued what he saw as the "racial traits" of Mexicans. He was complimentary of the Mexican luminary Juan Almonte, but seemed to ascribe his assets to being educated in the U.S.—though he had the earmarks of a "full blood Indian."[55]

---

50. Ibid., Report, 26 October 1865.
51. N.C. Kendall.
52. Report, 20 December 1865, Galveston Consulate.
53. Ibid., Report, 29 January 1866.
54. Ibid.
55. A.W. Terrell, 74, 75.

This was exemplary of a major problem the rebels faced in the borderlands: their contempt for Mexicans. Terrell's viewpoint was not his alone, for it was then in Corpus Christi that a U.S. military officer aligned with "colored troops" was moved to observe that "Mexicans are not classified there, in the common parlance of the country, as white men,"[56] the top rung on humanity's ladder, it was thought. In lockstep, the U.S. consul in Matamoros by the summer of 1866, while reporting that Carvajal [Carbajal] was in control of Tamaulipas—though Cortina was surging—mentioned in passing that "Mexicans are an excitable people."[57] This was echoed by yet another former rebel military man: N.C. Kendall was acerbic toward the "treachery of the Spaniard, Mexican and Indian (of which they are mostly an amalgamation)" which "shows itself in the female as well as male inhabitants of this 'God Forsaken Country.'"[58]

The soon-to-be infamous George Custer was then in command of a cavalry unit in the borderlands and he too found Euro-Americans generally to be "hostile and antagonistic…. in Texas…it would hardly be possible to find a man who has been strictly faithful to the Union," with murders so common by them as to be routine. Dangerously and curiously, he was asked what would be the reaction if the U.S. were to be "involved in a foreign war with Great Britain or France," hardly hypothetical given events in Mexico: "that question comes up in conversation," he said bewilderingly. This was just one more indicator that settlers remained up in arms: "I believe a white man has never been hung for murder in Texas, although it is the law. Cases have occurred of white men meeting freedmen they never saw before and murdering them merely from this feeling of hostility to them as a class…." In short, the settlers were continuing to affix the badges and indicia of slavery to Africans as many demanded "the right to transfer freedmen without their consent to another owner," and "they would inaugurate a system of oppression that would be equally as bad as slavery itself…." He had an inkling as to why, recalling Civil War battles—e.g., the Battle of Trevilian Station—where he was ordered to "attack the enemy in the rear," but "no man in my command knew the road," so "a negro guided me to the point I desired to reach. And this occurred in a large number of cases within my experience," where "almost invariably" there were

---

56. Report by Lieutenant Wilson Miller, 19 February 1866, in Joint Commission on Reconstruction.

57. Consul Lucius Avery to Sir, 9 August 1866, Despatches from U.S. Consuls in Matamoros, NARA.

58. N.C. Kendall.

"negro guides" pointing the way. "They would count the guns and troops...with remarkable accuracy."[59] This service to the state was hardly forgotten by those who had betrayed the state.

Major General Custer may have known what another soldier had noticed: the "boys in gray of the late CSA...still wear their uniform[s]...." Predictably, their red-hot animus was often directed toward Negro soldiers. "Another negro soldier was shot and instantly killed," said Texas rebel N.C. Kendall off-handedly in April 1866; "two negro soldiers were murdered last night and several more wounded.... collisions occur every day on the streets between the black and white soldiers"; then a "negro soldier was shot dead by a lawyer...." As he saw things, "negro soldiers in this state are a great annoyance to the inhabitants.... they are often insolent and insulting and in some cases have compelled ladies to leave the sidewalks"; it was "not uncommon for them to resort to firearms to resent an imaginary wrong done them by the whites...." Kendall thought he could answer the question of why the Lone Star State appeared to be more of a hellhole of bloodshed than other regions. "The people of this state have never seen the destruction of war, an invading army never having penetrated to the interior, consequently there are still a few bitter secessionists in the state...." Furthermore, he said, "people in this state have been growing rich during the war, while those of her sister states have lost millions in money and property," with Texas settlers less prone to compromise as a result. The bold rebels in Texas were paying musicians to repeatedly play their theme song: "Dixie." Cocking a snook, this effrontery was rendered, said Kendall, "in front of the Department Headquarters in the presence of federal soldiers and for no other purpose than to annoy the 'blue jackets'...." But it was Negro soldiers, above all, who inflamed his passions: the "sooner these troops are removed from the state," he huffed, "the better."[60]

Yet demonstrated insolence of Negro troops aside, it was also true that "Anglo criminals," according to one scholar, were "committing night robberies while disguised as negroes," and it was not unusual when a "group of whites in blackface beat and robbed a German...in his home near Brenham...." Then there were the documented complaints of rape or attempted rape of Negro women by

---

59. Report, Major General George Custer, 10 March 1866, in Joint Committee on Reconstruction.

60. N.C. Kendall.

Euro-American men, as if slavery had not ended. Little wonder there was palpable fear of "race war" during Reconstruction.[61]

One problem with such a conflict—from Washington's viewpoint—was the continuing heavy reliance on Negro soldiers in the border-lands, not an advantage in winning over settlers as a whole. In Texas's next door neighbor, New Mexico, soldiers were routinely expelled from the ranks. One example among many involved José Dolores Analla, an infantryman, who deserted and was sentenced to hard labor, "wearing a ball weighing twelve pounds attached to his left leg by a chain nine feet long...and at the expiration of his service," said officialdom, he was "to have his head shaved and be drummed out of the service...." A number of Spanish-surnamed soldiers were treated similarly, while Negro soldiers—with fewer options—found it necessary to remain enrolled in the military.[62] Faced with similar charges, Mauricio Arce hightailed it from New Mexico to Mexico. This was at a time when Negro troops were being ordered to the upper tributaries of the Arkansas River, presumably to confront Indigenes, which highlighted their importance.[63]

If it was any consolation, there were not just Spanish-surnamed soldiers who were being treated roughly. As Analla was veritably walking the plank, Corporal Gustave Lecroit—"a Frenchman and speaks the English language very imperfectly" was the official report—was found guilty of "neglect of duty...." This was occurring when the frightful spectacle of "mutiny" was invoked.[64] Negro soldiers too were accused of revolting, initially in Louisiana, then in San Antonio.

As ever, Cortina was on the march attracting numerous Mexicans to his banner (his family owned land on both sides of the border), who may have appreciated his unfurling the Mexican flag, even on the U.S. side of the border.[65]

But it was not just the recent past that was infuriating settlers and some of the soldiers from their families. As Major General Custer was providing testimony, a self-proclaimed Texas Indian fighter noticed a "Big Negro among the Indian band, who appeared to be

61. Smallwood, 92.

62. Report from Santa Fe, 10 January 1866, in Index of General Orders... New Mexico District, 1865-1868.

63. Ibid., Order from Brevet Brigadier General James H. Carleton, 15 August 1866 and 10 September 1866.

64. Report on Corporal Lecroit, 26 June 1866 in Index of General Orders... Department of Texas.

65. W.L. Richter, 56.

their chief [who] ordered a charge against the three ranch hands" and then went further to "answer...shots from his own pistol...." There were other Negroes and "three Mexicans" too but the "Big Negro" riveted their attention: he was "unusually large.... this large Negro...was in command...."[66]

Yet indicative of the perilous fate ahead for Negroes was the point that Major General Custer, like many officers, did not necessarily accept the simple notion of Negro equality. Most U.S. troops in the borderlands, at any rate, did not necessarily see as their top priority to protect the newly emancipated but to confront Indigenes, intimidate Mexicans and threaten French occupiers.[67]

Indeed, one potent implication of the end of the U.S. Civil War was that it provided a further rationale for upending Indigenes, especially those who backed the rebels. However, given the political and ideological underdevelopment in the still rapacious republic, even those who were loyal were punished, quite cynically. On the first day of spring in 1866, the Seminole Nation entered a treaty with Washington wherein it repudiated the 1 August 1861 pact it had brokered with the rebels—and forfeited more land as a result—though a number remained loyal. Still, Seminoles were compelled to relinquish over 2 million acres of land for a pittance: $352,262. As a sweetener designed to win over these Africans and, possibly, split the Nation, the agreement noted that "there are among the Seminoles many persons of African descent and blood, who have no interest or property in the soil," but this should now be rectified.[68]

At the same time, in one of the lengthiest treaties ever signed between the rapacious republicans and Indigenes, Cherokees too repudiated their "pretended treaty made with the so-called Confederate states" of 7 October 1861; this was not only "repudiated" but was "void" too. Yet the article that indicated there would be no compensation to "owners of slaves so emancipated" was bound to make some Cherokee as livid as former slaveholders in Texas then running amok.[69]

---

66. Captain John Elkins, *Indian Fighting on the Texas Frontier*, Amarillo: Russell & Cockrell, 1929, 46.

67. Smallwood, 112, 113.

68. "Treaty Between the United States of America and the Seminole Nation of Indians Concluded March 21, 1866...Proclaimed August 16, 1866," Huntington Library.

69. Treaty Proclaimed 11 August 1866, in "Treaties of the United States of America and the Cherokee Nation from 1785," Tahlequah, Cherokee Nation: National Printing Office, 1870, 119-138, 120, 123, Huntington Library.

Nevertheless, with U.S. troops fixated on the threat from Mexico, it was more difficult to focus on the challenge to settlers presented by Indigenes, many of whom were still reeling from the U.S. Civil War. Former rebel leader N.C. Kendall was bowled over when he spotted a band of "Tonkaways" [sic] who in his view "are the largest in stature and the most athletic and barbarous tribe of savages we have ever seen...."[70] But they too were on their last legs, despite playing a relatively minor role during the civil war.

And then there were Mexicans, who had the ear of Washington, who found distasteful this traitorous group of exiles leading what was termed sniffingly the "disaffected," dragging with them south of the border "their prejudices and their peculiar system of labor...." Aghast, this correspondent with Secretary Seward found it astonishing that "they have gone to the extreme of practically re-establishing a fact, in Mexico, the odious institution of slavery...a slavery so much the more odious because it is not restricted to color or determination of caste.... this slavery is hereditary...."[71]

This dispiriting analysis was echoed by an official of the Freedmen's Bureau, who found in mid-1866 that "it is too true that the conditions of the freedmen in the northern portion of this state is [sic] far worse than when they were slaves," mandating the "necessity for more troops" to overturn "the farce" then obtaining.[72]

Erstwhile enslavers were said to be "dyspeptic over the loss of their slaves," ready to turn back the hands of time by any means necessary. There was a "great scarcity of labor" in Texas, "notwithstanding during the war...vast numbers (thousands) of slaves... were run into this state from east of the Mississippi River...." This was a partial result of Africans resisting being treated in the old way. Consequently, said Major General J.B. Kiddo of the Bureau, there was an effort to "inaugurate a system of white emigration from Europe," for the "whole movement is based upon the assumption that negroes cannot be relied upon...and that they are destined to die out as a race...."[73]

An early scholar found that "the negroes' idleness and reluctance to sign contracts had led the planters to concoct a scheme

70. N.C. Kendall.

71. Mr. Romero to Secretary Seward, 5 October 1865, in U.S. Senate, 39th Congress, 1st Session, Ex. Doc., No. 8, VaHS-R.

72. William Sinclair, Galveston to John Morrison, Palestine, Texas, 23 June 1866, Reel 1, FBR.

73. Major General J.B. Kiddo to O.O. Howard, 23 July 1866, Reel 1, FBR.

to introduce immigrants...." To that end Thomas Affleck was dispatched to Europe to round up laborers.[74]

The Bureau could only operate effectively with troops nearby, but pressure mounted to withdraw them. Thus, Africans were not only being treated as if slavery had not ended, but planters, said a Bureau official, "would not feed old people who had formerly been their slaves. They were too old to earn their livelihood and the civil authorities would not receive and treat them as they did whites similarly situated." Hence "actual starvation" was looming—before "rations were issued."[75] It was not just imposed hunger that was battering Africans. From his prison cell former rebel Postmaster General John Reagan urged his fellow Texans at all costs to bar "'universal negro suffrage.'" As he spoke, there were 10,000 former rebels reportedly stationed in Mexico. Their presence cast a long shadow over the borderlands, making his ominous challenge all the more threatening.[76]

The double standard, which was to mark Jim Crow, was already flowering. At the observance of the national holiday on 4 July 1866 in Matagorda, the sheriff chose to "arrest" Africans "for carrying concealed weapons," while Euro-Texans were "not molested."[77]

Yet despite their overly ambitious plans, the rebel exiles faced insuperable obstacles. There was the internal opposition to Maximilian which was exacerbated by the massive deployment of foreign troops. There were the tens of thousands of U.S. troops lurking on the border and the material assistance to the Juárez forces. And there was the difficulty of adjusting to a foreign land, especially since many of these same men had been involved years earlier in conquering vast swaths of Mexican soil, which did not endear them to many of the local population.

When Henry Watkins Allen, one of the leaders of this treasonous bunch, expired in Mexico in the Spring of 1866, it was a deadly blow to traitorous pretensions. He was a brigadier general for the rebels and was wounded in epochal battles at both Shiloh and Baton Rouge, along with having served as the Pelican State's governor. Defiant to the end, in his casket he was laid out in his gray uniform draped

---

74. W.L. Richter, 205.

75. Major General J.B. Kiddo, Galveston to Commissioners and Generals, 11 July 1866, Reel 1, FBR.

76. W.L. Richter, 79. Cf., "The Minority Report in Favor of Extending the Right of Suffrage with Certain Limitation to All Men without Distinction of Race or Color Made in the Texas Reconstruction Convention by E. Degener," 24 February 1866, Austin: Southern Intelligencer Report, 1866, AAS.

77. William Sinclair to Captain, 25 July 1866, Reel 1, FBR.

with the bars and stars banner. Yet he was buried in the cemetery devoted to U.S. nationals—over the objection of U.S. entreaties: a final rebuke to Confederate aspirations.[78]

Allen was assuredly under stress, which may have hastened his death. Though he began a popular periodical, he was out of money yet too proud to beg. He thought he would receive relief in Paris, while noting that the "British Minister (Mr. Scarlett) has been very kind to me. I have received many courtesies at his hands...." Weeks before his passing, he was slated to depart Vera Cruz for Europe; he was also "determined to visit Jerusalem and the Holy Land" but, alas, death rudely interrupted his reverie.[79] This demise, and Allen's concomitant poverty, occurred though Maximilian had supplied a considerable $10,000 to his journalistic enterprise.[80]

Coincidentally, after Allen's expiration, Secretary Seward heard that "a great many southerners have left Mexico and returned to the United States"[81]—not necessarily good news for the newly emancipated. But it would have been premature to pop the corks on the champagne bottles, for just before Allen died, arriving in Galveston from his home in Georgia was one of the foremost rebel military leaders: James Longstreet.[82]

Interestingly, a former rebel sergeant who did not escape southward was not necessarily embracing some of these returnees. N.C. Kendall spoke with asperity of one rebel who "deserted the South and fled to Mexico" but was "too cowardly to come over to the North and take sides with us"; then they return and "prepare...the contract for furnishing the troops...with beef...." Kendall was no stranger in Texas, quite familiar with the area around the Brazos River: "in this valley are some of the finest cotton plantations in the Southern States and in fact is said to be the best land in the state for agricultural purposes...."[83] So, he likely knew of what he spoke.

By mid-1866, despite—or perhaps because of—declining fortunes, Paris had committed elite troops of the feared French Foreign Legion to Mexico, but this occurred in the midst of a yellow fever outbreak,

78. Consul Marcus Otterbourg to Secretary Seward, 5 May 1866, Reel 5, Despatches from U.S. Consuls in Mexico City, NARA.

79. S. Dorsey, 340, 341, 342.

80. *Mexican Times*, 22 January 1867.

81. Consul Otterbourg to Secretary Seward, 5 May 1866, Reel 5, Despatches from U.S. Consuls in Mexico City, NARA.

82. N.C. Kendall.

83. N.C. Kendall.

compromising their well-being.[84] Mexico was then reeling from the ravages of war, which included discharged soldiers from both sides of the border and various deserters, all of whom were as stable as nitro-glycerin. Fortunately for Mexico—but sadly for U.S. Negroes—many were headed to New Orleans; they were labeled authoritatively as "destitute and of the most dissolute habits...many such persons" of this type.[85]

This riffraff not only included dissolute rebels but refuse from the French forces.[86] Over the past few years these men—including the French—had attacked the U.S. consulate and despoiled the flag, which, it was said, they "despised."[87]

However, rebels had other options beyond Mexico that may have seemed more attractive. Unlike this southern neighbor, for example, there were Cuba and Brazil where support for enslavement of Africans was hardly ambiguous. Brazil, being farther from the U.S. than Cuba, was seen as a safer choice. Frank McMullen of Hill County, Texas, actually had lived in Mexico and had served in the region with the notorious William Walker before embarking for South America. But John Cardwell of Brazoria was symptomatic of the Texans who sailed to Brazil in that rather quickly he was disillusioned, deploring the "'inferior Africanized race'" to which he was expected to be sub-servient; the "'alarming decrease'" in the enslaved population; and the looming prospect of a "'thoroughly Africanized government.'" Besides, the original Portuguese settlers had "'blood [that] was deeply tinged with that of the Moor,'" facilitating "'thorough amalgamation'" which drove him from Texas in the first place. Of course, others more dis-traught about the collapse of their world simply committed suicide.[88]

Problematically, as the rebel redoubt in Mexico—then Brazil—weakened, like a seesaw, it provided more strength to the rebels in Texas. Ironically, when it was proclaimed that rebel rule in Texas had been restored as early as June 1866, it was complementarily an indi-cation that Maximilian's days were numbered.[89]

---

84. Report to Secretary Seward, 12 June 1866, Reel 9, Despatches from U.S. Consuls in Vera Cruz, NARA.

85. Consul Franklin Chase to Secretary Seward, 26 July 1866, Reel 4, Des-patches from U.S. Consuls in Tampico, NARA.

86. Ibid., Consul Chase to Secretary Seward, 22 August 1866.

87. Ibid., Consul Chase to Assistant Secretary F.W. Seward, 15 August 1866.

88. William Clark Griggs, "Frank McMullan's Brazilian Colony," M.A. thesis, TTU, 1974, iii, 50. 51.

89. W.L. Richter, 102.

U.S. Assistant Secretary of the Navy, Gustavus V. Fox, happened to be conferring with the man referred to as "the Emperor, Napoleon III" at the Tuileries Garden in Paris on the day in early July 1866 when his Austrian allies endured a crushing defeat at the hands of the Prussians. He sought to impress upon his French host that the U.S. had emerged strengthened from the war and that the "debt was already under the process of extinguishment..."—a subtle signal that the ongoing occupation of Mexico was doomed. But this was countered with equal subtlety by the host, who mentioned casually that rebel "General Beauregard, whom he had seen a few days since had also remarked on the increased development of the North...." But the Emperor conceded his own weakness when he warned Fox pointedly, "'do not be too friendly with Russia,'" which was bound to be rebuffed but underscored the challenges faced by Paris not only in North America but in Europe too.[90]

Nevertheless, rebels were heartened by the support they continued to receive from their own Lafayette, Polignac, who backed their efforts tirelessly.[91] The wider point was that Beauregard and Polignac aside, there were an insufficient number of Frenchmen to rescue the occupation of Mexico. But their original project—not secession necessarily but white supremacy surely—was destined to prevail in Texas.

Meanwhile, Matamoros—strategically sited cheek-by-jowl with Texas—was sieged in that about 150 U.S. nationals, mostly rebels, were rampaging. Yet, the U.S. envoy there had not ditched dreams of the past that had led to this fiasco, for he told Washington that the "better class of Mexicans" there "openly declare that their only hope of peace in this border is that the government of the United States will extend her protection over this part of Mexico."[92] "All the Spanish capitalists," said the U.S envoy in Tampico, "are now anxious to see this country annexed to ours to enable them to become citizens of the United States...."[93] This was echoed in the rebel organ, *Mexican Times*, which quoted favorably from like-minded reports in the *New York Herald Tribune* and *New York Times*, though presumably these

90. John D. Champlin, ed., *Narrative of the Mission to Russia in 1866, of the Hon. Gustavus Fox, Assistant Secretary of the Navy, from the Journal and Notes of J.F. Loubat*, New York: Appleton, 1873, 44, 45, 46.

91. *Mexican Times*, 1 October 1866.

92. Consul Avery to Secretary Seward, 28 September 1866, Reel 3, Despatches from U.S. Consuls in Matamoros, NARA.

93. Consul Franklin Chase to Assistant Secretary F.W. Seward, 22 September 1866, Reel 4, Despatches from U.S. Consuls in Tampico, NARA.

various rebel and loyal voices had different visions ultimately as to what would befall Mexico.[94]

Rebel exile John Edwards admitted that he was "half owner" of this "English Confederate weekly," which was no leisurely pursuit: "no man has ever worked harder than I have done in Mexico," he said wearily, "most of the time 16 hours a day." There were compensations, however: he had begun as a printer but now "I have a farm at Cordova…320 acres" at "25 dollars an acre." There his partner was "Dr. Tisdale from Missouri…a surgeon in the Confederate army. We own between us 640 acres of as fin[e] land as you ever saw," though the medic too "works like a negro. I live in Mexico [City], send him all the money I can raise and work like a negro too"—an inevitability when there were fewer enslaved Negroes around. Edwards sensed an impending storm though: "the Empire will not last—Maximilian will be forced out—anarchy and revolution will usurp the present order of stability and order." He had arrived at the bitter realization that "Americans…never know how little other people care for their country until they leave it. I know [Washington] despises this Empire as badly as the South hates the United States North; I know the Washington Cabinet don't [care] one straw for the so-called liberal Juarez, after they have used him as a cat's paw to draw the chestnuts out of the fire. I know that Grant would like to march from Brownsville to Monterrey with fifty thousand negroes," a real fear then driving events on both sides of the border. Still, he said, brightening, "Confederates are getting along very well here"; Jubal Early "spent a month here…he is proud, unyielding, a good hater and as much devoted to the poor, ruined South as ever…." An all-star team of rebel generals other than Early were present, including John McCausland, Cadmus Wilcox (a proud Texan), Joseph Shelby, Sterling Price, J.B. Magruder, Walter Stevens, Danville Leadbetter—"all here engaged in various pursuits" and "doing well." There were "many Confederate ladies" buzzing around. Fortunately, "the Empress and Emperor here are very favorably disposed to confederates." Still, Edwards remained seized with how Dixie was faring: "tell me all about how the forcing of the negroes [to] work and whether society is gradually elapsing into its old state again."[95] He would be pleased with responses to both queries.

---

94. *Mexican Times*, 5 November 1866.

95. John Edwards to "My Dear Darling Sisters," 6 April 1866, Morgan Collection.

Still, by September 1866 he remained optimistic about his newest home in that it contained "vast mineral resources…great agricultural wealth," compared to "desolated Virginia crammed with liberated negroes, preyed upon by Freedmen['s] Bureau agents"—and worse.[96] Happily, the presence in Mexico of M.F. Maury was heartening: he was "naturalized and made a Mexican…. Governor [Thomas Caute] Reynolds of Missouri is also here" and rebels had begun to penetrate the highest level of society. A son of the previous Mexican "Emperor," Agustín de Iturbide, had "married a lady in Georgetown, DC,"[97] yet another assurance of an impending rebel comeback.

---

96. John Edwards to "Darling Sister Fanny," 18 September 1866, Morgan Collection.

97. Undated newspaper article, ca. 1866, Morgan Collection.

Chapter 20

A Renewed Birth of Death, 1866-1868

By 1866 and continuing until 1867 Dixie was prostrate, on its knees—except for Texas. The state had been spared largely from the devastation endured by other parts of Dixie and benefited from an influx not only of rebels seeking greener pastures but others choosing to return north from temporary exile in Mexico. In early 1867 Governor James Throckmorton confirmed the obvious: "before the close of the late war," he said, "there was a large influx of...populations into Texas from the other southern states,"[1] including Africans and settlers alike. Their arrival reinforced his retrograde rule, leading General Sheridan to depose him later that year in favor of Elisha Pease, an oddball loyalist enslaver, who was able to displease all sides.

Throckmorton bollixed matters when he failed to bow out gracefully but, instead, grumbling that he was "now being removed from office in pursuance of an act of Congress, that is, in my judgment subversive of the rights of the states"—rehearsing the old states' rights dodge that continued to degenerate in the 20th century in order to uphold Jim Crow. "The charge is preferred," said the ousted governor, "that I am 'an impediment to the reconstruction' of this state...." He inflexibly stood by his claim that "appointing negroes on the board of registrars who are notoriously incompetent, when respectable white men could have been obtained" was—insensibly—beyond the pale, since they too "had been through the war and are loyal...." The Freedmen's Bureau irked him since it supposedly operated *ultra vires*: "its agents have made arrests...." The "town of Brenham was set on fire by United States soldiers" with no punishment, just as "freedmen charged by indictment with high crimes have been protected from arrest and trial. One charged with an attempt at rape upon a white girl of 14 years of age was taken from jail by the order of an agent for the

---

1. Governor Throckmorton to W. Wallace Davis, Boston, 6 February 1867, Box 4L-346, Throckmorton Papers.

Freedmen's Bureau...." Also troubling was that "property of citizens has been used without compensation...." As for the "frontier," it was "one continuous scene of butchery and devastation." The war ended officially in "May 1865...with the surrender of the Trans-Mississippi Department," and "every Southern State had already organized its state government except Texas," of course. Then he hoisted the victors on their own petard by mentioning, "inasmuch as many of the most intelligent communities at the North have continued to refuse the ballot to their colored population who are more or less educated, it was supposed that we could refuse it to the ignorant blacks in our midst without danger of incurring any penalty...."[2]

Herein Throckmorton lanced a postwar contradiction, insofar as Washington was pushing certain areas of Dixie ahead of where the North was willing to venture. On the one hand, Africans in Texas were armed in blue; on the other hand, part of their mission was to repress potential allies: Indigenes.[3]

Black churches, e.g., the African Methodist Episcopal religionists, lent their buildings to the Loyal League, which defended the rights of the emancipated, while Negro pastors often preached politics from the pulpit and led prayers for progressive victories. This was not greeted with equanimity by their opponents. In Fort Worth, for example, terrorists disrupted a Negro fete after it was determined that it was much too festive—they seemed to prefer Negroes in mourning mode. But this was effective insofar as Negroes began to halt the organizing of parties, dances, picnics and the like. Terrorist fury targeted Negroes who owned firearms, disarming them before a major offensive. Some Negroes moved out of their homes and slept in the woods.[4]

Negro schools were akin to a red flag to a bull as far as white supremacists were concerned. In early 1866, in Bosque and Hill counties, the newly emancipated were demanding the construction of schools.[5] But by the summer of 1866 the Freedmen's Bureau requested troops to protect teachers and these buildings; this was "attributable to the vulgar and uncommendable prejudice against educating the negro." Killings had become so frequent that this official, Major General J.B. Kiddo, said that this besieged community

2. J.W. Throckmorton, "To the People of Texas," 1867, Huntington Library.

3. Earl Henry Elam, "The History of the Wichita Indian Confederacy to 1868," Ph.D. dissertation, TTU, 1971.

4. Smallwood, 272, 334, 335.

5. Report by Philip Howard, Meridian, Texas, 19 March 1866, Reel 3, FBR.

"appear to have no family relations."[6] Like others, the Freedmen's Bureau was stunned by the energy expended in disarming Negroes,[7] making it easier to bludgeon them.

Retrospectively, it is dispiriting to track the reports of mayhem inflicted upon the emancipated in Texas. By 8 August 1866 Kiddo had visited Fort Bend, Colorado and Wharton counties and observed the "greatest trouble" was involved "in protecting the freedmen from lawless violence. Violence and murder are largely <u>on the increase</u>," he stressed, as "murders from one to five at a time of Negroes" was normative. More troops were requested,[8] but they were often busy battling Indigenes or monitoring the border in anticipation of a French-rebel incursion. Yet as many of these soldiers were peering southward for signs of an incipient invasion, if they had peered over their shoulder they may have spotted some of the suspects who killed Negroes then headed south to the border.[9]

Things got worse as August proceeded. "Outrages on the freedmen are constantly on the increase," lamented Kiddo; "murder and abuse of the freedmen and the virulent abuse of the female school teachers" were the hallmarks. Again, the press was in the vanguard in that it was "quite common for the newspapers to insinuate that the lady teachers cannot be looked upon in any other light than 'common prostitutes.'"[10] As planters presided over the slaying of Africans in Texas, a number headed east to recruit others, presumably more pliable—and, minimally, increasing labor supply to drive down the already pittance-like wages. R.H.D. Sorrel, an "extensive planter in this state," said Kiddo, "returns to Alabama to "procure freedmen to emigrate to this state as laborers...."[11]

He was not alone, as Africans were escaping Texas and dodging bullets; there was a "great scarcity of labor," said Kiddo at the end of August, and planters were headed not just to Alabama but to Georgia and South Carolina too "to procure labor...."[12] The Bureau "strongly urged immigration of free colored labor into this state,"[13] but if an African due east had made an objective analysis, Texas would not be high on the list to visit, let alone reside in.

---

6. Ibid., Major General J.B. Kiddo to O.O. Howard, 23 July 1866, Reel 1.
7. Ibid., William Sinclair to Captain, 30 July 1866.
8. Ibid., Major General J.B. Kiddo to O.O. Howard, 8 August 1866.
9. Ibid., William Sinclair to Captain in Houston, 10 August 1866.
10. Ibid., Major General Kiddo to O.O. Howard, 20 August 1866.
11. Ibid., Major General Kiddo to Major General Wagner, 28 August 1866.
12. Ibid., Major General Kiddo to O.O. Howard, 29 August 1866.
13. Ibid., Report to O.O. Howard, 29 September 1866.

Nonetheless, Bureau officials continued imploring Negroes elsewhere to move to Texas. A "great number of freed people in your state," said an aide to Kiddo to a Georgia military man, "are likely to become a burden," so the Lone Star State should be considered since "this state is wealthy and prosperous and laborers are much needed."[14] A similar plea was made to South Carolina,[15] North Carolina[16] and Alabama too.[17]Actually, the subtext of this plea was that Texas Africans were reluctant to accept the dire fate that had been thrust upon them and, as a result, were often in open rebellion, generating a cry for an infusion of laborers from elsewhere. In Jackson County, in an effort that was hardly atypical then, Kiddo described nervously how "some freedmen" were "suspected of burning or attempting to burn a house belonging to [the] plantation of J.B. Jones...."[18]

The frequent cause of outbreaks of violence featuring Africans contesting their oppressors was the reluctance of the latter to retreat from enslavement, "Juneteenth" notwithstanding. Such was the case in Cherokee County, not far from Nacogdoches. There, said an official, a major planter "never permitted the negroes formerly his slaves to leave him" and "that they are now held under contracts which they were forced to sign," then were "harshly treated," including "whipped several times" until he "forced them back to work." Then via "misrepresentation he had some children bound to him under the apprentice law."[19] Pursuant to an 1848 law, judges in Gainesville "bound several colored minors without parents or estate to their former masters who now have them in perfect bondage"[20]—such was the declaration of the Bureau in 1868.

14. Ibid., Aide to Kiddo to Major General Tilson, Georgia, 7 November 1866.

15. Ibid., Aide to Kiddo to Assistant Commissioner of Freedmen's Bureau of South Carolina, 21 November 1866.

16. Ibid., Major General Kiddo to Assistant Commissioner of Freedmen's Bureau, North Carolina, 20 December 1866.

17. Ibid., Aide to Kiddo to Major General W. Swayne, Alabama, 21 November 1866.

18. Ibid., Major General Kiddo to Captain Edward Miller, 13 November 1866.

19. Ibid., Report from J.T. Murray, County Attorney-Cherokee County, 13 March 1867, Reel 3.

20. Ibid., Report from J.E. Wheeler, County Judge, Cooke County, 12 April 1868.

A similar devilish plot unfolded in Clarksville in Red River County. There an African toiled for eight months post-emancipation for W.P. Dickson, his former master, who promised him a portion of the crop, but when he asked for his share he was refused; instead, he was threatened with "having his brains blown out," according to the Bureau. Then the malevolent oppressor "shot him in the head making an ugly wound."[21] It needs to be realized that these were not isolated cases and just as—the saying went—beating one slave served to keep the entire plantation work force in line, shooting one Negro through the head was sufficient to discipline a county. Thus, in nearby Jefferson in Marion County, the headline was stark: "Freedmen in that vicinity are being murdered."[22]

Despite the toxic perfidy of the planters, as was the case with the rebel army, this slaughter and persecution of Negroes was not at their hands alone. Kiddo told white supremacist Governor Throckmorton as much. These "outrages," he said, were "committed by a class of men who never owned property in negroes, who have been their competitors in labor to some extent and consequently have been their 'live long enemies' and particularly their enemies since their freedom."[23]

This is a crucial point not only for understanding what befell Africans before and after Appomattox but also in discerning the roots of U.S. fascism. Settler colonialism from its inception in what became North Carolina in the 1580s[24] was a multi-class project: poorer and more affluent European migrants across class lines joined hands for presumed mutual benefit. And by 1866 in Texas, poorer Europeans were loath to join hands with Africans or oppose depredations against Indigenes but instead—for the most part—took an opposing stance. This guaranteed a stony road ahead for Africans and Indigenes alike, complicated further by enslavement proclivities among the latter, while the former as a badge of citizenship joined the army in blue in routing Indigenes. All these factors were a recipe for disaster for Africans and Indigenes alike.

For already in Texas it was not difficult to espy the seeds of a germinating fascism, including its essential kernel: converting Africans into a prison labor force. In October 1866 the authorities in Houston were arresting "freedwomen," said the Bureau, "and compelling

---

21. Ibid., Report from J.W. Vanderburgh, 18 August 1867.

22. Ibid., Report from Stanton Weaver, Second Lieutenant, 5 April 1867, Reel 2.

23. Ibid., Major General Kiddo to Governor Throckmorton, 13 September 1866, Reel 6.

24. Horne, *Dawning*.

them to work on the streets of the city."[25] From Huntsville the message was that "a great number of freedpeople [sic] are confined in the penitentiary for very trivial offenses...."[26]

Tragically, Africans transitioned from the slave labor camps to prison labor camps—the latter bearing the insignia of an incipient fascism.

An instruction to keep in mind for the 21st century, insofar as Texas provides lessons, is how ineffectually Governor Pease, an ostensible ally of Africans, operated. "I knew that my appointment was distasteful to a large majority of the people who had participated in the rebellion," he said, conceding ground to the right in June 1868 as he was clearing his throat. "But the emancipation and enfranchisement of our colored population had infused [a] new element into the body politic," which was a reality on the way to dissolution. "Sheriffs have reported to this office that they were unable to obtain the aid of citizens to make arrests, because they feared personal violence from the parties and their friends...." When the state which presumably has a monopoly on violence is forced to retreat in the face of violence, it was indicative of a crisis hard to resolve. More to the point, he continued, "the great majority of the white population...still reject with scorn the mild terms offered them" by Washington.[27] Instead of compromise, this "great majority" pushed for repression of this "new element in...the body politic."

Preeminent among those uncompromisingly resistant was Louis Wigfall, the fire-eater who thought Jefferson Davis too liberal and namby-pamby for his hardboiled tastes. During the war he wanted to "'hang'" the maximum leader, hated Judah P. Benjamin, Davis's closest advisor ,and once counseled in a fit of bloodlust that the rebels "had to be filled with the spirit which inspired the Dutch when they inundated and destroyed their country to prevent its subjugation." He had vowed to destroy the Confederacy rather than end enslavement of Africans, and to prove his mettle was said to have walked from Georgia to Texas after Appomattox to make a last stand. By 1868, still tossing figurative hand grenades, he recommended the "bayonet instead of the ballot" be the ultimate political determinant,[28] anticipating authoritarian descendants in 20th-century Berlin and Rome.

---

25. Report to J.C. Delpress, 26 October 1866, Reel 1, FBR.

26. Ibid., Report from James Devine, 4 October 1866, Reel 23.

27. "Message of His Excellency Elisha M. Pease, Governor of Texas, to the Constitutional Convention, June 3, 1868," Austin: Daily Republican, 1868, Huntington Library.

28. E. King, Great South, 231, 330, 340, 359, 364.

And as would be the case in Wigfall's homeland in decades to come, with the hard right of Davis and Benjamin discredited, the harder right of Wigfall rose to the fore, those who saw compromise as moral incontinence.

Bucking this tidal wave of bile and bullets, Africans resisted. Another example occurred when in San Augustine the Negroes revolted, sent the planters packing—only to be subjected to a brutal counterattack by the burgeoning Ku Klux Klan, maturing into its instrumental role as the armed wing of the Democratic Party.[29] The response was swift and merciless. "Lynch law is proclaimed," cried the Bureau, a "negro has been hung"—but correspondingly "two white men have been shot."[30] The story was similar in Matagorda, where there was, according to the Bureau, "rumored insurrectionary feeling among the freedmen in the planting districts."[31] Why Africans were on the verge of an uprising was exposed when a number petitioned that they "hired ourselves as labourers" but were "nearly destitute" nonetheless because of wage theft: most signed with an "X,"[32] indicating a dearth of literacy.

Unfortunately, when such clashes materialized, the Africans were not triumphant. Such was the case in Bellville in early 1867 where the county judge detailed a "riot" or confrontation between the Negroes and their opponents; the result was that a "large part of the neighborhood are in arms hunting down the freedmen. Request troops for their protection" was the urgent plea,[33] though even if they could take time away from routing Indigenes, it was not discernible what the result would be.

In Centreville, a periodical appropriately named *The Conservative*, was horrified by the presence of a "number of negroes who were neither under the immediate control or protection of a white man"—so, they were shot and immolated. The deceased "made the experiment last year of living apart from the whites and the neighborhood was loud in their complaint against them," especially their demonstrated "insolence." They were influencing others and "had it not been for their influence and example," the influenced "might have been more contented with their lot and more useful to their employers,"

---

29. Lawrence Delbert Rice, "The Negro in Texas, 1874-1900," Ph.d. dissertation, TTU, 1968, 57 (abbrev. L.D. Rice).

30. Report from Lieutenant A.A. Metzner, 23 November 1867, Reel 3, FBR.

31. Ibid., Report by William Garretson, 26 June 1867.

32. Ibid., Petition, 30 April 1867, Reel 4.

33. Ibid., Report by County judge George W. Johnson, 30 April 1867, Reel 3.

a paramount objective. Unbendingly, this biased observer remonstrated: "the people of the South are not yet prepared for negro equality," and it was "absolutely necessary now to have a white to direct, superintend and protect them as it ever was, if not more so than while in slavery...."[34]

And there it was: enslavement may have been abolished, but the enslaver's mindset remained intact in various circles. Most Africans were unwilling to live in the old way, while many settlers were unwilling to adapt—which in a nutshell remains the case, albeit in different circumstances, to this very day.

Governor James Throckmorton was firmly in the grasp of his Democratic Party, which was unrepentant and unwilling to compromise. Symbolic of his party was Oran Milo Roberts, a former slaveholder, born in South Carolina with early years spent in Alabama. In 1866 he was in the vanguard of pushing for a "'white man government'" meaning no Negro suffrage or holding of state office or interracial marriage.[35] As Negro women in Houston were being rousted, Throckmorton was wailing that "Negroes [are] drilling" militarily; "there are meddling white men," he warned, "who have been inducing the negroes to believe they should prepare for a war," which meant his side should be "careful to keep a close look...."[36] Major General Kiddo sought vainly to reassure him that this "drilling" was "perfectly harmless" and for "display," he emphasized.[37] But for those accustomed to viewing Africans as subservient and certainly not involved in "drilling," this could not be "harmless" in any sense. Assuredly, Throckmorton shared this outlook: he continued to complain to the Bureau about this and demanded "that it be stopped."[38] Since Austin was critical to the larger ambition of routing Indigenes, his was a voice that was not easy to ignore.

For this was not the only war for which the governor was preparing. As for the Indigenes, he howled in a bloodcurdling cry, a "war of extermination will be waged against them."[39] He did not mention

34. Ibid., Clipping, 23 February 1867, Reel 4.

35. Yancey, 10, 57.

36. Governor Thorckmorton to James Gay, Esq., La Grange, Texas, 27 November 1866, Box 41-346, Throckmorton Papers.

37. Major General Kiddo to Governor Throckmorton, 8 January 1867, Reel 1, FBR.

38. Ibid., Report on Conversation with the governor, 13 November 1866, Reel 3.

39. Governor Throckmorton to Colonel Bishop, 28 November 1866, Box 41-346, Throckmorton Papers.

the war in Mexico then ongoing, but it was apparent that a war on three fronts was too much even for audacious settlers, so momentum increased to shut down backing for the French occupation—unhelpful in Washington, in any case, when aid to fight Indigenes was a high priority. For the governor, yet another priority ranked high: halting "negro suffrage."[40] Here he was responding to the demands of certain voters. By mid-1867 in Brenham, Africans were being coerced not to vote, under the threat of being "returned to slavery"; that planters thought "they can bribe the Bureau Agent," said an observer worryingly, "may be correct."[41]

The governor's ruthlessly relentless ability to coordinate the wiping out of Indigenes brought him leverage in Washington, which then made it difficult for the federals to rebuff his squashing of voting by Africans—even if they had a desire to do so. That Negro troops played a role in this denouement—as an emblem of citizenship—made it all the more tragic.

"Information is being received daily of Indian depredations," he blared in August 1866. "Their ravages are more serious than has been the case for years," while "loss of life has been alarming"; the "frontier line is rapidly receding," meaning the settler project overall was being threatened. "Thousands of cattle and horses are being driven off continually by a few bad white men and Mexicans, connected with the Indians, to New Mexico…and into Mexico…." Of course, the Tonkawa remained helpful to settlers, but this did not save them from diminishment, meaning more immigration from Europe was demanded.[42]

These poor Indigenes were being attacked from all sides. They were in a "deplorable and destitute condition," said the governor, though they "have always been friendly to the whites…." With the onset of civil war, he said, less friendly Indigenes were "determined to make war upon the white people and the Chickasaw and other friendly Indian Nations. The Tonkawa refused to engage" and, consequently, they were attacked by the warlike Indigenes, i.e., "Comanches, Caddoes" and—revealingly—"other remnants of tribes…."[43]

---

40. Ibid., Governor Throckmorton to N. Burford, Dallas, 7 December 1866.

41. Report by Edward Collins, 30 June 1867, Reel 4, FBR.

42. Message from Governor Throckmorton, 18 August 1866, Box 2H-28, Throckmorton Papers.

43. Ibid., Governor Throckmorton to Commissioner of Indian Affairs, 20 September 1866.

Paternalistically, by the Spring of 1867 the governor counseled the "removal of the Tonkawa Indians," who were to be "turned over to the care of the U.S. military forces."[44]

Throckmorton addressed President Andrew Johnson directly, sounding the alarm that "for a year past the whole line of the north-western frontier of this state, has been at one point and another been the object of Indian attacks" with "their usual ferocity."[45] Support for liquidation of Indigenes was bipartisan in Washington, salving the wound opened by treasonous rebellion, providing bargaining power to Austin that could then be used to further suppress Africans. The governor exposed what his true priority was when in the midst of alarmist whoops about Indigenes, he demanded that Negro troops be arrested.[46] Repetitively, he returned to the "ill feeling towards the soldiers....among our people," who "have much cause to fear outrages from the troops and especially the black ones...."[47]

The Freedmen's Bureau disagreed—adamantly. Their leader in Texas, Major General Kiddo, just as repetitively described "personal violence perpetrated on freedmen," especially in "northeastern Texas," specifically Marshall, a hotbed of anti-Negro fury.[48]

Plucking the heartstrings, the governor lamented that "quite a number of children have been carried into captivity and our defenseless women have been violated in the most shocking manner and afterwards horribly murdered...." But he had not lost sight of another preoccupation, encouraging European immigration and arguing that it would be "desirable that all military force and the agents of the Freedmen's Bureau should be withdrawn from the interior of the state."[49]

It was unclear if the governor was thinking hysterically or strategically. That is, was his hysteria about Negro troops actually a strategic realization that in the long run arming the emancipated was a major threat to white supremacy that could be assuaged by the deliverance

---

44. Ibid., Governor Throckmorton to Colonel Davis Gurley, 6 May 1867, Box 4L-346.

45. Ibid., Governor Throckmorton to President Johnson, 25 August 1866, Box 2H-28.

46. Ibid., Governor Throckmorton to Major General Heintzleman, 25 September 1866.

47. Ibid., Governor Throckmorton to Brigadier General Sturgis, 4 January 1867.

48. Major General Kiddo to O.O. Howard, 2 January 1867, Reel 1 FBR.

49. Message of Governor J.W. Throckmorton to the Legislature of Texas, Austin: State Gazette, 18 August 1866, Harvard U.

of the European immigration project? Or was this hysteria plain and simple, underestimating these troops' essential role in subduing Indigenes? Whatever the case, he did not cease in denouncing "wild tribes" who have executed a "general invasion of our border"; these "murderous Arabs of the plains" must be reduced to "beggary and want" and then "they might be made to observe treaties...." As far north as Kansas and due west in New Mexico there too was "suffering" from their alleged marauding. "We can have no permanent peace with them," he decried, "until a war of extermination is waged and they are taught to know and dread the power of the...government...."[50]

Then a settler and his son were killed—"after a most desperate struggle with the savages"—in Jack County, and the governor's burning ire knew no bounds. "We see," he intoned, "that treaties with these perfidious people are of no avail," with "retribution" the remedy and it was "not far distant...."[51]

Then Throckmorton appealed directly to General Sheridan,[52] who had the conflicting portfolios of repressing Indigenes and protecting Africans, with the former ineluctably assuming more importance and priority, not least since Negro troops lustily joined in the repressing fray. Sheridan was boxed in; he realized that "'reports are manufactured wholesale to effect the removal of troops from the interior to the frontier,'" swinging from protecting Africans to suppressing Indigenes. But the latter was also one of his chief priorities, so he created the conditions that allowed false stories of Indigenous depredations to flourish. Thus, at the end of the day, this priority was then coupled with runaway fear of what Negroes had in store, allowing for the pillaging of both oppressed groupings. Perversely, Negro troops moved from protecting their communities in East Texas from settler abuse to chasing down settler antagonists in West Texas—from the interior to the frontier in the parlance of the moment.[53]

Yet another turning point arrived in August 1866 when President Johnson—in light of the seeming success of mopping-up operations in Texas—declared the Civil War to be concluded[54]; this was preceded in April by yet another proclamation by him announcing that

---

50. Governor Throckmorton to General Getty, 3 October 1866, Box 2H-28, Throckmorton Papers.

51. Ibid., Governor Throckmorton to "Gentlemen of the Senate and House," 2 October 1866.

52. Roy Morris, Jr., *Sheridan: The Life and Wars of General Phil Sheridan*, New York: Vintage, 1993.

53. Shook, 329, 487.

54. *New York Times*, 21 August 1866.

the war of the rebellion had ended—except in Texas.[55] But actually, civil war shifted gears with a renewed focus on "ethnic cleansing" in North America with—perversely—Negro troops often at the tip of the spear.

"There is no part of the frontier from the Red River to the Rio Grande," said the governor, "that is not suffering…depredations…. every day brings the most distressing and heart rending accounts" as "settlements are rapidly being broken up…." He claimed that there was a Pan-Indigene consolidation in motion, a fond goal by many since the hallowed days of Tecumseh, earlier in the century. For the governor was "certain that the Cheyennes & Arrapahoes…tribes that live far beyond the borders of Texas," were "joined in their recent annual council by several other tribes and determined to continue their war upon Texas with redoubled vigor…." These two ethnicities were now "consort[ing] with the Kiowas, Northern Comanches & Lipan—all of which tribes are now concentrating their forces upon the border of Texas…."[56]

As time passed, the governor's rhetoric became more genocidal, referring to the "wild Comanches, Kiowas, Lipan who infect our borders," as if they were a virus. "These wild tribes do not know or recognize Texas as part of the U.S. government." Singled out were a "large band of Kickapoos [who] left Kansas & went to Mexico during the war" but now were "committing many outrages on our southwest frontier…." He insisted that "these rascals" be "remanded back to Kansas or make an exterminating war upon them…."[57]

Extermination, genocide, weighed heavily on the brain of Throckmorton. By early 1867 he commiserated with the governor of Mississippi, no slouch here: "like yourself," he began empathetically, "I despair of any just settlement of our troubles." There was "nothing ahead but misery and ruin" and "no other solution of the present fanatical and revolutionary tendencies except in blood—perhaps not just now but at no distant time,"[58] he added prophetically.

The governor demanded that the U.S. military "take steps at once to break up this den of thieves that shelter in Mexico," speaking of the Kickapoo, for it was "useless to call upon the Mexican authorities to

55. President Johnson, Message Proclaiming End to the Insurrection, 20 August 1866, Miller Center, UVa-C.

56. Governor Throckmorton to General Sheridan, 6 October 1866, Box 2H-28, Throckmorton Papers.

57. Ibid., Governor Throckmorton to B.H. Epperson, 16 November 1866.

58. Ibid., Governor Throckmorton to Governor of Mississippi, 10 February 1867, Box 4L-346.

deliver up or drive out these marauders...."[59] Out west in Eagle Pass, this small town was "in ruins," Washington was told. San Antonio was "thriving," according to this dispatch, but how long could that last— according to the bloodthirsty—if extermination failed to proceed?[60]

In sum, Austin was enmeshed in wars on many fronts, though those against Indigenes and Africans were existential in their minds. In this context, the French occupation of Mexico backed by rebels was a sacrificial lamb, destined for jettisoning. In 1867, Governor Throckmorton reached the old warhorse, Louis Wigfall, then cooling his heels in London—doubtlessly fretting about prosecution if he returned home to North America. It was a "real pleasure to hear from you," he beamed and then informed him of the grim news that his predecessor as governor, Pendleton Murrah, was "dead in Monterrey,"[61] as soon would be the project that brought him there.

Thus, while clamoring incessantly against Indigenes, the governor did not neglect the newly emancipated. He campaigned similarly against "the agents of the Freedman's [sic] Bureau" and the necessity of "relieving our citizens from fines and punishments [they] so often unjustly inflicted...."[62]

For the wily Texas governor was in the vanguard of devising the constitutional maneuver that was to hold white supremacists in good stead to this day: steer Negro suffrage away from the federal level and the constitution and simply render it a state matter.[63]

A volcano of violence had erupted in Texas, leaving few unaffected. Looking back from 1869, pro-Reconstruction delegates speaking to the U.S. Congress remonstrated that their plight in recent years had become "very desperate." Yes, there were 38 freedmen killed in 1865 and 165 in 1867 (conservative estimates) but there were 39 "whites" killed in the year of Appomattox and 166 by 1867. "Many persons have mysteriously disappeared, particularly individuals of the colored race," while "murder of negroes is so common as to render it impossible to keep an accurate count...." With blistering accuracy,

---

59. Ibid., Governor Throckmorton to Commander of the Military District of Texas, Galveston, 6 December 1866, Box 2H-28.

60. Report to Assistant F.W. Seward, 18 November 1867, Reel 1, Despatches from U.S. Consuls in Monterrey, NARA.

61. Governor Throckmorton to Louis Wigfall, 30 December 1867, Box 41-346, Throckmorton Papers.

62. Ibid., Governor Throckmorton to "Gentlemen of the Senate and House," 31 October 1866, Box 2H-28.

63. Ibid., Governor Throckmorton to "Dear Brown," 11 December 1866, Box 41-346.

it was said that "free speech and free press have never existed in Texas"; President Johnson was blamed for his "encouragement given the old confederate leaders...." One proposal, which was to recur, was to divide the state into separate pieces so as to dilute the potency of the white supremacists.[64]

Throckmorton's presence in the governor's chair evidenced the bitter reality that by 1866 the rebels had claimed what amounted to the complete control of Austin. In response, on the totemic date of 4 July 1867, a score of settlers and almost 60 Africans from about 20 key nodes assembled and sought to forge an organization that would redeem the promise of abolition[65]—to little avail in the long run.

* * *

Meanwhile south of the border, rebel exiles were continuing to endure difficulty, which would eventually force them to return to the nation they had fought. By mid-1866 there had been an "abduction" of 17 of them from their cosseted colony, blamed on Juárez's forces who were said by the U.S. consul to be "showing their displeasure of foreign immigration...."[66] By the end of the year it was evident that the occupation was coming apart at the seams, which did not bode well for the exiles. Frenchmen were being assassinated, and their property was being confiscated; many applied to U.S. consulates for citizenship—which did not bode well for Negroes, given the previous misdeeds of Polignac and Beauregard and Soulé and Maury and other men with roots in the hexagonal nation. As for the rapacious republic, the news was not all positive either; "the mere mention of [further] cession [of land] to the United States" was "fiercely denounced" as "traitor[ous]," and a cultural and rhetorical trait was developing, said this U.S. agent, to "deprecate the [purported] moral power of the United States" delivered, it was thought, by emancipation.[67] A telling sign occurred in December 1866 when

---

64. "Memorial to the Senators and Representatives of the Forty-First Congress. Memorial from the Commissioners Elected by the Reconstruction Convention of the State of Texas...," Washington, D.C.: Pearson, 1869, AAS.

65. "Statement and Memorial in Relation to Political Affairs in Texas, By Members of the Late Convention and Other Citizens of that State, Addressed to the Hon. B.F. Butler, Chairman of the Reconstruction Committee," Washington, D.C.: McGill & Witherow, 1869, AAS.

66. Consul Marcus Otterbourg to Assistant Secretary F.W. Seward, 2 June 1866, Reel 5, Despatches from U.S. Consuls in Mexico City, NARA.

67. Ibid., Consul Otterbourg to Assistant Secretary Seward, 1 December 1866.

Thomas Hindman, a former Major General in the rebel army, made a public statement stating his fervent desire to return to the U.S.[68]

Of similar symbolic resonance was what occurred in Acapulco in May 1866—the arrest and jailing by the authorities of John A. Sutter, son of the California pioneer and a U.S. Vice Commercial Agent, who had been a resident for a number of years.[69] He was accused of complicity in the smuggling of arms,[70] not minor in the context of a fierce battle against occupiers. Other U.S. nationals in Acapulco turned on Sutter, claiming he "purchased" his post at the consulate for $375; he was further portrayed as a "California German of ill repute [and] notorious bad character…compelled to leave California for an alleged attempt on the life of his father…." Worse, he was pictured as pro-Maximilian. In light of the Emperor's impending defenestration, failure to punish him "will compel every man having a white skin to leave this vicinity…."[71] Then the original pioneer, John Sutter, Sr., weighed in on behalf of his offspring, denying the above and reminding that the Sutters had roots in Switzerland, not Germany.[72]

Much to and fro occurred, then Sutter—opportunistically— announced that he was pro-Juárez (this was about two weeks before the execution of Maximilian); indeed, he floated the "rumor that the so-called Emperor Maximilian has been shot."[73]

Nonetheless, as to Maximilian, Sutter was premature but prescient. For in early 1867 it was reported that "the last of the French troops left" Mexico City en route for Vera Cruz and, it was thought, across the Atlantic.[74]

However, the threat to Washington presented by a European power, backed by thousands of traitors with military acumen, dissipated, and along with it the necessity to cater to Negro troops along the border. In some ways the demise of Maximilian represented the beginning of the end of Reconstruction, along with its antipode: the

---

68. Ibid., Statement by Thomas Hindman, 20 December 1866.

69. Gilbert Cole, Commercial Agent to State Department, 7 May 1866, Reel 3, Despatches from U.S. Consuls in Acapulco, NARA.

70. Ibid., Consulate to General Montenegro, Military Commander, 22 October 1866.

71. Ibid., Report from "Many Americans Resident in Acapulco," 6 December 1867.

72. Ibid., J.A. Sutter, Sr. to Assistant Secretary Seward, 9 January 1868.

73. Ibid., John Sutter to Secretary Seward, 4 June 1867.

74. Consul to Secretary Seward, 2 February 1867, Reel 10, Despatches from U.S. Consuls in Vera Cruz, NARA.

imminent and actual reenslavement of Africans in Texas en masse and elsewhere.

Then the other shoe dropped—this time in Africa. For by early June 1867 Secretary of State Seward was told that the battalion that had been dispatched from Alexandria during the apex of the U.S. Civil War to Mexico was back by 27 May—"after an absence of nearly four a half years" was the message; 470 had been killed in battle, 20 died from wounds, 28 died from disease, 63 were missing (descendants still in Mexico or Texas?), 2 deserted (ditto), and almost all spoke a language—French—that they did not previously, all indicative of their important role in propping up the occupation.[75]

Likewise, Washington had been aidful in propping up the soon-to-be victorious forces of Juárez. Supposedly this Mexican leader was suspicious of the fidelity of some of his comrades and often relied on a U.S. envoy—or so said the latter—as a result.[76] "If it were not for the presence of our vessels of war," said Consul Franklin Chase in Tampico, "I should now feel much concern for the security of life and property" nearby, as war raged all about.[77]

Finally, on 19 June 1867—in some sense, the most meaningful Juneteenth, insofar as it brought true emancipation closer as it closed off Mexico as a refuge for enslavers—Maximilian was executed summarily,[78] an appropriate end for a man not fluent in the language of those he supposedly ruled.[79]

Consider that as early as 1864, premier Texas settler "Rip Ford was queried about how to handle Negro property in light of the declining fortunes of secessionists; thus, enslavers were headed to Mexico with plans to "peon" the Negroes they dragged along in league with French occupiers.[80] The "Second Juneteenth"—minimally—slowed down this process.

75. Consul Charles Hale to Secretary Seward, 8 June 1867, Reel 4, Despatches from U.S. Consuls in Alexandria, NARA.

76. Consul Franklin Chase to State Department, 7 March 1867, Reel 5, Despatches from U.S. Consuls in Tampico, NARA. In the same collection and reel, see also Consul Chase to Assistant Secretary Seward, 23 March 1867.

77. Ibid., Consul Chase to Assistant Secretary Seward, 15 April 1867.

78. Shawcross.

79. José Luis Blasio, *Maximilian, Emperor of Mexico: Memoirs of His Private Secretary*, New Haven: Yale U Press, 1934, ix.

80. Irby, 136. Cf., Marisela Jiménez Ramos, "Black Mexico: Nineteenth Century Discourses of Race and Nation," Ph.D. dissertation, Brown U, 2009.

Revealingly, in June 1867 the Africans in Huntsville planned to mark the original "Juneteenth." They printed and posted handbills, but a wrongdoer by the name of Hillary Bowen scampered around town tearing them down as quickly as they were put up while proclaiming "Niggers will not be allowed to have anything of the kind...." James Button of the Freedmen's Bureau sought to dissuade him, but this scamp responded in what was termed a "contemptible manner making threats to shoot the party who told me," all the while "swearing and using very abusive language...." Bowen was enraged further when he was "informed...that I would fine him twenty five dollars for his contempt [of] my office," but "he refused to pay and defied me to collect it. I was on the point of arresting him but he had a number of other vagabonds waiting to rescue him...." So Button decided that the better part of valor was to retreat. A whopping 4000 celebrants were expected, and there were "about twenty young men of a disreputable character who have evinced a desire to mar the proceedings and create a riot."[81]

Another disturbing sign arose in Texas soon thereafter when it seemed that only Negroes marked the national holiday on 4 July. This was in the context of the bulk of settlers not surrendering to Washington, formal proclamations aside. It was also in the midst of a fevered flurry of massacres of Indigenes, as hunting them down became a kind of sporting event.[82] By 1868 Negroes and their allies were declaiming worriedly about a "'war of the races.'" Shockingly, the scholar Rebecca Kosary has found that "whites initiated more brutal and seemingly senseless violence toward blacks during Reconstruction in Texas than was ever the case in the days of slavery," with a new stamp being Euro-American women abusing their African counterparts.[83]

Black women were victimized repeatedly by violence at the hands of women settlers,[84] a legacy of their tormented relationship during slavery.

81. Report by James Button, Huntsville, 14 June 1867, Reel 4, FBR.

82. John Austin Edwards, "Social and Cultural Activities of Texans During Civil War and Reconstruction, 1861-1873," Ph.D. dissertation, TTU, 1985, 52, 254.

83. Rebecca Kosary, "To Degrade and Control: White Violence and the Maintenance of Racial and Gender Boundaries in Reconstruction Texas, 1865-1868," Ph.D. dissertation, TA&MU, 2006, 9, 56, 63.

84. B.C. Curtis, 97. See e.g., Stephanie E. Jones-Rogers, *They Were Her Property: White Women as Slave Owners in the American South*, New Haven: Yale U Press, 2019.

Remarkably, the onslaught against Indigenes was not by troops alone; in some cases, this was perpetrated by settlers and, as their prime chronicler put it, "without aid from the government." This was noticeably the case in Hamilton County, named, appropriately, after a former South Carolina governor who helped to finance the 1836 counter-revolution, and bounded, inappropriately, by Comanche County. The settlers were furious about what they saw as horse-thievery by the so-called "Red Devils," which was said to be at epidemic levels in the Upper Red River Valley; it was in 1868, said the genocidal historian J.W. Wilbarger, that the "last great raid was made [there] by a band of the Comanches, estimated at three hundred strong,"[85] as thereafter settlers responded forcefully. His challenger as the premier sadistically bellicose chronicler, M.L. Johnson, growled that the "only treaty of peace these redskins ever paid any attention to was a well placed bullet...."[86]

It bears repeating that there was a symbiosis linking anti-Indigene and anti-Negro violence. Thus, post-1865 may have induced a "new birth of freedom," but it also gave rise to a renewed birth of death, suitable to create a fertile womb for a subsequent emergence of fascism. The dynamic of U.S. settler colonialism was that even as reaction seemed to be retreating in the postwar period, it was actually advancing.

Another lesson of the past to keep in mind for today is how this barbarous context also gave rise to gangsterism. John Wesley Hardin, a thug and thief celebrated of late in song and cinema, was born in Bonham, Texas, in 1853, but at the age of 9 seriously considered fighting the "Yankees" during the war. Naturally, he considered President Lincoln to be a "demon." The "first man I ever killed," he boasted—and there were many more to come—was "the negro Mage" in 1868. "In those times," he asserted swaggeringly, "if there was anything that could arouse my passion, it was seeing impudent negroes lately freed insult or abuse old, wounded confederates...." In September 1871 alone he slew three more Africans in Austin, as he gloated about "putting down negro rule."[87]

It is likely that Hardin was uninvolved in the infamous "Millican Riot" of 1868, occurring far less than a marathon run from today's gigantic campus of Texas A& M University. But assuredly, those

---

85. Wilbarger, 382, 496, 586.

86. M.L. Johnson, *True History of the Struggles with Hostile Indians...*, Dallas: Publisher unidentified, 1923, Huntington Library.

87. *The Life of John Wesley Hardin from the Original Manuscript as Written by Himself*, Seguin, Texas: Smith & Moore, 1896, 9, 6, 13, 12, 15, 63, 74.

like him were at the controls as this area descended into violent anarchy when in response to the lynching of an African man, his comrades armed themselves for a showdown. Perhaps two dozen or more of them were slain, as once again Texas captured national headlines.[88]

Weeks after the "Second Juneteenth," in Tehuantepec—once crawling with Euro-Americans seeking a shortcut to San Francisco—Secretary Seward was told that there were "absolutely no American interests" present; "the only white man living in the place, a German, was murdered by the natives...."[89] Yet the definition of "American interests" was flexible, since a few weeks later a U.S. agent in nearby Acapulco sought to "order a vessel of war to this port" since "American interests at stake here are considerable...."[90]

In any event, Acapulco may have been more indicative of the postwar trans-border dispensation, at least as far as Northern Mexico was concerned. For it was then months after Maximilian's execution that Washington was instructed that "during the rebellion many men were driven from Texas into Tamaulipas, Chihuahua & Nuevo Leon" and a number had planted roots and were unlikely to depart.[91]

Still, after 19 June 1867, French residents of Tampico began lining up before the Tampico consulate of the U.S., seeking protection,[92] indebting themselves to the rapacious republic in case they wound up in New Orleans and were recruited to join in the repression of Africans or on the Texas frontier for the grimy task of "exterminating" Indigenes. In a contrasting note, just before the liquidation of Maximilian, Daniel Jenkins—described as a "colored man and barber by profession, aged from 35 to 40 years, born of free parents in the city of Charleston, South Carolina"—died in Monterrey. "This case of Jenkins is not of much importance,"[93] said the U.S. agent there haughtily, and the same could be said for the fate of his fellow Africans now bumpily en route to a satanic Jim Crow.

---

88. B.C. Curtis, 94, 95.

89. Consul John Ralph Lowe to Secretary Seward, 15 July 1867, Reel 3, Despatches from U.S. Consuls in Acapulco, NARA.

90. Ibid., Vice Commercial Agent John Sutter to Admiral H.K. Thatcher, Commanding North Pacific Squadron, 24 August 1867.

91. Report to Assistant Secretary Seward, 18 November 1867, Reel 1, Despatches from U.S. Consuls in Monterrey, NARA.

92. French residents to Consul Chase, 25 November 1867, Reel 5, Despatches from U.S. Consuls in Tampico, NARA.

93. Joseph Ulrich to Secretary Seward, 5 June 1867, Reel 1, Despatches from U.S. Consuls in Monterrey, NARA.

While Jenkins died in obscurity, rebels began the march back to acceptance in the state they had sought to overthrow. Hamilton Prioleau Bee, a former brigadier general in the militia of Texas before attaining the same rank in the rebel military—and coincidentally of French Protestant ancestry—showed up at the consulate in Monterrey where Jenkins was treated so dismissively and requested that the amnesty oath, allowing his return home, be administered. "I have declined," said the consul, although there were "very few officers here of the confederacy," most having abandoned ship earlier as the vessel of rebel exile was sinking.[94] Undeterred, Bee invested in a paper factory in Parras, Mexico.[95]

During the reign of Maximilian, the rebel journal *Mexican Times* was sailing along nicely with correspondents and agents in Havana, London, New York City and New Orleans[96]—who could moonlight as purveyors of intelligence—but soon they too had run aground as Maximilian was interred.

As Maximilian's star was descending, so were those from north of the border who had attached themselves to him. A.M. Hunt, formerly postmaster at Santa Fe, N.M., arrived in Mexico with a still considerable $3000 in gold—but then was robbed, taken prisoner by Juárez's forces, and faced imminent starvation and an uncertain fate.[97]

It was not clear how and why Hunt crossed the border with a small fortune, but it was clear that miscreants of various sorts at times sought to elude U.S. jurisdiction. One of these characters, a cotton gin owner in Fairfield, Texas, who was accused credibly, by one who knew, of having "brutally beaten freedmen" and "attempted to take the lives of others," and had hightailed it to New Orleans, headed to Honduras.[98]

However, the imminent arrival of the "Second Juneteenth" may have indicated that the promise of emancipation—i.e., non-slavery—was in motion, which was the extent of the optimism that could be afforded. In 1867 it would have been difficult to convince the Negro Dick Perkins that he should be optimistic. He was shot by his former master, and Perkins fired back—and was arrested and jailed. He escaped and fled to Houston, where the Bureau hospitalized

94. Ibid., Consul Joseph Ulrich to Secretary Seward, 20 October 1867.

95. Wahlstrom, 110.

96. *Mexican Times*, 11 December 1866.

97. U.S. Consular Agent, Puebla to Consul Otterbourg, 4 June 1867, Reel 5, Despatches from U.S. Consuls in Mexico City, NARA.

98. Report from C.S. Culver, 16 August 1867, Reel 3, FBR.

him—but there too he was arrested and jailed and remanded to a questionable destiny.[99]

Such was typical. There were "murderers now at large in Robertson County," was the news after Maximilian's execution; it was "utterly impossible to stem the tide of murder & disorder in this state," was the Bureau analysis. "The Bureau agents do not meet with aid in arresting criminals in ten counties in the state," it was said, as "over one hundred freedmen have been killed since January 1, 1867."[100] This county was indicative of the state as a whole. By late March 1867, a military man asserted that the "number of freedmen murdered in the state of Texas, since the surrender of the rebels…[is] as bad as represented."[101]

This county, not far from today's massive Texas A&M University campus, was known as having "few loyal men," while others were "maltreating and murdering" Africans as "the order of the day." Grimly, the Bureau was told that "the civil authorities affords [sic] them [Negroes] no protection and that they…are likely to be coerced by the whites at the ensuing election."[102]

The presence of Negro troops did not seem to hinder this marauding measurably, possibly because they were too busy throttling Indigenes. "I once belonged to a colored regiment which was stationed in Galveston," said Frank White, a Negro. What struck him was the "deep rooted prejudice…against colored soldiers," barring "fair and impartial trial" on the frequent occasions when they were subjected to ever harsher discipline.[103] White would have understood the plight of Robert Wright, alias Porter, who had been a private in the U.S. infantry. He was portrayed as a "colored man and nearly white" but that hue did not save him: he was murdered, in Brenham, Washington County, one example among many.[104]

It did seem the end of the French occupation marked a turning point, serving as an informal end to the Civil War, allowing Euro-Americans on both sides of the divide to focus more intently on dispossession of Indigenes, with the battering of Africans being collateral damage. Weeks after Maximilian's execution, an account from Sherman, Texas, sketched that a "set of lawless men commit

---

99. Ibid., Major General Kiddo to Governor Throckmorton, 8 January 1867, Reel 1.

100. Ibid., J.T. Kirkman to Lieutenant Colonel Albert, 23 July 1867.

101. Ibid., Report from Joseph Riley, Captain, 13th Infantry, 30 March 1867, Reel 3.

102. Ibid., Report from O.T. Hunsaker, Sterling, Texas.

103. Ibid., Report from Frank White, 26 July 1867, Reel 2.

104. Ibid., Report, 4 March 1867, Reel 4.

murders daily" and "killed several persons in cold blood...." But the guardians of the law felt they could "do nothing until the soldiers are better equipped" in that "soldiers have no arms for service...."[105]— at least as far as protecting Negroes was concerned.

An already bad situation was worsening. By July 1867 the infant Republic Party convened in Houston in sessions attended by Africans and settlers alike from 27 counties. However, the rebel press denounced this gathering as a "Radico-Congo" monstrosity.[106] Winfield Hancock eventually replaced Philip Sheridan in command of the military and also focused on combating Indigenes rather than protecting Africans, including sending troops comprised of the latter to the frontier. When Hancock was in turn supplanted by General Robert C. Buchanan, who had fought in the Black Hawk War, the Seminole War and the Mexican War, it was crystal clear that the policy of liquidating Indigenes first would not be altered. Negro troops who were not sent to the frontier were sent to the border, not close to where their community was mostly sited in East Texas, and there they came under strict scrutiny because in Brownsville there was a noticeable ferociously anti-Negro tendency, a holdover from the war with an organ that daily lambasted these armed men and openly had backed the French occupation. These soldiers had to be restrained from rebelling and destroying the organ that defamed them.[107] The watchers and antagonists of these troops may have had in mind what occurred in Brenham, where these armed men were blamed for pillaging and wielding arson against their defamers.[108]

As Negroes were clubbed and truncheoned in the midst of a wrenching transition away from slavery, unavoidably the bonds of society began to fray, impacting social relations: there was an emergence of what the Bureau called "taking other wives," and "evil that is being carried on" known as <u>adultery</u> [emphasis original]."[109] Still, there were unavoidable complexities in the transition from slavery to third-class citizenship. The Bureau wanted to know if "freedpeople who have cohabited for more than ten years are to be considered as man and wife."[110]

Making things worse was the arrival of the man who called himself "Dr. H. Parker," a "colored individual," as the Austin press described

105. Ibid., Report from A.W. Bryant, Sherman, Texas, 21 August 1867, Reel 3.
106. Richter, 117.
107. Ibid., 175-176.
108. Shook, 454.
109. Report from Dr. J.M. Donaldson, 9 June 1867, Reel 3, FBR.
110. Ibid., Report from D.S. Beath, 28 August 1868.

him. He was a "conservative orator, perambulating the country"; he was "highly endorsed" by Governor Throckmorton, quite suspectly, given his enmity toward the "colored." "Dr. Parker" was affluent, having "purchased two large farms...amounting to 1500 or 2000 acres," having "collected from" the governor and his patrons a "large amount of funds...." There were "several charges against him for adultery," leading to the suspicion that the authorities were sponsoring this violation of the anti-bigamy laws for tawdry reasons. He had consorted with a blind woman in Mobile before alighting in Texas, who believed that he had "killed" her spouse beforehand. Then he began "courting another...young widow"—then scurried to New Orleans. Depicted as a "robber and scoundrel," this man was "rather heavy set" and of "copper color" with a "full beard" and "very well spoken"; he was "five six or eight inches...one hundred and sixty pounds."[111]

But what was disturbing about "Dr. Parker," according to the Bureau, was that he was "speaking...in the interests of the Rebels" as he roamed through Texas,[112] with part of the payoff presumed to be his licentious misdeeds.

Then there were other martial battles reflective of an unsettled society in a twilight zone between slavery and emancipation. Anny Milstead, a Negro woman, had lived with Abram Milstead, a Euro-American man, in Florida. "Being a slave of his," she said in a sworn statement, this occurred though "his first wife Sally was then living," she was a "white woman." But she expired "about twenty four or five years ago," such was her estimate in 1867. A year later, "he took me for a wife, " she said clinically and she "lived with him in Florida" for "ten or twelve years having by him seven children. We then moved to the state of Texas...on the Colorado River" for "about six months," then to Mobile "about six years." There emerged "three children more...." Then he suggested she move to Mexico "in order to have us all set free," and so it was off to Matamoros—then Texas, "a place called Live Oak." Then the peripatetic crew were sited in Hidalgo County, with three children and Mr. Milstead. As late as December 1865 she was with him "as his wife"—until his death in February 1866. His estate included sums in a trunk and a "large amount of stock, cattle, horses and goats," now the subject of a bitterly contested inheritance battle—with Mrs. Milstead disfavored, given the unsettledness in Texas.[113]

111. Ibid., *Austin Republican*, 26 July 1867 and 7 July 1867, Reel 4.

112. Ibid., Report by A.E. Pratt, 15 September 1868, Reel 1.

113. Ibid., Sworn Statement by Anny Milstead, 13 January 1867, Reel 4.

Chapter 21

"For the First and Only Time in Texas History," 1868-1872

On 25 August 1868 a treaty was proclaimed between Indigenes—i.e., Cheyenne, Arapaho, Kiowa and those described as "Kiowa-Apaches"—and Washington, the last ever made with these groups.[1] This was significant, bringing the curtain down on an entire epoch, particularly since—per the genocidal caucus on the frontier—the only treaties worth pursuing were those propelled by bayonets and written in blood. With Indigenes in rapid retreat—a bipartisan cause in Washington—it became easier for Texas to promote its other priority: clobbering Negroes.

Yet as Washington could well attest, signing a treaty was one thing, having it reflect reality was quite another. After all, seven Indigenous leaders—two Comanche, one Apache and four Kiowa—earlier had been invited to Washington, where they signed a treaty on 6 April 1863,[2] and yet the bloodletting on the frontier continued. And it was in May 1871 that—according to a hyperbolically genocidal chronicler of Texas—150 "warriors under the leadership of…Kiowa chiefs" executed an "act of savage cruelty," rare in "recorded…history" on a scale "more barbarous and inhuman," than ever seen: "the unwarranted attack…upon Henry Warren's wagon train." This was a "dark period for West Texas," fumed J.W. Wilbarger. In sum, this treaty signaled that the curtain had come down on negotiating with Indigenes. It was viewed in Washington as their formal surrender—not so much among the intended victims,[3] though soon they would have to yield to fire and the sword.

Bilateral relations with Indigenes were not the only fork in the road reached postwar. With the "second Juneteenth" and the forcible

---

1. Wallace and Hoebel, 309, 332. See also "Treaty Between the United States of America and the Kiowa, Comanche and Apache Tribes of Indians," proclaimed 25 August 1868, Huntington Library.

2. Wallace and Hoebel, 332, 339.

3. Wilbarger, 555.

removal of Maximilian, Mexico became a more suitable site for export of U.S. capital, a trend that would accelerate in coming decades. It was also in 1868 that Secretary of State Seward was informed in rhapsodic terms that in Acapulco the "coming cotton crop promises fair," while "abundant wells of good petroleum have been discovered." The "necessary capital to work the same is furnished by San Francisco," while "coal, resembling in quality [that of] Pittsburgh [was] discovered...." That this report was penned by the scion of the Sutter family, a clan that had inaugurated the Gold Rush in California in the wake of Mexico's subjugation in the 1840s, made this report all the more poignant—and convincing.[4] Capital, representing the most potent wing of the ascendant Republic Party and the purported ally of Negroes, became even less interested in confronting anti-Indigene raids or even confronting the antagonists of Africans, as it was diverted into its primary preoccupation: profiteering. Coincidentally, after stepping down from office in 1869, William Seward promptly spent three months in Mexico, which did little to diminish the already considerable wealth of his affluent family.[5]

These capitalist interlopers were ensconced heavily along the border, leaving the impression that a de facto annexation was occurring. By early 1868, according to a dispatch sent to Seward from Monterrey, there were "more Americans living...on this frontier than in another section" of Mexico.[6] There were a reputed 100-200 U.S. nationals in Mexico City as of 1871 and they were concentrated in banking, "hardware," fine arts, education, mining and medicine.[7] They outnumbered U.S. nationals in Oaxaca where, according to official sources, there were "few citizens of the United States residing" as of 1870—though it was "transiently visited by a great many Americans."[8]

These officious visitors had brought with them their peculiar folkways too, as a number soon were accused of engagement in various robberies.[9] The response was predictable too; soon these exiles were

---

4. J.A. Sutter to Secretary of State Seward, 31 December 1868, Reel 2, Despatches from U.S. Consuls in Acapulco, NARA.

5. Baker, *Seward*, Volume V, 30.

6. Joseph Ulrich to Secretary Seward, 14 January 1868, Reel 1, Despatches from U.S. Consuls in Monterrey, NARA.

7. Consul Julius Skilton to Second Assistant Secretary of State, 30 September 1871, Reel 7, Despatches from U.S. Consuls in Mexico City, NARA.

8. Commercial Agent L.L. Lawrence to Secretary Fish, 30 June 1870, Reel 1, Despatches from U.S. Consuls in Oaxaca, NARA.

9. Consul Ulrich to Secretary Seward, 23 March 18 1869, Reel 1, Despatches from U.S. Consuls in Monterrey, NARA.

complaining of insecurity, the "general hatred that exists" against them, and how they were "badly treated."[10]

A similar scenario unfolded in Piedras Negras near the far west of Texas. The "feeling of...Mexicans here," said a U.S. official, "against the Americans is bitter," and "lower classes are taught and encouraged in this spirit of enmity...."[11] But even in central Mexico, San Luis Potosí, there remained a complement of rebel officers, according to a U.S. official, "full of enmity to our people and institutions," comfortably distant from the nation they despised.[12]

Nevertheless, the U.S. thought that there was so much hostility in Chihuahua to the recently installed President Juárez that—once again—Washington should contemplate "annexation" of its neighbor.[13] Instead, as early as 1871, Washington began leaning toward Porfirio Díaz, who assumed power six years later. Just as there was a commonality between the U.S. Civil War and the French occupation (which amounted in a sense to a Mexican civil war), the failure of the promise of Reconstruction contributed to and reflected the decades-long "Porfiriato." For the U.S. was exasperated with Juárez's seeming inability to halt attacks on U.S. nationals and, it was said, did little to curb those Mexicans who "seem to take pleasure...in insulting" and "robbing" them.[14]

Quite concerning was the developing trend of not only "Mexicans from the Texas side" marauding in Piedras Negras against U.S. nationals, but the fact that they were being joined by Negroes, which potentially could compromise the role of Negro troopers along the border.[15] All the while accounts continued to mount about the arrival of "hostile Indians" using Mexico as a sanctuary from which revenge could be sought in the U.S.,[16] intensifying calls to extend the U.S. border farther south.

This was self-serving insofar as pro-protectorate viewpoints were the norm in U.S. diplomatic circles. It was also a way to circumvent the stiff competition provided by peer nations in Mexico. For at this

10. Ibid., Santiago Hatchett to Consul Ulrich, 14 May 1869.

11. Ibid., Consul William Schuchardt to Secretary of State Hamilton Fish, 28 July 1869.

12. Ibid., Consul Ulrich to Secretary Seward, 19 April 1868.

13. Consul William Schuchardt to Secretary of State Hamilton Fish, 1 February 1870, Reel 1, Despatches from U.S. Consuls in Piedras Negras, NARA.

14. Ibid., J.H. Harrison, et al., to "My Dear Sir," 16 December 1871.

15. Ibid., Consul Schurchardt to State Department, 28 September 1872.

16. Ibid., Consul Schurchardt to Second Assistant Secretary of State, 26 December 1872.

same time in Acapulco, the analysis provided by a U.S. official was that commerce was "exclusively in the hands of German & English houses, established in Hamburg, Bremen, Liverpool and London," while "no American house of any importance has established itself as yet on the west coast of Mexico...." Thus "far all the attempts of San Francisco merchants to establish themselves on this coast have proved unsuccessful...." [17] A similar story obtained in Piedras Negras. "Import trade," said an official report, was "carried on by Germans, English and French," whose goods were "cheaper...than the American"—however, since many Mexicans journeyed to Eagle Pass to buy U.S. goods, this may have been overstated.[18]

It was also earlier in 1868 that another lack of success took place: a failed attempt was made to impeach and remove President Johnson, while afterwards peyote partaking among certain Indigenes accelerated, and that too may have been a product of the disoriented and altered political landscape. For the continuation of Johnson would mean in the shorter term further cudgeling of Indigenes and Africans too, and likewise in the longer horizon, post-1876, producing similar disorienting consequences.[19]

By June 1868 in Tyler, in the heart of the Texas cotton belt, the failure to oust Johnson was greeted with hosannas of joy; the planters and settlers alike recognized a victory when they saw one and knew how to capitalize on it. From Matamoros, the message to Secretary Seward was that among "thousands in the U.S." and in this vicinity, there were those who chose to "rejoice at the acquittal" of Johnson.[20] This was the message to the Freedmen's Bureau too. An informant shared the tidbit that in the aftermath of the "acquittal of the president," detractors of the Negro and Indigenes "exhibit a spirit as bitter and hostile as during the rebellion, that outrages with freedmen are becoming alarmingly numerous, that no day or night passes without some violence being committed upon them, that the ruffians are disguised," though even if they were unmasked consequence would generally be missing. "Children belonging to the

17. Report by J.A. Sutter, ca, August 1869, Reel 3, Despatches from U.S. Consuls in Acapulco, NARA.

18. Consul William Schuchardt to Secretary of State Hamilton Fish, 15 October 1870, Reel 1, Despatches from U.S. Consuls in Piedras Negras, NARA.

19. Brenda Wineapple, *The Impeachers: The Trial of Andrew Johnson and the Dream of a Just Nation*, New York: Random House, 2020.

20. Consul Thomas Scott to Secretary Seward, 27 May 1868, Reel 3, Despatches from U.S. Consuls in Matamoros, NARA.

freed school," in a continuing pattern, "have been beaten with clubs by grown persons," as the sight of a Negro willing to learn brought excoriating umbrage. "They threaten to burn the schoolhouse" and the attempt by Negroes to "organize a local militia" only inflamed these assailants further.[21]

In an exemplar of understatement, the Bureau found that in Travis County, the "sentiment of…many [of]…the white people concerning the education of the freedmen" was "hostile."[22]

Soon, in retaliatory response among Negroes in Tyler, threats to have a "head shot off" rose, along with "vicious other threats"—but this was in reference "to the case of John Crumb who was tried for raping a freedwoman and was acquitted…."[23] Sandy Point, site of cotton and sugar plantations, witnessed organized Africans and, said the Bureau, "they threaten the whites that they are headed by a freedman named Thomas Bolton who has from 1000 to 1500 men at his call," the kind of force that Throckmorton railed against repeatedly.[24]

Retaliation was swift and deadly: "bands of armed men," said the Bureau, "are raiding through the country shooting at every freedmen they meet."[25] "Freedpeople are suffering great injustice at the hands of the rebels" in Paris, Texas, said the Bureau; "many murders occur" and "perpetrators go unmolested…."[26] About thirty miles away in Clarksville, the Ku Klux Klan was creating one outrage after another.[27] In nearby Smith County, all within hailing distance of Dallas, Klansmen attacked and robbed the homes of the recently emancipated nearly every night for months.[28]

By early 1872 the Klan was reported to have a substantial membership of 15,000. Quite properly, Governor Edmund Davis asserted that this terrorist band "must be broken up before the next election or no fairness can be anticipated…." Davis found it necessary to

---

21. Report from Gregory Barrett, 6 June 1868, Reel 3, FBR.

22. Teacher's Monthly Report of the Freedmen's Bureau, April 1870, Box 1, Early African American Research Materials, Austin Public Library-Texas (abbrev. Early AARM).

23. Report from Gregory Barrett, 6 June 1868, Reel 3, FBR. (Although dated similarly, this is a separate report.)

24. Ibid., Report from Lieutenant Colonel George H. Bram, 13 June 1868.

25. Ibid., Report from Gregory Barrett, 14 August 1868.

26. Report from Charles Granger, 27 April 1868.

27. Report from S.F. Rand, 10 May 1868.

28. Whitney Nell Stewart, "The Racialized Politics of Home in Slavery and Freedom," Ph.D. Dissertation, Rice U, 2017, 204.

remove Austin's mayor "because of official persecution of colored people" which was suspiciously parallel to Klan policy.[29]

When General Sheridan was replaced by Winfield Hancock—a subsequent Democratic Party nominee for President—as Washington's administrator in Texas and Louisiana, matters deteriorated vertiginously. Before his arrival in 1868, murders averaged—officially—nine per month; this doubled upon his taking the reins of power and then tripled.[30] His arrival was a halfway house between the postwar glow with Republicans riding high and their post-1876 collapse.

In early 1868 the Houstonian John Augustus Ansley noted in his journal that it was "cold & clear" as Africans headed to the polls; the "first time," he said, "the freedmen had a chance to vote," an event to which he objected. "Loyal Leagues," he spat out, were "telling all sorts of lies & the negroes fearing they would be put back into slavery if they did not vote," so "all turned out to a man & went to the election...." Shockingly, he thought, they expected benefits from voting: "all expected mules & land if they voted the radical ticket and could not be held away from the ballot box" during this "rousing day."[31]

But instead of benefits, these voters were administered a poisonous dosage of pain. For in Houston the Ku Klux Klan had spawned a front group, the Teutonic Band of Brothers, also secretive, and demented specialists in shedding blood. Yet another KKK outgrowth was "The Roughs" and yet another was the "Knights of the White Camellia" as crushing the Negroes took on the fervency of a Holy Crusade with one group unable to contain the rampant enthusiasm. By August 1868—as certain Indigenes were proclaiming peace with Washington—Africans in the future "petro metro" were on the cusp of revolt. They were thought to be amassing northwest of the city with the aim of launching an attack. Conflict between Negro leadership and those denoted as "white radicals" did not help the overall cause.[32]

---

29. Governor Davis to Attorney General George H. Williams, 13 February 1872, Reel 1, Letters Received by the Department of Justice from the State of Texas, 1871-1884, NARA (abbrev. Letters Received).

30. "Winfield Hancock's Defiance of the Reconstruction Acts: Record from Official Sources of Hancock's Administration of Civil Affairs in 1867-1868 in Louisiana and Texas," 1868, AAS.

31. Entry, ca. February 1868, Ansley Journal.

32. Marion Mersebuger, "A Political History of Houston, Texas During the Reconstruction Period as Recorded by the Press: 1868-1878," M.A. thesis, Rice U, 1950, 28, 34, 52, 70, 140.

More to the point, Euro-American Republicans were split between Edmund Davis, a future governor, and the man to his right, Andrew J. Hamilton, a past chief executive.[33] These strange "radicals" often held private parties that excluded Negroes, and Davis at times entertained in the executive mansion but did not invite Negroes either.[34] Nevertheless, the Union League which had backing from both formulated an oath demanding affirmance to "removing all the concomitants of slavery...."[35]

This nonfeasance on Davis's part was distinctly dysfunctional since by 1870 about 11 of the 120 legislators were African and essential to the success of the governor's agenda. As the chief executive, Davis was depicted as presiding over the "armed enforcement of black civil rights," an unpopular goal among settlers requiring expert coordination. A sizable percentage of the state officers were African and the majority were Republicans, while most of those arrested—for a while—were Euro-Texan and, says scholar Robert Perkinson, "for the first and only time in Texas history, conservative Anglos found themselves complaining about police discrimination and criminal justice"; these "state police," he continues, "inspired such vitriol because it was the most racially integrated and most determinedly anti-racist law enforcement in Texas history...."[36]

Nonetheless, it was hardly reassuring when the Pease campaign for governor, as a GOP standard-bearer, declared that he chose to "acquiesce" to "abolishing slavery,"[37] as opposed to endorsing with enthusiasm.

The situation in Texas was worse than it looked. An official report authored by General J.J. Reynolds asserted that the Klan was active "in many part of Texas but are most numerous, bold and aggressive east of the Trinity River," where "civil law is almost a dead letter." In "some counties" the "civil officers" just happened to be "member[s] of the Klan"; hence, "the murder of Negroes is so common as to render it impossible to keep an accurate count." Problematically, this

33. Andress, 167. On the racist front reappearing also were the Knights of the Golden Circle, though they may been confused with the Klan: See e.g., Smallwood, 347.

34. Smallwood, 399.

35. "Ritual, Constitution and By-Laws of the National Council' of the Union League, Austin, 1868, Box 39, Pease, Graham, Niles Papers.

36. Robert Perkinson, "The Birth of the Texas Prison Empire, 1865-1915," Ph.D. dissertation, Yale U, 2001, 62, 64, 65 (abbrev. R. Perkinson).

37. Broadside of Pease Campaign for Governor, ca. 1868, Box 46, *Pease, Graham, Niles Papers.*

was "not discouraged by a majority of white people," just as this preponderance hardly objected to ongoing genocide against Indigenes. This deplorable state of affairs "could not otherwise exist" but for this preponderant acquiescence. Texas was primed for this scandal since "free speech and free press, as the terms are generally understood...have never existed in Texas...." General Reynolds espied a devolutionary spiral in that the "lawlessness of Eastern Texas" was "weaken[ing] the frontier posts to such an extent as to impair their efficiency for protection against the Indians," inducing more settler hysteria—and backlash. Thus, Reynolds thought the key was reducing "lawlessness" against Negroes, but that conflicted with settler priorities. This reduction was unlikely, meaning that Indigenes from "the Northwest, after having suffered defeat there, will make heavy incursions into Texas...."[38]

Indeed, there was an influential school of thought that argued that stationing U.S. troops in eastern Texas to slow down terrorizing of Negroes was actually hampering what was thought to be the wider and more crucial objective: liquidating Indigenes. So argued the Jacksboro cavalryman H.H. McConnell, who contended that by 1869 the "Texas frontier...was left almost entirely unprotected," since the "troops [were] pretty much being all engaged in the work of reconstruction in the interior," a boon to "bands of depredating Indians...." He was sarcastically contemptuous of the "benevolent civilizing policy so urgently advocated by...the Eastern States," which underestimated Indigenes who "have no more conception of gratitude than so many wolves,"[39] who too were on the fast track to evanescence.

North of Jacksboro, in Indian Territory in 1869, rumblings were such that would confirm McConnell's worst fears. Al Thompson was of Delaware ancestry and then was in today's Bartlesville. "I have heard the Osages chanting around a fire," he said chillingly, "'Kill the white man.' They, the Pawnees, the Delawares, the Kiowas," he explained, "were still hostile to the white man...." Of course, Osages "didn't permit marriage with a negro by any of the tribe," though this seemed to be limited to women: "if she married a negro, however, she would be shot from a horse," he pointed out, "usually by her father and the negro tied in a sack and drowned." The Choctaw Nation was hostile to railways crossing their land, which infuriated settlers. And Cherokees were skeptical when "some negroes from Alabama were going to prove that they were of Cherokee blood and take some land

---

38. Ibid., Official Report of General Reynolds, 4 December 1868.
39. H.H. McConnell, 173, 280.

in the Cherokee Nation," which did not endear them to the latter, just as their obstinance irked Africans,[40] all of which complicated any attempt to construct an anti-white supremacist front.

Nonetheless, as early as 1866 Texans petitioned Congress for the building of a railway through Indian Territory to connect the system of the Lone Star State with the rest of the nation.[41] It was then that Senator William Stewart of Nevada, a recent admittee to the union, echoed his congressional comrades when he claimed that "'the locomotive is the sole solution to the Indian Question,'"[42] which was shorthand for railways as a tool for liquidation, a thought that had occurred to Indigenes.

The Osage were also a concern of the man who called himself Colonel John Hunter, whose father—born in Virginia in 1823—shared with him stories about them. They were a "wild, treacherous tribe and would sneak up on the house in the night" and "would ride miles for a scalp," especially after a death of one of their crew, and at that point a "mourning party" would be launched. Their modus operandi, he thought, was "looking for trouble." Born in 1860, Hunter was no choir boy—heading "Hunter's Hell Hounds," rowdy teenage gangsters—who when he was fourteen "enlisted in the Indian war… to fight Cheyennes." He was "shot at many times by the Indians," he recalled decades later, "and had many narrow escapes…."[43]

But Indian Territory had an anomalous position in the heart of the U.S., amounting to a separate jurisdiction which—as occurred during slavery days—allowed arbitrage opportunities. Bass Reeves was born enslaved in Paris, Texas—or perhaps adjacent Arkansas—in 1838, but developed proficiency as a fighter and boxer, which was put to good use when he delivered a knockout blow to his "master." During the war he fled to Indian Territory, where he learned the languages of the Cherokee, Creek and Seminole and developed a fearsome reputation as a lawman—a post generally unavailable to Negroes in neighboring states, particularly after the fall of Reconstruction.[44]

From the southwestern corner of Texas, near Eagle Pass, events were consistent with the above—at least according to the U.S. consul in Piedras Negras. These border towns had assumed greater

40. Oral History, Al Thompson, 29 July 1937, IPP.

41. Stephen Franklin Shannon, "Galvestonians and Military Reconstruction, 1865-1867," Master's thesis, Rice U, 1975, 91 (abbrev. S.F. Shannon).

42. Hamalainen, 295.

43. Oral History, Colonel John Hunter, 23 November 1937, IPP.

44. John W. Ravage, *Black Pioneers: Images of the Black Experience on the North American Frontier*, Salt Lake City: U of Utah Press, 2008, 104.

importance during the Civil War for—like Matamoros-Brownsville—they became an outlet for cotton exports and resultant wealth. This led to cattle being expropriated with Kickapoo and "Lepan [Lipan]" accused of making "constant raids" into Texas from Mexico. The result was "few horses are left within eighty miles of the river on the Texas side," for fear of their being seized; inevitably there was "talking of entering Mexico to exterminate these tribes...."[45]

Howls and peals of outrage were emanating from this fraught border. "Depredations" by Indigenes were increasing, so the consul claimed. These purported marauders were "hostile to both the U.S. and Mexico," which may have been understandable but was strategically unwise. Targeted were the "Lepan [Lipan], Mescalero and Comanche," along with the "Kickapoo and Seminole." Unfortunately, strategically wise by the U.S. was to peel off the Seminoles and employing them as "scouts" against other Indigenes with the consul envisioning prophetically that this would prove to be "very useful."[46] Like so many factors tipping in favor of the traitors, the seeming inability of the men in blue to subdue Indigenes led to a demand for beefing up the savage Texas Rangers,[47] despite the Seminoles beginning to collar Kickapoo on behalf of the settlers.[48]

In fact, after 1870 these Indigenous scouts—recounts historian Kevin Mulroy—"killed, maimed, imprisoned and destroyed the villages and property of diverse bands of Kickapoo, Apaches, Cheyennes, Kiowas and Comanches...driving these bands onto reservations or deep into the Mexican interior and facilitating white expansion,"[49] a perverse chapter in the history of a group had been rooted in Florida before being compelled to move westward.

Bloodiness was anticipated, since by his own admission the U.S. consul counted 800 Kickapoo in Mexico with 300 "continually

45. Consul William Schuchardt to Secretary of State Hamilton Fish, 12 April 1869, Reel 1, Despatches from U.S. Consuls in Piedras Negras, NARA.

46. Ibid., Consul Schuchardt to Secretary of State Fish, 25 June 1870. Typically, the Seminole were treated shabbily by the settler regime. Their leader John Horse and his band returned to Texas in 1870 but were treated so horribly they retreated to Mexico: see Gassner, 110. See also James Alan Martin, "Drawing the Line: Dissent and Disloyalty in Texas, 1855 to 1874," Ph.D. dissertation, UT-A, 1985.

47. W.L. Richter, 299.

48. Consul Schuchardt to State Department, 4 January 1872, Reel 1, Despatches from U.S. Consuls in Piedras Negras, NARA.

49. Kevin Mulroy, *Freedom on the Border: The Seminole Maroons in Florida, the Indian Territory, Coahuila and Texas*, Lubbock: TTU Press, 2001, 131.

engaged in stealing stock from Texas...."[50] "Large bands of Kickapoo Indians from Mexico," said a U.S. official in Matamoros, "had crossed into Texas" and were busily "committing depredations"—"stealing stock and killing herdsmen...." Across the country in Piedras Negras, "evidence of Indian ravages increased," leaving Eagle Pass "in a state of alarm."[51]

"General Cortina" was fingered as the culprit when discussing the "armed bands of robbers from Mexico" that routinely crossed the border to perpetrate the "most wanton depredations"; he was said to be allied with Kickapoo from Laredo, although the "Indians had crossed in considerable numbers, accompanied by Mexicans disguised as Indians." This was a "frequent occurrence," as were "murder of the settlers." When not denouncing Cortina, the spotlight shifted to Kickapoo, who—it was thought—had not forgotten their expulsion from the U.S. that led to their current residence in Coahuila. Besides, said the U.S. agent gloomily, "authorities of the state of Coahuila protect these Indians and incite them."[52]

It wasn't just cattle that was seized. Mescalero Apaches and Comanches were accused of seizing "white captives...taken in Texas" and taken across the border, leaving the consul to ponder if he should "buy" them back.[53]

Llano, northwest of Austin and San Antonio, was said to have "suffered more at the hands of savage Indians" by early 1868 than comparable regions; these were the "darkest and saddest days that ever dawned upon the Legion Valley," said a mournful observer, all due to "atrocities committed by the Comanches...."[54]

Hundreds of miles away in Matamoros, a similar plaint arose. Cattle were said to be stolen from the Texas side of the border and taken to Mexico. These armed bands were said to be tied to Juan Cortina, who had yet to disappear. In Cameron and Hidalgo counties on the Texas side of the border, Washington was informed that "two thirds

50. Consul Schuchardt to Secretary Fish, 1 July 1869, Reel 1, Despatches from U.S. Consuls in Piedras Negras, NARA.

51. Consul Wilson to Assistant Secretary of State, William Hunter, 11 November 1871, Reel 4, Despatches from U.S. Consuls in Matamoros, NARA.

52. Ibid., Consul Wilson to Secretary Hunter, 17 November 1871.

53. Consul Schuchardt to Secretary Fish, 12 June 1869, Reel 1, Despatches from U.S. Consuls in Piedras Negras, NARA.

54. *The Bloody Trail in Texas: Sketches and Narratives of Indian Raids and Atrocities on our Frontier*, Bandera, Texas: J. Marvin Hunter, Huntington Library. See also John C. Duval, *The Adventures of Big-Foot Wallace, the Texas Ranger and Hunter*, Philadelphia: Claxton, Remsen & Haffelfinger, 1871.

of the inhabitants are Mexicans," and "all of these classes retain their Mexican feelings and customs," meaning exuding in the "hereditary dislike of their countrymen for Americans...." This was a commercial and national security concern compelling increased immigration from Europe in that it was "not probable they [Mexican-Americans] would be very active in furnishing information against their raiding countrymen and aiding otherwise their forays and capture them...."[55]

U.S. nationals were being murdered in Chihuahua—or so it was thought—but Emilio Velasco in Mexico was skeptical, reminding that "savage Indians received aid and encouragement from the American authorities for their depredations upon our soil and this was doubtless one of the reasons the Mexican government in 1848 insisted upon inserting in the Treaty of Guadalupe Hidalgo the clause making the American government responsible for the damages caused by Indian invasions."[56]

But it was not just Mexican Americans who presented a problem for Texas. Again, Cortina was at issue in that Washington was led to believe that "Mier" and the area "north of Monterrey" were "held by the forces of General Cortina...."[57]

As of early 1872 Cortina was thought to command about 600 men. He was also accused of "playing a double game," backing and opposing Juárez, which Washington believed was a replay of his "duplicity and treachery" during the French occupation; then he was charged with toggling between Juárez and Maximilian. But what concerned the U.S. most was his threat to their interests, going back to the 1850s when he "killed several of [Brownsville's] most prominent citizens and held the whole Texas frontier in the Lower Rio Grande in a state of siege for several months," reflective of his "known bitter animosity to all Americans."[58]

His "cattle stealing" demanded a strong cavalry force,"[59] continued the U.S. agent in Matamoros, but that could only bring further complexity in the form of more Negro troopers.

---

55. Consul Thomas Wilson to Assistant Secretary of State, William Hunter, 1 August 1871, Reel 4, Despatches from U.S. Consuls in Matamoros, NARA.

56. Emilio Velasco in *Siglo XIX*, 12 April 1872, Reel 7, Despatches from U.S. Consuls in Mexico City, NARA.

57. Consul Wilson to Assistant Secretary of State Hunter, 13 November 1871, Reel 4, Despatches from U.S. Consuls in Matamoros, NARA.

58. Ibid., Consul Wilson to Secretary Hunter, 10 February 1872.

59. Ibid., Consul Wilson to Secretary Hunter, 27 March 1872. On this same reel see also the Brownsville periodical *Daily Ranchero*, 26 March 1872, which details accusations against Cortina and Kickapoo. See also Translation of

At wits' end, Washington demanded the right of hot pursuit, to chase down these purported perpetrators even in Mexico and drag them across the border to stand trial—or worse.[60] The erosion of Mexican sovereignty was a kind of annexation of another sort.

But Washington thought violation of its sovereignty was precisely at issue, with a Brownsville official claiming that Mexicans had decided to "treat the Americans as enemies, that they claim the country between the Nueces and the Rio Grande and express a determination to drive the Americans from it...." It was "galling," said this unnamed leader, to see Cortina patrolling the frontier since "he has written the history of his career on this side of Rio Grande in...blood and fire...." He and his crew "had laid waste one hundred and twenty miles of frontier and [he] now occupies the double position of ranking officer of the Mexican army...and ranking cow and horse thief," and "received a large share of the plunder...." He "stocked four ranches mostly with cows and horses stolen from Texas"; since 1865 there had been "an average of five thousand cattle stolen...monthly and driven into Mexico," all in the Lower Rio Grande. "The total number is estimated at four hundred and twenty thousand and the actual value at six million three hundred thousand dollars," a still staggering sum. And this did "not include losses" at the hands of "Kickapoo Indians, naturalized citizens of Mexico...." U.S. officers seeking to disrupt this raiding were "killed...by armed Mexicans...." This was a "reign of terror," a "saturnalia of crime, violence and rapine" featuring "mercenary bands of marauders, Mexican officers and soldiers and Mexican outlaws and bandits." Wilting Texans had "become demoralized by half a century of war and internal convulsions...."[61]

* * *

Mexican document, 8 January 1872, that makes similar charges: Reel 7, Despatches from U.S. Consuls in Mexico City, NARA. See also Frank MacManus, District Attorney, 15th Judicial District, Brownsville, Texas, to Attorney General Amos T. Akerman, Washington, D.C., 2 October 1871, Reel 1, Letters Received: There was a "system of predatory warfare waged...by armed bands of Mexicans, organized for that purpose in the territory of Mexico" and "there finding asylum...."

60. Consul Schuchardt to Secretary Hunter, 13 December 1871, Reel 1, Despatches from U.S. Consuls in Piedras Negras, NARA.

61. Letter from Brownsville, March 1872, Letters Received. See also "Depredations on the Frontiers of Texas. Message from the President of the United States. Transmitting Report of the Commissioners for Inquiry into the Depredations...," 16 December 1872, 42nd Congress, House of Representatives, Ex. Doc. No. 39, UOk-N.

Bloodshed was not unique to Mexico but was influenced and tied to events in Texas. It was Governor Pease who in 1868 alerted the U.S. Congress with anxiety that "over 100 cases of homicide have occurred in Texas within the last 12 months," likely an understatement. But Pease was penetratingly accurate when he averred that the "large majority of the white population who participated in the last rebellion, are embittered against the government by their defeat"—and most crucially—the "loss of their slaves," a gargantuan social and financial penalty, little understood, even today. Thus, this multi-class grouping, many of whom did not own slave property, "regard the legislation of Congress on the subject of reconstruction as unconstitutional and hostile to their interests...." Similarly, "they look upon the enfranchisement of their late slaves and the disenfranchisement of [a] portion of their own class as an act of insult and oppression...." It was "extremely difficult to enforce the criminal laws in those portions of the state which are most densely occupied and often impossible to do so in those parts of the state which are sparsely settled...." This meant Texas was ungovernable, a precondition in the 20th century for counter-revolutionary upheaval. This unloosed majority decided to "redress their fancied wrongs and grievances by acts of violence" and, as in 1859, when Robert Neighbors was assassinated because of the perception that he was not sufficiently harsh toward Indigenes, by 1868 "United States officers and soldiers have been killed" because they were seen as overly protective of Negroes. And, as this indictment indicated, those that were "Mexican" and "white" as well were likewise slaughtered.[62]

Emancipation forced many planters into bankruptcy and unraveled a system whereby ownership of enslaved property was the beau ideal for numerous Euro-Texans.[63] Predictably, given the pre-existing white supremacy and dehumanization of Africans, violence to force them into an equivalent system was the response.

The impending replacement in the White House of Andrew Johnson by U.S. Grant did not curtail their lawlessness. By December 1868 Austin found that "many of the desperadoes of Northeastern Texas" were unbowed, harboring a "deep seated hostility" that "frequently exhibits itself in violence and terrorism towards loyal white and colored citizens...."[64]

---

62. Communication from Governor Pease of Texas "Relative to the Troubles in that State," 8 February 1868, Box 46, Pease, Graham, Niles Papers.

63. S.L. Watts, 60.

64. "Majority Report of Special Committee on the Condition of the State Reported in Convention," 23 December 1868, Box 46, Pease, Graham, Niles Papers.

By mid-1868 matters were deteriorating precipitously, or so thought Governor Pease: "My appointment was distasteful to a large majority of the people of Texas who had participated in the rebellion," meaning settlers overall. Then the latter felt power and prestige slipping from their grasp since "the loyal whites" along with the Africans "constitute a majority of the voting population," leading to enhanced violence against them both. Sheriffs were afraid to make arrests "because they feared violence"; thus "crime" was "never as prevalent in Texas as it is at this time." In the past six months there had been over 200 documented homicides in 67 of the state's 127 counties, leading to vigilantism and score settling. This was fueling a movement to divide Texas "into two or more states" which had "excited much discussion" among the population of 800,000. One idea was to sell territory west of the mouth of the Pecos River to the northwest corner of Hardeman County, except El Paso and Presidio counties. "This territory adjoins the territories set apart by the United States for the Indians and would be useful to them in carrying out their Indian policy," he said. As in the past, of greatest importance was to "encourage immigration" from Europe.[65]

That was not the only immigration from a continent in sight. A few weeks after the "first Juneteenth" a cry erupted for Chinese labor, seen as an alternative to the Negro variety.[66]

This was not an insubstantial matter in a land of white supremacy. Though Texas was well on its way to becoming the most populous state in Dixie, it was also the most sparsely settled. And in East Texas, about a third of the population was African—augmented by an influx pre-1865 from desperate enslavers.[67] Clearly, it would be easier to establish a firmer white supremacy if the population were augmented by an influx of those defined as "white." And Mississippi, in some ways Texas's mentor, was to show that even Chinese could be folded into a system of white supremacy.[68]

And then there was "immigration" from Mexico—rebel exiles disgruntled by the dislodging of Maximilian. Before his execution, rebel John Edwards in Mexico was upbeat: "another large immigration project is on foot. Dr. Cornelius Boyle, formerly of Washington City and during the war a provost marshal in Lee's army has visited,

---

65. Message of His Excellency Elisha Pease, Governor of Texas to the Constitutional Convention," 3 June 1868, Box 46, *Pease, Graham, Niles Papers.*

66. S.F. Shannon, 103-104.

67. Shook, 29.

68. James W. Loewen, *The Mississippi Chinese: Between Black and White,* Prospect Heights, Ill.: Waveland, 1988.

inspected and become favorably impressed with about 750,000 acres of uncultivated land on the Pacific Ocean.... families can be brought out. 160 acres are to be given gratis...." But even before the "Second Juneteenth," "mutual protection" was necessary to keep at bay Mexicans upset with these giveaways and sweetheart deals. "Times have changed badly," he lamented. But as he looked longingly northward he thought it was "only a question of time...before the Radicals triumph and commence their devastating work upon the South." He was downbeat about President Johnson, who "possesses neither the nerve, the virtue, nor the wisdom to make another Cromwell...." But with the pushback against the "Radicals," places like Texas became more attractive, sparing white supremacists the "greatest possible degree of social and political degradation"—although the "appeal again to the sword" clearly catalyzed this avoidable process.[69]

Yet in the halcyon days of Maximilian's rule, an observant journalist eagerly anticipated a "very large emigration...from the Southern States for thousands and thousands of men have lost everything they possessed on earth"; however, as matters evolved, it was unnecessary to move to Mexico when an unreconstructed Texas beckoned.[70]

Although the ouster of Maximilian was welcome, his departure also meant a surge of well-trained subverters due north. By early 1870 in Monterrey, the message to Washington was that "rebel generals" who "became enthusiastic imperialists, some of them even having positions under Maximilian" were unmoored since his dislodgement. They had little choice but to return to Dixie, Texas being in the unenviable position of being the closest port of call.[71]

Some subverters retained potency, however. It was also in 1870 that Consul Joseph Ulrich in Monterrey objected when a rebel politico from Texas who, during the war, was shipping cotton and other merchandise northward from Mexico to the Lone Star State, sought "using his influence to have me removed from position as consul"[72]—though it was Ulrich who had fled Texas because of his anti-secession views. Given the upsurge of rebel mastery, it would not be easy to predict an outcome.

It was good riddance, as far as Mexico City was concerned, when rebel exiles began departing. Looking back from 1870, U.S. consul

69. John Edwards to "Darling Sister Fanny," 18 September 1866, Morgan Collection.

70. Undated newspaper article, ca. 1866, Morgan Collection.

71. Consul Joseph Ulrich to Secretary of State Fish, 24 February 1870, Reel 2, Despatches from U.S. Consuls in Monterrey, NARA.

72. Ibid., Consul Ulrich to Secretary of State Fish, 19 March 1870.

Franklin Chase recalled without fondness a time when Tampico was "frequently thronged with Texas blockade runners composed of men of the worst class of society, belonging to various countries," though principally the U.S. Chase had resided there more or less since 1837 but had to flee to Havana on a British vessel, indicative of the threat posed by these rowdy roustabouts.[73]

They may have gone but were not forgotten. By 1870 Secretary of State Fish was told that French influence from Monterrey to Matamoros lingered and was manifested in continuing harassment of his countrymen: "practicing" of "outrages" was becoming a sport.[74]

Also beckoning was France, a land to which disgraced traitor Jefferson Davis journeyed after an all too brief detention. Just before his capture in the Spring of 1865, it was thought he would lead an army of 15,000 that would establish a base in Texas that could ally with the puppet French regime.[75] Unsurprisingly given his encouragement of Parisian ambition, he found that "officials were very courteous and gave all possible facilities" during his tour.[76]

In the prelude to the U.S. Civil War, a reactionary international brotherhood was forming with Confederates and Paris in the vanguard. The defeat of both in North America provided a stinging setback, but by late 1871 both were on the uptick with the rebels muscling their way back into influence in Dixie, while in France a menacing blow was administered to the Paris Commune, which anticipated the socialism that was to emerge in the 20th century. By 1871 Ambrose Dudley Mann, one of the rebels' most experienced diplomats, was in Paris, whence he informed Davis in ever bleaker terms about the "horrors of the siege and the Commune," which he thought sufficiently frightening to the European elite that it could be leveraged on "behalf of the Confederate States." That is, "Americans (by which I mean northerners) are in no favor at Versailles," while "the astute [Adolphe] Thiers," the butcher of communards, "has been equal to his position" in a "cunning" manner that impressed these butchers of Negroes: "he excites my interest in his success and all the more as a good hater of Yankeedom."[77]

---

73. Consul Franklin Chase to Senator Hannibal Hamlin, 25 June 1870, Reel 5, Despatches from U.S. Consuls in Tampico, NARA.

74. Consul Joseph Ulrich to Secretary of State Fish, 8 January 1870, Reel 2, Despatches from U.S. Consuls in Monterrey, NARA.

75. González-Quiroga, 234.

76. Jefferson Davis to R.S. Guernsey, 9 April 1870, in Ibid., Rowland, Volume VII, 266.

77. Ibid., A. Dudley Mann to Jefferson Davis, 5 December 1871, 298.

Among the tragedies of Reconstruction is that a primary victim—Africans—did not have a leadership or a party that could analyze and synthesize global trends for their betterment, while their antagonists were busily doing that, to Negro detriment. Instead, Washington under GOP rule sold weapons to Paris,[78] ostensibly to flummox an emerging Germany, which did not work when France was defeated, forging a trend that was to govern the global correlation of forces for decades to come.

To that end, when a constitution was drawn up for the abortive state of West Texas, one of the more detailed provisions concerned immigration, including "defraying the expenses" for same and the "support of agencies in foreign ports…and to the payment, in part, or in toto of the passage of immigrants from Europe to this state…."[79] The last thing Texas needed at this juncture was an influx of more reactionary Frenchmen, but this was a result this measure was designed to attain.

Augmenting the sector of the population designated as "white" was essential as what amounted to a war for Texas unwound during Reconstruction. Scholar Miguel Ángel González-Quiroga contends that in the 1870s "violence" in the borderlands "reached a level unmatched by anything that happened before or since," as Indigenes, Mexicans and Africans were summarily executed. Yet Texas's population ballooned from 818,579 in 1870 to 1,591,749 by 1880, largely because of an influx of those of European ancestry as the demographic portrait of the state was transformed. Ignacio Ramirez counseled, "'Have patience and procreate,'" but this proved insufficient, not least since Negro troopers who were almost 7% of the total U.S. population along the border during the 1870s at one juncture outnumbered their Euro-American counterparts three to one and were induced to do the heavy lifting of repression—contrary to their self-interest but a sign of their newly crafted citizenship.[80]

At Fort McKavett, about 150 miles northwest of San Antonio, beginning in 1870 the entire command, with the exception of officers, was comprised of 191 Africans, 144 defined as "mulatto," and one described as a "white negro" born in England; none of these men were from Texas, which may shed light on their ability to overlook the ferocity unleashed against Black Texans.[81]

---

78. Honeck, 184.

79. Constitution of the State of West Texas, 1869, Huntington Library.

80. González-Quiroga, 273, 278, 342.

81. Jerry Melton Sullivan, "Fort McKavett, Texas, 1852-1883," Master's thesis, TTU, 1972, 72 (abbrev. J.M. Sullivan).

Nevertheless, it was a combustible cocktail to arm the persecuted. Even when positing unfair prosecution, it is remarkable how many Negro soldiers were penalized for desertion, insubordination, theft and mutiny. At times they deserted en masse. In San Angelo, these men in blue had to be persuaded not to sack and burn the place. They sold weapons to Mexicans and, likely, Indigenes too. An interpreter for the Apache—John Glass—was a Negro who also spoke Spanish. Another Negro, Henry C. Turner of the Ninth Cavalry at Fort Duncan, fell asleep on guard duty, was jailed, then escaped to Mexico. As some "Seminole Negroes" were joining the U.S. in routing Kickapoo, it was feared that others would relocate to Mexico in the mountains if the government did not meet their demands; there they could obtain land, raid Texas and provide asylum for Negro deserters from the military. The fear that Indigenes and Africans would collaborate was a rationale explicating why the military brass was loath to assign detachments of the former to Negro regiments but, instead, to settler regiments. Similarly there were relationships of intimacy between Negro soldiers and women of Mexican origin, just as some of these men crossed the border and signed up with the Mexican military. This was notably the case in Piedras Negras, which during the enslavement era provided sanctuary for the enslaved in Texas and elsewhere. Other Negro soldiers adopted Spanish names, learned Spanish, converted to Catholicism.[82] The authorities, as a result of this flux, were reluctant to apply the harshly stringent Black Codes—regulations and laws designed to pulverize Negroes—to Africans who wielded weapons.[83]

These besieged soldiers had reason to know that they were hardly embraced in the borderlands, populated heavily by rebels.[84] Historian William Lee Richter found that "especially rough treatment was reserved" for these young men in blue.[85]

By January 1866 the number of federal troops had dwindled from a hefty 1 million months earlier (30% of whom were stationed in Texas) to a puny 87,500. Many of this number were rousting Indigenes and Mexicans, as opposed to protecting Negroes from depredations. The bulk of Negro troopers were in Texas by mid-1865, and their

---

82. Edward Valentin, Jr., "Black Enlisted Men in the U.S.-Mexico Borderlands: Race, Citizenship and Military Occupation, 1866-1930," Ph.D. dissertation, Rice U, 2020, 1, 64, 76, 105, 108, 112, 133, 136, 143, 146, 179.

83. S.F. Shannon, 154.

84. Shook, 230.

85. W.L. Richter, 265.

importance only increased with every passing year.[86] The fact that it was not unknown for Negro troopers to desert and join the Kiowa in attacking settlements did not necessarily enhance the future prospects of either community. What was needed was for these besieged communities to make joint appeals—perhaps via Mexico City—to London and St. Petersburg/Moscow or a rising Japan, but alas, that was seemingly beyond the ken of conventional thinking.[87]

An investigation revealed that "assaults with intent to kill, rapes, robberies, whippings of freedmen & other outrages" both "cruel & wanton" were uncontrollable in Texas, as these Negroes in blue rousted Indigenes and Mexicans. Assassinations were proliferating, ranging close to 1000 since Appomattox. A constitutional convention in 1868 uncovered a "frightful story of blood," punctuated by "plunder & robbery." Opportunistically, highways were "infested by bandits who will take life for a horse or a pistol or a purse...." Rebels were morphing into outlaws and gangsters in that "desperadoes with very few exceptions were either confederate officers or soldiers or bushwhackers." There was "much bad blood in this land" amongst those who were "intensely embittered against the freedmen on account of their emancipation and enfranchisement and on account of their devotion to the Republic Party...." Terrorized, the Negroes "can hold public meetings only supported by troops or armed men," with the latter in the process of being disarmed and former redeployed. Above all, the "dominant rebel element will not tolerate free discussion," displaying an "intolerance" that became the calling card of 20th-century fascism.[88]

As had been the case virtually since Appomattox—or the "first Juneteenth"—parts of Texas, notably in the east, were described by one scholar "as being in a state of racial war."[89] Yet another scholar uncovered the "prospect of a race war in Texas...during the summer of 1868" as the Klan entered its boost phase when a man named George Kennedy hit a "freedwoman with his cane for failing to yield the sidewalk to a white woman on a Tyler [Texas] street."[90]

---

86. Andrew F. Lang, "The Garrison War: Culture, Race and the Problem of Military Occupation During the American Civil War Era," Ph.D. dissertation, Rice U, 2013, 378, 384.

87. William H. Leckie with Shirley A. Leckie, *The Buffalo Soldiers: A Narrative of the Black Cavalry in the West*, Norman: U of Oklahoma Press, 2003. 105.

88. Report of the Special Committee on Lawlessness & Violence, Constitutional Convention of Texas, 30 June 1868, Box 46, Pease, Graham, Niles Papers.

89. A.D. Ivan, 149.

90. Yancey, 199.

That was not all. As 1868 was grinding to a savagely sanguinary close, it got worse, as the Bureau understood it. "School houses are being erected as fast as possible," though it was hard to find personnel "owing to the bitterness of the prejudice" against Negroes. Thus, it was difficult to find "boarding" for the "'nigger' teachers [as] they are termed...." Like the pre-1865 difference on enslavement between governors Throckmorton and Pease—i.e., no difference—as to education of Africans there was "but little difference in sentiment" between "those who are loyal and those who are not...." The suggested remedy would compound gender difference: "send us some male teachers as homes could be found with less difficulty and they would be less exposed to insult or outrage"—maybe. "Murder" of educators was common.[91]

Matters deteriorated as 1868 proceeded. "There is in fact no punishment for the perpetration of homicides when the guilty party is of the white race" was the grave announcement from Austin; there was a "total disregard for law and order, the intolerance of opinion differing from their own and the light value they place upon human life"—all markers of an emergent fascism. Typically for Texas, the "southern portion of the state," where those of Mexican origin predominated, was "much better than the north," where those defined as "white" were preponderant. "Killing of Union men or freedpeople" had been normalized.[92]

Thus, on the verge of the dawning of 1868, the Freedmen's Bureau delivered the dismaying news that "our freedmen who shipped their cotton last year got a much smaller return than those who sold for money on the ground and put the commission in their own pocket."[93] This too was a sign of worsening. In a firm rebuff to the first and second "Juneteenths," by August 1868 in Richmond, Texas, a "freed-woman," said the Bureau, "reported that her and her two brothers and two sisters have been kept without pay...since emancipation." Their overseer "has used them very badly...whipping her [with] a large whip...."[94] Things got so bad in Texas that Negroes left their hovels and began sleeping in the woods.[95]

---

91. Joseph Welch, Superintendent of Education to Major J.J. Reynolds, 17 October 1868, Reel 1, FBR.

92. Ibid., Report to O.O. Howard, 20 October 1868.

93. Ibid., J.J. Reynolds to O.O. Howard, 31 December 1867.

94. Ibid., Report from W.H. Rock, 14 August 1868, Reel 3.

95. Smallwood, 335. Cf., S.F. Shannon, 245: There was confusion as to the exact date of emancipation in Texas—which could have consequence if a

These punitive moves facilitated the rise of convict labor, a de facto slavery replacement, that took root notably on Texas sugar plantations with numerous deaths resulting from sunstroke, suggesting that in some ways this system was worse than slavery.[96] In a further rebuke to the traditional understanding of the "first Juneteenth," one African declared then that "'four years after freedom we didn't know we was free.'"[97]

Circumstances were becoming regressively worse to the point where balkanization was being contemplated. The most serious effort to divide the state of Texas occurred in 1868. At the time of 1845 annexation there had been an attempt to divide Texas into slave and non-slave states, then post-Appomattox there had been discussion of forming a Negro colony in Texas. A Houston writer said it "would...dismember the state as a means of dealing with the freed Negroes...[and] eliminate the negroes because the proposed reserve was inhabited by fierce Apaches and Comanches"[98]—knocking out two birds with one stone, as the mordant saying goes.

But white supremacists in Texas had bashing stones to spare, so there was little need to be parsimonious in their launching. Addressing this matter in early 1869, L.D. Evans—past "Know Nothing," then a Republican—conceded that in the Lone Star State "the difficulties are more formidable than in any other portion of the United States...." As he saw it, the problem was that "we are more diversified in races, languages, religions than any other division of the United States"— if so, this diversity is now national with obvious import for today. His "Know Nothing" slip was showing, however, when he cited Lincoln approvingly on the idea of "emancipation with colonization." He recalled speaking about this in early 1865 to Washington bigwig Thaddeus Stevens, who dissented but then, said Evans, admitted that Negroes in "distinct communities" was a neat idea. Since the Klan was most active where Negroes were most populous, it stood to reason that extracting this persecuted group from wider communities could reduce terrorism (actually, it might make it easier to find them—and persecute them more). Evans wanted to see "five states" on Texas territory, which was "guaranteed by express terms in the

---

litigant were "free" or not at the time of the cause of action—so the Supreme Court there selected 19 June 1865.

96. S.L. Watts, 67, 69.

97. R. Perkinson, 51.

98. Ronald Norman Gray, "The Abortive State of West Texas," Master's thesis, TTU, 1969, iii, 1.

resolution annexing Texas," and not "impaired by the cession of New Mexico to the United States in 1850." In light of the fact that Evans pronounced on women's suffrage—"I do not favor"—it becomes easier to question his proposal for a "Bantustan" for Africans in Texas (though the nascent Jim Crow was creating same organically).[99]

---

99. Speech of Hon. L.D. Evans on the Condition of Texas and the Formation of New States, Delivered in the Constitutional Convention of Texas, 6 January 1869, Huntington Library.

Chapter 22

Voter Suppression and the Roots of U.S. Fascism, 1872-1878

Though during the "Texas Spring," that brief era of reform featuring Black officialdom, the state continued to be marked by assassinations, murders, rapine, violence and worse, afterwards—post-1874—this preceding clamorous uproar seemed like calm personified, as Jim Crow and Democratic Party rule were entrenched.

Congressman De Witt Clinton Giddings served as an officer in the rebel military, then served in Congress as a Democrat and was seated by 1872 in an important election. He was seated in Congress over the stunned protestation of his opponent, William T. Clark, in a contest marked by ruthless savagery as counter-revolution was motoring. Giddings, rather slyly, accused his loyal opponents of being the evildoers and the same malefactors who "hounded loyal persons to death in 1861" as they compelled secession "and who drove Governor Sam Houston to his grave" during this rebellious election—though sticklers could argue that rebelliousness had continued since 1861 or even 1836. But according to Giddings, that is when voter fraud and intimidation was turbo-charged. Irately, he accused his opponents of all manner of misdeeds, but since he was allied with a Democratic Party that was tied to the terrorist Ku Klux Klan, one is left to wonder what Giddings and his camp were involved in. It was then in Limestone and Freestone counties, Giddings said, that his opponents "murdered innocent men, drove many from their homes, seized the registrars and Board of Election, took possession of the ballot-boxes, filled them with votes...and prevented qualified electors from voting...." This ungovernable mob of 600 men, he said, seized control of the counties, cut telegraph wires barring any calls for aid by their opponents—until they were declared victors in the "election."[1]

---

1. De Witt Clinton Giddings, "Third Congressional District of Texas: Giddings vs. W.T. Clark," 1872, AAS. See also Clipping, ca. March 1872, Reel 2, Letters Received: In Grimes County, Texas, "the vaults of the county [were]

This was an ultimately minor—though indicative—prelude to two movements of epochal significance. In late 1873, by means mostly malignant, the maniacally anti-Comanche candidate for governor, Richard Coke, prevailed over Edmund Davis, the Republican standard-bearer, who initially refused to relinquish his office. When this former rebel military officer arrived with his Democratic Party and Klan comrades to seize power on 12 January 1874, Davis was guarded by armed Negroes. However, Coke had the tailwinds of reaction at his back, not to mention the "Travis Rifles," who too were armed. President Grant did not back up Davis and, tremblingly, he backed down—and therein was inaugurated decade upon decade of Democratic rule in Texas, highlighting poll taxes, "white" primaries and disenfranchisement as primary features.[2]

There was a hiatus between the arrival of Governor Coke and the formalizing of U.S. apartheid or Jim Crow, though as ever praxis often preceded statute. Laws requiring racist segregation in transportation arrived in 1889, bars on interracial marriage came in 1881. A 1907 law allowed amusement facilities, roller rinks, movie theaters and especially public parks and libraries to segregate Negroes—or exclude them completely. A Black man who forgetfully entered a store in Apple Springs in Trinity County with his hat on was shot dead by the owner. A Black man, either rebellious or with a death wish, repeatedly entered the "wrong" door in Kreuz's Meat Market in Lockhart— and was beaten to a pulp and died. Even after the Democratic Party takeover in 1874, Negroes continued to vote—for a while.[3] Negroes served in the legislature until 1897, but by that date they were little more than ornaments of a past era.[4]

The ampler point is that in so many words, separate societies were created on the same soil, with proto-fascism on one side and bourgeois democracy on the other. Euro-Americans who protested could be branded as "N-word lovers" and executed, a deterrent to solidarity. Ineluctably, as movements against Jim Crow gathered steam and attainments, proto-fascism extended a wider snare. The point being that proto-fascism and bourgeois democracy cannot long co-exist, and in a settler colonial society grounded in white supremacy—absent

---

broken into by villainous robbers and the ballot boxes and election results all carried away!"

2. Otis A. Singletary, "The Negro Militia Movement During Radical Reconstruction," Ph.D. dissertation, LSU, 1949, 51.

3. Sitton and Conrad, 160, 164.

4. Smallwood, 411.

global currents and aid, the indispensable factor—the smart money is on proto-fascism.

It was also in 1873 that U.S. military man Ranald Mackenzie, with a bevy of armed men behind him, crossed into Mexico from Texas and obliterated an Indigenous encampment. The so-called "Seminole Negro Scouts" were with him as this punitive operation routed Kickapoo, Lipan and Mescalero, marking the beginning of the end of the most militant phase of their heroic resistance.[5] Then in 1874-1875 Mackenzie again led an army in the Red River War foiling the Comanche, Cheyenne and Kiowa as they sought to make real Tecumseh's earlier plan of Pan-Indian unity.[6] It was the "largest of the Indian wars," says one scholar, a formidable claim for a conflict that was fought in the panhandle and thus implicated Indian Territory. Like the "Seminole Negro" scouts, the Tonkawa remained prominent among the U.S. military and, says one scholar, consequentially were "hated by all Plains Indians."[7]

Mackenzie's initial foray was "one of the most daring exploits in the annals of Indian warfare," chortles one contemporary supporter of dispossession, as "Kickapoos and Potawatomies were persuaded [sic] to go to Indian Territory" and abandon Mexico.[8]

Yet another current writer described how Mackenzie's men "crept into the sanctuary, catching the Indians by surprise. The Indians—Comanches, Kiowas and Cheyennes—fled on foot." This was a defining moment," said Lawrence Wright, "at which the Texas frontier finally came to an end"[9]—though it might be fairer to depict this as the beginning of the end. The Kiowa, grouped with the Comanche as the fiercest of fighters,[10] wound up with a number of their

---

5. Richard A. Thompson, *Crossing the Border with the 4th Cavalry: Mackenzie's Raid into Mexico, 1873*, Waco: Texian Press, 1986, viii. See also Captain R.G. Carter, *On the Border with Mackenzie or Winning West Texas from the Comanches*, New York: Antiquarian, 1961.

6. Hahn, 379. Cf., Roger Hodge, *Texas Blood: Seven Generations Among the Outlaws, Ranchers, Indians, Missionaries, Soldiers and Smugglers of the Borderlands*, New York: Knopf, 2017.

7. Timothy H. Donovan, Jr., "The Red River War of 1874," Master's thesis, Rice U, 1972, 2, 14. See also Comar, 245: "During the 1860s and 1870s the Tonkawas worked as scouts and guides for U.S. soldiers at Fort Griffin and played an essential role against the Comanche and Kiowa during the Red River War of 1874-75. These groups had often attacked Tonkawas...."

8. J.M. Sullivan, 56.

9. L. Wright, 163. See also Edwin Eastman, *Seven and Nine Years Among the Comanches and Apaches*, Jersey City, N.J.: Clark Johnson, 1873.

10. Laura V. Hammer, *The No-Gun Man of Texas*, Amarillo: Author, 1935, 27.

leaders imprisoned in Fort Marion, Florida.[11] Left behind in Huntsville, Texas, was Satanta, who was said to have committed suicide.[12] The Seminole scouts proved essential in subduing the Comanche too,[13] whereas one of the most profound engagements between the heralded "Buffalo Soldiers," Negro men with guns, and Indigenous combatants occurred as Kiowa leaders were being jailed. It was then that the courageous Apache leader Victorio was cornered and defeated by these men fighting on behalf of settler hegemony, one of the most crucial episodes in the history of the Lone Star State,[14] as he and his hearty band were chased into Mexico, never to return.[15]

With a general dissipation prevailing in the borderlands as the Democratic Party brawled and bullied their way into power, the seams of society were sundered. Raids by Indigenes actually increased by 1875, belying the conceit that the homicidal Mackenzie had terminated resistance. Infantry troops were not the main force deployed against them, but cavalry were, which is where the Negro role was underscored. It was a "cavalryman's war," said scholar Arlen Lowery Fowler. However, the raiders not only encompassed Indigenes but also Mexicans and those described as "renegade whites." Moreover, the Negro infantry were involved with expeditions into Mexico, which did not enhance multiracial bonhomie either.[16]

There was a clear downside to entrusting Negro soldiers with weapons as Negroes at large were being pummeled. In late 1875, as Governor Coke was still settling in as governor, three Negro soldiers were accused of murder in Starr County, one of many incidents where men with guns were charged with various transgressions.[17]

---

11. Jennifer Graber, *The Gods of Indian Country: Religion and the Struggle for the American West*, New York: Oxford U Press, 2018; and Jenny Tone-Pah-Pah-Hote, *Crafting an Indigenous Nation: Kiowa Expressive Culture in the Progressive Era*, Chapel Hill: U of North Carolina Press, 2019.

12. Gray, Davis, 269.

13. See Reports, 25 April 1875, Box 27, Porter Papers. In this same collection, see also Box 24. See also Kenneth Porter, "The Seminole Negro-Indian Scouts, 1870-1881," *Southwestern Historical Quarterly*, 55 (No. 3, January 1952): 357-377.

14. Arlen Lowery Fowler, "The Negro Infantry in the West, 1860-1891," Ph.D. dissertation, Washington State U, 1968, 48 (abbrev. A.L. Fowler).

15. A.L. Fowler, 45.

16. Ibid., 25.

17. John Boyle, U.S. Attorney to Edward Pierpoint, 6 November 1875, Reel 1, Letters Received.

The audacity of Negroes in the borderlands, doubtlessly marked by those with guns, also trickled into Chihuahua in 1875 when a multi-racial gang from Silver City, N.M., arrived—including Africans—that began to maraud.[18] Near the same time in Runnels County, there was yet another multiracial gang, this one comprised of Negroes and Indigenes—"led by a big negro who appeared to be their chief," said an observer—that was involved in train robberies.[19] The specter of Negroes with guns proved to be noticeably provocative to settlers. Rumors about such were enough to enrage, e.g., the story from Houston in 1872 that the formerly enslaved had organized a militia and were storing arms.[20]

During this uproarious era, Texas—according to an Amarillo writer—not only continued to be the "impregnable rendezvous of the fugitive," reinforcing the state's role as a haven for wrongdoers, but as late as the 1870s the heroic Comanche continued to be fearfully regarded as "about the most bloodthirsty of all the Indian tribes."[21]

The U.S. thought it reasonable to vanquish the Comanche for as the 1870s unfolded they were combating settlers from the panhandle to the border. They were accused of stealing horses in Laredo, then crossing the border into Mexico, a major blow—if true—to the local economy.[22]

Washington was convinced that these groups—especially the Kickapoo—wanted to return to Kansas and they were just benevolently aiding them.[23] Just before then, Kickapoo—again—were being accused of all manner of peccadilloes from their domicile in Coahuila,

18. Report to Second Assistant Secretary of State, 18 May 1875, Reel 1, Despatches from U.S. Consuls in Chihuahua, NARA.

19. J.M. Franks, *Seventy Years in Texas: Memories of the Pioneer Days, Indian Depredations and the Northwest Cattle Trail*, Gatesville, Texas: Publisher Unclear, 1924, Huntington Library.

20. Mary Alice Pollard Lavender, "Social Conditions in Houston and Harris County, 1869-1872," Master's thesis, Rice U, 1950, 229-230. See also Victoria Lynne Brooks, "Crime and Violence in Frontier Houston: A Study of the Criminal District Court of Harris County, 1872-1876," Master's thesis, Rice U, 1974.

21. Roscoe Logue, *Tumbleweeds and Barbed Wire Fences*, Amarillo: Russell Stationery, 1836, 12

22. Commercial Agent Charles Winslow to William Hunter, Second Assistant Secretary of State, 26 September 1871, Reel 1, Despatches from U.S. Consuls in Guerrero, NARA.

23. Consul William Schuchardt to Second Assistant Secretary of State, 17 November 1873, Reel 1, Despatches from U.S. Consuls in Piedras Negras, NARA.

where they had received land grants after being expelled by settlers north of the border.[24] Once more, the apparently ubiquitous Cortina was said to be involved in their activity.[25]

Cortina was likely in mind when the U.S. delegate in Piedras Negras alleged that "many of the depredations committed lately by hostile... Kickapoo" were aided by official Mexico.[26] Customarily, one jaded analyst, after denouncing President Guerrero of Mexico for "provocative measures" leading to abolition in Texas decades later—"violating a treaty made with American colonists"—turned on the Kickapoo and celebrated that "half of them are dead" and "those who remain are terrible fellows" who were "born with the genius of murder and rapine...." The Comanche were "joining with them," referring to the "Bedouins of the West" who "have been a terror" that "acted like fiends." These two groups along with "Apaches and Mexicans have carried off immense herds and committed numberless murders."[27]

Cortina was likely in mind too when this writer said, "Indians have been aided and abetted by the Mexicans" for the wily Mexican leader was in the bullseye.[28] Cortina was said to be in the state of Guerrero when Mexican soldiers were charged with causing an uproar in Zapata County, Texas, extraordinary in retrospect given the almost 1000 miles that separated the two points.[29] Cortina also was spotted in his usual haunt of Matamoros, which almost prompted a U.S. intervention there since his very presence in the borderlands was a "menace" and "insult" to his powerful neighbor as "some years ago he had sacked Brownsville," said a U.S. agent angrily.[30] Cortina did not win plaudits among settlers when the former Texas governor, Andrew Jackson Hamilton, was said to be "protected" by him in Matamoros as he escaped the clutches of his foes, with the

---

24. Article by Emilio Velasco in *Siglo XIX*, 15 April 1872, Reel 7, Despatches from U.S. Consuls in Mexico City, NARA.

25. Ibid., Article by Emilio Velasco in *Siglo XIX*, 16 April 1872.

26. Consul William Schuchardt to Second Assistant Secretary of State, 20 February 1873, Reel 1, Despatches from U.S. Consuls in Piedras Negras, NARA.

27. E. King, *Great South*, 164, 179.

28. Edward King, *The Southern States of North America: A Record of Journeys...*, London: Blackie & Son, 1875, 169 (abbrev. E.King, *Southern States*).

29. Charles Winslow, Commercial Agent to Second Assistant Secretary of State William Hunter, 17 March 1872, Reel 1, Despatches from U.S. Consuls in Guerrero, NARA.

30. Consul Thomas Wilson to Assistant Secretary of State, William Hunter, 22 December 1873, Reel 4, Despatches from U.S. Consuls in Matamoros, NARA.

Mexican judge in the case fretting that he could be assassinated if he sought to extradite him.[31]

One of the first acts of incoming Governor Coke was to go after Cortina, who had been "depredating" for years, he said: "in 1857 Governor Houston had to send a military force to the Rio Grande"[32] and by 1874 this could not be ruled out—again.

The obsession with Cortina and his doings could not obscure that hostility in the borderlands to germinal U.S. imperialism could not be reduced to this hirsute Mexican leader. One of the many problems with this nascent two-party system was that the presumed progressives, the Republicans, too were not up to the task at hand. How could they rise to defend Negroes when they were more than willing to uproot Indigenes or miscomprehend Cortina for that matter? This weakened and hampered electoral turnout and destabilized the passion that was needed to overcome. In turn, white supremacists in the Democratic Party did not hesitate to point out that Republicans who were supporters of Reconstruction were also not averse to supporting a nakedly racist imperialism, that had its roots in the dispossessing of Indigenes and Mexicans earlier in the century.[33]

In the borderlands this insight would not have been seen as a surprise, and was refracted through how those seen as symbols of the U.S. were treated. That was the import of an 1877 petition from U.S. nationals in Chihuahua complaining bitterly about harassment from the locals.[34] José Eligio Muñoz also addressed "bad treatment," but he thought it was directed at "all foreigners" but "principally American citizens…in the state of Chihuahua…." He was "governor of the state" and had peculiar insight, notably concerning "some Americanized German subjects."[35] It was not just harassment. At times they were murdered in the vicinity of their property taken across the border to Mexico.[36] Seeking to arbitrage the discrepancies between

---

31. Ibid., Consul Thomas Wilson to Secretary Frederick Seward, 10 March 1874.

32. Governor Coke, Executive Office-Austin to Attorney General George Williams, 6 August 1874, Reel 1, Letters Received.

33. Erman, 30-31.

34. Petition, 5 March 1877, Reel 1, Despatches from U.S. Consuls in Chihuahua, NARA. See also J.M. Morgan, 395: "There is no race on earth that the Mexicans, high or low, hate as they do the Americans."

35. Report by José Eligio Muñoz, 19 August 1877, Reel 7, Despatches from U.S. Consuls in Mexico City, NARA.

36. Solomon Schutz to State Department, 6 March 1878, Reel 2, Despatches from U.S. Consuls in Paso del Norte, NARA.

two different nations, "many bad & desperate characters who seek refuge from justice on this frontier"[37] were arriving steadily, said a keen onlooker, while complicating further bilateral ties.

Hence, although the U.S. was increasingly unwilling to commit troops to protect U.S. nationals in East Texas, at the same time across the state there was a felt desire to cross the border in order to protect U.S. nationals beyond Washington's jurisdiction. In the future Ciudad Juárez, then Paseo del Norte, fear cascaded when the mayor expressed interest "to run every gringo out of the place [emphasis-original]," a threat—said the U.S. agent—mandating that "troops [be] sent to this neighborhood by the U.S. government...." Even "on the American side" of the border "armed bands of Mexicans have become alarmingly frequent...."[38] If history were to be the guide, Negro troops would be sent to repress Mexicans while their own community was unprotected. They would be sent, as well, because there was real fear that Mexican Americans were unreliable in patrolling the borderlands. But even that recruiting decision was questioned in 1870s when a group of Negro cavalrymen shot up a saloon patronized by settlers after a number of the latter attacked a Negro sergeant.[39]

This created a bind since there was also a gnawing fear in Austin that Cortina and those like him were aided by Mexican Americans. In 1875 there were raids into Texas by Mexicans, although a U.S. agent in Monterrey thought they were "Texas Mexicans," knowing it was "almost impossible to distinguish the Mexican people on our side of the river from those here." There was a "large body of Mexicans, said to be several hundred...gathering...to make an attack on the American settlement," and yet another rout was conducted between Laredo and Eagle Pass with "considerable damage done...." Next in the crosshairs were Edinburgh, then Corpus Christi, and although "plunder was the main object," simple "retaliation" in response to past and ongoing transgressions was also planned. Again, there was suspicion that a "false flag" operation was at play in that "ex-confederates" were also suspects. Still, continued Consul Joseph Ulrich, it would be a "great mistake" to "treat...with Mexico on terms of perfect equality"; instead the "'hard hand'" was recommended since "one half are Indians," speaking of those of Mexican origin, "only one remove from barbarism" and, not unrelated, "one

---

37. Ibid., Solomon Schutz to Second Assistant Secretary of State, 19 December 1878.

38. Ibid., Consul William Pierson to Second Assistant Secretary of State, 30 May 1877.

39. Levander, 21-48, 39.

quarter of mixed blood...." Given this, "treaties on the same bases as with entirely civilized peoples are sadly out of place. Those with Turkey, Siam and Morocco furnish a better model," he concluded.[40]

When a Negro was elected to the leadership body of the Cherokee Nation across the border in Indian Territory,[41] it tended to congeal such primitive sentiments.

What became Oklahoma was being viewed with suspicion by its southern neighbor as Reconstruction was being suffocated. "This superb country," said Edward King, "one of the most fertile on the globe, is a constant source of torment to the white men of the border," providing a distinct jurisdiction to which Negroes could escape.[42] As Governor Coke was forging his misrule, and Reconstruction was in its death throes, an alteration of the status of Indian Territory (IT) was being debated in Congress—and opposed by William Ross of the Cherokee Nation.[43]

This foretold the Anschluss of 1889 when this "fertile" soil was opened for settlers, then 1907, when IT was swallowed by Washington and spat out as the state of Oklahoma. This also foreshadowed the severe reduction in strength of Indigenes that was nothing short of breathtaking and not just in territorial loss and demographic disaster. As Ross was speaking before Congress, other Indigenes, including delegates from his own Cherokee, Creek, Seminole, Chickasaw and Choctaw, mounted opposition to other Washington measures designed to hamstring them all. By this point, Sitting Bull, the valiant Lakota leader, was "removed beyond your reach" in Canada, they chided. Perhaps now he and his people could thrive, since the "Five Civilized Nations" that they represented "were, before the war of the rebellion, unquestionably the richest people on the face of the

---

40. Consul Joseph Ulrich to William Hunter, Second Assistant Secretary of State, 27 April 1875, Reel 3, Despatches from U.S. Consuls in Monterrey, NARA.

41. Karen Coody Cooper, "Black Members of the Cherokee National Council," in Ty Wilson, et al., eds., *Oklahoma Black Cherokees*, Charleston: History Press, 2017, 84-91, 84.

42. E. King, *Southern States*, 199.

43. "Remarks in Opposition to Bills to Organize the Territory of Oklahoma by William P. Ross of the Cherokee Nation Before the Committee on Indian Affairs of the House of Representatives," 8 March 1876, Huntington Library. There were almost 30 "tribes...numbering about 80,000 persons.... less than a thousand in number are the descendants of Keokuk and Black Hawk" wars, dumped from Iowa and the Modoc, genocide victims from California.

globe…. for many years, before the war, these five nations were large exporters of beef cattle. In 1855 the Cherokees, alone, exported to California and the eastern markets, 90,000 head of beeves, worth at home $1,620,000." But, as matters evolved, they endured collateral damage from this titanic conflict and were among the biggest losers of the war, since at the war's close "there were probably not exceeding 200 cows and calves left within this Cherokee country."[44] In this land of ironies, settlers were complaining constantly about Indigenes expropriating livestock, when these complainers had initiated the process.

In a sense another "false flag" operation preceded this epic defeat in that raids in Texas attributed to Indigenes at times were actually settler desperados posing as Indigenes in order to generate the requisite fury. Once again, Texas was on the verge of a veritable "race war" and, again, President Grant was reluctant to intercede on behalf of those opposed to the "white united front," although they were Republicans like himself.

Likewise, Grant was seen as overly sympathetic to Juárez, with whom he had been yoked in recent years; he was eclipsed by the ascension of Porfirio Díaz, whose calcified rule extended for decades with an initial boost from Rutherford B. Hayes, Grant's successor,[45] a classmate of Texas Democratic Party leader, Guy Bryan at Kenyon College in Ohio.[46]

The prelude to the Hayes-Tilden race in Texas in 1876 was pockmarked with a steady stream of bloodletting. One analyst compared it to what befell the "Helots, slaves in Sparta," who were becoming intimidating because of "their numerical increase" and, consequently, were "reduced by general massacre…." Thus, on one tree in Gainesville, Texas, "forty unoffending Union men were held together…." As noted, there were not just Negroes, but allies of the Negroes who were subjected to rough measures—a trend to watch in the 21st century; thus, in Gillespie County hundreds of "unoffending Germans were shot down in cold blood…." Contemporaneous massacres in South Africa paled compared to the "wanton wickedness of brutality and

---

44. "The Indians Opposed to the Transfer Bill United Action of the Delegations of the Cherokee, Creek, Seminole, Chickasaw and Choctaw Nations in Opposition to the Measure…," Washington: Gibson, 1878, Huntington Library. Cf., Maurice Crandall, *These People Have Always Been a Republic*: *Indigenous Electorates in the U.S.-Mexico Borderlands, 1598-1912*, Chapel Hill: U of North Carolina Press, 2019.

45. M.G. Webster. On alleged "false flag" operations, see 110; for Grant-Hayes-Juárez-Díaz, see, e.g., 178.

46. Ibid., 178.

bloodthirstiness" that occurred in Robertson County alone, "in which a whole settlement of colored people—forty helpless and unoffending men, women and children—were mercilessly butchered...." One shaken eyewitness recounted that he "practiced law in Texas for now twenty six years and I know of no white person who has been punished for the killing of a negro either before or since the war. Public sentiment is against it," he added balefully. Hence, at a Democratic Party confab in the Fourth Congressional District, a nominator said that as an elderly Texan he had killed numerous Indigenes and he enjoyed doing so but, he confessed unashamedly, he would prefer to slay "two Negroes than one Indian." That the receipt of these unsettling reports by the U.S. Department of Justice did not bestir attorneys into action is the ultimate commentary on the distressing state of affairs.[47]

As so often happened, discord in Texas was of trans-border consequence. "Relations with Mexico were at their [worst] between 1871-1875," says historian Richard Tandy Marcum, "and during the latter year they reached a climax."[48] This was precisely the time when Coke was consolidating power, the Porfiriato was in gestation, and the promise of positive bilateral relations with the U.S. were fading as the memory of their joint undermining of the French occupation was hardly recalled.

As cruelly vicious unrest was erupting in Texas in 1876, Yucatan reflected same with harried reports of "disorders...owing to the late revolutionary movement...."[49] "This state has been in a chaotic condition," was the message to Washington, with "numerous revolutionary and counter-revolutionary movements.... Mérida has been closely besieged by the conservative forces...."[50]

Effectively, Reconstruction ended in Texas with Davis's unceremonious ouster, well before the vaunted "Compromise of 1876" that led to the presidency of Hayes. The path to wreckage was lubricated by the twin panics—severe economic downturns-of 1869 and 1873, which proved distracting to the elite base of the GOP and made it easier for them to toss Negroes from the dogsled into the jaws of the pursuing wolves.[51]

---

47. "The Republic-Weekly Edition," ca. 1876, Reel 2, Letters Received.

48. Richard Tandy Marcum, "Fort Brown and the Border Crises, 1846-1878," Master's thesis, TTU, 1960, 99.

49. Consul A.J. Lespinasse to Second Assistant Secretary of State, William Hunter, 5 October 1876, Reel 1, Despatches from U.S. Consuls in Mérida, NARA.

50. Ibid., Consul Lespinasse to Secretary Hunter, 8 January 1877.

51. D. Michael Bottoms, *An Aristocracy of Color: Race and Representation in California and the West, 1850-1890*, Norman: U of Oklahoma Press, 2013, 125.

To be sure, Davis was a shaky ally for freedom, given his intentional slights to his Negro base, his enthusiasm for subduing Indigenes, his promotion of European immigration—the fruits of which would ultimately undermine Indigenes and, likely, provide more votes for the Democratic Party. He was "not a Negrophile," says his sympathetic biographer accurately, as he "avoided the issue of social equality" for this persecuted group assiduously. But that was not enough for the Democratic Party base, as "few figures in Texas political history have been as unpopular and hated as passionately," says Ronald N. Gray.

Davis was eclectic, perhaps unstable politically, gyrating from the Whig Party in 1848 to an anti-Know Nothing in the 1850s to the GOP. But in context, was he worse than the unionist John Hancock, who said that he would accede to Negro suffrage after mules had been accorded the ballot? Although creating a Black "Bantustan" in West Texas was not seen as a progressive maneuver, when Davis advocated it he was portrayed as being party to a treasonous conspiracy, akin to Aaron Burr's earlier conspiracy. This episode illustrates why other than mass murder or involuntary mass deportation of Negroes, Jim Crow was the preferred "moderate" option. (This also illustrates why when a nation is as fundamentally right-wing as the U.S., traditional political labels tend to lose meaning.) Yet even here Davis's purpose— in his mind—was preferable to available alternatives insofar as he thought that an undivided Texas would be controlled by rebels and their allies, whereas his plan would create three loyal states. Like most Euro-Americans then—perhaps now—he elided the interests of Indigenes, offering settlers 160 acres at a giveaway $1 per acre, with further assets tossed in for railways. Yet Davis attracted the pestiferous ire of settlers when he chose not to oppose education for Negroes, which they opposed passionately. (Wiley College, one of today's Historically Black Colleges, was founded on his watch in 1873, while Huston-Tillotson, its peer, was founded shortly after he was ousted from office.) Every Negro appointment he made tended to irritate settlers, although few— if any—attained powerful posts. However, Davis's attempt to raise tax revenue by going where the money was—wealthy Euro-Americans— ignited the class collaboration ethos that animated settler colonialism, where poorer and wealthier joined hands. Still, 40% of the state police were Negroes, and this was a tossed-down gauntlet to the "white united front," spearheaded by the Klan, which by the end of his term had about 20,000 members in Texas.[52]

---

52. Gray, Davis, 440-441, 442, 9, 12, 89, 138, 153, 182, 214, 220, 222, 223. Cf., Dorsett, 168: The state police were "about 60 percent Negro...enough to

Possibly, Davis's enthusiasm for European immigration contributed to the rise in Klan membership and his electoral demise. Straggling into Texas from Mexico—and even from Brazil and Cuba too—were envenomed rebels, former enslavers now poverty-stricken and thirsting for revenge. "One of the saddest sights" in Galveston, said an observer in 1875, was the "daily arrival of hundreds of refugees from the older Southern States, seeking homes on the Texan prairies." This "flood" was "formidable," said Edward King, and was credited with Coke's gubernatorial triumph, converting this "Republican flood to Democratic ebb."[53]

As immigration increased, their numbers grew further after Davis left office, as the Negro population of the state declined from 31% in 1870 to 20.4% by 1900. Astoundingly, the Negro population in gross figures increased by 245% during this era—but the European-derived population soared by an astonishing 430%, all this as the Indigenous population was in decline. These figures also impacted party politics as the GOP in Texas, according to one study, "was more thoroughly dominated by negroes than in probably any other Southern State." Thus, at least 16 counties continued to contain Negro majorities between 1870 and 1900, and there were 13 more that averaged between 40% and 50%, 17 between 30% and 40%, and 23 between 20% and 30%. This would mean malign attention by settlers in order to bar Negro power and influence by any means available. Because the settler vote could be split, this left the frequently united Negro vote with the balance of power. Thus, in 1872 the entire Board of Aldermen in Huntsville and all of the County Commissioners in Walker County were Negroes. From 1868-1900 nearly 60 Negroes served in Texas legislatures or constitutional conventions. Building on the importation of the enslaved in the waning days of the Civil War—an estimated 100,000—between 1865 and 1876 at least 50,000 Negroes moved to Texas as labor agents were recruiting heavily due east in Mississippi and Alabama. With an eye on Austin, North Carolina passed a law inflicting severe penalties upon those seeking to attract "their" Negroes to depart, as the persecuted became desired simultaneously.[54]

---

make the force appear to be negro...." See also "To my Dear Sir," 3 December 1877, Box 1, Early AARM: "Methodism is so very strong among the colored people that it will tax all the energies of Mr. Tillotson and his friends to make his Institute the colored educational institution of Texas. But Fisk University thrives alongside of the Central Tennessee college."

53. E. King, *Southern States*, 99.

54. L.D. Rice,73, 147-148, 170, 191, 265.

Yet Texas had to recruit Negroes intensely, as so many were departing in a kind of "exodus fever," as it has been described: Kansas, Mexico, Liberia, Oklahoma were among the destinations. (According to one scholar, in 1879 alone, an estimated 12,000 Texas Negroes scurried to Kansas alone.[55]) Why? Consider that between 1870 and 1900 about 500 Negroes were slaughtered as a result of lynching and mob violence—by official figures, making the Lone Star State a leader in yet another ignominious category.[56]

The Justice Department in Washington was well aware of what was going on in Texas. In late 1873 the Deputy U.S. Marshal in Galveston warned his colleagues about the "leader of the local desperadoes," Jim Roan, who "murdered...two colored men" who were "industrious, peaceable men" but were slain nonetheless. The jury acquitted, then "several shots were fired" into Roan's abode. Violence was spiraling and "hostilities are possible all the time" since "many of the colored people" were also "heavily armed."[57] But the federals, so reliant upon Negroes for victory a few years earlier, were unable to meet the historical challenge and defend them, because of class and racist constraints.

One of the Negro leaders who sought to fill the political vacuum was Norris Wright Cuney. He was the son of an enslaved woman and a planter born in 1846. He was also of partial Indigenous ancestry. His father was one of Texas's richest men, owning 105 slaves. Cuney was close to Governor Davis and also had questionable ties to gamblers and other bilkers of Negroes. He also played a questionable role on the important docks of Galveston and was accused by some Negroes of sabotaging Republicans in favor of Democrats. During his heyday, Galveston, with a population of over 40,000, was the largest city in the state,[58] providing him with an impressive platform.

According to his daughter, Maud Cuney Hare, her father was of "Negro, Indian and Swiss descent"—with the former being "Potomac Indian...." She described him as a "slender figure, five feet, ten; straight black hair and mustache, black eyes; high cheek bones; a complexion more suggestive of Italy's sunny clime than of any portion of Africa's darkness," a revealing descriptor that could well be

55. John Gruesser, "Empires at Home and Abroad in Sutton E. Griggs' 'Imperium in Imperio,'" in Chakkalakal and Warren, 49-68, 55.

56. L.D. Rice, 58, 59, 69, 73, 147-148, 170, 191, 204, 265, 325, 329, 398, 399.

57. Deputy U.S. Marshal W.T. Canfield, Galveston to Hon. Thomas P. Ochiltree, U.S. Marshal, Eastern District of Texas, 20 October 1873, Reel 1, Letters Received.

58. Virginia Neal Hinze, "Norris Wright Cuney," Master's thesis, Rice U, 1965, 1, 14-15, 2, 26, 38, 122 (abbrev. Hinze).

applied to her as well. With apparent pride she cited a colleague who said her father "'resembles a Mexican.'" Perhaps that sheds light on the comment that there were few sites in Dixie where "black voters" were "to stick as closely to a black leader as those of Texas did to Norris Wright Cuney...."[59]

Cuney's father was also a Confederate supporter—his ownership of the enslaved reaching 115 by 1860—which may explain why the son was a lifelong insomniac.[60]

Admittedly, being a Negro leader of whatever stripe was no guarantee of extended life expectancy, especially since interracial fistfights were normative on the docks where Cuney ambled, along with the same occurring—more dangerously—in the military, still to be found in his Galveston.[61]

Another key Negro leader was George T. Ruby, also melanin-deficient (apparently settlers favored leaders who most resembled themselves physically). He was born in the U.S. Northeast and worked in Haiti before arriving in Texas. There he became a comrade of Governor Davis and, like Cuney, became influential on the docks of Galveston. Although he spoke French and Spanish, he exhibited a profound weakness of postwar Negro leadership: an inability or unwillingness to rally global support for the cause. This was needed since even Governor Davis recognized that terror against Negroes was supported by the "'majority of the people,'" meaning settlers. Moreover, after departing Texas—escaping may be the more apt verb—he was involved in New Orleans in rallying support for Mexico's Porfirio Díaz, although doing such for Juárez would have been time better spent.[62]

Serving alongside him in the ranks of Negro leaders was Matthew Gaines, born in Louisiana. A blacksmith, he reputedly was able to converse in seven different languages: he should have made a bee-line to Washington or Ottawa or Mexico City and put his fluency to the test on behalf of his beleaguered constituents. Like Ruby, he too served in the state legislature.[63]

At any rate, a new order was imposed in Texas from the barrel of a gun. The scholar Douglas Hales is not wrong when he asserts that

59. Maud Cuney Hare, *Norris Wright Cuney: A Tribune of the Black People*, New York City: Crisis, 1913, 1, 61, 227.

60. Douglas Hales, "The Cuneys: A Southern Family in White and Black," Ph.D. dissertation, TTU, 2000, 13, 22, 34.

61. S.F. Shannon, 164.

62. Carl H. Moneyhon, *George T. Ruby: Champion of Equal Rights*, Fort Worth: TCU Press, 2020, 12, 196, 210. 237. 274, 339.

63. Dorsett, 61.

"perhaps more than any other ex-confederate state, violence permeated Texas...."[64] This new order was formalized in 1875 at a Constitutional Convention in Austin. A spotlight was focused on "depredations...as to our Indian frontier" and whether such was "done...with the sanction or acquiescence of any foreign government," meaning Mexico. Railways too were a subject of intense discussion. A sign of the times was the "tender thanks to President Grant" for his aid in assisting the return of "a number of citizens of Texas, from Brazil," who likely would join the Democratic Party-Klan consensus. Ecumenically, their proceedings were printed in German, "Bohemian" and Spanish.[65]

Effective by 1876, this new counter-revolutionary charter reversed that of 1869 promulgated during the heyday of Reconstruction and, in large measure, remains in effect.[66] The "counter-revolution" against the Negro-influenced Republican Party, says scholar James Smallwood, "brought an end to Radical Reconstruction in Texas," which was cued by Coke's ouster of Davis a few years earlier in 1874.[67]

Despite the violence and dirty tricks involved, even in the mid-20th century, one Euro-Texan remained incandescent about what led to 1876. A disreputable "coalition of carpetbaggers, scalawags and negroes wrote the Constitution of 1869 and filled almost all state, district and county offices with members of the radical Republican Party," he said seething. He was gleeful about the imposition of a poll tax, designed to curtail voting in the "eastern part of the state where the negro population was centered," while in "other parts of the state the proposed restriction attracted little attention. Another measure which was aimed at 'Sambo,'" his derisive nickname for Africans, was changing the "makeup of judicial districts" to the detriment of the already persecuted.[68]

---

64. Douglas Hales, "Violence Perpetrated Against African Americans by Whites in Texas During Reconstruction, 1865-1868," Master's thesis, TTU, 1994, 42.

65. "Journal of the Constitutional Convention of the State of Texas Begun and Held at the City of Austin, September 6th, 1875," Galveston: News, 1875, 101, 752, Huntington Library.

66. "Constitution of the State of Texas, Adopted by the Constitutional Convention Convened at Austin, September 6th, 1875...Effective April 18th, 1876," Kansas City, Mo.: Riley, 1913, Huntington Library.

67. Smallwood, 408.

68. S.S. McKay, "Some Attitudes of West Texas Delegates to the Constitutional Convention of 1875," *West Texas Historical Association Yearbook*, 36 (October 1960): 109-115, 109, 112.

The Negroes of Austin were dazed and disoriented by this historical turn. One commentator was struck by what he saw in the capital: "sometimes he undertakes long journeys without the slightest idea where he is going," said Edward King, "and finding he has not enough money to return, locates anew…."[69]

Hopefully, these confounded Negroes did not wander into De Witt County, for there existed, said a keen observer, "many deeds of lawlessness and crimes" perpetrated by "men disguised by masks" operating in a "most cruel and bloody character…." There was the "loss of many innocent lives both colored and white," the Justice Department was told in early 1875, at the hands of the "murderous Ku Klux Klan confederation," a "secret conclave of midnight assassins" talented in "daring outrage and wanton insult."[70]

* * *

There continued to be a spillover in Texas from Mexico as rebels continued to depart, finding Juárez's rule unpalatable. Those described as "refugee Spaniards" from Cuba were flooding into Vera Cruz by 1873 in the wake of unrest on the island, helping to vitiate the need for any skills delivered by rebel exiles, mostly lacking fluency in Spanish in any case. At that point there were an estimated 227 U.S. nationals there but not a single mercantile firm: instead they were mechanics, laborers, teachers and clerks, along with the usual "migratory adventurers" seeking excitement. The competition from London was investing heavily in railways, said the U.S. envoy.[71]

Tampico continued to be a fortress of U.S. influence; southward along the Caribbean shore in Tuxpan, the "American colony" was the "largest in Mexico," said a close observer, with "75 families" and "250 souls" all told, "most engaged in sugar planting,"[72] providing both competition and coordination with the crop in Texas.

Across the water from Tuxpan was Mérida in still restive Yucatan, and there the U.S. national R.L. Stephen controlled a sugar plantation—at least until 1875 when he was murdered there. According to an official report, he was "murdered…by a band of savage Indians…." As was

---

69. E. King, *Southern States*, 132.

70. B.J. Pridgen to Attorney General George Williams, 5 February 1875, Reel 1, Letters Received.

71. Consul S.T. Trowbridge to State Department, 30 September 1873, Reel 10, Despatches from U.S. Consuls in Vera Cruz, NARA.

72. Consul to Secretary of State Hamilton Fish, 5 February 1874, Reel 5, Despatches from U.S Consuls in Tampico, NARA.

routine, the local authorities were deemed to be complicit, as they were "jealous."[73] His prominence was suggestive of a growing U.S. interest in this port city.[74] All this was taking place against the backdrop of an ongoing insurrection that was threatening "American interests" overall.[75]

The number of U.S. nationals in Mexico City had not diminished appreciably in the period leading up to Reconstruction's end in Texas, though cotton from there had decreased.[76] In Manzanillo there had been a telling transition from 1869 to 1873 from German and English vessels dominating the import of goods to those of the U.S., many in transit from Panama to San Francisco.[77]

Typically, dreams of seizing more Mexican land had failed to dissipate. By late 1872, reporting from across the border from El Paso, a U.S. agent was bracing for "war" and enthused since the "fertile soil of Texas will furnish more volunteers. The Texans are naturally soldiers," said William Pierson, and "the sight of blood and carnal knowledge of steel only excites them to bravery and greater deeds of valor and they owe Mexico a large debt," he added with a sulfurous twist, "for past injuries...." The plan then was "war with Mexico and a slicing off of the states of Chihuahua and Sonora," which "would heal the national gangrene and sink into oblivion the issues between North and South" in the U.S. "while at the same time the administration would become universally and deservedly popular and the Republican Party [would] receive thereby another decade in the annals of longevity."[78] This idea of waging war abroad to distract from travails at home became a staple of the U.S. in coming decades.

Washington was assured by this jingoistic envoy that he was "almost daily in receipt of communications from wealthy influential gentlemen of Chihuahua, Sonora and Texas regarding the absolute necessity of establishing a protectorate over Mexico or at least [he]

73. Consul A.J. Lespinasse to State Department, 25 October 1875, Reel 1, Despatches from U.S. Consuls in Mérida, NARA.

74. Ibid., Consul Lespinasse to Secretary of State Hamilton Fish, 6 January 1875.

75. Ibid., Consul A.J. Lespinasse to Second Assistant Secretary of State William Hunter, 10 March 1876.

76. "Commercial Report," 31 December 1873, Reel 7, Despatches from U.S. Consuls in Mexico City, NARA.

77. Consul Augustus Morrell to Second Assistant Secretary of State, 22 May 1873, Reel 1, Despatches from U.S. Consuls in Manzanillo, NARA.

78. Vice Consul William Pierson to Sir, 29 October 1872, Reel 2, Despatches from U.S. Consuls in Paso del Norte, NARA.

cherished hope that [Washington] will immediately take possession of Chihuahua and Sonora...."[79]

However, Washington was undergoing a transition, moving away from territorial aggrandizement to "dollar diplomacy" or "neo-colonialism," which was motivated as well by Mexico's pushback, rallying the hemisphere against aggression. Thus, Senator John Morgan of Alabama, formerly a fervent backer of snatching territory, began turning away from it. At the same time a tidal wave of U.S. investment flowed into Mexico, with Texas leading the way.[80]

Nonplussed, Pierson continued with his cheerleading, advising that a "war between the two countries...would be hailed with secret joy by...the Mexicans," albeit "received with holy horror by another class," with the "former [being] the people, the latter the officeholders,"[81] ripe for dislodging. Pierson was encouraged when an unnamed figure apprised him of an otherwise unknown "previous agreement with President Juarez" by which the U.S. was "to come into possession...of the states of Chihuahua and Sonora," Mexico's jewels.[82]

Unfortunately aiding this proposed war was the self-inflicted wound administered by Mexico. It was also in 1872 that the State Department was briefed on the "war with the savage Indians" precisely in Chihuahua,[83] which weakened national unity in a way that would benefit its voracious neighbor.

Actualizing the most belligerent fantasies of Washington was the New Yorker Ezekiel Steele, who was slain near Monterrey in a battle between the government and those described as "revolutionists"; he happened to be married to a Mexican woman, which in the eyes of some may have provided his venture with legitimacy.[84]

With the ascension of the Porfiriato, this leader's opponents regrouped in Texas and began lancing operations across the border,[85] which likely increased bilateral tension to the detriment of those like Steele.

Gathering on the Texas side of the border was a military force preparing for yet another invasion of Mexico, this one led by John "Rip"

---

79. Ibid., Vice Consul William Pierson to Sir, 4 November 1872.

80. M.G. Webster, 283, 278.

81. Vice Consul Pierson to Sir, 29 November 1872, Reel 2, Despatches from U.S. Consuls in Paso del Norte, NARA.

82. Ibid., Unnamed to Pierson, 18 October 1872.

83. J.C. Huston, Vice Consul to Second Assistant Secretary of State, 31 December 1872, Reel 1, Despatches from U.S. Consuls in Chihuahua, NARA.

84. Consul Joseph Ulrich to Second Assistant Secretary of State, 29 July 1872, Reel 2, Despatches from U.S. Consuls in Monterrey, NARA.

85. Ibid., Vice Consul to State Department, 15 June 1878, Reel 3.

Ford of Brownsville, described accurately as a "man of military experience,"[86] given his notoriety as a rebel traitor. Simultaneously, there was another invasion bruited, this time from Mexico to Texas, but with voting, not military conquest, in mind—or such was the message to the Attorney General in Washington, D.C. In anticipation of what was to emerge full-blown in the 21st century, the idea was that certain Texans had come to Mexico and were "engaged in procuring aliens to come from Mexico for the purpose of voting in the coming congressional election...." The problem was that it was not easy to distinguish Mexicans from Mexican Americans, since in the borderlands the "great majority of the population being of Mexican origin," it was "difficult to distinguish between permanent & transient people...."[87]

Like the vampire that would not die, rising from the grave in the wake of Reconstruction's end in Texas was the discredited idea of a "Sierra Madre Republic" centered in Monterrey. This notion was "entertained by many," said the U.S. agent there, although the "very unfriendly feeling towards the Texans on the part of the greater part of intelligent Mexicans" was bollixing the project. Forwarded for consumption was the Monterrey periodical *El Mequetrefe* which spoke of open conspiracy in Texas to engineer secession.[88]

Yet another periodical in Nuevo León spoke of Texas's sinister intentions, as if yet another annexation were contemplated. This soured further many Mexicans on both Texas and the U.S. although, said Consul Joseph Ulrich, the plot was "looked on more favorably [by] the ranchers and farmers" of Mexico "than by the people of the larger cities...."[89] Certainly, as a Mexican official argued, the attraction to his nation on the part of U.S. real estate speculators eager to capitalize on the latest property boondoggle had increased since 1848.[90]

This macabre trend was proceeding in 1876 as the moment was arriving for the formal strangulation of Reconstruction. As with the Coke-Davis battle in 1874, President Grant deemed it unworthy to intervene against the "white united front" that was driving events. As his presidential term was expiring, the U.S. Marshal in Galveston

---

86. U.S. Attorney, Galveston to Charles Devens, Attorney General, 17 January 1878, Reel 2, Letters Received.

87. Ibid., Telegram to U.S. Attorney General, 24 October 1878.

88. Consul Ulrich to Second Assistant Secretary of State, 6 October 1874, Reel 3, Despatches from U.S. Consuls in Monterrey, NARA.

89. Ibid., Consul Ulrich to Second Assistant Secretary of State, 18 October 1874.

90. Mexican document, ca. 1872, Reel 7, Despatches from U.S. Consuls in Mexico City, NARA.

indicated that a five-alarm fire was raging in Texas. Members of the Republican Party were being "murdered" routinely. "Military aid" from Washington was requested in order to insure a "successful investigation" in what amounted to an extension of a civil war thought to have been resolved. "Martial law is the only and surest way to protect the loyal citizens of the South," was the battle cry that fell on uncomprehending ears. As was to be expected, the recently emancipated bore the brunt of this inflicted savagery. Of the party members slain in Wharton County, for example, in one month there were "14 colored men and one white man...."[91] However, the garroting of the latter was sufficient to send an important message that supporting justice presented a mortal danger—a precondition for the rise of fascism.

Wharton County, dozens of miles southwest from Houston, was a hotbed of this carnival of assassination. But soon the outgoing U.S. Attorney General was informed of the unavoidable: "Negroes were preparing to murder" in retaliation, supposedly at the behest of a Euro-American Republican, Isaac Baughman, a native of Indiana who moved there in 1867. He was "arming the negroes and inciting them to insurrection...." At first the roughnecks and evildoers approached him "holding their hands under their coats to conceal pistols...." But soon they were sufficiently emboldened as about a dozen of these terrorists surrounded his house, "killing him in his bed." The upshot was predictable: "not only did Governor Coke refuse protection" but the "courts have done nothing...."[92]

The executive was asleep at the switch, the judiciary was somnolent, while the legislature had been handcuffed. The new constitution in Texas, hurriedly proclaimed, projected fear and disgust with popular rule insofar as it delimited anxiety about the reach of elected officials: it was a backup plan in case the poll tax and voter suppression proved ineffective. The scholar C. Vann Woodward saw it as an expression of "overweening disgust of legislatures. Of the fifty-eight sections in the chapter of the Texas constitution dealing with the legislature, over half of them place limitations on its authority...."[93]

It was true that Euro-American men across class lines constituted the preponderance of the terrorist brigades who imposed forcibly their diktat in Texas. However, the scholar Robert Walter Shook

91. U.S. Marshal to Alphonso Taft, Attorney General, 12 October 1876, Reel 1, Letters Received.

92. Ibid., Robert Kyle to Attorney General Alphonso Taft, 23 December 1876.

93. C. Vann Woodward, *Origin of the New South, 1877-1913*, Baton Rouge: LSU Press, 1974, 65.

points out that "women and preachers were perhaps the most violent in their expression of hostility for the conquerors,"[94] referring to federal forces whose diminishment was a prerequisite to the efflorescence of terrorism.

As federal forces retreated, advancing were the Texas Rangers.[95] As the so-called Salt War of 1877 exploded in the far west of the state in a conflict over this valuable commodity, the Rangers were provided with a pretext for brutal assaults on those of Mexican origin and the Indigenes known as the Tiguas. This was nothing new for the latter, who had fled to Mexico during the Civil War to avoid persecution by rebels.[96] As so often happened then, this latest "war" raised the disturbing circumstance of "race war."[97]

The same can be said about what Washington considered mopping-up operations against Indigenes elsewhere. Postwar the Lakota, an equivalent of the Comanche in their battle readiness, were paid the ultimate compliment *cum* insult by settlers in that they were conflated with rebellious Negroes. George Custer, formerly of the borderlands, quite infamously made his last stand northward against the Lakota in 1876; accompanying him was a Negro, Isaiah Dorman, ironically wed to a Hunkpapa Lakota woman, and he too lost his life on the battlefield.[98]

Dorman made for strange company with Custer, he of the flowing blond locks, for the man who died with his boots on, while in Texas a decade earlier, opposed what he strangely called the "'slave vote'" since he argued that if the GOP were to become dependent upon the Negro vote it was doomed to failure.[99] The conundrum was that without the Negro vote—as the GOP soon was to discover—this party would become a nullity in Texas.

94. Shook, 459.

95. See, e.g., N.A. Jennings, *A Texas Ranger*, New York: Scribner's, 1899.

96. Comar, 192.

97. M.G. Webster, 233.

98. Hamalainen, 342, 365.

99. Shook, 73.

Chapter 23

The Roots of Jim Crow and U.S. Fascism in Oklahoma and Texas, 1879-1921

As early as 1880, as a result of an exodus from Dixie and immigration from Europe, Texas had become the most populous state in the Old South, a distinction it has not relinquished today.[1] Tens of thousands arrived and joined revanchists already present in a mass revolt against what was termed contemptuously the "'Africanization of our beloved commonwealth.'" In 1865 Africans constituted about 35% of the state's population, but that turned out to be the beginning of a slippery slide downward—in terms of percentage, even as gross numbers increased. In that context the lily-white Texas Rangers battled Mexican Americans to the death, joined white supremacist violence against Africans, and broke the first strikes of the Knights of Labor. They were akin to an aboveground version of the Ku Klux Klan—with overlapping directorates at times—both allied to a revenge-seeking Democratic Party.[2]

The political climate in Texas, awful in the best of times, skidded further into darkness after the rise of these revanchists. Mance Lipscomb, the bluesman born in 1895 in Navasota—basking uneasily in the shadow of the sprawling campus of Texas A&M University—captured the anger and alienation of Black Texans too numerous to mention. "'That's the dirtiest place in the world, Navasota. More niggers killed there'n any place in the world...they killed niggers for the fun of it. Specially if a man tried to hold up for his rights, they gonna kill him, get rid of him.'"[3]

Slavery, said travel writer F.L. Olmsted, involved the "'authority of all white people over all black [people],'" converting each among the latter into a potential cop.[4] Post-1865 there were beefed-up

---

1. Andrew Rolle, *The Lost Cause: The Confederate Exodus to Mexico*, Norman: U of Oklahoma Press, 1992, 8.

2. R. Perkinson, 79, 80.

3. Sitton and Conrad, 158.

4. Bolton, *Fugitivism*, 183.

police forces, the Klan and other terrorists—and, still, freelance Euro-Americans, often termed "Karens."[5]

It bears repeating that when Texas Negroes were knocked down, they often went down swinging, an unnerving reputation that they took with them as they scampered away. Thus, by 1900 the man known as Kid Gardener found himself in Cape Town, South Africa, well on the way to the horrors of apartheid, and after being hassled he blurted out tempestuously, "'You trying to class me with your Cape Town nigguhs? I'm from Texas,'" he boasted, "'and I ain't to be tampered with.'"[6] Predictably, the early Black heavyweight champion Jack Johnson had roots in Galveston.[7]

It may have been the case that Lipscomb was unaware of W.C. Brann, the fire-breathing white supremacist with roots in Austin and Waco who crusaded vitriolically against the Negro—before being murdered in 1898. Before that day, prayed for his by his multiple antagonists, he savaged Africans, claiming "we have tried the restraining influence of religion and the elevating force of education…without avail…. we have…incarcerated the offenders for life at hard labor and hanged them by the neck…. we have hunted the black rape-fiend to death with hounds, bored him with buckshot; fricasseed him over slow fires and flayed him alive," yet "these brutal imps of darkness and the devil" persisted. For he fulminated, "the baleful shadow of the black man hangs over every Southern home like the sword of Damocles…." What to do? Preemptive violence was on his mind in that it was "much better to shoot a negro before he commits an irreparable crime against the honor of a family than to hang him afterwards…." Perhaps it was inevitable that after the many cries to "exterminate" Indigenes that Negroes would be next in line for genocide. "We do not want to re-enslave him," he assured haughtily—since "he is not worth it. And if we desired to do so, the world, which is crazed with its own foolish cackle of 'equality and fraternity' would not permit it."[8] So, steady but sure grinding the Negro down to dust was the preferred option.

Still, consider this: "the world…would not permit it." Here Brann captured pithily the lesson that few post-Reconstruction Negro leaders seemed to grasp: given the adverse balance of forces domestically,

---

5. *St. Louis Post-Dispatch,* 30 November 2021.

6. Nadia Nurhussein, *Black Land: Imperial Ethiopianism and African America,* Princeton: Princeton U Press, 2019, 101.

7. Gerald Horne, *The Bittersweet Science: Racism, Racketeering and the Political Economy of Boxing,* New York: International, 2021.

8. Brann, Volume I, 25, 26.

lengthening the battlefield, rallying the international community to the banner, was the way out.

Intriguingly enough, in the midst of the flowering of this violence, the important Black Texas writer Sutton Griggs was born in 1872. By 1899 he had published his premier novel, *Imperium in Imperio*, which—reflecting the unparalleled thunderous clamor of his state— featured a secret organization sited in Texas and aimed at destroying racism by any means at hand. This could involve an armed takeover of the state in league with the antagonists of the U.S.,[9] a Black strategy with a lengthy genealogy, stretching back to the origins of settler colonialism[10] to relatively recent times.[11]

In a sense, Griggs and his avid Negro readers were reflecting the times in that in 1894 the so-called lily-white convention in Texas proposed that a section of the continent be set aside for Negroes. His proposal would effectuate this idea in a manner most advantageous to his community.[12] Then in the 1880s the notion was afloat that Negroes should form Black agricultural colonies in the state. John Rayner, a man of African descent from Texas, became a leader of Texas populists thereafter.[13]

* * *

As noted, U.S. incursions into Mexico postwar took the form mostly of "dollar diplomacy" or neo-colonialism, or developing imperialism or the export of capital. The brother of the influential Confederate James Morris Morgan by the late 1870s was a U.S. envoy in Mexico. P.H. Morgan, in concert with Alexander Shepherd, organized a mining expedition in Mexico and, said J.M. Morgan, the idea was to "'get rich quick,'" which he thought could occur given "notoriously lazy Mexicans."[14]

9. Finnie D. Coleman, *Sutton E. Griggs and the Struggle Against White Supremacy*, Knoxville: U of Tennessee Press, 2007; Sutton E. Griggs, *Imperium in Imperio*, Cincinnati: Editor, 1899; Andrew R. Graybill and Adam Arenson, eds., *Testing the Limits of the United States*, Berkeley: U of California Press, 2015.

10. Horne, *Dawning*.

11. Gerald Horne, *Black Revolutionary: William Patterson and the Globalization of the African American Freedom Struggle*, Urbana: U of Illinois Press, 2013.

12. Hinze, 115.

13. Gregg Cantrell, *Kenneth and John B. Rayner and the Limits of Southern Dissent*, Urbana: U of Illinois Press, 1993.

14. J.M. Morgan, 383, 387.

As capital moved, so did labor. Reviving an older trend, U.S. Negroes began discussion of forming a settlement of sorts in Mexico by 1889.[15] Similarly, Texans were then headed for the mines of Sierra Mojada in Coahuila.[16]

As capital flowed across borders, Londoners invested in Texas, notably in the cattle industry. A pioneer here was John Adair, who joined with U.S. cattleman Charles Goodnight to form a cattle empire, and they were quickly joined by other foreign investors.[17]

Facilitating the influx of capital and labor were railroads, which in the 1880s were being constructed as far south in Mexico as Zacatecas, and which also were bringing more U.S. nationals there—"workmen, adventurers, toughs," all "claiming American citizenship," according to the consul there.[18]

*   *   *

As had been the case for some years, eruptions in Texas and Dixie more generally were of consequence in the separate jurisdiction that was Indian Territory (IT). Thus, Africans were also on the move. Nick Gramlick was born in 1877 in Kansas, but arrived in what is now Oklahoma by 1890 and recalled the upsetting event of 1892, when about 500 Negroes straggled there from Memphis: "all were hungry."[19] Wilson Randle, a Negro born in 1859, also recalled when hundreds from Memphis fled to Oklahoma.[20]

Bill Gilliam was born in 1849, but when queried was in Watonga, Okla. He was of African and Cherokee ancestry and by 1888 was in Memphis. He witnessed "trouble" when "five colored men were hung without a trial" and "others were killed without a chance." Then "we heard of this land where we could get free homes and decided to form a colony" and traipsed 97 days to Indian Territory,

15. *Cleveland Gazette*, 29 June 1889.

16. Consul David Strother to Second Assistant Secretary of State, 10 October 1879, Reel 8, Despatches from U.S. Consuls in Mexico City, NARA.

17. Kenneth D. Rose, *Unspeakable Awfulness: America Through the Eyes of European Travelers, 1865-1900*, New York: Routledge, 2014, 242.

18. Consul A.M. Kimball to John Davis, Assistant Secretary of State, 5 May 1884, Reel 1, Despatches from U.S. Consuls in Zacatecas, NARA.

19. Oral History, Nick Gramlich, 24 December 1937, IPP.

20. Oral History, Wilson Randle, 10 March 1938, IPP. Cf., Ibid., Oral History, Willis Sidney Monroe, 14 March 1938: "One of the things I remember the most is when the group of negroes walked...from Memphis.... they had been bribed into coming to Oklahoma...[to] get free homes...."

500 strong with 150 being "women and large girls" with "forty small children."[21]

This was occurring as wholly Black towns in the vicinity became more prevalent, including what became Boley and Langston, Okla.[22] This was occurring when IT had it own uniqueness: 39 nations with their own languages, reportedly more than spoken in Europe.[23]

Fanny F. Allen, born enslaved in Sardis, Miss., in 1841, told an inquirer of a time when "hundreds of negroes from the south had been persuaded to come to the new town," speaking of Langston, "which was to be negroes' own city."[24] As for Boley, Louis Mann noted that they flipped the script against so-called "sundown towns" popular among Euro-Americans: "they had a sign and law," he said, "not to let the sun go down on a white man in Boley...."[25]

Madison McLeod was born in 1878 in Coldwater, Miss., but he was unaware of the true nature of Boley upon arrival. "The man... at the train to meet me and to my surprise he was a negro.... I was introduced to the mayor and found he was a negro"; this he "did not know" beforehand—"that Boley was a negro town."[26]

As suggested by Boley and Langston, in IT there was a steady commotion: the "Green Peach War" of the 1880s was among the anti-dispossession insurrections there in the run-up to Oklahoma's statehood in 1907.[27] It was primarily a "rebellion among the Creeks," said Will Robinson, born in those environs in 1865.[28] Also implicating the Creek Nation was the "Crazy Snake Uprising," which also involved so-called "Creek Freedmen" in conflict with settlers. M.C. Hickman, born in 1862 and then a resident of Henryetta, Okla., said

---

21. Ibid., Oral History, Bill Gilliam, 10 February 1838.

22. Kenneth Marvin Hamilton, *Black Towns and Profit: Promotion and Development in the Trans-Appalachian West, 1877-1915*, Urbana: U of Illinois Press, 1991. See also Kendra Field, *Growing Up with the Country: Family, Race and Nation After the Civil War*, New Haven: Yale U Press, 2018.

23. Cobb, 41.

24. Oral History, Fanny F. Allen, 12 October 1937, IPP.

25. Ibid., Oral History, Louis Mann, 17 September 1937. At the same site, see also Oral History, Ransome Ferris, 28 March 1938. Born in 1871, this resident of Quapaw, Okla., averred: "we have never had any permanent negro residents in this country and it was about this time that the men from Baxter Springs began to hire negroes" and then appeared a "sign in large letters" blaring "'Darkies don't let the sun go down on you in this town....'"

26. Ibid., Oral History, Madison McLeod, 25 June 1937.

27. Burton, *Black*, 22.

28. Oral History, Will Robinson, 24 February 1937, IPP.

that "Crazy Snake wanted to get his country back" with "no white people in here at all"; his movement had "about five hundred" adherents. "Crazy Snake had told all who joined him," said Hickman, "that when they got the country back they would [all] be considered citizens of the Creek Nation, regardless of color and have the rights of an Indian...,"[29] which was contrary to the Jim Crow praxis in Oklahoma. "Snake Indians," said Peter Maytubby, Jr., then of Caddo, Okla., "did not want the government to divide the land," i.e., allotment of the 1880s, but contradictorily, the "United States sent negro soldiers to keep order" as a result.[30]

Jim Guin was born in 1893 in the Creek Nation and he too remembered "Chitto 'Crazy Snake' Harjo, Creek Indian-Warrior-Statesman," who "fought against the law of the white man; he was the leader of several rebellions, the last in 1907.... these 'Crazy Snake' Indians who often had more negro blood than Indian" were on the march. Once "about ten negro 'Snake' Indians on horses entered the circle of their camp fire. One of these negroes sang out: 'Hello, white man! We burn you before day.'"[31]

One analyst has asserted that "'[many negroes] could talk Creek and Creeks like negroes better than they did whites.'" The famed Black lawman in the region, Bass Reeves, spoke Creek among other Indigenous languages.[32]

Jake Simmons was born in 1865 near Fort Washita in IT; his father had arrived there in 1851 as an adopted Cherokee citizen. His ancestry included Creek and African, and "most" of the former group, he said, were supportive of the rebels during the war—including his father who wore the gray uniform. This war was "disastrous" for the Creek "from start to finish" as they were "more pitiable than the rest of the nation of the five tribes" post-1865.[33] But what may have been a disaster for Creeks increased pressure upon them by Washington, and

---

29. Ibid., Oral History, M.C. Hickman, 17 August 1837.

30. Ibid., Oral History, Peter Maytubby, Jr., 24 August 1937. He adds, "Girls at the Tuskahoma College were all excited when they heard the soldiers were coming, for they thought they might find sweethearts among them but were greatly disappointed when the negro soldiers arrived...."

31. Ibid., Oral History, Jim Guin, 2 May 1938.

32. Burton, *Black*, 180, 170. See also Diary Entry, 18 April 1863, Stephen Foreman Collection: "I do not suppose there is one Creek in the Nation who knows anything of the grammar of the language. A grammar of the language I would like to see. It might give a clue to the grammar of the Cherokee language, which to this day is involved in darkness."

33. Oral History, Jake Simmons, ca. 1937, IPP.

may have opened more doors of opportunity for Negroes—including Simmons himself who, his admiring biographer says, established an "African-American Oil Dynasty" that included considerable wealth.[34]

Joining Simmons in the ranks of the affluent was Zack Foreman, who was spoken of eloquently by J.J. Cape, then of Mill Creek, Okla. Cape, born in 1867 and hailing from Texas, where a man like Foreman would be hard to conjure, spoke admiringly of this man as a "very wealthy...Cherokee Freedman," indeed the "wealthiest cattleman in the Cherokee Nation" and "the only negro in the United States at that time who privately owned a railroad."[35]

Thus it was unsurprising when in the early days of Okmulgee in the Creek Nation, as Dicey Stakes recalled matters, "one day a train load of negroes came. Everyday more negroes were brought until there were many."[36] At a certain point, according to Joe Grayson, born in 1873 in Arkansas, in Okmulgee "negroes...almost owned the town at one time and even had a negro postmaster," all this "before allotment" in the 1880s[37] when Washington disrupted collective ownership of the land. A.E. Dixon arrived in Okmulgee in 1902 at the age of 32 and he too remembered that "Jim Roper [was] a negro postmaster then."[38]

This wealth in turn necessitated a withering blow to Negro and Indigenous strength, softening up both for the emergence—at some point—of fascism.

This apprehension about Negroes and Indigenes reclaiming the land in Oklahoma continued to generate angst and animate ambition. Jim Simpson of Henryetta, Okla., recollected what occurred there in 1907: "Some negroes were also there from Texas and...expected to take the land away from the whites."[39]

For as the towns of Langston and Boley indicated, Negroes foresaw more opportunity in Indian Territory than elsewhere within the bounds of the U.S. When Forest Lee, a Negro born in 1879, arrived

---

34. Jonathan D. Greenberg, *Staking a Claim: Jake Simmons and the Making of an African-American Oil Dynasty*, New York: Atheneum, 1990.

35. Oral History, J.J. Cape, 4 March 1938, IPP. See also "Cherokee Advocate," 27 June 1874, Folder 4, Chickasaw Nation Collection, UOk-N: Herein is an editorial on the recently emancipated among Choctaw and Chickasaw and what is to become of them.

36. Oral History, Dicey Stakes, 23 June 1937, IPP.

37. Ibid., Oral History, Joe M. Grayson, 17 December 1937.

38. Ibid., Oral History, A.E. Dixon, 8 June 1937.

39. Ibid., Oral History, Jim Simpson, 20 April 1938.

in what became Oklahoma, he detected there were a "good many negroes in Chickasha when I first came...."[40]

Consequently, when Samuel Coffelt—born in 1862—arrived in 1889 in what was to become Oklahoma, he noticed that "Negro troops were stationed there to keep 'Sooners,'" meaning European land grabbers, "and settlers" at bay.[41] J.H. Simmons, born in 1877, recalled a time when "the Indian Department sent about two hundred negro soldiers to quell the hostile Indians,"[42] which did not endear them to the latter, though their being weaponized was a sign of strength.

Generally, a significant sector of the police in Muskogee were Negroes.[43] M.J. Burton arrived in IT and encountered a U.S. Marshal with "a couple of guns in his belt.... we were from Texas," he said wondrously, "where such a thing as a negro officer was unheard of."[44] John Pedford was born in 1864 in Arkansas and arrived in IT in 1887. He recalled a time in the town of Fort Gibson when "negro men went to the stores...and purchased guns and ammunition for a fight."[45]

Jones Louis Puckett arrived in IT in 1883, and then a "negro by the name of Dick Glass was a terror." This was during a time of intense conflict in the Creek Nation, and Puckett "saw more negroes than I had ever seen before or have since. Some had shotguns, some had muskets and some had Winchesters."[46]

There were other aspects to Negroes being there. Jennie Williams Hoskins Christy was born in France in 1857, but her father was German. She recalled without fondness a time when in Fort Reno near her residence, "those negro soldiers would come to town and practically take Nigger Town. They would ride right through the houses if they happened to find the doors open, a shootin' and a cussin'."[47] The presence of these boisterously empowered soldiers then attracted other Africans.

---

40. Ibid., Oral History, Forest Lee, 21 September 1937.

41. Ibid., Oral History, Samuel Coffelt, 27 June 1937.

42. Ibid., Oral History, J.H. Simmons, 3 August 1937.

43. Burton, *Black*, 132.

44. Oral History, M.J. Burton, 22 March 1938, IPP. See also Nudie Eugene Williams, "A History of the American Southwest Black United States Deputy Marshals in the Indian Territory, 1875-1907," Master's thesis, Oklahoma State U, 1973: Because many Negroes knew Indigenous languages, they were recruited to this post.

45. Oral History, John Pedford, 15 December 1937, IPP.

46. Ibid., Oral History, Jones Louis Puckett, 21 July 1937.

47. Ibid., Oral History, Jennie Williams Hoskins Christy, 26 October 1937.

As time passed, it did seem that ties between Indigenes and Africans were friendlier than those between settlers and the latter. Daniel Jackson, born in 1859, then residing in Elk City, Okla., recalled that the "negro Britt ran a train from Jacksboro to Fort Griffen. This train was made up of five or six wagons and teams…. Indians surrounded them and killed all of the drivers but negro Britt…."[48]

James Small was born in 1841 in Tennessee and recalled decades later that "after the close of the war, the descendants of the negro slaves intermarried with the Creeks" and "descendants of the negro slaves who had no Indian blood were allowed forty acres of land," unlike Texas and Dixie generally. By the 1890s in Coweta, IT, a "citizen of the more than half negro blood was postmaster and also owned the largest mercantile establishment" that was "employing white, negro and Indian clerks; he also owned a cotton gin and had extensive land holdings and large herds of cattle."[49]

Unlike in Texas and Dixie generally, Choctaw leader Green McCurtain, a former enslaver, called in the 1890s for the formerly enslaved to receive "'forty acres of land.'" By 1906, on the eve of statehood, IT had a Negro population of over 80,000; some Indigenes of African descent, who in the peculiar U.S. system were defined as Negro ultimately, primarily spoke Choctaw, Creek and related languages.[50]

M.J. Burton of Texas moved to what became Speer, Okla., but, he said, it was "originally called Cooksville" because an "old Mississippi freedman, Albert Cook, owned the land around here." There had "always been lots of negroes around here," he reminded, "and that about three miles west of here there was once a negro academy called Oak Grove"—but then reaction set in and it was "burned several years ago and was never rebuilt."[51]

De'Leslaine Davis arrived in IT in 1880 because he thought it was there that the Negro was "given a fair chance."[52] In this context, it was unavoidable that Negroes from Texas would stream across the border and, alternatively, an attempt would be made to convert IT into a land resembling its southern neighbor.

With Indian Territory as a separate jurisdiction, this created arbitrage opportunities and not just for Negroes. James Armstrong, a

---

48. Ibid., Oral History, Daniel Jackson, 27 May 1937.

49. Ibid., Oral History, James Small, 18 August 1937.

50. Christina Dickerson-Cousin, *Black Indians and Freedmen: The African Methodist Episcopal Church and Indigenous Americans, 1816-1916*, Urbana: U of Illinois Press, 134, 135, 136.

51. Oral History, M.J. Burton, 22 March 1938, IPP.

52. Ibid., Oral History, De'Leslaine Davis, 11 October 1937.

Choctaw born in 1876, remembered that "some white folks told the Indians they could run off down into Texas and the law couldn't get them as [IT] had no jurisdiction over them in Texas...."[53] John Barr arrived in the Chickasaw nation about 1871 and remembered subsequently that "full blood Indians" did not welcome settlers, especially those from Texas, but they arrived anyway since this territory was "an ideal stomping ground for renegades and outlaws from other states."[54]

Fannie Blythe Marks, then of Vinita, Okla., recounted that "desperadoes" from "the States" flocked to IT because of problematic extradition pacts, and this outlawry included the notorious Belle Starr.[55] Victor M. Locke shot a Negro in Louisiana and then, according to O.L. Blanche, fled to "Shawneetown" in IT where he worked for the Choctaw millionaire Robert Jones before decamping to Clarkville, Texas.[56]

When barbed wire fenced off the Texas plains by 1885, it was kind of an enclosure movement, driving away "surplus" settlers,[57] at times to the north. By 1888, arriving in El Reno was Annie Hutchinson, born in 1856 in Georgia and reaching Texas by 1878. She was not the kind of settler that Negroes would have welcomed in that she acknowledged "my father owned a large plantation and nearly four hundred slaves."[58]

Historian Arthur T. Burton has found that "the white outlaw, completely free of any legal responsibility in this area, ran wild. He abused the Indian women...[thus] the Indians in the interior developed a deep distrust of all white men. They reasoned that all white men were exactly like the outlaws." However, the "scenario for Indian and black outlaws was a little different than for the white

---

53. Ibid., Oral History, James Armstrong, 22 December 1937.

54. Ibid., Oral History, John Barr, 13 January 1938.

55. Ibid., Oral History, Fannie Blythe Marks, 9 September 1937. Cf., Shirley Glenn, *Belle Starr and Her Times: The Literature, the Facts and the Legend*, Norman: U of Oklahoma Press, 1982.

56. Oral History, O.L. Blanche, 21 May 1937, IPP.

57. L. Wright, 165.

58. Oral History, Annie Hutchinson, 20 July 1937, IPP. At the same site, see also Oral History, Fannie Borden, 19 October 1937: She was born in 1863 on her father's 600-acre plantation but wound up in Texas, then Altus, Okla. See also Oral History, Lucinda Hickey, 25 March 1937: She was born in the Cherokee Nation in an enslaving family. See also Oral History, Mary James, 3 August 1937: This resident of Fairland, Okla., mentioned that her grandfather owned 36 enslaved Africans and Confederate leader Stand Watie was "our friend."

outlaws. The Indian and black outlaws would prey on the white set-tlements along the border and whites traveling through the Indian nations...."[59]

P.P. Hammer arrived in IT from Texas in 1892 and mentioned later that there were "many Indians here" and a "goodly number of negroes," with the latter "depending largely on stealing and robbing for their living."[60] It would not be unfair to see this alleged criminality as a form of rebellion against the encroachment of settler colonial-ism,[61] the latter carried the seeds of both Jim Crow and fascism.

Negroes had much to protect north of Texas. Another "benefit" that materialized was that of the "wealthy negroes who had Indian blood from their mothers,"[62] and were able to reap assets as a result. An outgrowth of these familial ties was pointed to by Maud E. Smith, born in 1881 in El Reno. Once she met a Negro accompanied by Indi-genes who was "taken captive when he was a little child and knew no people other than the Indians among whom he was raised. He did not know who he was. He had married an Indian squaw [sic]."[63]

The fluidity of IT facilitated the rise of various inchoate revolts, among which was the one symbolized by Crawford Goldsby, alias "Cherokee Bill." He was born in San Angelo, Texas, ca. 1874 of mixed Cherokee, African and European ancestry; his mother provided the first two strains and his German father the latter. As with slavery, he was able to find sanctuary in the Creek Nation after various rob-beries and killings—before meeting his executioner in 1896.[64] Jim Vaughn of Paden, Okla., later recalled that Cherokee Bill "terror-ized the country around Fort Gibson, Tahlequah and the Cookson Hills. His brother, Clarence...was another bad one...." What riled them was a significant change for "during those early days, the Indi-ans, Negroes and whites bunked in the same bunkhouses, ate at the same table and thought nothing of mingling." But then malcontents "stirred up the feelings" and "made a law that the negroes were

59. Burton, *Black*, 163, 164.

60. Oral History, P.P. Hammer, 23 November 1937, IPP.

61. Eric J. Hobsbawm, *Primitive Rebels, Studies in Archaic Forms of Social Movement in the 19th and 20th Centuries*, New York: Norton, 1965.

62. Oral History, Louis Rentie, 23 August 1937, IPP.

63. Ibid., Oral History, Maud E. Smith, 29 June 1937.

64. "A Short Sketch of the Life of Cherokee Bill Given by Mrs. E.H. Whit-mire Presented to W.J.B. Bigby, Field Worker," 14 April 1937, IPP. At the same site, see also Oral History, Frank Gill, 20 July 1937: Cherokee Bill's father was "an Irishman," while his "mother was a coal black negro...."

to be a separate class from the whites and Indians and were not to mix...."[65] igniting revolt.

Cherokee Bill attracted negative attention from J.W. Rice of Tulsa, who opined that he "inherited seemingly the worst features of his mixed Indian, white and negro descent" in that his "whole story is one of outlawry." His "very appearance was menacing," which Rice knew since he "saw him after the cruel killing of a white man."[66] Yet when the stoic and feared Cherokee Bill mounted the scaffold to be executed and was asked if he had anything to say, he replied gruffly, "'I did not come here to make a talk but came to be hanged [emphasis-original]."[67]

This was the denouement of a betrayal. John Hannon arrived in IT in 1881 and commented later that a "negro named Rogers who was Deputy U.S. Marshal, finally betrayed Bill. He invited him into his home as a friend, entertained him...until he got his confidence, then knocked him in the head with a fire poker and captured him. He was hanged at Fort Smith, Arkansas,"[68] in early 1896.

Henry Clay too was born in Texas, 1864 in his case, but wound up in Chickasha, Okla., with aims not unlike that of Cherokee Bill. "Being a Negro," he recounted, "I saw the possibility of making easy money, running a gambling and drinking house," taking advantage of "lots of work being done by negroes and they were paid good wages...." As a result, it "wasn't unusual to see a man get killed over some small remark...."[69]

John Rice, born in 1875 but then speaking from El Reno, Okla., recalled a time when "finding of dead bodies of unidentified people was not...uncommon...."[70]

These fatalities may have been at the hands of "Buck's Gang." These outlaws, said Benton Callahan, were a mélange of "mixed negroes, Indians and whites. Rufus Buck a Euchee [Yuchi]-negro was the leader," and "Lucky Davis, a negro" was leading those who "terrorized," as they were the "meanest and dirtiest band of outlaws that ever existed...."[71] Carrie Marshall Pitman was born in Texas in 1871; her

65. Ibid., Oral History, Jim Vaughn, 30 November 1937.

66. Ibid., Oral History, J.W. Rice, 7 December 1937.

67. Ibid., Oral History, John Humberd, 11 May 1937.

68. Ibid., Oral History, John Hannon, ca. 1938. A Negro man, Isaac C. Morris, was interpreter of the Choctaw and Chickasaw languages at the federal court in Fort Smith: *Cleveland Gazette*, 29 June 1889.

69. Oral History, Henry Clay, 16 June 1937, IPP.

70. Ibid., Oral History, John L. Rice, 14 April 1938.

71. Ibid., Oral History, Benton Callahan, 27 August 1937. On Buck see Burton, *Black*, 88.

father was a Seminole Freedman and she baked for the Cole Younger gang. The "Rufus Buck gang were five in number," she recalled, "three colored men and two Indian boys...."[72]

Then there was the man that H. Lee Jackson, then of Poteau, Okla., called the "notorious negro renegade" known as "Booly July." He was a "desperate character who had gathered around him quite a number of renegade negroes"; he also was "part Indian by blood" and "with the assistance of influential Indian friends [he] always escaped conviction...." His specialty was preying on settlers traveling through Texas en route to the presumed riches of California.[73] And there was the Cook Gang, comprised heavily of Negro men, the majority being Cherokee Freedmen.[74] C.H. Eberle, born in Arkansas in 1858, had not forgotten the "bad negro" known as "Coon Van" when queried in the 1930s. He was part of a "mob of six or seven hundred" comprised heavily of Cherokee Freedmen who "attacked" a "pay office" in 1897.[75]

Pete Cole observed that postwar "the negroes from adjoining states moved in on the Choctaws and the Chickasaws on the banks of the Red River," nearby Texas, "and formed their own settlement"; they "depended upon stealing for a living," which created momentum to import the rigor of Texas across the river.[76] "We were harassed and robbed by the 'Pin Indians,'" said Susan Riley Gott referring to the so-called "full-blood" Cherokee; born in 1857, she referred indignantly to these "full bloods whose sole business was to steal and pilfer...."[77]

W.C. Mead, then of Altus, Okla., had a differing memory, though he may not have been referring to Cherokee. "The only law we had in those days was the United States marshals and...they had their hands full. The Indians did not give so much trouble but as usual it was the half-breeds; sometimes half-negro and half white, sometimes half negro and Indian, sometimes half white and Indian and bad white men. You seldom found a full blood Indian bad."[78]

This malice was all-sided, according to the settler Marshall Clark, born in 1848 and a resident of what became Duncan, Okla. Postwar he knew of a "bunch of negroes settled up and down the creek. Something happened and the cowboys took seven of these negroes

72. Oral History, Carrie Marshall Pitman, 12 April 1938, IPP.
73. Ibid., Oral History, H. Lee Jackson, 22 April 1938.
74. Burton, *Black*, 45.
75. Oral History, C.H. Eberle, ca. 1937, IPP.
76. Ibid., Oral History, Pete Cole, 22 October 1937.
77. Ibid., Oral History, Susan Riley Gott, 15 February 1937.
78. Ibid., Oral History, W.C. Mead, 17 January 1938.

and hanged them all to a limb of one tree...."[79] Edna Hunt Osborne recollected the area known as "Buck Tree Council...that was where Indians and negroes were treated, executed and whipped...stood them against the wall to shoot them...."[80]

Anderson Bean, a Negro, was born in 1851 in Arkansas, but wound up in Muskogee. "It was not safe for us 'niggers' to go out on the streets at night," he said, referring to an undefined period characterized by an "uprising of the negroes, that was started by Coon Vann...."[81] B.K. McElhannan may have been aware of the latter. Born in 1881 in Alcorn, Miss., he referred obliquely to the "race riot" of 1907 when "the Okmulgee and Muskogee negroes were going to help wipe Henryetta [Okla.] off the map...."[82]

Jim Simpson, born in 1887, was of partial Cherokee ancestry and he remembered the uproar in Henryetta about 1907 when a Negro was lynched and "about three days later...the Negroes were all driven out of town.... the ones who wouldn't leave were beaten until they were glad to leave...." Then "volunteer guards kept negroes from coming back...."[83] Ben Williams, born in 1840 and living at the time of his interview in Idabel, Okla., said "[Indians] would shoot at a 'nigger' just to see him jump and run...."[84]

On the other hand, Bettie Perdue Woodall, then of Welch, Okla., had an incompatible experience. Her roots were in Georgia, and her father was a "half breed Cherokee" who headed first to IT, then to Texas during the Civil War since "Pin Indians were getting too bad...." Her uncle there was a "large slave owner" and "was just as mean to them as he could be. He could whip them at the least excuse" with a "long black snake whip." The "poor negro was screaming with all his might, when an Indian rode up, unnoticed by either my uncle or the negro. He gave a loud war whoop, lunged his horse at my uncle, hit him across the eyes with his quirt momentarily blinding him, snatched the poor bleeding negro up behind him and rode off...." This "made my uncle so mad at the whole Indian race that he said they were no better than the negro...." Understandably, when emancipation finally arrived this uncle was "almost like a mad man"[85]—and the same could be said for Texas slaveholders as a class.

---

79. Ibid., Oral History, Marshall Clark, 23 March 1937.

80. Ibid., Oral History, Edna Hunt Osborne, 3 September 1937.

81. Ibid., Oral History, Anderson Bean, 22 February 1937.

82. Ibid., Oral History, B.K. McElhannan, 22 April 1937.

83. Ibid., Oral History, Jim Simpson, 20 April 1938.

84. Ibid., Oral History, Ben Williams, 12 July 1937.

85. Ibid., Oral History, Bettie Perdue Woodall, 20 September 1937. At the same site, see Oral History, David Gillis, 20 May 1937. It was in 1883

Chaney McNair, born enslaved in the Cherokee Nation in 1852, would have understood this disturbing story. "I was told," he said later, "that down in Texas the slave owners set a rule that each slave was to do so much work each day and any who failed to come up to their rule received so many lashes when night came."[86]

Yet as some Indigenes were cozying up to Africans—and vice-versa—their animus toward settlers was not disintegrating and reached the sensitive realm of religion. Travis Ely was born in 1860 and recollected that Cheyenne told him that "'white men had funny religion. They kill Jesus Christ and then cry about it and expect Indian[s] to cry too and we're not going to do it.' The Arapaho...wondered why white people and negroes shout so about their religion. They said 'is god deaf?'"[87]

Jeff Randolph was born in Kentucky in 1862, then moved west. He was of Cherokee, Creek and Negro ancestry and brought with him unforgiving memories that colored his perceptions of his new homeland. For in Kentucky "many whites had their heads cut off and put on a picket fence as a warning to others for teaching the negroes during this time." This was an incentive for forging the "white united front" that served to undergird proto-fascism. Randolph was also aware of the system of communication that allowed Indigenes to send messages over vast plains. Cheyenne and Arapaho knew of Custer's death, for example, "the next morning.... they used as methods of rapid communication throughout the country by signal hills, by flaming arrows and by tom tom beats, one tribe would signal another tribe."[88]

*   *   *

This was all part of a trend whereby Europeans were arriving in Texas and Africans were departing the Lone Star State for Indian Territory. However, the continuing accusations of outlawry in IT—especially spearheaded by Negroes—and the rapacity of settlers lusting for Indigenous land, created momentum for statehood by 1907.

---

that he spotted Bob Dalton harass a Negro youth eating an apple: "thinking it would be funny to scare the negro, Dalton called to the negro to halt, which he did and quickly." Dalton then said, "'Put that apple on your head and I will show you some fancy shooting.'" The youth balked and Dalton's response was that if he did not comply he would shoot him anyway—so he put the apple on his head and Dalton plugged it as the trembling youth avoided—physical—damage.

86. Ibid., Oral History, Chaney McNair, 11 May 1937.

87. Ibid., Oral History, Travis Ely, 19 March 1938.

88. Ibid., Oral History, Jeff Randolph, ca. 1938.

Interestingly, although Jim Crow was a primary initiative after statehood and notwithstanding the poisonous legacy of enslavement in IT,[89] Mack Harris—born in the Choctaw Nation in 1871 and then residing in Haileyville—claimed that during his youth and early adulthood, "Indians and Negroes and all went to what schools were near us...."[90] This process may have led to the development of premier historian of the 20th century, John Hope Franklin. His father, Buck Franklin, recalled that "my people came from Mississippi" and his mother was owned by Choctaw: "they raised my mother and allowed her every privilege of their own people...."[91]

This was considerable since Frank Tucker spoke at length about Robert Hill, who "owned so many slaves he did not know them all and did not know how much money he was worth. He was reputed to be the first full blood Choctaw Indian millionaire."[92] Andrew Willhite, born in 1869 and at the time of his speaking residing in Henryetta, Okla., noted that the "Choctaw Nation was the best part of the whole territory as it was very good for farms, stock raising and hunting"—besides, there were "Indians with negro wives."[93]

Sally Henderson Ross was born in 1882 in Hartshorne, Okla., a legacy of the Choctaw Nation. There was a "good sized community of negroes and Indians there," she recalled. "Most the negroes were

89. Ibid., Oral History, William Nail, 21 April 1838: The Chickasaw says this man born in 1860 and then residing in Poteau, Okla., were "reluctant in recognizing the emancipation of the slaves and continued to hold them in slavery for some after the close of the war." He also saw slaveholding Choctaw as being more pro-Negro than Chickasaw. At the same site, see also Oral History, Charles Culter Torrey, 28 February 1938: "The Cherokee language is very difficult.... I learned a few words of Choctaw much more quickly and readily than the same amount of Cherokee.... Choctaw and Chickasaw... resemble each other closely."

90. Ibid., Oral History, Mack Harris, 25 March 1938: He concedes, however, that his "father, being from Missouri, didn't want me to go to school with the negroes...."

91. Ibid., Oral History, B.C. Franklin, 4 February 1938.

92. Ibid., Oral History, Frank Tucker, 4 February 1937. At the same site, see also Oral History, Gomer Gower, 22 March 1938: Purported benevolence of wealthy Indigenes toward Negroes was not universal. By 1890, he says, "not a single negro was employed in the Indian Territory mines"—until "negro strikebreakers from Kansas" arrived in the coal mines of Alderson, Okla.

93. Ibid., Oral History, Andrew Willhite, 11 January 1938. At the same site see Oral History, Charles Moore Brown, 24 June 1937: Of African and Choctaw ancestry, he asserted that "when I was growing up there were no white people in this country much."

freedmen and owned land"; her stepfather was a "freedman and had the right to land under the Choctaw land," and "all the negroes could understand that language then...."[94]

Grant Fowlks was born in 1867 in Arkansas, so he had a basis of comparison with the Choctaw Nation, where his family moved by 1890. "We never had any trouble with the Indians here," he recalled later. "We had lots of dealings with them...they were honest.... I never lived among better people than the Indians.... if you would let them alone and attend to your own business you would never have trouble with them...."[95]

There were those who could have commented upon what he sensed. Emma Thompson Hampton's mother was born enslaved in the Chickasaw Nation, and she was born in 1880 in the Choctaw Nation. She recalled that Box Springs, a hamlet there, was "made up of negroes."[96]

Edna Hunt Osborne, born in 1881, recalled that in IT, "the Choctaw Indian children went free to the school and white ones had to pay tuition...." There was another form of segregation at "Indian weddings" that featured "two ministers...one white man for the benefit of the white guests and a full blood Indian minister" too.[97]

This practice was an outgrowth of the past. Granny Wolfe was Cherokee and spoke little or no English, employing a "negro girl" as an interpreter. Wolfe argued that "slaves preferred living in the Cherokee Nation to residence in the United States," a trend which continued postwar.[98]

Eliza Whitmire concurred. Formerly enslaved, she was born in Georgia and owned by a Cherokee slaveholder. "Slaves who belonged to the Cherokees fared much better than the slaves who belonged to the white race," she said. "When allotment came," speaking of the postwar plan by Washington to divide the land and disrupt collective control, "they gave us an equal right with them in land drawings"— though she added pointedly, "the United States government forced them to do this...."[99]

---

94. Ibid., Oral History, Sally Henderson Moss, 15 April 1938.

95. Ibid., Oral History, Grant Fowlks, 29 July 1937.

96. Ibid., Oral History, Emma Thompson Hampton, 15 February 1938.

97. Ibid., Oral History, Edna Hunt Osborne, 3 September 1937.

98. Ibid., Oral History, Granny Wolfe, 1 February 1938.

99. Ibid., Oral History, Eliza Whitmire, 14 October 1938. By the time of the interview she was 102 years old: "I was about five years old," she said, "when Andrew Jackson ordered" expulsion of the Cherokee. Then

This "Indian Territory Exception" was doomed to run aground given its proximity to Texas, which accelerated with the illicit land rush of 1889 (which actually began before this instrumental date) and culminated in 1907 with statehood. Not only did this new state predate Virginia in defining legally the so-called "one drop rule," which regarded any hint of African ancestry as a kind of pollutant that obliterated all other ancestries, mandated Blackness by law, but its antipode "whiteness"—according to scholar Alaina E. Roberts—*could* include "Native peoples, as well as Asian, Mexican, mixed Native and white and other non-Black peoples...."[100] [emphasis-author]

The driving motivation was to punish and isolate the descendants of enslaved Africans in a manner congruent with that of the Lone Star State, while disrupting the anti-white supremacist front. The crowning blow occurred in 1921, when Tulsa Negroes were looted, plundered and driven from the state. Evidently the elite effort to disrupt class solidarity worked in that according to one close study of the massacre, "most of the white combatants were oilfield workers."[101]

The results were, in a sense, unavoidable. A.F. Adkins, born in 1882 and described as a "quadroon negro," had an uncle who "decided that he would claim he was an Indian, a mixed breed Creek.... his hair was fairly straight anyway, so he let it grow long and wore it in two braids with beads and bright colored strings and ribbons braided in them and a beaded band around his head. He got a big hat...posed as a Creek Indian. They called him Chief Dillahunty.... he married a big old yellow negro woman who beat him up at will."[102]

In short, the consequence was a form of psychological warfare whereby Negroes were compelled to avoid their African ancestry and, indeed, to despise it. And, yes, psychological warfare was waged as well against Indigenes.[103]

Euro-Americans descended in pillaging mobs; they "even rifled the graves for any jewelry," then homes, and drove "off their cattle...."

100. A.E. Roberts, 122.

101. Krehbiel, 18. See also Oral History, Major Frank van Voorhis, 25 October 1937, IPP: The interviewee was in charge of the National Guard in Tulsa in 1921 and witnessed "firing back and forth between blacks and whites.... maddened armed whites were our worst problem...in a state of frenzy" more manic than "negro snipers...in the belfry of the [A.M.E.] church at Greenwood and Cameron...." It was "surprising," he said, to see the "number of negroes in army attire World War uniforms," along with the fact that they were "well supplied with long range Winchesters...."

102. Ibid., Oral History, A.F. Adkins, 12 February 1938.

103. Ibid., Oral History, Ben Beckley, 9 August 1937. Domiciled in Monahans, Texas, and born in 1881, he spoke German, English, and understood

But propelling the demented process was what C.E. Wakefield, then of Duncan, Okla., noticed. Born in 1880 in Cook County, Texas, he observed, "we were so afraid of Negroes...we were afraid he would kill us at night...."[104] This pervasive atmosphere of violence may have borne psychological meaning and influenced what Williams Thompson Jones of Fort Towson, Okla., and born in 1867, noticed early on: "the Indians and native born mixed negro Indians were mean. They'd just kill each other at the drop of a hat...."[105]

At the same time, the embittering postwar legacy of enslavement had yet to be purged—or confronted—which, to a degree, remains the case. E.H. Lookabaugh was born in 1871 and arrived from Kansas in 1898 in what became Watonga, Okla. A Euro-American "made the remark that he had been the owner of a slave who were of more than account than these two men," referring to a Negro and a Mexican looking on with mounting resentment. "They did not like his remark," so they killed him.[106]

Even after statehood and the attempt to affix polecat status to the Negro, this besieged and persecuted group refused to surrender easily. John Mahoney was born in 1865 and arrived in IT by 1889, the beginning of the illicit land grab by settlers. By 1909 he was in Guthrie, Okla., later recollecting that "negroes of the town were arming themselves and a race war would have been on. I could not sleep for several nights afterwards."[107]

They had reason to arm considering the memories of Minnie Jones Himes, born in 1875; she wound up in what became Duncan, Okla., and recalled a time when "a bunch of these negroes were run out, seven of them being hanged" and subjected to the further indignity of a continuing message as they were "left there for a long time...."[108]

Osage and "Mexican languages": "much has been said and written about the Indians being unemotional.... their emotions have been restrained for so many generations that this restraint is a sort of second nature with them. They are repressed from babyhood.... had the children been permitted to laugh and cry they could not have kept their whereabouts secret from their enemies." At the same site see Oral History, Joe M. Grayson, 17 December 1937: "When an Indian was whipped he wouldn't 'grunt' nor groan if it killed him.... you could hear a negro who got the same amount of punishment screaming for four miles...."

104. Ibid., Oral History, C.E. Wakefield, 27 April 1937.
105. Ibid., Oral History, Williams Thompson Jones, 9 March 1938.
106. Ibid., Oral History, E.H. Lookabaugh, 8 April 1938.
107. Ibid., Oral History, John Mahoney, 20 October 1937.
108. Ibid., Oral History, Minnie Jones Himes, 13 May 1937.

Then there was the quotidian fraud spoken of by Ellen Donahoe of Tulsa, but born in Wisconsin in 1855: settlers by the 1890s were seeking to "buy all the negro [land] claims.... that was permitted but you could not buy a white person's claim."[109]

However, there had been a sharp change in the transition from Indian Territory to Oklahoma. In the former regime there was a significant concentration of Negro peace officers, but this changed dramatically after statehood, as Jim Crow was implanted forcibly.[110] Subsequent attempts to reverse the tide of reaction, though exhibiting promise, proved unavailing and illustrate a theme of this work: because resistance often was so formidable, reaction doubled down and became ever fiercer in Texas and Oklahoma, outstripping in magnitude and reach underlying proto-fascist sentiment anywhere else.[111]

Jim Carr of Frederick, Okla., saw this phenomenon materialize before his very eyes. The authorities bluntly decided to "order the negroes to leave," fomenting a "general exodus" helter skelter. It was 26 May 1910, he said, when "'Nigger Town'" was emptied, and though during better times Africans had migrated northward from Texas, now they returned there. The outgoing "Frisco platform resembled a large plunder shop, with all the negroes' household goods and personal effects piled high, waiting to be shipped out...."[112] Something similar happened near the same time in Geary, Okla., when—according to John Dean, born in 1869—"all the negro element was run out with the exception of one Charlie Marshman, a cook."[113]

From what seemed to be a promised land, postwar IT was converted into the charnel house of post-1907 Oklahoma. Beginning as early as 1908, about 1000 Black Oklahomans fled northward to Saskatchewan and Alberta.[114] On a single day in 1909 the entire Negro population of Sapulpa, Okla., was expelled; near Muskogee, a Black neighborhood was obliterated and then buildings were burned down where it was thought the victimized were hiding. Oklahoma was justifiably seen as both a variation of Texas and the nation's pancreas. This trend put paid to the talk about Oklahoma becoming

---

109. Ibid., Oral History, Ellen Donahoe, 20 May 1937.

110. Burton, *Black*, 164.

111. Charles Bush, "The Green Corn Rebellion," U of Oklahoma, Master's thesis, 1932. See also James R. Green, *Grass Roots Socialism: Radical Movements in the Southwest, 1895-1943*, Baton Rouge: LSU Press, 1978.

112. Oral History, Jim Carr, 11 May 1937, IPP.

113. Ibid., Oral History, John Dean, 22 June 1937.

114. R. Bruce Shepard, "North to the Promised Land: Black Migration to the Canadian Plains," *Chronicles of Oklahoma*, 66 (Fall 1988): 306-327.

the nation's first Black state, an update of Indian Territory.[115] By 1914 some Black Oklahomans were headed to West Africa.[116]

Black Texans were also seeking sanctuary, notably after the "Slocum Massacre of 1910," described as an "act of genocide in East Texas" in the wake of a "race war." An inflamed Dallas journalist charged that "Negroes were preparing to rise and kill all of the white people." What resulted was "one of the largest mass murders of blacks in American history," exceeding contemporaneous conflicts in Tulsa and Rosewood, Fla., according to one study. Ultimately, 23 Africans and four settlers were killed—by one estimate. Seizing property of Africans was the underlying motivation, as they were "'hunted... down like sheep.'" It was just "coon hunting," said one observer. Incongruously, Palestine, Texas—the home of Confederate major-domo John Reagan—was implicated in the slaughter, while the *Jewish Herald* in Houston rationalized the impending slaughter: "the people make the laws and the people can suspend the laws."[117]

However, given the dialectic of repression generating resistance—and vice versa—it was also during this same period that Jack Johnson, the heavyweight champion from Galveston, was forced into exile in order to elude spurious charges and wound up in Mexico City during the revolutionary decade. There he sought to establish a beachhead against Jim Crow. It was also then that the monumental "Plan of San Diego" was crafted, which was said to involve retaking the land seized improperly by the U.S. during the war of aggression of the 1840s and establishing in its stead independent Black and Indigenous polities.[118]

Jack Johnson was simply one of a series of prominent Black personalities who exhibited a fascination with Mexico, a lengthening list that came to include W.E.B. Du Bois, Langston Hughes, Katherine Dunham and Elizabeth Catlett.[119]

It was not just northern Texas that was aflame. The borderlands continued to be unsettled too. Again, Texas dissidents—and

115. Cobb, 85, 86, 99, 106.

116. William E. Bittle and Gilbert Geis, *The Longest Way Home: Chief Alfred Sam's Back-to-Africa Movement*, Detroit: Wayne State U Press, 1964.

117. E.R. Bills, 11, 13, 16, 19, 31, 51, 1, 115-116. See also *Dallas Morning News*, 1 August 1910; *Palestine Daily Herald*, 30 July 1910; *Jewish Herald*, 17 March 1910; *El Paso Herald*, 1 August 1910.

118. Gerald Horne, *Black and Brown: African-Americans and the Mexican Revolution, 1910-1920*, New York: NYU Press, 2005.

119. Theodore W. Cohen, *Finding Afro-Mexico: Race and Nation after the Revolution*, Cambridge: Cambridge U Press, 2020.

reactionaries too—had an advantage of bordering a regime that was not altogether friendly. Thus, in 1880 in Laredo, 17 prisoners overwhelmed their guards and tried to swim to freedom in Mexico; eight were killed or drowned, three went missing and may have been successful in escape, and the balance were recaptured. From the Mexican side of the border, shots were fired at the Texas pursuers.[120]

Something similar occurred once more in 1880, this time involving Indigenes raiding in Texas, then crossing the border with deadly fire aimed at their pursuers from Mexico.[121] A few years later, after a body was found decapitated, said a U.S. official in Nuevo Laredo, "great excitement was produced," featuring "hostile demonstrations by the mob toward all Americans," i.e., "the outcome of the old spirit of hostility to the United States exists in the minds of a class of people."[122] A continuing attribute of the borderlands—through the 1880s—was the persistent presence of Chiricahua Apaches, many of whom knew the Spanish language and were unreconciled to a settler presence.[123] It would require massive firepower and heavy dosages of bigotry to subdue them, both of which laid the groundwork for a further flowering of reaction.

At the same time, despite the earlier idea that Kickapoo had been subdued a few years earlier, by 1879 there was a report that "the only band of Mexican Indians which of late years have committed any outrages on U.S. territory from this state," meaning Chihuahua, was precisely this theretofore unsubdued group. Understatedly, Washington was told, this "caused considerable annoyance to the [ranches] on the Texas side of the Rio Grande...." Apaches were accused of the capital crime of horse stealing, calling for intensifying stringent measures.[124] There was an unnamed "Indian chief" accused of "raiding from Mexico into New Mexico and Arizona; "he and his bucks," said the U.S. emissary, "have killed...white people and some negros."[125]

120. Vice Consul John Jenne to Second Assistant Secretary of State William Hunter, 12 August 1880, Reel 1, Despatches from U.S. Consuls in Nuevo Laredo, NARA.

121. Ibid., Clipping, ca. August 1880.

122. Ibid., Report, 27 July 1883.

123. John G. Bourke, *An Apache Campaign in the Sierra Madre*, Lincoln: U of Nebraska Press, 1987, 83.

124. Report to Second Assistant Secretary of State, 20 July 1879, Reel 1, Despatches from U.S. Consuls in Chihuahua, NARA.

125. Ibid., Report to Second Assistant Secretary of State, 7 November 1879.

* * *

In between abolition and an embryonic fascism, there emerged the system of Jim Crow or U.S. apartheid. Rather than the 1860s scheme favored for a time by the likes of the now sainted Abraham Lincoln—emancipation then deportation—there arrived instead a kind of internal exile for Negroes, a funhouse mirror image of what rebels chose for themselves postwar in Mexico, Cuba and Brazil. There was a not unsuccessful attempt to create a "separate but unequal" Negro society within the borders of the former slaveholders' republic. But, alas, this apartheid was compromised when, owing to its growing global obligations in competition with the socialist camp, the U.S. had to retreat from the more egregious aspects of Jim Crow in an attempt to win "hearts and minds" in a colonized Africa and the Caribbean, then moving toward sovereignty in the mid-20th century.

But beginning in 1989 the socialist camp began to disintegrate, and correspondingly, there was lessened pressure on U.S. imperialism to undermine the tangled legacies of slavery and Jim Crow. However, as this 1950s offensive was unfolding, strategically weakened were the forces most keen to pursue a global agenda and, as well, build working-class coalitions with the grit and strength to confront those on the other side of the barricades.[126]

* * *

In order to understand the persistence of conservatism—indeed, fascist inclinations—in the U.S., it is necessary to understand the "Indigenous Question" in the West, beginning with Oklahoma and spreading westward to the Pacific Northwest and due northward to the Dakotas and Montana. And one must also understand what used to be called the "Negro Question," spreading eastward from Texas through Dixie. Actually, Texas is the linchpin insofar as it illustrates the lengths to which settlers reached in order to "resolve" the Indigenous Question and the depths to which they sank in order to bludgeon the population now known as "African-American"—which, if not careful, can in coming decades endure the obliterative fate of the proud Comanche, once hailed as the "Lords of the Plains."

---

126. Horne, *Communist*.

Epilogue

The Struggle Continues

It is telling that in a book detailing the awfulness of the "Trail of Tears," the expulsion of Indigenes from the southeast quadrant of North America to an uncertain fate in what became Oklahoma, the author chose to cite the notorious quotation from Adolf Hitler wherein he equated the expelled Indigenes with those of Eastern Europe and declaimed ghoulishly, "'the Volga must be our Mississippi.'"[1] This was illuminative of the horrid reality that in a number of ways, Berlin in the 1930s and 1940s emulated Washington in the 1830s and 1840s. The failure to halt or even slowdown the latter served to lubricate the path for the former.[2]

The Bulgarian Communist Georgi Dimitrov, who fought fascism toe-to-toe during its rise and was one of the first to theorize this monstrosity, spoke of it as the open terrorist dictatorship of the most reactionary, chauvinistic and imperialist wing of the ruling elite.[3] In practice and befitting an apartheid system, the U.S. operated on two tracks, with fascist-like methods deployed against the enslaved and Indigenes and those so bold as to stand with them or act in rebellion like them, while a kind of bourgeois democracy was accorded settlers that qualified. What needs to be considered today is this: with the retreat of Jim Crow in the 1950s, not least in revulsion flowing from the anti-fascist war, and the concomitant erosion of the socialist camp of which those like Dimitrov were a constituent element, will fascism be extended more broadly, beyond the boundaries of its 19th-century precursors?

Preliminary signs are not encouraging and it is not simply because the parallels with high fascism are so foreboding—genocide, mass dispossession, demagogy, chauvinism, wars of aggression, religion instrumentalized, runaway patriarchy, class collaboration especially in the Pan-European community, and as a direct result labor subdued

1. Saunt, xvi.

2. John Whitman, *Hitler's American Model: The United States and the Making of Nazi Race Law*, Princeton: Princeton U Press, 2017.

3. Stella D. Blagoeva, *Dimitrov: A Biography*, New York: International, 1934.

along with its complement, the left-wing. Encouraging, however, is that the model for fascism that is Texas illustrates that resistance persists. The lingering question is whether the international climate will provide tailwinds—or headwinds.

The horrid parallels between the 1930s and today were prefigured by the desperate gambit of slaveholding rebels who sought to reaffirm the construction of a state built on a towering mountain of African corpses victimized by enslavement and the ongoing cry to "exterminate" Indigenes. These maniacal obsessions did not die in 1865. Appropriately, Francis Lubbock, the Texas governor during this brutal war, carries a name that disgraces a major city in the western part of the state: he accompanied Jefferson Davis as he scurried from arrest in 1865—en route to Texas—and by 1905 asked to be buried in his gray military uniform, symbolizing the struggle to perpetuate slavery forevermore.[4]

Just before Lubbock expired, the oil gusher known as "Spindletop" adjacent to Beaumont was uncovered. It was the "El Dorado of its time," says one scholar, creating fortunes that were to subsidize reactionary politics for decades to come. Unsurprisingly, as late as 1940 Black oil workers accounted for 0.5% of all employees in U.S. oil exploration and production and 3.0% of all refinery workers. Also predictable was that East Texas would develop some of the more garish lynchings and naked terrorism targeting Black people,[5] including a horrid 1916 episode when the teeth of a victim were sold for $5 apiece: a mob of 15,000 viewed the spectacle as the man was torched.[6]

Thus, in the 1920s Dallas was widely regarded as "the most racist city" in the nation. The modern scholar Andrés Tijerina went a step further and called Texas "the most brutally racist place in the United States."[7] These notorious credentials were cemented by the fact that Dallas reportedly had the largest Ku Klux Klan chapter in the nation in the 1920s and decades later had a thriving branch of the John Birch Society.[8]

---

4. Flusche, 87.

5. Darren Dochuk, *Anointed with Oil: How Christianity and Crude Made Modern America*, New York: Basic, 2019, 104, 113 (abbrev. Dochuk).

6. Jane Wolfe, *The Murchisons: The Rise and Fall of a Texas Dynasty*, New York: St. Martin's, 1989, 31.

7. Burrough, 187, 290.

8. Edward H. Miller, *The Nut Country: Right Wing Dallas and the Birth of the Southern Strategy*, Chicago: U of Chicago Press, 2015, 70 (abbrev. E.H. Miller). See also Alexander Charles Comer, Jr., "Invisible Empire in the Southwest:

Contributing to the overall lawlessness was the reality that cities like Galveston devolved from smuggling of enslaved Africans into the smuggling of moonshine in the early 20th century, which laid a foundation for a resurgence of organized crime[9]—not a force for equal opportunity.

These formidable obstacles notwithstanding, Texas by the 1930s developed one of the more vibrant branches of the U.S. Communist Party. In the preceding decade, Lovett Fort-Whiteman, born in 1894 in Dallas, was regarded widely as the "first Black member" of the U.S. Communist Party.[10] Then Emma Tenayuca and her spouse, Homer Brooks of that same party, contributed significantly to a theoretical viewpoint that sought to comprehend the population of Mexican origin in Texas and due west.[11]

At the same time El Paso—as distant from the fields of blood that characterized East Texas as Chicago was from New York—developed an important pole of resistance against Jim Crow that culminated in voting rights successes in the 1940s that had national impact.[12]

Even then, however, the preponderance of the state's population resided due east, meaning Texas continued to be a bulwark for Dixiecrats, the ascension of Lyndon B. Johnson and Ralph Yarborough notwithstanding.[13]

During this era, Roy Cullen of Houston was regarded as probably the richest man in the U.S. His mother had moved from South Carolina to Texas after the family's plantation was immolated; his grandfather fought in the secession war against Mexico. His competitor in this dubious race for filthy lucre, H.L. Hunt, had a father who fought alongside the Dixie secessionists in 1861. He was often dubbed the richest man in the world. The other member of this Texas troika, Clint Murchison, like the other two, had a penchant

---

The Ku Klux Klan in Texas, Louisiana, Oklahoma and Arkansas, 1920-1930," Ph.D. dissertation, UT-A, 1962.

9. Kimber Fountain, *The Maceos and the Free State of Galveston: An Authorized History*, Charleston: History Press, 2020.

10. *New York Amsterdam News*, 12-18 August 2021.

11. Emma Tenayuca and Homer Brooks, "The Mexican Question in the Southwest," *The Communist*, (No. 3, 1939): 257-268.

12. Darlene Clark Hine, *Black Victory: The Rise and Fall of the White Primary in Texas*, Millwood, N.Y.: KTO, 1979.

13. David A. Bateman, et al., eds., *Southern Nation: Congress and White Supremacy after Reconstruction*, Princeton: Princeton U Press, 2020. Cf., Patrick Cox, *Ralph W. Yarborough, the People's Senator*, Austin: U of Texas Press, 2002.

for employing "Negro servants"—a throwback to slavery perhaps? Virtually every radical right-wing movement in the U.S. during the 1950s was propped up by these Texas oilmen—including virulent anti-Semitism and the shenanigans of Senator Joseph McCarthy of Wisconsin. Their placeman, Governor R. Allan Shivers of Texas, proposed that Communist Party membership be just cause for imposing the death penalty, while Cullen was the largest individual donor to U.S. politicians in 1952 and 1954.

The relationship of these "oiligarchs" with the state was cemented by the reality that the U.S. Navy was likely the largest purchaser of oil in the world. Their parasitical tie to Mexico was embodied in Murchison owning a half million acres there. By 1963, the phone number of Hunt's son was found in the pocket of Jack Ruby, assassin of the accused assassin of President John F. Kennedy. Naturally, Hunt was briefed about the findings of the investigation into these foul crimes—before Earl Warren himself, the titular head of the commission and Chief Justice of the U.S. Supreme Court. Hunt's putrid spewing was broadcast on 500 radio stations at its height, which aided his food sideline which—while tainted—was dumped in Black communities. Even William F. Buckley, scion of yet another Texas oil fortune and patron saint of modern conservatism, felt that Hunt gave "'capitalism a bad name....'"[14]

As early as 1902 Texas oil production outstripped that of the rest of the world combined. So, not only was Murchison a major landowner in Mexico, he also had a 300,000-acre ranch he never visited. Not only did Hunt command the radio airwaves, his newspaper column was printed in 1800 newspapers. Not only did Murchison back McCarthy, he regarded him as a brother.[15] Cullen was not just a conservative but a donor to the leading Dixiecrat and ultra-right candidate for president in 1948, J. Strom Thurmond of South Carolina. And Hunt's maunderings were often filtered through the proliferating Christian anticommunist networks.[16]

Not only were these men avid backers of Senator McCarthy, he was also considered Texas's "third U.S. Senator." Hunt's backers included leading movie star John Wayne and premier cleric Norman Vincent Peale.[17]

---

14. Bryan Burrough, *The Big Rich: The Rise and Fall of the Greatest Texas Oil Fortunes*, New York: Penguin, 2009, 19, 20, 56, 82, 126, 135, 221, 229, 232, 241, 255, 308, 309, 336, 343, 354, 389.

15. Jane Wolfe, *The Murchisons: The Rise and Fall of a Texas Dynasty*, New York: St. Martin's, 1989, 26, 141, 194, 197.

16. Dochuk, 359, 361.

17. E.H. Miller, 31, 52.

By the 1970s Texas had created the biggest, most profound punishment system in the history of the U.S. and was a leader in imposing the death penalty besides, disproportionately exacted against the descendants of enslaved Africans. Coincidentally, this was occurring as Texas was becoming one of the most diverse regions nationally in the country, as if this were a response to multiculturalism.[18]

By the 21st century, Texas had the most sizable Black population in the U.S.,[19] a demographic reality which—as history indicates—often generated fierce Negrophobic reaction, as this prison-industrial complex suggests.

This contributed to a major trend of the current century: Texas is to the U.S. as the U.S. is to the world—suggesting that if you want to change the U.S., then the world: start in the Lone Star State. Trends in Austin influenced other state capitals, from the death penalty to circumscribing the reproductive freedom of women. Washington has played a pivotal role in the 20th century by igniting a global movement against socialism, which amounted to a movement against wealth redistribution, that reached a bloodstained apex during the genocidal war in Indo-China, but also encompassed support for the status quo in the land of apartheid.[20] The impetus for this ill-fated turn was distilled in Texas with the hysterical reaction to abolition, that amounted to one of the more profound chapters in wealth redistribution in world history, when the enslavers were expropriated without compensation, plunging many a settler family into penury, sparking enragement of a kind rarely seen. At the same time the enslaved were poised to reclaim the fruits of their labor from this very same process. Out of this vortex was generated an ongoing attempt to turn back the clock, which today could lead to an antebellum heir: fascism.

Moreover, with regard to anti-labor crusades,[21] Texas, because of its size and population density, has been in the vanguard, which in turn has provided fertile soil for all manner of outrages. As ever, the population diversity of the state, with a still sizable population of Mexican origin, provided even more targets for white supremacists to target.[22]

---

18. R. Perkinson, viii.

19. Christine Samir, "The Growing Diversity of Black America," Washington, D.C.: Pew Research Center, 2021.

20. Horne, *White Supremacy.*

21. Bruce A. Glasrud and James Maroney, eds., *Texas Labor History*, College Station: TA&MU Press, 2013.

22. Nicholas Villanueva, Jr., *The Lynching of Mexicans in the Texas Borderlands*, Albuquerque: U of New Mexico Press, 2017; Monica Muñoz Martinez,

When the man who became the 45th U.S. president began in 2015 his campaign for this high office, he singled out Mexico and Mexicans for censure and obloquy.[23] His tempestuous reign garnered major support in Texas. After the Attorney General of the State of New York sued his ally, the gun-crazy National Rifle Association, President Donald J. Trump instantly proposed that the group "'should move to Texas and lead a very good and beautiful life.'"[24]

Months later came the attempted coup of 6 January 2021, when Trump supporters stormed Capitol Hill and sought to prevent the peaceful transfer of power. In the hubbub following this cataclysm, the Attorney General of the State of Texas—Ken Paxton—was the only person in the 50 states holding this august position who declined to condemn this outrage; he actually spoke at the rally in Washington, D.C., preceding the putsch.[25] Ineluctably, Texas supplied more arrestees on 6 January than any other jurisdiction,[26] including next-door Virginia, which had led the nation into Civil War but whose lightning rod role has been supplanted by its former Confederate comrade.

Participation in this enragement of 6 January was not necessarily a cause for marginalizing—it may have been a badge of honor. Thus, Mark Middleton, who was accused of assaulting police officers on this fateful day, is—as I write—running for a seat in the legislature in Austin on the Republican Party ticket with an emphasis on "Texas sovereignty."[27] (Of late, secession talk has again arisen in Texas and, instead of the Democratic Party being in the vanguard, it has been replaced by the GOP—as the former lost the settler vote in the 1960s when it moved against Jim Crow.)

Texas is also in the vanguard of seeking to move the nation rightward on matters such as "Critical Race Theory" or providing an accurate account of Texas's bloodstained history in classrooms, voting rights and other fraught matters. The latter led to the recent blaring headline: "Texas gerrymandering is about keeping a grip

---

The Injustice Never Leaves You: Anti-Mexican Violence in Texas, Cambridge: Harvard U Press, 2018.

23. Raúl Hinojosa-Ojeda and Edward Teller, *The Trump Paradox: Migration, Trade and Racial Politics in U.S.-Mexico Integration*, Oakland: U of California Press, 2021.

24. *New York Times*, 7 August 2020.

25. *Houston Chronicle*, 14 January 2021.

26. *Houston Chronicle*, 28 May 2021. Cf., *Houston Chronicle*, 11 December 2021: More arrestees came from Florida on 6 January.

27. *The Hill*, 30 November 2021.

on white power,"[28] a resonant theme since 1836. This is a long-term trend causing one scholar to speak credibly of "America's Lone Star Constitution,"[29] insofar as too many decisions by the U.S. Supreme Court dragging the nation rightward have involved Texas litigants. Current governor Greg Abbott has spoken of "Texas Exceptionalism" as an analog to so-called "American Exceptionalism." Just as Washington's foreign policy has sought to impose its assumed uniqueness on the planet as a whole, Austin is acting similarly with regard to the nation.[30]

Amid the gloom and doom, there remains room for optimism. Early in 2021 Martin Luther King III, son of the slain Nobel Laureate, arrived in Oaxaca for the 190th anniversary of the death of Mexican President Vicente Guerrero, who in 1829 unleashed abolition of slavery, which then sparked Texas secession, then civil war, then delivering to us to the complicated present. He was accompanied by President Andrés Manuel López Obrador and was welcomed in turn by the population of African descent, which was estimated at about 5% in Oaxaca and 2% nationally.[31] In extending the hand of friendship across the border, this development of a foreign policy "from below" is a surefire way to block the ascendancy of a recrudescent fascism.

---

28. *Los Angeles Times*, 8 December 2021.

29. Lucas A. Powe, Jr., *America's Lone Star Constitution: How Supreme Court Cases from Texas Shape the Nation*, Oakland: U of California Press, 2018.

30. *New York Times*, 13 December 2021.

31. *New York Amsterdam News*, 18-24 August 2021.

Abbreviations and Sources

N.B. Only archival collections and titles cited more than once are included in the following lists. As the reader is more likely to search out the full description of the source by the abbreviation provided, this list is in alphabetical order by abbreviation. In cases where a title has been published in multiple volumes, this fact has been noted, with only the date of the first cited title in the series.

Archival Collections

AAS: American Antiquarian Society, Worcester, Massachusetts.

Anderson Papers: Gary Anderson Papers, UOk-N.

Ansley Journal: John Augustus Ansley Journal, UT-A.

APL: Austin Public Library.

Bacon Papers: Edward W. Bacon Papers, AAS.

Barker Collection UT-A: Eugene Barker Collection, UT-A.

Baylor U: Baylor University, Waco, Texas.

Bolton Papers: Herbert Bolton Papers, UC-B.

CCSC: College of Charleston, South Carolina.

CFR: Committee on Foreign Relations, South Carolina Department of Archives and History-Columbia.

Early AARM: Early African American Research Materials, APL.

FBR: Records of the Assistant Commissioner for the State of Texas, Bureau of Refugees, Freedmen and Abandoned Land, 1865-1869, U of Houston-Texas.

Galveston Consulate: Galveston Consulate, Diplomatic Archives-Paris, France.

Graybill Papers: Levi Graybill Papers, Huntington Library.

Green Papers: Thomas Jefferson Green Papers, UNC-CH.

Hamilton Correspondence: John and William Hamilton Correspondence, Library of Congress, Washington, D.C.

Heflin Papers: Cleon Eugene Heflin Papers, UOk-N.

Historic New Orleans: Williams Research Center, Historic New Orleans Collection.

Huntington Library: Huntington Library, San Marino, California.

Index of General Orders: "Index of General Orders, Department of Texas, 1865," Huntington Library.

IPP: Indian Pioneer Papers, UOk-N.

Jefferson Davis Papers: Jefferson Davis Papers, Emory U, Atlanta.

Kendall Papers: William Kay Kendall Papers, UOk-N.

Letters Received: Letters Received by the Department of Justice from the State of Texas, 1871-1884, NARA.

LSU: Louisiana State University.

Mason Correspondence: Richard Barnes Mason Correspondence Regarding Texas Indians, Huntington Library.

Mayhall: M.P. Mayhall, "Indian Relations in Texas, 1820-1835," n.d., Box 2 B 112, Eugene Barker Papers, UT-A.

MoHS: Missouri Historical Society-St. Louis.

Morgan Collection: Mrs. L.N. Morgan Collection, UOk-N.

Mugarrieta Papers: José Marcos Mugarrieta Papers, UC-B.

NARA: National Archives and Records Administration, College Park, Maryland.

NARA-DC: National Archives and Records Administration-Washington, D.C.

NYHS: New-York Historical Society, Manhattan.

NYU: New York University.

Pease, Graham, Nile Papers: Pease, Graham and Nile Families Papers-APL.

Porter Papers: Kenneth Wiggins Porter Papers, Schomburg Center for Research in Black Culture, Harlem, New York Public Library.

Rice U: Rice University [Institute], Houston.

Rickard Papers: James Helme Rickard Papers, AAS.

Riddell: John Leonard Riddell Manuscripts, Tulane U, New Orleans.

Robey Collection: Roberta Robey Collection, UOk-N.

Ross Collection: John Ross Collection, Division of Manuscripts Collection, UOk-N.

Saligny: Alphonse Du Bois de Saligny Translation Project Records, APL.

Sam Houston Papers: Governor Sam Houston Papers, Texas Archives.

SMU: Southern Methodist University.

Stephen Foreman Collection: Stephen Foreman Collection, UOk-N.

Stoes Papers: Kathleen Stoes Papers, New Mexico State U-Las Cruces.

TA&MU: Texas A&M University.

TCU: Texas Christian University.

Terrell Papers: Alexander Watkins Terrell Papers, UT-A.

Texas Archives: Texas State Archives-Austin.

Texas Legation: Records of Texas Legation to U.S., Texas State Archives-Austin.

Texas Republic SoS: Records of Texas Republic Secretary of State, Texas State Archives-Austin.

Throckmorton Papers: James Throckmorton Papers, UT-A.
TTU: Texas Tech University, Lubbock.
UC-B: University of California-Berkeley.
UNC-CH: University of North Carolina-Chapel Hill.
UNT: University of North Texas.
UOk-N: University of Oklahoma-Norman.
UT-A: University of Texas-Austin.
UT-Arl: University of Texas-Arlington.
UT-EP: University of Texas-El Paso.
UT-PA: University of Texas-Pan American.
UVa-C: University of Virginia-Charlottesville.
VaHS-R: Virginia Historical Society-Richmond.
Ward Papers: Thomas William Ward Papers, APL.
Wigfall Papers: Louis Wigfall Papers, UT-A.

Books, Pamphlets, Journal Articles, Dissertations and Theses

Abel 1993: Annie Heloise Abel, *The American Indian and the End of the Confederacy, 1863-1866*, Lincoln, Neb.: Bison Books, 1993.

Abel and Klingberg: Annie Heloise Abel and Frank J. Klingberg, eds., *A Side Light on Anglo-American Relations, 1839-1858, Furnished by the Correspondence of Lewis Tappan and Others with the British and Foreign Anti-Slavery Foreign Society*, Lancaster, Pennsylvania: Association for the Study of Negro Life and History, 1927.

Abert: John Galvin, ed., James W. Abert, *Through the Country of the Comanche Indians in the Fall of the Year 1845, the Journal of a U.S. Army Expedition...*, San Francisco: Howell, 1970.

A.D. Ivan: Adrien D. Ivan, "Masters No More: Abolition and Texas Planters, 1860-1890," Ph.D. dissertation, UNT, 2010.

A.E. Roberts: Alaina E. Roberts, *I've Been Here All the While: Black Freedom on Native Land*, Philadelphia: U of Pennsylvania Press, 2021.

A. Jones: Anson Jones, *Memoranda and Official Correspondence Relating to the Republic of Texas, its History and Annexation*, New York: Appleton, 1859.

A.L. Fowler: Arlen Lowery Fowler, "The Negro Infantry in the West, 1860-1891," Ph.D. dissertation, Washington State U, 1968.

Ames and Lundy: Julius Rubens Ames and Benjamin Lundy, *The Anti-Texass Legion Protest of Some Free Men, States and Presses Against the Texass Rebellion Against the Laws of Nature and Nations*, Albany, 1844, NYHS.

Anderson: W. L. Anderson, et al., eds., *Guide to Cherokee Documents in Foreign Archives*, Metuchen, N.J.: Scarecrow Press, 1983.

Andress: Elsye Drennan Andress, "The Gubernatorial Career of Andrew Jackson Hamilton," M.A. thesis, TTU, 1955.

Annexation of Texas: Opinions: "Annexation of Texas: Opinions of Messrs. Clay, Polk, Benton & Van Buren on the Immediate Annexation of Texas," Washington, D.C.?, 1844, MoHS.

Annual Report of the Secretary of the Interior, 1859: "Annual Report of the Secretary of the Interior to Congress, of December 1, 1859," Box 1, Heflin Papers.

Appleton and Palfrey: "Correspondence Between Nathan Appleton and John G. Palfrey Intended as a Supplement to Mr. Palfrey's Pamphlet on the Slave Power," Boston: Eastburn, 1846, MoHS, also NYHS.

A Report and Treatise: "A Report and Treatise on Slavery and the Slavery Agitation...printed by Order of the House of Representatives of Texas, December 1857," Austin: Marshall, 1857, Huntington Library.

A. Smith: Ashbel Smith, "Reminiscences of the Texas Republic, Annual Address Delivered Before the Historical Society of Galveston," 15 December 1875, Huntington Library.

Audain: Mekala Shadd-Sartor Audain, "Mexican Canaan: Fugitive Slaves and Free Blacks on the American Frontier, 1804-1867," Ph.D. dissertation, Rutgers U, 2014.

Austin Papers: Eugene Barker, ed., *The Austin Papers, October 1834-January 1837*, Washington: Government Printing Office, 1924-1928, multiple volumes.

A. Waters: Andrew Waters, ed., *I Was Born in Slavery: Personal Accounts of Slavery in Texas*, Winston-Salem: Blair, 2003.

A.W. Terrell: Alexander Watkins Terrell, *From Texas to Mexico and the Court of Maximilian in 1865*, Dallas: Book Club of Texas, 1933.

Bacha-Garza, *Civil War*: Roseann Bacha-Garza, et al., eds., *The Civil War on the Rio Grande, 1846-1876*, College Station: TA&MU Press, 2019.

Baker, Seward: George E. Baker, ed., *The Works of William H. Seward*, New York: Redfield, 1853, multiple volumes.

Barba: Paul Andres Barba, "Enslaved in Texas: Slavery, Migration and Identity in Native Country," Ph.d. dissertation, U of California-Santa Barbara, 2016.

Barbee: James Edward Barbee, "A Brief History of the Early Barbee Families of Smith County, Texas," n.d., CCSC.

Barr: Alwyn Barr, "Freedom and Slavery in the Republic: African American Experiences in the Republic of Texas," in Howell and Swanlund.

Bassett: John Spencer Bassett, ed., *The Correspondence of Andrew Jackson*, Washington, D.C.: Carnegie, 1926.

Baumgartner: Alice Baumgartner, "Abolition from the South: Mexico and the Road to U.S. Civil War, 1821-1867," Ph.D. dissertation, Yale U, 2018.

B.C. Curtis: Bearington Cecil Curtis, "A Sisyphean Task: Reevaluating Reconstruction in Texas Under the Command of Major General Charles Griffin," M.A. thesis, TA&MU, 2020.

Bell: William H. Bell, "Knights of the Golden Circle, Its Organization and Activities in Texas Prior to the Civil War," M.A. thesis, Texas College of Arts and Industries, 1965.

Bielski: Mark F. Bielski, *The Mortal Blow to the Confederacy: The Fall of New Orleans, 1862*, El Dorado Hills, California: Savas Beatie, 2021.

Bigelow: John Bigelow, *France and the Confederate Navy, 1862-1868*, New York: Harper & Bros., 1888.

Blaufarb: Rafe Blaufarb, *Bonapartists in the Borderlands: French Exiles and Refugees on the Gulf Coast, 1815-1835*, Tuscaloosa: U of Alabama Press, 2005.

Bolton: S. Charles Bolton, *Fugitivism: Escaping Slavery in the Lower Mississippi Valley, 1820-1860*, Fayetteville: U of Arkansas Press, 2019.

Bonham: Milledge Bonham, "The French Consuls in the Confederate States," in *Studies in Southern History and Politics*, New York: Columbia U Press, 1914.

Booker: Charles Albro Booker, ed., *Memoirs of Elisha Oscar Crosby, Reminiscences of California and Guatemala from 1849 to 1864*, San Marino: Huntington, 1945.

Bradley: Ed Bradley, "Forgotten Filibusters: Private Hostile Expeditions from the United States into Spanish Texas, 1812-1821," Ph.D. dissertation, U of Illinois, 1999.

Brann: William Cowper Brann, *A Collection of Writings of W.C. Brann*, Waco: Herz, 1905, multiple volumes.

Brice: Donaly E. Brice, *The Great Comanche Raid: Boldest Indian Attack on the Texas Republic*, Austin: Eakin, 1987.

Buckingham: James Silk Buckingham, *The Slave States of America*, London: Fisher, 1842, multiple volumes.

Buenger: Walter Louis Buenger, "Stilling the Voice of Reason: Texas and the Union," Ph.D. dissertation, Rice U, 1979.

Bugbee, Slavery: Lester Gladstone Bugbee, "Slavery in Early Texas," *Political Science Quarterly*, 13 (1898).

Burrough: Bryan Burrough, et al., *Forget the Alamo: The Rise and Fall of an American Myth*, New York: Penguin, 2021.

Burton, *Black*: Arthur T. Burton, *Black, Red and Deadly: Black and Indian Gunfighters of the Indian Territories*, Fort Worth: Eakin, 1991.

Butler Correspondence: *Private and Official Correspondence of General Benjamin F. Butler, During the Period of the Civil War*, Norwood, Mass.: Plimpton, 1917, multiple volumes.

Carrigan: William Dean Carrigan, "Slavery on the Frontier: The Peculiar Institution in Central Texas," in Bruce A. Glasrud and Deborah M. Liles, eds., *African Americans in Central Texas History: From Slavery to Civil Rights*, College Station: TA&MU, 2019.

Caughfield: Adrienne Helene Caughfield, *Mothers of the West: Women in Texas and their Roles in Manifest Destiny, 1820-1860*, TCU, 2002.

C.F. Adams: Charles Francis Adams, ed., *Memoirs of John Quincy Adams Comprising Portions of His Diary from 1795 to 1848*, Philadelphia: Lippincott, multiple volumes.

Chakkalakal and Warren: Tess Chakkalakal and Kenneth W. Warren, eds., *Jim Crow, Literature, and the Legacy of Sutton E. Griggs*, Athens: U of Georgia Press, 2013.

Chambless: Beauford Chambless, "The First President of Texas: The Life of David Gouverneur Burnet," Rice U, Ph.D. dissertation, 1954.

Cobb: Russell Cobb, *The Great Oklahoma Swindle: Race, Religion and Lies in America's Weirdest State*, Lincoln: U of Nebraska Press, 2020.

Comar: Scott C. Comar, "The Tigua Indians of Ysleta Del Sur: A Borderland's Community," Ph.D. dissertation, UT-EP, 2015.

"Condition of Texas": "Condition of Texas...Message from the President of the United States...," 22, 24 December 1836, U.S. Congress. House of Representatives, 24th Congress, 2nd Session, Doc. No. 35, Huntington Library.

Connors and Muñoz: Thomas G. Connors and Raúl Isaí Muñoz, "Looking for the North American Invasion in Mexico City," *American Historical Review* 125 (No. 2, April 2020).

Conquest of Santa Fe: *The Conquest of Santa Fe and Subjugation of New Mexico by the Military Forces of the United States...*, Philadelphia: H. Packer, 1847, Huntington Library.

Cox: Keith William Cox, "Conflicts of Interest: Race, Class, Mexicanidad and the Negotiation of Rule in U.S. Occupied Mexico, 1846-1848," Ph.D. dissertation, U of California-Riverside, 2007.

Crenshaw: Ollinger Crenshaw, "The Knights of the Golden Circle," *American Historical Review*, 47 (No. 1, October 1941).

Crews: James Robert Crews, "Reconstruction in Brownsville, Texas," M.A. thesis, TTU, 1969.

Cutrer: Thomas Cutrer, "'My Wild Hunt Indians': The Journal of Willis L. Lang, First Lieutenant, Waco Rangers, 23 April-7 September," n.d., UOk-N.

Cutts: James Madison Cutts, *The Conquest of California and New Mexico, by the Forces of the United States in the Years 1846 & 1847*, Albuquerque: Horn & Wallace, 1965 [originally published 1847].

Daddysman 1976: James William Daddysman, "The Matamoros Trade, 1861-1865," Ph.D. dissertation, West Virginia U, 1976.

Daniel Webster: *The Writings and Speeches of Daniel Webster...*, Boston: Little Brown, 1903, multiple volumes.

Dean: Christopher C. Dean, *Letters on the Chickasaw and Osage Missions...*, Boston: Massachusetts Sabbath School Union, 1831.

de Courcy: Anne de Courcy, *The Husband Hunters: American Heiresses who Married into the British Aristocracy*, New York: St. Martin's, 2017.

DeLay: Brian DeLay, *War of a Thousand Deserts*, New Haven: Yale U Press, 2008.

De León: Arnoldo De León, *The Tejano Community, 1836-1900*, Dallas: SMU, 1997.

Dewees: W.B. Dewees, *Letters from an Early Settler of Texas*, Louisville: Morton & Griswold, 1852.

de Wit: Tim de Wit, "Land of Conspiracies: Pan-Indian Conspiracy Fears in the Union Government and the American Civil War in the Indian Territory, 1861-1866," date unclear, Faculty of Humanities, Vrije Universiteit van Amsterdam, Box 13, Division of Manuscripts Collection, UOk-N.

D.G. Wright: Mrs. D. Giraud Wright, *A Southern Girl in '61: The War-Time Memories of a Confederate Senator's Daughter*, New York: Doubleday, Page, 1905.

Dirkmaat: Gerrit John Dirmaat, "Enemies Foreign and Domestic: U.S. Relations with Mormons in the U.S. Empire in North America, 1844-1854," Ph.D. dissertation, U of Colorado, 2010.

Dochuk: Darren Dochuk, *Anointed with Oil: How Christianity and Crude Made Modern America*, New York: Basic, 2019.

Dorsett: Jesse Dorsett, "Blacks in Reconstruction Texas, 1865-1877," Ph.D. dissertation, TCU, 1981.

Downs: Fane Downs, "The History of Mexicans in Texas, 1820-1845," Ph.D. dissertation, TTU, 1970.

Drum: Stella M. Drum, ed., *Down the Santa Fe Trail and Into Mexico: The Diary of Susan Shelby Magoffin, 1846-1847*, Lincoln: U of Nebraska Press, 1962.

D. Stanley: Dorothy Stanley, ed., *The Autobiography of Sir Henry Morton Stanley*, Boston: Houghton Mifflin, 1909.

E.D. Adams: Ephraim Douglas Adams, ed., *British Diplomatic Correspondence Concerning the Republic of Texas, 1838-1846*, Austin: Texas State Historical Association, ca. 1918.

E.H. Miller: Edward H. Miller, *The Nut Country: Right Wing Dallas and the Birth of the Southern Strategy*, Chicago: U of Chicago Press, 2015.

E. King, *Great South*: Edward King, *The Great South...*, Baton Rouge: LSU Press, 1972 [originally published in 1874; this version edited by W.M. Drake and R.R. Jones].

E.King, *Southern States*: Edward King, *The Southern States of North America: A Record of Journeys...*, London: Blackie & Son, 1875.

Elam: Earl Henry Elam, "Anglo American Relations with the Wichita Indians in Texas, 1822-1859," M.A. thesis, TTU, 1967.

Ellis: George Edward Ellis, ed., *Letters Upon the Annexation of Texas, Addresses to Hon. John Quincy Adams, as Originally Published in the Boston Atlas Under the Signature of Lisle*, Boston: White, Lewis & Porter, 1845.

Erath: *Memoirs of George Erath*, Austin: Texas State Historical Association, 1923.

E.R. Bills: E.R. Bills, *The 1910 Slocum Massacre: An Act of Genocide in East Texas*, Charleston, S.C.: History Press, 2014.

Erman: Sam Erman, *Almost Citizens: Puerto Rico, the U.S. Constitution and Empire*, New York: Cambridge U Press, 2019.

Everett: Edward Everett, ed., *The Writings and Speeches of Daniel Webster...*, Boston: Little Brown, 1903, multiple volumes.

Examination and Review: Examination and Review of a Pamphlet Printed and Secretly Circulated by M.D. Gorostiza, Late Envoy Extraordinary from Mexico: Previous to His Departure from the United States and by Him Entitled 'Correspondence Between the Legation Extraordinary of Mexico and the Department of State of the United States Respecting the Passage of the Sabine, by the Troops Under the Command of General Gaines*, Washington, D.C.: Force, 1837, NYHS.

Faulk: Odie B. Faulk, "The Last Years of Spanish Texas, 1778-1821," Ph.D. dissertation, TTU.

Ferrell: Robert Ferrell, ed., *Monterrey Is Ours! The Mexican War Letters of Lieutenant Dana, 1845-1847*, Lexington: U Press of Kentucky, 2014.

F.J. Scott: Florence Johnson Scott, *"Old Rough and Ready" on the Rio Grande*: San Antonio: Naylor, 1935.

Flusche: Raymond Paul Flusche, "Francis Richard Lubbock," M.A. thesis, TTU, 1947.

Foreman, *Traveler*: Grant Foreman, ed., *A Traveler in Indian Territory: The Journal of Ethan Allen Hitchcock*, Norman: U of Oklahoma Press, 1996.

Fornell: Earl Wesley Fornell, "Island City: The Story of Galveston on the Eve of Secession, 1850-1860," Ph.D. dissertation, Rice U, 1955.

Franklin: Jimmie Lewis Franklin, *Journey Toward Hope: A History of Blacks in Oklahoma*, Norman: U of Oklahoma Press, 1982.

Frazier: Donald Shaw Frazier, "Blood and Treasure: Confederate Imperialists in the American Southwest," Ph.D. dissertation, TCU, 1992.

Froebel: Julius Froebel, *Seven Years' Travel in Central America, Northern Mexico and the Far West of the United States*, London: Bentley, 1869.

From Virginia: From Virginia to Texas 1835: Diary of Col. William F. Gray, Giving Details of His Journey to Texas and Return in 1835-1836 and Second Journey to Texas in 1837*, Houston: Young, 1965 [originally published 1909].

Gaff and Gaff: Alan D. Gaff and Donald H. Gaff, eds., *From the Halls of the Montezumas: Mexican War Dispatches from James L. Freaner, Writing Under the Name 'Mustang,'* Denton: UNT Press, 2019.

Garrison: George P. Garrison, *Diplomatic Correspondence of the Republic of Texas*, Washington: Government Printing Office, 1911, multiple volumes.

Gassner: John C. Gassner, "African American Fugitive Slaves and Freemen in Matamoros, Tamaulipas, 1820-1865," M.A. thesis, UT-PA, 2004.

Giddings: Joshua R. Giddings, *The Exiles of Florida*, Columbus, Ohio: Follett, Foster, 1858.

Gleason: Mildred S. Gleason, *Caddo: A Survey of Caddo Indians in Northeast Texas and Marion County, 1541-1840*, Jefferson, Texas: Marion County Historical Commission, 1981.

G. Nelson: George Nelson, *The Alamo: An Illustrated History*, Uvalde, Texas: Aldine, 2009.

González-Quiroga: Miguel Ángel González-Quiroga, *War and Peace on the Rio Grande Frontier, 1830-1880*, Norman: U of Oklahoma Press, 2020.

Govenar: Alan Govenar, compiler, *The Blues Come to Texas: Paul Oliver and Mack McCormick's Unfinished Book*, College Station: TA&MU Press, 2019.

Grandin: Greg Grandin, *The End of the Myth: From the Frontier to the Border Wall in the Mind of America*, New York: Holt, 2019.

Gray, Davis: Ronald N. Gray, "Edmund J. Davis: Radical Republican and Reconstruction Governor of Texas," Ph.D. dissertation, TTU, 1976.

Grear: Charles David Grear, "Texans to the Front: Why Texans Fought the Civil War," Ph.D. dissertation, TCU, 2005.

Green, *Calendar*: Michael R. Green, ed., *Calendar of the Papers of Mirabeau Buonaparte Lamar*, Austin: Texas State Library, 1982.

Gregg: Josiah Gregg, *Commerce of the Prairies or the Journal of a Santa Fe Trader During Eight Expeditions Across the Great Western Frontier and a Residence of Nearly Nine Years in Northern New Mexico*, New York: Langley, 1845, multiple volumes.

Guardino: Peter Guardino, *The Dead March: A History of the Mexican-American War*, Cambridge: Harvard U Press, 2017.

Hahn: Steven Hahn, *A Nation Without Borders: The United States and Its World in an Age of Civil Wars, 1830-1910*, New York: Penguin, 2017.

Hale: Edward Everett Hale, "How to Conquer Texas Before Texas Conquers Us," Boston: Redding & Co., 17 March 1845.

Hamalainen: Pekka Hamalainen, *Lakota America: A New History of Indigenous Power*, New Haven: Yale U Press, 2019.

Hammack: Maria Esther Hammack, "The Other Underground Railroad: Hidden Histories of Slavery and Freedom Across the Porous Frontiers of Nineteenth Century United States, Mexico and the Caribbean," M.A. thesis, East Carolina U, 2015.

Hampton: Neal McDonald Hampton, "A Dark Cloud Rests Upon our Nation: Lipan Sovereignty and Relations with Mexico, the United States and the Republic of Texas," M.A. thesis, U of Central Oklahoma, 2015.

Haynes, Somervell: Sam W. Haynes, "The Somervell and Mier Expeditions: The Political and Diplomatic Consequences of Frontier Adventurism in the Texas Republic, 1842-1844," Ph.D. dissertation, U of Houston, 1988.

Herrera: Jose Maria Herrera, "The Blueprint for Hemispheric Hegemony: Joel Roberts Poinsett and the First United Diplomatic Mission to Mexico," Ph.D. dissertation, Purdue U, 2007.

H.H. McConnell: H.H. McConnell, *Five Years a Cavalryman, or Sketches of Regular Army on the Texas Frontier, 1866-1871*, Norman: U of Oklahoma Press, 1996 [originally published Jacksboro, Texas: Rogers, 1889], Huntington Library.

Himmel: Kelly Frank Himmel, "Anglo-Texans, Karankawas and Tonkawas, 1821-1859: A Sociological Analysis of Conquest," Ph.D. dissertation, UT-A.

Hinze: Virginia Neal Hinze, "Norris Wright Cuney," M.A. thesis, Rice U, 1965.

H.M. Pease: Helen Marie Pease, "Elisha Marshall Pease (A Biography)," B.A. thesis, Incarnate Word College, May 1937, Box 112, Pease, Graham, Nile Papers.

Honeck: Mischa Honeck, 'We Are the Revolutionists': German Speaking Immigrants and American Abolitionists after 1848, Athens: U of Georgia Press, 2011.

Horne, Communist: Gerald Horne, Communist Front? The Civil Rights Congress, 1946-1956, New York: International, 2021.

Horne, Confronting Black Jacobins: Gerald Horne, Confronting Black Jacobins: The U.S., the Haitian Revolution and the Origins of the Dominican Republic, New York: Monthly Review Press, 2015.

Horne, Counter-Revolution of 1776: Gerald Horne, The Counter-Revolution of 1776: Slave Resistance and the Origins of the United States of America, New York: NYU Press, 2014.

Horne, Dawning: Gerald Horne, The Dawning of the Apocalypse: The Roots of Slavery, White Supremacy, Settler Colonialism and Capitalism in the Long 16th Century, New York: Monthly Review Press, 2020.

Horne, Negro Comrades: Gerald Horne, Negro Comrades of the Crown: African Americans and the British Empire Fight the U.S. Before Emancipation, New York: NYU Press, 2013.

Horne, Race to Revolution: Gerald Horne, Race to Revolution: The United States and Cuba During Slavery and Jim Crow, New York: Monthly Review Press, 2014.

Horne, White Supremacy: Gerald Horne, White Supremacy Confronted: U.S. Imperialism and Anticommunism vs. the Liberation of Southern Africa, from Rhodes to Mandela, New York: International, 2019.

Howell and Swanlund: Kenneth W. Howell and Charles Swanlund, eds., Single Star of the West: The Republic of Texas, 1836-1845, Denton: UNT Press, 2017.

Irby: James Arthur Irby, "Line of the Rio Grande: War and Trade on the Confederate Pioneer, 1861-1865," Ph.D. dissertation, U of Georgia, 1969.

Jacobus: Penelope Lea Jacobus, "The Scramble for Texas: European Diplomacy and Imperial Interest in the Republic of Texas, 1835-1846," Ph.D. dissertation, UT-EP, 2020.

Jameson: J. Franklin Jameson, ed., Correspondence of John C. Calhoun, Washington, D.C., 1899.

J.A. Slover: "Autobiography of James Anderson Slover...," 1860, UOk-N.

J.B. Moore: John Bassett Moore, ed., The Works of James Buchanan, Comprising His Speeches, State Papers and Private Correspondence, 1813-1830, London: Lippincott, multiple volumes, 1908.

J.D. Richardson, *Messages and Papers of Jefferson Davis*: James D. Richardson, ed., *The Messages and Papers of Jefferson Davis and the Confederacy, Including Diplomatic Correspondence, 1861-1865*, New York: Chelsea House, 1966.

J.D. Riley: John Denny Riley, "Santos Benavides: His Influence in the Lower Rio Grande, 1823-1891," Ph.D. dissertation, TCU, 1976.

J. Edwards: John Edwards, *Shelby's Expedition to Mexico: An Unwritten Leaf of the War*, Kansas City, Mo.: Kansas City Times Steam Book and Job Printing, 1872.

Jewett: Clayton E. Jewett, "On Its Own: Texas in the Confederacy," Ph.D. dissertation, Catholic U, 1998.

J.H. Smith: Justin H. Smith, *The Annexation of Texas*, New York: Baker and Taylor, 1911.

J.M. Morgan: James Morris Morgan, *Recollections of a Rebel Reefer*, Boston: Houghton Mifflin, 1917.

Joint Commission on Reconstruction: "U.S. Congress, Joint Commission on Reconstruction, Report: Florida, Louisiana, Texas," Washington, D.C., 1866.

J.M. Sullivan: Jerry Melton Sullivan, "Fort McKavett, Texas, 1852-1883," M.A. thesis, TTU, 1972.

Joseph Allen Stout, Last Years: Joseph Allen Stout, "The Last Years of Manifest Destiny: Filibustering in Northwestern Mexico, 1848-1862," Ph.D. dissertation, Oklahoma State U, 1971.

Joseph Allen Stout, *Liberators*: Joseph Allen Stout, *The Liberators: Filibustering Expeditions into Mexico, 1848-1852 and the Last Thrust of Manifest Destiny*, Los Angeles: Westernlore, 1973.

Joseph and Henderson: Gilbert M. Joseph and Timothy Henderson, eds., *The Mexico Reader: History, Culture, Politics*, Durham: Duke U Press, 2002.

Junius: Junius, "Annexation of Texas," New York: Greeley & McElrath, 1844, Oberlin College.

Kattner: Lauren A. Kattner, "Ethnicity Plus: Historical Roots of Slavery for the Germans of Louisiana and East Texas, 1719-1830," Ph.D. dissertation, UT-A, 1997.

Kennedy: William Kennedy, Esq., *Texas: The Rise, Progress and Prospects of the Republic of Texas*, London: Hastings, 1841, multiple volumes.

K.H. Jones: Kelly Houston Jones, *A Weary Land: Slavery on the Ground in Arkansas*, Athens: U of Georgia Press, 2021.

Kievit: Joyce Ann Kievit, "Dissension in the Cherokee Nation, 1860 to 1866," M.A. thesis, U of Houston-Clear Lake, 1992.

Kilbride: Daniel Kilbride, *Being American in Europe, 1750-1860*, Baltimore: Johns Hopkins U Press, 2013.

Kimball: J.P. Kimball, translator, *Laws and Decrees of the State of Coahuila and Texas in Spanish and English to which is added the Constitution of Said State: Also the Colonization Law of the State of Tamaulipas and Naturalization*

Law of the General Congress. By Order of the Secretary of State, Houston: Telegraph Power Press, 1839.

Kinard: Jeff Kinard, *Lafayette of the South: Prince Camille de Polignac and the American Civil War*, College Station: TA&MU Press, 2001.

King: Alvy Leon King, "Louis T. Wigfall: The Stormy Petrel," Ph.D. dissertation, TTU, 1967.

Kite: Jodella Dorothea Kite, "A Social History of the Anglo-American Colonies in Mexican Texas, 1821-1835," Ph.D. dissertation, TTU, 1990.

Klos: George Klos, "Blacks and the Seminole Removal Debate, 1821-1835," *Florida Historical Quarterly*, 68 (No. 1, 1989).

Koch: Lena Clara Koch, "The Federal Indian Policy in Texas, 1845-1860," *Southwestern Historical Quarterly*, 28 (No. 4, April 1925).

Krehbiel: Randy Krehbiel, *Tulsa, 1921: Reporting a Massacre*, Norman: U of Oklahoma Press, 2019.

Lack: Paul Dean Lack, "Urban Slavery in the Southwest," Ph.D. dissertation, TTU, 1973.

Lagarde: François Lagarde, ed., *The French in Texas: History, Migration, Culture*, Austin: U of Texas Press, 2003.

Lahti: Janne Lahti, *Wars for Empire: Apaches, the United States and the Southwest Borderlands*, Norman: U of Oklahoma Press, 2019.

Lanehart: David T. Lanehart, "The Navajos and the Peace Commission of 1867," M.A. thesis, TTU, 1981.

L.D. Rice: Lawrence Delbert Rice, "The Negro in Texas, 1874-1900," Ph.D. dissertation, TTU, 1968.

Lee: Nelson Lee, *Three Years Among the Comanches: The Narrative of Nelson Lee, the Texas Ranger*, [originally published Albany: Baker Taylor, 1859], Norman: U of Oklahoma Press, 1957.

Levander: Caroline Levander, "Sutton Griggs and the Borderlands of Empire," in Tess Chakkalakal and Kenneth W. Warren, eds., *Jim Crow, Literature, and the Legacy of Sutton E. Griggs*, Athens: U of Georgia Press, 2013.

Lewis: Felice Flanery Lewis, *Trailing Clouds of Glory: Zachary Taylor's Mexican War Campaign and His Emerging Civil War Leaders*, Tuscaloosa: U of Alabama Press, 2010.

L.S. Hudson: Linda Sybert Hudson, "Military Knights of the Golden Circle in Texas, 1854-1861," M.A. thesis, Stephen F. Austin U, 1990.

L. Thomas: Lately Thomas, *Between Two Empires: The Life Story of California's First Senator, William McKendree Gwin*, Boston: Houghton Mifflin, 1969.

L. Wright: Lawrence Wright, *God Save Texas: A Journey into the Soul of the Lone Star State*, New York: Random House, 2018.

Maillard: N. Doran Maillard, *The History of the Republic of Texas....*, London: Smith, Elder, 1842.

Maissin: Eugene Maissin, *The French in Mexico and Texas, 1838-1839*, Salado, Texas: Anson Jones Press, 1961.

Mann: Horace Mann, *Horace Mann's Letters on the Extension of Slavery into California and New Mexico: And on the Duty of the Congress to Provide the Trial by Jury for Fugitive Slaves*, Washington, D.C.: Buell and Blanchard, 1850, Huntington Library [reprinted Yellow Springs: Antioch Press, 1935].

Manning: William Manning, ed., Diplomatic Correspondence of the United States, Inter-American Affairs, 1831-1860, Washington, D.C.: Carnegie Endowment, 1939, multiple volumes.

Marryat: Captain Marryat, *Narrative of the Travels and Adventures of Monsieur Violet in California, Sonora and Western Texas*, New York: Harper & Bros., 1843.

Martelle: Scott Martelle, *William Walker's Wars: How One Man's Private American Army Tried to Conquer Mexico, Nicaragua and Honduras*, Chicago: Chicago Review Press, 2019.

Mayo: Robert Mayo, *Political Sketches of Eight Years in Washington; in Four Parts with Annotations to Each...*, Baltimore: Lucas, 1839.

McConnell, *Negro Troops*: Roland McConnell, *Negro Troops of Antebellum Louisiana: A History of the Battalion of Free Men of Color*, Baton Rouge: LSU Press, 1968.

M.C.F. Long: Mary Cole Farrow Long, *Stranger in a Strange Land: From Beaufort, South Carolina to Galveston Island, Republic of Texas, A Biography of Judge James Pope Cole*, Belton, Texas: Bear Hollow, 1986.

McReynolds: James M. McReynolds, "Family Life in a Borderland Community: Nacogdoches, Texas, 1779-1861," Ph.D. dissertation, TTU, 1978.

M.D. Brown: Marjorie Denise Brown, "Diplomatic Ties: Slavery and Diplomacy in the Gulf Coast Region, 1836-1845," Ph.D. dissertation, Vanderbilt U, 2017.

Meade: George Meade, *The Life and Letters of George Gordon Meade, Major General United States Army*, Scribner's, 1913, multiple volumes.

Messages of the President, 1848: "Messages of the President of the United States: with the Correspondence, Therewith Communicated Between the Secretary of War and Other Officers of the Government Upon the Subject of the Mexican War: 30th Congress, 1st Session: Executive Document No. 56, House of Representatives, 1845-1849," Washington: Wendell and Benthuysen, 1848, Huntington Library.

M.G. Webster: Michael G. Webster, "Texan Manifest Destiny and the Mexican Border Conflict, 1865-1880," Ph.D. dissertation, Indiana U, 1972.

M.K. Nelson: Megan Kate Nelson, *The Three-Cornered War: The Union, the Confederacy and Native Peoples in the Fight for the West*, New York: Scribner, 2020.

Morrison: Lynda Sanderford Morrison, "The Life and Times of José Canuto Yela: Yucatecan Priest and Patriot (1802-1859)," Ph.D. dissertation, U of Alabama, 1993.

M.R. Moore: Michael Rugeley Moore, "Settlers, Slaves, Sharecroppers and Stockhands: A Texas Plantation Ranch, 1824-1896," M.A. thesis, U of Houston, 2001.

Naylor: Celia E. Naylor, *African Cherokees in Indian Territory: From Chattel to Citizens*, Chapel Hill: U of North Carolina Press, 2008.

N.C. Kendall: Sergeant N.C. Kendall, *Reminiscences of the Closing Scenes of the Great American Rebellion*, 1866, TTU.

Newcomb: W.W. Newcomb, Jr., *Indians of Texas*, Austin: U of Texas Press, 1961.

Newlin: Deborah Lamont Newlin, "The Tonkawa People: A Tribal History, From Earliest Times to 1893," M.A. thesis, TTU, 1981.

Newsome: Zoie Odom Newsome, "Antislavery Sentiment in Texas, 1821-1861," M.A. thesis, TTU, 1968.

Nichols 2012: James David Nichols, "The Limits of Liberty: African Americans, Indians and Peons in the Texas-Mexico Borderlands, 1820-1860," Ph.D. dissertation, State U of New York-Stony Brook, 2012.

Nichols 2018: James David Nichols, *The Limits of Liberty: Mobility and the Making of the Eastern U.S. Mexican Border*, Lincoln: U of Nebraska Press, 2018.

Niles: John Niles, *History of South America and Mexico...*, Hartford: Huntington, 1839.

Official Reports of Battles: *Official Reports of Battles*, Richmond: Smith, 1864.

Oldham and White: Williamson S. Oldham and George W. White, compilers, *A Digest of the General Statute Laws of the State of Texas...which were in Force Before the Declaration of Independence...*, Austin: Marshall, 1859.

Olmsted, *Cotton*: Frederick Law Olmsted, *The Cotton Kingdom: A Traveler's Observations on Cotton and Slavery in the American Slave States...*, New York: Mason, 1861, multiple volumes.

Olmsted, *Journey*: Frederick Law Olmsted, *A Journey Through Texas; or a Saddle Trip on the Southwestern Frontier with a Statistical Appendix*, New York: Dix, Edwards, 1857.

Original Reports: "Original Reports...State Department...", 29th Congress, 1st Session, 8 December 1845-7 August 1846," NARA-DC.

Origins and Objects: "Origins and Objects of the Slaveholders' Conspiracy Against Democratic Principles as well as Against the National Union—Illustrated in the Speeches of Andrew Jackson Hamilton, in the Statements of Lorenzo Sherwood, Ex-Member of the Texas Legislature and the Publications," New York: Baker & Godwin, 1862, Huntington Library.

Parker, *Notes*: W.B. Parker, *Notes Taken During the Expedition Commanded by Captain R.B. Marcy, USA, Through Unexplored Texas in the Summer and Fall of 1854*, Philadelphia: Hayes & Zell, 1856.

Paschal: Kristopher Paschal, "'Texas Must be a Slave Country:' The Development of Slavery in Mexican Texas and the Institution's Role in the Coming of Revolution, 1821-1836," M.A. thesis, SMU, 2010.

Phillips: Stephen C. Phillips, "An Address on the Annexation of Texas and the Aspect of Slavery in the United States in Connection therewith; Delivered in Boston, November 14 and 18, 1845," Boston: Crosby and Nichols, 1845, Oberlin College-Ohio.

Pierce: Edward Pierce, ed., *Memoir and Letters of Charles Sumner*, London: Low, Marston, Searle & Rivington, 1878, multiple volumes.

Pike: Corporal James Pike, *The Scout and Ranger: Being the Personal Adventures...as a Texas Ranger in the Indian Wars...*, Cincinnati: Hawley, 1865.

Pollard: Edward A. Pollard, *The Lost Cause: A New Southern History of the War of the Confederates*, New York: E.B. Treat, 1866.

Pridgen: H. McBride Pridgen, "People of Texas on the Protection of Slave Property," Austin, 1859, Harvard U, Cambridge, Mass.

Probus: "Probus," *The Texan Revolution...a Letter from Washington on the Annexation of Texas and the Late Outrage in California*, 1842, Huntington Library.

Quaife: Milo Milton Quaife, ed., *The Diary of James K. Polk During His Presidency, 1845 to 1849*, Chicago: McClurg, 1910, multiple volumes.

Ray: Kelly Ray, "Houston in Chains: Slaves and Free Blacks in the Texas Courts, 1845-1867," M.A. thesis, U of Houston, 2011.

Rejected Treaty: U.S. Congress, House of Representatives, 28th Congress, 1st Session, Doc. No. 271, Texas. Message from the President of the United States..., Rejected Treaty for the Annexation of the Republic of Texas to the United States..., [1844], Huntington Library.

Report of Operations: "Report of Operations of the United States Forces and General Information on the Condition of Affairs in the Military Division of the Southwest and Gulf and Department of the Gulf...from May 29, 1865...Major General Philip H. Sheridan...," Huntington Library.

Report of the Committee of Investigation 1873: *Report of the Committee of Investigation Sent in 1873 by the Mexican Government to the Frontier of Texas*, New York: Baker & Godwin, 1875.

R.E. Ruiz: Ramón Eduardo Ruiz, ed., *An American in Maximilian's Mexico, 1865-1866: The Diaries of William Marshall Anderson*, Huntington Library, 1959.

Richards: Thomas W. Richards, Jr., "The Texas Moment: Breakaway Republics and Contested Sovereignty in North America," Ph.D. dissertation, Temple U, 2016.

R.N. Richardson: Rupert Norval Richardson, *The Frontier of Northwest Texas, 1846 to 1876: Advance and Defense by the Pioneer Settlers of the Cross Timbers and Prairies*, Glendale: Clark, 1963.

Robbins: Fred Robbins, "The Origin and Development of the African Slave Trade in Galveston, Texas and Surrounding Areas from 1816 to 1836," *East Texas Historical Journal*, 9 (No. 2, October 1971).

Rowland: Duncan Rowland, ed., *Jefferson Davis, Constitutionalist: His Letters, Papers and Speeches*, Jackson: Mississippi Department of Archives and History, 1923, multiple volumes.

R. Perkinson: Robert Perkinson, "The Birth of the Texas Prison Empire, 1865-1915," Ph.D. dissertation, Yale U, 2001.

R. Taylor: Richard Taylor, *Destruction and Reconstruction: Personal Experiences of the Late War*, New York: Appleton, 1879.

Sainlaude: Stève Sainlaude, *France and the American Civil War: A Diplomatic History*, Chapel Hill: U of North Carolina Press, 2019.

Saunt: Claudio Saunt, *Unworthy Republic: The Dispossession of Native Americans and the Road to Indian Territory*, New York: Norton, 2020.

Scobie: John Scobie, "Texas: Its Claims to be Recognized as an Independent Power by Great Britain; Examined in a Series of Letters," London: Harvey and Darnton, 1839, Huntington Library.

S. Dorsey: Sarah A. Dorsey, *Recollections of Henry Watkins Allen, Brigadier-General Confederate States Army, Ex-Governor of Louisiana*, New York: Doolady, 1866.

Sedgwick: John Sedgwick, *Blood Moon: An American Epic of War and Splendor in the Cherokee Nation*, New York: Simon & Schuster, 2018.

S.F. Shannon: Stephen Franklin Shannon, "Galvestonians and Military Reconstruction, 1865-1867," M.A. thesis, Rice U, 1975.

Shawcross: Edward Shawcross, *The Last Emperor of Mexico*, New York: Basic, 2021.

Shelton: Robert Stuart Shelton, "Waterfront Workers of Galveston, Texas, 1838-1920," Ph.D. dissertation, Rice U, 2001.

Sheridan, *Memoirs*: *Personal Memoirs of* Philip *Henry Sheridan, General United States Army*, New York: Appleton, 1904, multiple volumes.

Shook: Robert Walter Shook, "Federal Occupation and Administration of Texas," Ph.D. dissertation, UNT, 1970.

Shuck: Sheri Marie Shuck, "Voices from the Southern Borderlands: The Alabamas and Coushattas, 1500-1859," Ph.D. dissertation, Auburn U, 2000.

Simpson: "A Bloody Christmas Eve: How the Death of Richards Fields and Lauerac Caused the Collapse of the Fredonian Republic," from Memoirs of John P. Simpson 1838-1841, originally from Steen Library, Stephen F. Austin State U, Box 4, Anderson Papers.

Sitton and Conrad: Thad Sitton and James H. Conrad, *Freedom Colonies: Independent Black Texans in the Time of Jim Crow*, Austin: U of Texas Press, 2005.

Slaveholders' Rebellion: "The Slaveholders' Rebellion Against the Democratic Institutions as well as Against the National Union, As set Forth in the Speech of the Hon. Lorenzo Sherwood, Ex-Member of the Texan Legislature, Delivered at Champlain in Northern New York, October 1862...," New York: Westcott, 1862.

S.L. Watts: Sandra Lee Watts, "A History of the Sugar Cane Industry with Special Reference to Brazoria County," M.A. thesis, Rice U, 1969.

Smallwood: James M. Smallwood, "Black Texans During Reconstruction, 1865-1874," Ph.D. dissertation, TTU, 1974.

S. Page: Sebastian Page, *Black Resettlement and the American Civil War*, New York: Cambridge U Press, 2021.

Stevens: Kenneth R. Stevens, ed., *The Texas Legation Papers*, Fort Worth: TCU Press, 2012.

Stiff: Colonel Edward Stiff, *The Texas Emigrant: A Narration of the Adventures of the Author in Texas....*, Cincinnati: Conclin, 1840.

Stout: Jay A. Stout, *Slaughter at Goliad: The Mexican Massacre: The Massacre of 400 Texas Volunteers*, Annapolis: Naval Institute Press, 2008.

Swanson: Doug J. Swanson, *Cult of Glory: The Bold and Brutal History of the Texas Rangers*, New York: Viking, 2020.

Tanner: Helen Hornbeck Tanner, *The Territory of the Caddo Tribe of Oklahoma...*, New York: Garland, 1974.

Texas Annexation Bill: "Texas Annexation Bill[,] Speech of Mr. Benton of Missouri in Reply to Mr. McDuffie, Delivered in the Senate of the United States, June 15, 1844," Washington, D.C.: Gideon's Office, 1844, MoHS.

Texas Constitution 1861: "The Constitution of the State of Texas as Amended in 1861...of the Confederate States of America...," Austin: Marshall, 1861, CCSC.

Thompson: Waddy Thompson, *Recollections of Mexico*: New York: Wiley and Putnam, 1846.

Thompson and Jones: Jerry Thompson and Lawrence T. Jones III, *Civil War and Revolution on the Rio Grande Frontier: A Narrative...History*, Austin: Texas State Historical Association, 2004.

Thompson, "...Santos Benavides and...Cortina": Jerry Thompson, "Colonel José de los Santos Benavides and General Juan Nepomuceno Cortina: Two Astounding Civil War Tejanos," in Bacha-Garza, *Civil War*.

Tilley, *McIntyre*: Nannie F. Tilley, ed., *Federals on the Frontier: The Diary of Benjamin F. McIntyre, 1862-1864*, Austin: U of Texas Press, 1963.

Torget, *Cotton*: Andrew John Torget, "Cotton Empire: Slavery and the Texas Borderlands, 1820-1837," Ph.D. dissertation, U of Virginia, 2009.

Torget, *Seeds*: Andrew J. Torget, *Seeds of Empire: Cotton, Slavery and the Transformation of the Texas Borderlands, 1800-1850*, Chapel Hill: U of North Carolina Press, 2015.

Tyler and Murphy: Ronnie C. Tyler and Lawrence R. Murphy, eds., *The Slave Narratives of Texas*, Austin: Encino, 1974.

V.M. Rose: Victor M. Rose, *Ross' Texas Brigade...*, Louisville: Courier-Journal, 1882.

Wagner: Leslie Alice Jones Wagner, "Disputed Territory: Rio Grande/Rio Bravo Borderlands, 1838-1840," M.A. thesis, UT-Arl, 1998.

Wahlstrom: Todd W. Wahlstrom, *The Southern Exodus to Mexico: Migration Across the Borderlands after the American Civil War*, Lincoln: U of Nebraska Press, 2015.

Waite: Kevin Waite, "The Slave South in the Far West: California, the Pacific and Proslavery Visions of Empire," Ph.D. dissertation, U of Pennsylvania, 2016.

Wallace and Hoebel: Ernest Wallace and E.A. Hoebel, *The Comanches: Lords of the South Plains*, Norman: U of Oklahoma Press, 1952.

War of the Rebellion: *The War of the Rebellion, A Compilation of the Official Records of the Union and Confederate Armies*, Washington, D.C.: Department of War, 1900, multiple volumes.

Watson: Tom V. Watson, "A Study of Agriculture in Colonial Texas, 1821-1836," M.A. thesis, TTU, 1935.

W.C. Gaines: W. Craig Gaines, *The Confederate Cherokees: John Drew's Regiment of Mounted Rifles*, Baton Rouge: Louisiana State U Press, 1989.

W.E.H. Gramp: W.E.H. Gramp, *The Journal of a Grandfather*, St. Louis: W.E. Hughes, 1912.

Wharton: Clarence R. Wharton, *The Republic of Texas: A Brief History of Texas from the First American Colonies in 1821 to Annexation in 1846*, Houston: Young, 1922.

Wilbarger: J.W. Wilbarger, *Indian Depredations in Texas. Reliable Accounts of Battles, Wars, Adventures, Forays, Murders, Massacres, etc. Together with Biographical Sketches of Many of the Most Noted Fighters and Frontiersmen of Texas*, Austin: Hutchings, 1889.

William Fairfax Gray: Paul Lack, ed., "The Diary of William Fairfax Gray: From Virginia to Texas, 1835," Dallas: De Golyer Library, Clements Center, SMU, 1997.

Williams and Barker: Amelia W. Williams and Eugene Barker, eds., *The Writings of Sam Houston, 1813-1863*, Austin: Pemberton, 1970, multiple volumes.

Wilson and Thompson: John P. Wilson and Jerry Thompson, eds., *The Civil War in West Texas and New Mexico: The Lost Letterbook of Brigadier General Henry Hopkins Sibley*, El Paso: Texas Western Press, 2001.

Winfrey: Dorman H. Winfrey, ed., *Texas Indian Papers, 1825-1843, Edited From the Original Manuscript Copies in the Texas State Archives*, Austin: Texas State Library, 1959.

Winkler: E.W. Winkler, ed., *Manuscripts, Letters and Documents of Early Texians, 1821-1845*, Austin: Steck, 1937.

W.J. Hughes: William John Hughes, "'Rip' Ford, Texan: The Public Life and Services of John Salmon Ford, 1836-1883," Ph.D. dissertation, TTU, 1958.

W. Johnson: Walter Johnson, *The Broken Heart of America: St. Louis and the Violent History of the United States*, New York: Basic, 2020.

W.L. Richter: William Lee Richter, "The Army in Texas During Reconstruction, 1865-1870," Ph.D. dissertation, LSU and Agricultural and Mechanical College, 1970.

W.P. Johnston: William Preston Johnston, *The Life of General Albert Sidney Johnston*, New York: Appleton, 1878.

W.P. Snow: William Parker Snow, *Southern Generals, Their Lives and Campaigns*, New York: Richardson, 1866, Huntington Library, multiple volumes.

W. Watson, *Adventures*: William Watson, *The Adventures of a Blockade Runner or Trade in Times of War*, London: Unwin, 1898.

Yancey: William C. Yancey, "The Old Alcalde: Oran Milo Roberts, Texas' Forgotten Fire-Eater," Ph.D. dissertation, UNT, 2016.

Index

About The Author

Gerald Horne is Moores Professor of History and African American Studies at the University of Houston. He has published more than three dozen books including "White Supremacy Confronted: U.S. Imperialism and Anticommunism vs. the Liberation of Southern Africa from Rhodes to Mandela" and "The Apocalypse of Settler Colonialism: The Roots of Slavery, White Supremacy and Capitalism in Seventeenth-Century North America and the Caribbean."